Handbook of Globalization and the Environment

PUBLIC ADMINISTRATION AND PUBLIC POLICY

A Comprehensive Publication Program

Executive Editor

JACK RABIN
Professor of Public Administration and Public Policy
School of Public Affairs
The Capital College
The Pennsylvania State University—Harrisburg
Middletown, Pennsylvania

Assistant to the Executive Editor
T. Aaron Wachhaus, Jr.

Available Electronically

PublicADMINISTRATION*netBASE*

Handbook of Globalization and the Environment

Khi V. Thai
Florida Atlantic University
Boca Raton, Florida, U.S.A.

Dianne Rahm
University of Texas at San Antonio
San Antonio, Texas, U.S.A.

Jerrell D. Coggburn
University of Texas at San Antonio
San Antonio, Texas, U.S.A.

CRC Press
Taylor & Francis Group
Boca Raton   London   New York

CRC Press is an imprint of the
Taylor & Francis Group, an informa business

CRC Press
Taylor & Francis Group
6000 Broken Sound Parkway NW, Suite 300
Boca Raton, FL 33487-2742

© 2007 by Taylor & Francis Group, LLC
CRC Press is an imprint of Taylor & Francis Group, an Informa business

No claim to original U.S. Government works
Printed in the United States of America on acid-free paper
10 9 8 7 6 5 4 3 2 1

International Standard Book Number-10: 1-57444-553-7 (Hardcover)
International Standard Book Number-13: 978-1-57444-553-4 (Hardcover)

Library of Congress Cataloging-in-Publication Data

Handbook of globalization and the environment / editors, Khi V. Thai, Dianne
    Rahm, and Jerrell D. Coggburn.
        p. cm. -- (Public administration and public policy ; 130)
    Includes bibliographical references and index.
    ISBN-13: 978-1-57444-553-4 (alk. paper)
    ISBN-10: 1-57444-553-7 (alk. paper)
    1. Environmental policy--International cooperation. 2.
Globalization--Environmental aspects. I. Thai, Khi V., 1941- II. Rahm, Dianne.
III. Coggburn, Jerrell D. IV. Title. V. Series.

GE170.H3663 2007
363.7'0526--dc22   2006023243

Visit the Taylor & Francis Web site at
http://www.taylorandfrancis.com

and the CRC Press Web site at
http://www.crcpress.com

Preface

In the past few decades, worldwide social, political, legal, ethical, cultural and technological forces have led to a globalization movement. Indeed, many efforts have been made in globalizing various economic areas, including global environmental protection, world trade agreements, global sustainable development, etc. However, there are many debates on globalization and its effects on the environment and/or sustainable economic growth around the globe. Some argue that globalization protects the global environment from environmental degradation and promotes sustainable economic growth in the world, especially in developing countries. But some others, particularly those in developing countries, believe that globalization is a threat to economic growth and sustainable development. This handbook will address these major issues: globalization, development, and the environment. We hope that the book will enrich this debate.

Khi V. Thai
Dianne Rahm
Jerrell D. Coggburn

The Editors

Khi V. Thai, PhD, is professor of public administration at the Florida Atlantic University (FAU) in Fort Lauderdale, Florida. Currently, he serves as director of the Public Procurement Research Center, created under a partnership agreement between FAU and the National Institute of Governmental Purchasing, Inc. His research interests are in public finance management, health care, and public procurement. He has authored or co-authored, and edited or co-edited over 80 refereed articles, book chapters and technical reports, journal symposia, and nine books including *Introduction to Public Procurement* (2004), *Developing and Managing Requests for Proposals in the Public Sector* (2004), *Advancing Public Procurement: Practices, Innovation and Knowledge Sharing* (co-editor) (2006), *Public Budgeting: A Managerial Perspective* (co-author) (Forthcoming), and *Handbook of Public Procurement* (Editor) (forthcoming). He is also an editor, *Journal of Public Budgeting, Accounting & Financial Management*, editor-in-chief, *Journal of Public Procurement*, and managing editor, *International Journal of Organization Theory and Behavior*. He has organized a variety of training programs and study tours, including the advanced leadership and management program for high-ranking government officials from third world countries. He also has provided consulting services in public procurement (including, most recently, Sierra Leone's procurement reform, Canada's federal government procurement review, and Uganda's procurement transparency).

Dianne Rahm, PhD, is professor of public administration at The University of Texas at San Antonio. Dr. Rahm received her PhD from the Syracuse University's Maxwell School of Citizenship and Public Affairs. Her research interests are in environmental policy, energy policy, and science and technology policy. She has authored or co-authored, and edited or co-edited over 50 articles, book chapters, and reports and five books including *Sustainable Energy and the States: Politics, Markets, and Leadership,* (2006), *United States Public Policy: A Budgetary Approach* (2004), *Toxic Waste and Environmental Policy in the*

21ˢᵗ Century United States, (2002), *University-Industry R&D Collaboration in the United States, the United Kingdom, and Japan* (2000), *and Technology and U.S. Competitiveness: An Institutional Focus*, (1992).

Jerrell D. Coggburn, PhD, is an associate professor in the Department of Public Administration at The University of Texas at San Antonio, where he also serves as chair. His primary research interests are in human resources management, public management, and public procurement. He is a past recipient (with Sandra K. Schneider and William G. Jacoby, 1997) of the William and Frederick Mosher Award for the best *Public Administration Review* article written by an academician. Coggburn serves on the editorial board of the *Review of Public Personnel Administration* and the executive board of the American Society for Public Administration's Section on Personnel Administration and Labor Relations. His research has appeared in *Public Administration Review*, *Review of Public Personnel Administration, Journal of Public Administration Research and Theory, Public Performance & Management Review, International Journal of Public Administration, Public Administration Quarterly*, and other scholarly outlets. Coggburn received the BA degree (1992) in political science from Oklahoma State University and MPA (1994) and PhD (1999) degrees from the University of South Carolina.

Contributors

Steffan Bauer
German Development Institute (DIE)
Bonn, Germany

Kathi K. Beratan
Duke University
Durham, North Carolina

Frank Biermann
Nicholas School of the Environment
    and Earth Sciences Levine Science
    Research Center
Environmental Policy Analysis
Vrije University
Amsterdam, The Netherlands

R. Michael Bireley
Department of Public Administration
The University of Texas
San Antonio, Texas

Bruce Bjork
Department of Public Administration
The University of Texas
San Antonio, Texas

Jerrell D. Coggburn
Department of Public Administration
The University of Texas
San Antonio, Texas

David Howard Davis
Political Science and Public
    Administration
University of Toledo
Toledo, Ohio

Ilhom Esanov
Tashkent Institute for Irrigation
    and Melioration
Tashkent, Republic of Uzbekistan

Kyle Farmbry
School of Public Affairs and
    Administration
Rutgers University
Newark, New Jersey

Michael J. Gaffney
Institute for Environmental Studies
Vrije University
Amsterdam, The Netherlands

Joyeeta Gupta
Institute for Environmental Studies
Vrije University
Amsterdam, The Netherlands

Jennifer E. Horan
Department of Political Science
University of North Carolina
Wilmington, North Carolina

Catherine Horiuchi
College of Professional Studies
University of San Francisco
San Francisco, California

Wendy A. Kellogg
Levin College of Urban Affairs
Cleveland State University
Cleveland, Ohio

Madina Khalmirzaeva
Tashkent Institute for Irrigation
and Melioration
Tashkent, Republic of Uzbekistan

W. Henry Lambright
The Maxwell School of Citizenship
and Public Affairs
Syracuse University
Syracuse, New York

Nicholas P. Lovrich
Division of Governmental Studies
and Services
Washington State University
Pullman, Washington

Donna L. Lybecker
Department of Political Science
and Environmental Studies
Pennsylvania State University
Altoona, Pennsylvania

Tetyana Lysak
Department of Political Science
Washington State University
Pullman, Washington

Aroon Manorahan
School of Public Affairs and
Administration
Rutgers University
Newark, New Jersey

Erica M. Matheny
Levin College of Urban Affairs
Cleveland State University
Cleveland, Ohio

Dayna R. Matthews
School of Urban Studies and
Public Administration
Old Dominion University
Norfolk, Virginia

Michael J. Mortimer
Department of Forestry
Virginia Polytechnic Institute
and State University
Blacksburg, Virginia

Celeste Murphy-Greene
School of Urban Studies and
Public Administration
Old Dominion University
Norfolk, Virginia

Lisa Nelson
Department of Political Science
California State Polytechnic
University
Pomona, California

Anna Ya Ni
Center for Technology and
Information Policy
The Maxwell School of Citizenship
and Public Affairs
Syracuse University
Syracuse, New York

Brian Pangrle
Lee & Hays, PLLC
Spokane, Washington

Laura E. Pasquale
Florida Department of Environmental
Protection
Tallahassee, Florida

Ross Prizzia
Public Administration
University of Hawaii, West Oahu
Pearl City, Hawaii

Dianne Rahm
Department of Public Administration
The University of Texas
San Antonio, Texas

Kristi L. Ross
Political Science Department
Geology Department
Northern Arizona University
Flagstaff, Arizona

Zachary A. Smith
Northern Arizona University
Flagstaff, Arizona

Brent S. Steel
Department of Political Science
Oregon State University
Corvallis, Oregon

Mark Stephan
Department of Political Science
Washington State University
Pullman, Washington

Katrina Darlene Taylor
Department of Political Science
Florida Atlantic University
Fort Lauderdale, Florida

Khi V. Thai
Florida Atlantic University
Fort Lauderdale, Florida

Dang Tran
Department of Economics &
    Statistics
California State University
Los Angeles, California

Rebecca L. Warner
Department of Sociology
Oregon State University
Corvallis, Oregon

Edward P. Weber
Department of Political Science
Washington State University
Pullman, Washington

Fariborz Zelli
Tyndall Centre for Climate
    Change Research
Coordinator MOSAIC Research
    Group
University of East Anglia
Norwich, United Kingdom

Table of Contents

PART I: GLOBAL ENVIRONMENTAL ISSUES AND POLICIES

6 The Environmental Frontier of Space 95

W. Henry Lambright and Anna Ya Ni

7 Human Rights to Water... 115

Zachary A. Smith and Kristi L. Ross

PART II: GLOBAL ENVIRONMENTAL ORGANIZATIONS AND INSTITUTIONS

11   United Nations Conferences and the Legitimization of Environmental NGOs 217

Kyle Farmbry and Aroon Manorahan

17   Sustainability Issues in Public Procurement 359

Brian Pangrle

18   Managing Nuclear Waste 381

Catherine Horiuchi

Chapter 1

Globalization and the Environment: an Introduction

Khi V. Thai
Florida Atlantic University

Dianne Rahm and Jerrell D. Coggburn
The University of Texas at San Antonio

1.1   Overview

There are many debates on globalization and its effects on the environment and/or sustainable economic growth around the globe. Proponents of globalization argue that it protects the global environment from environmental degradation and promotes sustainable economic growth in the world, especially in developing countries. Opponents, on the other hand, contend that globalization is a threat to sustainable development. According to these opponents, global corporate business enterprises are responsible for environmental catastrophes that hinder sustainable economic growth. This chapter will briefly review the literature on globalization, the environment, and sustainable economic growth. We close with an overview of the book.

1.1.1 The Conceptual Meaning of Globalization

Globalization is viewed as a step toward a fully integrated world market [1,2] and as a key ingredient of a global society [3]. Globalization is also seen by some academics as a "borderless world" [4]. Brown [5] expounds on globalization as large-scale openness of borders accomplished by loosening state regulations to promote rapid financial transactions, trade, communications, and other social and cultural activities. More precisely, globalization is a phenomenon that encourages international integration through free trade and communication across borders [6,7].

Matteis [8] defines globalization as the process of progressive growth of economic activities which transcends any kind of geographical border. According to this definition, globalization can be seen as the increasing movement of goods and services as well as human resources through trade and investments among nations. Trade liberalization policy and international trade are perceived as important ingredients of globalization.

1.1.2 Perspectives on Sustainable Economic Growth

The World Commission on Environment and Development defines sustainable development simply as "development that meets the needs of the present without compromising the ability of future generations to meet theirs" [9]. From this definition, sustainable economic growth can be explained as sufficient economic growth for the present generation without harming the ability of future generations to attain their needs. The 1992 Rio Earth Summit provided a framework for moving towards sustainable development. The summit was rooted in the notion that efforts to protect the environment must consider eradication of poverty and the need for economic development while at the same time economic development programs should reflect consideration of long-term environmental impacts. The Rio framework reaffirmed the principles of sustainable development provided by the World Commission on Environment and Development [10]. The Earth Summit emphasized that the international economy should provide a supportive international climate for achieving environmental and development goals by promoting sustainable development through trade liberalization [10,11].

The World Bank [12] holds a complementary view on sustainable development [10]; it holds that environmental degradation, if extreme enough, can destroy societies, making whatever level of development previously achieved unsustainable. The World Bank emphasizes the need for control of population growth and the use of technology in developing countries to promote sustainable development [10,13].

1.1.3 Globalization, the Environment, and Sustainable Economic Growth

Will globalization lead to a sustainable environment and a sustainable economy? Researchers have disagreed on the various and multiple impacts of globalization on the environment and on economic growth.

1.1.3.1 Globalization and Sustainable Economic Growth

According to Matteis [8], globalization will have both positive and negative consequences with respect to sustainable economic growth. The positive aspects of trade liberalization in a global marketplace include competition, increased productivity, economic growth, and increased access to foreign capital. By creating competitive global markets, trade liberalization maximizes resources with consequent reduction of production costs and helps increase productivity. Similarly, the United Nations' World Commission on Environment and Development [9] views the free market economy and trade liberalization as indicators of promoting sustainable economic growth. Free market access for products of developing countries, lower interest rates, technology transfer, and larger capital flows—the main ingredients of the global economy—have been identified by the United Nations as essential to sustainable development and poverty reduction. The World Bank [12] also focuses on the need for a free market economy and trade liberalization to reduce poverty and achieve sustainable growth. Globalization has provided the power of technology, especially information technology, to bolster the path of sustainable development for many nations; and has driven the world into a state of greater openness, interdependence, and integration that will bring about new development opportunities [14].

In addition, transnational corporations play a significant role in promoting sustainable economic growth within developing nations [15]. Halme, Park, and Chiu [16] explain the diverging impacts of globalization on sustainable economic growth. They argue that in spite of economic crisis in the late 1990s, countries in the Asia-Pacific region have attained the fastest rate of economic growth in the world over the past quarter century. Although the absolute number of poor remains high due to rapid population growth and other factors, the percentage of Asians who live in poverty has been reduced from 50 to 25% over the same period of time.

However, globalization imposes exogenous constraints on economic growth and contributes to strengthening economic dependence on international demand. It increases vulnerability to the fluctuations of international markets [8]. Indeed, according to Pronk [2], globalization will increase consumption and production, which will be coupled with unequal access to resources. Pronk emphasizes the need for creating new sustainable production and consumption patterns, as well as redirecting economic growth toward labor-incentive and bottom-up development which reduces poverty.

For example, the structural adjustment reforms in the 1980s and the influence of the North American Free Trade Agreement (NAFTA) in the 1990s manufacturing sector in the Caribbean island states failed to create a sustained path towards economic growth and have reduced the competitiveness of regional assembly-based manufacturers in the island states [17]. In addition to manufacturing, Caribbean service exports also continue to be affected by incompatibilities among global and local structures and institutions. Unfortunately, according to Mullings [17], individual island states have little power to challenge the trade or policy-based lending requirements of powerful global institutions like the World Trade Organization (WTO) or the International Monetary Fund (IMF).

Holliday, Schmidheiny, and Watts [18] emphasize the need for corporate social responsibility, that is, "commitment of the business to contribute to sustainable development, working with employees, their families and local community and society at large to improve their quality of life." Unfortunately, although globalization is purported to create "trickle-down" gains for all, it has all too often resulted in gains for just a few—most of whom are wealthy [19,20]. Concerns over equity issues are plentiful.

1.1.3.2 Globalization and a Sustainable Environment

Researchers also disagree on the impact of economic growth helped by globalization on the environment. The United Nations [11] argues that environmental degradation can be reduced through reduction of poverty. Holliday, Schmidheiny, and Watts [18] believe that producing more goods and services with fewer resources will reduce waste and pollution while promoting sustainable growth. In this respect, they argue that free and open markets are essential for sustainable economic growth. Jeppesen and Hansen [15] found that transnational corporations in collaboration with enterprises in developing nations play an important role in environmental affairs for at least two reasons. Transnational corporations have environmental standards, monitoring, and pollution control mechanisms in place. Moreover, transnational corporations provide technical assistance and training to businesses in developing countries, which in turn promotes environmentally friendly economic development.

However, Castro [10] rejects the idea that economic growth is achieved by free trade, that economic growth reduces poverty, and that if poverty is reduced environmental degradation will be reduced. Castro argues that despite the partial success in reducing poverty, rapid economic growth, coupled with increasing urban population, has surpassed antipollution investments and has resulted in deteriorating air and water quality as well as loss of biodiversity and natural resources.

Major pollution threats to the environment in the age of globalization come from economic activities, such as agriculture, mining, manufacturing, and transportation [21]. For instance, deforestation rates in East Asia were the highest of any region in the early 1990s. The World Bank [22] reports that Indonesia alone lost 20 million hectares of forest between 1985 and 1998, while almost 90% of productive old-growth forests have been destroyed in the Philippines since 1990. Halme, Park, and Chiu [16] further argue that globalization is a challenge to sustainable development in Asia because the wealthy northern countries consume 80% of the world's production while developing countries bear the burden of environmental and social impacts caused by that consumption. Moreover, threats to the environment in developing nations are more severe than in the developed world, due to cheap labor, access to inexpensive raw materials, poor environmental regulations, and other investment-friendly incentives offered by the governments of the host countries.

A positive trend has emerged recently: sustainability reporting and environmental information disclosure. For example, the sustainability reports published by the Fortune Global 250 indicate that the largest most visible multinational companies are very active in disclosing information on their environmental and social policies as well as their performance. Data show that European countries and Japan maintain a certain level of sustainability reporting, both in quantity and quality. Many multinational companies have also started disclosing economic aspects of sustainability [23], which indicate that global corporations are conducive to sustainable development.

Assessing the full impact of globalization on poverty reduction, economic development, and environmental quality is difficult to do. The phenomenon called globalization continues to transform as time goes on. Likewise, ecosystems respond to more than just globalization. Climate change, population growth, the use of new technologies, changes in patterns of consumption, alterations in production processes, civil conflict, and variations in the use of natural resources each play a role in environmental outcomes. Some are independent of globalization; others are intertwined with it. In this tightly coupled complex scenario, prediction of outcomes may be more art than science. Nevertheless, deepening our understanding of these phenomena is critical if we are to move to a more effective policy that seeks to end poverty and create economic growth, while at the same time protecting the environment. That is the purpose of this book.

1.2   Book Contents

The book is divided into four parts. Part One focuses on global environmental issues and policies. Part Two looks at global environmental organizations and institutions. Part Three addresses environmental management and accountability. Part Four discusses controversies in globalization and the environment. Further detail on the contents of each part is provided below.

1.2.1   Part One: Global Environmental Issues and Policies

Global environmental issues and policies are the subject of Part One. The term "sustainable development" only entered the global environmental lexicon about 20 years ago with the 1987 publication of *Our Common Future* by the UN's World Commission on Environmental Development. Since that time, efforts have been made to bring meaning to the term and to pursue strategies that integrate economic, environmental, and other social considerations. Ross Prizzia's chapter considers sustainable development from an international perspective. In the first part, he explores the challenges of simultaneously promoting development and the environment. As noted, many developing countries focus on rapid economic growth in the short-term at the expense of the environment, with the idea that environmental problems can be fixed "later." In contrast, the UN's Conference on the Environment and Development and its Agenda 21 have spurred some countries to develop specific sustainable development strategies. In the second part of the chapter, Prizzia uses "good practices" guidelines for national sustainable development strategies, as outlined by the Organization of Economic Cooperation and Development (OECD) and the UN, to examine OECD countries' performance. These good practices fall into eight categories: policy integration, intergenerational timeframe, analysis and assessment, indicators and targets, coordination and institutions, local and regional governance, stakeholder participation, and monitoring and evaluation. Finally, Prizzia concludes by calling for more meaningful measures of sustainability, arguing that traditional measures of economic welfare, such as gross national product (GNP), eschew important aspects of human and environmental well-being, hence obfuscating true welfare, and calling for far more international cooperation.

David H. Davis's chapter examines the evolution of global warming policy with a special emphasis on the European Union and its member countries. Davis provides an overview of the environmental policy framework in Europe, including an account of the prominent role played by scientific and technical staff in the various environmental bureaucracies. Environmental staffers were, for example, instrumental in pushing the European Union to assume a leadership role in global carbon reduction efforts. Davis shows not only the United States' reluctance to embrace global agreements like the Kyoto Protocol, but also the bargaining and compromise (e.g., on emissions trading) that has typified the progress that has been made on global warming policy. The chapter concludes by drawing contrasts and similarities between European countries and the United States in this important facet of global environmental policy.

Zachary A. Smith and Katrina Darlene Taylor provide a detailed look at transborder air pollution and its relationship to globalization. The authors argue that the rise in environmental degradation associated with transborder air pollution is linked to and probably caused by the increase in globalization. The chapter examines several framework international agreements or regimes that have been created to deal with air pollution. The authors conclude that for international environmental regimes to be effective, they must be enforced, transparent, and held accountable. They also suggest that trade agreements, including environmental provisions, might be the logical instrument for future negotiations to control transborder pollution issues.

Steffan Bauer's chapter focuses on the interlinkages between the process that has come to be called desertification with global development, poverty eradication, and global warming. Arguing that dryland degradation is a better concept with which to describe the local and regional processes at work, Bauer reminds the reader that desertification is not the encroachment of existing deserts on fertile lands, as is commonly thought. In that sense, desertification is not a global commons phenomenon like global warming or stratospheric ozone depletion. Despite the fact that desertification occurs locally and needs to be primarily addressed at local and regional levels, Bauer contends that desertification has evolved as a globalized concept that has achieved significant status in the governance of North–South relations. The global governance approach to dryland degradation is outlined by the United Nations Convention to Combat Desertification, which the author contends reflects two decades of environmental politics in which development concerns have taken precedence over environmental issues.

While the other chapters in this section focus on "global" environmental issues, the chapter by W. Henry Lambright and Anna Ya Ni explores a different environmental frontier: space. The chapter is framed around the development of space technology and the subsequent policy change associated with efforts to realize positive uses of space technology and mitigate potential negative impacts. The authors examine three areas of space technology and policy, each with environmental dimensions: space-based observation of Earth, near-earth orbit, and deep space. First, the writers illustrate how technological advances witnessed the development of satellites used for space-based obser-vations of Earth's weather, atmospheric conditions (especially ozone levels—something that solidified NASA's environmental role in the United States), and land resources. Second, their section on near-earth orbit demonstrates, in what may be surprising to some, the exhaustible nature of space resources, including desirable orbital positions for communications satellites and workable frequen-cies. This section also discusses the increasingly serious environmental problem—both on Earth and in space—of space debris. Finally, their section on deep space discusses policy efforts related to forward (from Earth to other planets) and backward (from other planets back to Earth) contamination. On the whole, the chapter effectively demonstrates that global environmental concerns extend well beyond Earth's atmosphere.

There is little disagreement that access to clean, safe drinking water is a necessity, but there is also little agreement over how best to ensure that states provide that access to their citizens. This topic, human rights to water, is the subject of the chapter by Zachary A. Smith and Kristi L. Ross. They illustrate how the demand for freshwater has grown rapidly in recent decades, along with a rise in global population and in industrial and agricultural production, all of which strain the supply of the resource. Smith and Ross argue that the fundamental problem is one of access, something that is itself affected by a host of direct (e.g., distance to sources, cost, supply) and indirect (distribution and demand) factors. The authors discuss the shift in efforts to resolve water access issues from national and collaborative water management strategies to a focus on governance. One such example, viewing water as a human right, as articulated in declarations by various international organizations, is a shift that has not come without controversy or concern. Some parties argue that water should be viewed as a common good to which humans have a right (e.g., the right to a certain daily amount of water), while others view water as an economic good (i.e., something that is economically valued and, as such, will (should) be conserved and protected). This chapter weighs the merits of several approaches to addressing the problem of water access, concluding that ultimate solutions will be difficult given the increasing interconnectedness of the world and that any effective approach must be one devised within regional and local contexts.

1.2.2 Part Two: Global Environmental Organizations and Institutions

Part Two looks at global environmental organizations and institutions. It begins with Frank Biermann's chapter on global environmental governance regimes. Biermann begins by defining the term "global governance" as new forms of regulation that differ from traditional hierarchical state activity ("government"). Governance, the author suggests, implies self-regulation, public–private cooperation, and new forms of multilevel policy efforts. The chapter reviews some of the disagreement in terms of how governance is defined, with normative approaches differing from phenomenological ones. From a phenomenological framework, global governance is an emerging new phenomenon in world politics that can be described and analyzed. From a normative framework, global environmental governance is a political program that is coping (or failing to cope) with contemporary problems associated with modern environmental issues. Biermann describes three features that make global governance different from traditional international relations: increased segmentation of policy making, increased participation of nonstate and intergovernmental actors, and increased influence of private organizations in policy making. The chapter concludes with two examples of reform in the existing system of global environmental governance: the United Nations Environment Organization and institutionalizing civil society involvement.

In "The Role of the United Nations: From Stockholm to Johannesburg," Lisa Nelson explores the role the United Nations has played as the world moved toward globalization and began to consider seriously the interconnection between development and environmental deterioration. The author argues that the UN first recognized the potential conflict between development and the environment in the early 1970s, and since then has woven a concern for the environment into all development programs and a concern for development into all environment programs. In addition, acknowledgment of global interdependence and transnational environmental issues has led to a series of international conventions or treaties that are administered by the UN. Despite the lack of enforcement capability, Nelson suggests that the UN has successfully constructed a world environmental regime that addresses long-term issues of environmental degradation. In addition, the UN has not only been the force behind defining sustainable development, it also has served as the driving force for demanding an integration of social, economic, and environmental factors. The chapter reviews the sustainable development efforts undertaken by the UN from the 1972 meeting in Stockholm to the 2002 meeting in Johannesburg.

One obvious manifestation of globalization is trade, and with trade comes environmental impact. Helping to shape these issues are international institutions like the WTO—the focus of Fariborz Zelli's contribution to this handbook. The relationship between trade and the environment and the role of the WTO in mediating that relationship is not all at once clear. Skeptics contend that the WTO and international trade liberalization will harm the environment by, for example, creating a race to the bottom in environmental standards, shifting environmental risks to less-developed countries, and encouraging economic growth and the concomitant exploitation of resources. On the other hand, those holding more optimistic views suggest that the WTO can positively affect environmental performance in global trade by raising environmental awareness and facilitating the dissemination of environmentally preferable technologies and products. Zelli's chapter provides a comprehensive examination of this trade–environment nexus. First, he presents various (and, at times, conflicting) assumptions about trade–environment compatibility. Next, he reviews the WTO's environmentally-related organizational arrangements and their record, to date, in handling environmentally related trade disputes. The chapter concludes with a discussion of potential strategies for improving WTO compatibility with environmental law. In its totality, Zelli's chapter vividly illustrates the complexity of sorting out the relationship between global trade and the environment, as well as the need for additional empirical evidence to serve as the basis for future informed action.

Nongovernmental organizations, or NGOs, are playing increasingly important roles in a variety of policy domains, including environmental. Kyle Farmbry and Aroon Manorahan examine this emergence of NGOs in their chapter "United Nations Conferences and the Legitimization of Environmental NGOs." The authors describe the confluence of events that served to increase the legitimacy and prominence of NGOs during the latter part of the twentieth century. Using the framework of the United Nations' environmental conferences, the evolutionary development of NGOs' roles is explicated. The authors argue that this development now places NGOs at a critical juncture in terms of the scope of their roles and activities relative to other legitimate players. They suggest that a model of NGOs as partners in change, as opposed to drivers of change, may be emerging. Building on this suggestion, Farmbry and Manorahan develop a prescriptive framework for furthering the discourse on the nongovernmental sector, with emphasis placed on issues of capacity development and long-term sustainability, and ensuring states maintain their environmental responsibilities.

Brent S. Steel and Rebecca L. Warner's chapter analyzes the state of global environmental knowledge and awareness from an international and comparative perspective. They begin by noting contributing factors (e.g., socioeconomic status, sources of environmental information, formal environmental educational) to a perceived knowledge gap in worldwide ecological science literacy. Next, Steel and Warner assess the current state of global environmental awareness and knowledge. They present survey data that suggest both are high regardless of type of country (i.e., developing, current/former communist, industrial/postindustrial), a finding that augers well for global environmental education efforts. Speaking of such efforts, the authors submit that a one-size-fits-all approach to environmental education will be ineffective. Some countries (e.g., postcommunist countries with high literacy and education participation rates but underdeveloped civil societies) may benefit most from formal education approaches through schools, while others (e.g., developing countries) may benefit most from "hybrid" approaches that combine both formal and informal elements, including indigenous knowledge. Whether the approach be formal, informal, or hybrid, the authors note the existing general agreement that environmental education should contain four components: providing information on ecological concepts, raising awareness of how human behavior affects the environment, offering opportunities for investigating and evaluating environmental solutions, and developing skills to implement those solutions. Steel and Warner conclude by posing the challenge of translating environmental awareness, knowledge, and education into behavior supporting sustainability if the "attitude–behavior gap" is to be closed.

1.2.3 Part Three: Environmental Management and Accountability

Environmental management and accountability is the theme of Part Three. Concerns over environmental degradation and environmental sustainability have pushed governments to search for new ways to combat environmental problems. Jerrell D. Coggburn and Dianne Rahm's chapter addresses one such approach: green procurement. Green procurement attempts to address environmental challenges by taking advantage of a government's vast purchasing power to create strong markets for environmentally friendly (i.e., "green") products and services. Coggburn and Rahm first review the policy framework for green procurement in the United States. Next, they explore developments in green procurement at the national, state, and local levels. The chapter presents several broad strategies governments and procurement professionals can pursue in implementing green procurement, such as, creating price preferences, developing green product and service specifications, and forming green teams. The chapter concludes by identifying several challenges facing governments implementing green procurement policies and offering guidance on overcoming them.

Laura Pasquale's chapter on environmental management begins with an overview of U.S. environmental regulation and the current range of pollution prevention mechanisms, both voluntary and mandatory, in use. She argues that despite the fact that we spend billions of dollars each year trying to prevent pollution, relatively little is known about how and why pollution prevention efforts work. After reviewing the weakness of the current media-based (air, water, and waste) regulatory structure, Pasquale argues that to improve environmental quality, policy makers and regulators need to view the environment and the cultures within it as complex systems. The complex system here refers to the constant interaction of individuals and groups, plants and animals, and local and global ecosystems. The awareness of this complexity results in the attempt to move away from "command and control" regulatory structures towards more flexible options, including social marketing, financial incentives, integrative regulation, sustainability projects, pollution prevention, promotion of new technologies, and self-certification. The chapter then introduces the environmental management system (EMS) and shows how the EMS is effective in addressing that complexity. The chapter concludes with recommendations for sustaining participation in the EMS.

In "Sustainable Waterfront Development in the Great Lakes Basin," Wendy Kellogg and Erica Matheny focus on the role globalization has played in the economic function of cities—specifically the cities of Canada and the United States that historically have depended on the Great Lakes basin to fuel their urban cores. In the last several decades, many of these cities have sought to reverse the loss of a population and industrial base that came with globalization through a reinvestment in their waterfronts. For some of the cities, this reinvestment has primarily been in industry. For other cities, the investment has been in quality of life amenities and ecological restoration. The chapter describes efforts in four cities to create urban sustainability by making their waterfront the centerpiece.

In their exploration of public policy efforts aimed at promoting both agricultural productivity increases and environmental sustainability, Edward Weber, Madina Khalmirzaeva, Mark Stephan, Tetyana Lysak, and Ilhom Esanov look at the role of water user associations in Uzbekistan. They argue that a more refined understanding of institutional and social dynamics is required for good public policy to be forged. They emphasize the importance of substantive citizen participation in the policy process, collaborative decision processes, and distributed decision-making authority as key to success of sustainable agricultural practices in Uzbekistan.

In "Sustainability Issues and Public Procurement," Brian Pangrle provides a two-prong approach highlighting the issues that need to be confronted to establish a sustainable procurement model. Emphasizing the differences between "green procurement" and "sustainable procurement," Pangrle argues that green measures, while useful, fall short of the goal of sustainable practices. The practical issues that confront governments as they establish and try to implement sustainable procurement codes are discussed.

Catherine Horiuchi's chapter focuses on the management of nuclear waste. After briefly reviewing the types and characteristics of radioactive wastes that need to be managed, she turns to a discussion of the planned U.S. permanent repository at Yucca Mountain. Over budget and many years behind expected completion, the failure of the government to provide a repository to receive both civilian and military radioactive waste has had enormous consequences. These include the problems presented to the nuclear industry of how to continue to store spent fuel rods in temporary on-site facilities, the contamination problems at nuclear weapons production facilities, as well as the potential for terrorists gaining access to nuclear materials. Horiuchi discusses the routes that other countries have taken to handle their nuclear waste, including reprocessing and mixed oxide fuel (MOX) technologies to reduce the mass of waste needing permanent storage. She closes on a note of uncertainty, pointing out that while global warming is making production of electricity via nuclear power more attractive, the problems of disposal are still not tractable, and waste continues to amass without a solution in sight.

In their chapter, Nicholas P. Lovrich, Michael J. Gaffney, Edward P. Weber, R. Michael Bierley, Dayna R. Matthews, and Bruce Bjork examine a collaborative community-based approach to environmental regulatory compliance. In particular, the authors examine salmon recovery efforts in the Pacific Northwest within the regulatory context of the United States Endangered Species Act. The chapter contrasts two cases, Methow Valley and the Walla Walla Basin, where efforts have succeeded in achieving legal compliance and protecting endangered species. While both efforts were successful, the authors point to the advantages of pursuing the proactive collaborative enforcement model, referred to as Resource-Oriented Enforcement (ROE), exemplified in Walla Walla. Cited advantages of ROE include it being less polarizing, while promoting trust between citizens and government regulatory agencies, and forming a foundation for future cooperative compliance efforts. The model holds promise for resource protection efforts generally, but requires attention to training regulators in proactive approaches and appreciation for factors that can mitigate success like history and relationships from jurisdiction to jurisdiction. Success is more likely where regulatory agencies are consistent, predictable, and reliable and where communities exhibit high levels of social capital.

1.2.4 Part Four: Controversies in Globalization and the Environment

The book concludes with a discussion of the controversies in globalization and the environment. Michael Mortimer's chapter, "Ecoterrorism: A Natural Reaction of Violence?" explores the behavior of radical environmentalists in their efforts to prevent environmental degradation. After discussing the common definitions, syntax, and semantics of direct action, ecoterrorism, environmental terrorism, and ecotage, Mortimer reflects on environmental activists' differentiation of the use of violence against property versus the use of violence against people. Direct action tactics against property (such as arson; tree spiking; or sabotage to equipment, vehicles, buildings, and laboratories) is compared to intimidation campaigns (harassing letters and telephone calls) versus direct physical violence (assault). Mortimer discusses the concern that growing links exist between ecoterrorists and antiglobalist activists. In the antiglobalism context, direct action tactics often result in street violence and chaos that, according to the author, is hard to dismiss as nonviolent even if no assaults against individuals occur. The author agues that the merging of ecoterror groups with antiglobalization efforts may move ecoterrorists more in the direction of crimes against persons than property. The author concludes with a concern that if such a shift does occur, it will signal a new chapter in direct environmental action in the United States.

Joyeeta Gupta addresses the issues associated with globalization, environmental challenges, and North–South disputes. After exploring these concepts separately, she links the ideas together. She argues that North–South friction has arisen out of the colonial past, a past that is largely ignored by the North but is a vital issue in the South, which seeks to reorganize itself away from the colonial forms. The author argues that it is in this context that environment and development issues become complex. The chapter explores much of this complexity.

Achieving equal protection from environmental and health hazards is the focus of Celeste Murphy–Greene's chapter on environmental justice. The chapter traces the historical development of environmental justice in the United States, where interest in environmental justice first developed, and reviews the current literature on the subject. Her discussion draws parallels between environmental justice issues and causes in the United States and other countries around the world. For example, she cites research showing that the location of hazardous waste facilities is strongly correlated with communities' racial minorities and, to a lesser degree, socioeconomic status; similar results are reported in other countries. Generally, these communities have different perceptions of and tolerance for risk and are less well equipped to respond to any perceived risk. She notes further that, globally, many less-developed countries are willing to accept the short-term economic benefits of harboring other countries' hazardous waste or opening foreign-owned, high-polluting facilities over the long-term costs to environmental conditions and health. The chapter's final section explores these issues in more depth with three cases exemplifying forms of environmental injustice: Nigeria, South Africa, and the United States–Mexico Border Region. Murphy–Greene concludes with a call for support of an international environmental court that would serve as an impartial decision maker for those impacted by unjust environmental conditions.

Dang T. Tran's chapter examines the promotion of economic growth through globalization in less-developed countries (LDCs). Tran discusses the requisite economic development forces for industrialization and development including, among other things, market economies and governments active in both framing rules for economic activity and developing technological capacity. He argues that vertical specialization (that is, specializing on a particular aspect of the production process) allows LDCs to operate successfully in the global arena without requiring firms to master an entire production process. This, along with technological upgrades, can set the stage for LDCs to move on to more sophisticated production. Importantly, as the author mentions, environmental problems often accompany development efforts in LDCs, including untreated waste polluting water supplies, increased production of greenhouse gases, acid rain, and soil erosion. These problems grow in intensity, and occur in a compressed amount of time, as LDCs move from agriculture- to industry-based economies, ebbing only as they move from industry- to service-based economies. This creates the need for LDCs to integrate environmental policy considerations into their overall development strategy. Finally, the chapter shifts from supply issues to a consideration of demand conditions. Here, Tran develops a growth model intended to identify goods to be produced and policies to be adopted in order for LDCs to be successful in the global environment.

In "Managing the Science–Policy Interface in a Complex and Contentious World," Kathi Beratan explores the relationship between science and the ability of scientists to communicate so that policy makers can use science in decision making. She asks: How can we modify the science–policy interface so that we more effectively put knowledge to work towards addressing significant problems? The chapter begins with an exploration of our coupled social and ecological systems, which the author contends are complex and adaptive. The author argues that in these coupled systems, a change to any part of the system will be reflected in the system as a whole. These changes may result in major shifts in system conditions and behaviors, which might occur abruptly and with very little advanced warning. These changes are likely to be irreversible. When dealing with these kinds of problems, decision makers usually turn to scientists. But there is a boundary between scientists and policy makers that must be bridged if science is to be brought to the decision maker's assistance. The rest of the chapter explores how this border might be bridged.

The Horan and Lybecker chapter titled "Multiparty Environmental Negotiations: The Democratizing Nations of Mexico and Ecuador," focuses on the issue of multiparty communication in nations' transitioning to greater democracy. The authors use the cases of Mexico and Ecuador to explore the intricacies of environmental negotiations within the context of increasing grassroots and international pressure for transparency in environmental decision making. Mexico, a relatively wealthy developing nation with NAFTA ties to the United States and Canada, and Ecuador, a geographically small and poor nation, illustrate the diversity of progress toward open multiparty environmental negotiation within the democratizing states of Latin America.

Acknowledgments

The authors wish to thank Dr. Rafique Islam, Research Associate in the Public Procurement Research Center at Florida Atlantic University, for his research assistance. The authors wish to gratefully acknowledge the able editorial assistance of Alexandra Voigt, Research Assistant in the Department of Public Administration at The University of Texas at San Antonio. Finally, we wish to thank all the authors who contributed to the volume as well as the excellent professionals at Taylor and Francis Group.

References

1. Falk, R., States of siege: will globalization win out? *International Affairs*, 73(1), 1997.
2. Pronk, J., Sustainability, poverty, and climate, Presented at 9th Greening of Industry Network Conference, Bangkok, Thailand, 2001.
3. Buttel, F.H., Some observations on states, world orders, and the politics of sustainability, *Organization and Environment*, 11(3), 261, 1998.
4. Ohmae, K., *The Borderless World*, Harper-Collins, London, 1990.
5. Brown, S., *International Relations in a Changing Global System: Towards a Theory of World Polity*, Westview Press, Boulder, CO, 1992.
6. Leaders: Is globalization doomed? The hubris of the West *The Economist*, 360(8241), 14, 2001.
7. Survey: Globalization and its critics *The Economist*, 360(8241), 3, 2001.
8. Matteis, A.D., International trade and economic growth in a global environment, *Journal of International Development*, 16(4), 575, 2004.
9. World Commission on Environment and Development, *Our Common Future*, Oxford University Press, New York, 1987, 8.
10. Castro, C.J., Sustainable development: mainstream and critical perspectives, *Organization and Environment*, 17(2), 195, 2004.
11. United Nations Conference on Environment and Development, Agenda 21, Available at: http://www.un.org/esa/sustdev/documents/agenda21/ (accessed on April 26, 2006).

12. World Bank, *World Development Report 1992: Development and Environment*, Oxford University Press, New York, 1992.

13. World Bank, *World Development Report 2003: Sustainable Development in a Dynamic World*, Oxford University Press, New York, 2003.

14. Panitchpakdi, S., Asia, environment and the future of development, Presented at 9th Greening of Industry Network Conference, Bangkok, Thailand, 2001.

15. Jeppesen, S. and Hansen, M.W., Environmental upgrading of Third World enterprises through linkages to transnational corporations: theoretical perspectives and preliminary evidence, *Business Strategy and the Environment*, 13(4), 261, 2004.

16. Halme, M., Park, J., and Chiu, A., Editorial: managing globalization for sustainability in the 21st century, *Business Strategy and the Environment*, 11(2), 81, 2002.

17. Mullings, B., Globalization and the territorialization of the new Caribbean service economy, *Journal of Economic Geography*, 4(3), 275, 2004.

18. Holliday, C., Schmidheiny, S., and Watts, P., *Walking the Talk: The Business Case for Sustainable Development*, Berrett-Koehler, San Francisco, CA, 2002.

19. Cavanagh, J., Mander, J., Anderson, S., Kimbrell, A., Barker, D., Korten, D., *et al. Alternatives to Economic Globalization: A Better World is Possible*, Berrett-Koehler, San Francisco, CA, 2002.

20. Barnett, M.L., Are globalization and sustainability compatible? A review of the debate between the World Business Council for Sustainable Development and the International Forum on Globalization, *Organization and Environment*, 17(4), 523, 2004.

21. Aparakkakankanamage, A., Globalization, sustainable development, and environmental problems in the Third World: a case of Sri Lanka, A Doctoral Dissertation Submitted to University of Maryland, College Park, 2005.

22. World Bank, *Regional Strategies—East Asia and Pacific*, Available at: http://web.worldbank.org/WBSITE/EXTERNAL/TOPICS/ENVIRONMENT/0,,contentMDK:20268711~menuPK:547580~pagePK:148956~piPK:216618~theSitePK:244381,00.html (accessed on April 26, 2006).

23. Kolk, A., Trends in sustainability reporting by the Fortune Global 250, *Business Strategy and the Environment*, 12(5), 279, 2003.

GLOBAL ENVIRONMENTAL ISSUES AND POLICIES

I

Chapter 2

Sustainable Development in an International Perspective

Ross Prizzia
University of Hawaii

2.1 The Movement toward Sustainable Development

2.1.1 Definition

The term "sustainable development" was introduced into the language of international environmental diplomacy by the United Nations' World Commission on Environment and Development in its widely circulated 1987 report, *Our Common Future*. Sustainable development referred to "development that meets the needs of the present without compromising the ability of future generations to meet their own needs" [1]. The 1987 report, known as the Brundtland Commission Report, contained two key concepts: (1) *needs* to which overriding priority should be given, particularly to the world's poor, and (2) *limitations* imposed by the state of technology and social organization on the environment's ability to meet present and future needs [1]. This approach to sustainable development requires conservation of the resource itself, and not mere alleviation of immediate environmental harms. The resource base is comprehensive, including water, air, minerals, land, and all the complex interrelationships woven in ecology, including humans in their cultural and social systems. The Brundtland Report emphasized reconciling global environmental protection, social welfare, and national economic development.

Subsequent definitions of sustainable development proliferated, but in practice it has come to mean development that achieves a balance among economic, environmental, and social objectives for present and future generations. Sustainable development requires that priority be given to maintaining the value of renewable resources and ecosystems more generally. It does not require that every tree harvested must be replaced, but it does not allow development to impair future output. It supports activities that do not disadvantage future generations, and, thus, it is a concept that will also maintain intergenerational equity. The optimal definition of sustainable development recognizes and incorporates the social, economic, and ecological objectives of multi-generations.

2.1.2 From Stockholm to Rio, Kyoto, and Beyond

The 1972 Conference on the Human Environment in Stockholm, Sweden, attended by 113 states and representatives from 19 international organizations, was the first truly international conference devoted exclusively to environmental issues. The major tenets of this conference were the basis of the 1987 Brundtland Report, *Our Common Future*. It placed environmental issues on the global agenda, created a set of principles and an action plan for environmentally sound management, and led to the creation of the United Nations Environmental Program (UNEP). This conference played a catalytic role in promoting the subsequent adoption of international agreements concerned with ocean dumping, pollution from ships, and the endangered species trade [2]. It also adopted the "Stockholm Declaration on the Human Environment," which included forward-looking principles, such as Principle 13, that declared the need for integration and coordination in development planning to allow for environmental protection [3].

However, the Stockholm conference was limited in its effectiveness because environmental protection and the need for development, especially in developing countries, were seen as competing needs and thus were dealt with in a separate, uncoordinated fashion. Birnie [4] concluded that the conference was more concerned with identifying trade-offs between environment and development than with promoting harmonious linkages between the two. Even UN documents acknowledged after the Stockholm conference that little was accomplished to concretely integrate environmental concerns into development policies and plans [5]. A more integrated perspective that incorporated both economic development and environmental sensitivities was clearly needed.

While the concept of sustainable development can be grasped at a conceptual level, it has proven more difficult to apply concretely. The Brundtland Report advised that qualitative development must replace quantitative growth in achieving sustainable development. Underlying conditions that could promote the process were described. These include: (1) broad citizen participation, (2) an economic system that produces sustainable surpluses and technical knowledge, (3) systems and processes for resolving disputes, (4) a system of production based on preserving the ecological base, (5) international economic and social systems that foster sustainable trade and finance, and (6) a flexible administrative system [1].

The Brudtland Report recognized, however, that even if all of these conditions were in place, the transition to a sustainable society would be difficult. Many existing institutions and practices would need to change. The report asserted that "painful choices have to be made. Thus, in the final analysis, sustainable development must rest on political will" [1]. Clear paradigm shifts were identified as essential to sustainable development, but debate remained over the nature of these paradigm shifts and what they implied for the economic and social organization of a sustainable world [6].

In December 1989, the United Nations General Assembly passed Resolution 44/228 that called for a conference that should "elaborate strategies and measures to halt and reverse the effects of environmental degradation in the context of increased national and international efforts to promote sustainable and environmentally sound development in all countries" [5]. In response, the UN Conference on the Environment and Development [7] was held in Rio de Janeiro, Brazil, during the summer of 1992, unprecedented historical event with the largest gathering of 114 heads of state, including 10,000 representatives from 178 countries and 1400 non-governmental organizations represented by additional thousands.

The commitment of leaders from around the world to sustainable development was clearly articulated in Agenda 21, the key document of the summit. Agenda 21 activities are organized under environmental and development themes: quality of life, efficient use of natural resources, protection of the global commons, management of human settlements, and sustainable economic growth. Agenda 21 recognizes that the persistence of severe poverty in several parts of the world alongside a standard of living based on wasteful consumption of resources in other parts is not a sustainable model, and that environmental management must be practiced in developing and industrial countries alike. During the 1992 conference it was agreed that to implement Agenda 21, countries should prepare a national sustainable development strategy.

While sustainable development was the unifying principle for the entire Rio conference, there was disagreement about its meaning and implications. The UNCED process attempted to provide guidance in implementing sustainable development by laying out a set of principles and a plan of action based on the concept. Indeed, Rio was less about debating the definition of sustainable development than it was about developing approaches to ensure its implementation. A meeting of international legal scholars concluded that sustainable development "is as much about process and institutional arrangements as about sustainable norms" [8]. Implementing the principles of equity and living within ecological limits can only be accomplished if social, political, and economic systems have the flexibility to be redirected toward sustainability as well as integrated with each other and the environment. Lang [8] argued that the main challenge to sustainable development is integration.

In the 1997 Kyoto conference on climate change, developed countries agreed on specific targets for cutting their emissions of greenhouse gases, resulting in a general framework, which became known as the Kyoto Protocol, with specifics to be detailed over the next few years. The U.S. proposed to stabilize emissions only and not cut them at all, while the European Union called for a 15% cut. In the end, there was a trade off, and industrialized countries were committed to an overall reduction of emissions of greenhouse gases to 5.2% below 1990 levels for the period 2008–2012. However, the complexity of the negotiations created considerable confusion over compliance even after the Kyoto Protocol itself was adopted because it only outlined the basic features for compliance but did not explain the all-important rules of how they would operate. Although 84 countries signed the Protocol, indicating their intent to ratify it, many others were reluctant to take even this step.

While there is consensus that government policies around the world have neglected the environment, there are no reliable standard measures for evaluating a country's environmental policies. Reflecting both policies and outcomes, one recently developed indicator, "genuine saving," measures the rate of saving after accounting for investments in human capital, depreciation of produced assets, and depletion and degradation of the environment [9]. Such measures, however, are still experimental.

There has been some progress in agreements reached on international environmental issues. Many countries have completed a country environmental profile, formulated conservation and biodiversity strategies, and participated in global treaties. However, this limited movement provides only a governmental declaration of good intentions. Moreover, measures are only weakly related to environmental outcomes [10].

Generally, environmental degradation is most devastating for the poor and most vulnerable, who often depend on natural resources for their incomes and have few possibilities for substituting other assets. This is especially the case in the long run, where growth policies focus on accumulation, investment, and economic growth. Countries throughout the world have overexploited their forests, fisheries, and mineral wealth and have polluted their water and air in order to accelerate short-term economic growth.

2.1.3 Growth as a Challenge to Sustainable Development

Evidence to the contrary has not dispelled the perception that the environment is a luxury good that can be demanded as incomes rise with economic growth. As a result, developing countries tend to ignore environmental concerns as policy-makers focus almost exclusively on accelerating economic growth. By doing so, they ignore the potential enormity of economic, social, and ecological costs and the reality that sometimes the damage incurred is irreversible. For example, while air and water pollution levels appear to be reversible, their impacts on human well being often are not, and promises of future remedial action can hardly compensate for health and safety losses by the present generation.

Belying East Asia's phenomenal record of economic growth and poverty reduction is its poor environmental record. In 1995, China was home to 15 of the 20 most polluted cities in the world, as measured by the concentration of total suspended particulates [11]. Air pollution, especially high levels of total suspended particulates, resulted in premature deaths and severe health damage in several cities in China and outside China in urban areas such as Bangkok,

Jakarta, and Manila. Countries that experienced rapid growth in the context of economic reforms in the 1980s—China, Korea, Malaysia, and Thailand—saw carbon dioxide emissions per capita double or triple after reforms that had led to accelerated economic growth.

However, it is not just rapid growth that leads to problems of natural capital degradation. Neither rapid nor slow growth is automatically a predictor of the degradation of natural capital [12]. While air pollution is not as widespread a problem in Central and South America as in Asia, in part because of the relatively low growth of industrialization, pollution is a serious concern in Mexico City, Rio de Janeiro, and Santiago. Because of low growth, highly skewed income distributions, inadequate investments in education and health, and political instability, poverty has remained stubbornly high, creating vicious cycles of increasing natural resource degradation and further loss of income. In another example, measured in the 1980s, differences in air pollution and traffic congestion between slow-growing Manila and fast growing Bangkok were minimal [13]. Fast-growth, with increasing urbanization, industrial expansion, and exploitation of renewable and nonrenewable resources, place pressure on the environment such that many indicators show a decline in the quality of natural capital during growth periods. However, growth creates conditions for environmental improvement by creating demand for better environmental quality and making resources available for improvement.

Not all indicators show worsening environmental conditions among the fast growing economies in Asia. Access to clean water and sanitation increased rapidly in China, Korea, Malaysia, and Thailand. In 1995, the share of the population with access to safe water rose from 71% in 1982 to 89% in Malaysia, from 66 to 89% in Thailand, from 39 to 65% in Indonesia, and from 65 to 83% in the Philippines. Similarly, sanitation service availability rose from 46 to 96% in Thailand, from 30 to 55% in Indonesia, and from 57 to 77% in the Philippines [11]. Though still at low levels in Cambodia, the Lao People's Democratic Republic, and Vietnam, access to safe water and sanitation has been steadily increasing with economic growth [9,11].

While countries embarking on a path of sustainable development can incorporate environmental policies directly into their economic strategy at any time, most countries have followed the grow-now-and-clean-up-later approach. The fast growers among developing countries, such as China, Indonesia, Korea, and Thailand, have paid severely in terms of deteriorating environmental quality. This has recently become an even greater problem for Thailand and Indonesia. When recovering from the economic crisis of 1996–1997, both countries made environmental protection a low funding priority for implementation of even existing environmental policies. Although the economies in the region slowed during 1998 and gradually recovered during 1999 and 2000, the environmental impacts did not follow a similar fluctuating trend and were more or less persistent. For example, the levels of pollution in coastal waters showed no incremental reduction during the 1997–2000 period [14]. Economic growth in the region was, and continues to be, strongly tied to export-oriented policies, high savings rates, sound macroeconomic policies, and strong institutional frameworks [15].

Despite claims that the region contains a "wealth of natural resources" [16] environmental degradation in Asia is indicated by a precipitous decline in living and non-living resources; loss of habitat, species and environmental services; and growing levels of pollution and waste production. Environmental problems are increasingly regional in nature, either because they are common and shared problems, or because their causes or consequences cross borders. The Asia's changing political economy and modes of production contribute to environmental problems. Also subsistence lifestyles, which remain heavily dependent on the direct exploitation of natural resources and environmental services, still constitute the basic means of survival for over half the region's population. However, the leading cause of environmental decline and resource depletion has been the "industrialization of Asia within the world economy" [17]. From an economic perspective, private gains have come at the expense of the public or common good embedded in environmental systems. The environment continues to be exploited in the process of economic activity [18]. The damaging environmental consequences have been and continue to be extensive while the region is becoming "dirtier, less ecologically diverse and more environmentally vulnerable" [19].

Deforestation, desertification, land degradation and the loss of arable land have become enduring features of environmental decline in East Asia. According to the Asian Development Bank [18], "pressure on land in the Asia and Pacific region is most severe…compared to other regions of the world." Deforestation offers some of the most "visible evidence of the rate of environmental change" [17]. Primary forests have been severely depleted and forest cover continues to be lost at a rate of approximately 1 per cent per year [18]. About 20% of vegetated land in East Asia suffers soil degradation from water logging, erosion, and overgrazing. Severe land degradation in China, Thailand, and Vietnam threatens several ecosystems with irreversible damage [11]. Biodiversity in 50%–75% of coastlines and protected marine areas in East Asia is classified as highly threatened.

In this region the rule of law, political stability, and historical context cumulatively play an important role in defining a country's growth. Despite some variability from country to country, Asia has certain commonalities, including, colonial rule accompanied by a lasting influence from Europe and/or the U.S., and political instability, which impact economic growth and the ability to compete in regional and global economic activity [14].

Under the auspices of the Environmental Protection Agency (EPA), the United States has negotiated a number of government-to-government bilateral agreements and has established a series of bilateral environmental programs. It has also supported a feasibility study on the establishment of an Association of South East Asian Nations (ASEAN) network for the assessment and promotion of environmentally sound technologies. However, in spite of growing global demands that the "new" world environmental order should be based on solidarity and collective responsibility, neither U.S. environmental policy towards the region nor the regional consequences of its international environmental policy meets this test. The results of recent research have revealed that the U.S. is fundamentally "self-regarding" rather than "other-regarding" in the various dimensions of its environmental relationship with the region and suggest that the consequences for both the region and for the U.S. may be substantial. Continued environmental degradation in the region has the potential to undermine other U.S. policy goals in terms of its reputation, economic objectives, and even its more orthodox geopolitical security objectives [20]. Moreover, the ASEAN countries have made it quite clear that they wish to see the U.S. reconsider its position on Kyoto in view of the global nature of climate change [21].

Controlling the common causes of global environmental degradation seems daunting because it originates with a large number of economic activities considered essential to growth. Moreover, factors that contribute to environmental degradation differ from nation to nation, depending on the stage of development. For example, most developing nations depend on fossil fuel combustion for economic production and are unlikely to switch to cleaner, but more expensive fuels. While stricter environmental regulations force developed nations to use cleaner and more efficient energy sources, other industrial practices like the use of synthetic fertilizers in modern agri-businesses contribute to the destruction of the ecosystem [22].

In fast and slow growing economies, developing and developed nations, evidence of the declining quality of natural capital indicates heavy costs and diminished prospects for future growth. Segments of the population that are already multiply disadvantaged—the poor, women, and young children—are forced to bear the brunt of environmental degradation. For example, when industrial toxic effluents degrade water quality, the poor often lack access to purified municipal water supplies or the resources to invest in water filters and other purification systems. As a result, human damage may be irreversible, including the loss of genetic material.

The complex causes and effects of global environmental degradation demand development strategies that require adherence to standards of growth that promote sustainability of natural capital and compatibility with domestic and external economic stability. This translates into growth that does not excessively degrade the natural environment and includes the support of the poor and vulnerable. Typically, the state is responsible for development strategies that orchestrate economic growth and environmental management, and, in this role, should focus on collaborative approaches with local communities and the private sector that balance economic and social performance. Global environmental problems, while challenging, do offer opportunities to address national problems if international cooperation can be secured, which in return balances economic and social measures of success [23,24].

While development strategies and plans are essential for highlighting important environmental issues, they are less effective in identifying priorities for action and making explicit the process of necessary policy reform. As a result, policy matters, documentation, and dissemination of successful cases and specific experiences in environmental management take on added importance [23,24]. Therefore, various national, regional, and international agencies have striven to document and share evidence of specific cases of good practices in sustainable development. Yet, the record shows that attempts to reach consensus, set a standard for good practices in sustainable development, and obtain compliance have been less successful in the United States than in Europe.

2.1.4 Sustainable Development in the United States

Serious consideration of sustainable development in American political practice and public policy is relatively recent. Although recognition of its importance is widespread, efforts to translate its implicit principles into political practice have been uncoordinated and inconsistent. At the federal, state, regional, and local levels, however, accumulating evidence shows that many of the ideas advocated by proponents of sustainability are being applied, often experimentally, in different policy domains.

As early as 1993, the National Commission on the Environment, a prestigious group of private individuals including four former heads of the U.S. EPA, called for rethinking environmental policies and urged that "U.S. leadership should be based on the concept of *sustainable development*, and the merging of economic and environmental goals in the concept of sustainable development can and should constitute a central guiding principle for national environmental and economic policymaking" [25].

In 1997, President Clinton took up the challenge by appointing a new President's Council on Sustainable Development. The council, consisting of some twenty-five leaders from industry, government, and the environmental community, met over a period of six years and issued several reports [25]. However, after 1997, the Republican-dominated Congress was indifferent or hostile to the idea of sustainability, and the council's work was largely disregarded by other federal agencies. The EPA did introduce some new community-based environmental protection programs to encourage state and local governments to adopt sustainable development projects, and other departments attempted to define sustainability goals and to remediate environmental degradation caused by federal agencies including the Department of Defense [26].

The federal government continues to promote the concept of sustainable development through incremental, modest innovations in its own structure, such as the Interagency Working Group on Sustainable Development Indicators and numerous study initiatives within virtually all major federal departments. For example, in 2002 and 2003 the EPA initiated several important reforms of innovative community-based approaches to environmental management that focus on citizen participation [27–29]. Several state governments in the U.S. have adopted environmental policy innovations in the management of hazardous waste. These state-sponsored, non-federally mandated initiatives to protect the environment support the general principles of sustainable development [30].

Among federal agencies, the ecological precepts on which sustainability ideas are grounded are being tested and implemented by the major land management agencies—the Bureau of Land Management, the Forest Service, the National Park Service, and the Fish and Wildlife Service—through the development of *ecosystem management*. For the most part, however, sustainable development has been regarded as "someone else's problem" and has remained outside the vocabulary of U.S. politics, particularly at the national level [31].

Since 2001, President George W. Bush has not supported the concept of sustainable development, preferring instead the older concept of environmental "stewardship." His policies appear to assume that scientific and technological advances brought about by global economic growth will allow humans to overcome or adapt to future environmental challenges. As in the Reagan Administration, environmental concerns have been relegated to the margins of policymaking.

In fact, empirical evidence indicates that the U.S. does not fare well on measures of environmental sustainability. One quantitative index, developed at Yale and Columbia Universities, ranks the U.S. 45th out of 146 countries studied—behind nations such as Japan, Germany, Russia, and even Botswana, Croatia, and Estonia [32]. Further, the fact that the U.S. has not ratified international environmental treaties such as the Kyoto Protocol (1997), the Convention on Biological Diversity (1992) and its Biosafety Protocol (2000), the Basel Convention on transboundary movement of hazardous wastes (1989), the Stockholm Convention on persistent organic pollutants (2001), and the Convention on the Law of the Sea (1982) does not speak well of U.S. global environmental stewardship.

President George W. Bush's rejection of the Kyoto Protocol, which entered into effect on February 16, 2005, has isolated the U.S. from virtually all of the rest of the world on climate change diplomacy. More than 140 other nations have ratified the protocol, including all other industrialized nations, except Australia. Moreover, the U.S. has attempted to block negotiations on targets for further greenhouse gas reductions following the end of the Kyoto period in 2012 [33]. President Bush's separate plan for gradually reducing U.S. greenhouse gas "emission intensity" (the volume of emissions per unit of economic output) by inviting companies to voluntarily submit data to a national emissions registry is not likely to have much effect. According to one estimate, under Bush's policy, total U.S. greenhouse gas emissions will *rise* 14% over 2000 levels and 30% above 1990 levels by 2010 [34]. However, Bush's support for new technologies such as vehicles powered by hydrogen fuel cells and zero-emissions coal-fired power plants may help to provide solutions in the decades beyond that [35].

Several climate change bills have been introduced in the U.S. Congress. The Climate Stewardship Act of 2003, sponsored by Senators Joseph Lieberman (Democrat, Connecticut), and John McCain (Republican, Arizona), failed to get passed by a 43–55 vote on October 30, 2003. This bipartisan legislation, which is likely to be considered again in the 109th Congress (2005–2007), would cap greenhouse gas emissions from electricity generation, transportation, industrial, and commercial sectors in the United States at 2000 levels in 2010 and at 1990 levels in 2016 [36,37].

The European Union has already created a cap-and-trade program covering about half of its industrial carbon dioxide emissions, beginning in 2005. Because many multinational corporations are subject to these and other national restrictions (e.g., in Japan and China), pressure will likely mount for a similar

U.S. system that might be linked to an international trading regime in the future [38]. In the meantime, many state and local governments in the U.S. are taking actions to stem greenhouse gas emissions without waiting for the federal government to act [39,40].

The governments of many countries, particularly those associated with the Organization for Economic Cooperation and Development (OECD), have adopted many of the international standards for sustainable development in their national strategies and practices. However, the U.S. remains one of only six of the thirty OECD countries that do not have a national sustainable strategy. The U.S. has instead adopted a decentralized approach and emphasized public/private sustainable development partnership to promote economic growth, social development and environmental "stewardship" [41].

2.2 National Strategies and Good Practices in OECD Countries

Most OECD countries have developed and implemented national strategies for sustainable development (NSSD) in accordance with the 1992 mandate of *Agenda 21*. The sustainable development strategy process offers an opportunity to build on complementary programs in the economic, environmental, and social spheres to improve the long-term effectiveness of government policy agendas. In 2001, the OECD Development Assistance Committee (DAC) developed a set of guidelines to assist developing countries in formulating their national strategies for sustainable development [42]. These guidelines were based on a number of key principles, such as broad consultation, country ownership, and realistic targets. In 2002, the UN Department of Economic and Social Affairs also developed guidelines for preparing a national sustainable strategy [43]. These guidelines focused on five precepts: (1) integrating economic, social, and environmental objectives, and ensuring balance across sectors, territories and generations; (2) ensuring broad participation and effective partnership; (3) promoting country ownership and commitment; (4) developing capacity and an enabling environment; and (5) focusing on outcome and means of implementation. Comparisons show that the UN and OECD guidelines are very similar with regard to a number of criteria (Table 2.1).

The main principles of good practices recognized by the UN and OECD include:

Policy integration—national strategies should give consideration to economic, social and environmental concerns in integrated approaches and plans.

Intergenerational timeframe—national strategies should adopt a long-term timeframe that enables inclusion of intergenerational principles and indicators.

Analysis and assessments—integrated assessment tools should be used to identify the environmental, economic, and social costs and benefits of policy and strategy options.

Indicators and targets—strategies should be based on structured indicator systems to assist in monitoring progress and to serve as quantitative targets.

Table 2.1 Comparison of UN and OECD Principles for National Strategies for Sustainable Development (UN DESA 2002 OECD 2001)

Main Principles	OECD	United Nations
Policy Integration	Integrate economic, social and environmental objectives comprehensive and integrated strategy	Integrate economic, social and environmental objectives link different sectors
Intergenerational timeframe	Consensus on long-term vision	Shared strategic and pragmatic vision link short-term to medium/long term
Analysis and assessments	Base on comprehensive and reliable analysis build on existing processes and strategies	Anchor in sound technical and economic analysis build on existing mechanisms and strategies
Indicators and targets	Targeted with clear budgetary priorities	Realistic, flexible targets
Coordination and institutions	High-level government commitment and influential lead insitutions	Strong institution or group of institutions spearheading the process
Local and regional governance	Link national and local levels	Link national, regional, and global levels
Stakeholder participation	Effective participation people centered	Access to information for all stakeholders transparency and accountability partnership among government, civil, society, private sector, and external institution
Monitoring and evaluation	Incorporate monitoring, learning, and improvement	integrated mechanisms for assessment, follow up, evaluation and feedback

Coordination and institutions—a wide range of government departments and agencies should be involved in the formulation and implementation of national strategies, with overall responsibility in the office of the Prime Minister or equivalent.

Local and regional governance—local and regional authorities should be fully involved in the development of national strategies, with certain delivery aspects assigned to sub-national levels.

Stakeholder participation—stakeholders (e.g., businesses, unions, non-governmental organizations) should participate with government representatives in commissions responsible for developing and implementing national strategies.

Monitoring and evaluation—independent bodies or processes should be established to act as watchdogs monitoring implementation of national strategies and providing recommendations for their improvement.

Table 2.2   Good Practices by Selected OECD Countries (EEAC 2005 UN DESA 2004)

Good Practices	OECD Countries
Policy integration	New Zealand, Norway, Sweden
Integenerational timeframe	Finland, Germany, Sweden
Analysis and assessments	European Union, Switzerland, United Kingdom
Indicators and targets	Austria, Czech Republic, Ireland
Coordination and institutions	Finland, France, Germany
Local and regional governance	Korea, Netherlands, United Kingdom
Stakeholder participation	Czech Republic, Portugal, Slovak Republic
Monitoring and evaluation	Canada, France, United Kingdom

A review of the OECD countries' national strategies shows that many lack the basic design and implementation elements recommended by both the OECD and the UN [44]. There is no single method, specific entry point, or ideal coordinating mechanism for these strategies that will reflect the economic, environmental, social, and cultural specificities of countries. However, the practices in the strategies of the OECD countries that are more likely to yield positive results can be identified, and these, in turn, can inform further analysis and refinement of existing guidelines. The extent to which the OECD countries have followed the guidelines for good practices is reviewed in the remainder of this chapter (Table 2.2).

2.2.1   Policy Integration

The integration of economic, environmental, and social objectives of sustainable development is one of the most difficult balances to achieve in formulating a national strategy. In practice, most national strategies focus on environmental issues with some attempts to incorporate economic aspects. The social dimension has been the most neglected. Seldom are social goals and their relevant indicators woven into a comprehensive strategy. Most commonly, social objectives are simply listed alongside other objectives. As a result, few national strategies develop processes and mechanisms for considering and making trade-offs among economic, environmental, and social objectives in overall policy-making. Moreover, there exist striking differences across countries in how they interpret social objectives—from a focus on the health consequences of environmental policies, to concerns about ethnic minorities and gender balance, to broader considerations about the quality of life, sustainable consumption, and social relations (e.g., poverty, crime, employment, education).

New Zealand gives equal weight to social sustainable development in relation to the economy and environment, with special attention to demographic trends, new roles of women in society, improvements in health and housing, and better integration of Maori communities. Norway includes quantitative targets for enhancing social conditions at home and abroad, particularly human capital, such as level of education, life expectancy, and long-term employment. In Sweden, social considerations are well integrated into the Swedish *National Strategy for Sustainable Development,* including the fight against poverty, sustainable consumption and production, population and public health, social cohesion, welfare and security, employment and learning, and regional and community development [45].

2.2.2 *Intergenerational Timeframe*

In addition to balancing economic, environmental, and social objectives, a basic tenet of sustainable development mandates "meeting the needs of the present generation without compromising the ability of future generations to meet their own needs" [1]. The ever depleting stocks of assets (e.g., man-made, natural, human, and social capital) that underpin sustainable development must be preserved over time. This calls for national strategies that support intergenerational equity by setting long term timeframes in their sustainable development plans.

The national strategies of most countries have specific short-term timeframes (e.g., 2000–2005). Others have medium-term timeframes of ten years, such as the Czech Republic Strategy for Sustainable Development that covers the years 2004–2014. While short and medium-term timeframes facilitate monitoring progress on specific goals and dealing with change within those time periods, they leave national strategies vulnerable to political whims. Although some strategies include an inherent renewal expectation or periodic renewals required by law, they may still be subject to the ideological or political agendas of successive governments. Strategic planning frameworks are more likely to be successful when they are based on long-term vision backed by strong and lasting political commitment.

To this end, Germany and Sweden have adopted timeframes of 18–30 years in their national strategies for sustainable development. Sweden's strategy has a 25 year planning perspective, while allowing that measures taken in accordance with the strategy may need to be reassessed more frequently. The German strategy developed in 2002 contains quantified and time-bound indicators extending to 2020 [46].

While a longer timeframe allows for better incorporation of intergenerational considerations, these are difficult to define and quantify. Finland, Sweden, and Germany have included indicators addressing intergenerational concerns in their strategies. In economic terms, these might relate to relieving public debt; in environmental terms, concern for the preservation of resources; and in social terms, the provision of adequate retirement incomes. Related to the environmental dimension, for example, the Swedish strategy emphasizes that "the overall objective of environmental policy is to hand over a society to the next generation in which the major environmental problems have been solved" [45]. Finland includes intergenerational indicators, such as government financial liabilities and preservation of biodiversity in monitoring its sustainable development. Germany supports intergenerational equity by avoiding high public debt and short-term economic decisions that could increase burdens on future generations.

2.2.3 Analysis and Assessments

Sound analysis and ongoing assessments that utilize existing tools and data, including environmental assessments, cost-benefit analyses, and accounting frameworks play crucial roles in providing information on changing economic, environmental, and social conditions, pressures and responses, and their correlations with strategy objectives and indicators. In the evaluation process, those underlying trade-offs among economic, environmental, and social objectives are identified that can assist in priority setting and policy making for sustainable development. However, with the exception of a few countries, most national strategies lack provisions for systematically assessing the costs and benefits of alternative actions and informing trade-offs across the full range of sustainable development issues.

The most commonly used assessment tools come from the environmental policy field. Environmental Impact Assessments (EIA) attempt to gauge the potential ecological effects of policies before they are implemented. In Canada, the cabinet Directive on the Environmental Assessment of Policy Plan and Program Proposals requires that government agencies incorporate environmental considerations in their reviews of various proposals, including positive and negative effects, and report these to the public. Other countries—including Denmark, Greece, Italy, and Spain—use strategic environmental assessment (SEA) to discern potential outcomes. Ireland and Portugal employ strengths, weaknesses, opportunities, and threats (SWOT) analysis for sustainable assessments and priority setting.

Budget mechanisms that show links between spending decisions and sustainable development impacts are also useful assessment tools. In the Netherlands, each ministry is requested to give an overview of its contribution to sustainable development in its annual budget that is discussed in Parliament. Sweden, Norway and a few other countries have similar green budgeting approaches that outline the potential sustainable development impacts related to public spending on proposed policies and programs.

More sophisticated analytical tools are now being tried in some countries. For example, the United Kingdom's *Sustainable Development Strategy* adopted Integrated Policy Appraisal (IPA) to assess the potential impact of policy proposals in the following categories: public expenditure and economic impacts, regulatory impacts, rural proofing, health impact assessment, environmental appraisal, policy appraisal for equal treatment, and climate change. The assessments are used to better understand linkages among economic, social, and environmental systems and to assist government departments in assessing the total sustainability impacts of policy proposals [47]. Switzerland uses a newer tool, Strategic Sustainability Assessments (SSA), in its planning processes to review sustainable development linkages and the overall effects of potential policies and actions. For example, SSA is used to evaluate the impact of draft legislation and development projects on economic, environmental, and social dimensions of sustainable development and to identify potential deficiencies early enough in the process to influence the direction taken [48]. Similarly, the *European Union Strategy for Sustainable Development* established that all major legislative proposals should undergo Sustainability Assessments, meaning "an assessment of the potential economic, environmental and social benefits and costs of action or lack of action, both inside and outside the EU" [49]. Proposals should include, where relevant, the effects of gender equality and equal opportunities and should identify the groups who bear the burden of change so that policy makers can judge the need for measures to help these groups adapt.

2.2.4   Indicators and Targets

The development and incorporation of quantitative indicators can help to minimize the discrepancies between the intended outcomes set forth in national strategies and what is or can be realized in practice. Statistics and indicators make it easier to identify and assess trade-offs among the economic, environmental, and social dimensions of sustainable development. Indicators can be used to track progress along sustainable paths and define performance targets. They also contribute to policy transparency and accountability in sustainable development strategies.

Most OECD countries have developed a set of indicators as part of their national strategies. These indicators vary widely across countries and are generally organized according to specific themes and sub-themes. Some strategies specify relatively few, mostly environmental, indicators. Others adopt large indicator systems. The New Zealand Program of Action is based on 40 indicators that provide insight on the themes of population changes, environmental and ecosystem resilience, economic growth and innovation, skills and knowledge, living standards and health, consumption and resource use, and social cohesion. Switzerland monitors sustainable development according to the MONET indicator system, which includes 115 indicators for 26 themes, allowing it to track the current situation and trends as well as the country's position relative to other countries [48].

A few countries are refining their structural approaches and choice of indicators as they revise their national strategies. In Norway, a special commission proposed a new indicator set to monitor the Norwegian Action Plan for Sustainable Development, *National Agenda 21*. This includes 16 indicators that identify and assess the welfare effects of the various components of national wealth: financial capital, real capital, human capital, natural capital and environmental capital. Finland developed its first set of indicators in 2000 and revised and broadened them in 2004 to include 68 indicators in eight categories and three sustainable development dimensions.

Some countries regularly track their progress on the basis of sustainability indicators, and a few have established quantified time-bound targets. For example, the German strategy uses indicators in fiscal, economic, education, research, housing, special planning, crime prevention, energy, and environmental areas as targets. The U.K.'s new strategy, *Securing the Future*, contains 68 indicators, 20 of which are linked to specific quantifiable goals. Progress on indicators is reported annually, and a "traffic light" approach is used to show areas of improvement and deterioration [47].

However, the most comprehensive and overall Good Practices of Indicators and Targets are found in Austria, Czech Republic, and Ireland. The Austrian *Strategy for Sustainable Development* specifies 52 indicators in four action fields—Austria's quality of life, Austria as a dynamic business location, Austria as a living space, and Austria's global responsibility—and includes 20 key objectives with quantified time-bound goals. The Czech Republic strategy outlines two sets of indicators, each organized according to six categories: economic, environmental, social, research and development and education, European and international context, and good governance. One set (116 indicators) is used to monitor progress on specific elements, while the other set (24 indicators) is used in communications with policy makers and the public. In Ireland, the government's work program to develop indicators of sustainable development to implement the *Strategy for Ireland* includes the formulation of green national accounts and satellite accounting approaches to supplement economic accounts.

2.2.5 Coordination and Institutions

Achieving sustainable development depends heavily on high-level political commitment, well-functioning government institutions, and overcoming coordination failures in public policies. Involving and coordinating a wide range of government departments compel strategists to take a broad view of issues, give voice to a range of dispersed interests, and develop trade-offs across policy areas. However, more important than all-inclusiveness is placement of responsibility for overseeing the different participating agencies and coordinating strategy implementation to achieve maximum coherence. Assigning responsibility for implementation of a national strategy to a department that lacks authority over other agencies it will oversee will not be effective. The best approach is to assign overall coordination to a prime minister's or president's office which has greater authority than line ministries to demand inputs and resolve conflicts, which is the case in France, Finland, Portugal, and Germany. The national implementation mechanisms of each country varies and reflects whether its sustainable development strategy provides an overarching framework for action or is a less effective collection of existing or fragmented strategies.

In most OECD countries, overall responsibility for strategy implementation is housed in the Ministry of Environment, either directly or indirectly, through a coordinating committee which it oversees. This is true for Austria, Belgium, Denmark, Greece, Italy, Ireland, Luxembourg, the Netherlands, and the U.K. Although the U.K. replaced its Green Cabinet with a Sustainable Development

Cabinet, the Department of Environment, Food and Rural Affairs (DEFRA) leads the preparation of sustainable development strategies and manages implementation across the government. In 2005, Sweden changed its Environment Ministry into the Ministry of Sustainable Development, responsible for coordinating the government's work on sustainable development.

Another approach is to assign responsibility for national sustainability strategies to finance ministries that can assure that strategic management is linked to fiscal priority setting, national expenditure, and revenue generation. Norway has placed responsibility for its sustainable development plan in the Ministry of Finance, while in the Czech Republic, the Governmental Council for Sustainable Development is chaired by the Deputy Minister for Economic Affairs.

In some countries, individual ministries or agencies are responsible for preparing and implementing strategies that remain largely uncoordinated. Canada has a system in which each governmental department develops its own sustainable development strategy and approach; however, it is now attempting to formulate an overall national plan and related coordinating mechanism.

The most comprehensive overall Good Practices in Coordination and Institutions are found in Finland, France, and Germany. In Finland, the National Commission on Sustainable Development is responsible for the preparation and implementation of the national strategy and is chaired by the Prime Minister. Similarly, in France, the inter-Ministerial Committee for Sustainable Development, chaired by the Prime Minister, has overall responsibility for France's sustainable development strategy. And in Germany, the Federal Chancellery is formally in charge of both the formulation and implementation of the national strategy for sustainable development, overseeing the input of various Ministries and retaining the last word in inter-ministerial disagreements.

2.2.6   Local and Regional Governance

Sustainable development strategies should involve local authorities and be a two-way interactive process between national and local governmental entities. The main strategic principles and directions should be set at the central level, but the more detailed planning, implementation and monitoring can also be undertaken at a decentralized level, with appropriate transfer of resources and authority. Under the best of conditions, orchestrating sustainable development initiatives is not easy, but when different geographical jurisdictions have competing agendas, the task can be onerous. Only a few OECD governments have attempted to fully coordinate with the sustainable development efforts at sub-national government levels.

Coordination among different levels of government is inherently more difficult in federal states (e.g., Australia, Belgium, Canada, and Switzerland) where powers over sustainable development policies are divided among various levels of government. The decentralized institutional structure in federal countries often requires special procedures to leverage change and implement sustainable development strategies. Canada's lack of a national strategy is in part attributed to the enormous time-consuming joint effort it would take to coordinate its federal and provincial governments.

Some countries have developed separate but equal approaches for devolved regions. The United Kingdom developed a U.K. strategic framework for sustainable development, but with emphasis on delivery at the regional level in Scotland, Wales, and Northern Ireland. France devotes attention to the "territories" in its sustainable development strategy that encompasses both regional and sub-regional levels of government [47].

Countries such as France and Portugal have fully included local and regional authorities in the preparation of their national sustainable development strategies. The U.K. also has a strong local component in its strategy, including Local Strategic Partnerships and Sustainable Community Plans. Some countries (e.g., Denmark, Iceland, Ireland, Korea) are coordinating national and local implementation of sustainable development strategies through local Agenda 21 processes. Chapter 28 of Agenda 21 contains guidance for local initiatives in support of their overall goals where local authorities are asked to develop their own sub-strategies to suit their economies and specific circumstances.

The overall most comprehensive Good Practices in Local and Regional governance are found in Korea, Netherlands, and the U.K. In Korea, in accordance with its *National Environmental Vision for the New Millennium*, regional governments have adopted a Local Agenda 21 which is coordinated by the Korean Council for Local Agenda 21. In the Netherlands, the *National Strategy for Sustainable Development* gives general guidance for sustainability processes at sub-national levels that are to be tailored to the local situation. The U.K.'s shared framework for sustainable development, *One Future—Different Paths*, establishes common goals for England, Scotland, Wales and Northern Ireland without compromising the strengths offered by regional delivery and a diversity of approaches.

2.2.7 Stakeholder Participation

Active stakeholder participation (e.g., businesses, trade unions, non-governmental organizations, indigenous peoples) should be an inherent feature in the development and implementation of national strategies for sustainable development. Sustainable development involves trade-offs among economic, social, and ecological objectives that should not be determined by governments alone. Decisions and value judgments, which involve and affect the public, require participatory approaches that should engage this same public through effective communication. Ultimately, the extent of stakeholders' involvement in policy processes depends upon national institutional settings and preferences. Structures vary widely across OECD countries in terms of the status, timing, and breadth of involvement of stakeholders.

Several countries have implemented ad hoc participation processes, in which stakeholders are consulted in the development of national strategies, but less so in implementation and subsequent development phases. Public surveys of varying magnitudes have been used to solicit comments on draft strategies.

For example, in Belgium, the Preliminary Draft Plan for sustainable development was placed on a public website and subsidies were given to public interest associations to support information projects related to the consultation. In Finland, stakeholder groups were asked to prepare their own sustainable development strategies in tandem to the government strategy, as part of the National Sustainable Development Partnership Process; this led to a number of partnerships, for example, on sustainable transport solutions, protection of the Baltic Sea, and others.

Some countries include stakeholders on special commissions and councils that provide advice to but are separate from the government bodies that implement the strategies. These include the Federal Sustainable Development council in Belgium, the National Council for Sustainable Development in France, the Council on Sustainable Development in Germany, the National Sustainable Development Council in Ireland, and the Sustainable Development Commission in the U.K.

Other countries include stakeholders alongside government bodies as part of their overall coordination structure for sustainable development. These include the Committee for a Sustainable Austria, the Government Council for Sustainable Development in the Czech Republic, the National Commission on Sustainable Development in Finland, the National Sustainable Development Council in Ireland, the Board of Sustainable Development in Poland, the Council for the Environment and Sustainable Development in Portugal, and the Commission for Sustainable Development in the Slovak Republic.

Ideally, national strategies for sustainable development should be implemented by bodies with wide representation from social partners and other stakeholders in order to promote consultation, dialogue, and more innovative approaches. The overall Good Practices in Stakeholder Participation are found in the Czech Republic, Portugal, and the Slovak Republic. In the Czech Republic, the Government Council for Sustainable Development includes the government, businesses, academics, NGOs and other stakeholders and serves as the umbrella group for developing, implementing, and revising the national sustainable development strategy. In Portugal, one of the four principles of the national strategy is to progress towards a society of solidarity and knowledge. This principle includes interventions to strengthen the citizen components of education and greater access to information and participation in decision-making, which is exemplified in the Council for the Environment and Sustainable Development. The Slovak Republic has broad consultations with stakeholders in the development of its national strategy and includes the main business and non-governmental groups on the *Slovakian Commission for Sustainable Development* to oversee implementation.

2.2.8 *Monitoring and Evaluation*

National strategies for sustainable development are not meant to be static plans, but rather dynamic processes that evolve as more information becomes available about priorities, technological options, policy cost-effectiveness, and viable problem-solving techniques of implementation. Learning, adaptation, and continual improvement should be characteristics of national strategies. This ideally requires an external, independent agency or process to monitor the implementation of national sustainable development strategies, as well as feed back for necessary adjustments and improvements.

Both Canada and the U.K. have opted for an independent auditing process as learning tools for sustainable development. In Canada, the Commissioner of the Environment and Sustainable Development (CESD) in the Office of the Auditor General is responsible for reporting to the parliament on the extent to which departments are implementing and achieving the goals and objectives laid out in their sustainable development strategies. These strategies must be reviewed, revised, and retabled every three years, in order to provide a regular opportunity for learning and adaptation. In the U.K., the role of the Sustainable Development Commission, established in 2000, was strengthened in 2005 so that it moved from "critical friend" to "watchdog"; it utilized both the National Audit Office and the Audit Commission to oversee implementation of the national strategy. New Zealand has appointed a similar but more limited Parliamentary Commissioner for the Environment, who primarily audits the Environment Ministry.

France developed a methodology for a unique peer review process to promote experience sharing with other countries in support of the continual improvement of its national strategy. In February 2005, France subjected its own national strategy to a peer review by a group of four peer partner countries—Belgium, Ghana, Mauritius and the U.K. The peers made 13 general and 42 specific recommendations, including how to promote sustainable development partnerships with developing countries, establish more participatory processes, and ensure effective monitoring of the national sustainable development strategy. The French hope "that this approach will be found to have generic value that can be used (and developed further) by other countries through similar exercise" [50].

Other countries are also developing oversight bodies. Belgium assigned this task to the Federal Planning Bureau in which a task force periodically reports on the quality of the federal government's sustainable development policies and programs. In 2004, Germany established a Parliamentary Committee for Sustainable Development that calls for plenary debates and gives recommendations to the federal government regarding strategy implementation.

Overall, the most comprehensive Good Practices in Monitoring and Evaluation are found in Canada, France, and the U.K. In 1995, Canada established a Commissioner of the Environment and Sustainable Development (CESD) to audit the sustainable development strategies of different government departments and report each year to Parliament on progress and challenges in implementation. France initiated peer reviews of national strategies for sustainable development involving civil society, international organizations, and other countries that make recommendations on the process, content, indicators and implementation. In the U.K., the Commissioner on Sustainable Development (CSD) has been assigned a reinforced "watchdog" role beginning in 2006, whereby it will monitor implementation of the U.K. strategy and report regularly to the Prime Minister on strengths and weaknesses [47].

2.3   Conclusion

The concept of sustainable development as a constraint to unchecked growth is gaining support from governments, corporations, and environmental groups around the world. It is foolhardy, even dangerous, to ignore the precaution that growth should not exceed levels consistent with the health and well being of future generations. However, this happens in the frenzy to be competitive in the world economy when nations follow a globalization process founded upon an upward, unlimited, and unchecked economic growth model that seriously threatens our global future. The process inevitably leads to the exhaustion of many of the world's natural resources, such as fauna, flora, and non-renewable sources of energy, as well as to the deterioration of natural processes that are crucial for any ecosystem's viability of life on the planet. Kenneth Boulding, a leading pioneer of sustainability, sarcastically quipped, "Anyone who believes that exponential growth can go on forever in a finite world is either a madman...or an economist" [52]. Others who understand the gravity of unbridled growth point also to the growing awareness of the social unsustainability of the current style of development, that is, globalization, taking place in the midst of increasing social inequality and exclusion, a reality which certainly precedes but also has been exacerbated by the very process of globalization [51].

The concept of sustainable development itself has many meanings and requires much more discussion and research than it has had so far in the U.S. However one defines sustainable development, concrete indicators are still urgently needed to measure progress toward it in different sectors. Traditional measures of economic welfare are just no longer adequate. Standard national accounting indices that measure gross national product or gross domestic product in monetary terms fail to capture many facets of human and environmental well being. For example, these indices count all expenditures for pollution control and cleanup as part of the output of goods and services but do not subtract the economic value of losses caused by environmental degradation and depletion of nonrenewable resources. Increased pollution thus counts positively rather than negatively, whereas depreciation of environmental capital is ignored. A number of scholars and international agencies, including the World Bank, have been developing alternative measures of welfare that more accurately value environmental goods and services and overall quality of life. The U.S. does considerably worse on some of these scales than on conventional economic indices.

Beyond economic indicators, the development not only of better measures of environmental quality per se—that is, the health of ecosystems and the limits to the stresses we can place on them—but also of improved gauges of progress in human activity to reduce society's impacts on natural systems is essential. For example, all nations need to focus on trends in energy consumption, green house gas emissions, land use, waste generation, recycling, and reuse of materials, agricultural practices, and driving habits. However, broad social and cultural factors, such as income inequality, population growth, educational patterns, political representation, and access to information, can also be considered important indicators of sustainability. Many governmental and nongovernmental organizations are working on such indicators, including the EPA and other federal agencies and state and local bodies [52]. Until we begin to think differently and creatively about basic indicators of success, we are unlikely to make genuine progress toward sustainable development.

Although significant changes do not require that we change the whole world all at once, they do require that we draw more complex connections between sustainability and our everyday habits and behaviors, that we act politically at the local level to infuse sustainability within the civic life of communities, and, more importantly, that we recognize an allegiance to our global community. The movement toward a sustainable world requires far more international cooperation and governance than we now have [53]. The challenges we face are ultimately human and political—meeting basic human needs, limiting population growth, restricting consumption of nonrenewable resources, building a sense of world community, and negotiating mutually beneficial agreements among nations. These global sustainable goals can be achieved only within an extended, intergenerational timeframe with a collaborative, enlightened, and powerful political leadership at the helm.

References

1. World Commission on Environment and Development (WCED). *Our Common Future*, Oxford University Press, Oxford, 1987.
2. Cicin-Sain, B., Sustainable development and integrated coastal management, *Ocean and Coastal Management*, 21, 11, 1993.
3. Matsui, Y., The road to sustainable development: Evolution of the concept of development in the UN, in *Sustainable Development and Good Governance*, K. Gunther *et al.*, Eds., Kluwer Academic Publishers, Amsterdam, 1995, 67–83.
4. Birnie, P.W., The law of the sea and the united nations conference on environment and development, in *Ocean Yearbook*, E. Mann-Borghese, Ed., University of Chicago Press, Chicago, 1993, 77–85.
5. Chasek, P., The story of the UNCED process, in *Negotiating International Regimes: Lessons Learned from the United Nations Conference on Environment and Development*, G. Sjostedt *et al.*, Eds., Graham and Trotman, London, 1994, 45.
6. Caldwell, L.K., *International Environmental Policy: Emergence and Dimensions*, 2nd ed., Duke University Press, Durham, NC, 1990.
7. United Nations Conference on Environment and Development (UNCED). *Agenda 21: Program of Action for Sustainable Development*, United Nations Department of Public Information, New York, 1992.
8. Lang, W., How to manage sustainable development? in in *Sustainable Development and Good Governance*, K. Gunther *et al.*, Eds., Kluwer Academic Publisher, Amsterdam 1995, 94.
9. World Bank, *World Development Indicators*, World Bank Publications, The World Bank Group, Washington, D.C., 1999.
10. World Bank, *The Quality of Growth*, Oxford University Press, New York, 2000.
11. World Bank, Environmental implications of the economic crisis and adjustment in East Asia, *East Asia environment and social development unit discussion paper*, Vol.1, World Bank Publications, The World Bank Group, Washington, D.C., 1999.
12. Thomas, V. and Belt, T., Growth and environment: Allies or foes, *Finance and Development*, 34, 22, 1997.

13. Hammer, J. S. and Shelty, S., East Asia's environment: Principles and priorities for action, *World Bank discussion paper*, Vol. 287, World Bank, Washington, D.C., 1995.
14. Adeel, Z., *Introduction to environmental governance concepts in East Asian context* East Asian Experiences on Environmental Governance, United Nations University Press, New York, 2003.
15. Weder, B., *Model, Myth, or Miracle? Reassessing the Role of Governments in East Asian Experience*, United Nations Press, Tokyo, 1999.
16. Rabasa, A., The changing political-military environment: Southeast Asia, in *The United States and Asia: Towards a New US Strategy and Force Posture*, Z. Khalilzad *et al.*, Eds., RAND, Santa Monica, CA, 2001, 3.
17. Vervoorn, A., *Re-orient: Change in Asian Societies*, Oxford University Press, Oxford, 1998.
18. Asian Development Bank., *Southeast Asia Sub-Regional Report for the World Summit on Sustainable Development*, Asian Development Bank Publications, New York, 2001.
19. Asian Development Bank. *Emerging Asia: Changes and Challenges*, Asian Development Bank, Manila, 1997.
20. Elliott, L., Environmental protection and US–Asia relations: A policy of disconnect, *The Pacific Review*, 17, 291, 2004.
21. ASEAN Secretariat. *Report to the World Summit on Sustainable Development*, ASEAN Secretariat, Jakarta, 2002.
22. Tilman, D., Forecasting agriculturally driven global environmental changes, *Science*, 292, 281, 2001.
23. Prizzia, R., The impact of development and privatization environmental protection: An international perspective, *Environment, Development, and Sustainability*, 4, 315, 2002.
24. Prizzia, R., Globalization, privatization, and environmental protection: An international perspective, *The ICFAI Journal of Environmental Economics*, 1, 7, 2003.
25. President's Council on Sustainable Development (PCSD). *Sustainable America and sustainable development: A new consensus*, US Government Printing Office, Washington, D.C., 1996. President's Council on Sustainable Development (PCSD). *Building on consensus: A progress report on sustainable America*, President's Council on Sustainable Development, Washington, D.C., 1996.
26. Prizzia, R., Natural attenuation as a viable remediation method, *Environmental Management and Health*, 2, 428, 2001.
27. Prizzia, R., Citizen participation in environmental administration: The role of restoration advisory board, *National Resources and Environment Administration*, 25, 1, 2004.
28. Prizzia, R., Community involvement in protecting the environment, *The Innovation Journal: The Public Sector Innovation Journal*, 10(1), 2005, (Special Issue on Citizen Engagement and Empowerment), 1–6, 2005.
29. Irvin, R.A. and Stansbury, J., Citizen participation in decision making: Is it worth the effort? *Public Administration Review*, 64, 55, 2004.
30. Sapat, A., Devolution and innovation: The adoption of state environmental policy innovations by administrative agencies, *Public Administration Review*, 64, 141, 2004.
31. Bryner, G.C., The United States: "Sorry—not our problem", in *Implementing Sustainable Development: Strategies and Initiatives in High Consumption Societies*, M.W. Lafferty and J. Meadowcroft, Eds., Oxford University Press, Oxford, 2000, 273.
32. Esty, D.C., Levy, M., Srebotnjak, T., and de Sherbinin, A., *Environmental Sustainability Index: Benchmarking National Environmental Stewardship*, Yale Center for Environmental Law & Policy, New Haven, CT, 2005.
33. Rohter, L., U.S. waters down global commitment to curb greenhouse cases, *New York Times*, December 19, 2004.
34. Claussen, E., Climate change solutions: A science and policy agenda, December 6, 2004, available at www.pewclimate.org/press_room/speech_transcripts/climatechange.cfm (accessed on February 28, 2005).

35. Department of Energy (DOE), Department of energy FY2006 Congressional Budget Request: Budget Highlights, February, 2005, available at www.mbe.doe.gov/budget/06budget/Content/Highlights/06_highlights.pdf (accessed on February 28, 2005).

36. Seelye, K.Q., McCain and Lieberman office bill to require cuts in gases, *New York Times*, January 9, 2003.

37. Pianin, E., Senate rejects mandatory cap on greenhouse gas emissions, *Washington Post*, October 31, 2003.

38. Lander, M., Mixed feelings as treaty on greenhouse gases takes effect, *New York Times*, Business Section, February 16, 2005.

39. Sanders, E., Rebuffing bush, 132 mayors embrace kyoto rules, *New York Times*, May 14, 2005.

40. Pew Center for Global Climate Change (PCGCC), Learning from state action on climate change, December, 2004, available at www.pewclimate.org/policy_center/policy_reports_and_analysis/states/index.cfm (accessed on February 28, 2005).

41. European Environment and Sustainable Development Advisory Councils (EEAC), *Sustaining sustainability: A Benchmark Study on National Strategies Towards Sustainable Development and the Impact of Councils in Nine EU Member States*, EEAC series, Background Study Vol. 2, Lemma Publishers, Utrecht, 2005, available at http://www.eeac-net.org/workgroups/sustdey_SDBenchmark.htm (accessed on February, 2005).

42. OECD, *The DAC guidelines: Strategies for sustainable development: Guidance for development cooperation*, Development Assistance Committee, 2001, available at http://www.oecd.org/dataoecd/34/10/266958.pdf (accessed on May 10, 2006).

43. UN Department of Economic and Social Affair (UN DESA), *Guidance in Preparing a National Sustainable Development Strategy: Managing Sustainable Development in the New Millennium*, 2002, available at http://www.un.org/esa/sustdev/publications/nsds_guidance.pdf (accessed 2005).

44. Cherp, A., George, C., and Kirkpatrick, C., A methodology for assessing national sustainable development strategies, *Environment and Planning C: Government and Policy*, 22, 6, 2004.

45. Swedish Government, A summary of government communication 2001/02.172 Sweden's national strategy for sustainable development 2002, Stockholm, Sweden, 2002.

46. Federal Government of Germany (FGG). *Perspectives of Germany: Our Strategy for Sustainable Development*, Federal Government of Germany, Berlin, 2002.

47. U.K. Government (U.K.G), Sustainable development commission: About the commission, available at http://www.sd-commission.gov.uk/commission/index.htm (accessed on February 2004).

48. Swiss Federal Council (SFC). *Sustainable Development Strategy 2002*, Berne, Switzerland, 2002.

49. Organization for Economic Cooperation and Development (OECD), Environmental Performance Reviews—Poland, Paris, Mexico, 2003.

50. French Government, The French national strategy for sustainable development: Report on a peer and shared learning process, Ministry of Ecology and Sustainable Development and Ministry of Foreign Affairs, 2005.

51. Stiglitz, J., *Globalization and its Discontents*, WW. Norton & Co., New York, 2002.

52. Kates, R.W., Parris, T.M., and Leiserowitz, A.A., What is sustainable development? *Environment*, 47, 8, 2005.

53. Dunn, S. and Flavin, C., Moving the climate change agenda forward, in *State of the World*, Worldwatch Institute, Washington D.C., 2002, 24.

Chapter 3

European Global Warming Policy

David Howard Davis
University of Toledo

3.1 Introduction

Two years ago, the Kyoto Protocol entered into force, to the surprise of many observers, who believed the American rejection doomed it to oblivion. Because the limits to carbon affect all industry, it is potentially the most influential environmental treaty that has ever been drawn. In the fourteen years since the Rio Earth Summit and the nine years since the Kyoto conference, the United States (U.S.) and Europe have taken divergent roles. Indeed, they now stand on opposite sides. The U.S. and Europe differ on the Kyoto Protocol in terms of governmental structure, the role of bureaucracy and attitude. Moreover, since the Rio Summit in 1992, the European Union has emerged as a body capable of uniting the diverse policies and agencies of twenty-five countries. The European Union and the climate change program have evolved together.

3.2 The European Union Commission

Compared to the U.S., Europe, in both its unified and pre-unified forms, has depended more on bureaucratic agencies. Today, the key player in climate policy is the EU Commission, located in Brussels. More specifically, the lead agency is the Directorate General for the Environment, with secondary roles played by the Directorates General for Enterprise and for Energy and Transport.

Their rivalries and competing interests parallel the U.S. situation with respect to the Environmental Protection Agency (EPA) versus the Treasury, Commerce and Energy Departments. The Commission is staffed by career civil servants drawn from all member states. Upon becoming employees, they take an oath to serve the Council only, and not to represent the interests of their home countries.

The Commission's two main duties are (1) to initiate and define new environmental legislation, and (2) to ensure that measures, which have been agreed upon, are actually put into practice in the member states. Unlike most legislatures, civil servants, not elected politicians, propose the exact text of a bill. Of course, they have already been negotiating for as long as a year, with the key members of Parliament, the Council of Ministers and interest groups before actually introducing the bill. The first step in the legislation process occurs in the Parliament, and if approved, the second step takes place in the Council of Ministers.

The European Parliament consists of 732 members elected directly by the citizens of the member countries. The size of a country's delegation is tied roughly to its population, ranging from ninety-nine for Germany to six for Luxembourg. The Parliament has a Committee on the Environment, Public Health and Consumer Policy with fifty-eight members. Officially, the seat of the Parliament is Strasbourg, but it often meets in Brussels where it holds most committee sessions. Over the years, the role of the Parliament has been evolving from merely advisory to acting more like a real legislature. The Parliament has authority in certain areas, but not others. For example, it cannot legislate on matters of a common foreign policy or defense, but it can do so on matters of the environment or health or safety. It is organized into Groups (that is political parties) who consult with the Directorate General staff. Coordination comes from a rapporteur from the largest Group, as well as shadow rapporteurs from the other Groups. While usually the Groups are the key to support and opposition, this is not always true. Sometimes the parliamentarians choose to vote by nationality.

All but a few parliamentarians belong to a Group, such as the Christian Democrats or the Socialists, which are trans-national political parties. Forty-two parliamentarians are Greens, making it a medium sized Group. Its co-president is Daniel Cohn-Bendit of France, who, a quarter of a century ago, won international fame as a student revolutionary during the Events of May in Paris. At that time he won the nickname of Danny the Red for both the color of his hair and his leftist politics. Other parliamentary Groups also are sympathetic to the environment, such as the United Left-Nordic Green Left Group. The Greens consider their first priority supporting sustainable development. With respect to climate change, they believe that the EU proposals are too weak, and they have pushed for prompt adoption of the Kyoto Protocol. The Greens have other interests besides the environment, and recently have added the term Free Alliance to their name to reflect their concerns with the Iraq War and economic development in the Third World, as well as environmental ones like clean air and water and genetically modified food. In 2004 all the green parties in Europe founded a combined party to coordinate campaigns for the Parliament. Like the American Congress, the European Parliament asks its lobbyists to register, and in so doing have produced a list of hundreds. While a few of them are pro-environmental, many more are pro-industry.

Once the proposed legislation is passed by the Parliament, it goes to the Council of Ministers in one of its nine configurations. The Council consists of ministers of the governments of each of the EU member states. One of its configurations is for environmental issues, in which case it consists of the environmental ministers of the twenty-five member states. For hammering out the details, the Council of Ministers convenes a Working Group, consisting of two or three civil servants from each of the member states, in other words not the EU bureaucrats. On average, Working Groups are able to resolve about 70% of the problems. The next step is that the proposed legislation is up for consideration by the Committee of Permanent Representatives (COREPER), which consists of the ambassadors or their deputies from member states stationed in Brussels. They are usually able to resolve another 10–15% of the problems. At this stage the legislative proposals go up to the full Council of Ministers (in its environmental configuration). The proposal now returns to the Parliament for its agreement. When agreement is not possible, both the Parliament and the Council of Ministers appoint members to a Conciliation Committee.

With respect to climate change policy, the Commission staffs the EU delegations to the annual Conferences of the Parties established by the Framework Convention on Climate Change signed at the Rio Summit in 1992. Delegates come from a range of Directorates General. The Environmental branch is always represented, but so are the Enterprise and the Energy and Transport branches, assuring that business has its say. Others come from the planners in Economy and Finance, as well as experts from Research and from Development. Members of the Parliament, which are often part of the delegation, but they do not serve as negotiators [1]. In comparison to the U.S., career civil servants are much more important.

The Environment Directorate General has a staff of 550. Its current Action Programme, the sixth, will run to 2011. It concentrates on climate change, biodiversity, health, natural resources and waste. In the last decade or so, its programs have shifted from command and control to market based solutions, following the trend in Britain, the U.S. and elsewhere. Critics of the Commission claim that it sometimes makes arbitrary decisions. Unlike the situation in a single country, these Brussels bureaucrats can impose detailed requirements with little control by an elected parliament. This "democracy deficit," as it is called, causes resentment.

The European Union traces its history back to the Coal and Steel Community, established in 1951, a genesis that would seem to be the antithesis of an effort to reduce carbon. It consisted of France, West Germany, Italy, Belgium, Luxembourg, and the Netherlands. Six years later, the Treaty of Rome united these same six countries into the Common Market. Its goals were economic integration through eliminating tariffs and allowing workers and investment to move freely. Environmental protection was not included. It was only twelve years since the end of World War II, and the continent was still recovering industrially. Moreover, public and elite awareness about the environment was minimal, a situation mirrored on the other side of the Atlantic.

The European Community, as it styled itself at that time, passed its first environmental directive in 1967, setting standards for classifying, packaging and labeling dangerous substances. The aim, however, was more to facilitate trade than to protect the environment. Twelve years later, it promulgated detailed regulations to control hazardous chemicals. In 1972, the Community began to write a formal policy and established the Environment and Consumer Protection Service as part of its Industrial Policy Directorate. The Service was later moved out of the Industrial Directorate. Although regulations and standards were issued piecemeal, by 1987 there were a total of 150. Most were concerned with water and air pollution. The Commission on the Rhine River, established in 1816, was brought under the EC aegis. The Rhine had been polluted by salt, heavy metals, and chemicals, and the Danube had suffered from similar pollution. Other water problems were found in the Mediterranean, Baltic, and North Seas.

In 1973, the Environment Directorate set out its first Action Programme, which might be classified as pre-environmental since it declared its goal was quality of life. This reflected the limited authority under the Treaty of Rome; however, this shifted as time went on as the Directorate issued a new Action Programme about every five or ten years. In 1981 the organization became a Directorate General with a staff of one hundred fifty. Today, it is one of thirty-six Directorates General and specialized service agencies which make up the Commission.

Under the Treaty of Rome, environmental protection had to be justified under provisions for trade, but the Single European Act, signed in 1986, included a title on environmental protection, designated Articles 130 r–t. The articles listed the objectives of protecting the environment and ensuring a prudent and rational utilization of natural resources. It enumerated the principles of preventive action and declared that damage should be rectified at the source, and that the polluter should pay for any damage. Voting would be on the basis of a qualified majority, not unanimity. This would prevent a veto by allowing passage by a majority, albeit greater than a simple majority of half. This qualified majority does not operate for taxes, which must be passed unanimously. By this point the original six countries were joined by six others: Britain, Ireland and Denmark in 1973, Greece in 1981, and Spain and Portugal in 1985. Later, three more joined: Sweden, Finland and Austria.

Another environmental bureaucracy exists, but one with little policy importance. The European Environment Agency, which was established by the Council in 1990, is charged with gathering technical data. The Environment Agency got off to a slow start, not beginning operations until 1994. It manages the European environment information and observation network (EIONET), and considers its role to be restricted to data collection and analysis. It denies that it is a regulator, a policy maker, or a research body. From time to time, the suggestion is made that it should inspect the inspectors—in other words, it should audit the environmental agencies of the member states—but in the view of most on the Council, this would give the agency too much power. Agency membership extends beyond the Union by including Switzerland and several Balkan countries. It has a budget of 25 million euros (US $30 million) and a staff of one hundred. Its headquarters are located in Copenhagen.

3.3   Climate Change Treaty Structure

In 1992, the United Nations sponsored the Earth Summit in Rio de Janeiro, where 160 nations signed the Framework Convention on Climate Change. Seven years earlier, at a technical workshop in Villach, Austria, the scientific consensus had established with certainty that the earth was warming, and that greenhouse gases were the cause, the primary gas being carbon dioxide. Only three years later, 340 scientists and government officials meeting in Toronto recommended a solution. First and foremost, the industrial First World should reduce its output of greenhouse gases by 20%. Furthermore, all countries should agree to a comprehensive treaty, and the industrial countries should establish a fund to pay compensation to the developing ones. The rationale for this financial aid was that the First World had had more than a century to gain the benefits of industrialization, whereas the Third World had not. Forcing them to meet the higher standard would condemn them to permanent poverty.

After signing the Framework Convention in Rio, the parties agreed to confer annually to develop specific solutions to the problem. For several years the Conferences of the Parties labored, but in 1997 they proposed a treaty, known as a protocol, for signature at the meeting in Kyoto, Japan. This established quotas for each industrial country, expressed in terms of a percentage reduction of greenhouse gases from their 1990 levels. (A list of them appeared in Annex B of the treaty, hence they were known as Annex B countries.) The developing countries were exempt. This included China, which was the world's second largest emitter of greenhouse gases, as well as India, and other developing nations that emitted large amounts. Russia and Ukraine got quotas based on their emissions seven years earlier, which was before their economies had collapsed and when they were at a high point of burning coal and oil in old fashioned, inefficient factories and electric generating plants. The industrial countries signed the Protocol, and the developing countries, of course, were pleased.

After agreeing to the Kyoto Protocol, the industrial countries had to ratify it. This meant actually trying to meet the quotas, which put pressure on industry. Although the Europeans had taken the lead in agreeing to the quotas, it took them a long time to ratify the Protocol. Although virtually all announced they intended to ratify it, none of the bigger industrial countries did so until just before the Third Earth Summit held in Johannesburg, South Africa, in 2002. The EU as a collectivity also ratified at this time. The U.S. had signed the protocol at the Kyoto Conference in 1997, but held off ratification. President Clinton was ambivalent. While he had supported it and Vice President Al Gore was enthusiastic, Clinton postponed sending it to the Senate for its consent. The reason was that the senators felt the pressure of industry. They had two objections: first, it would harm the American economy, and second that it was not fair because it exempted China. In the end, Clinton never sent the Protocol to the Senate, even though he claimed it was a good idea.

After his inauguration in 2001, President George W. Bush waited only a few weeks to announce that the U.S. would reject the Protocol. The news stunned the Europeans. It seemed to be a death blow. The Protocol had a provision that in order for it to enter into force, it needed ratification of countries that contributed 55% of the greenhouse gases. The U.S. contributed 25%. Moreover, these had to be from the industrial countries, which collectively contributed 75%, with the other 25% coming from the underdeveloped countries. Russia, which contributed 17%, claimed it was not interested in ratifying. The U.S. stood alone in opposition (with the single exception of Australia). Then, unexpectedly in 2004, the Europeans promised the Russians to support their admission to the World Trade Organization as a quid pro quo. Russia ratified it, and the Protocol entered into force in February 2005.

3.4 EU Involvement

The European Community (after 1992, styled the EU) became deeply interested in global warming in 1988 following the conference in Toronto. The Commission's environmental staff prepared a report for the Council meeting that November that suggested the EC take a leadership role. It seemed important to move forward without waiting endlessly for more scientific evidence. It was a "no regrets strategy," that is, at a minimum doing enough to prevent a permanent problem. The plan was to put a tax on carbon, which was very similar to a tax on energy. This met strong internal opposition from the Commission's Energy Directorate, which wanted low cost fuels and an assured supply. The Continent had remained vulnerable after the oil boycott of 1973. The bureaucratic compromise at the time did little to move beyond the status quo. Nevertheless, the environmental staff continued to advocate a position of leadership on the warming issue. Within a few years, the Commission moved to a position that the EC should lead the world in reducing carbon emissions. It developed more detailed plans for a tax on carbon, with the revenue going to the national governments to be spent on environmental projects. There remained the obvious task of getting economic competitors like the U.S. and Japan to adopt a similar carbon tax; otherwise, Europe would be at a disadvantage in exporting products. In order to make the tax less onerous for exports, the Commission gave exemptions to six industrial sectors that were highly energy intensive; however, these were concessions that gave away much of the benefit sought. In 1991, the Council adopted a policy of stabilization at 1990 levels by 2000 and toyed with the idea of carbon reductions.

In preparation for the Rio Summit, the EC Commission developed a proposal to tax carbon in energy. This fit the aim of European leadership, which was a goal of the Environmental Directorate General, under the leadership of its head, Carlo Ripa di Meana, and of the entire commission, led by Jacques Delors. The Energy Directorate General objected that it would skew energy policy. Yet, both sides could see possible commonalities. The energy team was concerned with limited supplies and recognized that taxing BTUs would conserve them. Moreover, both sides came to believe that energy efficiency would yield benefits in greater overall efficiency and lower costs. Thus, a compromise emerged. The tax would be based half on the energy value of fuels and half on their carbon content, and it would eventually be set at $10 a barrel of oil. Nuclear energy would be liable only for the Btu portion since it did not emit carbon, and renewable fuels would be completely exempt. The new tax would replace other taxes such as sales and income, so the net effect on consumers would be neutral. If not offset, the carbon Btu tax would produce excessive revenues for national governments. The tax proposal won support elsewhere in the Commission in Brussels; for example, the Economic Directorate General liked the idea of a tax rather than old fashioned command and control regulations.

The immediate reaction of heavy industry toward the proposed tax was hostile. Several oil and chemical companies like Shell and Dow, with extensive facilities in the Netherlands, threatened the Dutch government with a move to Kazakhstan in central Asia. Because the EC lacked authority to impose taxes, all it could do was suggest that the member states impose the carbon tax in their own countries.

Although heavy industry opposed this carbon—energy tax proposal, on many environmental issues big business supports EU action. The most influential interest group is the European Round Table of Industrialists, organized in 1983 by the head of the Volvo Corporation. He organized the heads of fifteen other corporations, including ICI, Unilever, Nestlé, Philips and Fiat. Members are the chief executive officers personally, not their corporations. The roster has now grown to forty-five members. The Round Table has sought to harmonize government policies and regulations on trade throughout the Continent. This would enable the big companies to take advantage of economies of scale in their manufacturing and sales. Over the years the group has advocated the construction of the tunnel under the English Channel, the bridge from Denmark to Sweden, high speed trains and more highways, all of which it got. Next, it advocated a common currency: the Euro. Still later when the Eastern countries sought to join the EU, the Round Table pushed for guarantees that they would reduce their taxes, facilitate privatization, permit foreign investors to buy land, and not give special privileges to local companies. Although the Round Table wants to avoid environmental restrictions in general, it is agreeable if the burden is uniform, and competing American and Japanese companies will not have an advantage.

As the EU began to develop its unified bargaining position on global warming, it had to face the conflicting interests of its various members. The Netherlands had a lot of natural gas, and its people were very pro-environmental. Denmark was in a similar situation. France, with a large nuclear industry, saw benefits. Germany, Britain and Spain, all with coal reserves, worried that a carbon tax would make their mines uncompetitive. Portugal and Greece, each with weak economies, believed that the short term effects would be crippling. Furthermore, if the U.S. and Japan did not establish a carbon tax at the same time, they would enjoy a competitive advantage over Europe. Indeed, it would be important for big developing countries like China to do so also. Within weeks the Commission Directorate General Environment watered down its proposal due to pressure from industry. Its stance when it got to Rio was merely that a carbon tax was a good idea, one that deserved study. The concept was kicked around for a few years, until it eventually faded away. The defeat of President Clinton's similar proposal for an American Btu tax further damaged its prospects.

For the next decade, the European view dominated world policy on global warming. The Berlin Mandate, issued by the first Conference of the Parties in 1995, accomplished most of the European objectives, even though the Americans were strongly opposed. At the second Conference of the Parties, the Europeans pressed for making the deadlines sooner, and were accommodating to the desires of the developing countries not to have to meet any targets. To support the effort, the Conference of the Parties established a secretariat located in Bonn. Since the 1980s, technical support had come from the Intergovernmental Panel on Climate Change (IPCC).

3.5 The Kyoto Conference

Leading up to the Conference, the Europeans met frequently to coordinate their position. The fact that they were exceeding their reduction targets inspired them to press for a higher target of 15%. Of course, the reason was not due to their own efforts, but a combination of the British dash for gas from the North Sea, the closing of obsolete and dirty factories in the former East Germany, and the widespread economic recession that kept down energy usage. The offer of 15% was also conditioned on the U.S. and Japan following suit. In March the EU environmental ministers roughed out a deal for different quotas for each member state. This would be placing a bubble over the entire Continent. Reductions would be as high as 30% for Luxembourg. Germany, Britain, Austria, Belgium, Italy, Denmark, and the Netherlands would also be required to reduce their emissions. France and Finland would freeze emissions. Sweden, Ireland, Spain and Greece could increase their emissions. Finally, Portugal would have the biggest increase: 40%. The figures reflected the member states' success in reducing carbon, as well as their needs for economic development. The allotments became known as burden sharing.

Six weeks before the conference, the EU sent a delegation of top officials to Washington to persuade Clinton that the American proposal to cut emissions to 1990 levels within fifteen years was inadequate. Furthermore, the officials hoped to counter U.S. demands that China and the developing countries be included. When experts and mid-level diplomats from 131 countries met in Bonn to try to reach detailed agreement in anticipation of the Kyoto Conference, the negotiations stalled.

Once the parties arrived in Kyoto, it was apparent that their differences were extreme. The Europeans began with the position that they would not accept higher cuts than other industrial nations, but this gave way to the practicalities of reaching an agreement. They also backed off their pledge of 15% cuts when it became obvious that the U.S. and Japan would not do the same. They began by opposing loopholes, primarily the American proposal for carbon sinks (forests) or for flexibility mechanisms of emission trading, Joint Implementation and Clean Development Mechanisms. By the end of the acrimonious eleven days, the Europeans had conceded these points. The EU's efforts to coordinate on a daily basis were exhausting. The fifteen member countries met up to three times a day, sometimes for a total of six hours, lasting until 3:00 am.

The final target for the European Union was an 8% reduction, 7% for the U.S. and 6% for Japan. The EU later negotiated final numbers for the bubble among its members, resulting in a different level for each one, that is burden sharing. Among the big countries, Germany and Denmark cut the most, 21%, and Britain cut 12%. Portugal got the biggest increase, 27%, Greece got 25%, Italy got 15%, and Ireland got 13%. The Netherlands, usually regarded as an environmental leader, was required to cut only 6% [2]. This was a concession to its oil and chemical industries. In tonnage rather than percentages, the German reduction would be 260 million tons, and the British would be almost 100 million tons. With its small base, Portugal would add only 20 million tons.

After Kyoto the EU moved forward to promote the Protocol and have it ratified both by the Union collectively and by the (then) fifteen member states. Through its Commission Directorate General, periodic meetings of the member environmental ministers, and the semi-annual meetings of the European Council (Summit), the EU managed to present a fairly unified position toward the non-European parties to the Kyoto Protocol, although often arrived at after difficult internal bargaining. Ratification by the Union and its members took longer than expected. The EU did not ratify the Protocol until 2002. During the same period, it found itself drifting away from the U.S. At first, the division was mild while Clinton remained president, but after George W. Bush became president, the chasm widened.

Besides checking with its member governments, the EU took into account the opinions of interest groups. The Climate Action Network maintains a European office in Brussels, with a staff of six, where it monitors the EU Climate Change Programme, burden sharing among its members, emissions trading, renewables, efficiency, and other programs. The Network also has its own representatives in most countries. Its eighty-three European affiliates include international ones like the World Wildlife Federation and Friends of the Earth, as well as those unique to a country like the Danish Naturfredningsforening and the Portuguese Association for Nature Conservation.

The EU also considered the goals of business. The Round Table of Industrialists laid out several. It sought a stable, predictable and flexible investment environment and a target setting which would reflect the particular characteristics of individual industries. It wanted voluntary action, which would pay attention to cost effectiveness and utilize cost benefit analysis when evaluating any recommendations [3]. The Union of Industrial and Employers' Confederations of Europe (UNICE) follows EU developments in detail. Within the Commission, business finds a sympathetic ear in the Directorate General for Enterprises and the Directorate General for Energy and Transport.

Although an overwhelming number of industries are unsympathetic toward regulations limiting carbon dioxide emissions, a few see its benefits. The European Business Council for a Sustainable Energy Future, based in Brussels, has about forty members who would benefit from the Kyoto Protocol. These range from railways and natural gas companies to engineering and financial consultants. The World Alliance for Decentralized Energy, based in Edinburgh, has about twenty members, ranging from national organizations to individual companies manufacturing co-generation equipment.

Several big businesses have chosen the role of environmental good citizen. Under the personal leadership of Sir John Browne, BP pursued a green path. In 1998 Sir John pledged to cut its greenhouse gas emissions by 10% rather than the lower Kyoto target. In an additional step, he withdrew his American subsidiary, Amoco, from the notorious Global Climate Coalition. (The Coalition was an anti-environmental lobbying group in the U.S. in existence in the later 1990s, until it became discredited.) During the next year, BP began pollution auditing as the basis for a company wide trading system. In a symbolic gesture, the corporation changed its logo to a sunburst, and announced it visualized a future beyond petroleum.

The bi-national Royal Dutch Shell corporation was a close second to BP in its efforts to become more environmentally friendly. After a slight delay, it also withdrew its American subsidiary from the Global Climate Coalition. It invested in a plant to turn wood shavings into green fuel for automobiles and opened a hydrogen fuel station in Iceland, using geothermal power from geysers to manufacture the hydrogen. Its chairman, Sir Philip Watts, gave a speech in Texas, calling for the global warming skeptics to get off the fence and accept that action needs to be taken "before it is too late." He said "we can't wait to answer all questions beyond reasonable doubt," adding "there is compelling evidence that climate change is a threat." Sir Philip lamented the growing animosity across the Atlantic [4]. Shell also has established a fifth major business division: International Renewables. It began an internal greenhouse gas emissions trading system. The greening of the Royal Dutch Shell marked a change from the mid-1990s when it had attracted criticism for dumping an old drilling platform into the North Sea and had condoned human rights violations connected with its operations in Nigeria. Today, it joins BP to serve as a model for other businesses that want to support the environment.

Throughout Europe, business is adjusting to the demands for controlling greenhouse gas emissions with more or less grace. The Germans appear to be most accepting. Yet, virtually everywhere industrialists seem to believe that there will be no restrictions in excess of those for 2008–2012, the first commitment period. The idea of a second and a third commitment period with tighter and tighter limits seems beyond their ken. After the first period, nearly all the easy fixes will be used up. These include the dash to gas, decreases due to the collapse of East German and Eastern block economies, greater efficiency with new factories, and so forth. Even trading will lose its allure. While environmentalists and government experts foresee a second commitment period, business does not.

After the sixth Conference of the Parties at the Hague collapsed, the Europeans blamed the American demands for flexibility mechanisms (in U.S. terminology) or loopholes (in the view of the Europeans). One such mechanism was carbon sinks in the form of forests, both at home and in developing countries. Of course, Europe has little potential for adding to its forests, and therefore is unenthusiastic.

The Europeans were outraged when Bush renounced the Kyoto treaty. When Margot Wallstrom, head of the environmental Directorate General, flew to Washington to protest, she got an unsympathetic hearing. The Senate environment sub-committee chairman, Robert Smith, canceled a meeting with the delegation. The State Department arranged for the delegation to talk to only middle ranking officials. EPA Administrator Christine Todd Whitman was the only one who expressed any sympathy, and she was unable to do much. The EU officials followed up the visit to Washington with visits to Russia and Japan to encourage ratification. To do so they offered concessions and aid. They also visited China.

The following year, in preparation for the seventh Conference of the Parties in Marrakesh, Morocco, the EU persuaded nearly all countries except the U.S. to undertake reductions. Unfortunately, this involved compromises that lowered the amount of carbon dioxide reductions by the top thirty-seven industrial countries to about 2% rather than the 6% goal articulated in the Kyoto Protocol. Developing countries were to get $500 million in aid as an incentive.

With an eye on its public image, the EU was able to ratify the Protocol three months before the Earth Summit in Johannesburg in 2002, the tenth anniversary of the Rio Summit that signed the Framework Convention. At Johannesburg, the U.S. came under widespread criticism, led by the EU delegations. Along with fifteen other delegations, the Europeans issued a statement pledging to exceed the Kyoto targets. Many saw the American position on global warming as part of a pattern of unilateral and disruptive action, including the invasion of Iraq, failure to pay United Nations dues, renunciation of the Anti-Ballistic Missile Treaty, and revival of the Star Wars missile defense system.

Over the next few years, little progress was made. The basic concepts and most of the details were in place. The annual Conferences of the Parties in New Delhi, Milan and Buenos Aires involved merely tinkering with details, like how to calculate the value of afforestation. With the intransigence of the Americans, it seemed unlikely that the Protocol would ever be ratified. Some Europeans began to speculate on the possibility of an alternative treaty to replace the Kyoto Protocol. The reasoning was that under European leadership, enough countries could limit their greenhouse gas emissions to have a positive impact and reduce global warming. As it turned out, this was not necessary with the Russian ratification and the entry of the Kyoto Protocol into force. The Europeans deserve credit for enticing Russia with the promise of entry into the WTO. Yet, without the U.S., this was only a marginal improvement over a Europe led alternative. At present, the industrial countries that have ratified the Protocol account for 62% of emissions of greenhouse gases.

3.6   Trading

After the Johannesburg summit, the EU put an emissions trading system in place, which began in 2005. This was a reversal of the European negotiating position at Kyoto, which had opposed the American proposal on trading. Looking at the high cost of compliance led to the change of heart. The European Parliament and the Council of Environmental Ministers approved the Emission Trading Scheme (ETS). It covers twenty-eight countries: the twenty-five member states plus Norway, Switzerland and Liechtenstein. The goal is for emitters to make cuts where they are the cheapest, thereby generating the greatest savings for the total economy. A further goal is to foster innovation. Companies have an incentive to reduce their greenhouse gases. The scheme does not include all emissions, however. It covers facilities for energy, ferrous metals, cement, glass, pulp, paper and boards, which will amount to 40% of emissions, but it does not cover aluminum, chemicals, transportation or household use. Transportation and domestic use are hard to regulate, and the aluminum and chemical industries have powerful political lobbies.

Implementation uses permits for each facility that entitle the holder to emit one ton of carbon dioxide or its equivalent, called an allowance. This is done by the member states. The value of an allowance for a single ton is predicted to be in the range of $5–$30. Early trades were for $10 a ton. The first period of trading is 2005–2007, and the second is to end with the Kyoto dates of 2008–2012. The allowances, which are granted free of charge, can be traded across the entire twenty-eight nation region. It became apparent at once that the number of allowances was too generous, so there was no real pressure to reduce carbon emissions.

Several aspects remain unresolved. Member states may apply to exclude particular facilities temporarily. Supposedly, they will make equivalent reductions in greenhouse gases by alternative techniques and will be carefully monitored. Member states may provide that allowances canceled in the first period be reissued in the second period, a form of banking. Member states may use Emission Reduction Units from Joint Implementation projects under the Kyoto Protocol toward meeting their targets under the treaty. This will also be true for Certified Emission Reductions from Clean Development Mechanisms and Removal Units from forest sinks. A concern with both the basic scheme and its links with the Protocol flexibility mechanisms is the transaction costs, that is the expense for actually making the trade in terms of identifying allowances and buying or selling them at a reasonable cost in a timely fashion.

The EU designed the scheme to avoid giving an unfair advantage to any one member state. It believed that having a diversity of methods for assigning the initial quantities of the allowances, both by grandfathering and auctions, would avoid giving special advantage to existing companies.

The EU does not want its member states to compete in offering the most lenient situation. There will be a temptation for poorer countries to lower their pollution standards to entice factories to move there. A further problem is that a company may move facilities to places not covered. An obvious location is Russia or the Ukraine. The EU planners considered it important to expand the scheme to cover all of western and central Europe by adding three non-members. Of course, facilities can also move to developing countries not covered by Kyoto. If these problems are resolved, the European scheme will be a logical worldwide model. Unfortunately, when the deadline of March 31, 2004, arrived for the countries to submit their national plans, none did. Seven submitted preliminary plans, and the rest submitted nothing.

The EU emissions trading scheme is designed to allow some trading outside of the country of origin of the emissions. The Kyoto Protocol provides for two methods: Joint Implementation and the Clean Development Mechanism. The former is between two industrial countries (that is Annex B), and the latter is between an industrial country and a developing one. This is also a change from the European bargaining position at the Kyoto Conference. Again, the realities of actually meeting the limits prompted backtracking. Aside from the differing partners, Joint Implementation and the Clean Development Mechanism both provide for implementation in a different country and then trading the reduced emissions. For example, a European corporation will reduce greenhouse gas emissions in a different country, perhaps Romania or Indonesia, then trade them for credits at home. One method would be simply to buy an old inefficient factory and close it. Another method would be to assist in constructing a new plant in Rumania or Indonesia so that it will emit fewer gases. The problem with this latter method, however, is that a new plant virtually always has newer and more efficient engineering, so the question becomes how much is a plant eligible to trade to the European facilities of the corporation.

3.7 The Individual European Countries

Although the EU now dominates climate policy, the roles of the individual countries have not disappeared. Fifteen or twenty years ago, before the EU was so strong and unified, their policies were crucial in negotiating the Framework Convention in 1992 and the Kyoto Protocol in 1997.

During the 1980s it seemed that Britain would be on the side of industry and burning more oil and carbon. Margaret Thatcher became prime minister in 1979 on a free market platform for the Conservative Party. She was a great advocate of a smaller role for government, blaming the kingdom's economic stagnation on nationalized industries like coal and steel, heavy handed state regulation, and a lack of free enterprise incentives. Her policies paralleled and indeed led those of Ronald Reagan in the U.S. Early on, she began to sell state owned corporations, including the North Sea oil and gas corporations.

Thatcher's remedy began to work, and the economy picked up. Unlike Reagan, however, she was concerned about the environment. In particular she worried about the greenhouse effect. By training, she was a chemist, having taken a degree in the subject at Oxford University. She was also persuaded by the scientific work of the IPCC. In 1988 she gave a speech to the Royal Society, in which she outlined environmental dangers, and the following year she addressed the UN General Assembly, calling for protocols on climate change, ozone depletion, and the preservation of plant species. Thatcher also hosted an international conference on saving the ozone layer. British scientific agencies, such as the Hadley Center for Climate Prediction and Research in Exeter, are among the best in the world. British scientists have held influential positions in international agencies. For example John Houghton chaired the technical section of the IPCC.

British support for controlling greenhouse gases continued under Thatcher's Conservative Party successor as prime minister, John Major. When the Labor Party won control of the government in 1997 and Tony Blair became prime minister, the government's support for the Kyoto Treaty was even stronger. Yet, a strange thing happened with Blair. He lost his enthusiasm for the Kyoto Protocol. In 2005, he said that he was changing his thinking about this. He no longer believed that negotiating international treaties was going to help. The truth is, he observed, "no country is going to cut its growth or consumption substantially in light of a long-term environmental problem" [5]. The only hope he saw was new science and technology. In October he said:

> We also have to recognize that while the Kyoto Protocol takes us in the right direction, it is not enough. We need to cut greenhouse gas emissions radically but Kyoto doesn't even stabilize them. It won't work as intended, either, unless the U.S. is part of it… We have to understand as well that, even if the U.S. did sign up to Kyoto, it wouldn't affect the huge growth in energy consumption we will see in India and China [6].

Even more than Britain, Germany has been a leader in the movement to control greenhouse gases. In 1990, Chancellor Helmut Kohl and his Cabinet announced that Germany intended to reduce its carbon dioxide emissions by 25% of the 1987 level by 2005. Besides the environmental improvements, Kohl and his Christian Democratic Party believed this was a way to help the nuclear power industry, which had been under attack since the Chernobyl accident. Nuclear reactors emitted no carbon. Also, the Christian Democrats believed that a pro-environmental policy might take support away from the Green Party and might undermine the Socialist-Green coalition government [6]. The Cabinet Resolution established an inter-ministerial working group and five study groups. Unlike the U.S., in Germany most scientists work directly for government agencies, and they do not have the tradition of taking positions in opposition to their employers.

Germany continued to develop its policy of big reductions in carbon dioxide, and this was the position that it took to the Rio Summit two years later. In fact, the closing of inefficient and unprofitable factories in East Germany allowed the newly reunited country to reduce carbon emissions by 13% in just five years. Two further factors were the decline of the coal industry due to mine depletion and an economic recession that occurred during the period. Finally, in response to the guilt remaining from World War II, Germany likes to be seen as a leader on moral issues. Its new constitution of 1994 includes environmental rights. At home, the anti-warming policy was not universally applauded. The Economic Ministry and the Transportation Ministry did not consider it achievable and worried about harm to the economy. Trade unions considered it a threat to jobs. Within Europe, Germany pushed for a strong stance by proposing the bubble, whereby less developed members like Portugal and Greece would get lenient targets of 20 to 30% increases, to be made up for by even bigger reductions by Germany and Britain.

Recently, scientists at the Max Planck Institute in Germany have discovered that living plants, dried leaves and grass emit methane. Methane is a greenhouse gas like carbon dioxide. The quantity is significant, amounting to 10 and 30% of all annual global emissions of methane. This new finding fits with other satellite studies that show increased methane correlated with deforestation and unexplained plumes of methane over old tropical forests. The consequences are worth noting because so far scientists have believed that planting more trees would decrease the amount of carbon dioxide in the atmosphere, but this may be canceled out by the methane. The Max Planck Institute is in fact a collection of eighty nonprofit research centers sponsored by federal and state governments.

France has strongly supported limits to greenhouse gases. Unlike Germany and Britain, it sees nuclear power to be a key ingredient. Furthermore, the government sees this to be a route to independence from foreign oil supplies, and has connected it to its defense policy of an independent nuclear strike force. Furthermore, the utility, Electricité de France, was a government corporation. The French polity is highly centralized, depends on experts, and has a long tradition of planning. France generates 77% of its electricity from the atom, plus 13% from falling water. It has a total of fifty-nine reactors. Thus, due to its energy mix, the country emits only a small amount of carbon dioxide.

Leading up to the Rio Summit, France strongly supported the draft treaty that became the Framework Convention on Climate Change. A French diplomat, Jean Ripert, chaired the negotiations at the United Nations headquarters. Under pressure from the George H. W. Bush Administration, he was forced to water down the draft. When questioned on this, he diplomatically replied, "We've got to start somewhere" [7].

Five years later, in preparation for the Kyoto Conference, France advocated firm controls, committing itself to a 15% reduction. A week before the Conference, the government announced a comprehensive plan that encompassed taxes, public transportation, renewables, and afforestation. Quotas for industry would be voluntary. The environment minister, Dominique Voynet, declared she would rather see no agreement than one watered down to meet the demands of the Americans. Once the sessions started in Kyoto, the French delegates held firm to their position, but on the last night they compromised, at the urging of the British, in order to prevent the collapse of the conference. While the European target was an 8% reduction, after burden sharing adjustments, the French target was zero, that is, stabilization at the 1990 level.

The government did not actually decide on its own plan to meet the Kyoto targets for three years. The left wing coalition that governed under Prime Minister Lionel Jospin was divided on several issues. Environment minister Voynet opposed emissions trading, but finally had to concede on this point. The key instrument would be the ecotax on fuels used by industry, utilities and households. Gasoline and diesel fuel for automobiles and trucks would be taxed. In fact, France was the only European country actually to reduce its carbon dioxide emissions, due to its nuclear power plants and a sluggish economy. France toyed with the idea of getting credits under the Protocols

Clean Development Mechanism by helping a developing country build a nuclear power reactor, a concept frightening both to environmentalists and those worried about weapons proliferation. Although it did not pursue this at the time, recently it agreed to help Libya to develop a civilian nuclear program. Libya did promise to give up nuclear, chemical and biological weapons. Yet, this was still the same country that sponsored terrorism in the 1980s, including bombing civilian airlines over Scotland and Niger. Furthermore, it hardly seemed to need more sources of energy in view of all its oil.

When President Bush declared in 2001 that the U.S. would not adhere to the Kyoto Protocol, France led the outrage. Voynet called it a scandal. The foreign minister warned the U.S. it could not ignore the problem if it wanted to be a world leader. The president, Jacques Chirac, said, "I appeal solemnly to all states and first and foremost the industrialized countries to implement the Kyoto protocol on climatic change in its totality and without delay" [8]. Righteous anger united all parts of the political spectrum. Chirac was a conservative, the prime minister and the foreign minister were Socialists, and the environment minister was a Green. In July the US–EU split on global warming fired debate at the annual Group of 8 meeting in Genoa, Italy, but Bush was unrepentant. The session was marred by riots by protesters, some concerned about the environment and others about the more general threat of globalization to the Third World. The city became a battle zone, and one protester was killed. While most of the demonstrations were peaceful, a few hundred anarchists, mainly from Germany and Britain, hurled firebombs and set cars, stores and banks on fire, resulting in $25 million damage.

In 2002, France joined the other EU countries in ratifying the Kyoto Protocol. The impetus was the upcoming Environmental Summit at Johannesburg. President Chirac attended and told the delegates, "If the whole of humanity behaved like the northern countries, it would take two more planets to satisfy our needs" [9].

The following summer a severe heat wave concentrated French attention on global warming. A few months previously the new conservative government had reviewed the country's climate plan, finding that although France was right on target for controlling emissions overall, its transportation and construction industries were polluting too much. The government reiterated its support for the nuclear industry, in spite of criticism from environmentalists and the example of Germany's planning to phase out nuclear plants. Most French citizens were opposed. A public opinion poll found 67% of French people believed—wrongly—that nuclear energy triggered climate change [10].

Denmark signed the Framework Convention in Rio, and then came home to do something about it, unlike many other countries. It announced that it would cut emissions by 20% by 2005, at a time when the Netherlands and Belgium mumbled about a 5% cut, and Britain proposed mere stabilization. During its rotating EC presidency, the Danes put first priority on ratifying the Framework Convention and introducing carbon taxes. The country began its own carbon tax, the first and only one to do so. By this action, its advocates intended to set an example for the rest of Europe. At the Kyoto Conference of the Parties, a Dane, Ritt Bjerregaard, was the chief negotiator for the EU. In her outspoken manner, she publicly complained about the weak proposals coming from the U.S. and from Japan. Unfortunately, by the end of the conference, her delegation had to accept a weaker position in order to have any agreement at all.

In 1981, the government energy plan had set a target of producing 10% of its energy from wind, and it seems on schedule to meet this goal. The generators are owned by electric utilities, municipalities, farm cooperatives and even individuals. In the first years, the government paid a subsidy of 30%, which went down to 15% as costs fell. Some of the early windmills, which many local residents called ugly and noisy, seemed to be environmental blights themselves. Improved engineering helped, and for esthetic reasons, they are now concentrated in wind farms rather than near neighbors.

From 1982 to 2002, the Danish parliament supported the environment strongly, but in 2002, the voters gave the Liberal Party (actually conservative) and its allies enough seats to form a new coalition government. It was conservative in policy and less eager to favor Danish leadership in environmental matters. In a controversial appointment, it named Bjorn Lomborg, author of *The Skeptical Environmentalist*, to direct the Environmental Assessment Institute. His book makes a strong argument against the scientific evidence of global warming and of techniques to prevent it. Upon his appointment, the Institute rewrote its official policy to match Lomborg's. First, the Institute advocated getting the most for the money. Second, it noted that most of the Danish proposals are expensive to implement, such as ending electricity exports, which would cost the nation $263 million. Third, the high cost of earlier efforts was due to the fact that Denmark focused on reducing its own carbon dioxide emissions. It would be cheaper to carry out reductions in other countries by using the flexible mechanisms of the Kyoto Protocol [11]. This was a big change from prior Danish policy.

Lomborg's colleagues did not all take well to his critique of global warming. The Danish Committee on Scientific Dishonesty, a branch of the national Research Agency that draws together some of the country's most senior scientists, condemned his work. The committee's 6,640 word judgment concluded that his book "is deemed to fall within the concept of scientific dishonesty" and that it "is deemed clearly contrary to the standards of good scientific practice." The committee said that "The defendant, …based on customary scientific standards and in light of his systematic onesidedness in the choice of data and line of argument, has clearly acted at variance with good scientific practice" [12]. This followed blasts from major international scientific journals. *Nature* printed a review that compared Lomborg to maverick academics who deny the Holocaust [13]. *Scientific American* devoted eleven pages to an attack in which Lomborg is accused of "egregious distortions" and of being "ignorant" and "muddled" [14]. Later, the Science Ministry, reflecting the views of the elected political leaders, overturned the dishonesty verdict. Lomborg himself left the directorship after less than two years. Indeed, the situation was unusual by European standards, both in Lomborg's naked imposition of right wing policy on an agency, and in the other scientists' attacks on him for dishonesty.

3.8   Conclusion

In comparison to the U.S. situation, European agencies are similar in that they are key players. They are the source of expertise, and by devoting their full time attention to global warming for many years, they shape policy. Another similarity is that different agencies promote different interests. In virtually every country and in the EU, rivalry exists between the environmental agency and those concerned with industry, trade and transportation. In contrast to the U.S. situation, policy in general is more worried about the dangers of global warming. With the present Bush Administration, U.S. government agencies are pressured to belittle the threat and to look for alternatives to controlling carbon emissions. The European bureaucrats are more in harmony with their political superiors. Except in Denmark, warming is seen as a danger, and the Kyoto Protocol is seen as a solution. A further difference is the absence of the "democracy deficit," meaning excessive control by unelected bureaucrats in Brussels. While U.S. environmentalists may not be happy with many current policies, few disagree that that is what the president and a majority of Congress want.

References

1. Interview with Artur Runge-Metzger, EU Commission Directorate General Environment, Unit on Climate Change, Ozone and Energy April 13, 2004.
2. Bartsch, Ulrich and Muller, Benito, *Fossil Fuels in a Changing Climate*, Oxford University Press, Oxford, 2000, Table 2.1 Kyoto Protocol Commitments, 17.
3. European Round Table of Industrialists, *Climate Change: How Government and Industry Can Work Together*, ERT, Brussels, 2000, 8, 10.
4. MacAlister, Terry, Shell chief delivers global warming warning, *The Guardian*, March, 2003.
5. Dyer, Gwynne, Global accord on emissions still a crisis away, *The Blade*, December, 2005.
6. Blair, Tony, Get real on climate change, *The Observer*, October 30, 2005.
7. Mouat, Lucia, U.S. wins concessions on global warming but Loses Goodwill, *Christian Science Monitor*, May, 1992.
8. Chirac Criticizes U.S. over Kyoto Global Warming Treaty, *Agence France Presse*, March, 2001.
9. South African Press Association Two more planets needed if all behave like North, *Financial Times*, September, 2002.
10. Bryant, Elizabeth, Heat wave renews the nuclear debate, *United Press International*, August, 2003.
11. Danish Environmental Assessment Institute, Climate Change, 2006. Available at www.imv.dk. Accessed May 12, 2006.
12. McCarthy, Michael, Best selling scourge of the greens accused of dishonesty, *The Independent*, January, 2003.
13. Pimm, Stuart and Harvery, Jeff, Review, *Nature*, November, 2001.
14. Schneider, Stephen, Global warming: Neglecting the Complexities, *Scientific American*, January, 2002.

Chapter 4

Transborder Air Pollution

Zachary A. Smith and Katrina Darlene Taylor
Northern Arizona University

4.1 Introduction

This chapter will explore the relationship of transborder air pollution to globalization. It will also discuss the environmental regimes that have been formed to address this issue. The rise in environmental degradation due to transborder air pollution is directly correlated and likely caused by the increase in economic globalization. In this chapter, we will address the effects of international trade agreements on environmental commodities. Additionally, we will discuss the successes and failures of the environmental regimes created by the international agreements dealing with air pollution. Finally, we will offer suggestions for the improvement of future regimes so that they may better accomplish their goals.

International regimes have been studied by many scholars to determine their efficacy in finding solutions to the problems for which they were formed [1,2]. This chapter will focus on the countries affected by transborder air pollution, its connection to international trade agreements, and the regimes that have been created to alleviate the problem. Whether or not these regimes have been completely successful has yet to be determined due to the temporal nature of the problem and its solutions. Regardless, we will use data that has been collected to examine the solvency of these regimes up to the present time.

Regimes are an important focus of study because of the nature of transborder air pollution. Often when transborder air pollution occurs, it is difficult for the country receiving the pollution to influence the country exporting the pollution. Given the common pool nature of transborder air pollution, countries that are exporting pollutants have little incentive to restrict their polluting activities. Consequently, effective international pollution control requires a transparent environmental agreement, or regime, which will hold the polluting country or countries accountable. Ideally, such an arrangement will be politically and economically beneficial for all of the countries involved.

As the effects of globalization find their way into the culture and lifestyles of people across the world, we are becoming increasingly aware of our interdependence on the same resources. The implications of poor environmental stewardship are becoming more evident. Borders have little influence on the transport of pollutants or toxins from one country to another. Despite the existence of borders, we are all subject to the limitations of the "Global Commons" that we must rely on for our survival.

These limitations are often caused by the phenomenon known as "The Tragedy of the Commons," which refers to the tendency of rational individuals to take personal advantage of a common pool resource until it is eventually destroyed or left useless for everyone. The common pool resources that are shared internationally include but are not limited to the atmosphere, air, and the oceans. The rise in globalization has led to an increase in worldwide demand for these resources. Consequently, globalization has caused the addition of more negative externalities, such as pollution, to the shared environment. Globalization has also led to an increase in international trade, which in turn has resulted in the rise in the production of goods by industrial means and an increase in associated pollution. This occurs all over the planet in developed and developing nations. This chapter focuses on the common pool resource of air.

Societies across the world have been encountering the problems associated with air pollution for centuries. Air pollution is mostly attributable to rising industrial production, the increased dependence on the automobile and other activities that require the use of fossil fuels. Governments across the world have established regulations to mitigate air pollution. With the rise of air pollution domestically came policies that addressed the problem by sending pollutants into the atmosphere and away from the country of origin. This led to an awareness of the notion that the atmosphere is a common pool resource and must be treated as one.

4.2 Air Pollution

This section will discuss the causes of air pollution and the early responses of countries to address the problems associated with it. These early responses will then be connected to the occurrence of transborder air pollution. Acid deposition that was discovered and linked with transborder air pollution will then be discussed.

4.2.1 Causes

Historically, the causes of transborder air pollution have ranged from volcanic eruption to forest fires. In recent decades, the main source of air pollution in developed countries has been the direct result of increased production within industrialized nations [3]. Industrial air pollution has been facilitated in part by increased industrial output due to globalization [4,5].

Since the 1970s, air quality standards developed by the United States have been adopted by developed nations worldwide. The initial response by industries to air quality regulation was to build tall smoke stacks so that ambient air quality in the area of the polluting facility met standards imposed by regulations. This practice, known as the "tall smoke stack policy," did reduce the pollutants in the immediate area [3]. It did not take long for communities to become aware that this practice was causing the deposition of air pollutions far from the source of emission. Often this deposition was acidic and is now referred to as acid deposition, commonly known as acid rain.

4.2.2   Acid Deposition

Acid deposition is composed primarily of sulfur dioxide, nitrous oxides, volatile organic compounds, and ozone. Acid deposition begins with emissions of these chemicals primarily from industrial plants and automobile exhaust. The chemicals then interact with water vapor and sunlight in the upper atmosphere to form acidic compounds. These acidic substances then fall to the earth in the form of rain, snow, sleet, fog, dew, and even as dry particulate matter and gas. The impact of acid deposition over the long term can be devastating. Scientific studies have linked transborder acid deposition with declining forest productivity and the acidification of tens of thousands lakes and rivers (which has resulted in the decline of fish stocks and can affect the reproductive capabilities of both fish and amphibians), deterioration of historical buildings and monuments, as well as numerous human health problems [6].

4.3   Countries Significantly Affected by Transborder Air Pollution

The implications of air pollution and acid deposition have been felt by countries worldwide. The following section will discuss the experiences with these effects of specific countries especially as they relate to transborder air pollution. While there are many more countries that are experiencing the consequences of transborder air pollution, we will discuss in detail those most heavily impacted. We will be focusing on areas where extensive research has been completed, including Europe, Russia, the United States, Canada, Mexico, China, and Japan.

4.3.1   Europe

Recognition of the problem of transborder air pollution in Europe began in 1968 when the Swedish scientist Svante Oden published his findings on a study of precipitation in Scandinavia. He argued that acidic precipitation was causing damage to fish and lakes and was largely caused by industrial emissions traveling from Britain and Central Europe [7]. By the late 1970s countries like

Austria, Switzerland, and all of the Nordic states, with the exception of Iceland, were importing significantly more sulfur than they were producing.

Forest decline due to acid deposition has been most prevalent in Europe, especially in Germany and Scandinavia, where much of the pollutants that cause acid deposition were imported from other countries [8]. This was largely due to the West–East wind pattern and variations in regional ecosystem sensitivity [9]. In Norway and Sweden, thousands of lakes contain no fish and have lost their acid neutralizing capabilities [8].

4.3.2   Russia

Russia's first national air protection policies began in 1980 with the adoption of the Law of Air Protection Act [1]. This was after they had signed the Convention on Long Range Transborder Air Pollution (CLRTAP). CLRTAP is the first regime in the region to address the problem on transborder air pollution. The Law of Air Protection Act was primarily designed for the reduction of transborder air pollution rather than for the protection of air within its own borders. Currently, domestic air protection policies in Russia have placed a major emphasis on emissions from mobile sources.

Russia's involvement in 1979 in CLRTAP and the passage of the Law of Air Protection Act was designed to satisfy external political concerns rather than to change domestic environmental conditions. Ironically, Russia was a net importer when it entered into the Long Range Transboundary Air Pollution agreement with the majority of transborder air pollution entering its country from Poland, East and West Germany, Finland, Czechoslovakia, and Hungary [1]. Russia also imports more heavy metals from Europe than it exports [10]. Nickel smelters on the Kola Peninsula are the exception; however, these emissions are causing significant transborder air pollution in Scandinavia [1].

4.3.3   United States and Canada

In the first documented incidence of transborder air pollution between the United States and Canada, the U.S. was on the receiving end. Current trends, however, now show that about one half of all acid deposition in Canada comes from the United States. This gives Canada the highest proportion of acid deposition from another country of any country in the world [11]. This has caused a decline in forest productivity in Eastern Canada due to the pollution imported from U.S. Midwest industrial firms [12]. Additionally, as of 1994, thousands of Canadian lakes are fishless due to acidification, and thousands more are in danger of losing their fish stocks. It should be noted, however, that between 1975 and 1990, partly due to the success of the U.S. Clean Air Act, sulfur dioxide emissions in the United States decreased by 30% [13].

In return, Canada is responsible for only 20% of the United States' acid deposition. The Eastern U.S. forests are experiencing the second worst decline due to acid deposition. Although Canadian air pollution contributes to this decline, the majority of the loss of productivity is due to domestic industrial air pollution from the same industrial processes that are polluting Canadian forests.

4.3.4 United States and Mexico

The close proximity of border towns on the U.S.–Mexico Border has made it difficult over the years to determine what proportion of pollutants is traveling across the border from the various cities. In the most congested areas, mobile and stationary sources are contributing to contamination on both sides of the border [14]. Additionally, over 2500 factories in the Maquiladora zone, a 65 miles wide free trade zone established along the border, have led to increased environmental impacts in both countries. Air pollution in this area has gone unregulated for years, partially due to the fact that the factories are jointly owned by the United States and Mexico. Restrictions due to the U.S. Constitution, which gives sole power to the federal government to regulate foreign affairs, limit the ability of border states to legally and effectively work towards solutions to the transborder pollution problems.

Efforts to address the problem of transborder air pollution are encompassed in new initiatives by the Mexican Government. Currently, Mexico holds the reduction of environmental impacts high in priority when taking on new international economic endeavors. In 1996, the Amendment to the General Law of Ecological Balance and Environmental Protection established environmental accountability for industrial firms in Mexico [15].

4.3.5 China and Japan

Japan imports as much as 48% of its air pollutants [16]. China is the main contributor to Japan's imported air pollution [17]. In 1990, China accounted for 37% of sulfur in Japan [18]. Left unchecked, Chinese emissions could cause a serious decline in air quality in Japan over the next few decades [19]. Currently, no agreements have been made to directly mitigate the problem of transborder air pollution between these nations [20]. National plans to reduce sulfur dioxide, however, have been adopted by China within the last decade [21]. As a result, sulfur dioxide emissions in China have been on the decline since the late 1990's [22]. Currently, Official Development Assistance (ODA) programs of Japan are offering low interest loans to China for environmental projects [21]. These loans are cited as an indirect cause of reductions of transborder air pollution originating in China [21].

4.4 The Globalization Effect

As mentioned in the introduction, rapidly growing industrial development and production due to globalization is a key factor in the increasingly negative externalities on the environment [23]. Scholarly analyses that consider globalization and the environment have generally focused on globalization as a "process of trade liberalization and the growth of global capital" [24]. Trade agreements that promote trade liberalization are a direct effect of globalization on the world economy. While debate among scholars is still deadlocked as to the advantages and disadvantages of these practices, it is helpful to discuss the various positions on this topic. This section will begin with a look at the World Trade Organization (WTO), followed by a discussion of the North American Free Trade Agreement (NAFTA) and will conclude with some general, but differing views of the effects of international and free trade on the environment.

4.4.1 WTO

The General Agreement on Tarriffs and Trade (GATT), which was initiated in 1947, was the predecessor to the WTO. The WTO is an international trade agreement that was ratified by members of the GATT in 1995 and now boasts a membership of over 130 countries. Both agreements created trade liberalization among their members. Although many of the trade agreements made through the WTO allow its members to influence the environmental regulatory practices of their trading partners, the WTO contains no enforcement measures or legal mechanisms for even the most powerful countries to affect the environmental regulatory standards of other signatories [25]. This lack of enforcement of environmental quality standards is of concern to academics and activists alike.

4.4.2 NAFTA

NAFTA has been considered a "green trade agreement" because it addresses environmental concerns within its charter. It was ratified with an environmental side agreement, the North American Agreement on Environmental Cooperation (NAAEC). The NAAEC was negotiated and signed on September 13, 2003 and went into force on January 1, 1994. The preamble of the NAAEC makes reference to protecting the environment, including the promotion of sustainable development and the need to protect and strengthen environmental laws [26]. The NAAEC promotes open access and transparency to information regarding each NAFTA country's pollution emissions and their strategies for effective environmental policy. Article 14 of the NAAEC provides a procedural mechanism and process for the submission of complaints towards the intent of the NAAEC. Under article 14 any person or NGO residing within the NAFTA trading bloc can file a submission, asserting that any one of the signatory parties to NAFTA is insufficiently upholding its environmental laws according to the NAAEC agreement. An investigation of the complaint is then conducted. There is a strong argument for the effectiveness of this process due to its transparent nature [27].

4.4.3 Viewpoints of the Relationship between Trade Liberalization and the Environment

Although there is a fear that trade liberalization will weaken the environmental regulations of countries involved in the agreement, some evidence suggests otherwise. It has been found that the majority of trade agreements have required the country with lower regulatory standards to raise its standards to meet those of the country with higher standards. This is in contrast to popular belief that a country with more stringent regulations will lower its standards in order to promote trade with another country. This is often called the "California Effect" in which the "powerful and wealthier 'green' political jurisdictions promote a regulatory 'race to the top' among its trading partners" [25]. Trade liberalization, it is argued, gives green countries leverage over countries they might not have been able to influence otherwise.

Additionally, the expansion of international trade over the last 50 years has ultimately improved global environmental quality, according to some scholars. While the former could be considered a benefit of the increasing occurrence of global trade, the latter is a statement that deserves further reflection. Although there are many trade agreements that have promoted environmental regulations in countries that might not have implemented them in the first place, a number of the most significant regulations have occurred as a result of increasing international environmental cooperation that is unrelated to trade negotiations.

Furthermore, Emery Roe and Michel J. G. van Eeten argue that two other viewpoints regarding the globalization of trade run in opposition to this argument and further negate the positive effects of trade liberalization. Most critics of economic theory tend to subscribe to one or another of these common viewpoints. The first viewpoint, which has gathered much attention in the media and academia since the WTO protests in Seattle in 1999, holds that "Economic globalization is the number one threat to the survival of the natural world...because the WTO rules do not consider the value of such elements as clean air and fresh water..." Because the WTO supports and pursues agreements that enhance trade liberalization, this viewpoint argues that it will "bring on a global environmental collapse." The second viewpoint addressed by Roe and van Eeten is centered on "the precautionary principle." It argues that ecosystems are so complex, it is difficult to read the signs and know for sure if they are in danger. Because of the abruptness of environmental damage, "it is necessary that we act in a precautionary way..." [24]. The authors present an original third outlook, which recognizes the need for further research of globalization on environmental processes but advocates sensitivity to real time and the need to take action now [24]. The argument of this third viewpoint could in fact be realized by the advancement and study of international environmental regimes.

4.5   International Environmental Regimes

This section will first examine the historical case of the Trail Smelter Dispute, which is considered by many to be the first, albeit unsuccessful, environmental regime. The ruling in this dispute created the *Trail Smelter Principle* and the "visible damage" requirement. Following the examination of the historical basis for regime formation in the area of transborder air pollution, we will address the development, successes, and failures of three of the most established regimes in this area. The longevity of these regimes has allowed for the study of their effects on the problem of transborder air pollution. First, we will discuss CLTAP and the formation of the Long Range Transboundary Air Pollution (LRTAP) agreement. Then, we will look at the U.S.—Canada Memorandum of Intent (MOI). Finally, we will address the La Paz Agreement between the United States and Mexico.

According to Jørgen Wettestad, regimes are "social institutions consisting of agreed-upon principles, norms, rules, procedures and programmes that govern the interactions of actors in specific issue areas" [2]. In this case, the social institutions stem from international agreements which establish the rules and procedures for the reduction of transborder air pollution among various countries. As mentioned earlier, because of the common pool nature of transborder air pollution, regimes are becoming the most popular and arguably useful method for reducing emissions multi-laterally. Because transborder air pollution is a fairly recent issue to concern countries, most environmental regimes that address this problem are young, and it is difficult to assess the impacts of such agreements. The international environmental regimes we will discuss are among the oldest and have already demonstrated results.

4.5.1 Trail Smelter Dispute

The first international dispute over transborder air pollution that led to international cooperation to address the problem is significant because it marks the first recognition of transborder air pollution. The famous Trail Smelter dispute began in 1927 and lasted until 1941. It began when it was discovered by farmers in Northport, Washington that the emissions from Consolidated Smelter and Mining Company (C.S. & M.) in Trail, Canada were causing crop damage [12]. Unfortunately, at this time in history, the sensitive high-tech equipment that was required to detect acid deposition was yet to be developed and employed in studies relating air pollution to crop damage. With the Trail Smelter Dispute, the "visible damage" requirement made it difficult for U.S. scientists to prove damage was linked to the transborder air pollution. This was because the pollution is undetectable by the naked eye and requires measurements of the chemicals in the soil, on the leaves of trees, and in the water. As a result, the Arbitral Commission, a three judge panel that oversaw the proceedings, made the final decision that the C.S.& M. plant would have to pay a negligible amount in reparations to the farmers of Northport. The "visible damage" requirement would set back the abatement of transborder air pollution for decades. Not only would Canada continue to pollute the United States, but also the precedent would allow U.S. mid-western factories to pollute Ontario for decades to come. Additionally, Arizona and Texas Smelters would proceed to send damaging air pollution to Mexico for more than 50 years [12]. Fortunately, science and technology would make the establishment of "clear and convincing evidence" as required by the visible damage standard easier in the future when the problem of transborder air pollution was again brought to the forefront of international environmental concerns.

Although this agreement is considered to be unsuccessful by many theorists, it extended the "polluter pays" notion and laid down a very important principle in international law for future cases [12]. This principle, known as the *Trail Smelter Principle*, states: "No State has the right to use or permit the use of its territory in such a manner as to cause injury in or to the territory of another State or the properties or the persons therein, especially when the injury has serious consequences and is established by clear and convincing evidence" [28].

The Trail Smelter Dispute did not deal with the effects of acid deposition nor did it acknowledge that acid deposition was even occurring. This oversight would allow for fifty more years of unchecked emissions in the international environmental community. Not until the effects of acid deposition were too severe to ignore would the issue of transborder air pollution be addressed by the international community.

4.5.2 LRTAP

Prior to the Convention on Long Range Transboundary Air Pollution of 1979, the Swedish scientist Svante Oden had initiated the Scandinavian response to transborder air pollution. This prompted the Organization for Economic Cooperation and Development (OECD) to commission a study of the phenomenon in 1969. This was the first international recognition of transborder acid deposition. The first international effort to cooperatively monitor the occurrence of acid deposition agreed upon at the 1972 Stockholm Convention by the OECD soon followed. The scientific efforts of the OECD were consolidated in 1978 under the Cooperative Program for the Monitoring and Evaluation of the Long Range Transmission of Air Pollutants in Europe (EMEP). Once it was confirmed that transborder air pollution was resulting in acid deposition with harmful impacts on the environment, the Convention on Long Range Transboundary Air Pollution (LRTAP) convened. In 1979, the LRTAP agreement was signed by most of the Eastern and Western European countries, the United States, Canada and the USSR in Geneva under the auspices of the United Nations Economic Commission for Europe (ECE). This would become the first multilateral agreement on air pollution.

The agreement created the LRTAP organization, which consisted of an institutional framework, including an executive body, a secretariat, and a bureau. These bodies were responsible for the administrative tasks and decisions necessary to contribute to the success of the agreement. Also, the organization coordinated scientific research efforts through the creation of Subsidiary Working Groups. These groups would use scientific data to make regulatory proposals for the Executive Body. The Subsidiary Working Group was further divided into research and monitoring groups that specialized in the measurement of pollutant levels, technology recommendations, effects of pollution and strategies incorporating economic concerns.

Initially, the agreement did not contain strong commitments for emissions reductions. This was due to resistance by the United Kingdom and Germany to sign a treaty with binding pollution abatement commitments. A strong enough scientific link between the emissions of one country and damage in another country had not yet been established. Meanwhile, research and monitoring continued under the LRTAP organization. In 1982, a meeting on acidification of the environment in Europe revealed that forests were also being severely damaged by acid deposition, especially German forests. The German scientists who discovered the occurrence have referred to this phenomenon as Waldsterben. The revelation of Waldsterben caused a dramatic shift by Germany to a position of being in favor of mandatory emissions reductions.

The first regulatory step of the LRTAP agreement was proposed in 1983 by the Nordic countries. The plan proposed a 30% reduction in Sulfur Emissions by 1993, using 1980 as a base year. Although Germany now supported such a measure, the United Kingdom, France and Italy failed to back the proposal. Despite this lack of consensus, the First Sulfur Protocol was adopted by the LRTAP organization and opened for signature. The three largest sulfur producers, the United Kingdom, Poland and Spain, did not adopt the protocol.

In 1988, the LRTAP member countries adopted the next regulatory measure, the Nitrogen Oxide (NO_x) Protocol. Unlike the first Sulfur Protocol, the NO_x Protocol called for a freeze of NO_x emissions at the 1987 level from 1994 onward. The next major protocol was the Volatile Organic Compounds (VOCs) Protocol, signed in 1991 and called for a 30% reduction of VOC emissions between 1988 and 1999 based on 1988 levels. The 1988 levels could be national levels or within specific tropospheric ozone management areas (TOMA). And in 1994, the Second Sulfur Protocol was signed to further reduce sulfur emissions based on the "critical loads approach." The goal of this approach, as opposed to across the board reductions, was to promote cost efficient policies that would reduce sulfur emissions to levels that were not malignant to the environment or human health. The Regional Acidification Information and Simulation (RAINS) Model was used to help determine the most cost efficient pollution abatement strategies. Two other protocols were signed in 1998, including a protocol to reduce heavy metal pollutants and persistent organic pollutants (POPs). Additionally, a multi-effects and multi-pollutants protocol was adopted in 1999 to further reduce NO_x, VOCs, sulfur dioxide (SO_2), and ammonia (NH_3) pollution. It was hoped that the effects of acidification, tropospheric ozone formation and eutrophication would be reduced. These agreements marked the continued commitment of LRTAP members to reduce emissions that contributed to transborder air pollution.

One of the most important aspects of the LRTAP agreement is its institutional framework. This framework, however, did not provide for any enforcement mechanism or consequences for non-compliance with its regulations. This was especially evident with the first sulfur protocol in which several nations never signed the agreement, much less complied with its requirements. The provision that called for countries to report their efforts to reduce pollution and the results created public transparency and accountability. This may have contributed to the attempts by the member states to reduce emissions.

The reduction of most emissions in the LRTAP states is not attributed to the agreement. Although the reduction in emissions by Britain and Russia would have been unlikely without the establishment of the LRTAP regime, much of the perceived success in other countries is believed by many scholars to be endogenous and could be attributed to a plethora of other variables [1].

Implementation studies indicate that factors such as energy switches motivated by lower costs and a reduction in industrial pollution due to economic decline have been more influential in the alleviation of acid deposition in Europe than the LRTAP agreement [2]. Because the Nordic states and Canada were importing air pollution as well as creating it, it was in their own best interests to reduce emissions to prevent severe environmental degradation. It is likely that these countries would have created national initiatives on their own to alleviate the problem [1]. Additionally, the LRTAP agreement has failed in that many of the member countries are having problems achieving their targeted reductions [1]. This has caused a controversy among LRTAP member states over the RAINS model.

The costs of emissions reductions suggested by RAINS are still too high for many of the Eastern European states. Additionally, the RAINS model is being criticized because it is the only model used. This makes its results more vulnerable to challenge by member states. Currently, lobbyists and other special interest groups are working to discredit the model [29]. Discrediting the model and its findings could lead to years of additional research and a freeze on emissions reductions. In the meantime, EANET, the regional monitoring group in South East Asia, has adopted its own version of the RAINS model [30]. The same controversy could arise among the EANET states where acid deposition has the potential to become a larger problem than in Europe. These factors make it difficult to assess the LRTAP agreement as anything more than a medium success [2].

4.5.3 MOI

The Bilateral Research Consultation Group on the Long Range Transport of Air Pollutants was established in 1978 by the Canadian and U.S. governments. This was after significant harms to the environment in Canada were linked with industrial emission in the United States. Less than 2 years after the establishment of the joint Research Consultation Group, the 1980 Memorandum of Intent on Transboundary Air Pollution was signed. The agreement was comprised of four phases; the first three consisted of research on the various effects of acid rain. In the fourth phase the two countries were to begin negotiations on an agreement to reduce the emissions that contributed to transborder air pollution.

After the first three phases were complete, the United States continued to push for additional research rather than sign an agreement to reduce emissions. In 1984, the Canadian government decided to go it alone. They introduced a controls program that would reduce national emissions by 50%. After dragging its feet for several more years, the U.S. finally signed the United States–Canada Agreement on Air Quality in 1991. This agreement committed the U.S. and Canada to a reduction in SO_2 and NO_x emissions by 50%.

While both countries are on target to reduce emissions by the target dates specified in the agreement, other variables contributed to the reduction of emissions by the United States. For similar and different reasons to LRTAP, the U.S.—Canada MOI is also not viewed as an entirely successful regime. This agreement may have been partially responsible for the decrease in U.S. contributions to transborder air pollution. However, after the MOI agreement, the U.S. government was responsible for settling the domestic dispute over interstate air pollution in the Northeast. Emissions were reduced more for that reason than to appease Canada.

Like LRTAP, the MOI lacks any serious enforcement mechanisms. This oversight allowed the United States to stall commitment to emissions reductions for several years. This means that there are no consequences for any increase in pollution that may occur as a result of the policies of the George W. Bush Administration. This administration has cut enforcement funding of the EPA by 13%, which has caused a drop of fifty cases where the agency was investigating violations of the Clean Air Act [31]. Potentially, this means that fifty more firms will be permitted to operate without meeting national air quality standards.

4.5.4 La Paz

The La Paz Agreement of 1983 was the first transnational agreement between the United States and Mexico to address the problem of transborder pollution caused by both countries. The agreement addressed urban air pollution and mobile pollution sources that were contributing to environmental degradation in congested areas along the border. It did this by setting up a cooperative network of air quality monitoring stations. Emissions reduction targets were set for smelters along the border, and air quality standards were implemented for border cities.

The outcome of the La Paz agreement may be viewed by some as slightly more effective than the MOI, though it is not without its shortcomings. A reduction in SO_2 emissions by smelters on the Mexican side of the border can be directly attributed to the La Paz agreement. Ambient air quality is no longer affected by smelter emissions because of this reduction [14]. Much is still to be accomplished, however, especially in regard to mobile source emissions. Neither the San Diego–Tijuana nor the El Paso–Ciudad Juarez border cities have met air quality standards by the target date. Visibility in U.S. National Parks is still a concern as SO_2 emissions from Mexico are contributing to the reduced visibility across the U.S. border. Again, the lack of an enforcement mechanism is cited as the major cause of this failure. Like the Eastern European States, Mexico lacks the financial resources to fully comply with the La Paz Agreement.

4.6 Conclusion: Future Trends in Transborder Air Pollution Control

All three of the agreements mentioned above have a recurring theme. They lack a direct enforcement mechanism or body. This fact contributes the most to these regimes' failures to substantially reduce transborder air pollution. While economic leverage may seem like a viable solution to enforcement of environmental regime regulations, the reality is that member states must first become willing participants of an agreement. Connecting protectionist trade policies to environmental regimes has a potential to prevent countries from signing the agreement altogether. Potential member states must feel that the regime is beneficial to them over all. An effective, if indirect, form of enforceability in a regime is transparency and accountability [1]. The LRTAP agreement was the most successful of the three agreements in this area because it required regular reporting from its member states of actions they were taking to comply with the agreement and the effects these actions were having on that country's air pollution problem. Because of the multi-lateral efforts to cooperate scientifically, this made false reporting undesirable. It was unlikely that an LRTAP member country could submit a false report without being caught [1].

Additionally, transparency of regimes is essential because it allows for the involvement of international civil society [27]. International civil society consists of scientists, non-governmental environmental organizations, the media, and other interest groups. By making the information available about the level of involvement and compliance of member states with regime regulations, international civil society is empowered with the knowledge to apply pressure to non-compliers. This can be an effective tactic in affecting the behavior of non-complying countries.

Another solution is to stop the problem at the source with agreements that are already in place. There is no denying that trade and the environment are inherently linked. Trade liberalization encourages production, which can increase environmental degradation. A poorly managed environment will ultimately lead to more expensive inputs or, worse, fewer inputs for the various modes of production required to make trade profitable. Therefore, it is essential that trade liberalization agreements incorporate environmental quality standards into their provisions. Amendments to these trade accords to follow NAFTA standards could eventually prevent the need for the formation of additional international environmental regimes. The problems would be mitigated before the need for such an organization arose.

The literature in favor and against linking trade benefits to compliance with environmental regulations is sizable. In the case of Eastern Europe and Mexico, trade restrictions may hinder rather than help the efforts to reduce emissions. This is because these countries are already experiencing economic difficulties that prevent them from complying with agreements in the first place. Adding to this problem with trade restrictions would have a counter effect. Using models like RAINS, which takes into account least cost solutions and cost benefit analysis, is a step in the right direction. Still, more needs to be done in the development of better models for assessing low cost alternatives. In the case of developing nations, it is important for countries like the United States, Western Europe and other developed nations involved in these regimes to provide assistance in order to achieve the target reductions agreed upon. This assistance could come in the form of low interest loans, like the ODA programs of Japan. These low-interest loans have been instrumental in the development of Chinese environmental projects that have led to reductions in acid deposition [21].

Another solution that needs to be explored is the development of cleaner technology. Continuing with green technology transfer and development between countries is an essential element for success. Many regimes provide for low cost technology transfer but not development. Additionally, there is little emphasis on multi-lateral development of alternative technologies that may reduce dependence on fossil fuels, the main contributor to air pollution. Again, members of these three regimes could stand to learn from the cooperative efforts of China and Japan. They have set up a joint fund to cover pollution abatement technologies. The success of the joint scientific studies of these regimes to identify transborder air pollution causes and effects indicates that additional collaborative efforts to develop technology could prove very effective.

The costs of adopting such technology, regardless of the development costs saved through multilateral cooperation, could prevent the economic viability of these alternatives in the current market economy. That is why when considering almost any environmental solutions, whether those developed through regime involvement or domestically, it is necessary to consider the true value of inputs and outputs. While traditional economics puts value on labor and capital, economic models often fail to account for the negative externalities of production and the less tangible, but no less important, market effects. Essentially, regime recommendations will not be considered economically viable by member countries until the values of economic indicators are changed to account for the true cost of unchecked pollution. This is because the costs of production in the market economy seem significantly lower when money does not have to be invested into pollution abatement or alternative energy technologies. The theories for applying quantitative values to environmental externalities are unfortunately beyond the scope of this paper. We do want to point out, however, that until previously ignored quantifiable costs (i.e., negative externalities) are fully incorporated, and important non-quantifiable costs and benefits are somehow included in market transactions any international pollution regime will, ultimately, fail.

Finally, the success of these regimes in combating transborder air pollution is essential if formation of other international regimes to alleviate global environmental problems is to follow. While the majority of international regimes have been formed to address regional transborder air pollution, the discovery of and research into intercontinental transport (ICT) of air pollutants may lead to the development of environmental regimes on a hemisphere or even global scale [22]. This is because the only way to effectively reduce the occurrence of ICT air pollutants is for countries to engage in multi-lateral agreements. This relates back to the common pool nature of air. It is imperative that successful regime characteristics be identified and followed if the formation of such a regime is to be successful.

While the LRTAP, the U.S.—Canada MOI and the La Paz agreements have not completely mitigated the problems associated with transborder air pollution, they definitely have the potential to become successful regimes. Maintaining transparency and accountability are essential elements for the compliance of member states. Amending trade agreements to combat environmental degradation at its source could eventually absorb the need for further regime formation. Additionally, recognizing the economic hardship of developing nations and accounting for that in these agreements through low interest loans or aid could help bring these nations up to par with global environmental standards. Also, adjusting economic indicators to reflect the true cost of pollution will show the real economic consequences and the necessity of adopting regime regulations. Finally, international regimes are in a unique position to benefit from collaboration on the development of alternative technologies that would reduce their dependence on the energy sources that are the main contributors to transborder air pollution. These elements are necessary if regimes to address other global atmospheric issues are to have a successful model to follow.

References

1. Young, O.R., *The Effectiveness of International Regimes*, MIT Press, Cambridge, 1999.
2. Wettestad, J., Designing effective environmental regimes: The conditional keys, *Global Governance*, 3, 317, 2001.
3. Brimblecombe, P., Environmental acidification, in *Global Atmospheric Chemical Change*, C.N. Hewitt and W.T. Sturges, Eds., Elsevier Applied Science, London, 1993, 236.
4. Pacific Institute, Economic Globalization and the Environment, 2004, Available at http://www.pacinst.org/topics/globalization_and_environment (accessed on May 12, 2006).
5. Yale Global Online, Environment, 2005. Available at http://yaleglobal.yale.edu/environment/ (accessed on May 12, 2006).
6. National Expert Group on Transboundary Air Pollution (NEGTAP), Report on transboundary air pollution: Acidification, eutrophication and ground level ozone in the U.K., Centre for Ecology and Hydrology, Edinburgh, 2001.
7. Wettestad, J., The ECE convention on long-range transboundary air pollution: From common cuts to critical loads, in *Science and Politics in International Environmental Regimes* S. Andresen, Eds., Manchester University Press, Manchester, 2000, 95.
8. Smith, Zachary A., *The Environmental Policy Paradox*, Princeton Hall, Upper Saddle River, 2004.
9. Darst, R.G., *Smokestack Diplomacy: Cooperation and Conflict in East–West Environmental Politics*, The MIT Press, Cambridge, 2001, 93.
10. Odintsov, D.I., Forestry problems related to air pollution in Central Asia, in *Air Pollution and the Forests of Developing and Rapidly Industrializing Countries*, J.L. Innes and A.H. Haron, Eds., CABI Publishing, Wallingford, 2000, 111.
11. Mentz, Fredric C., Transborder emissions trading between Canada and the United States, *Natural Resources Journal*, 35, 803, 1995.
12. Wirth, J.D., *Smelter Smoke in North America: The Politics of Transborder Pollution*, University Press of Kansas, Lawrence, 2000, 1.
13. Clarkson, J. and Schmandt, J., The role of air pollution in forest decline, in *Emerging Issues in Forest Policy*, 1st ed., P.N. Nemetz, Ed., UBC Press, Vancouver, 1992, 50.
14. Bureau of National Affairs, *Overview of the Environmental Laws of Mexico*, BNA Plus, Washington DC, 1992, III-13.
15. Luna, J.C., Legal framework for environmental protection in Mexico, in *International Environmental Law and Regulations*, Vol. 3, D. Campbell and S. Cotter, Eds., Wiley, Chichester, 1999, 175.
16. Maeda, T., Wang, Z., Hayashi, M., and Huang, M., Long-range transport of sulfur from Northeast Asia to Chengshantu, Shandong Peninsula: Measurement and simulation, *Water, Air, and Soil Pollution*, 130, 1793, 2001.
17. Murano, K., Mukai, H., Hatakeyama, S., Jang, E.-S., and Uno, I., Transboundary air pollution over remote islands in Japan: Observed data and estimates from a numerical model, *Atmospheric Environment*, 34, 5139, 2000.

18. Zarsky, L., Energy and the environment in Asia-Pacific: Regional cooperation and market governance, in *The Global Environment in the Twenty-First Century: Prospects for International Cooperation*, P.S. Chasek, Ed., United Nations University Press, Tokyo, 2000, 277.

19. Ohara, T., Uno, I., Wakamatsu, S., and Murano, K., Numerical simulation of the springtime trans-boundary air pollution in East Asia, *Water, Air and Soil Pollution*, 130, 295, 2001.

20. Alagappa, M., Environmental governance-the potential of regional institutions: Introduction, in *The Global Environment in the Twenty-First Century: Prospects for International Cooperation*, P.S. Chasek, Ed., United Nations University Press, Tokyo, 2000, 26.

21. Lai, H., Kawashima, H., Shindo, J., and Ohga, K. Stages in the history of China's acid rain control strategy in the light of China–Japan relations, *Water, Air and Soil Pollution*, 130, 1843, 2001.

22. Holloway, T., Fiore, A. and Galanter-Hastings, M., Intercontinental transport of air pollution: Will emerging science lead to a new hemispheric treaty? *Environment Science and Technology*, 37, 4535, 2003.

23. Statement from the International Conference on Alternatives to Globalization, Approved November 9, 1998. Available at http://www.earthisland.org/news /news_sage3.html (accessed on May 12, 2006).

24. Roe, E. and van Eeten, M.J.G., Three-not two-major environmental counter narratives to globalization, *Global Environmental Politics*, 4, 37, 2004.

25. Vogel, D., *Trading Up: Consumer and Environmental Regulation in a Global Economy*, Harvard University Press, Cambridge, 1995, 7.

26. Block, A., Trade and environment in the Western Hemisphere: Expanding the North American on environmental cooperation into the Americas, *Lewis and Clark Law School*, 33, 501, 2003.

27. von Moltke, K., Institutional interactions: The structure of regimes for trade and the environment, in *Global Governance*, O.R. Young, Ed., MIT Press, Cambridge, 1997, Chapter 9.

28. Ainsa, F. Jr., International cooperation in the abatement of environmental air pollution in the El Paso–Juarez area, in *Air Pollution Along the United States–Mexico Border*, H.G. Applegate and C.R. Bath, Eds., Texas Western Press, El Paso, 1974, 128.

29. Tuinstra, W., Hordijk, L., and Amann, M., Using computer models in international negotiations, *Environment*, 41, 32, 1999.

30. Wangwongwatana, S., Step-by-step approach to establish acid deposition monitoring network in East Asia (EANET): Thailand's experiences, *Water, Air and Soil Pollution*, 130, 151, 2001.

31. Moan, J.L. and Smith, Z.A., Bush and the environment, in *A Bird in the Bush: Failed Policies of the George W. Bush Administration*, C. Dowling, Ed., Algora Publishing, New York, 2005, 91.

Chapter 5

Desertification

Steffan Bauer
German Development Institute

5.1   Introduction

The issue of desertification is intriguing to study for both scholars who perceive of globalization as a recent phenomenon with a decidedly new quality of global interdependencies and for those who are more skeptical about its distinctiveness and novelty [1]. To begin with, the very question whether desertification is, after all, a global issue or not is a matter of heated debate among scientists as well as policy makers. Much like globalization, desertification has evolved as a complex, multifaceted phenomenon, and much like globalization, it is contested both as a concept and as a process [2,3]. I shall argue in the following that desertification is as much a product of globalization as it circumscribes a local environmental phenomenon that occurs across the globe and that is interlinked with several processes of global scope. Hence, the phenomenon of desertification itself does not necessarily require encompassing the whole globe in order to be associated with the phenomenon of globalization [4].

The chapter is organized in two main sections. The first is concerned with the key characteristics and underlying concepts of desertification. In this section, I will discuss the extent to which desertification actually constitutes a global issue. As a first step, I will address desertification from a geographical angle, thereby relating it to concepts of dryland degradation and drought. Secondly, I take a historical perspective on dryland degradation to show that, while there have always been deserts, desertification is a rather recent issue. In a third and final step of this section, I will highlight some global issues that are related to desertification in that they are indicative of global interdependencies that affect the world's dryland regions. To this end, I will elaborate in particular on the examples of agricultural trade liberalization as well as climate change and biological diversity. Having thus established that desertification can indeed be perceived as a global issue, in the second main section, I turn to the global political responses vis-à-vis the desertification phenomenon. First, I will trace how desertification has been globalized politically. Second, I will outline recent efforts to govern global desertification by way of an international legal commitment, the United Nations Convention to Combat Desertification (UNCCD). The latter sub-section will both describe the international institutional arrangements to halt desertification and discuss the instrumental status that is attributed to the convention in the global pursuit of sustainable development and poverty eradication. The chapter concludes with a brief outlook pertaining to the relevance of desertification for both global environmental governance and future research on globalization and the environment.

5.2   Desertification as a Global Issue

A glance at the plethora of definitions that seek to capture the essence of desertification is helpful to underscore just how contested the concept of desertification remains to this day in the fora of public policy as well as in academic circles [5–10]. Far more than one hundred definitions are dispersed throughout the literature of the natural and social sciences, thereby reflecting the prevalent taxonomic confusion as much as promoting it [11]. Much of the current debates about what desertification is and how it should be addressed as a global policy issue converge, however, around the definition provided in the UNCCD. Although this definition is inevitably disputed in its own right, it provides a useful point of reference. In the following, I will use the convention's definition, in which desertification is defined as "land degradation in arid, semi-arid and dry sub-humid areas resulting from various factors, including climatic variations and human activities" [12].

5.2.1   The Issue at Stake: Dryland Degradation

A look at the biophysical characteristics of arid and semi-arid lands as well as the geo-ecological processes that supposedly cause their desertification reveals why the very term is so contested. To begin with, the commonly envisaged image of encroaching deserts, i.e., wandering sand dunes that spread over hitherto fertile land to irretrievably bury it, grossly distorts the phenomenon that is actually occurring. Instead, desertification is first and foremost about the degradation of drylands. This, however, does not equal an expansive movement of existing deserts (although the latter arguably provides for a useful illustration of the potentially transboundary nature of ecological deterioration).

In terms of spatial scale, some 40% of the world's land mass can be classified as dryland and thus as potentially at risk of desertification [13]. It stands to reason that this risk is significantly higher for sub-humid and semi-arid zones compared to the arid and hyper-arid zones (comprising actual deserts), which have little to lose in terms of natural productivity. From the perspective of human livelihoods, the trajectory of desertification is, for the same reason, much more severe in semi-arid regions where there is a relatively high population density compared to scarcely inhabited deserts. The total population of the world's drylands inhabitants amounts to roughly two billion, about half of which dwell in rural livelihoods [13]. How many of these really are affected by dryland degradation and to what extent ultimately depends on the concepts and indicators that are applied to assess the vulnerability of these livelihoods and the extent and quality of dryland degradation [14,15]. Accordingly, available estimates vary widely. While various sources consider 70% and more of the world's drylands as degraded, the Millennium Ecosystem Assessment (MA) suggests a much more conservative 10%–20%. Even so, the livelihoods that need to be considered as severely affected amount to at least 250 million and probably up to 1.2 billion people, while many more are threatened by the prospect of desertification [7,13,16–21]. For instance, household members may as a consequence of desertification become economic refugees to supplement family income by way of sending remittances, or even whole families may be uprooted and forced to migrate in order to survive [22]. Again, while the general dynamic is well documented for parts of Africa, Asia, Latin America and the Middle East, precise quantification of desertification-related migration is highly uncertain on a global scale [22].

Uncertainty and variation in data estimates are symptomatic of the wide definition of desertification as it has been internationally established through the UNCCD. Conceptually employed to encapsulate a number of causes, effects, symptoms and interactions of a highly complex phenomenon, it almost inevitably brings with it a variety of arbitrary interpretations with potentially substantial implications. These will depend on who is referring to desertification, in which context, and, crucially, to what end. While this is widely acknowledged to be problematic, it is also pragmatically accepted that an unambiguous definition will not emerge in the foreseeable future [23]. Hence, instead of referring to desertification, experts often prefer to relate to the environmental process that is at the heart of the desertification discourse, namely dryland degradation. In a sense, dryland degradation provides the common denominator within the plethora of interpretations. Pertaining to the quality of land, a process of degradation always implies a loss in biological and economic productivity of soil as a natural resource. Again, however, judgments on soil productivity may lie in the eye of the beholder. As Herrmann and Hutchinson observe, what is a loss of productivity from the perspective of a peasant farmer might actually constitute a gain from the perspective of a livestock herder [11]. Once more, the text of the UNCCD provides for a widely used definition. Land degradation "means reduction or loss in arid, semi-arid and dry sub-humid areas, of the biological or economic productivity and complexity of rain fed cropland, irrigated cropland, or range, pasture, forest and woodlands resulting from land uses or from a process or a combination of processes, including processes arising from human activities and habitation patterns such as (i) soil erosion caused by wind and/or water; (ii) deterioration of the physical, chemical and biological or economic properties of soil; and (iii) long-term loss of natural vegetation" [12].

Two key terms that are inextricably linked to debates about desertification and dryland degradation are aridity and drought. While they are explained at length elsewhere, a basic awareness of these concepts is needed to grasp both the complexity and ramifications of desertification [6,8,11]. Crucially, these terms refer to distinct conditions and must not be used interchangeably. Aridity is the major climatic condition that defines the physical characteristic of drylands and deserts by way of a permanent rainfall deficit in association with high variability and unpredictability of precipitation. Drought, to the contrary, is a temporary event that is defined by rainfalls that are well below average over an extended period of time (typically more than one year) in a given region [11]. Moreover, episodes of drought may occur in any environment, not just drylands. In contrast to aridity, there is also a distinct social component to drought in as much as its impact on affected livelihoods tends to accumulate and often persist beyond an immediate drought period. For instance, conditions of drought-induced food insecurity may trigger migration even as precipitation patterns are returning to normal. In short, while aridity and drought are strikingly similar in their appearance, they both are fundamentally different natural phenomena [11].

Against these externally given natural background conditions, human land use activities have been the focus of policy debates and research on the causes and consequences of desertification. Yet, controversies typically arise about the extent to which the causes of desertification are natural or anthropogenic [24]. Evidently, the natural and human drivers of desertification can hardly be disentangled. This analytical problem is compounded by the highly politicized debates about the anthropogenic nature of global warming. Notwithstanding these delicate problems, natural and social scientists tend to agree that the immediate causes of dryland degradation result from a mixture of unsustainable human activities at the local level, namely the exploitation of soil and water resources beyond the limited carrying capacity of ecologically vulnerable drylands. The overgrazing and trampling of pastures, deforestation due to firewood consumption and commercial logging, expansive crop cultivation in fragile marginal lands, and intensive, often mono-cultural crop-cultivation are only some typical examples for the stress humans place on drylands. Often these are aggravated by accompanying increases in population pressure, which is exceptionally high in dryland regions [25]. Where these anthropogenic factors are at work, recurring droughts, desiccation, extreme weather events and global warming will inevitably exacerbate the exhaustion and erosion of soil as well as the depletion of water sources, but these factors are unlikely to trigger desertification by themselves. Hence, geographer Monique Mainguet cautions that the observation of land degradation makes for "a useful alarm signal from the environment to indicate when human activities have reached the threshold of tolerance" [21]. Of course, land degradation can affect any geographical region. Typically a short term process, it can be easily halted and even reversed, at least in theory. It is precarious, however, for the drylands in the world's arid and semi-arid regions where the capacities to attend to land degradation are typically severely compounded by endemic poverty. In addition, political and economic structures have proven unfavorable for sustainable land management in many of the affected countries, notably in Africa [26]. Consequently, in these regions land degradation is particularly prone to worsen incrementally, thus eventually amounting to full-fledged and irreversible desertification.

5.2.2 A Brief History of Desertification

Again like globalization, desertification is not necessarily a new phenomenon. Humankind has had a stake in the availability and accessibility of arable land and pastures ever since it started to cultivate crops and to herd livestock. Arguably, then, processes of anthropogenic land degradation are just as old. In fact, anecdotal evidence for an early human awareness of desertification is dispersed throughout literature. Plato is said to have deplored the vanishing of fertile soil in ancient Attica, Sumerian literature illustrates the adverse impact of deforestation in Mesopotamia, and the region of today's Argentina purportedly suffered from considerable land degradation at the time of the Spanish conquest. France and Great Britain installed a joint Anglo-French Forestry Commission to advise their colonial administrations on natural resource management [27]. This did little to prevent them, however, from spurring considerable dryland degradation in vast parts of West Africa through colonial plantations in the early 20th century. For instance, the areas west of today's Senegal and south of today's Niger were particularly affected by large-scale groundnut monocultures. The social conse-quences of land degradation in the North American "Dust Bowl" have found expression in American art and literature of the 1930s.*

The case is not settled, however, over who established desertification as a subject for systematic academic research, although natural scientists, geogra-phers and cultural anthropologists evidently were concerned with the respective issues as early as the 1920s. For instance, the aforementioned Anglo-French Forestry Commission also investigated evidence of an advan-cing desert in the West African colonies [27]. Several scholars attribute the coining of the term "désertification" to the French colonial geographer André Aubréville. While Aubréville's seminal *Climats, forêts et désertification de l'Afrique tropicale* (1949) assessed the progressive loss of vegetation cover and soil erosion in African drylands, he stopped short, however, of defining desertification [28]. A more systematic scientific inquiry into environments under arid and semi-arid climatic conditions only commenced in 1951 when the United Nations Educational, Scientific and Cultural Organization (UNESCO) established its Arid Zone Research Program. Commissioned through this program, Peveril Meigs eventually provided the taxonomic basis for most contemporary efforts to define arid conditions [11,29]. These pioneering achievements notwithstanding, the history of desertification *as a global issue* only really began with the 1977 United Nations Conference on Desertification, which followed the experience of the Great Sahelian Drought of the late 1960s and early 1970s. Its contribution to the globalization of

---

* See, but for two outstanding examples, *An American Exodus: A Record of Human Erosion in the Thirties* by photographer Dorothea Lange and agronomist Paul Taylor as well as John Steinbeck's novel *The Grapes of Wrath*, both originally published in 1939.

desertification and subsequent implications for the political responses to it will be addressed below.

5.2.3 Desertification and Global Interdependence

Considering that most historical examples of desertification, as well as recent ones, typically relate to local occurrences of dryland degradation, it would appear that the phenomenon is global merely in the sense that it can be observed all around the world. Moreover, there is considerable regional variation in the causes, appearance, and consequences of aridity. For instance, geographers distinguish four basic categories of deserts according to the dryland zones where they are found. These are the trade wind deserts beneath the subtropical atmospheric high-pressure zones, the continental deserts in the interior drainage basins of the mid-latitudes, the rain shadow deserts typically found on the lee side of mountain ranges, and the coastal deserts found at those continental edges that are affected by cold ocean currents [11]. Also, land degradation is higher both in extent and severity in some parts of Europe and North America than it is in those regions that are commonly associated with deserts and desertification, namely Africa and Asia [30]. Yet, the peoples of the latter regions are much more severely affected by desertification by way of complex interlinkages within their regional context, notably poverty, population pressures, governance issues and ensuing questions of food security. From this perspective, desertification might hence be considered as a predominantly regional affair.

The global scope and significance of desertification is immediately apparent when taking into account the global interdependencies that are evidently interlinked with desertification, even if the complexity of these interlinkages is only partly understood today. In fact, "a complex but plausible chain of causation between Western driving habits, Western transport and energy policies and the changing agricultural fortunes of Bangladesh or sub-Saharan Africa and their internal politics" can be established without much difficulty [31]. This relates in particular to the tangible interlinkages between desertification and two genuine global common problems that will be addressed below, namely climate change and the loss of biological diversity.

Moreover, from a perspective of political economy, the structuralist argument can be made that desertification is a global issue in as much as the supply and demand for arable land has become increasingly transnationalized. By definition, land degradation decreases both the quality and absolute availability of arable land. Land rights granting people access to (potentially) useful pastures and arable soil have always been a crucial determinant for socio-economic development and equity. Historic examples for local uprisings and violent conflicts about the use of land abound were often charged with ethnic or other pretexts. Yet, free market globalization and its inherent tendency to increase privatization does not stop short of land ownership. Hence, even more land is turned from a state controlled public good into private commodities, an increasing share of which is directly or indirectly managed by transnational enterprises. In conjunction with an eventual breakthrough in the liberalization of world trade in agricultural commodities, in itself an epitome of globalization, this trend is likely to intensify. To be sure, public ownership does not necessarily preclude the marginalization of rural population as can be witnessed in many poorly governed countries around the world. Nor does it guarantee properly functioning markets at macroeconomic and sector levels [32]. However, the appropriation of private land is clearly out of the reach of the rural poor, who predominantly inhabit the world's dryland regions. Consequently, the so-called anti-globalization movement, rather ironically a highly transnational phenomenon in its own right, has duly enlisted the cause of the landless among its objectives.

Not least, the issue of desertification is inherently linked to global political ambitions, namely the fight against world poverty and the promotion of sustainable development, both of which are again intertwined with the economic issue of agricultural trade liberalization. In the following, I will briefly discuss the global interdependencies between desertification and agricultural trade liberalization as well as among desertification, global warming and biological diversity to illustrate the actual globalization of the desertification phenomenon.

5.2.3.1 Agricultural Trade Liberalization

On many counts, the liberalization of world trade epitomizes the common understanding of globalization. If they provide a reliable and realistic barometer, the vivid and at times militant protests of the aforementioned anti-globalization movement routinely address the governmental conferences convening under the auspices of the World Trade Organization (WTO). In the realm of agricultural trade, liberalization has so far been comparatively modest due to persistent protectionist measures on behalf of developed countries, notably represented by the United States' farm bill and the European Union's common agricultural policy. Subsequent distortions of the world food markets seriously affect the terms of trade to the disadvantage of food producers in many poor dryland countries [13]. Accordingly, agricultural trade liberalization continues to be a bone of contention in protracted trade negotiations among a significant number of stakeholders with very different stakes. Yet, the history of the world trade regime and the agenda of the WTO's ongoing Doha Round suggest that further liberalization of agricultural trade is pending rather than stagnating [33]. The interdependencies of agricultural trade liberalization and desertification are two-fold. On the one hand, agricultural trade liberalization is supposed to substantially promote economic growth in the developing world and thus provide a powerful instrument in the fight against poverty. Indeed, the marginalization of developing country farmers in the world trade system is commonly perceived as a major driver of poverty [34]. This, it is further assumed, would in turn alleviate the pressures exerted on the world's drylands by the rural poor. On the other hand, the extension and intensification of agricultural production that is likely to ensue from agricultural trade liberalization is expected to accelerate dryland degradation, thus further compounding the scarcity of usable land

[13,34]. Export-oriented crop cultivation is typically accompanied by water shortages due to large scale irrigation, water pollution through the use of pesticides and fertilizers, and soil degradation both by sterilization and saliniza-tion. Either of these ecological impacts can be a driver of land degradation and accordingly increases the risk of desertification in dryland regions. Moreover, large-scale agricultural production for the world market bears the risk that rural populations may be further marginalized in terms of access to both land and markets, thus potentially off-setting whatever alleviation might be achieved through economic growth. Indeed, the globalizing aspects of the political economy would arguably benefit some stakeholders while others are left behind and unable to improve their lot in the globalization process [2].

5.2.3.2   Climate Change and Loss of Biological Diversity

Although estimations about the magnitude of recent global warming vary considerably, it is by now well established that it is indeed occurring, first, at an alarming rate and, second, mostly driven by anthropogenic factors [35]. First and foremost, anthropogenic climate change is linked to the large-scale emission of carbon dioxide and other greenhouse gases that follow from the tremendous energy consumption we find ingrained in the economic structures and sub-sequent behavioral patterns of the industrialized world [31]. Despite a lack of similarly robust knowledge on global precipitation patterns, it can reasonably be assumed that anthropogenic-induced global warming has serious consequences for desertification [36]. For one thing, natural scientists expect climate-related biological feedback loops to affect global desertification [37,38]. In particular, so-called carbon fertilization is hypothesised to boost plant growth by way of a carbon-dioxide enriched atmosphere. The latter is assumed to enhance photo-synthesis as well as water use efficiency in plants [11]. However, recent research cautions that the positive effects of carbon fertilization may be offset by an ensuing loss in soil nutrients [11]. More importantly, rising temperatures are certain to lead to increasing evapo-transpiration. This, in turn, further intensifies the feedback between global warming and desertification. Given no substantial changes in rainfall, increasing evapo-transpiration, in combination with continuous pressure from human land use under drier conditions, could ultimately cause the desertification of degraded drylands. This would then intensify global warming through the release of ever more carbon dioxide from cleared vegetation and the subsequent reduction of carbon sequestration potential of the degraded land [11]. The magnitude of this feedback is considerable. At the current rate of desertifica-tion, it is estimated that an annual average of 300 million tons of carbon are released into the atmosphere from drylands, which equals about 4% of all global greenhouse gas emissions [13].

A further dimension of the global ecology, biological diversity is deeply ingrained in most ecosystemic services that drylands potentially provide. It is adversely affected both by global warming, which tends to perturb the stability of ecosystems, and desertification, which directly compounds the loss of species as reductions in vegetation cover affect both flora and fauna. However, vegetation and its diversity of physical structures are instrumental in soil conservation, as well as the ability to fulfill crucial regulatory functions pertaining to rainfall infiltration, surface runoff and local microclimates. The disruption of these and other related ecosystemic services that are provided through dryland flora are found to be key drivers of desertification and accompanying manifestations, such as the loss of important habitats of a wide variety of species and reduced capacities of carbon sequestration [13]. Taken together, the strong interlinkages between desertification, biological diversity and climate change, underscore the globalization of desertification in spite of its local appearance.

5.3   Governing Global Desertification

In response to ongoing global transformations, the political world has turned to new governance approaches in order to adjust its problem-solving capacity to the magnitude of global challenges. The global governance of desertification can therefore be understood as a political process that involves a multiplicity of actors who interact at multiple levels and through a variety of institutional mechanisms [39,40]. Today, this process is contained, as well as guided, by a global convention that has evolved and is being implemented under the auspices of the United Nations.

5.3.1   *The Political Globalization of Desertification*

The issue of desertification eventually entered the arena of international politics in 1973, following a particularly severe drought and ensuing famine in the Sahel region (1968–1973). As an immediate response, several countries of the Sahel region stepped up their cooperative efforts by establishing an Inter-State Permanent Committee on Drought Control in the Sahel, to which the United Nations duly responded with the creation of a Sudano-Sahelian Office. Soon thereafter the United Nations Environment Program (UNEP) called for a United Nations Conference on Desertification (UNCOD), although the issue of desertification had not been addressed by the 1972 United Nations Conference on the Human Environment that had established and originally mandated the UNEP. UNCOD was eventually held in Nairobi in 1977 and has been lauded as one of the best scientifically prepared conferences of the 1970s [41]. At the conference, representatives of ninety-four governments actually produced a Plan of Action to Combat Desertification (PACD), albeit to little avail [5,41,42]. Notably, the UNEP-led Inter-Agency Working Group on Desertification proved unable to generate the necessary financial support from governments. However, the PACD, administered and monitored by the UNEP's Desertification Control/Program Activity Center, effectively established desertification as an issue of international environmental politics. From a normative perspective, desertification was no longer to be viewed as an exclusive problem of the Sahel region. At the same time, the ineffectiveness of the PACD in terms of substantive policy making fostered the notion that "if anything meaningful were ever to be done about desertification, the issue would have to attain higher international profile as a truly global issue" [43].

Thus, in association with the persistent demands of African governments, the UNEP and the PACD were instrumental in galvanizing the political globalization of desertification [43,44]. Even so, tangible efforts to address the phenomenon at the global level did only materialize in the wake of the United Nations Conference on Environment and Development, held in Rio de Janeiro in 1992 [5]. It was at this so-called "Earth Summit" that, at the insistence of developing countries, governments finally agreed to negotiate an international legal convention with the objective of halting the degradation of the world's drylands. The United Nations General Assembly duly established an intergovernmental negotiating committee that first convened in January 1993.* Ensuing intergovernmental negotiations came to an exceptionally swift close when the *UNCCD in those Countries Experiencing Serious Drought and/or Desertification, Particularly in Africa*, to quote its cumbersome full name, was formally adopted in Paris on June 17, 1994. Although most parties were explicitly unhappy with diverse elements of the treaty, the convention legally entered into force in 1996 after a comparably swift ratification process.† Today, 191 signatories are members to the convention, which equates to the closest approximation to universal membership of any comparable international legal agreement that has been achieved to date. Oddly, this impressive manifestation of the political globalization of desertification comes in conjunction with an explicit prioritization of Africa as well as several regional annexes, which underscore the divergent expectations concerning the convention's implementation [12].

Despite the universal endorsement of the convention and the extraordinary brevity of the negotiations preceding it, the UNCCD process is second to none in exposing fundamental political tensions between the developed and the developing world, notably concerning state obligations and financial provisions. In addition, the negotiation process unveiled unprecedented stark tensions within the coalition of the global South, which were overcome by the developed countries' reluctance to concede to a convention on desertification in the first place [43,45]. In fact, attaining the UNCCD has widely been interpreted as a token of the bargaining power that developing countries might derive from an increased global awareness of ecological interdependence [45–50]. Namely, the developed countries' approval to negotiate a convention on desertification at the UNCED was a price on which the G77 and China insisted for their acceptance of the Northern-driven Convention on Biological Diversity (CBD) and UN Framework Convention on Climate Change (UNFCCC) respectively, both of which were opened for signature at Rio.

There is by now an increasingly substantive amount of literature on the negotiation process that led to the convention. In the most comprehensive assessment to date, Elisabeth Corell scrupulously examined the UNCCD's evolution, thereby bringing to the fore the inherently political nature of the prevailing desertification discourse [5]. A chief witness, long-term UNCCD Executive Secretary Hama A. Diallo, underscores this reading by observing

---

* See UNGA Resolution 47/188 of December 22, 1992.
† After receiving from Chad its 50th ratification on December 26, 1996.

that "desertification has a political appeal that land degradation does not have" [5]. Indeed, the framing of desertification enshrined by the convention bears strong implications for its interpretation by policy makers as well as the general public with crucial repercussions for the translation of its objectives in terms of policy implementation. Notwithstanding plausible scientific objections as to the elusiveness of desertification as a concept, in the realm of international politics desertification has thus undeniably become a global issue.

5.3.2 The UNCCD Process in its First Decade

One decade after its entry into force, the UNCCD remains an intriguing case to study, not only in a view of globalization but also in terms of global environmental governance. However, owing to the relative youth of the UNCCD process, no studies are yet available to evaluate the achievements of the UNCCD in a manner that could possibly match the insights of the case studies available for many other multilateral environmental agreements. In the following section, I will outline how the UNCCD has thus far been implemented and how this relates to the global political issue that desertification has become in the two decades preceding the adoption of the convention. As is to be expected, the implementation of the UNCCD strongly reflects its genesis in the context of the UNCED and the ensuing ubiquity of the sustainable development paradigm in global environmental policy making. In fact, as the only one of the so-called Rio Conventions that was actually spawned, as opposed to being opened for signature at the Rio Summit, the UNCCD gives ample reference to the norms and principles that dominated debates at the UNCED [47,51,52]. In particularly notable distinction from the time-honored international environmental agreements of the 1970s and 1980s, the UNCCD places a strong and explicit emphasis on the involvement of nongovernmental stakeholders, particularly community based organizations, thereby reflecting the UNCED's emphasis on participatory approaches to policy making and implementation. The relative success in this endeavor is reflected by a growing number of studies that scrutinize the influence exerted by non-state participants in the UNCCD process [5,27,53–55]. Moreover, the "spirit of Rio" has also transpired to respective provisions in the convention that are meant to further decentralize modes of governance and to appropriately appreciate local knowledge in the combat against desertification [52,56–59].

Consequently, many professionals engaged in the implementation of the convention, both at national and international levels, do not necessarily perceive the UNCCD as an environmental treaty. This reading of the convention is prominently underscored by UNCCD officials, who like to promote the UNCCD as "the sustainable development convention" in order to distinguish it from the plethora of multilateral environmental agreements. In fact, highlighting once more the complexity of desertification, implementation of the UNCCD is also intended to be instrumental in the global fight against poverty [12]. Poverty, it is recognized, can be both a cause and a consequence of dryland degradation.

Consequently, measures to combat desertification should ideally address poverty and sustainable land management simultaneously [60]. Many have subsequently considered the UNCCD as a development convention and its primary objective as fighting poverty, thereby reflecting salient differences of opinion that protracted the negotiations of the convention between developing and developed countries. The underlying desire, mostly on part of developing countries, to fashion the UNCCD's implementation in a manner that prioritizes poverty reduction over environmental protection is as apparent as it is politically legitimate. It is for this precise reason, however, that developed countries have been reluctant to acknowledge desertification as a global commons problem and to commit themselves to substantive legal obligations. Hence, the future success or failure of the UNCCD will arguably depend on the effective mediation of divergent perspectives on the environment-poverty-nexus [61].

Thus far, the implementation of the UNCCD has been predominated by its formal institutionalization at the international level and within the geographical regions specified in the respective annexes to the convention [12]. Formally, this process began with the first Conference of Parties (COP), which convened in Rome in the fall of 1997, although some institutional provisions had already been taken in the interim period following the adoption of the convention and during which the negotiations committee continued to meet. Constituted by all signatories of the convention, the COP is the political core around which the UNCCD regime is built. It convenes every two years and acts as the principal governing body of the convention. In this function, the parties are seconded by a Committee on Science and Technology (CST) and, since 2002, a Committee for the Review of the Implementation of the Convention (CRIC).* The former is designed to promote the coordination of scientific research on desertification related issues and to facilitate the transfer of relevant technologies between the parties, thereby paying special attention to local know-how and practices. The latter is meant to meet on an annual basis to provide for a continual review of the implementation of the convention and to develop policy recommendations accordingly. All of these bodies are serviced by the UNCCD Secretariat that, after an interim period at the UN offices in Geneva, took its permanent offices alongside the UNFCCC Secretariat in Bonn, Germany, in 1999 [62]. Although considerably smaller than the latter, the UNCCD Secretariat operates on equal footing in terms of international protocol, which implies an elevated status compared to the majority of environmental treaty secretariats, at least formally [63]. One manifestation thereof, the UNCCD Executive Secretary is ex officio Assistant Secretary-General to the United Nations. As the administrative hub within the UNCCD regime, the secretariat also maintains the interlinkages of the UNCCD with other international agencies, notably the United Nations headquarters, the World Bank, the Food and Agricultural Organization (FAO), the International Fund for Agricultural Development (IFAD) and the United Nations Environment Program (UNEP), the climate change and biodiversity conventions as well as a number of regional organizations and a range of banks

---

* The CRIC was formally established by COP-5 in Geneva in October 2001 (ICCD/COP(5)/L.15.).

and funding agencies [64]. Due to their placement, perhaps, within this complex institutional setting, procedural and institutional matters dominated the first couple of COP meetings. Again reproducing the compromises of the original negotiations, much time has been spent in particular debating the financing of UNCCD implementation. In this respect, the convention provides for a global mechanism, which is administered through the IFAD and is meant to liaise between UNCCD related development projects and the appropriate multilateral donor agencies [65]. Yet, developing countries made it clear that they felt short-changed by lack of a genuine UNCCD funding mechanism. The issue proved to be a major bone of contention at virtually every COP gathering, but has meanwhile been ameliorated, if not entirely solved, by the incorporation of sustainable land management into the portfolio of the Global Environment Facility (GEF) as of 2003 [66]. This has been perceived by many as an overdue step, which developing countries, notably from Africa, had aspired to ever since the establishment of the GEF in 1994. Not least, GEF eligibility in its own right signifies the globalization of desertification because the facility is exclusively mandated to fund projects pertaining to the protection of the global commons. Following this breakthrough in the international institutionalization of the UNCCD, governments eventually turned to the substantive aspects of on the ground policy implementation at their sixth COP, which was held in Havana, Cuba, in 2003. Yet, the issue of financing the convention process and the UNCCD's eligibility for GEF funds is exemplary for the many issues that had proven insurmountable throughout the negotiations and which basically remained unresolved at the time the UNCCD was adopted. Hence, time and again these issues return to haunt the parties, thus arguably inhibiting a more efficient implementation of the convention. Indeed, it appears uncertain whether the challenges associated with the transition from formal institutionalization to substantive operationalizing will effectively be solved in the immediate future [67].

Thus far, serious judgments of the UNCCD's effectiveness in terms of tangible impacts on the ground can hardly be made. As might be expected, however, the few qualitative case studies that are available indicate marked discrepancies between regime intentions and local implementation [56,58]. Although the high-flying sustainable development principles laid out in the convention transpire to national discourses on land development policies, they have a long way to go to eventually converge with the realities of local communities affected by desertification. Analytically, an assessment of the UNCCD's impact on the ground is further exacerbated by the fact that links between local land management policies and national applications of UNCCD provisions often remain vague. Even if these links could be clearly identified, the separation of the specific outcomes of the UNCCD from the background noise of general political and socio-economic developments will remain problematic [68]. Indeed, a satisfactory solution is not in sight as to how certain observable effects may be causally attributed to the implementation of the UNCCD amidst myriad variables that are potentially interfering with the complexity of desertification [69].

5.4 Summary and Outlook

Profound interlinkages with the global development agenda notwithstanding, desertification and dryland degradation are concepts that relate first and foremost to global environmental change. Specifically, desertification circumscribes processes of environmental degradation in the roughly 40% of the Earth's land masses that are climatically arid, semi-arid or sub-humid. Contrary to popular belief, desertification neither relates to an encroachment of existing deserts nor is it a genuine global commons issue in the sense that global warming or stratospheric ozone depletion are. Despite significant global interlinkages, desertification as such, occurs locally and accordingly, needs to be primarily addressed at local and regional levels where it may be halted or reversed. Yet, desertification has evolved as a globalization concept that has achieved considerable status, both symbolically and substantially, in the intricate governance of north–south relations. Besides, the process by which the political globalization of desertification has been advanced undergirds the notion that global policy making is no longer an exclusive domain of nation states. Academic experts, international bureaucrats, multinational enterprises and civil society actors at local, national and transnational levels have all had a part to play in shaping the ways in which desertification is perceived, and, subsequently influence the outcomes of global desertification politics. The global governance approach to dryland degradation has found its expression manifested in the UNCCD. Although the latter evidently evolved as a product of two decades of international environmental politics, it simultaneously reflects a global paradigm shift in which development concerns have arguably taken precedence over environmental issues since the 1992 United Nations Conference on Environment and Development and, even more so, since the global endorsement of the Millennium Development Goals in 2000 and the 2002 World Summit on Sustainable Development. Part and parcel of the global discourse on sustainable development, the UNCCD process in its first decade has indeed contributed to highlighting the interlinkages among desertification, environmental protection and poverty. Hence, the global response to desertification embodied by the UNCCD can in parallel be seen as a manifestation of the globalization of the sustainable development paradigm [52].

Against this background, some argue that the implementation of the UNCCD epitomizes postmodern global governance [70]. Skeptics caution, however, that the establishment of a global convention was a wrong strategic choice to address the manifold problems associated with drylands development and that the UNCCD evades the real challenges that people affected by desertification are facing [42]. Arguably, now that the UNCCD process at last seems prepared "to move from its initial conceptual phase to a much awaited implementation phase" it finds itself at a crossroad [34]. Whichever path it may take, the global magnitude of both the severe socio-economic and environmental ramifications of desertification is not to be denied. What remains to be seen, however, is whether the "combat" against desertification can and will be effectively fought by global means or whether humankind would be better advised to de-globalize desertification and resort to addressing land degradation on the ground. In this context, the policy relevance of competing conceptual understandings of desertification must not be forgotten. While the United Nations definition does provide useful relief from the taxonomic haggling preceding the UNCCD, it does not actually solve the problems that are ineluctably attached to a definition that is neither scientifically precise nor politically unambiguous. Clearly, a solution to this dilemma is not in sight. Alas, the limitations of the prevalent concept of desertification and its implications in terms of how it is employed academically as well as politically always need to be borne in mind as we strive for a better understanding of desertification as both a product and a driver of global environmental change.

References

1. Keohane, R.O. and Nye, J.S., Globalization: What's new? What's not? (and so what?), *Foreign Policy*, 118, 104, 2000.
2. Kütting, G. and Rose, S., The environment as a global issue, in *International Environmental Politics*, M.M. Betsill, K. Hochstetler, and D. Stevis, Eds., Macmillan/Palgrave, Basingstoke, 2005, 113–141.
3. Robertson, R. and Scholte, J.A. Eds., *Encyclopedia of Globalization*, Routledge, London, forthcoming.
4. Prakash, A. and Hart, J.A., Globalization and governance: An introduction, in *Globalization and Governance*, A. Prakash and J.A. Hart, Eds., Routledge, London, 1999, 1–24.
5. Corell, E., The negotiable desert, expert knowledge in the negotiations of the convention to combat desertification, in *Linköping Studies in Arts and Sciences*, Linköping University, Routledge, 1999, 191.
6. Dregne, H.E., *Desertification of Arid Lands*, Harwood, London, 1983.
7. Middleton, N.J. and Thomas, D.S.G., *World Atlas of Desertification*, Edward Arnold Publishers/UNEP, London, 1992.
8. Mainguet, M., *Desertification, Natural Background and Human Mismanagement*, 2nd ed., Springer, Berlin, 1994.
9. Reynolds, J.F., Desertification, in *Encyclopedia of Biodiversity*, S. Levin, Ed., Academic, San Diego, CA, 2001, 61–78.
10. Glantz, M.H. and Orlovsky, N., Desertification: A review of the concept, *Desertification Control Bulletin*, 9, 15, 1983.
11. Herrmann, S.M. and Hutchinson, C.F., The Scientific Basis: Linkages Between Land Degradation, Drought, and Desertification, in *Governing Global Desertification, Linking Environmental Degradation, Poverty and Participation*, P.M. Johnson, K. Mayrand, and M. Paquin, Eds., Ashgate, Aldershot, 2006, 11–25.
12. UNCCD. *United Nations Convention to Combat Desertification in Those Countries Experiencing Serious Drought and/or Desertification, particularly in Africa, Text with Annexes, and a Preface by the UNCCD Secretariat*, UNCCD, Bonn, 2002.
13. MA, Millennium Ecosystem Assessment. *Ecosystems and Human Well-Being: Desertification Synthesis*, World Resources Institute, Washington DC, 2005.
14. Downing, T.E. and Lüdeke, M., International desertification: Social geographies of vulnerability and adaptation, in *Global Desertification, Do Humans Cause Deserts?* J.F. Reynolds and D.M. Stafford Smith, Eds., Dahlem University Press, Berlin, 2002, 233–252.
15. Vogel, C.H. and Smith, J.R., Building social resilience in arid ecosystems, in *Global Desertification, Do Humans Cause Deserts?* J.F. Reynolds and D.M. Stafford Smith, Eds., Dahlem University Press, Berlin, 2002, 233–252.

16. Katyal, J. and Vleg, P., Desertification: Concept, causes and Amelioration, ZEF discussion Paper Nr. 33, Zentrum für Entwicklungsforschung, Bonn, 2000.

17. Reynolds, J.F. and Stafford Smith, D.M., Eds., Global desertification, Do humans cause deserts? J. Lupp, Ed., *The Dahlem Konferenzen*, Dahlem University Press, Berlin, 2002, 88.

18. UNEP, United Nations Environment Programme. *GEO-3, Global Environment Outlook*, UNEP/Earthprint, Stevenage, 2002.

19. UNCCD. Desertification secretariat. *Down to Earth, A Simplified Guide to the Convention to Combat Desertification, Why it is Necessary and What is Important and Different About It?* UNCCD, Bonn, 1995.

20. UNCCD. *Preserving Our Common Ground: UNCCD 10 Years On*, UNCCD, Bonn, 2004.

21. Thomas, D.S.G. and Middleton, N.J., *Desertification: Exploding the Myth*, Wiley, Chichester, 1994.

22. Leighton, M., Desertification and migration, in *Governing Global Desertification, Linking Environmental Degradation, Poverty and Participation*, P.M. Johnson, K. Mayrand, and M. Paquin, Eds., Ashgate, Aldershot, 2006, 43–58.

23. Stafford Smith, D.M. and Reynolds, J.F., Desertification, a new paradigm for an old problem, in *Global Desertification, Do Humans Cause Deserts?* J.F. Reynolds and D.M. Stafford Smith, Eds., Dahlem University Press, Berlin, 2002, 403–424.

24. Reynolds, J.F. and Stafford Smith, D.M., Do humans cause deserts? in *Global Desertification, Do Humans Cause Deserts?* J.F. Reynolds and D.M. Stafford Smith, Eds., Dahlem University Press, Berlin, 2002, 1–21.

25. Johnson, P.M., Mayrand, K., and Paquin, M., Eds., *Governing Global Desertification, Linking environmental degradation, poverty and participation*; Kirton, J. and von Moltke, K., Eds., *Global Environmental Governance*, Ashgate, Aldershot, 2006.

26. AMCEN/UNEP, African Ministerial Conference on the Environment and United Nations Environment Programme. *Africa Environment Outlook. Past, Present and Future Perspectives*, Earthprint/UNEP, Stevenage/Nairobi, 2002.

27. Long Martello, M., Expert advice and desertification policy: Past experience and current challenges, *Global Environmental Politics*, 4, 85, 2004.

28. Aubréville, A., *Climats, Forêts et DéSertification de l'Afrique Tropicale*, Societé d'éditions géographiques, maritime et coloniales, Paris, 1949.

29. Meigs, P., in *World Distribution of Arid and Semi-Arid Homoclimates*, United Nations Educational Scientific and Cultural Organization, Ed., UNESCO, Paris, 1953, 203–210.

30. UNEP in *UNEP's Strategy on Land Use Management and Soil Conservation, A Strengthened Functional Approach*, UNEP Division of Policy Development and Law, Ed. in *Policy Series*, UNEP, Nairobi, 2004, 4.

31. Held, D., McGrew, A., Goldblatt, D., and Perraton, J., Catastrophe in the making: Globalization and the environment, in *Global Transformations*, D. Held, A. McGrew, D. Goldblatt, and J. Perraton, Eds., Stanford University Press, Stanford, 1999, 376–413.

32. Harou, P.A., What is the role of markets in altering the sensitivity of arid land systems to perturbation? in *Global Desertification, Do Humans Cause Deserts?* J.F. Reynolds and D.M. Stafford Smith, Eds., Dahlem University Press, Berlin, 2002, 437.

33. WTO, World Trade Organization, Ministerial Declaration. Doha, Qatar, 14 November 2001, WT/MIN(01)/DEC/1, World Trade Organization, Geneva, 2001.

34. Mayrand, K. and Paquin, M., Agriculture, trade, and desertification: Implications for UNCCD, in *Governing Global Desertification. Linking Environmental Degradation, Poverty, and Participation*, P.M. Johnson, K. Mayrand, and M. Paquin, Eds., Ashgate, Aldershot, 2006, 177–193.

35. IPCC, Intergovernmental Panel on Climate Change, Climate Change 2001: Synthesis Report. Summary for Policymakers, IPCC Plenary XVIII, Wembley, UK, 24-29 September 2001, IPCC Secretariat, Geneva, 2001.

36. Nicholson, S.E., What are the key components of climate as a driver of desertification?, in *Global Desertification, Do Humans Cause Deserts?* J.F. Reynolds and D.M. Stafford Smith, Eds., Dahlem University Press, Berlin, 2002, 41–57.

37. Schlesinger, W.H., Reynolds, J.F., Cunninghmn, G.L., Huenneke, L.F., Jarrell, W.M., Virginia, R.A., and Whitford, W.G., Biological feedbacks in global desertification, *Science*, 247, 1043, 2004.

38. Xue, Y. and Fennessy, M.J., Under what condition does land-cover change impact regional climate? in *Global Desertification. Do Humans Cause Deserts?* J.F. Reynolds and D.M. Stafford Smith, Eds., Dahlem University Press, Berlin, 2002, 59–74.

39. Biermann, F., Global governance and the environment, in *International Environmental Politics*, M.M. Betsill, K. Hochstetler, and D. Stevis, Eds., Palgrave Macmillan, Basingstoke, 2005, 237–261.

40. Dingwerth, K. and Pattberg, P., Global governance as a perspective on world politics, *Global Governance* 12, 185, 2006.

41. McCormick, J., *The Global Environmental Movement. Reclaiming Paradise*, Indiana University Press, Bloomington, 1989.

42. Toulmin, C., Combating desertification: Encouraging local action within a global framework, in *Green Globe Yearbook of International Co-operation on Environment and Development*, H.O. Bergesen and G. Parmann, Eds., Oxford University Press, Oxford, 1994.

43. Najam, A., Negotiating desertification, in *Governing Global Desertification. Linking Environmental Degradation, Poverty and Participation*, P.M. Johnson, K. Mayrand, and M. Paquin, Eds., Ashgate, Aldershot, UK, 2006, 56–72.

44. Corell, E., Dryland degradation—Africa's main environmental challenge: International activities from the 1970s to the 1990s and the future of the United Nations convention to combat desertification, in *International Environmental Law and Policy in Africa*, B. Chaytor and K.R. Gray, Eds., Kluwer, Dordrecht, 2003, 1–29.

45. Najam, A., Dynamics of the southern collective: Developing countries in desertification negotiations, *Global Environmental Politics*, 4, 128, 2004.

46. Agarwal, A., Narain, S., and Sharma, A., *Green Politics: Global Environmental Negotiations*, Centre for Science and Development, New Delhi, 1999.

47. Chasek, P.S., The convention to combat desertification: Lessons learned for sustainable development, *Journal of Environment and Development*, 6, 147, 1997.

48. Chasek, P., *Earth Negotiations: Analyzing Thirty Years of Environmental Diplomacy*, United Nations University Press, Tokyo, 2001.

49. Sell, S., North–south environmental bargaining: Ozone, climate change, and biodiversity, *Global Governance*, 2, 97, 1996.

50. Gupta, J., Global environmental governance: Challenges for the south from a theoretical perspective, in *A World Environment Organization: Solution or Threat for Effective International Environmental Governance?* F. Biermann and S. Bauer, Eds., Ashgate, Aldershot, 2005, 5783.

51. Toulmin, C., Combating desertification by conventional means, *Global Environmental Change*, 5, 455, 1995.

52. Bruyninckx, H., Sustainable development: The institutionalization of a contested policy concept, in *International Environmental Politics*, M.M. Betsill, K. Hochstetler, and D. Stevis, Eds., Palgrave Macmillan, Basingstoke, 2005, 265–298.

53. Corell, E. and Betsill, M.M., A comparative look at NGO influence in international environmental negotiations: Desertification and climate change, *Global Environmental Politics*, 1, 86, 2001.

54. Knabe, F., Civil society's role in negotiating and implementing the UNCCD, in *Governing Global Desertification. Linking Environmental Degradation, Poverty and Participation*, P.M. Johnson, K. Mayrand, and M. Paquin, Eds., Ashgate, Aldershot, 2006, 89–107.

55. Bauer, S., Does bureaucracy really matter? The authority of intergovernmental treaty secretariats in global environmental politics, *Global Environmental Politics*, 6, 23, 2006.

56. Bruyninckx, H., The convention to combat desertification and the role of innovative policy-making discourses: The case of Burkina Faso, *Global Environmental Politics*, 4, 107, 2004.

57. Oettlé, N., Knowledge and the UNCCD: The community exchange and training programme, in *Governing Global Desertification, Linking Environmental Degradation, Poverty, and Participation*, P.M. Johnson, K. Mayrand, and M. Paquin, Eds., Ashgate, Aldershot, 2006, 163–175.

58. Pearce, R., Decentralisation and sustainable resources management in West Africa: A line of action for revising national action programmes, in *Governing Global Desertification. Linking Environmental Degradation, Poverty, and Participation*, P.M. Johnson, K. Mayrand, and M. Paquin, Eds., Ashgate, Aldershot, 2006, 147–162.

59. Poulsen, L. and Lo, M., Promoting good governance through the implementation of the UNCCD, in *Governing Global Desertification, Linking Environmental Degradation, Poverty, and Participation*, P.M. Johnson, K. Mayrand, and M. Paquin, Eds., Ashgate, Aldershot, 2006, 109–130.

60. Way, S.A., Examining the linkages between poverty and land degradation: From blaming the poor towards recognising the rights of the poor in marginal dryland areas, in *Governing Global Desertification. Linking Environmental Degradation, Poverty and Participation*, P.M. Johnson, K. Mayrand, and M. Paquin, Eds., Ashgate, Aldershot, 2006, 29–42.

61. WBGU, German Advisory Council on Global Change. *Fighting poverty through environmental policy.* World in Transition Series, Earthscan, London, 2004.

62. Bauer, S., The United Nations and the fight against desertification: What role for the UNCCD secretariat? in *Governing Global Desertification, Linking Environmental Degradation, Poverty, and Participation*, P.M. Johnson, K. Mayrand, and M. Paquin, Eds., Ashgate, Aldershot, 2006, 73–87.

63. Bauer, S., Busch, P.-O., and Siebenhüner, B., Bureaucratic organizations in international environmental governance: Administering "our common future", Paper read at SCORE Conference "Organizing the World: Rules and rule-setting among organizations", 13–15 October 2005, at Handelshogskolan Stockholm, 2005.

64. Chasek, P.S. and Corell, E., Addressing desertification at the international level, the institutional system, in *Global Desertification, Do Humans Cause Deserts?* J.F. Reynolds and D.M.S. Smith, Eds., Dahlem University Press, Berlin, 2002, 275–294.

65. Falloux, F., Tressler, S., and Mayrand, K., The global mechanism and UNCCD financing: Constraints and opportunities, in *Governing Global Desertification. Linking Environmental Degradation, Poverty and Participation*, P.M. Johnson, K. Mayrand, and M. Paquin, Eds., Ashgate, Aldershot, 2006, 131–145.

66. Johnson, P.M., Mayrand, K., and Paquin, M., *Conclusion: The UNCCD at a crossroad*, Governing Global Desertification, Linking Environmental Degradation, Poverty, and Participation, Ashgate, Aldershot, 2006.

67. Biermann, F. and Bauer, S., Assessing the effectiveness of intergovernmental organisations in international environmental politics, *Global Environmental Change*, 14, 189, 2004.

68. Wettestad, J., The effectiveness of environmental policies, in *International Environmental Politics*, M.M. Betsill, K. Hochstetler, and D. Stevis, Eds., Palgrave Macmillan, Basingstoke, 2005, 373–410.

69. Rechkemmer, A., Postmodern Global Governance. The United Nations Convention to Combat Desertification, Stiftung Wissenschaft und Politik, Ed. in *Aktuelle Materialien zur Internationalen Politik Nr. 71*, Nomos, Baden-Baden, 2004.

70. Toulmin, C., *Lessons from the Theatre: Should this be the Final Curtain Call for the Convention to Combat Desertification, IIED Opinion—World Summit on Sustainable Development*, International Institute for Environment and Development, London, 2001.

Chapter 6

The Environmental Frontier of Space

W. Henry Lambright and Anna Ya Ni
Syracuse University

6.1   Introduction

Space, "the Final Frontier," is surely a technological frontier. But it is also an environmental frontier. It is an environmental frontier in at least three ways. First, the vantage point of space can be used to monitor planet Earth and its environmental problems, whether natural or man-made. Second, near-Earth orbit is a place that is occupied and used by human beings and their machines. This place has certain unique features that make it a valuable, exploitable, and scarce resource. It is also getting crowded and thus polluted with debris. Third, the exploration of deep space—the Moon, Mars and beyond—presents opportunities, but also potential dangers of environmental contamination, forward to other celestial bodies, backward to Earth. Moreover, there are conflicts involving environmental values at this third frontier. As space is opened up for human use, conflicting visions arise between those who see space, especially Mars, as the next place to be conquered and developed and those who see it as a special, pristine place to be protected.

This essay tracks these three "frontiers" of space as an environmental policy concern. Most policy activity has been about the first frontier, using space in relation to the home planet. There has been some policy development concerned with the second. The third frontier has received minimal attention from policymakers. Environmental policy has evolved with the development and application of space technology. This essay analyzes each of the three faces of space-environment policy. The emphasis is on policymaking by the National Aeronautics and Space Administration (NASA) and the United States, the world's dominant space power. However, the roles of other agencies and nations are discussed as relevant. They have become more significant from a space and environmental standpoint as the years have passed.

6.2   Conceptual Framework

To discuss space and environment, we use the lens of policy change in relation to technology. A new technology comes into being, for example, space technology in 1957 with the launch of Sputnik. Actors (national, sub-national, international) became aware of the possible uses of space technology. They advocate policies that favor using space for particular purposes in their interests. As space technology is developed and implemented, it provides a push for policy and opens new options. Some of these relate to positive environmental uses of the technology. So also are negative environmental impacts envisioned. Over time, policies to deal with the positive and negative environmental dimensions of space technology are enacted.

In the three areas of space/environment studied—earth observation, near-earth orbit, deep space—technology and policy have advanced unevenly. Earth observation is a direct environmental application of space technology. Hence, it has seen the most space-environment interaction and policy development. Earth satellites can "see" environmental change and monitor the impacts of environmental treaties. This is not to say that the Earth observation front is all well in terms of policy. There are unresolved policy problems in the transition of satellite technology from research and development (R&D) to use. In near-Earth orbit, the environmental policy dimensions are essentially related to negative impacts of the long-term use of a place. There are issues of crowding and also of debris from past use. These policy matters are much less developed than those in the first realm. In deep space, there was environmental policy in connection with Apollo and speculation about what comes next with using the Moon and especially Mars.

6.3   Space and the Home Planet

National Aeronautics and Space Administration is a space agency with an environmental mission. That mission was implicit in the 1960s and has become ever more explicit subsequently. Formed in 1958, NASA then and now has emphasized manned space flight and missions *from* Earth. But it has always had Earth as an "applications" emphasis via its satellites. The initial environmental application proved extraordinarily significant—the weather satellite.

The first weather satellite, Tiros, went up in 1960. Quickly, meteorologists saw how it could help the science of weather forecasting. The unprecedented views of advancing weather systems gave them a powerful new tool, an instrument they wanted and needed. One of the most spectacular uses was tracking hurricanes. In 1961, Tiros spotted Hurricane Carla as it approached the Gulf Coast. Its early warning enabled 350,000 people to evacuate. Again and again, weather satellites literally saved lives, especially in 1969, when it alerted the United States to a giant storm, Camille, as it approached the country from afar [1].

This weather satellite was successful not only because of its obvious relevance to meteorology, but also because a policy regime was constructed in the mid-1960s that enabled it to be put to use effectively. NASA was an R&D agency and its role was to develop ever more sophisticated satellites. The Weather Bureau, absorbed into the National Oceanic and Atmospheric Administration (NOAA) in 1970, was a user. There were sharp conflicts between NASA and the Weather Bureau in the 1960s, but that decade ended with an agreement between the two agencies. NASA would develop technology. As satellites became operational, they would pass to the Weather Bureau/NOAA to use. NASA paid for the R&D and the Weather Bureau/NOAA subsequently paid for operations. To the extent that NASA created satellites that were more advanced (and expensive) than NOAA needed, those satellites had an alternative user—the scientific community or possibly the military. With NASA paying the bill, the space agency worked with the atmospheric science community to learn more about the upper atmosphere [2,3].

The weather satellite represented the earliest direct connection between NASA and the Earth environment. Another connection, albeit indirect, were the pictures of Earth from Apollo, which proved to be an inspiration to the environmental movement. Earthrise from the Moon, photographed by Apollo 11 astronauts in 1969, energized the environmental movement and provided a symbol for its first Earth Day in 1970.

6.3.1 Space in the Environment—Energy Decade

Space, per se, declined sharply as a policy priority in the 1970s, while environment and energy concerns rose. James Fletcher, NASA Administrator from 1971 to 1977 (and again from 1986 to 1989) was personally interested in the environment and no doubt also understood it as a way to keep NASA relevant to the nation's needs. He explicitly stressed NASA's environmental mission and sought to broaden it. He told Congress in 1973 that NASA was "an environmental agency" and that "everything we do... helps in some practical way to improve the environment of our planet and helps us understand the forces that affect it" [4].

In 1972, NASA launched Landsat, a satellite intended to do for land resources what meteorological satellites were doing for weather and atmosphere. There was not one user agency for Landsat, but many potential users, both public and private. NASA launched a number of demonstrations of Landsat in the 1970s that were aimed at enticing various users to become interested in taking over Landsat once it was operational. The Carter White House, in 1979, transferred management of Landsat to NOAA in hopes of stimulating its use. NASA, meanwhile, continued to look for ways to show relevance at a time when it was developing the Shuttle and manned spaceflights were not taking place. The Landsat story takes on a life of its own, mostly tangential to NASA after 1979. It is a troubled life, owing to the issue of uncertainty as to "who" were its users and who would take it over if NASA gave it up once it passed from R&D.

Meanwhile, energy exploded as an issue in the 1970s, and NASA sought to relate to it, while strengthening and diversifying its environmental credentials. Along with the Department of Energy, NASA studied the notion of solar power satellites (SPS). These would entail an array of solar cells of enormous scale—perhaps the size of Manhattan—positioned in space to pick up solar rays and beam them in the form of microwaves to Earth. They would go to large receiving stations on Earth and be transferred to the electrical grid [5]. The sheer scale and cost of this enterprise, coupled with the end of the energy crisis in the early 1980s, meant that SPS never got beyond studies.

Also, as energy shortages were linked with environmental concerns, the notion of "limits to growth" gained prominence in the 1970s, aided by a book of the same name [6]. One of the more imaginative ways space, energy and environment converged in the 1970s was the concept of communes in space. Gerard O'Neil, a noted Princeton physicist, published a visionary article in the journal *Physics Today* in 1974. There, he outlined a scheme for human migration beyond planet Earth.

He proposed colonies situated in huge structures at "Lagrangian" points in space where gravity between Earth and Sun would hold the required structures in balance and provide stability. His ideas caught on with a number of people, as these colonies would be eco-friendly, rely on solar energy, and employ recycling. O'Neil was a serious scientist who received NASA support to develop his ideas. He gave rise to a movement called the L5 society, i.e., people seeking utopia in space. Although the movement continued in the 1980s, it never gained enough momentum to become viable in influencing policy. O'Neil died in 1992, his vision unfulfilled [7].

National Aeronautics and Space Administration's greatest success in the 1970s, in terms of environmental policy, lay in acquiring a specific mandate to pursue research on an emerging environmental issue—one that became pivotal in the global environmental movement in the succeeding decade—the stratospheric ozone. With NASA actively lobbying, Congress in 1975 directed NASA "to conduct a comprehensive program of research, technology, and monitoring of the phenomena of the upper atmosphere." In 1977, the year Fletcher stepped down as NASA Administrator, Congress directed NASA to issue biennial reports to Congress on the status of the ozone depletion problem. Together, the 1975 and 1977 acts legitimized an expansion of NASA's environmental role.

National Aeronautics and Space Administration moved ahead in a related area at the same time. In 1978, NASA launched Seasat, a satellite to test the uses of remote sensing to the oceans. Although it operated only 3½ months, Seasat revealed that space could assist in dealing with ocean-related environmental concerns [8].

The idea of combining NASA's atmospheric, land and ocean satellites into a larger, comprehensive environmental monitoring system appealed to James Beggs when he became NASA Administrator in 1981. In 1982, Beggs proclaimed NASA's desire to lead "an international cooperative project to use space technology to address natural and man-made changes affecting habitability of Earth." The proposal fell flat politically at the time. It was premature, especially in the Reagan administration. If anything, the Reagan White House wished to lower the government's environmental profile, which it equated with regulation [9].

For NASA, this rebuff meant shifting into an extensive planning mode, enlisting the scientific community, as well as other agencies, to build support for the idea. What NASA needed was some catalyst that would allow it to promote its larger environmental claims. It soon got the catalyst from the environmental issue where it was best positioned to take a "lead agency" role.

6.3.2 The Ozone Hole

In 1985, a group of British scientists, using ground-based techniques, discovered extraordinary and unexpected ozone depletion over Antarctica. There had been theories propounded about the impacts of commonly used chemicals called chlorofluorocarbons (CFCs) on ozone depletion in the stratosphere. Such depletion could lead to skin cancer and other effects. Yet, there lacked convincing evidence of human impacts on depletion, as well as a sense of urgency. Antarctica provided the urgency. NASA followed up the British Antarctic findings with alarming satellite images that confirmed what quickly became known as the "ozone hole." Environmentalists, media, and politicians throughout the world demanded action. With NASA largely funding the enterprise and NOAA a leading partner, an interagency, international expedition went to Antarctica. It determined that the likely cause was indeed man-made chemicals rather than some "natural" change. In 1987, the Montreal Protocol was concluded, with NASA and NOAA scientists critical in providing technical support to the diplomats. These macro-events provided the stimuli NASA needed to proclaim publicly it had a "Mission to Planet Earth (MTPE)." By the end of the decade, NASA was ready to turn its plans into a program [10].

6.3.3 Mission to Planet Earth and Earth Observation System

In 1989, President George H. W. Bush publicly endorsed NASA's new program, officially called MTPE. The key element was the Earth Observation System (EOS), projected to cost $30 billion over a 15 years span. EOS would provide long-term data sets. It would use a large range of land, sea, and atmospheric sensors built on two huge platforms in space, and it would provide comprehensive and simultaneous measurements of global change. The next year, just as implementation of MTPE got underway, the program ran into a financial barrier. Because of exploding federal budget deficits, Bush and Congress agreed on budget caps for discretionary expenditures, including space. NASA could not have both the Space Station and EOS growing rapidly in expense at the same time. Something had to give, and it was EOS [10].

Earth Observation System subsequently went through downsizing and restructuring, becoming primarily a climate change-oriented program. When

Republicans took control of Congress in 1995, they attacked EOS as "political" science linked to unproven claims about global warming voiced by Vice President Al Gore. EOS survived, but what emerged from a decade of upheaval for the program was a set of three moderate-sized satellites, launched sequentially as they became ready, emphasizing different aspects of environmental (especially climate) change. The cost of developing the EOS system, including a data dissemination component, was approximately $6.8 billion [11]. The first satellite, Terra, went up in 1999; the second, Aqua, in 2002; the third, Aura, in 2004.

Earth Observation System was not the system that had been planned in the late 1980s, but was a significant leap forward in environmental observation. In addition, NASA launched a number of more specialized environmental satellites. Meanwhile, many other nations (Europe, Japan, Russia, Canada, India, China, and others) launched satellites to monitor their own regional environmental problems. In 2003, these spacefaring nations met under U.S. State Department auspices and agreed to link their national systems into a "system of systems" that would coordinate diverse measurements. Everyone, it was now argued, had a common interest in knowing how the planet, especially its climate, was changing. There was also an interest in how satellites could help better assist all people in coping with national disasters in general. The United States said it would play a lead role in developing such a "system of systems" [12].

6.3.4 Landsat

With NASA, the Earth observation history is one of R&D—advancing technology as a mission. It was not NASA's mission to maintain operational systems. In weather satellites, a policy regime had been established in the 1960s. While there were many tensions and issues subsequently, the regime of development-use and who paid for what was largely sustained. There was a natural user agency that provided a market pull on the technology. Landsat proved much more problematic.

Landsat in the 1970s was shown to be useful to researchers, as well as operating agencies such as NOAA, the Department of Agriculture, the Department of Interior, and others [13]. But none of these agencies wanted Landsat enough to pay for its long-term maintenance. With the success of the communications satellite (discussed below), there was a model of utilization and hope in the Carter Administration that Landsat might be "privatized." The transfer of control of Landsat to NOAA in 1979 was seen as temporary. The commitment of the Reagan Administration to privatization of Landsat was even stronger for ideological reasons.

In 1984, Congress passed legislation that set policy for transfer of Landsat to the private sector [14]. A joint venture of Hughes and Radio Corporation of America (RCA), called Earth Observation Satellite (EOSAT), won a competition to be the designated agent for use and operational control. NASA continued to advance the technology. Meanwhile, government policy for use lagged. As old Landsats reached the end of their lives, new ones came on orbit. EOSAT received a federal subsidy for the transition to private control, which it supplemented with private fees from customers.

By the time George H. W. Bush became president in 1989, it was clear that EOSAT would not make enough money to take over from the government. No one agency wanted to finance the operating system. NASA was wondering why it should pay for advancing Landsat when the whole question of user control and operation was in limbo.

In 1991, Department of Defense (DOD) found Landsat images useful to planning and executing maneuvers during the 1991 Gulf War. This was in spite of the fact that Landsat resolution had not advanced as it might have, because it was held back by national security restrictions during the Cold War. DOD and spy agencies did not want the U.S.S.R. to know how strong was the resolution capability the United States possessed for its spy satellites, so it restricted resolution of civilian satellites. But other countries, especially France, had taken advantage of Landsat's "lag," to develop satellites with stronger resolution and were in a position to capture technological and commercial leadership in the field. With France showing ever better resolution, and the Cold War ending, the resolution restriction was lifted.

Hence, policy was made to keep Landsat going, make it more competitive, and full control was returned to the public sector. The Land Remote Sensing Policy Act of 1992 put Landsat 7 and beyond under joint control of NASA and DOD, with the two agencies splitting the bill in half. Practically everyone agreed the Landsat's continuing data sets were valuable, now going back 20 years. However, in 1993 DOD and NASA disagreed strongly on the next Landsat to be developed, Landsat 7, in terms of requirements and budget. DOD dropped out of the partnership, agreeing to pay only a modest separation cost.

In 1994, the Clinton Administration developed yet another policy regime, involving NASA, NOAA, and the Department of Interior [15]. Landsat was folded into NASA's "MTPE" and the three agencies' roles in the inter-agency U.S. Global Change Research Program. By now, a commercial remote sensing sector had emerged that was able to make money translating and selling data from Landsat and other public systems via licenses from the government. Landsat 7 thus was justified as useful for NASA's R&D mission and the other agencies' user missions. It went up in 1999.

The Landsat issue came on the agenda of President George W. Bush in connection with a multi-purpose weather satellite system set in motion by Clinton that was called the National Polar-Orbiting Operational Environmental Satellite System (NPOESS). It was decided to guarantee data continuity beyond Landsat 7 by putting Landsat-type sensors on NPOESS, a DOD–NOAA–NASA satellite system being developed primarily to provide operational weather information for both military and civilian needs.

However, it became clear in 2005 that NPOESS would not be launched in time to prevent a serious gap in Landsat data, since Landsat 7 was soon reaching the end of its useful life. In this year, the White House decided to replace the NPOESS policy with a new policy that directed NASA and the Department of Interior (U.S. Geological Survey) to build and launch a dedicated Landsat-type satellite that could go into orbit by 2009, much sooner than NPOESS.

What the Landsat saga illustrates is a policy quandary still not resolved. NASA has the mandate for R&D in Earth observational satellites. The issue has to do with expensive operational satellite systems. The weather field is well-established. Landsat, on the other hand, has always been an orphan from a user-agency perspective—too valuable to let go, but apparently not valuable enough to make it the priority of a specific user agency to run. Meanwhile, NASA goes beyond R&D, developing and also operating.

National Aeronautics and Space Administration plays this dual role in more than one field of Earth observation. Due to its legislated activity in the upper atmosphere area, and historic lead agency role in the ozone depletion field, it has assumed a de facto monitoring role for global compliance with the Montreal Protocol. It determines whether the ozone health of the planet is improving or not as a result of that treaty.

Hence, the Landsat story is tortuous from a policy standpoint. It reveals graphically a larger question: who should run (and finance) long-term operating systems in Earth observation technologies outside the weather field? The issue has not been resolved. It is not just a challenge for space policy; it is an environmental policy challenge also, as environmental policy increasingly comes to rely on the monitoring of the planet's health from space.

6.4 Near-Earth Orbit

A second frontier of the space-environmental policy is near-Earth orbit. Near-Earth orbit is a special place, in more than one way. It provides an unusual vantage point for monitoring the Earth, as discussed above. It is also a place from which to look outward, as the Hubble Space Telescope does. Moreover, it is a place where humans now circle the Earth via the International Space Station (ISS). Once finished, ISS is to be an international laboratory for science and possible manufacture, making use of zero gravity.

The most important use of ISS is going to be studying the impact of long-duration stays in space on human physiology and psychology. The present goal of the manned space program is to go back to the Moon for extended periods and eventually go on to Mars. That goal requires more knowledge of the effects of space on astronauts. Near-Earth is thus an orbit that can be put to use for many purposes, looking down, looking up, or staying in place. Like all special places, it can be subject to over-use. Environmental impacts can be deleterious to machines and life-threatening to humans who inhabit it.

6.4.1 The Commercial Significance of Geosynchronous Orbit

If there is one part of near-Earth orbit that is exceptionally worrisome from a space-environmental perspective, it is geosynchronous orbit. This is an orbit that is at a specific distance from Earth that allows an object in orbit to rotate with the Earth. Within this orbit an even more precise location makes objects geostationary. They stay in one specific place all the time. The geosynchronous orbit has proven indispensable for the geostationary communications satellite, the single most successful economic spin-off from the space program. Needless to say, it is equally of significance to military communication and navigation. Consequently, there has been a need for policy development to protect this critical part of the space environment.

It was Arthur Clarke in 1945 who published the first article detailing how this special orbit could be extraordinarily useful. By putting three satellites in geosynchronous orbit, he wrote, at just the right places, it would be possible to have global telecommunications coverage. Clarke pointed out that the curvature of the Earth's surface and atmospheric interface place limits on ground-based transmissions. Hence, the geosynchronous orbit would allow a huge breakthrough in global communications. For these insights, Clarke is frequently called the "Father of Satellite Communications."

Clarke's ideas had to await man's ability to escape the Earth's gravity. That came in 1957 with the Soviet Union's launch of Sputnik. Sputnik triggered a number of U.S. space initiatives and ushered in the new era of satellite communication, particularly after NASA was created in 1958. The Defense Department was similarly active. The first U.S. communications project, known as Signal Communication by Orbital Relay Equipment (SCORE), was launched by DOD as a broadcast-only satellite in December, 1958. SCORE lasted only twelve days and could only send to Earth a pre-recorded message from President Eisenhower: "Peace on Earth, good will toward men" [16].

Meanwhile, the private sector, such as AT&T and Hughes Aircraft Company, also moved into R&D on communications satellites. In August 1960, the first artificial satellite that actually replayed a real-time voice message from Earth to orbit and back, the Echo 1, was launched by NASA. In October, the first artificial communications satellite that foreshadowed today's active satellite technology, Courier 1B, was designed and launched by the U.S. military.

As technology of communications satellites sped ahead, policy development lagged. For example, in 1960, AT&T filed with the Federal Communications Commission (FCC) for permission to launch an experimental communications satellite with a view to rapidly implement an operational system. The U.S. government reacted with surprise because there was no policy in place to help execute the many actions related to the proposal. During 1961 and 1962, an intensive debate took place in the U.S. about public vs. private ownership and operations. This led to the passage of the Communications Satellite Act, which created a new entity known as the Communications Satellite Corporation (COMSAT) with ownership divided fifty–fifty between the public and the various telecommunications corporations.

Communications Satellite Corporation's initial capitalization of $200 million dollars was considered sufficient to build a system of dozens of satellites, as offered by a joint AT&T/Radio Corporation of America proposal. However, NASA recognized that the geosynchronous orbit, which was higher and would soon be attained by launch rockets, would require fewer satellites, as Clarke had forecast. Hence, it looked with favor at a more advanced satellite, the geosynchronous satellite proposed by Hughes, for the initial system. A policy difference lay with the fact that AT&T/RCA were willing to put more of their own money into their system in order to get "positioned" literally, in the lead of a new industry. To go to geosynchronous orbit meant more time and money had to be spent by the government to advance the launch and satellite technology. NASA, under its administrator, James Webb, was able and willing to make the public investment, with Hughes as a contractor, in an experimental system. In December, 1963, Syncom 2, built by Hughes, developed by both company and NASA funding, was launched as a prototype. It demonstrated the advantage of the geosynchronous orbit. In April, 1965, COMSAT's first satellite, and also the first operational geosynchronous communications satellite, Early Bird [known officially as International Telecommunications Satellite Consortium 1 (INTELSAT 1)], was launched. The age of communications satellites had begun.

Although COMSAT and the initial launch vehicles and satellites were American, other countries had been involved from the beginning in the new technology. By the time Early Bird was launched, communications earth stations already existed in the United Kingdom, France, Germany, Brazil, and Japan. Negotiations in 1963 and 1964 resulted in a new international organization. Evolved from COMSAT, the U.S. manager of the emerging global system, the INTELSAT, was formed in August 1964. From a handful of members in 1965, INTELSAT has grown to a present day international consortium with over 110 nations and operates powerful communications satellites, using the geosynchronous and more specialized orbits. INTELSAT provides services to the entire globe, not just the industrialized nations.

While using the international system, many countries have developed domestic communications satellites with orbits appropriate to particular uses. The Soviet Union developed their first domestic satellite system, Molniya, in 1965 using a non-geosynchronous orbit. In 1972, Telesat Canada launched its first domestic communications satellite, Anik, to serve the vast Canadian continental area. The first U.S. domestic communications satellite was Western Union's Westar I, launched in April 1974. These countries have been joined by Indonesia in 1976, Japan in 1978, India in 1982, Brazil in 1985, Mexico in 1985, and many others. Each year from 10 to 20 communications satellites are launched into the increasingly crowded near-Earth space environment [17].

6.4.2 Policy Problems of Geosynchronous/Geostationary Orbit

As noted, a special type of geosynchronous orbit is a geostationary orbit. A geostationary satellite stays over the same point on the surface of the Earth at all times. While all geostationary orbits must be geosynchronous, not all geosynchronous orbits are geostationary. Unlike all other classes of orbits, there is only one geostationary orbit. The advantage of a satellite in a geostationary orbit is that it remains fixed relative to the Earth's surface. This makes it an ideal orbit for communications. Users on Earth always know where to point an antenna. However, the fact that there is only one geostationary orbit presents serious policy problems. There are a limited number of places to put satellites without the risk of interference with other satellites. Regulating the geosynchronous/geostationary orbit has been found necessary.

Geostationary satellites can only orbit over the equator. Most geostationary satellites rarely can stray beyond a 30 km band that encompasses the nominal altitude of the geostationary position [18]. They are confined to an extremely small area in comparison to other regions of near-Earth space. For example, each satellite is usually kept in its position with an accuracy of approximately one-tenth of one degree. This situation allows no more than 1800 satellites to be positioned in geostationary orbit without posing a navigational hazard to one another [19]. Still, this theoretical maximum overestimates the possible number of desirable positions. The physical as well as economical values of various satellite positions are not equal. Only a subset of slots within the band of operations is best suited for communications.

Orbital positions, in general, that have broad coverage of continental regions are more desirable than those that can access only smaller portions of those land masses. In addition, the orbital slots over industrialized areas are in much more demand than in less developed areas. Slots over less developed countries with a location that would give a satellite coverage of industrial countries are also in demand. Hence, there is a "pecking order" in near-Earth space orbits, and nations compete for a share of this space environment.

6.4.3 *Electromagnetic Spectrum*

Another serious concern is interference, always a thorny issue for radio communication. The issue is the matter of frequency. Interference occurs when two different transmissions are made in the same geographic area at the same frequency. Such transmissions may lead to deterioration or even loss of signals. To coordinate a large number of users in a certain geographic area, communication systems are required to use different frequencies to avoid interference.

The interference problem arises both as a matter of physics and a matter of economics. Some frequencies simply cannot penetrate the layers of the Earth's atmosphere or magnetic field, making them unsuitable for a space-based relay system. Other frequencies, despite their technical availability, have been set aside for conducting astronomical research [20]. Moreover, unlike many other services that can reallocate the same frequency in other regions due to their limited power and geographic coverage, geostationary communications can hardly reuse the same frequency by the very nature of its broad coverage and high power. In addition, the demand for communications services increases at a rapid rate. Terrestrial communications and broadcast services, space based services unrelated to geostationary communications, as well as mobile satellite services have taken up wide swaths of the spectrum and even made inroads into frequencies previously set aside for geosynchronous systems. Competition for the allocation of frequencies among various users limits the ability of services to expand greatly through the acquisition of additional spectra. The fixed communications satellite services are limited to three frequency bands: the C band, Ku band, and Ka band [21]. Despite the physical and economical limitations of geostationary satellite systems, demand for them continues to grow, a fact bringing about the need of spacefaring nations to negotiate for use of an increasingly insufficient resource in space.

6.4.4 The Role of International Telecommunications Union

Currently, the United Nations (UN) agency that regulates the use of geosynchronous orbits is the International Telecommunications Union (ITU), which is a large specialized organization with a voting membership that very nearly mirrors that of its parent organization, the UN. The ITU's financing is derived from voluntary contributions of its members. As with all agencies of the UN, the principle of "one state, one vote" applies to the ITU.

In 1988, ITU acknowledged that all countries have an equal right to orbital slots. However, Article II of the Outer Space Treaty forbids any claim of sovereignty by any country in space, a circumstance which would not allow countries to establish dominion over the orbital places above their territory. To ensure at least some access to geostationary orbits to all countries, the ITU gave countries rights to an orbital slot directly over their territory at conferences in 1985 and 1988. With some consideration given to the country making the request, the ITU dispenses the orbital slot based on a "first come, first served" basis. There is no mandatory system to deal with disputes over orbital slots. In addition to orbital slots, the ITU also regulates satellite broadcast frequencies.

The ITU has only power granted by sovereign nations; it does not regulate officially. The role played by the ITU is that of an "efficiency-enhancing resource" for avoiding potential usage conflicts and resolving disputes among sovereign states [22]. Therefore, a number of policy challenges are present in this existing governing situation.

As the ITU cannot enforce its rulings, states and firms can launch satellites into orbit regardless of orbital slot or frequency issues. In 1994, China launched a satellite into orbit without the approval of the ITU. This Chinese satellite has the potential to interfere with neighboring satellites [23].

Due to the fact that each country is assigned the right to positions in space, some governments, which do not have the technological or economic ability to launch satellites, can take natural advantages of their terrestrial locations to gain economic benefits. For example, Tonga secured the rights to six orbital slots and then auctioned them off to private firms [24]. Other countries, such as Gibraltar and Papua New Guinea, have also auctioned off orbital slots or are considering such plans [25].

6.4.5 Space Debris

Complicating the use of near-Earth space is space debris. A half century has passed since Sputnik went up. Many nations now use space for civilian and military intelligence purposes. Not all material put into space comes down. For ISS, communications satellites, Earth-monitoring satellites, and space telescopes, space pollution is a present and growing danger. Space debris is associated with extremely high kinetic energies as it speeds around the planet. A collision with a piece of space debris only 1 cm in diameter can destroy a spacecraft in low-Earth orbit [26]. Even the smaller particulates can degrade spacecraft operations or seriously damage them. In geostationary orbit, the potential threat of debris is of a different nature as velocities among active spacecraft and debris tend to be lower, due to the relatively slow velocity of objects and the confined direction and orbital angle of working satellites, derelicts, and other forms of debris [27]. Nonetheless, the unique physical characteristics that make the geostationary orbit so desirable have resulted in high concentrations of satellites. Consequently, there is more debris located there and, thus, a greater chance of collision with valuable space satellites. Moreover, debris in low-Earth orbit, impacting the upper reaches of the atmosphere, may gradually disintegrate and disappear, but geosynchronous debris tends to remain a continual threat in the orbit area.

In 1989, ground trackers reported around 7500 spent rocket stages, dead satellites, screwdrivers and other man-made objects orbiting around the Earth [28]. Currently, The U.S. Satellite Catalog recorded that more than 9000 pieces of orbiting debris, larger than 10 cm in lower-Earth orbit and 1 m in geosynchronous orbit, are tracked by the U.S. Space Surveillance Network [29]. Moreover, the amount of debris keeps growing steadily larger, due both to increased space activities and the fact that each piece of debris involved in a collision can produce still more debris. Although NASA and other space agencies track debris large enough to be seen in telescopes, there is still much debris too small to track. A recent *Science* article warns that "[t]he current debris population in the [Low Earth Orbit] LEO region has reached the point where the environment is unstable" and "[a]n average of 18.2 collisions (10.8 catastrophic, 7.4 noncatastrophic) would be expected in the next 200 years" [30].

In August 1996, a piece of suitcase-sized debris struck a French Ministry of Defense satellite, marking the first time that two objects previously catalogued by ground radar have collided [31]. In August 2000, two metal balls of fire, which were boosters from a Delta II rocket, fell over the western cape of South Africa [32]. Falling debris obviously presents different policy concerns from debris in orbit. Both are increasingly serious issues.

A variation of the debris issue pertains to "nuclear debris." For years, spacecraft sent to places in space, where solar or chemical propulsion have been inadequate, have used nuclear batteries called radioisotope thermoelectric generators (RTGs) for electricity needs. They use the power of radioactive decay from plutonium. There have been protests on the part of environmentalists and anti-nuclear groups about the launch of such spacecraft. A major protest took place in Florida when the Cassini Saturn probe was launched in 1997. More recently, the Pluto launch in 2006 was protested. Opponents worry that if the spacecraft exploded on launch or while near Earth, it would spread radioactive debris. No protest has yet stopped a launch. But there is well-justified wariness. U.S. launches require special precautions and international coordination in the event of a launch accident [33]. It was a matter of luck that when Columbia disintegrated in 2003, over East Texas and Louisiana, and rained debris, there were no human casualties on the ground.

6.4.6 The Outer Space Treaty

Currently, the fundamental policy instrument guiding space activity is the Outer Space Treaty of 1967 [34]. Its major purpose in the 1960s was for arms control. Its provisions focused on ensuring freedom of access and forestalling the exercise of national control. Outer space was treated as a global common.

The treaty provides that weapons of nuclear or mass destruction may not be placed in orbit around the Earth or on celestial bodies. It limits the use of the Moon and other celestial bodies exclusively to peaceful purposes and expressly prohibits their use for establishing military bases, installations, or fortifications, testing weapons of any kind, or conducting military maneuvers. However, it does not ban totally the military use of space.

When the treaty was drafted, space activity was still extremely rare. Therefore, the treaty paid little attention to the possibility of pollution of the near-space environment or other issues of crowding, especially in the geosynchronous/geostationary locale. Policy lags behind technology and growing space-environment issues. In 2002 an 11-member Inter-Agency Space Debris Coordination Committee (IADC), whose members include all the major spacefaring nations, established guidelines to try to limit the build-up of orbital garbage, but a recent report noted considerable non-compliance by satellite operations in the critical geo-stationary orbit [35].

6.5   Deep Space as Environment

The third environmental frontier of space technology lies with deep space—"the Moon, Mars, and beyond." That was the phrase President George W. Bush used when he launched the NASA Space Exploration Vision in 2004. This is the ultimate space and environmental frontier, although it begins with a return to one abandoned in 1972 when Apollo lunar missions concluded.

The major current environmental issue here is protection from contamination—forward to other planets and backward to Earth. A future issue has to do with developing the planet Mars through a technology called terraforming, in effect, planetary engineering. Yet another is the mining of asteroids and protection of Earth from asteroid collision.

6.5.1   The Moon

By sending probes to the Moon and other planets, there have been fears of contaminating them with earthly organisms. By returning them (and people) to Earth, there may be a threat of bringing alien species back to Earth that would infect its citizens and wipe out humanity. Michael Crichton's book and movie, *The Andromeda Strain*, conjured just such a possibility.

As with most issues involving space, at least in the United States, Apollo was a genesis. While there were some scientists who were concerned about "forward contamination," the major worry of Apollo scientists was backward contamination. The Moon was lifeless, but there was worry over the very remote chance that Apollo astronauts could pick up some unknown infection from a lunar source and bring it back to Earth.

National Aeronautics and Space Administration began sterilizing robotic surveyors sent to the Moon to look for launching sites. There was a debate among technical specialists about whether and how much sterilization was necessary to prevent forward contamination. NASA decided to create contamination facilities for Moon samples (rocks, soil, etc.) brought back by astronauts; they even "decontaminated" the astronauts themselves.

These concerns helped stimulate a new scientific field in the 1960s called initially "exobiology," later "astrobiology." Funded by NASA, this field aimed primarily at the discovery of extraterrestrial life [36]. Worried about the contamination issue (forward and backward), exobiologists and their allies pushed for an international policy to head off problems. In 1967, the Outer Space Treaty included this statement:

> "...parties to the treaty shall pursue studies of outer space, including the Moon and other celestial bodies, and conduct exploration of them so as to avoid their harmful contamination and also adverse changes in the environment of the earth resulting from the introduction of extraterrestrial matter and, where necessary, shall adopt appropriate measures for their purpose...." [37]

The Outer Space Treaty was signed by many nations, including the Soviet Union and the United States.

When Apollo astronauts returned to Earth, they were quarantined briefly, along with Moon rocks and paraphernalia. Suitably decontaminated, they were released. No harm came to them or planet Earth form lunar life forms. There were none. The astronauts certainly added human pollution to the Moon, but the lunar surface was already cratered with much worse environmental impacts from space. Apollo ended, but exobiology as a field was stimulated and continued, as did a small office at NASA that concerned itself with planetary protection as a long-term issue.

6.5.2   Mars

After Apollo, manned journeys to the Moon ceased, but the planetary program of robotic probes continued. In 1976, NASA's largest and most ambitious planetary mission up to this time, Viking, was launched. Viking's connection to planetary protection was explicit. Its most publicized goal was to land equipment on Mars and conduct experiments to determine if life might exist there. NASA went to great lengths to sterilize the equipment so that it would not take bacteria to Mars, thereby obviating the experiments. However, while the mission succeeded in landing equipment on Mars, the tests were inconclusive and, for many, negative on the issue of Martian life [38].

The issue of life on Mars faded after Viking, but was revived dramatically in 1996. What helped in rejuvenating interest was the claim by some scientists that a meteorite discovered in Antarctica contained fossilized bacteria from the Red Planet. In the next year, NASA's Pathfinder probe landed successfully on Mars, and its Sojourner rover crawled along the surface, sending pictures back to Earth that were riveting. After two mishaps with Mars missions, NASA subsequently sent Spirit and Opportunity, two more probes, which landed successfully in 2003 and revealed credible evidence of past water on the surface. Where there was water, there was the possibility of life as we know it. Exobiologists, now called astrobiologists, had new hope.

The "Holy Grail" of the unmanned space program is now a mission to Mars that would return a sample of soil to Earth. The various reconnaissance and landing missions underway in the early 21st century would ultimately lead to this demanding mission. Earlier missions hope to find the places with signs of previous water, those most likely to have spawned life in the past. In the late 1990s, NASA planned a sample return mission for launch as early as 2005. When the two Mars missions launched in 1999 failed, the Mars Sample Return goal slipped to 2011 and was postponed again subsequently for financial reasons. When that mission does eventually take place, the issue of forward and especially backward contamination—from Mars to Earth—will surely be raised.

Among advocates of human spaceflight to Mars, the most emotional issue for those with environmental values concerns the very distant future. There will come a time when human settlement will commence, but even before then, we may wonder: what will man do to Mars to make it less hostile an environment?

Various members of the Mars Society, the principal private advocacy group for Mars exploration, have idealistic goals for the Red Planet. Like the L5 Society mentioned earlier, they seek utopian settlements beyond Earth as a way for the human species to start over again. This time humanity would create the perfect society in a pristine place, a place that it would keep pristine. They see Mars as a "New Eden."

But others in the Mars Society speak of "terraforming" Mars. Terraforming refers to planetary engineering, building an artificial environment, and making Mars safe for man. This is technology development on a grand scale, creating a new environment compatible with human comfort.

The two competing visions of a future Mars divide the activists. On the one side are those who see Mars as the next frontier, much as the New World was a frontier after Columbus or the Western U.S. was a frontier in the nineteenth century. They use terms such as "manifest destiny." The other side sees Mars as a pure, almost sacred place to be conserved and protected. Visions also divide variously on the role of government, with one group wanting as little as possible, and the other seeing government as a necessary force, whether to stimulate planetary engineering or protect the planet from such action.

It is remarkable how basic values and disputes carry forward from Earth to space, even space policy far ahead in distance and time. Space is indeed a frontier, but it is also an environment. "Frontier" and "environment," as terms, evoke a vast range of values and political agendas, many incompatible with one another. They have in the past, and will continue in the future [39].

6.5.3 Beyond

Issues in the "beyond" category vary with one's imagination. However, at this point in history, the most significant "beyond" issue that has attracted policy attention is asteroids. Most of the attention is speculative, but it is about important matters, nonetheless [40].

One aspect is the mining of asteroids for resources of one kind or another. Such a possibility was discussed in the 1970s and early 1980s when energy and other mineral resource scarcities were experienced or anticipated. Space visionaries developed various schemes for exploiting asteroidal resources and sending them back to Earth. Others saw possibilities of using asteroidal resources in space, possibly in the making of giant solar energy systems noted earlier in this chapter. Those who foresaw colonies in space also looked upon asteroids as sources of construction material.

These schemes did not disappear in the 1990s but by then had certainly declined in prevalence. Exploiting asteroids commercially or governmentally depended on breakthroughs in the ease and expense of access to space. The cost of getting into orbit, especially for putting people into space, was so high that the very expense put a damper on many ideas about using asteroids. However, in the 21st century, it is likely that asteroids as a resource will reemerge as space technology advances.

The other major issue involving asteroids is collision, perhaps the ultimate natural environmental disaster. Asteroids have hit Earth with great impact in the past and will again. Sixty-five million years ago a large asteroid is believed to have hit Earth and caused the demise of the dinosaurs. Asteroid collision is one of those very-low-probability-very-high-risk disaster events. There may have been five more extinctions of species in Earth's history due to asteroid collision. In addition to these major collisions, there have been collisions from smaller objects that have been quite damaging and could have been disastrous if they had hit cities. A collision in Siberia, far from humanity, in 1908 is believed to have caused an explosion equivalent to 10 megatons of TNT.

The U.S. government (NASA, DOD) tracks the course of asteroids, but it is not a high priority. The prevailing view is that if an asteroid is found to be headed toward Earth, there will be time (years) of warning. Exactly what must be the appropriate response is an interesting question. There have been movies about asteroid threats and counter attacks. Strategies include blowing asteroids up or nudging them from their Earth trajectory. Maybe these are plausible strategies; maybe they are not. Clearly, if and when an asteroid headed toward Earth is spotted, there will almost certainly be an attempt to avoid or mitigate what could be environmental disaster on an awesome scale. The threat of asteroid collision could have the beneficial effect of bringing nations together in the name of planetary security.

6.6 Conclusion

Discussed have been three frontiers of environmental policy as they relate to space: (1) space-based observations of Earth for understanding and predicting large-scale environmental change; (2) near-Earth space as a place increasingly used for commercial, scientific, military, and other practical purposes, and consequent issues of regulation for crowding and debris; and (3) deep space—the moon, Mars, and beyond- as humanity reaches to explore, settle, exploit and protect itself from outer space. Policy has set in motion technological advancement. Technology's advancement has linked space with environmental policy.

Space-based observations are the most obvious and self-conscious application of space technology to environmental policy. They began in the 1960s and have expanded enormously since. With increased concern for global warming, they are likely to be even more central to environmental policy for the future. Communications satellites and their use of geostationary near-Earth orbit also began in the 1960s and have been continually driven by commercial and military interests. The environmental impacts of communications satellites have been an after-thought, but they are becoming more salient with the growth of users of near-Earth orbits. In the case of deep space, the major environmental issue to date has been contamination—forward and backward. That it was perceived in the 1960s as a concern speaks well of policymakers of that era. It is also an issue likely to gain importance in the 21st century.

It is fair to say that environmental considerations have evolved unevenly and slowly and have had mixed influence on space policy. These considerations have obviously moved further with Earth observation than other areas. But even here, there is unevenness, with a serious lack of policy to govern operational Earth observation systems other than weather prediction. Environmental policy has been a late-arriving "overlay" on policies pursued for economic and other reasons in near-Earth orbit. But it is rising on the agenda of policymakers who are concerned with the use of particular orbits in near-Earth space. It has had to do so for reasons of crowding in a limited resource place. Environmental policy in relation to deep space received early attention owing to Apollo and contamination issues. Since the 1960s, it has been an episodic policy concern. However, it is likely to grow also in the future as Mars is explored continuously with robotic devices to find life, and as man revisits the Moon.

The most serious, and immediate, unresolved problem in the nexus of space and environment is arguably that of debris in near-earth orbit, especially in the orbit favored for communications satellites. More and more nations seek to use this special place for practical needs, both civilian and military. As this limited resource becomes steadily more crowded and polluted, it requires regulation. Policies to protect near-Earth space appear weak or not in place at all. Most people do not think of space as environment. They will when the first debris-related accident destroys a major satellite of significance, or worse, if a piece of debris hits the ISS or Space Shuttle and takes human life. When that happens, there will be widespread acknowledgement that space is not only a final frontier of technology but of environment as well.

References

1. Hughes, P., Weather satellites come of age, *Weatherwise*, 69, 1984.
2. Newell, H., *Beyond the Atmosphere: Early Years of Space Science*, NASA, Washington, DC, 1980, 321.

3. Mack, P. and Williamson, R., Observing the weather from space, in *Exploring the Unknown: Selected Documents in the History of the US Civil Space Program*, J. Logsdon, Ed., in Using Space, Vol. III, NASA, Washington, DC, 1998, 160.

4. Launius, R.D., A western Mormon in Washington, D.C.: James C. Fletcher, NASA, and the Final Frontier, *Pacific Historical Review*, 64(2), 236, 1995.

5. Goodstein, D., *Out of Gas: The End of the Age of Oil*, Norton, New York, 2004, 111–112.

6. Meadows, D.H., Meadows, D.L., Randers, J., and Behrens, W.W. III, *The Limits to Growth*, University Books, New York, 1972.

7. Maher, N., Neil Maher on shooting the Moon, *Environmental History*, 121, 2004.

8. NASA, Seasat 1978 Overview, Feb. 10, 1998. Available at http://southport.jpl.nasa.gov/scienceapps/seasat.html. Accessed May 22, 2006.

9. Edelson, E., Laying the foundation, *Mosaic*, 19, 6, 2005.

10. Lambright, W.H., The origins of NASA's mission to planet earth, in Entrepreneurship and space technology: The ups and downs of 'mission to planet earth,' *Public Administration Review*, 97, 1994.

11. Lambright, W.H., The rise and fall of interagency cooperation: The US global change research program, *Public Administration Review*, 41, 1997.

12. Berger, B., Reversing course, *Space News*, 10, 2005.

13. Mack, P.E. and Williamson, R.A., Observing the earth from space, in *Exploring the Unknown* J.M. Logsdon, et al., Eds., NASA SP-4407, Vol. III, National Aeronautics and Space Administration, Washington, DC, 1988.

14. Land Remote-Sensing Commercialization Act of 1984, Public Law 98-365, July 17, 1984.

15. The White House, Presidential Decision Directive/NSTC-3, Landsat Remote Sensing Strategy, May 5, 1994.

16. Pelton, J.N., The history of satellite communications, in *Exploring the Unknown*, John M. Logsdon, et al., Eds., NASA SP-4407, Vol. III, National Aeronautics and Space Administration, Washington, DC, 1988.

17. Whalen, D.J., Communications Satellites: Making the Global Village Possible, NASA History Division, NASA Headquarters, Washington, DC, 2005. Available at http://www.hq.nasa.gov/office/pao/History/satcomhistory.html (accessed on November 1, 2005).

18. Martinez, L., *Communications Satellites: Power Politics in Space*, Artech House, Inc., Dedham, MA, 1985.

19. Smith, M.L., *International Regulation of Satellite Communication*, 9, 1990.

20. National Research Council, Views of the Committee on Radio Frequencies Concerning Frequency Allocations for the Passive Services at the 1992 World Administrative Radio Conference.

21. Dichmann, D.J. and Thrash, T.A., The GEO–LEO connection, *Launchspace*, Feb–Mar, 1998.

22. Kennedy, C.H. and Pastor, M.V., *An Introduction to International Telecommunications Law*, Artech House, Boston, MA, 1996.

23. Holley, D., Tokyo says new Chinese satellite violates pact, *Los Angeles Times*, July 25, B5, 1994.

24. Price, M.E., Satellite broadcasting as trade routes in the sky, *Public Culture*, 11, 387, 1999.

25. Roberts, L.D., A lost connection: Geostationary satellite networks and the international telecommunication union, *Berkeley Technology Law Journal*, 15, 2000.

26. Baker, H.A., *Space Debris: Legal and Policy Implications*, 8, 1998.

27. Leinberg, G., Orbital space debris, *Journal of Law and Technology*, 93, 98, 1989.

28. Sawyer, K., Orbiting litter poses risk to space ventures, *The Washington Post*, A3, 1989.

29. Johnson, N.J., Whitlock, D.O., Anz-Meador, P.D., et al., *History of On-Orbit Satellite Fragmentations,* SC-62530, NASA Johnson Space Center, Houston, TX, 13, 2004.

30. Liou, J.-C. and Johnson, N.L., Risks in space from orbiting debris, *Science*, 311, 340, 2006.

31. David, L., Space debris damages French defense satellite, *Space News*, 19, 1996.

32. Great balls of fire, *Spaceflight*, 42, 311, 2000.

33. Covault, C., Warpspeed, *Aviation Week and Space Technology*, January, 48, 2006.

34. Outer Space Treaty, 1967. Available at http://www.state.gov/www/global/arms/treaties/space1.html (accessed on May 22, 2006).

35. de Selding, P.B., Debris mitigation improves, but more work urged, *Space News*, January, 6, 2006.

36. See Dick, S. and Strick, J., in *The Living Universe: NASA and the Development of Astrobiology*, Rutgers, New Brunswick, NJ, 2004,, chap. 3.

37. Treaty on Principles Governing the Activities of States in the Exploration and Use of Outer Space, Including the Moon and Other Celestial Bodies, Signed at Washington DC, London, Moscow, January 27, 1967.

38. Dick, S.J. and Strick, J.E., Vikings to mars, in *The Living Universe: NASA and the Development of Astrobiology*, Rutgers University Press, New Brunswick, NJ, 2004, chap. 4.

39. Lambright, W.H., The quest for mars, in *Space Policy in the 21st Century*, W.H. Lambright, Ed., Johns Hopkins, Baltimore, MD, 2003, 173–197.

40. Deudney, D., High impacts: Asteroidal utilization, collision avoidance, and the outer space regime, in *Space Policy in the 21st Century*, W.H. Lambright, Ed., Johns Hopkins, Baltimore, MD, 2003, 147–172.

Chapter 7

Human Rights to Water

Zachary A. Smith and Kristi L. Ross
Northern Arizona University

"There is an eternal dispute between those who imagine the world to suit their policy, and those who correct their policy to suit the realities of the world."

—attributed to Albert Sorel

7.1 Introduction

As the human population increases, our world is effectively becoming smaller, leading to the globalization of companies, markets, economies, and government. It is no surprise then that issues concerning human rights and freshwater issues are quickly emerging on this global front. It has been estimated that over 1 billion people are without access to clean, safe drinking water, while 2.5 billion people live without adequate sanitation [1–3]. Water supply, demand, distribution, and pollution issues have become the focus of international discussion on freshwater. One result of globalization has been an increased tendency toward deriving international solutions to local and regional problems like access to clean, safe drinking water. Early approaches to addressing water access issues involved the recommendation of national water management strategies, the implementation of which has proven difficult. Though better water management strategies are necessary for improving access, recent discussion has turned toward the enactment of international human rights legislation to declare a right to a daily per capita minimum amount of water. This suggestion has sparked debate over whether and how rights to water should be defined through human rights language.

In this chapter, we explore the variables that weigh most heavily in the freshwater supply problem and how they relate to water management practices in a global context. Next, we examine the evolution of human rights to water and the challenges and advantages of such an approach to the freshwater supply problem. We then discuss the financial and organizational implications of human rights to water on developing nations. Finally, we explore some alternatives to a human rights based approach that recognize water as a fundamental right while simultaneously acknowledging a need for better and, in some cases, innovative management strategies to improve access. Ultimately, the freshwater problem is one of global proportions; nevertheless, the solution to the problem is unique to each watershed and is therefore limited in scope to the local and regional scales.

7.2   Addressing the Variables that Affect Access

Since the major issue driving the freshwater supply problem is access, we should consider the variables that affect access. Access to clean, safe drinking water is inhibited by no less than four direct factors: distance to the source, denial of access, cost, and supply; and no less than two indirect factors: distribution and demand. These variables are tightly woven, creating complex interdependencies where one variable is affected by change in another. For example, if the distance to the source is reduced by bringing services into the home, cost may become the prohibitive factor. In the context of globalization, access to water is everyone's problem; pollutants dumped into the Ganges River in Nepal will eventually prevent access for downstream users in India, for instance. Development of urban areas to attract foreign businesses may result in reduced infiltration of water into local aquifers. As the trend of globalization pushes forward, the interdependence of these variables among and within nations will only continue to become stronger, affecting—and being affected by—international relations. This section will take a closer look at these variables and the complex interactions that exist between them on local, regional, and global scales.

7.2.1   Distribution, Supply, and Demand

Perhaps the most important variables that affect water availability on regional and global scales are distribution, supply, and demand. Global and regional climate patterns result in differential distribution of water resources over the globe and regionally. Within this climate framework exists a regional dynamic of distribution that is attributable to infrastructure. When services are not equitably distributed amongst users, access is inhibited for those outside the service area. This issue is most prominent in rural areas of developing countries, as most water infrastructure is concentrated near urban centers and agricultural regions, but it also affects the urban poor in cases where service to wealthier neighborhoods is given priority. Another major effect on urban supply is development; as the surface area of paved land increases, runoff also increases, while the infiltration of rainfall into the water table decreases. This is especially important in arid urban areas where groundwater is the principle water source.

As mentioned above, supply is as much a function of demand as it is a function of distribution. For this reason, demand management is important in the consideration of solutions to the problem of access. Water demand management entails reducing the demands on freshwater through conservation and pollution abatement. Pollution is important to demand management because polluted water places a demand on freshwater as a carrier of pollutants [4]. Conservation can be utilized in both the household and agricultural sectors to reduce demand. The logic of demand management theory is that by decreasing supply inhibitors (pollution and over consumption/overuse), we can effectively decrease demands on freshwater. Use of this terminology is risky though, as it could be interpreted to mean that by increasing supply we effectively decrease demand. This is not the case, however, as increasing supply in this model requires a reduction in demand before an increase in supply can be achieved. We must also be aware that using language that connotes an increase in supply may lead to inefficient use of water by giving the impression that a supply surplus exists. Full-cost water pricing may be the best method for reducing household use, but we should note that this method should only be employed in conjunction with subsidization for those who cannot afford to pay the full cost.

Demand is not limited to local populations, either. Many watersheds cross state and national boundaries, complicating the political aspects of demand. Collaborative management techniques may help to solve transboundary disputes that not only create more demand for resources, but that also affect regional and local distribution and supply. The collaborative watershed management model seeks to increase the efficiency of and coordination among the many interests for a given watershed. By increasing stakeholder participation, decentralizing the decision making process, and adopting the watershed as the water management unit, the collaborative effort should, in theory, result in more successful and more sustainable management of the watershed. Mostafa Dolatyar and Tim Gray demonstrate that collaborative management techniques are especially applicable in the Middle East, where most of the major water sources cross jurisdictional boundaries and many stakeholders are involved [5].

With a nearly exponential increase in global demand over the past 40 years, freshwater supplies are being pushed to their limits more than ever. This is especially critical in arid regions, such as the southwestern U.S., most of Africa, parts of Europe and Asia, and the Middle East. Figure 7.1 shows the increase in global population from 1950 to 2000. Figure 7.2 shows the increase in global water usage from 1950 to 2000. Notice that the rate of increase, or slope, of the two curves is nearly identical. This suggests a strong correlation between population and water consumption; however, this correlation is not as straightforward as it may seem at first. The majority of water use takes place in the industrial sector, followed by the agricultural and domestic sectors, respectively. Nevertheless, as population increases, industrial and agricultural production also increase, so there is an indirect correlation at the very least. We should note, of course, that as industrial and agricultural production increase, so do both surface and groundwater pollution.

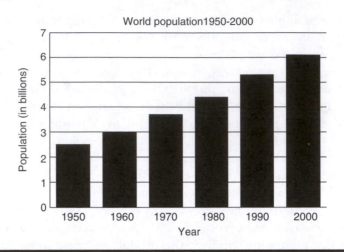

Figure 7.1 World population by year from 1950 to 2000 (Data from United Nations Department of Economic and Social Affairs Population Division, World Population Prospects: The 2004 Revision, available from http://www.un.org/ esa/population/unpop.htm, 2004. With permission.)

7.2.2 Pollution

Access to clean, safe drinking water is further inhibited by pollution—this is true even in non-arid regions, where water supplies are seemingly plentiful. Pollution abatement is inhibited by lack of sanitation in many areas, creating a circular problem. There are two types of pollution: point source pollution and

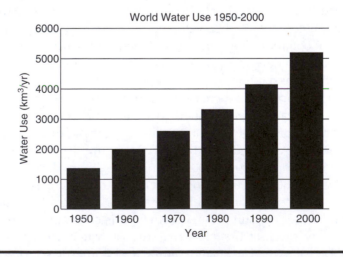

Figure 7.2 World water use by year from 1950 to 2000. Includes data from the continents of Asia, Africa, North America, South America, Europe, and Oceania (Data from Dolatyar, M. and Gray, T., *Water Politics in the Middle East*, 1st ed., St. Martin's Press, Inc., New York, 2000. With permission.)

non-point source pollution. Point source pollution can be traced to a specific, known source, such as a leak in a sewage pipeline. Non-point source pollution has more diffuse origins, such as agricultural pesticides. The exact originating location of such non-point source pollution is difficult to determine. It often originates upstream, sometimes in neighboring states or countries, adding another variable to transboundary disputes. Once again, collaborative management practices may hold the answer to solving transboundary disputes involving pollution, as well as distribution, supply, and demand.

The infrastructure required to treat and deliver water is costly, and in the case of developing nations where many people cannot pay the economic price for water, it is nearly impossible for the government to provide this infrastructure without outside help. As discussed later, many developing nations have turned to private, often international, water companies to provide the infrastructure that is so critical for clean, safe drinking water. At least one author has suggested that international funding may be required to meet the infrastructure needs of many developing countries [6]. In the context of globalization, this suggests that solving the freshwater problem may further the interdependence of countries upon one another, which may complicate attempts to solve problems on local and regional scales. The next section will explore the historical context of international solutions to the freshwater problem. Though there has always been a focus on management issues, recent discourse in the international community has placed a greater focus on governance issues.

7.3   Toward Human Rights to Water

The concept of human rights to water is one that has been evolving since 1948, when the United Nations (UN) General Assembly penned the International Bill of Human Rights—comprising, among others, the Universal Declaration of Human Rights and the International Covenant on Economic, Social, and Cultural Rights (ICESCR). Article 25 of the Declaration states that "[everyone] has the right to a standard of living adequate for the health and well-being of himself and of his family" [7]. Such a statement implies a fundamental right to water since it is necessary for health. Subsequent international covenants attempted to define the parameters of the freshwater supply problem by approaching it from the perspective of improving access to clean water and outlining management strategies to do so. Nevertheless, more recent discourse has concerned the establishment of explicit human rights to water, while establishing a global policy through which such rights can be recognized and ensured on the national level. This approach has not been met with agreement from all international participants, however. Several reasons for not using a human rights based approach to improve water access have been cited. The following sections will explore the historical and current approaches to the problem and evaluate the challenges of the human rights based approach to water policy.

7.3.1 Integrated Water Resources Management

Early approaches to improving access to clean, safe drinking water involved assessing the state of water resource management policies and practices around the world. The first major assessment came in 1977 at the UN Conference on Water, held in Mar del Plata, Argentina. The conference resulted in the Mar del Plata Action Plan, which assessed the worldwide state of water resources management and noted the lack of data available for the formulation of effective water resources planning. Muhammad Rahaman and Olli Varis write that the Action Plan was "the first internationally coordinated approach to [integrated water resources management (IWRM)]," and that the conference "considered water management on a holistic and comprehensive basis" [8]. The Plan outlined some of the water resource management issues that were identified as affecting both international and national policy. Perhaps the most important contribution of the conference was its discussion of issues at all levels, from local to international, and its inclusion of representatives from developing nations. Later conferences would build upon the advancements made at the Mar del Plata conference.

The 1992 International Conference on Water and Environment was held in Dublin and resulted in the establishment of the following four guiding principles for local, national, and international water resources management:

1. Fresh water is a finite, vulnerable, and essential resource that must be managed in an integrated manner.
2. Water development and management should be participatory, involving users, planners and policymakers at all levels.
3. Women are central to the provision, management, and safeguarding of water and should be included in decision making and implementation processes.
4. Water has an economic value and should be treated as an economic good in order to encourage conservation and protection of water; while considering the basic right of all people to have access to clean, safe water at an affordable price [9].

Both the Mar del Plata Action Plan and the Dublin Principles made a lasting impression on international water resources planning. Together, they brought forth the idea of IWRM and, though the Dublin conference did not include participation from the developing world [8], both conferences brought attention to the need for such participation in international conferences. We should note that the fourth Dublin Principle, that water should be treated as an economic good, is a hotly debated issue in international forums on water resources management. The idea has met with particularly stiff resistance from many proponents of explicit human rights to water, who have asserted that water must be treated as a common good rather than an economic good.

The Second World Water Forum was held in The Hague, The Netherlands in 2000. The major contribution of this conference was that it involved stakeholders from all levels, including those from developing nations. The recommendations of this conference included a continued focus on the development of IWRM, including cooperation amongst stakeholders in transboundary water resources management. Most notably, and most subject to debate, the conference recommendations included a push for full-cost water pricing and the use of fully privatized systems or public-private partnerships to achieve conference objectives. The UN General Assembly adopted the Millennium Declaration in the same year, declaring: "We resolve…to halve, by the year 2015…the proportion of people who are unable to reach or to afford safe drinking water" [10]. It is notable that the Millennium Declaration did not outline any measures by which this goal is to be achieved. Even so, that statement has been quoted in the literature as the motivation for many different approaches to solving the problem of access to clean, safe drinking water.

The above approaches attempted to improve access through better management practices. Nevertheless, Rahaman and Varis have noted that there are still several problems with national, regional, and local implementation of IWRM practices [8]. Larry Swatuk and Dianne Rahm have demonstrated the challenges that Botswana faces in implementing IWRM policies amidst the country's push for economic development. Among the factors impeding implementation in Botswana are governance issues, public education issues, lack of water monitoring, use of supply-side water policy, and the existence of power relations that favor international actors over local actors. As the authors state: "[Money] has drawn all segments of society into unsustainable forms of water resource use, openly suggesting to them that technological solutions are never far away" [11]. These problems with internationally-derived management approaches may be the reason that some interested parties feel that explicit human rights to water must be proclaimed in order to place the focus of international concern on law and governance issues.

The paradoxical relationship between sustainable management and rapid economic development is one that all developing nations face, and this must be kept in mind when formulating any international guidelines or policy regarding water resources management. As one author points out, international agreements create political accountability, but they do not create legal accountability [12]. It has been argued that using human rights language to establish rights to water creates legal accountability [1,3,12,13], though this legal accountability can be seen as counterproductive. As Marcus Moench notes, a government that fails to provide for the minimum basic water needs of its citizens, for whatever reason, could potentially be held legally accountable for human rights violations [14]. Whether or not this is true may ultimately depend upon how a human right to water is defined.

7.3.2 *What is a Human Right to Water?*

In 2003, the UN Committee on Economic, Social and Cultural Rights released General Comment No. 15, which states: "…the Committee has previously recognized that water is a human right contained in article 11, paragraph 1 [of the ICESCR]...The right should also be seen in conjunction with other rights enshrined in the International Bill of Human Rights, foremost amongst them the right to life and human dignity" [2]. Thus, the General Comment took a step in the direction of explicit human rights to water. Several other international covenants and agreements have included statements that explicitly protect rights to water for specific marginalized groups. Rights to water have been proclaimed through human rights documents concerning women's rights and children's rights, and through humanitarian law. Article 14 of the 1979 Convention on the Elimination of All Forms of Discrimination Against Women requires states to eliminate discrimination against women in rural areas to ensure that they enjoy adequate living conditions, particularly in relation to housing, sanitation, electricity, and water supply [3]. Article 24 of the 1989 Convention of the Rights of the Child requires states to provide the highest standard of attainable health, particularly in the provision of adequate food and clean drinking water [3]. The 1977 Protocols to the Geneva Conventions established humanitarian laws that provide explicit protection for drinking water supplies and installations, as well as for irrigation works [15].

Such right to water assertions naturally lead to the question: if rights to water are protected by other human rights, why should they be defined as separate human rights? It is important to note that the aforementioned human rights protections do not apply to marginalized groups that fall outside of the specific categories covered by those rights. It is also noteworthy that, though several countries have relatively recently adopted constitutions that protect rights to clean, safe drinking water (e.g., Uganda and South Africa), many others have not. Perhaps the best justification for explicit human rights to water is to improve access for those who have little or no access to clean, safe drinking water. Many of the countries in which these needs are not being met have shown negligence in managing water resources, resulting in inequitable distribution and unsustainable management of what little resources are available. Some have turned to private water companies to supply water infrastructure and services, which has presented a conflict of interest for the poor and for conservation measures where regulations have fallen short. Ashfaq Khalfan lists the following additional justifications for legally binding, explicitly defined human rights to water:

■ To create a focus on lack of access to water caused by discrimination and failure to address the needs of marginalized communities;
■ To address process issues and require involvement of relevant communities in the planning process; and
■ To place an emphasis on monitoring and accountability, especially where services are privatized, and implement penalties for non-compliance [13].

Other justifications that have been cited by Peter Gleick include: sharpening the focus on international watershed disputes and resolving conflicts over shared water resources; creating international legal obligations; and setting specific priorities for water policy [1].

Another question that naturally arises is: what are the obligations of States parties? General Comment No. 15 specifically outlines the obligations of parties to the ICESCR to *respect*, *protect*, and *fulfill* the right to water. The obligation to *respect* includes "refraining from engaging in any practice or activity that denies or limits equal access to adequate water…[and] unlawfully diminishing or polluting water," among many others. The obligation to *protect* includes "adopting the necessary and effective legislative and other measures" to prevent third parties from denying access; and not polluting or over extracting resources, "including natural sources, wells and other water distribution systems." Also, "[where] water services (such as piped water networks, water tankers, access to rivers and wells) are operated or controlled by third parties, States parties must prevent them from compromising equal, affordable, and physical access to sufficient, safe and acceptable water. To prevent such abuses an effective regulatory system must be established, in conformity with the Covenant and this General Comment, which includes independent monitoring, genuine public participation and imposition of penalties for non-compliance" [2]. The obligation to *fulfill* includes adopting a national water strategy; recognizing rights to water through national legal systems; ensuring that water is affordable for everyone; facilitating improved and sustainable access to water; and providing for the needs of those who cannot provide for themselves. Effectively, General Comment No. 15 has set forth the language of explicit human rights to water by clarifying that such rights were never excluded from the ICESCR in the first place. Nevertheless, there does not seem to be complete agreement as to whether explicit human rights to water are the appropriate solution to the problem of access.

7.3.3   Challenges

There is little disagreement that access to clean, safe drinking water is a necessity. There is, however, little agreement as to how a fundamental right to water should be claimed, protected, and enforced. At the same time that we discuss the justifications for language that establishes explicit human rights to water, we must also acknowledge that several authors have expressed reservations about using human rights as an avenue to guarantee access to clean, safe drinking water. Moench notes that "arguments about the denial of human rights are most often associated with acts of commission—such as murder, torture, and genocide—as opposed to acts of omission—such as the failure of a government to provide for the basic needs of its people" [14]. This reflects the disparity in the way that human rights to water are perceived by different parties; the spectrum of interpretations runs the gamut from individual legal rights to common good rights. One reservation that some authors have expressed with regard to explicit human rights to water is that they may come into conflict with other human rights, such as cultural rights, individual rights, or ecological rights. Further, there are several inconsistencies in the language of General Comment No. 15 that foreshadow some of the potential problems with a human rights based global water policy. Another problem presented by a human rights based approach to water policy is that of enforcement.

Concerns that explicit human rights to water may conflict with other rights are justified by the following language of General Comment No. 15: "Water is essential for enjoying certain cultural practices (right to take part in cultural life). Nevertheless, priority in the allocation of water must be given to the right to water for personal and domestic use" [2]. This prioritization of water could potentially create conflict with other rights. Tom Greaves cites the importance of water to the culture of the American Lummi Indians in Washington State, who rely on the salmon from the Nooksack River for their cultural survival. He writes: "The Lummi Nation's right to cultural perpetuation is a human right guaranteed not only in the UN covenants but also in the Point Elliott Treaty of 1855 between the Lummi and the territorial government [of Washington]" [16]. The oldest recognized users of Nooksack River water, the Lummi also employ sustainable water management practices to ensure sufficient water supply for future Lummi generations. The policy practices outlined in General Comment No. 15 possess the potential to create conflict with the cultural, environmental, and legal water rights of the Lummi. No doubt, there are numerous other indigenous, and other groups, to whom this language may be problematic. Concerns about such conflicts are most prominent amongst regional participants in global water policy discussions, reflecting the fact that human rights-based international water policy may not be able to satisfy the needs of all interested parties.

For that matter, it may be true that no form of international water policy will be able to satisfy all interested parties. Gleick's assertion that an explicit human right to water will help to set specific priorities for water policy [1] may also be true, but an internationally enforced national water policy may also serve to complicate the picture at regional and local levels. This may be the reason that IWRM has faced implementation problems at the national level. Leonard Hammer, in reference to the national implementation strategy of General Comment No. 15, states that "there are times when it is better to look within the State system to make the assessment rather than impose mandated and pre-determined policy from the outside" [17]. Just as Zachary Smith and Grenetta Thomassey have suggested that a national water policy presents a conflict of interest for local and regional water managers in the U.S. [18], a global water policy could present a conflict of interest if it requires the development of such national water policy.

Additionally, the national implementation strategy outlined in Section V of General Comment No. 15 raises the possibility of several contextual problems. While stating that "priority in the allocation of water must be given to the right to water for personal and domestic use" [2], it goes on to state that: "Any national measures designed to realize the right to water should not interfere with the enjoyment of other human rights"[2]. It is hardly foreseeable that there is any way to avoid stepping on other rights to water while giving priority to water for "personal and domestic use." At the same time, it is difficult to imagine how to provide for the minimum basic needs of everyone without establishing such priorities. Nevertheless, such contradictory language could certainly create interpretational inconsistencies in international and national adjudication and litigation.

For example, Dinah Shelton notes that the language of the International Covenant on Civil and Political Rights (ICCPR—a third covenant under the International Bill of Human Rights) and its accompanying General Comment No. 23 has made it difficult for individuals to assert their cultural rights through complaints to the UN Human Rights Committee (HRC) [19]. She asserts that the following loopholes in the ICCPR language have resulted in decisions against complainants: (1) the ICCPR requires the complainant to exhaust all local remedies, regardless of expense, before coming to the HRC; (2) the HRC allows States to file for exemption from the ICCPR's applicable Article 27 stipulations if they have established laws to protect against inequality and discrimination; (3) the HRC requires that the complainant establish that the act presents a "serious deprivation of cultural life;" and (4) the HRC strictly interprets what constitutes a minority in a given state. Thus, it appears in this example that the burden of proof falls on the complainant—and when the complainant is a poor urbanite or rural villager with little or no resources, legal recourse is moot.

This brings us to the topic that has troubled international human rights legislation for many years: enforcement. The call for explicit human rights to water has centered on creating legal recourse through which States parties can be held accountable for providing a minimum amount of safe, clean drinking water to the more than 1 billion people who are lacking such access. There is considerable debate among jurists of the International Court of Justice as to whether international human rights legislation carries any weight of legal enforcement in international court [20]. In most cases, the only actions taken by member nations against states that are in violation of human rights agreements are trade embargoes and threats. Trade embargoes sometimes result in a lack of access to food for the poor, in addition to an existing lack of water. Further, the burden of enforcement falls on member states, which sometimes do not act against the violating state for political reasons. Nagendra Singh writes: "If the legal link of enforcement is missing the word of law would degenerate to a moral recommendation to be ignored at will" [20]. This is the worst possible scenario where access to clean, safe drinking water is concerned.

7.3.4 International Trade

Another arena in which international water policy could be harmful is international trade. Some authors have expressed reservations about the relationship between international trade agreements and the protection of national water rights, particularly where private international water corporations are concerned [4,6]. For example, a California based water company is currently suing Canada under the auspices of the North American Free Trade Agreement (NAFTA) for the right to export water from British Columbia, where water exports are not allowed by law [21]. Shiney Varghese warns that if "water services are included in [the General Agreement on Trade in Services (GATS)]…the water crisis will be aggravated, especially in the developing countries, where privatization is likely to be poorly regulated" [4]. The widespread support of water privatization in international agreements and the encouragement of privatization by the World Bank and the International Monetary Fund could potentially lead to unsustainable practices, such as large-volume, international out-of-basin transfers.

The question of whether or not to privatize water services is one that many nations are attempting to address in the context of the global economy and in light of the freshwater problem. There are strong arguments both for and against explicit human rights to water, and discussion on the topic is far from complete. As the global community continues to grow, access to clean, safe drinking water will become an increasingly prominent issue. The questions discussed here are of the utmost importance, and there are no easy answers to them. Regardless of whether or not explicit human rights to water are declared, there still remain questions regarding how to go about making access to clean, safe drinking water possible. Therefore, these newly unearthed issues of governance do not alone solve the issues of management. The next section will explore the implications of human rights to water on management of water resources; specifically, it will examine the problem of organizing and financing water services, especially in developing nations.

7.4 Implications of a Human Right to Water

Another question raised by explicit human rights to water is: how are developing nations with limited economic resources to provide for minimum needs? A human rights based approach to issues of water access has many implications for the financing of water resources in developing nations. Some have already turned to privatization, hoping that large, international water corporations with the capital to invest in the infrastructure can save the day. Under a human rights mandate, developing nations will be forced to take whatever short-term measures are necessary to get the required infrastructure in place. In the context of globalization, the tendency of developing nations to rely on foreign water companies to provide water infrastructure and services is dangerous at best. If water services are included in global trade agreements, large-scale privatization could result in a monopolistic state in which municipalities are unable to compete, leaving foreign, private services as the only option. As mentioned previously, it would be both bad economics and bad science to allow foreign companies to decide the fate of a nation's water resources. Therefore, outside funding would almost certainly be necessary for most developing nations to get the infrastructure in place and avoid being held in violation of human rights.

Though there have been some success stories involving private water companies, privatization of water services has not met with success across the board. A good example of privatization gone badly is that of Buenos Aires, Argentina. In 1993, with a loan of US $30 million from the World Bank, the government of Argentina contracted water services for the city of Buenos Aires to the French conglomerate Aguas Argentinas. By 1997, the World Bank issued another US $911 million in loans to Aguas Argentinas. While Aguas Argentinas was successful in bringing water services to 700,000 homes by 2000, the government failed to regulate the water company's activities, resulting in huge connection fees (US $800) and rate hikes that many poor people could not afford. In addition, the promised water treatment plant was never built and sewage services were never completed. By 2002, Aguas Argentinas had defaulted on over US $700 million in loans, and over 1 million people were still without the running water and sewage that they had been promised [22]. As Nickson points out, organization of urban water supply must be strong enough to support self-financing, regardless of who controls or owns the supply [23].

This is not to say that private companies have nothing to offer in the provision of water services, however. As General Comment No. 15 asserts, effective regulation must be in place if private services are to be used. The Buenos Aires situation is a perfect example of the need for such a requirement. Private sector participation comes in many forms, and there have been several success stories involving public–private partnerships (PPP) that may provide other avenues for involvement of the private sector. There are two major forms of PPP: corporatization and joint venture. Because corporatization relies heavily on investment in bonds, it is not feasible in many developing countries where the bond market is either absent or weak. The joint venture model may be useful in many areas where the government does not have the funds to create the infrastructure alone, but where full privatization might create a conflict of interest for the poor. Shared ownership in this model results in the public partner's retaining a largely regulatory role, while the private partner performs daily operations. The public partner is also a shareholder in the company, giving it a vested interest in maintaining political acceptability of the company's actions [24]. Anton Earle asserts that this mutual interest could potentially facilitate conflict resolution. Nevertheless, he also points out that conflicts of interest can arise as the public partner tries to maintain its regulatory role while simultaneously trying to maximize returns. Also, productivity can be impeded as public and private partners approach project development from different perspectives and with different timetables [24].

Mike Muller has highlighted the struggle South Africa faces in meeting the constitutional rights of its citizens to safe water and adequate sanitation in light of the "gross inequalities inherited with the end of apartheid in 1994" [6]. He explains that the emphasis on the ends over the means has resulted in many private water interests taking hold; without which, he notes, South Africa could not have achieved as much improvement as it has since 1994. Through public–private partnerships, the South African government has been able to provide a free basic water supply of 25 l per person per day to the poor. Nevertheless, Muller notes that international trade agreements such as the GATS should not mandate private services, as it would have long-term ill effects on the water management systems in developing countries. He also notes that, due to huge disparities in South Africa's distribution of wealth, the provision of public services in many areas will require outside funding at the regional and global levels.

Perhaps an even better answer for some, especially in rural areas, may be the water cooperative. In Bolivia, several cities have formed water cooperatives, most notably the Cooperativa de Servicios Públicos "Santa Cruz" Ltda, or SAGUAPAC. The cooperative has been operating in the City of Santa Cruz, with a population of 1 million, since 1979. The 96,000 customers of the cooperative are all automatically members, and the system is divided up into nine water districts. The members of each district elect the administrative board, which appoints the general manager. The members also elect a separate supervisory board, which evaluates the performance of the administrative board. Andrew Nickson of the University of Birmingham reports that the water system has a low level of unaccounted-for water, 100% metering, a 96% bill collection rate, 80% water coverage, and a 24-hour supply. He concludes that the success of SAGUAPAC can be attributed to two key factors:

■ The bottom-up structure of the cooperative facilitates the implementation of projects faster and more efficiently than in public sector companies; and
■ The cooperative structure helps to protect the general manager from political interference [25].

The water cooperative may work best in areas where population is somewhat limited or where several cooperatives operate over a larger population. However, cooperatives have their problems, as well. Paul Constance notes that SAGUAPAC faces serious long-term challenges in the extension of its services because cooperatives must find their own sources of funding. The decision to abstain from political interference hurts them when they lobby for public funding. He attributes SAGUAPAC's success in large part to the fact that most of its customers are in the middle- to high-class ranks. He notes that SAGUAPAC customers pay as much as 50% more than customers in areas with public services. Nevertheless, he says that participation in the decision making process gives customers a sense of ownership. He also cites governance as a key factor in the success of SAGUAPAC, noting that several Bolivian cooperatives have failed to insulate themselves successfully from political interference [26].

Eduardo Chilundo and Joel das Neves Tembe have examined the centralized public water management system in Mozambique. Observing water use in three similar towns, they conclude that though Mozambique has been able to provide for the basic needs of its citizens, some reform is needed [27]. Centralized water management consists of maintenance, repair, and operation of water supply systems. Though metering is in place, costs cover no more than operation, repair, and maintenance. Lump sum fees are charged for use of public water systems, and water from the river is free. The result is overuse by irrigators and domestic users alike. The authors propose the following reforms: development of a national irrigation policy; enactment of water pricing; more equitable distribution of water resources; adoption of the river basin for irrigation planning; involvement of all stakeholders in planning; strengthening coordination among water institutions; arrangement for cooperation with Swaziland, the upstream country; and investment in irrigation research. Though the government of Mozambique has taken a step in the right direction, it may benefit from a more structured and locally managed system.

The problems cited in these examples are representative of the water management problems that many nations around the world are facing. As Mike Muller states, "South Africa's inequalities are mirrored on a global scale and its experience is thus relevant to the global water policy debate" [6]. Even so, it is important that the international community recognize that similar problems do not necessarily have identical solutions. Several authors have recognized the need for alternative approaches to solving the freshwater problem, many of which are presented in specific contexts. The following section explores some of these alternatives, noting their strengths and weaknesses.

7.5   Alternatives

Documents of the UN and WHO imply that a fundamental right to water is equated with what should be an explicit human right to water for all [2,3]. However, while acknowledging water as a fundamental right, other authors have outlined policy and management strategies that they argue would improve access without employing human rights language to do so. The following examples offer alternative interpretations of rights to water without neglecting the fundamental right of all people to a minimum amount of clean, safe drinking water.

M. Ramón Llamas has suggested applying a universal ethics to water policy and management practices [28]. Drawing on existing social ethical principles, he applies these principles to basic water management variables. For example, he applies the ethical principle of solidarity to balancing the needs of the many stakeholders involved in transboundary water disputes. Additionally, he applies the ethical principle of stewardship to sustainable development practices, which he notes need not exclude responsible use of dams and groundwater development. He notes that technology and conservation do not have to be mutually exclusive and that hydrogeological data, along with technology and education, "improve stakeholder participation and lead to efficient use of the resource." He also emphasizes the importance of water resource managers to honor the intrinsic, as well as the utilitarian values of water. Llamas' principles may sound a bit idealistic; however, his principles are flexible enough to honor the cultural, environmental, and individual rights that some have claimed may be compromised by explicit human rights to water.

Leonard Hammer has asserted that context is the greatest problem in defining human rights. He argues that the popular anthropocentric and eco-centric approaches to a human right to water create individual-group dichotomies that cannot be resolved [17]. Citing the "somewhat overbearing" nature of the General Comment No. 15 implementation strategies, he presents a framework that incorporates an individual human right to water with "a more holistic approach to water that accounts for broader social, cultural, and economic considerations as well." By "recognizing the environmental link with indigenous peoples and the importance of accounting for indigenous peoples in the sustainable development equation," he argues for an approach that incorporates indigenous rights, thereby protecting cultural, environmental and individual rights. The major drawbacks of Hammer's proposal are: (1) indigenous groups are difficult to define, and (2) it creates the potential for neglecting disadvantaged non-indigenous people. Nevertheless, Hammer's emphasis on a "local-based understanding of the needs and desires of the population" through indigenous participation is noteworthy when taken in its own context.

Marcus Moench has addressed the debate over whether water should be treated as a common good or as an economic good. He notes: "Debates over water rights have become particularly intense over the past decade as the concept of water as an economic good has gained prominence and come in conflict with the concept of water as a social good" [14]. He proposes an ethical approach to water policy, involving water as both an entitlement and as a public trust, to provide "a vehicle for granting water the status of a human right" [14]. Moench asserts that the first priority must be to provide access to water for all, i.e., water as a common good. He cites Garrett Hardin's "Tragedy of the Commons" as an argument for not treating water as a common good across the board, however; the premise of such an argument is that people tend to take for granted resources that are treated as common goods. Similar to the fourth Dublin Principle, Moench argues that individual rights to water encourage responsible use; therefore, they should not be excluded from water policy. Thus, he suggests that by combining an ethical approach with private rights notions, it is possible to create a framework to balance public interests and private incentives. As he says: "In most instances this is quite different from common conceptions of human rights" [14].

7.6 Conclusions

Globalization has had a far-reaching impact, affecting the way that nations, businesses, and individuals operate on a daily basis. It has touched every part of our lives through its influence on the economy; on market and trade dynamics; on cultural change; on governance; and on natural resource management, to name just a few ways. As the world continues to become more interconnected through globalization policies, the international community becomes more intimately involved in the policies of individual nations. Likewise, as the world's population continues to grow, regional freshwater issues will become more prominent in the eyes of the international community. Thus, the community will continue to seek solutions to these problems, whether as recommendations, as international law, or as global policy. From a perspective of management or a perspective of governance, the issue of access to clean, safe drinking water is a problem of global proportions.

Whether enforced through human rights to water or approached through ethical means, solutions to access problems caused by inequitable distribution, pollution, supply, and demand must be devised within regional and local contexts. Though international IWRM plans suffer from implementation problems, the real problems may be due to governance issues within the state rather than any shortcoming of the IWRM model. Therefore, such plans must be designed and implemented at regional and local levels with only minimal guidance from the international and national levels. Sustainable management practices such as IWRM, when properly implemented, serve to improve access by improving stakeholder participation, water quality, water quantity, and the long-term health and sustainability of the watershed.

Regarding human rights language as a solution to the problem of access, Moench notes that there may be some truth to the following quote from *The Economist*: "The new rights would have to be defined in the vaguest, most general terms if they are to be plausibly universal in scope. These rights will either mean nothing, if they are regarded as only empty platitudes; or, if the intention is to move from stating rights to enforcing laws, they will be constitutionally dangerous" [14]. Nevertheless, a human rights based approach to water does not have to be formulated through new human rights language that could potentially alienate some members of the global community. The right exists by implication as a prerequisite for the right to life, and that alone should carry the legal force necessary to protect the right to water to any extent that human rights language will.

Though ethical approaches lack legal force, similar to management approaches, they provide a flexible framework within which different cultural and social values can be weighed in the development of national, regional, and local policies and programs. Whether water is treated as an economic good, a common good, or both, it is in the best interests of developing nations to limit the use of privatized water systems. Where privatization is necessary or preferred, it would be best implemented along with strict regulations on pricing, distribution of services, and sustainable management practices. This includes limiting interbasin transfers to only what is absolutely necessary, allowing the sale of water to outside users only when it will not have adverse short- or long-term effects on the watershed. Further, internationally mandated or conditional privatization should not be allowed—the choice of whether or not to privatize should be left up to the stakeholders. We should also note that subsidization of water costs might be necessary in poor urban or rural areas.

Regardless of the hesitations of some international participants, the UN and other international agencies are moving ahead with their plans to implement an international endorsement of human rights to water. The first step came with the penning of General Comment No. 15, but whether the next step will consist of explicit human rights language to set water aside as a human right separable from the right to life remains to be seen. Either way, the challenges facing the international community to address the problems of access, implementation, and enforcement are many. Perhaps the greatest challenge will be to address the freshwater problem without resorting to language that is, in the words of Leonard Hammer, "overbearing."

References

1. Gleick, P.H., The human right to water, *Water Nepal*, 10, 117, 2003.
2. United Nations, Substantive issues arising in the implementation of the International Covenant on Economic, Social and Cultural Rights, General Comment No. 15, Twenty-ninth session of the United Nations Committee on Economic, Social and Cultural Rights, Geneva, Switzerland, 2002, 2–3, 9–10, 15.
3. World Health Organization. *The Right to Water*, 1st Ed., World Health Organization, Geneva, Switzerland, 2003.
4. Varghese, S., Transnational led privatization and the new regime for the global governance of water, *Water Nepal*, 10, 77, 2003.
5. Dolatyar, M. and Gray, T., *Water Politics in the Middle East*, 1st Ed., St. Martin's Press, Inc., New York, 2000.
6. Muller, M., Public-private partnerships in water: A South African perspective on the global debate, *J. Int. Dev.*, 15, 1115, 2003.
7. United Nations, Universal Declaration of Human Rights 1948, *United Nations Online*, Article 25, available at http://www.un.org/Overview/rights.html (accessed on November 2, 2005).
8. Rahaman, M., Varis, O., Integrated water resources management: Evolution, prospects, and future challenges, *Sustainability: Science, Practice, and Policy*, 2005, 2, available at http://ejournal.nbii.org (accessed on November 1, 2005).
9. Young, G.J., Dooge, J.C., and Rodda, J.C., *Global Water Resource Issues*, 1st Ed., Cambridge University Press, Cambridge, 1994.
10. United Nations, The Millennium Development Goals report, *UN Millennium Development Goals*, 2005, available at http://www.un.org/millenniumgoals/ (accessed on November 12, 2005).
11. Swatuk, L.A. and Rahm, D., Integrating policy, disintegrating practice: Water resource management in Botswana, *Phys. Chem. Earth*, 29, 1357, 2004.
12. Water Aid and Rights and Humanity, Right to water: Introduction to human rights, RighttoWater.org, 2006, available at http://www.righttowater.org.uk/code/homepage.asp (accessed on January 11, 2006).
13. Khalfan, A., The right-based approach to water governance: Rhetoric or real contribution? *The Forum*, 11, 6, 2004.
14. Moench, M., Searching for balance: Water rights, human rights, and water ethics, *Water Nepal*, 10, 117, 2003.
15. World Health Organization, Legal recognition of the right to water, *World Health Organization*, 2005, available at http://www.who.int/water_sanitation_health/humanrights/en/index1.html (accessed on June 28, 2005).
16. Greaves, T., Water rights in the Pacific Northwest, in *Water Culture, and Power, Donahue*, J.M. Donahue and B.R. Johnston, Eds., Island Press, Washington DC, 1998, 35–46, chap. 3
17. Hammer, L., Indigenous peoples as a catalyst for applying the human right to water, *Int. J. Minor. Group Rights*, 10, 131, 2004.
18. Smith, Z.A. and Thomassey, G., *Fresh Water Issues*, 1st ed., ABC-CLIO, Inc., Santa Barbara, CA, 2002.
19. Shelton, D., Human Rights Committee's decisions, *Hum. Rights Dialogue*, 2, 31, 2005.
20. Singh, N., *Enforcement of Human Rights*, 1st Ed., Kluwer Academic Publishers, Hingham, MA, 1986, 10.
21. Barlow, M., Report summary: Blue gold: The global water crisis and the commodification of the world's water supply, *International Forum on Globalization*, 1999, available at http://www.ifg.org/analysis/reports/TMP1037743184.htm (accessed on July 1, 2005).

22. Santoro, D., The "Aguas" tango: Cashing in on Buenos Aires' privatization, *The Water Barons*, 2003, available at http://www.publicintegrity.org/water/report.aspx?sID=ch&rID=50&aID=50 (accessed on November 6, 2005).

23. Nickson, A., Pipe dreams: Does privatized water offer poor urban neighborhoods a better supply? *The Water Page*, 1998, available at http://www.thewaterpage.com/ppp_debate.htm (accessed on November 6, 2005).

24. Earle, A., Public private partnerships in water and sanitation, *The Water Page*, 2001, available at http://www.thewaterpage.com/ppp_new_main.htm#types (accessed on June 30, 2005).

25. Nickson, A., Organizational structure and performance in urban water supply: The case of the SAGUAPAC co-operative in Santa Cruz, Bolivia, Paper No. 38, The Economic and Social Research Council of the Department for International Development, U.K., 2005.

26. Constance, P., Are cooperatives a better way to solve Latin America's water problems? *IDBAmérica online*, 2005, available at http://www.iadb.org/idbamerica/index.cfm?thisid=3497 (accessed on November 18, 2005).

27. Chilundo, E. and das Neves Tembe, J., Community management of water: The case of Umbeluzi Basin, Mozambique, *Water Nepal*, 10, 369, 2003.

28. Llamas, M.R., Ethical considerations in water management systems, *Water Nepal*, 10, 13, 2003.

GLOBAL ENVIRONMENTAL ORGANIZATIONS AND INSTITUTIONS

II

Chapter 8

Global Environmental Governance

Frank Biermann

Vrije University

8.1   Introduction

"Global governance" has become a key term of the discourse on world politics at the dawn of the 21st century. While an Internet search conducted in 1997 revealed only 3418 references to "global governance" and in January 2004 less than 90,000, in January 2005 the World Wide Web listed 1,780,000 pages that mentioned the term. Global governance became a rallying call for policy advocates who hail it as panacea for the evils of globalization; a global menace for opponents who fear it as the universal hegemony of the many by the powerful few; and an analytical concept that has given rise to much discussion among scholars of international relations.

This chapter shall explore the concept of global governance of the environment.* I will first sketch different current uses of the term "global governance" in the literature. In the second section, I highlight three key characteristics of global governance that make it different from traditional international relations. The last section offers the reader two examples from recent policy debates on the reform of the existing system of global environmental governance.

---

* This chapter draws on my article "Global Governance and the Environment", in *The Study of International Environmental Politics*, Michele Betsill, Kathryn Hochstetler and Dimitris Stevis, Eds., Palgrave Macmillan, Basingstoke, UK, forthcoming.

8.2 The Concept of Global Environmental Governance

The concept of global governance builds on a substantial pedigree of studies that have analyzed international environmental cooperation long before, starting with the 1972 Stockholm Conference on the Human Environment, which led to a first wave of academic studies on intergovernmental environmental cooperation and organization [1–3]. The most relevant precursor of the concept of global governance is the debate on international environmental regimes of the 1980s and 1990s [4–7], including the discussions on the creation of environmental regimes, on their maintenance, and on their eventual effectiveness [8–17]. Important earlier research also addressed intergovernmental environmental organizations [18,19] and non-state environmental organizations [20–23], both of which have received new attention in the global governance discourse.

The modern discourse on global environmental governance builds on these earlier debates. The concept of "governance" was developed first within the field of domestic politics [24] for new forms of regulation that differed from traditional hierarchical state activity ("government"). Here, "governance" generally implies notions of self-regulation by societal actors, of private–public cooperation in the solving of societal problems, and of new forms of multilevel policy, especially in the European Union. In the discourse on development policy, the term has also received some relevance in the 1990s, frequently with the contested qualifier "good governance" [25].

The more recent notion of "global governance" tries to capture similar developments at the international level. Clear definitions of "global governance" have not yet been agreed upon: global governance means different things to different authors [26,27]. There are essentially two broad categories of meanings for "global governance", one phenomenological, one normative: global governance as an emerging new phenomenon of world politics that can be described and analyzed, or global governance as a political program or project that is needed to cope with various problems of modernity (the affirmative–normative perspective) or that is to be criticized for its flaws and attempts at global domination of weak states through the powerful few (the critical–normative perspective). Other differentiations seem to be less relevant, for example between governance as a system of rules, an activity, or a process [28,29].

Within the group of writers who employ a phenomenological definition of global governance, definitions differ regarding their scope. Some restrict the term to problems of foreign policy and more traditional forms of world politics. Oran Young, for example, sees global governance as "the combined efforts of international and transnational regimes" [15]. Lawrence S. Finkelstein defines the concept as "doing internationally what governments do at home" and as "governing, without sovereign authority, relationships that transcend national frontiers" [29]. The problem with these narrow phenomenological understandings of global governance is the need to distinguish the term from traditional international relations because it is often not clear what is gained by using the term "global governance" instead of "international relations" or "world politics".

Other writers try to address this problem by broadening the term to encompass an increasing number of social and political interactions. James Rosenau, for example, writes that "the sum of the world's formal and informal rules systems at all levels of community amount to what can properly be called global governance" [30]. In an earlier paper, Rosenau had defined global governance equally broadly as "systems of rules at all levels of human activity—from the family to the international organization—in which the pursuit of goals through the exercise of control has transnational repercussions" [31]. The United Nations (UNs) Commission on Global Governance [32] described governance similarly vague as "the sum of the many ways individuals and institutions, public and private, manage their common affairs. It is a continuing process through which conflicting or diverse interests may be accommodated and cooperative action taken. It includes formal institutions and regimes empowered to enforce compliance, as well as informal arrangements that people and institutions either have agreed to or perceive to be in their interest." When transferred to the global level, such all-encompassing definitions hardly leave room for anything that is not global governance. Given the increasing international interdependence at all levels, few political rules will have no repercussions beyond the borders of the nation state. In this broad usage, the term threatens to become synonymous with politics.

A different strand of literature views global governance as a political program or "project", mainly in an affirmative sense that demands the construction of a "global governance architecture" as a counterweight to the negative consequences of economic and ecological globalization. Typically, this involves the call for the creation of new institutions, such as multilateral treaties and conventions, of new and more effective international organizations, and of new forms of financial mechanisms to account for the dependence of current international regimes on the goodwill of national governments. The UN Commission on Global Governance [32] adhered also to this understanding of the term and elaborated a plethora of more or less far-reaching reform proposals to deal with problems of modernization: global governance is seen here as a solution, as a tool that politicians need to develop and employ to solve the problems that globalization has brought about. Several authors have adopted the programmatic definition of global governance, yet without its affirmative connotation. These authors can be divided into three broad camps, which all share the same concern: that increasing global governance is subduing national sovereignty through some form of supranational hierarchy. First, some neoconservative writers see global governance as the attempt of the UN and others to limit the unilateral freedom of action of powerful states (typically with reference to U.S. power). A second group of writers view global governance through the lens of north–south power conflicts. The Geneva-based South Centre, for example, cautioned in 1996 that in "an international community ridden with inequalities and injustice, institutionalizing 'global governance' without paying careful attention to the question of who wields power, and without adequate safeguards, is tantamount to sanctioning governance of the many weak by the powerful few" [33].

Which definition or conceptualization is then preferable? All definitions offered in the current debate have pros and cons, depending on the context in which they are used. Given the increasing complexity and interdependence of world society in the face of economic and ecological globalization, more effective global regimes and organizations are needed, and there is nothing wrong in calling this political reform program "global governance". Also, today's international relations differ from the 1950s and 1960s in many respects, and it seems appropriate to denote these new forms of international regulation as "global governance". The term should be restricted, however, to qualitatively new phenomena of world politics. Not much analytical insight can be expected if all forms of human interaction, or all forms of interstate relations, are relabelled as "global governance". Instead, I argue that empirically, "global governance" is defined by a number of new phenomena of world politics that make the world of today different from what it used to be in the 1950s.

First, global governance describes world politics that is no longer confined to nation states, but is characterized by increased participation of actors that have so far been largely active at the subnational level. This multiactor governance includes private actors, such as networks of experts, environmentalists, human rights lobby groups and multinational corporations, as well as new agencies set up by governments, including intergovernmental organizations and international courts. Second, this increased participation has given rise to new forms of institutions in addition to the traditional system of legally binding documents negotiated by states. Politics are now often organized in networks and in new forms of public–private and private–private cooperation. Third, the emerging global governance system is characterized by an increasing segmentation of different layers and clusters of rule-making and rule-implementing, fragmented both vertically between supranational, international, national and subnational layers of authority and horizontally between different parallel rule-making systems maintained by different groups of actors.

None of this is entirely new. Some non-state actors, such as the Catholic Church, have been influential and engaged in treaty-making with governments for centuries. Politics among nations has always been a multilevel process, with governmental delegations being forced to seek support from domestic constituencies. Also, not all areas of politics follow the new paradigm of global governance, and the term may not aptly describe quite a few real world conflicts especially in the area of war and peace. On the other hand, global governance is there. It is more frequent, and it is on the rise. It is a reaction to the complexities of modern societies and to increasing economic, cultural, social and ecological globalization. Whereas globalization denotes the harmonization and mutual dependence of once separate, territorially defined spheres of human activity and authority, global governance catches the political reaction to these processes. New degrees of global interdependence beget the increasing institutionalization of decision-making beyond the confines of the nation state, with a resulting transformation of the ways and means of global politics. Quantity—the increasing number of functional areas that require global regulation and of international regulatory regimes—creates shifts in quality: new types of actors have trod on the stage; new types of institutions have emerged; with new types of interlinkage problems as a result.

Trade integration, for example, has required international regulation of more and more "trade-related" issue areas beyond the key concerns of custom liberalization; the impacts of this drive for institutionalization then brought the world trade regime on the radar screen of a variety of new actors beyond the traditional world of interstate politics: unions, business associations or environmentalists pay close attention to the emergence of the world trade regime and become actors of global governance in their own right. The globalization of environmental problems, from global climate change to the loss of biodiversity, creates new interdependencies among nation states that require new regulatory institutions at the global level. These institutions, however, do not remain isolated from the continuing debates within nation states, a situation which results in governance systems that stretch from local environmental politics to global negotiations and back. I will now elaborate on the key characteristics of global environmental governance.

8.3   Characteristics of Global Environmental Governance

8.3.1   *Increased Segmentation: Complexity through Fragmentation*

Global environmental governance is marked, first, by a new segmentation of policy-making, both vertically (multilevel governance) and horizontally (multipolar governance). The increasing institutionalization of world politics at the global level does not occur, and is indeed not conceivable, without continuing policy-making at national and subnational levels. Global standards need to be implemented and put into practice at the local level, and global norm-setting requires local decision-making to set the frames for global decisions. This results in the coexistence of policy-making at the subnational, national, regional and global levels in more and more issue areas, with the potential of both conflicts and synergies among different levels of regulatory activity. The international regulation of trade in genetically modified organisms serves as a prime example for such multilevel governance [34,35].

Likewise, the increasing institutionalization of world politics at the global level does not occur in a uniform manner that covers all parts of the international community to the same extent. In the case of the 1987 Montreal Protocol on Substances that Deplete the Ozone Layer, for example, various recent amendments have provided for new standards and timetables that are not accepted by all parties to the original agreement from 1987. This leads to a substantial multiplicity of sub-regimes within the overall normative framework. The most prominent example of such horizontal fragmentation of policies is humankind's response to the global warming problem. Here, we observe the emergence of parallel policy approaches that include equally important segments of international society and may develop into divergent regulatory regimes in global climate governance.

Divergent policy approaches within a horizontally and vertically segmented policy arena pose significant challenges. Lack of uniform policies may jeopardize the success of the segmented approaches adopted by individual groups of countries or at different levels of decision-making. Regarding climate policy, for instance, the global emissions trading regime as envisaged by the 1997 Kyoto Protocol may create perverse incentives if the United States is not party to the mechanism. The possibly strong economic implications of a stringent climate policy adopted by one group of states may have severe ramifications for other policy arenas, such as the world trade regime [36]. On the other hand, a segmented policy arena may also have advantages. Distinct policy arenas allow for the testing of innovative policy instruments in some nations or at some levels of decision-making, with subsequent diffusion in other regions or levels [37–39]. Also, sensible international policies could mitigate the negative political consequences of a horizontally and vertically segmented governance architecture, and innovative policies may assist in the step-by-step convergence of parallel approaches.

These challenges of interlinkages within a segmented governance system, however, have only poorly been addressed by students of global governance. Most scholars have focused on the emergence of international regimes and on their effectiveness in particular issue areas. The interlinkages of regimes in different environmental policy areas have been addressed but only recently [40–44]. Yet, interlinkages of parallel policies and regimes within a horizontally and vertically segmented governance system in the same issue area have hardly been studied; there is a need to explore the consequences of divergent policies in global environmental governance and to analyze what sets of compatible or diverging norms and rules exist, how they predetermine the political opportunities for coordination, and of what response strategies policymakers could avail themselves. This research will also require better collaboration among distinct communities of researchers, especially those focusing on the international level and on international relations, and those concentrating on the national level and on comparative environmental politics [45,46].

8.3.2 Increased Participation: Diversity through Inclusion

Second, global environmental governance departs from international politics because of the degree of participation by different actors that were earlier confined to the national sphere. The Westphalian system of international politics was characterized as politics among states. Non-state actors were either non-existent or lacked sufficient power to influence affairs beyond territorial borders. There have been exceptions—such as the Catholic Church with its highly centralized system of authority or the transnational antislavery movement in the 19th century—yet those remained rare and confined to specific historic circumstances. The notion of global governance departs from traditional state-centred politics in accepting a host of non-state entities as new influential actors in transnational relations. The field of environmental policy provides ample illustrations for this evolution of a "multi-actor governance system".

The new role of nongovernmental lobbying organizations in world politics, for example, has been acknowledged and analyzed for decades. Activist groups, business associations and policy research institutes now provide research and policy advice, monitor the commitments of states, inform governments and the public about the actions of their own diplomats and those of negotiation partners, and give diplomats at international meetings direct feedback [20–23,47]. Carefully orchestrated campaigns of environmentalists have proved capable of changing foreign policy of powerful nation states—markedly in the campaign against the dumping of the Brent Spar—or initiating new global rules, such as the global campaign on banning anti-personnel landmines.

Second, networks of scientists have assumed a new role in providing complex technical information that is indispensable for policy-making on issues marked by both analytic and normative uncertainty. While the new role of experts in world politics is evident in many policy areas, it is particularly prevalent in the field of global environmental policy [48]. New international networks of scientists and experts have emerged, in a mix of self-organization and state-sponsorship, to provide scientific information on both the kinds of environmental problems at stake and the options for decision-makers to cope with them. Such scientific advice for political decision-making is not new in world politics; negotiations on fishing quotas for example have long been assisted by the International Council for the Exploration of the Sea. These early examples, however, have significantly increased in both number and impact, which is mirrored in the substantial academic interest in global scientific networks in recent years [49,50–54].

Third, business has taken a more prominent direct role in international decision-making. Again, the influence of major companies on international affairs is not new, and in some social theories, such as Marxism, business actors have been granted center stage in global affairs. However, this "old" influence by the corporate sector was mainly indirect through its influence on national governments. Today, many corporations take a more visible, direct role in international negotiations as immediate partners of governments, for example in the framework of the UNs and of the Global Compact that major corporations have concluded with the world organization [55–57].

Fourth, global governance is marked by an increasing influence of inter-governmental organizations [58]. In the field of environmental policy, more than two hundred international organizations have been set-up in the form of secretariats to the many international environmental treaties concluded in the last two decades. Whether the creation of a new United Nations Environment Organization (UNEO) would help or harm global environmental governance has been debated for more than thirty years, with no conclusive answer (see the related discussion below).

Fifth, global governance is characterized by new, more powerful forms of supranational jurisdiction. While the International Court of Justice in The Hague has been available for the settlement of interstate disputes for almost eighty years without ever being involved in major conflicts, new tribunals have been established recently, with a considerable and unprecedented degree of compliance by state governments. These include the international criminal tribunals in

The Hague, the dispute settlement body under the World Trade Organization, the International Tribunal for the Law of the Sea, as well as the new International Criminal Court. While states remain the eventual sources of authority through their power to alter the legal standards that international courts may apply, and through their remaining option to reject a court's judgment or jurisdiction, current evidence suggests that even powerful nations accept international jurisdiction on sensitive issues, notably in the area of trade.

8.3.3 Increased Privatization: Negotiation through Partnerships

Finally, global environmental governance is also defined by new forms of cooperation beyond the traditional intergovernmental negotiation of inter-national law. The influence of non-state actors is not confined to lobbying in such negotiations; more and more, private actors become formally part of norm-setting and norm-implementing institutions and mechanisms in global govern-ance, which denotes a shift from intergovernmental regimes to public–private and increasingly private–private cooperation and policy-making at the global level [55–57,59]. Private actors became partners of governments in the implementation of international standards, for example as quasi-implementing agencies for many programs of development assistance administered through the World Bank or bilateral agencies. At times, private actors venture to negotiate their own standards, such as in the Forest Stewardship Council or the Marine Stewardship Council, two standard-setting bodies created by major corporations and environmental advocacy groups without direct involvement of govern-ments. The new institutions set up by scientists and experts to advise policy, while formally often under governmental control, also enjoy a large degree of private autonomy from state control.

At times it seems that traditional intergovernmental policy-making through diplomatic conferences is being replaced by such networks, which some see as being more efficient and transparent. Yet the distribution of global public policy networks is often linked to the particular interests of private actors that have to respond to their particular constituencies, and serious questions of the legiti-macy of private standard-setting remain. For example, the World Commission on Dams has been hailed as a new and effective mechanism that has quickly generated widely accepted standards, which had earlier been difficult to negotiate due to the persistent resistance of affected countries. Yet, this success of private standard-setting gives rise to other voices pointing to the inherent problems of legitimacy that are part and parcel of private policy-making, which cannot relate back to democratic elections or other forms of formal representation [60].

8.4 Current Reform Debates

Global governance is a political response to economic, cultural, social and ecological globalization. It is not initiated and developed by some centralized decision-making body, but by an amalgam of centers of authority at various levels. The efficacy of the current system of global governance has been the subject of intense debate. It is not only a normative discussion on "more global governance", but likewise a debate on "better global governance". I will sketch two of these reform debates in this section; both are related to environmental policy, and each attends to a particular aspect of global governance that has been highlighted above.

8.4.1 Segmentation: the Debate on a United Nations Environment Organization

One reform debate in the field of global environmental governance concerns the organizational and institutional fragmentation of global environmental policy. Many observers have pointed to the paradoxical situation that strong and powerful international bodies oriented towards economic growth—such as the World Trade Organization, the World Bank or the International Monetary Fund—are hardly matched by UNEP, the modest UN programme for environmental issues. The same imbalance is revealed when UNEP is compared to the plethora of influential UN specialized agencies in the fields of labor, shipping, agriculture, communication or culture. As a mere programme, UNEP has no right to adopt treaties or any regulations upon its own initiative, it cannot avail itself of any regular and predictable funding, and it is subordinated to the UN Economic and Social Council. UNEP's staff hardly exceeds 300 professionals—a trifle compared to its national counterparts, such as the German Federal Environment Agency with 1043 employees and the United States Environmental Protection Agency with a staff of 18,807.

This situation has led to a variety of proposals to grant the environment what other policy areas long had: a strong international agency with a sizeable mandate, significant resources and sufficient autonomy. The debate on such a world environment organization—or a global environmental organization, as it is sometimes being referred to (e.g., [61])—has been going on for some time. Magnus et al. [62] have reviewed no less than 17 recent proposals for a new organization, and they have not even covered all proposals that can be found in the literature, which dates back 34 years to George Kennan ([1]; see [63–65] for an overview). France has now taken the lead of reform proponents in its recent call for UNEO. However, in recent years many opponents of a new agency have also taken the floor [66–69].

Most proponents of such a UNEO can be divided into more pragmatic and more radical approaches. The more radical strand in the literature demands the abolition of major agencies such as the World Meteorological Organization (WMO), the creation of a new agency with enforcement power—e.g., through trade sanctions—or the creation of a new agency in addition to UNEP, which would have to transfer many of its functions to the new organization [70]. Most of these radical designs are both unrealistic and undesirable. Abolishing UN agencies has been rare in post-1945 history and seems politically unfeasible or unnecessary for most agencies today. Trade sanctions to enforce environmental treaties would unfairly focus on less powerful developing countries while leaving the big industrialized countries sacrosanct [71]. Establishing a new agency in addition to UNEP would create new coordinating problems while attempting to solve them and would likely result in an imbalance between supposedly global issues—to be addressed by a new global environmental organization—and local issues, which would then be addressed by the remaining UNEP.

Pragmatists, instead, propose maintaining the current system of decentralized, issue-specific international environmental regimes along with existing specialized organizations active in the environmental field, while strengthening the interests of environmental protection by upgrading UNEP from a mere UN programme to a full-fledged international organization. This UNEO would have its own budget and legal personality, increased financial and staff resources, and enhanced legal powers. In this model, a UNEO would function among the other international institutions and organizations, whose member states might then be inclined to shift some competencies related to the environment to the new agency. Additional financial and staff resources could be devoted to the fields of awareness raising, technology transfer, and the provision of environmental expertise to international, national and sub-national levels. The elevation of UNEP to a UNEO of this type could be modeled on the World Health Organization (WHO) and the International Labor Organization (ILO), that is, independent international organizations with their own membership.

There are three chief arguments brought forward in favor of a new agency. First, upgrading UNEP to a UNEO could ameliorate the coordination deficit in the global governance architecture that results in substantial costs and sub-optimal policy outcomes. When UNEP was set-up in 1972, it was still a comparatively independent player with a clearly defined work area. Since then, however, the increase in international environmental regimes has led to considerable fragmentation of the system. Norms and standards in each area of environmental governance are set up by distinct legislative bodies—the conferences of the parties—with little respect for repercussions and for links with other fields. While the decentralized negotiation of rules and standards in separate functional bodies may be defensible, this is less so regarding the organizational fragmentation of the various convention secretariats, which have evolved into medium-sized bureaucracies with strong centrifugal tendencies. In addition, most specialized international organizations and bodies have initiated their own environmental programs independently from each other and with little policy coordination among themselves and with UNEP.

Streamlining environmental secretariats and negotiations into one body would especially increase the voice of the South in global environmental negotiations. The current system of organizational fragmentation and inadequate coordination causes special problems for developing countries. Individual environmental agreements are negotiated in a variety of places, ranging from Vienna to Montreal, Helsinki, London, Nairobi, Copenhagen, Bangkok, Nairobi, Vienna, San José, Montreal, Cairo, Beijing and Ouagadougou, and on various issues, for example ozone policy. This nomadic nature of a "travelling diplomatic circus" also characterizes most sub-committees of environmental conventions. Developing countries lack the resources to attend all these meetings with a sufficient number of well-qualified diplomats and experts [72]. The creation of a UNEO could help developing countries build up specialized "environmental embassies" at the seat of the new organization, which would reduce their costs and increase their negotiation skills and respective influence.

Second, if UNEP were upgraded to a UNEO, the body would be better poised to support regime-building processes, especially by initiating and preparing new treaties. The ILO could serve as a model. ILO has developed a comprehensive body of "ILO conventions" that comes close to a global labor code. In comparison, global environmental policy is far more disparate and cumbersome in its norm-setting processes. It is also riddled with various disputes among the UN specialized organizations regarding their competencies, with UNEP in its current setting unable to protect environmental interests adequately. A UNEO could also approve—by qualified majority vote—certain regulations, which would then be binding on all members, comparable to articles 21 and 22 of the WHO Statute. The UNEO Assembly could also adopt draft treaties that have been negotiated by sub-committees under its auspices and would then be opened for signature within UNEO headquarters. The ILO Constitution, for example, requires its parties in article 19(5) to process, within one year, all treaties adopted by the ILO General Conference to the respective national authorities and to report back to the organization on progress in the ratification process. Although governments remain free not to ratify an ILO treaty adopted by the ILO assembly, the ILO mandate still goes much beyond the powers of the UNEP Governing Council, which cannot pressure governments in the same way as ILO can.

Third, upgrading UNEP to a UNEO could assist in the build-up of environmental capacities in developing countries. Strengthening the capacity of developing countries to deal with global and domestic environmental problems has become one of the most essential functions of global environmental regimes [11]. The demand for financial and technological north–south transfers is certain to grow when global climate, biodiversity and other policies are more intensively implemented in the South. Yet, the current organizational setting for financial north–south transfers suffers from an adhocism and fragmentation that does not fully meet the requirements of transparency, efficiency and participation of the parties involved. At present, most industrialized countries strive for a strengthening of the World Bank and its recent affiliate, the Global Environment Facility (GEF), to which they will likely wish to assign most financial transfers. Many developing countries, on the other hand, view this development with concern, given their perspective of the Bank as a northern-dominated institution ruled by decision-making procedures based on contributions. Though the GEF has been substantially reformed since 1994, it still meets with opposition from the South. A way out would be to move the tasks of overseeing capacity building and financial and technological assistance for global environmental policies to an independent body that is specially designed to account for the distinct character of north–south relations in global environmental policy, that could link the normative and technical aspects of financial and technological assistance, and that is strong enough to overcome the fragmentation of the current multitude of inefficient single funds. Such a body could be a UNEO.

An organization, as opposed to a program, could allow for a system of regular, predictable and assessed contributions of members, instead of voluntary contributions, as is the case with UNEP. A more comprehensive reform that leads to the creation of a new agency could also involve the reassembling and streamlining of the current system of independent (trust) funds, including the ozone fund under the Montreal Protocol and the GEF of the World Bank (jointly administered with UNEP and UNDP). The norm-setting functions of the GEF, for example regarding the criteria for financial disbursement, could be transferred to the UNEO Assembly in a system that would leave GEF the role of a "finance ministry" under the overall supervision and normative guidance of the UNEO Assembly. This would unite the economic and administrative expertise of GEF's staff with the "legislative" role of a UNEO.

In sum, creating a UNEO would pave the way for the elevation of environmental policies on the agenda of governments, international organizations and private organizations; it could assist in developing the capacities for environmental policy in African, Asian and Latin American countries; and it would improve the institutional environment for the negotiation of new conventions and action programs, as well as for the implementation and coordination of existing ones.

8.4.2 Participation and Privatization: Institutionalizing Civil Society Involvement

A second example of a reform debate deals with the increased participation of non-state actors in global environmental governance. This participation has not been without friction. Developing countries, in particular, often object to increases in the influence of non-governmental organizations in international forums because they view these groups as being more favorable to northern agendas, perspectives and interests. Developing countries argue that most associations are headquartered in industrialized countries, that most funds donated to their cause stem from northern organizations, both public and private, and that this situation influences the agenda of these groups to be more accountable to northern audiences [33]. However, these suspected biases in the work of non-governmental actors should not lead to a decrease in the participation of civil society, but rather to the establishment of mechanisms that ensure a balance of opinions and perspectives.

I offer as an example the recent institutionalization and formalization of the advice of scientists and other experts on climate change. The key institution here is the Intergovernmental Panel on Climate Change (IPCC). The evolution of the IPCC is typical for the functioning of global governance; it has been initiated not by governments but by international organizations—the WMO and the UNEP. It is compriseed of private actors—experts, scientists and their autonomous professional organizations—that are nonetheless engaged in a constant dialogue with representatives from governments. The final summary conclusions of IPCC reports are drafted by scientists, but are submitted to a line-by-line review by governmental delegates. The reports from the IPCC are partially commissioned by public institutions—the UN climate convention—but are structured and organized by the expert community itself.

Typical for global environmental governance has been the continuous struggle for influence in this body, especially between industrialized and developing countries [52,73–77]. When IPCC was set up in 1988, only a few experts and scientists from developing countries were actively involved. This has led, as many observers from developing countries argued, to a notable lack of credibility, legitimacy and saliency of these reports in the South. Continuous complaints from delegates from developing countries has led to a number of reforms since 1989, which resulted in an increasing institutionalization of the involvement of private actors in this subsystem of global governance [74]. For example, current IPCC rules of procedure now require each working group of scientists to be chaired by one developed and one developing country scientist. Each chapter of the assessment reports must have at least one lead author from a developing country. IPCC's governance structure now has a quota system that rather resembles public political bodies, such as the meetings of parties to the Montreal Protocol, the executive committee of the ozone fund or the GEF, all of which are governed by north–south parity procedures.

These changes have ameliorated, yet not abolished, existing inequalities between the north and south in global governance. Financing, in particular, remains a problem. Most research institutions in developing countries lack funds to send their scientists to professional conferences abroad. This has been addressed for direct participation in IPCC working groups. Still, general communication between southern and northern scientists is scarce compared to transatlantic or intra-European cooperation [74,78]. Nonetheless, the institutionalization of the involvement of scientists in IPCC has helped to increase the legitimacy of the panel in the South.

8.5 Conclusion

The current global governance discourse reveals that more theoretical debate as well as empirical research is needed. I will emphasize three needs for further discussion.

First, the debate on the very term "global governance" and its conceptualization is not yet sufficiently concluded. There are a number of conceptual approaches, which in part have been reviewed in this chapter. Yet, none of these has mustered sufficient support within the community. The second main section of this chapter has argued for an empirical understanding of global governance as a concept to denote essentially new phenomena in world politics that cannot be analyzed adequately in the framework of traditional concepts such as international relations. This does not deny that global governance is also an important political program. Yet, it remains crucial to demarcate clearly the use of the term and to state whether any given analysis employs the phenomenological or the normative notion of the term "global governance".

Both uses of the term also suggest the need for further research. The phenomenological conceptualization directly defines a research program: first, multi-actor governance requires us to understand better the behavior and the influence of the new actors of world politics. While environmentalist lobbyist groups and scientists have been studied in some detail as actors of global environmental governance, significantly less knowledge is available regarding the increasing role of intergovernmental organizations and of business actors. This is one of the exciting new research frontiers in this field.

Second, the new mechanisms of global governance, such as private–public partnerships, also point to a new research program that helps us to understand better the emergence, maintenance, effectiveness and, finally, the legitimacy of these new regulatory mechanisms. Some work on private–public and private–private cooperation in the field of global environmental governance has already been done, yet what is needed is a larger research effort that equals the substantial series of comparative studies on international environmental regimes in the 1980s and 1990s.

Third, the increasing segmentation of world politics is, again, also an empirical development in need of more research. We need to better understand in what ways governance between different levels occurs. This, in particular, requires new approaches of linking academic sub-disciplines that have been apart for a long time, i.e., international relations and comparative politics. Research programs on the international climate regime, for example, must be better integrated with comparative work on national or local energy politics. This requires a number of essentially new research programs on "interlinkages" and on the "interplay" within global environmental governance.

All this eventually needs to feed back into the actual reform debates, which have been exemplified in this chapter by the institutionalization of expert advice and the strengthening of the existing system of global environmental governance through the creation of a new world environment organization. However, these reform efforts toward a more effective and more legitimate system of environmental institutions and environmental organizations require, first and foremost, a better basic understanding of the set of phenomena that have been conceptualized in this chapter as global environmental governance.

References

1. Kennan, G.F., To prevent a world wasteland: A proposal, *Foreign Affairs*, 48 (3), 401, 1970.
2. Johnson, B., The United Nations institutional response to Stockholm: A case study in the international politics of institutional change, *International Organization*, 26 (2), 255, 1972.
3. Caldwell, L.K., *International Environmental Policy: Emergence and Dimensions*, Duke University Press, Durham, NC, 1984.
4. Krasner, S.D., Ed., in *International Regimes*, Cornell University Press, Ithaca, NY, 1983, 273.
5. Young, O.R., International regimes: Problems of concept formation, *World Politics*, 32 (4), 331, 1980.

6. Young, O.R., International regimes: Toward a new theory of institutions, *World Politics*, 39, 104, 1986.

7. Young, O.R., *International Cooperation: Building Regimes for Natural Resources and the Environment*, Cornell University Press, Ithaca, NY, 1989.

8. Bernauer, T., The effect of international environmental institutions, *International Organization*, 49 (2), 351, 1995.

9. Brown Weiss, E. and Jacobson, H.K., Eds., in *Engaging Countries. Strengthening Compliance with International Environmental Accords*, MIT Press, Cambridge, 1998, 475.

10. Haas, P.M., Keohane, R., and Levy, M.A., Eds., in *Institutions for the Earth: Sources of Effective International Environmental Protection*, MIT Press, Cambridge, 1993, 14.

11. Keohane, R.O. and Levy, M.A., Eds., in *Institutions for Environmental Aid: Pitfalls and Promise*, MIT Press, Cambridge, 1996, 167.

12. Mitchell, R.B. and Bernauer, T., Empirical research on international environmental policy: Designing qualitative case studies, *Journal of Environment and Development*, 7 (1), 4, 1998.

13. Young, O.R., *International Governance: Protecting the Environment in a Stateless Society*, Cornell University Press, Ithaca, NY, 1994.

14. Young, O.R., Ed., in *Global Governance: Drawing Insights from the Environmental Experience*, MIT Press, Cambridge, 1997, 364.

15. Young, O.R., in *Governance in World Affairs*, Cornell University Press, Ithaca, NY, 1999, 11.

16. Young, O.R., Levy, M.A., and Osherenko, G., Eds., in *Effectiveness of International Environmental Regimes: Causal Connections and Behavioral Mechanisms*, MIT Press, Cambridge, 1999.

17. Zürn, M., The rise of international environmental politics, *World Politics*, 50 (4), 617, 1998.

18. Kay, D.A. and Jacobson, H.K., Eds., in *Environmental Protection: The International Dimension*, Allenheld, Osmun & Co, Totowa, 1983, 6.

19. Bartlett, R.V., Kurian, P.A., and Malik, M., Eds., in *International Organizations and Environmental Policy*, Greenwood Press, Westport, CT, 1995.

20. Conca, K., Greening the United Nations: Environmental organizations and the UN system, *Third World Quartely*, 16 (3), 441, 1995.

21. Princen, T., Finger, M., and Manno, J., Nongovernmental organizations in world environmental politics, *International Environmental Affairs*, 7 (1), 42, 1995.

22. Raustiala, K., States, NGOs, and international environmental institutions, *International Studies Quartely*, 42 (4), 719, 1997.

23. Wapner, P., *Environmental Activism and World Civic Politics*, State University of New York Press, Albany, NY, 1996.

24. van Kersbergen, K. and van Waarden, F., "Governance" as a bridge between disciplines: Cross-disciplinary inspiration regarding shifts in governance and problems of governability, accountability and legitimacy, *European Journal of Political Research*, 43 (2), 143, 2004.

25. Hewitt de Alcántara, C., Uses and abuses of the concept of governance, *International Social Science Journal*, 155, 105, 1998.

26. Dingwerth, K. and Pattberg P., Global governanceas a perspective on world politics, *Global Governance*, 12(2), 185, 2006.

27. Gupta, J., Global environmental governance: Challenges for the south from a theoretical perspective, in *A World Environment Organization: Solution or Threat for Effective International Environmental Governance?*, F. Biermann and S. Bauer, Eds., Ashgate, Aldershot, UK, 2005, 57.

28. Smouts, M., The proper use of governance in international relations, *International Social Science Journal*, 155, 81, 1998.

29. Finkelstein, L.S., What is global governance? *Global Governance*, 1 (3), 367, 1995.
30. Rosenau, J.N., *Globalization and Governance: Sustainability Between Fragmentation and Integration*. Paper presented at the Conference on Governance and Sustainability: New Challenges for the State, Business, and Civil Society, Berlin, September 30, 2002, 4.
31. Rosenau, J.N., Governance in the twenty-first century, *Global Governance*, 1 (1), 13, 1995.
32. Commission on Global Governance, *Our Global Neighbourhood. The Report of the Commission on Global Governance*, Oxford University Press, Oxford, 1995, 2.
33. South Centre. *For a Strong and Democratic United Nations: A South Perspective on UN Reform*, South Centre, Geneva, 1996, 32.
34. Gupta, A., Governing trade in genetically modified organisms: The Cartagena protocol on biosafety, *Environment*, 42 (4), 23, 2000.
35. Gupta, A., When global is local: Negotiating safe use of biotechnology, in *Earthly Politics: Local and Global in Environmental Governance*, S. Jasanoff and M. Long-Martello, Eds., MIT Press, Cambridge, 2004, 127.
36. Biermann, F. and Brohm, R., Implementing the Kyoto Protocol without the United States: The strategic role of energy tax adjustments at the border, *Climate Policy*, 4 (3), 289, 2005.
37. Vogel, D., *Trading Up: Consumer and Environmental Regulation in a Global Economy*, Harvard University Press, Cambridge, 1995.
38. Jänicke, M. and Jörgens, H., Strategic environmental planning and uncertainty: A cross-national comparison of green plans in industrialized countries, *Policy Studies Journal*, 28 (3), 612, 2000.
39. Kern, K., Jörgens, H., Jänicke, M., *The Diffusion of Environmental Policy Innovations: A Contribution to the Globalisation of Environmental Policy*, Discussion Paper FS II 01-302 of the Social Science Research Centre Berlin, Social Science Research Centre Berlin, Berlin, 2001.
40. Velasquez, J., Prospects for Rio+10: The need for an inter-linkages approach to global environmental governance, *Global Environmental Change*, 10 (4), 307, 2000.
41. Chambers, W.B., Ed., in *Inter-Linkages: The Kyoto Protocol and the International Trade and Investment Regimes*, W.B. Chambers, Ed., United Nations University Press, Tokyo, 2001, 119.
42. Rosendal, G.K., Impacts of overlapping international regimes: The case of biodiversity, *Global Governance*, 7 (1), 95, 2001.
43. Rosendal, G.K., Overlapping international regimes: The case of the Intergovernmental Forum on Forests (IFF) between climate change and biodiversity, *International Environmental Agreements: Politics, Law and Economics*, 1 (4), 447, 2001.
44. Stokke, O.S., Managing straddling stocks: The interplay of global and regional regimes, *Ocean and Coastal Managament*, 43 (2), 205, 2000.
45. Biermann, F. and Dingwerth, K., Global environmental change and the nation state, *Global Environmental Politics*, 4 (1), 1, 2004.
46. Young, O.R., *The Institutional Dimension of Environmental Change: Fit, Interplay and Scale*, MIT Press, Cambridge, 2002.
47. Betsill, M. and Corell, E., NGO influence in international environmental negotiations: A framework for analysis, *Global Environmental Politics*, 1 (4), 65, 2001.
48. Hisschemöller, M., Hoppe, R., Dunn, W.N., and Ravetz, J., Eds., in *Knowledge, Power and Participation in Environmental Policy Analysis*, Transaction Publishers, New Brunswick, NJ, 2001.
49. Haas, P.M., *Saving the Mediterranean: The Politics of International Environmental Cooperation*, Columbia University Press, New York, 1990.
50. Jäger, J., Current thinking on using scientific findings in environmental policy making, *Environmental Modeling and Assessment*, 3, 143, 1998.

51. Mitchell, R.B., Sources of transparency: information systems in international regimes, *International Studies Quartely*, 42, 109, 1998.

52. Biermann, F., Institutions for scientific advice: Global environmental assessments and their influence in developing countries, *Global Governance*, 8 (2), 195, 2002.

53. Mitchell, R.B., Clark, W.C., and Cash, D.W., Eds., *Global Environmental Assessments: Information, Institutions and Influence*, MIT Press, Cambridge, 2006.

54. Jasanoff, S. and Long-Martello, M., Eds., in *Earthly Politics: Local and Global in Environmental Governance*, MIT Press, Cambridge, 2004.

55. Cutler, C., Haufler, V., and Porter, T., Eds., in *Private Authority and International Affairs*, State University of New York Press, Albany, NY, 1999.

56. Higgot, R.A., Underhill, G.D, and Bieler, A., Eds., in *Non-State Actors and Authority in the Global System*, Routledge, London, 1999.

57. Hall, R.B. and Biersteker, T.J., Eds., in *The Emergence of Private Authority in Global Governance*, Cambridge University Press, Cambridge, 2002.

58. Biermann, F. and Bauer, S., Assessing the effectiveness of intergovernmental organizations in international environmental politics, *Global Environmental Change*, 14 (2), 189, 2004.

59. Pattberg, P., *The Institutionalisation of Private Governance: Conceptualising an Emerging Trend in Global Environmental Politics*, Global Governance Working Paper No 9, The Global Governance Project, Amsterdam, Berlin, Oldenburg, Potsdam, 2004.

60. Dingwerth, K., The democratic legitimacy of public–private rule making: What can we learn from the World Commission on Dams? *Global Governance*, 11 (1), 65, 2005.

61. Runge, C.F., A Global Environment Organization (GEO) and the world trading system, *Journal of World Trade*, 35 (4), 399, 2001.

62. Lodewalk, M. and Whalley, J., Reviewing proposals for a World Environmental Organisation, *The World Economy*, 25 (5), 601, 2002.

63. Charnovitz, S., A world environment organization, *Columbia Journal of Environmental Law*, 27 (2), 321, 2002.

64. Charnovitz, S., Toward a World Environment Organization: Reflections upon a vital debate, in *A World Environment Organization. Solution or Threat for Effective International Environmental Governance?* F. Biermann and S. Bauer, Eds., Ashgate, Aldershot, UK, 2005, 89.

65. Bauer, S. and Biermann, F., The debate on a World Environment Organization: An introduction, in *A World Environment Organization: Solution or Threat for Effective International Environmental Governance?* F. Biermann and S. Bauer, Eds., Ashgate, Aldershot, UK, 2005, 1–23.

66. Juma, C., Stunting green progress, *Financial Times*, 6 July, 2000.

67. von Moltke, K., The organization of the impossible, *Global Environmental Politics*, 1 (1), 23, 2001.

68. von Moltke, K., Clustering international environmental agreements as an alternative to a World Environment Organization, in *A World Environment Organization: Solution or Threat for Effective International Environmental Governance?* F. Biermann and S. Bauer, Eds., Ashgate, Aldershot, UK, 2005, 175–204.

69. Oberthür, S. and Gehring, T., Reforming international environmental governance: An institutional perspective on proposals for a World Environment Organization, in *A World Environment Organization. Solution or Threat for Effective International Environmental Governance?* F. Biermann and S. Bauer, Eds., Ashgate, Aldershot, UK, 2005, 205–234.

70. Kanie, N. and Haas, P.M., Eds., in *Emerging Forces in Environmental Governance*, United Nations University Press, Tokyo, 2004.

71. Biermann, F., The rising tide of green unilateralism in world trade law: Options for reconciling the emerging north–south conflict, *Journal of World Trade*, 35 (3), 421, 2001.

72. Rajan, M.G., *Global Environmental Politics: India and the North–South Politics of Global Environmental Issues*, Oxford University Press, Delhi, 1997.

73. Agrawala, S., Context and early origins of the Intergovernmental Panel on Climate Change, *Climatic Change*, 39, 605, 1998.

74. Agrawala, S., Structural and process history of the Intergovernmental Panel on Climate Change, *Climatic Change*, 39, 621, 1998.

75. Siebenhüner, B., How do scientific assessments learn? Part 1. Conceptual framework and case study of the IPCC, *Environmental Science and Policy*, 5, 411, 2002.

76. Siebenhüner, B., How do scientific assessments learn? Part 2.Case study of the LRTAP assessment and comparative conclusions, *Environmental Science and Policy*, 5, 421, 2002.

77. Siebenhüner, B., The changing role of nation states in international environmental assessments: The Case of the IPCC, *Global Environmental Change*, 13 (2), 113, 2003.

78. Kandlikar, M. and Sagar, A., Climate change research and analysis in India: An integrated assessment of a south–north divide, *Global Environmental Change*, 9 (2), 119, 1999.

Chapter 9

The Role of the United Nations: from Stockholm to Johannesburg

Lisa Nelson

California State Polytechnic University

"Thirty years ago, in Stockholm, we agreed on the urgent need to respond to the problem of environmental deterioration. Ten years ago, at the United Nations Conference on Environment and Development, held in Rio de Janeiro, we agreed that the protection of the environment and social and economic development are fundamental to sustainable development, based on the Rio Principles. …The Johannesburg Summit has also confirmed that significant progress has been made towards achieving a global consensus and partnership among all the people of our planet."

—From the Johannesburg Declaration on Sustainable Development [1].

9.1   Introduction

The United Nations is one of humanity's greatest achievements, and at the same time it is a dream, a work in progress, challenged by the social and environmental impacts of economic globalization and by persistent national policies and choices that undermine agreed on goals and objectives. What role does the United Nations play in protecting, maintaining, and restoring environmental quality in this age of globalization? The United Nations, primarily organized to prevent wars and promote peaceful conflict resolution and political stability, has also, since its beginning, been a key player in the effort to promote social and economic development in countries attaining independence since World War II [2]. The connection (and initial perception of a conflict) between development and the environment was recognized in the early 1970s, and ever since, the UN has been weaving environmental awareness into its development programs, and a concern for development into its environmental programs. In addition, the widespread recognition of global interdependence and transnational environmental issues has led to a number of international conventions (treaties) that are administered through the UN. In combining concerns for development with environmental awareness, the UN has served as a leading reference point for the definition and global pursuit of sustainability, encompassing economic, social, and environmental elements. Despite the UN's lack of enforcement capabilities, the several international conventions that are housed within it serve as reference points for national, regional, and local policies that are enforceable. Myer and colleagues note the UN's integral position within a world environmental regime that has developed over the last several decades from informal discourse among scientific associations to more formal intergovernmental communications. In particular, the UN is foundational for addressing issues of long term environmental degradation in the absence of other strong collective actors [3].

The UN has reported that approximately 70% of its efforts are devoted to economic and social progress and development, and that it is well positioned to do so because it represents no single national nor business interest, and has a global presence. All countries have a voice in its major policy decisions [4]. Currently, the UN is working to help nations decentralize their development programs, and it is using the internationally agreed on Millenium Development Goals (MDGs) as a focal set of targets and accompanying criteria to attract funding and shape its programs. Goal 7 of the eight MDGs is to achieve major improvements in environmental sustainability. Presentations of the MDGs in publications and on the Internet emphasize the interconnectedness of all goals. In particular, the UN has stressed the importance of environmental protection to achieving development goals and to connecting the alleviation of poverty to environmental sustainability. The mode of operation for implementing the environmental programs of the United Nations is to develop project-focused partnerships with donor and host country governments, specific government agencies, private sector trade groups and corporations, the World Bank, and civil society organizations. The UN administrative units with the lead environmental roles are the UN Environmental Programme (UNEP) and the UN Development Programme (UNDP), in addition to the secretariats administering the various conventions. United Nations Educational, Scientific, and Cultural Organization (UNESCO) also houses some environmental programs and has declared 2005–2014 the decade of Education for Sustainable Development.

Globalization heightens the role of the UN as a clearinghouse and forum for the protection, maintenance, and restoration of the environment, as the interconnections between the quality of life across the planet become increasingly apparent. Globalization has many faces: internationalization, border openness, a process of capital accumulation, ideology, and a variety of transborder phenomena, such as the Internet [5,6]. As globalization alters the nature and character of governance at all levels, the UN becomes a more significant institution, an obstacle for some aspirations and an opportunity for others. Farazmand argues that the UN itself has been a major factor in globalization, although he focuses primarily on the economic structural adjustments required by the affiliate World Bank, International Monetary Fund, and World Trade Organization. Stiglitz agrees that international finance institutions are dominated "by commercial and financial interests in the wealthiest industrial countries" [2].

The UN, in contrast, provides a platform for bringing nations together to discuss common concerns, and it has the administrative structure to network and partner with all sectors to bring global aspirations of peace and sufficiency within reach, and to address global environmental issues and ecological sustainability [7]. The UN and its affiliates have themselves contributed substantially to the documentation of how the role of government is shifting in response to these new circumstances [5,8].

How has the United Nations, originally organized with the goal of preventing armed conflict around the world, come to include environmental protection in its portfolio of concerns and programs? The history of UN environmental interest is highlighted by five major events, each of which has served to energize international commitment to the environment, far beyond the funding of specific UN programming. These are the Stockholm Convention on the Human Environment (1972), the Brundtland Report (1987), The UN Conference on Environment and Development (also known as the Earth Summit), which produced the Rio Declaration and Agenda 21 (1992), The Millenium Declaration and MDGs (2000), and the World Conference on Sustainable Development (held in Johannesburg, 2002).

The Stockholm Convention on the Human Environment of 1972 is widely perceived as the initial step in the organization of international efforts to protect the environment through the instrument of the United Nations. However, in the prior year, the Man and the Biosphere program (MAB) was instituted within the UNESCO. This was primarily conceived of as a scientific research venture to better understand the details of specific different ecosystems around the world, and has led to the enrollment of a number of sites into the international network of biosphere reserves. Research units were established in many developing countries [9].

The MAB program itself grew out of the work and experience with the International Biological Programme (IBP) and the International Council of Scientific Unions (ICSU) [9]. The latter is now known as the International Council for Science, a non-governmental organization formed in 1931 to foster international cooperation on the advancement of science. United Nations, Educational, Scientific, and Cultural Organization, in partnership with ICSU, the Food and Agriculture Organization (FAO), the World Health Organization (WHO) and the World Meteorological Organization (WMO), organized a

Biosphere Conference in 1968. The MAB program has since been harnessed to serve the implementation of Agenda 21, and related Conventions, especially the Convention on Biodiversity. It has thus shifted from its focus on research to a means for reconciling resource use and conservation at the field level [10]. These early research-based international gatherings built a strong foundation for subsequent developments in international environmental governance.

9.2   Stockholm, 1972: Convention on the Human Environment

The report issued by the Convention on the Human Environment held in Stockholm is the foundational document and reference point for subsequent advancements toward protection of the global environment made in Rio de Janeiro and Johannesburg.

Farazmand [11] describes prior UN development concerns as focusing entirely on economic development based on the model of the industrial West. Western support for UN development programs was primarily motivated by the desire to compete with Communist regimes for the loyalty of the developing countries [11]. The environment has only been a concern of the public and national and international law and institutions for the past 40 years [12,13]. The Stockholm Conference represented a shift in the understanding of global needs, responsive to growing public awareness of environmental deterioration and its causes. The international think tank Club of Rome published its highly influential study, *Limits to Growth*, in 1972, sparking awareness and debate over the question of whether the earth could sustain the rising economic expectations of the world's populations, and predicting that current growth rates could not be sustained for another 100 years [14]. With rising environmental awareness, Western countries began to be interested in the manner and the trajectory of development in the less developed countries.

The Stockholm Convention in June 1972 led to UN General Assembly Resolution 2997, which established the UNEP. This Convention was the first "serious international attempt to grapple with global environmental problems" and also led to treaties to save endangered species (Convention on International Trade in Endangered Species (CITES)) and reduce pollution [14].

9.2.1   Creation of the UNEP

UN Environmental Programme (UNEP) is credited with major contributions in developing the Montreal Protocol, the Convention on Biodiversity and the Convention to Combat Desertification, and for helping over 100 countries develop their own environmental legislation and institutions. UNEP has also been important in the monitoring, analysis and publication of global environmental trends [14]. Although UNEP is the UN's lead agency on the environment, there are many other UN bodies with environmental responsibilities, so UNEP's authority and agenda-setting capacity is limited. Additionally, UNEP is typically funded at a much lower level than the environmental programs within the World

Bank, UNDP, the Global Environment Facility (GEF), "and even some environmental NGOs" [14]. UNEP posts the motto on its website, "Environment for Development." The website also presents key milestones in the progress of international environmental initiatives (Table 9.1).

9.2.2 Initial Multilateral Environmental Agreements, 1972–1987

A number of small environmental treaties were established prior to 1972, mostly dealing with hunting, fishing, and protecting wildlife and fisheries, but over 60% have been signed since the Stockholm Conference and are administered by a United Nations authority [14]. The CITES is one of the first major environmental treaties, which are also referred to as Multilateral Environmental Agreements (MEAs). Its purpose is to protect endangered species of plants and animals from over-exploitation so that they are able to survive in the wild. Adopted in 1973

Table 9.1   UN Environmental Programme Milestones (UNEP, 2005a)

1972—UN Conference on the Human Environment recommends creation of UN Environmental Organization

1972—UNEP created by UN General Assembly

1973—Convention on International Trade in Endangered Species (CITES)

1975—Mediterranean Action Plan first UNEP-brokered Regional Seas Agreement

1979—Bonn Convention on Migratory Species

1985—Vienna Convention for the Protection of the Ozone Layer

1987—Montreal Protocol on Substances that Deplete the Ozone Layer

1988—Intergovernmental Panel on Climate Change (IPCC)

1989—Basel Convention on the Transboundary Movement of Hazardous Wastes

1992—UN Conference on Environment and Development (Earth Summit) publishes Agenda 21, a blueprint for Sustainable Development

1992—Convention on Biological Diversity

1995—Global Programme of Action (GPA) launched to protect marine environment from land-based sources of pollution

1997—Nairobi Declaration redefines and strengthens UNEP's role and mandate

1998—Rotterdam Convention on Prior Informed Consent

2000—Cartagena Protocol on Biosafety adopted to address issue of genetically modified organisms

2000—Malmö Declaration—first Global Ministerial Forum on the Environment calls for strengthened international environmental governance

2000—Millennium Declaration—Environmental Sustainability included as one of eight Millennium Development Goals

2001—Stockholm Convention on Persistent Organic Pollutants (POPs)

2002—World Summit on Sustainable Development

2004—Bali Strategic Plan for Technology Support and Capacity Building

2005—World Summit outcome document highlights key role of Environment in Sustainable Development

Source: From United Nations Environment Programme, *Milestones*, 2005, http://www.unep.org/Documents.Multilingual/Default.asp?DocumentID=287&ArticleID=3313&l=en

and entering into force in 1975, it has 162 parties signed on, or 84% of the world's nations. Convention on International Trade in Endangered Species is governed by the UNEP and the CITES Secretariat, based in Geneva.

The international treaties that have resulted in United Nations tracking and management of resources have long been controversial for United States partisans wishing to protect U.S. "consumer" interests. Payne and Roberts provide an example of casting international governance of seabed mineral rights as a "threat" of wealth redistribution [15]. On the other hand, international treaties can also provide legitimacy for the politically more difficult implementation of rules and enforcement at the national and subnational levels [16].

The Montreal Protocol, signed in 1987, is widely considered to be one of the most successful MEAs on record. Industrialized countries have been very successful in phasing out ozone-depleting chemicals. In addition, 1987 saw the signing of the Basel Accord, which controls transboundary movement of hazardous waste and prohibits its export from developed to developing countries [17].

Proclamation 4 of the Stockholm Resolution stated that most of the environmental problems in the developing countries were caused by under-development. In the developed countries, the resolution stated that environmental problems were "generally related to industrialization and technological development." This tension between development and environment created a dilemma for both development specialists and environmentalists that eventually led to the effort to synthesize these interests in the Brundtland Commission Report.

9.3 Brundtland Report, 1987

Between 1972 and 1987, the developed nations evolved sets of pollution control and natural resource protection regimes. The oil crisis of the early 1970s led to the exploration of alternative energy production, consumption, and land use patterns. Chemical and nuclear accidents such as Love Canal, Three Mile Island, Bhopal, and Chernobyl raised public concerns and led to stricter controls on chemical and nuclear production and waste disposal. At the same time, leaders of the developing countries expressed a sense of injustice that they should be restricted from patterns of development that the developed countries had enjoyed since the industrial revolution, and the search began for ways to help these countries develop without such a high cost to local environmental quality and to the world's climate and biological diversity.

Following a "Stockholm +10" conference in Nairobi organized by the UNEP, the World Commission on Environment and Development was established and charged in 1983 to report on global environmental problems and recommend strategies for sustainable development. The Commission's report, "Our Common Future" was transmitted to the UN General Assembly in 1987, and also became known as the Brundtland Report after its chair, Gro Harlem Brundtland of Norway. The report argued against the previous dilemma of environment vs. development, stating instead that the activities that needed to be taken on behalf of the environment would actually aid development, not hinder it, and that in fact the old conventional approaches to both social development and environmental protection would lead to instability [17]. This report contains the definition of sustainability that has become nearly universally accepted: "Development that meets the needs of the present without compromising the ability of future generations to meet their own needs."

Sustainable development and the definition given it in the Brundtland report became much more widespread as an articulating principle during and following the 1992 Earth Summit in Rio de Janeiro. In fact it was the Brundtland report that provided the impetus for the General Assembly to convene the 1992 Conference on Environment and Development. An interesting modification in the language appeared in Principle 3 of the Rio Declaration: "The right to development must be fulfilled so as to equitably meet developmental and environmental needs of present and future generations."

9.4 Rio De Janeiro, 1992: the Earth Summit and Agenda 21

This UN Conference on Environment and Development was convened by the UNCED Secretariat to investigate means to integrate environmental concerns into national-level economic planning and decision-making. Research for the program and the proposals for Agenda 21 began in 1989. Ultimately, compromises weakened some of the proposals, but the scope and direction of what remained was unprecedented at the international level.

Also known as the Earth Summit, this conference was remarkable for the number of countries that participated (172) and especially the large number of NGOs represented (2400) at a parallel conference in the same location at the same time. Over 10,000 journalists attended as well. The key documents produced here were The Rio Declaration and the plan for sustainable development known as Agenda 21. Leaders from 100 nations also signed the Convention on Climate Change and the Convention on Biological Diversity. In addition, the UN formed the Commission on Sustainable Development (CSD) to ensure effective implementation of the Agenda 21 principles [18].

9.4.1 The Rio Declaration

The Rio Declaration sets out the fundamental principles underlying Agenda 21 (Appendix A). It reaffirms commitments to human rights, national sovereignty, the eradication of poverty, the special circumstances facing developing countries, and peace. It supports free trade and public participation in decision making, and specifically calls for the inclusion of women, youth, and indigenous peoples.

9.4.2 Agenda 21

Agenda 21 is a 300-page document that details commitments to a wide range of environmental improvements grounded in the goal of improving life for humanity. Agenda 21 has had a wide impact on developed countries. Many large and small European cities and some in North America adopted the principles of Agenda 21 as planning guidelines for future growth and the redesigning of transportation, water and waste treatment, and habitat protection [19–21]. This is a prime example of how ideas first expressed in UN venues designed to improve conditions in developing nations were found to inspire changes in developed areas as well. For example, in the mid-1990s, a director of the Toledo, Ohio Metroparks distributed copies of Agenda 21 to people attending a meeting of the Black Swamp Conservancy, an organization intended to protect and restore natural areas in the Maumee River watershed of northwest Ohio. The Clinton administration established a President's Council on Sustainable Development to study and recommend applications of Agenda 21 to U.S. policies and programs [22].

The direct impact of Agenda 21 is that over 6,000 cities and towns worldwide had adopted versions of it for themselves, and over 80 countries, mostly among the developing nations, had set up multi-stakeholder bodies to develop national plans by 2002 [23].

9.4.3   The Convention on Climate Change

The Convention on Climate Change was another important agreement made at the Rio Summit, and has been signed by 165 countries. It conveyed the intention that countries voluntarily reduce their emission of greenhouse gases to 1990 levels by 2000, but most industrialized countries did not meet that goal. The Kyoto Protocol of 1997 addressed this challenge by setting up legally binding targets of ratcheting emissions of greenhouse gases to 5% below 1990 by the years 2008–2012. Only two industrialized nations have ratified this Protocol [23].

9.4.4   The Convention on Biodiversity

This convention has been more successful in gaining ratification, as 183 nations have signed on to preserve habitat and use other means to protect animal and plant species. It has since been expanded to address the risks of transboundary movement of genetically-altered organisms and biotechnology practices in the Cartagena Protocol on Biosafety. The Johannesburg Summit took up the issue of how the benefits of genetic resources will be shared with the people of their country of origin [23]. In other words, if a multinational corporation gains benefits from developing a medicine from a plant or animal from a tropical rainforest, how can these benefits be shared with the people of the country where that rainforest is located?

9.4.5   Commission on Sustainable Development

The Commission on Sustainable Development (CSD) was formed by the UN General Assembly to ensure implementation of the agreements made in Rio de Janeiro. The CSD conducts annual reviews of the implementation of Agenda 21 and works to support governments, businesses and NGOs in their efforts to promote and achieve sustainable development. It relies primarily on reports submitted by governments and on meetings held among parties seeking to work together. The CSD's establishment following Rio was accompanied by the formation of the Inter-Agency Committee on Sustainable Development, for the function of achieving coordination for sustainable development among existing UN agencies, and by the formation of the High-level Advisory Board on Sustainable Development, intended to advise the Secretary-General and the CSD on issues related to implementation [18]. The Secretariat for the CSD is the UN's Division of Sustainable Development, within the UN's Department of Economic and Social Affairs.

9.4.6   Rio +5

In 1997, a special session of the General Assembly was called to review progress toward implementing Agenda 21. The session became known as "Rio +5." The report of the session reaffirmed commitment to the goals of Agenda 21 but remarked on the worsening conditions that the goals are meant to address. As areas of urgent action, the programme for further implementation of Agenda 21 called for renewed commitments of international partnership outlined in Principle 7 of Agenda 21, and called for greater measurable progress by the time the next review of progress was scheduled for 2002 [24].

9.4.7   Summary of Rio Conference

Despite the good intentions of Agenda 21 and its achievements in raising global awareness about the urgency of establishing sustainable development and modifying the consumption practices of developed countries, a variety of indicators showed that environmental conditions and the hardships faced by a large proportion of the world's population have continued to deteriorate. The UN held another gathering in 2000 that resulted in the Millenium Declaration and the consolidation of the agenda for change into the MDGs.

9.5   The Millennium Development Goals, 2000

Farazmand, discussing trends in development administration, found the endeavor highly influenced by globalizing corporate elites, and the UN, in some respects, a tool of United States hegemony [11]. Simultaneously, however, the development profession has also become much friendlier to indigenous cultures, human rights, gender equality, and meaningful democratization. These concerns have been integrated into an international Millenium Declaration passed in the United Nations in 2000, and are now being acted on through the mechanism of the MDGs, as listed below:

> Goal 1: Eradicate extreme poverty
> Goal 2: Achieve universal primary education
> Goal 3: Promote gender equality and empower women

Goal 4: Reduce child mortality
Goal 5: Improve maternal health
Goal 6: Combat HIV/AIDS, malaria and other diseases
Goal 7: Ensure environmental sustainability
Goal 8: Develop a global partnership for achieving the goals

UN websites and publications, as well as others, assert that the problems and solutions for each goal are highly interrelated with each of the other goals, and, indeed, the interdependence of the MDGs is readily apparent. To the extent that environmental stress and deterioration are linked to overpopulation, it becomes obvious that women's reproductive health and freedom of choice must be improved. In Nepal, resource-poor in heating and energy resources, deforestation has led to soil erosion and further impoverishment [2,8,25].

The following discussion will focus on Goal 7, ensuring environmental sustainability. Each goal has specified targets and indicators (Table 9.2). One can see that neither the targets nor the indicators fully capture the scope of the goal. However, they are individually meaningful and are aligned with current data collection and analysis capabilities at the UN and the World Bank. This is a telling example of how the drive for measurable accountability affects selections made in implementation decisions. Fortunately, civil society organizations are able to address the resulting omissions, although they too, in seeking funding from UN-led projects, have opportunities to align themselves to affect

Table 9.2   Millenium Development Goal 7 Targets and Indicators

Target 9. Integrate the principles of sustainable development into country policies and programmes and reverse the loss of environmental resources

Indicators for Target 9 and organization tracking the data

  25. Proportion of land area covered by forest (FAO)

  26. Ratio of area protected to maintain biological diversity to surface area (UNEP-WCMC)

  27. Energy use (kg oil equivalent) per $1 GDP(PPP)(IEA, World Bank)

  28. CO_2 emissions per capita (UNFCCC, UNSD) and consumption of ozone-depleting CFCs (ODP tons) (UNEP-Ozone Secretariat)

  29. Proportion of population using solid fuels (WHO)

Target 10. Halve, by 2015, the proportion of people without sustainable access to safe drinking water and sanitation

Indicators for Target 10

  30. Proportion of population with sustainable access to an improved water source, urban and rural (UNICEF-WHO)

  31. Proportion of population with access to improved sanitation, urban and rural (UNICEF-WHO)

Target 11. By 2020, to have achieved a significant improvement in the lives of at least 100 million slum dwellers

Indicators for Target 11

  32. Proportion of households with access to secure tenure (UN-HABITAT)

Source: From Millenium Project, *Goals, Targets, and Indicators*, 2005, http://www.unmillenniumproject.org/goals/goals03.htm

these indicators rather than others. In addition, the UNDP is encouraging national governments to decentralize measurement and reporting, as well as implementation, in ways that are locally appropriate and consistent with local priorities.

The Economist expressed the opinion in September 2005 that the MDGs could not be met [26]. One can see from the table of targets and indicators for Goal 7 that even the effort to identify means for measurable progress does not state what constitutes the achievement of the goal. In some cases it is not clear which direction might be considered an improvement (i.e., energy use).

Unfortunately, this sustainable development target is the least specific and the least understood of all the MDG targets by nations, making it easy to pass over in favor of targets that are simpler to understand and measure, such as the provision of safe drinking water, or the reduction of infant mortality. In addition, no specific measures of governance (with the exception of measuring the tenure security of urban slum dwellers) are included in the sustainable development target, so the essential tie between a healthier environment and the governance of natural resources is missing.

Furthermore, the idea that the sustainable development goal is basic to the achievement of all the other goals and central to lasting progress against poverty is acknowledged in the MDG structure, but it is not elaborated in a way that guides nations to act or gives them adequate measures of how well they are integrating sustainable development principles in their work to meet the other MDGs [25]. Addressing these important lacks requires clearer guidance on the links among ecosystems, governance, and each MDG, as well as an expanded slate of indicators that better encompasses the governance dimension of these goals.

Nevertheless, these targets and indicators support a wide range of meaningful initiatives and efforts, especially as programmatic efforts seek to decentralize. Decentralization is a key tenet of governance, as opposed to centralized bureaucratic governments [8]. It is worth noting here that UNDP has piloted some innovative local capacity building and leadership training activities in several locations around the world to promote the idea of decentralizing the MDGs. This program, called "Social Artistry," creatively combines individual human development processes with collective visioning of the future and the steps needed to move together in that direction. It utilizes the creative arts and cultural resources of the country to vitalize and integrate the individual, communicative, group, and societal elements [27].

The United Nations promotes the MDGs in many venues and has integrated their simple and direct message into the organizational purposes and programs throughout its agencies. It strongly encourages its national offices to promote the MDGs in the field.

Another step taken by the UN Economic and Social Council in 2000 was the establishment of the UN Forum on Forests, aimed at promoting forest sustainability [28]. This was seen as follow-up to Chapter 11 of Agenda 21 and a longer document of Forest Principles. Developing the language to promote sustainability was politically challenging because of the divided opinion among developed and developing countries over forest sustainability.

As the UN has developed and integrated its implementation of the MDGs into its programs, the interest in the environment and sustainable development was maintained by the scheduling of the Earth Summit. Ten years after Rio, gaps in Agenda 21 had been detected, some problems had worsened, and some new problems had been identified. In addition, the role of energy production and use had emerged as an important issue to address.

9.6   Johannesburg, 2002: Renewal of Commitments

The World Conference on Sustainable Development met in Johannesburg in 2002, with over 20,000 registered participants [13]. The Summit was designed to examine progress in implementing the goals of the Rio conference that had been held ten years earlier. The Johannesburg Plan of Implementation (JPOI) is the major result of that conference.

The JPOI fills some gaps in the Agenda 21 and the MDGs and addresses some newly emerging issues, including "to halve the proportion of people without access to basic sanitation by 2015; to use and produce chemicals by 2020 in ways that do not lead to significant adverse effects on human health and the environment; to maintain or restore depleted fish stocks to levels that can produce the maximum sustainable yield on an urgent basis and where possible by 2015; and to achieve by 2010 a significant reduction in the current rate of loss of biological diversity" [29].

As a result of the directive for the WCSD to promote partnerships, the UN Department of Economic and Social Affairs, Division of Sustainable Development now lists 311 partnerships in its online database, defined as "Voluntary multi-stakeholder initiatives contributing to the implementation of Agenda 21, Rio + 5 and the JPOI" [30]. The Johannesburg Summit has been found by some to fall short of steps necessary to reverse or modify the impacts of economic globalization on the world's people and environment, a shortcoming shared by other intergovernmental political governance structures [31].

9.7   Additional Conventions and Secretariats, 1993–2002

There are over 500 MIAs, but about 300 are regional rather than global [13]. The tendency over the last 30 years has been to develop broader multi-issue rather than single-issue treaties. Today, there are six major Secretariats implementing international treaties, or Conventions: Biological Diversity, International Trade in Endangered Species of Wild Fauna or Flora (CITES), Ozone, the Montreal Protocol, Migratory Species of Wild Animals, and the Control of Transboundary Movements of Hazardous Wastes and Their Disposal. UN Environmental Programme also implements the Convention on Persistent Organic Pollutants, and several additional Secretariats implement treaties on climate change, prior informed consent (providing information on the risks associated with importing various chemicals), desertification, and regional seas.

9.8   Beyond the 2002 Earth Summit

The increasing pace of globalization demands international attention to equalizing its effects by raising the living standards of the poor. Policies for sustainable, equitable, and democratic growth are critical for global and local environments, and they will require a change in institutions and mind-sets [2].

These are exciting times for the world and the United Nations. Programs within its agencies and the burgeoning number of civil society organizations are being steered toward the consensus of what is needed. Even at the time of the Rio Summit, more than ten thousand NGOs maintained liaisons with the UNEP headquarters in Nairobi, Kenya [32]. The MDGs are a very straightforward, easy to communicate vision, and grounded on years of discussion and experience going back to Stockholm in 1973. Subsequent dialogues and summits have built on them and fine-tuned targets and strategies. What is truly exciting about the interrelatedness of the goals is that while the problems they refer to are interrelated, so are the solutions. If something is done to improve education for women, the environment is made more sustainable. If the spread of HIV/AIDS is slowed and halted, social and economic systems can be stabilized. Better governance achieves better equity, and participation and accountability become sturdier [13].

The UN faces some significant challenges. Specific United Nations programs as well as the institution as a whole contend chronically with financial commitments made by member nations that are not met. An example from the environmental area is that of the trust funds of the Convention on Biological Diversity. The Convention maintains a website that displays the numbers for pledges, collections, and unpaid commitments for the current and past years [33].

In addition, there are political issues. The United States proposed 450 changes to the United Nations Summit action agenda in the fall of 2005, most of them hostile to international governance and the implementation of the MDGs [34]. The U.S. Ambassador to the UN explained that the reason he was seeking removal of references to the MDGS was that although the U.S. supported the goals, it did not support the specific targets and indicators that had been developed later by UN administrators [26].

The United States has also been a reluctant partner on specific environmental agreements, most notably the Kyoto Treaty. Its unwillingness to shoulder the burden of potential costs is the consequence of both corporate influence on policy and the lack of political will to take any action that might reduce its international competitiveness or domestic economic growth. Leaders of both major political parties have advocated free trade policies that lift restrictions on the exploitation of workers and the environment. This consensus is ideological in a way that serves the goals of neoliberals. The ideology of globalism makes five claims, according to Steger [35]. The following discussion explores Steger's critique of these claims and examines how they affect the United Nations and its environmental declarations and programs.

■ *Globalization is about the liberalization and global integration of markets.* This pro-market viewpoint claims everyone benefits from instantaneous capital flows. Yet, Steger and even Friedman have shown clearly that the hyper-responsive finance market "herd" has devastated local, regional, and national currencies and economies. These are conditions that promote the problems that the United Nations and other relief programs are assigned the task of mitigating. Steger suggests markets should be made accountable to international political institutions.

■ *Globalization is inevitable and irreversible.* This deterministic claim undermines the remaining strands of safety nets and accountability, and warns that people and their institutions must get on board or suffer the consequences of being left out.

■ *Nobody is in charge of globalization.* Steger argues that the "Washington consensus" of the WTO, World Bank, and IMF, backed by the U.S. military, privileges the leadership of the United States. The U.S. has the only effective veto at the IMF [2].

■ *Globalization benefits everyone.* Global inequality has increased. Inequality has increased within countries as well, in rich and poor countries.

■ *Globalization furthers the spread of democracy in the world.* Steger argues this is a fundamental neoliberal equation of democracy with free markets, completely neglecting the question of how public agendas are framed and discussed. Recent questions raised about the validity of election results in the United States erode the legitimacy of voting as an indicator of the spread of democracy.

Steger suggests that the most likely future scenario is for the neoliberal free market forces to continue to consolidate their position, using improved public relations to smooth over criticisms. Increasingly violent backlashes are another possibility. The third alternative Steger discusses is a "global New Deal" along the lines proposed by financier-philanthropist George Soros and many others in the civil society sector. Many aspects of the following recommended measures would expand the role of the UN in a future global economy:

■ Forgiveness of all third world debt
■ Taxes on international financial transactions to finance a new world development institution administered largely by the global South
■ Elimination of off-shore tax havens
■ Implementation of stringent global environmental agreements
■ Implementation of a more equitable global development agenda
■ International labor protection standards
■ Greater transparency and accountability by national governments and international institutions
■ Gender-sensitive governance [35].

United States support for the UN and the internationally agreed on mechanisms for improving environmental sustainability is vital to the rapid implementation of the near-global consensus on what needs to be done. It is also vital that environmental sustainability become a central driver and criterion for the economic policy decisions made at all levels [13].

As the leading institution for international governance, there are several types of environmental and natural resource issues that the United Nations is uniquely able to address:

- Monitoring global biodiversity
- Protecting the global commons
  - □ Forging agreements on protecting the climate
  - □ Governance of Antarctica and its resources
  - □ Governance of the oceans
  - □ Governance of space
- Promoting and implementing international law and dispute resolution
  - □ Addressing the ecological impacts of war and terrorism
- Promoting sustainability and development
  - □ Monitoring and advancing the condition of women and children
- Coordinating disaster relief

The United Nations' capacity and effectiveness in addressing the above issues will depend to a great extent on the taming of global economic institutions and practices. The World Trade Organization, World Bank, and regional economic organizations can assist the UN in all its missions. In 1993, Haas and colleagues concluded that overall, the effectiveness of existing institutions was lacking, especially in comparison to the rapidly expanding claims on it [36]. More positively, they suggested that some problems were being tamed, while the formation of new ones might be slowing. Twelve years later, one may ask if the situation has improved. The UN has facilitated an enormous number of initiatives that have been undertaken and expanded by the civil society sector, such as Local Governments for Sustainability (the ICLEI), and its Cities for Climate Protection Program (CCP) [37]. In 1993, the UN hosted the first meeting of local governments interested in climate protection, leading to the formation of the organization, which now has over 650 member cities on its roster. This organization was recently highlighted for its intent to assist cities in reducing carbon dioxide emissions at the Clinton Global Initiative conference. Betsill found that active participants gain financial and political rewards, as well as legitimacy, for the adoption of local climate protection measures through their association with CCP, beyond simple communication and information [38]. Rodriguez also analyzes the political efficacy of civil society sector networks, noting their success at national and international levels, but calling for greater attention to local community involvement [39].

The UN as a civil/civic organization is a weak force in comparison to its more powerful pro-globalizing economically-focused siblings, the World Bank, IMF and WTO [2,35]. To the extent that the neoliberal policies demanded by these institutions are blind to their environmental impacts and population disruptions, the agreements and programmes set in place by the UN and its partners are vulnerable. Many argue that these economic organizations are to blame for much of the inequity and structural poverty around the world, and that they must be replaced with financing institutions that do a better job of addressing the needs of borrowing nations rather than lending corporations. Current practices destabilize rather than assist.

Yet, the rising internationalism of transnational institutions and social movements represented by the burgeoning network of civil society organizations represents a countervailing power [35,40,41]. For those groups, the UN is a well-established platform for international discussion and cooperation in response to environmental problems. "The UN system is the only universal device for reacting to new global threats of environmental degradation, global terrorism, and transnational organized crime" [42]. If the people of the world are to restore, maintain, and protect the global environment, the United Nations and its programs will be valuable components of the growing network of organizations dedicated to a world that works for everyone.

The UN's weaknesses are ultimately a reflection of the fact that economic power today is greater than political power, and economic power now directs governments and international institutions at a scale never before experienced on the planet, with inadequate attention to widespread social and environmental costs. The UN's role is thus only as strong as those with economic power will permit it to be. Currently, the most important and hopeful actions taken by UN agencies lie in promoting the MDGs at the local level because these are capable of being replicated village by village. Change will have to occur in global finance and trade institutions before the UN will be able to effectively carry out its many assignments.

Appendix A   Rio Declaration

REPORT OF THE UNITED NATIONS CONFERENCE ON ENVIRONMENT AND DEVELOPMENT* (Rio de Janeiro, 3–14 June 1992).

Annex I

RIO DECLARATION ON ENVIRONMENT AND DEVELOPMENT.
The United Nations Conference on Environment and Development,
Having met at Rio de Janeiro from 3 to 14 June 1992,

---

* Report of the United Nations Conference on the Human Environment, Stockholm, 5–16 June 1972 (United Nations publication, Sales No. E.73.II.A.14 and corrigendum), chap. I.

Reaffirming the Declaration of the United Nations Conference on the Human Environment, adopted at Stockholm on 16 June 1972, and seeking to build upon it,

With the goal of establishing a new and equitable global partnership through the creation of new levels of cooperation among States, key sectors of societies and people,

Working towards international agreements which respect the interests of all and protect the integrity of the global environmental and developmental system,

Recognizing the integral and interdependent nature of the Earth, our home,

Proclaims that:

Principle 1. Human beings are at the center of concerns for sustainable development. They are entitled to a healthy and productive life in harmony with nature.

Principle 2. States have, in accordance with the Charter of the United Nations and the principles of international law, the sovereign right to exploit their own resources pursuant to their own environmental and developmental policies, and the responsibility to ensure that activities within their jurisdiction or control do not cause damage to the environment of other States or of areas beyond the limits of national jurisdiction.

Principle 3. The right to development must be fulfilled so as to equitably meet developmental and environmental needs of present and future generations.

Principle 4. In order to achieve sustainable development, environmental protection shall constitute an integral part of the development process and cannot be considered in isolation from it.

Principle 5. All States and all people shall cooperate in the essential task of eradicating poverty as an indispensable requirement for sustainable development, in order to decrease the disparities in standards of living and better meet the needs of the majority of the people of the world.

Principle 6. The special situation and needs of developing countries, particularly the least developed and those most environmentally vulnerable, shall be given special priority. International actions in the field of development should also address the interests and needs of all countries.

Principle 7. States shall cooperate in a spirit of global partnership to conserve, protect and restore the health and integrity of the Earth's ecosystem. In view of the different contributions to global environmental degradation, States have common but differentiated responsibilities. The developed countries acknowledge the responsibility that they bear in the international pursuit of sustainable development in view of the pressures their societies place on the global environment and of the technologies and financial resources they command.

Principle 8. To achieve sustainable development and a higher quality of life for all people, States should reduce and eliminate unsustainable patterns of production and consumption and promote appropriate demographic policies.

Principle 9. States should cooperate to strengthen endogenous capacity-building for sustainable development by improving scientific understanding through exchanges of scientific and technological knowledge, and by enhancing the development, adaptation, diffusion and transfer of technologies, including new and innovative technologies.

Principle 10. Environmental issues are best handled with the participation of all concerned citizens, at the relevant level. At the national level, each individual shall have appropriate access to information concerning the environment that is held by public authorities, including information on hazardous materials and activities in their communities, and the opportunity to participate in decision-making processes. States shall facilitate and encourage public awareness and participation by making information widely available. Effective access to judicial and administrative proceedings, including redress and remedy, shall be provided.

Principle 11. States shall enact effective environmental legislation. Environmental standards, management objectives and priorities should reflect the environmental and developmental context to which they apply. Standards applied by some countries may be inappropriate and of unwarranted economic and social cost to other countries, in particular developing countries.

Principle 12. States should cooperate to promote a supportive and open international economic system that would lead to economic growth and sustainable development in all countries, to better address the problems of environmental degradation. Trade policy measures for environmental purposes should not constitute a means of arbitrary or unjustifiable discrimination or a disguised restriction on international trade. Unilateral actions to deal with environmental challenges outside the jurisdiction of the importing country should be avoided. Environmental measures addressing transboundary or global environmental problems should, as far as possible, be based on an international consensus.

Principle 13. States shall develop national law regarding liability and compensation for the victims of pollution and other environmental damage. States shall also cooperate in an expeditious and more determined manner to develop further international law regarding liability and compensation for adverse effects of environmental damage caused by activities within their jurisdiction or control to areas beyond their jurisdiction.

Principle 14. States should effectively cooperate to discourage or prevent the relocation and transfer to other States of any activities and substances that cause severe environmental degradation or are found to be harmful to human health.

Principle 15. In order to protect the environment, the precautionary approach shall be widely applied by States according to their capabilities. Where there are threats of serious or irreversible damage, lack of full scientific certainty shall not be used as a reason for postponing cost-effective measures to prevent environmental degradation.

Principle 16. National authorities should endeavor to promote the internalization of environmental costs and the use of economic instruments, taking into account the approach that the polluter should, in principle, bear the cost of pollution, with due regard to the public interest and without distorting international trade and investment.

Principle 17. Environmental impact assessment, as a national instrument, shall be undertaken for proposed activities that are likely to have a significant adverse impact on the environment and are subject to a decision of a competent national authority.

Principle 18. States shall immediately notify other States of any natural disasters or other emergencies that are likely to produce sudden harmful effects on the environment of those States. Every effort shall be made by the international community to help States so afflicted.

Principle 19. States shall provide prior and timely notification and relevant information to potentially affected States on activities that may have a significant adverse transboundary environmental effect and shall consult with those States at an early stage and in good faith.

Principle 20. Women have a vital role in environmental management and development. Their full participation is therefore essential to achieve sustainable development.

Principle 21. The creativity, ideals and courage of the youth of the world should be mobilized to forge a global partnership in order to achieve sustainable development and ensure a better future for all.

Principle 22. Indigenous people and their communities and other local communities have a vital role in environmental management and development because of their knowledge and traditional practices. States should recognize and duly support their identity, culture and interests and enable their effective participation in the achievement of sustainable development.

Principle 23. The environment and natural resources of people under oppression, domination and occupation shall be protected.

Principle 24. Warfare is inherently destructive of sustainable development. States shall therefore respect international law providing protection for the environment in times of armed conflict and cooperate in its further development, as necessary.

Principle 25. Peace, development and environmental protection are interdependent and indivisible.

Principle 26. States shall resolve all their environmental disputes peacefully and by appropriate means in accordance with the Charter of the United Nations.

Principle 27. States and people shall cooperate in good faith and in a spirit of partnership in the fulfillment of the principles embodied in this Declaration and in the further development of international law in the field of sustainable development.

Appendix B Excerpt from the Johannesburg Declaration on Sustainable Development [1]

"…From Stockholm to Rio de Janeiro to Johannesburg.

Thirty years ago, in Stockholm, we agreed on the urgent need to respond to the problem of environmental deterioration. Ten years ago, at the United Nations Conference on Environment and Development, held in Rio de Janeiro, we agreed that the protection of the environment and social and economic development are fundamental to sustainable development, based on the Rio Principles. To achieve such development, we adopted the global programme entitled Agenda 21 and the Rio Declaration on Environment and Development to which we reaffirm our commitment. The Rio Conference was a significant milestone that set a new agenda for sustainable development.

Between Rio and Johannesburg, the world's nations have met in several major conferences under the auspices of the United Nations, including the International Conference on Financing for Development, as well as the Doha Ministerial Conference. These conferences defined for the world a comprehensive vision for the future of humanity. At the Johannesburg Summit, we have achieved much in bringing together a rich tapestry of peoples and views in a constructive search for a common path towards a world that respects and implements the vision of sustainable development. The Johannesburg Summit has also confirmed that significant progress has been made towards achieving a global consensus and partnership among all the people of our planet" [1].

References

1. United Nations, *Johannesburg Declaration on Sustainable Development*, 2005, Available at: http://www.un.org/esa/sustdev/documents/WSSD_POI_PD/English/POI_PD.htm (accessed on May 2, 2006).
2. Stiglitz, J.E., *Globalization and Its Discontents*, W.W. Norton, New York, 2002.
3. Myer, J.W., Frank, D.J., and Hironaka, A., The structuring of a world environmental regime, 1870–1990, *International Organization*, 51, 623, 1997.
4. UN, *Overview: UN in Brief*, 2002, Available at: http://www.un.org/Overview/brief5.html (accessed on May 2, 2006).
5. Farazmand, A., Globalization and public administration, *Public Administration Review*, 59, 509, 1999.
6. Friedman, T., *The Lexus and the Olive Tree*, Anchor (Random House), New York, 2000.
7. Garcia-Zamor, J. and Khator, R., *Public Administration in the Global Village*, Praeger, Westport, CT, 1994.
8. Klay, W.E., Trends and paradoxes affecting the present and future environments of public organizations, *Public Administration Quarterly*, 22, 160, 1998.

9. UNESCO. *Man Belongs to the Earth: International Cooperation in Environmental Research*, UNESCO's Man and the Biosphere Program, Paris, 1988.

10. MAB, *The MAB Programme*, 2005, Available at: www.unesco.org/mab (accessed on May 2, 2006).

11. Farazmand, A., Development and comparative administration: Past, present and future, *Public Administration Quarterly*, 20, 343, 1996.

12. Kates, R.W., Parris, T.M., and Leiserowitz, A.A., What is sustainable development? Goals, indicators, values, and practice, *Environment*, 47, 8, 2005.

13. World Resources Institute. *World Resources 2002–2004: Decisions for the Earth; Balance, Voice, and Power*, World Resources Institute, Washington, DC, 2003.

14. Club of Rome, *Limits to Growth*, 1973.

15. Payne, R.J. and Roberts, F.J., Bureaucratic politics on the seabed: A plea for systematic research on proposed U.N. management, *Southern Review of Public Administration*, 7, 43, 1983.

16. Alley, R., The South Pacific's environmental policy tensions, *Public Administration and Development*, 19, 137, 1999.

17. Runyan, C. and Norderhaug, M., *The Path to Johannesburg*, World Watch Institute, Washington, DC, 2002.

18. UN, *Briefing Papers Homepage*, 2000, Available at: http://www.un.org/geninfo/bp/worconf.html (accessed on May 2, 2006).

19. Priemus, H., Sustainable cities: How to realize an ecological breakthrough: A Dutch approach, *International Planning Studies*, 4, 213, 1999.

20. Beatley, T., *Green Urbanism: Learning from European Cities*, Island Press, Washington, DC, 2000.

21. Aall, C., Municipal environmental policy in Norway: From 'mainstream' policy to 'real' Agenda 21, *Local Environment*, 5, 451, 2000.

22. Sitarz, D., *Sustainable America: America's Environment, Economy and Society in the 21st Century*, Earthpress, Carbondale, IL, 1998.

23. Johannesburg Summit, *Facts About Progress Since the Earth Summit*, 2002, Available at: http://www.johannesburgsummit.org/html/media_info/pressreleases_factsheets/wssd2_progress_rio.pdf (accessed on May 2, 2006).

24. UN, *Five Years After Rio: Where Do We Stand?* 1997, Available at: www.un.org/ecosocdev/geninfo/sustdev/5years_2.htm (accessed on May 2, 2006).

25. World Resources Institute, *The Wealth of the Poor: Managing Ecosystems to Fight Poverty*, World Resources Institute, Washington, DC, 2005, Available at: http://population.wri.org/pubs_content.cfm?PubID=4073 (accessed on May 2, 2006).

26. The Economist, Aspirations and obligations, *Economist*, 376, 13, 2005.

27. Houston, J. and Sanders, J., *Social Artist's Fieldbook: Book One; Developing Your Inner Capacities*, International Institute of Social Artistry, Ashland, OR, 2004.

28. United Nations Economic and Social Council, *About UNFF*, 2005, Available at: http://www.un.org/esa/forests/about.html (accessed on May 2, 2006).

29. Johannesburg Summit, *The Johannesburg Summit Test: What Will Change?* 2002, Available at: http://www.johannesburgsummit.org/html/whats_new/feature_story41.html (accessed on May 2, 2006).

30. United Nations Division for Sustainable Development, *Partnerships for Sustainable Development*, 2005, Available at: http://www.un.org/esa/sustdev/partnerships/partnerships.htm (accessed on May 2, 2006).

31. Pallemaerts, M., Is multilateralism the future? Sustainable development or globalisation as a comprehensive vision of the future of humanity, *Environment, Development and Sustainability*, 5, 275, 2003.

32. Trzyna, T. and Childers, R., *World Directory of Environmental Organizations*, Institute of Public Affairs, Sacramento, CA, 1992.

33. Convention on Biological Diversity, *Parties to the Convention on Biological Diversity/Cartegena Protocol on Biosafety: Financial Information*, 2005, Available at: www.biodiv.org/world/parties.asp?tab=1&menu=home (accessed on November 14, 2005).

34. Bennis, P., *A Declaration of War*, 2005, Available at: www.TomPaine.com (accessed on August 31 2005).

35. Steger, M.B., *Globalism: The New Market Ideology*, Rowman and Littlefield Publishers, Inc., Lanham, MD, 2002.

36. Haas, P.M., Keohane, R., and Levy, M., *Institutions for the Earth*, MIT Press, Boston, MA, 1993.

37. Cities for Climate Protection, *About CCP*, 2005, Available at: www.iclei.org/index. php?id=811 (accessed on May 2, 2006).

38. Betsill, M.M., Transnational networks and global environmental governance: The Cities for Climate Protection program, *International Studies Quarterly*, 48, 471, 2004.

39. Guadalupe Moog Rodrigues, M., Advocating for the environment, *Environment*, 46, 13, 2004.

40. Barber, B., *Jihad/McWorld*, Times Books, New York, 1995.

41. Capra, F., *Hidden Connections: Integrating the Biological, Cognitive, and Social Dimensions of Sustainability*, Doubleday, New York, 2002.

42. Arystanbekova, A., The UN in an age of globalization: Adapting to a widening spectrum of threats, *UN Chronicle*, 41, 45, 2004.

Chapter 10

The World Trade Organization: Free Trade and Its Environmental Impacts

Fariborz Zelli

University of East Anglia

"I see no conflict between trade and the environment.
Countries and international institutions must simply ensure that they pursue their various policies coherently."

Pascal Lamy, WTO-Director General, 28 March 2006

10.1   Introduction

At first glance, Pascal Lamy's statement is a highly optimistic expression of the classical win–win hypothesis, reflecting belief in co-existence, mutual support and synergism between trade liberalization and environmental protection. However, the second phrase introduces an important qualification, wherein Lamy concedes that the untouched state of nature between both fields is not *that* free of conflicts [1]. Taken at face value, the quote implies that there is no inherent harmony between free trade and the environment; rather, such harmony needs to be constructed (i.e., brought about by active policy coordination). As a major source of this coordination Lamy names "international institutions" such as the World Trade Organization (WTO). This view of a constructed coherence also implies an important distinction which is often ignored: the WTO's impact on the environment and free trade's impact on the environment are not necessarily the same. In fact, through its regulatory efforts, the WTO might significantly alter the consequences of free trade for the global ecology.

Thus, in three aspects, the above quotation by the WTO Director-General has marked out the course of this chapter. I will start out with an overview of common assumptions on the impact of free trade on the environment—assumptions which, very much like the first part of Lamy's statement, are all-encompassing and deterministic. From there, I will narrow the scope of examination to specific and immediate hardware-to-hardware impacts: akin to the second part of the above statement, the emphasis shall be put on the WTO's efforts to actively ensure coherence between international trade law and environmental regulations. Finally, I will take into account the role of countries in these coordinative efforts, which is a third factor named by Lamy. As will be shown, the ongoing deadlock among WTO members on ecological questions has so far prevented a more comprehensive approach, thereby leaving the momentum to the organization's dispute settlement system.

10.2   What Impact and How to Assess It?

10.2.1   Classical Assumptions about the Impact of Trade Liberalization

Major controversies about the (in-)coherence between trade liberalization on the one hand and environmental protection on the other date back to the early 1970s, particularly instigated by the 1972 United Nations Conference on the Human Environment (UNCHE) in Stockholm. In the pre-negotiations for this conference, both representatives of developed and developing countries for the first time discussed the trade-environment nexus in a larger setting. Another forum for such early debates was the Organization for Economic Cooperation and Development (OECD) which adopted "guiding principles concerning the international economic aspects of environmental policies" in May 1972. Also, the General Agreement on Tariffs and Trade (GATT) tried to join the party, and establishing in 1971 the Group on Environmental Measures and International Trade (EMIT). In these various settings, the compatibility question was raised out of the emerging awareness that new transboundary environmental challenges had to be tackled within an international setting.

Parallel to this debate among practitioners, academics from various disciplines, such as international economics, international law, and political science sparked off similar discussions, most noteworthy in the aftermath of the 1972 "Limits to Growth" Report of the Club of Rome [2]. Political theorists came up with a multitude of mostly normative models discussing how the objectives of sustainability and growth could be reconciled, or whether such reconciliation was even possible. Even when ignoring the more utopian blueprints of these earlier debates, and instead concentrating on more realistic models, it is still possible to paradigmatically distinguish the protagonists of a win–win hypothesis from an eco-fundamentalist position.*

At the occasion of the WTO's establishment, these two groups voiced major assumptions and predictions about the environmental impact of the new organization. The only expectation which both sides, skeptics and optimists, had in common was that the WTO would bring about a further intensification and liberalization of global trade. Bernauer [3] summarizes the perspective of the trade-skeptical group [4–7] along the following well-known lines of argument:

1. Intensified international trade will promote economic growth across the globe, thus accelerating the current rate of environmental exploitation.
2. Further trade liberalization will exploit and freeze the low environmental standards of certain countries, in particular least developed countries (LDCs). With re-imports of end-products facilitated, developed countries will be given further incentive to outsource ecologically detrimental industries into LDCs, along with the relocation of hazardous goods, e.g., wastes or pollutants. In short, the WTO will promote the transfer of risks to the global South, leading to a faster depletion of its rich environmental assets.
3. Correspondingly, stronger trade liberalization will threaten previously high environmental standards in other countries, in particular industrial-ized countries. Through the adjustment and abolition of commercial barriers, it will spark off a race to the bottom, severely obstructing domestic environmental policies and safety standards as well as local, environmen-tally sound ways of life.

On the other side of the spectrum of opinions, proponents of a harmony hypothesis [8,9] and advocates of "Free Market Environmentalism" [10,11] stress the considerable synergy between environmental and commercial objectives. Naturally, major representatives of the world trade regime adopted their position and repeatedly stressed the win–win situation (e.g., Pascal Lamy, as quoted above, or former GATT Director-General Arthur Dunkel).† Their key tenets include [12]:

1. Intensified international trade will promote economic growth and welfare across the globe, thus raising the international awareness of post-material, long-term goals such as environmental protection.

---

* This is not to disregard positions which occupy middle ground between both extremes, e.g., the proponents of green trade such as Daly (Beyond Growth: The Economics of Sustainable Development, 1996); Gray (Beyond New Rights: Markets, Government and the Common Environment 1993); or Norton (Toward Unity Among Environmentalists 1991). Clearly the below lists of arguments shall provide a paradigmatic introduction to the issue and are far from being exhaustive.

† Arthur Dunkel: "International trade and the protection of the environment are at heart natural allies" (quoted from Eglin 1998: 253).

2. Further trade liberalization will enhance the dissemination of environmentally sound products and technologies. By the same token, it will challenge protectionist policies which favor environmentally harmful production methods.

3. International trade appears un-ecological because it has so far not been applied appropriately and thoroughly. The WTO has the potential to set things right on a global scale: conflicts between environmental protection and economic globalization can now be solved in a comprehensive manner, for example, by integrated accounting which internalizes ecological costs [13–15].

10.2.2 Looking for a Signpost: the WTO's Effect on Domestic and International Environmental Policies and Standards

The deterministic nature of these and other classical assumptions strongly suggests the need for profound empirical evidence. *But how to provide this evidence—that is, how to reliably assess the WTO's impact on the environment?* A closer look at the aforementioned hypotheses might at least help to distinguish possible research endeavors from impossible ones. In fact, any clear-cut corroboration of the respective first item on both lists—each one focusing on economic growth, though under reversed premises—seems unfeasible. The causal chain from free trade to ecological degradation (or improvement) is simply too complex and too long for precise forecasts concerning the influence of the numerous third factors on the environment, let alone side-effects and unintended consequences.* These difficulties notwithstanding, several efforts have been made to develop and apply tools for a comprehensive environmental impact assessment of the international trade regime. However, "empirical studies of the social and ecological effects of free trade are still in their early days" and first need further methodological development [16,17].[†]

Regarding the second win–win assumption (i.e., trade liberalization curbs ecologically harmful subsidies), the avenue of causation from the WTO to a potentially positive environmental impact appears significantly shorter. And indeed, in the fisheries sector, the link between depleted fish stocks and trade-distorting subsidies is well accepted. Likewise, subsidies in the agrarian sector may encourage intensive farming, and, subsequently, overgrazing, land conversion and the loss of forests [17]. Moreover, subsidies on carbon-intensive

---

* Moreover, since economic growth assumes the status of an intervening variable in such a research design, one would additionally have to substantiate the causality between free trade on the one side and economic growth on the other.

† Since 1999, a very promising instrument for Sustainability Impact Assessment (SIA) has been designed and partially tested on behalf of the European Commission (e.g., for the forest sector, cf. Katila and Simula (Sustainability Impact Assessment of Proposed WTO Negotiations 2005)). However, critics complain about a pro-liberalization bias of the original SIA design, since the conceptions do not include scenarios of less or no trade liberalization (Santarius et al. 2003: 41). Further studies of environmental impact assessment were announced by Canada and the United States (see also Section 10.6.3).

polluting sources, as they currently exist in a number of OECD member states, hamper the expansion of renewable energies in these countries. However, as plausible as these arguments might sound, it is too early to praise the WTO's role in removing global subsidies. As is well known, controversies about agricultural subsidies are still at the core of WTO's internal disputes, and they are far from being solved. Similarly, lengthy discussions in different WTO forums on the removal of fisheries subsidies have not yet produced significant results.* The same goes for the debate on the export of domestically prohibited goods (DPGs) which present a danger to the environment or the health of humans, plants or animals.[†] As will be shown in Section 10.3.2, this stagnation or idleness goes back to the fact that the relevant organs have no authority to develop a proper WTO environmental policy. All in all, these current observations about ineffectual efforts at subsidies removal indicate that the above assumption remains tenuous, at best.[‡]

Finally, the third win–win assumption about the need for adequate ecological accounting is even less helpful for the WTO's outlook. Such ideas—in their most modest forms like environmental taxing which rather runs counter to WTO principles—have at best been realized in a handful of national economies of highly industrialized countries. And they certainly play no role whatsoever in current WTO negotiations.

When bearing in mind these methodological or empirical obstacles to investigation of most of the above assumptions, what is left for a more reliable examination are but two of the listed predictions voiced by trade skeptics (items 2 and 3). Both hypotheses—risk transfer and race to the bottom—share a focus on environmental standards and rules. But it is particularly the race-to-the-bottom assumption whose causal inference stops at these standards, treating them as dependent variables. In other words: this third assumption does not focus on end-of-the-pipe impacts on the environment, but rather on the WTO's more immediate effects on particular environmental policies and norms, both multilateral and domestic. This immediacy should allow for more

---

* Discussion on fisheries subsidies are taking place in the context of the Agreement on Subsidies and Countervailing Measures (SCM) in the Negotiating Group on Rules. Furthermore, such subsidies have been discussed at length in the CTE under item 6 of its work program (http://www.wto.org/English/tratop_e/envir_e/envir_backgrnd_e/c4s1_e.htm [23 April 2006]).

† The GATT had taken up this subject as early as 1982 and established a notification system which, however, proved unsuccessful and was abolished after 8 years. Though the DPG issue was included into the Marrakesh Agreement, further attempts to revive the notification system have failed; apparently, the WTO has left the matter to multilateral agreements which were originally designed for the issue, e.g., the Basel Convention on the Control of Transboundary Movements of Hazardous Wastes and their Disposal (http://www.wto.org/English/tratop_e/envir_e/envir_-backgrnd_e/c4s3_e.htm [23 April 2006]).

‡ Moreover, the WTO Secretariat anyway voiced concerns about the extent to which the positive ecological impact of the removal of subsidies could be correctly assessed. In a 1997 background note on "Environmental Benefits of Removing Trade Restrictions and Distortions", the secretariat pointed out that these benefits are likely to be indirect and not readily identifiable in general terms (Doc. WT/CTE/W/67, http://docsonline.wto.org/imrd/directdoc.asp?DDFDocuments/t/wt/cte/w67.wpf [23 April 2006]).

dependable—though far from exhaustive—findings about the international trade organization's environmental role. In the terminology of international regime theory, such an approach corresponds with an *output* level perspective [18–20]. This perspective implies that the ensuing sections will focus on the institutional hardware (*output*), i.e., the bodies and norms produced by an international regime (in case of the trade regime: the WTO and the agreements under its auspices, as explored in Section 10.3) and their respective influence on the output of other institutions—for our purpose: domestic environmental policies and standards (Section 10.4) as well as multilateral environmental agreements (Section 10.5).*

10.3 The WTO's Environmentally Relevant Institutions

Right from the start in 1995, the WTO has addressed the compatibility of international trade and environmental protection—both through the establishment of specific bodies (see Section 10.3.2) and via particular rules in some its agreements, most prominently by recognizing the objective of sustainable development in the preamble of the WTO Agreement (see Section 10.3.3). However, one should not misinterpret this initial inclusion of environmental concern as either brand-new or issue-specific: on the one hand, during the Uruguay Round (1986–1993), negotiators made efforts to integrate a variety of issue-areas such as international finance, development assistance, health and

---

* Besides the *output*-level, two further levels of effectiveness grasp the less immediate consequences of a regime (which in turn are harder to be assessed in a clear-cut manner). These levels are: the *outcome*-level where a regime exerts behavioral effects on relevant actors, e.g., states parties, and the *impact*-level of the ultimate consequences of a regime on a given subject matter, e.g., biological diversity (cf. Underdal 2004).

NB: Given that the remainder of this chapter will focus on one level, namely the *output* effectiveness of the WTO, the term "impact" will not be used in the narrow sense of this typology, but in a general sense, i.e., interchangeably with terms like "effect" or "consequence." Moreover, regime theorists have come up with other well-cited typologies of regime effectiveness. For instance, Young and Levy (See The Effectiveness of International Regimes: Causal Connections and Behavioral Mechanisms, 1999: 4ff.) distinguish between five possible approaches to the concept of regime effectiveness:

(1) *Problem-Solving Approach* (degree to which the problem that prompts regime creation is eliminated).
(2) *Legal Approach* (degree to which contractual obligations are met).
(3) *Economic Approach* (compliance [i.e., legal approach] + degree of economic efficiency).
(4) *Normative Approach* (degree of achievement of normative principles, e.g., fairness, participation, etc.).
(5) *Political Approach* (degree of causing changes in the behavior/interests of actors and in the policies/performances of institutions).

Whereas the *output*-level as such is not covered by any of these categories, types 2 and 5 correspond with a regime's *outcome* effectiveness, and type 1 clearly equals the *impact* effectiveness of the above typology.

civil aviation;* on the other hand, the old, pre-WTO GATT had not completely ignored the trade implications of environmental policies.

10.3.1 The Old GATT and the Environment

It took the GATT no less than 24 years to explicitly address the connection between international trade and the environment. In November 1971, on the verge of the 1972 Stockholm Conference on the Human Environment, the GATT Council of Representatives established the Group on Environmental Measures and International Trade (EMIT). Nonetheless, it would be quite an overstatement to speak of a continuous environmental agenda from the early 1970s onwards; in fact, the EMIT never convened in the first twenty years after its establishment. And it took up to 1989, until another "organ" with an environmental subject—a working group on trade in hazardous substances—was set up.[†] It was thus only the late 1980s and early 1990s that a second environmental debate took place within the architecture of the GATT, clearly instigated by key events such as the publication of the Brundtland Commission's report on "Our Common Future" [21] and the 1992 UN Conference on Environment and Development in Rio. This second debate "came at an awkward time for GATT signatories, since the Uruguay Round entered a deep crisis in the early 1990s and the agricultural dispute between the U.S.A. and the EU threatened to scupper the talks" [16]. Though advocated by major industrialized countries, any comprehensive approach to ecological standards was blocked by developing countries who interpreted them as a disguise for protectionist measures [22] (see Section 10.3.2).

Given the rather sporadic and mostly consultative nature of these initiatives (due to the controversies among member states), the baseline for the old GATT's environmental agenda is not to be found in the activities of its political bodies. Instead, this agenda has mostly been externally imposed by some of the states' parties, namely when invoking the GATT Panel in order to solve disputes about national environmental policies. It is thus the dispute settlement system, where the old GATT repeatedly shaped and broadened its environmental role—a tradition which was well picked up by the WTO, though as will be shown, with more favorable implications for environmental concerns. The importance of these judicial decisions notwithstanding, the next section will focus on a more obvious novelty of the WTO, namely bodies particularly designed for the trade-environment nexus.

---

* Among the WTO bodies dealing with these issues are the Trade and Finance and Trade Facilitation Division, the Training and Technical Cooperation Institute, the Committee on Trade-Related Investment Measures, the Committee on Trade and Development, the Sub-Committee on Least-Developed Countries, the Committee on Trade in Civil Aircraft, etc. cf.http://www.wto.org/English/tratop_e/envir_e/envir_backgrnd_e/c1s1_e.htm (14 April 2006).

[†] The EMIT should convene at the request of Contracting Parties, with participation being open to all. However, this only happened in 1991; again, an upcoming global conference, the 1992 UN Conference on Trade and Environment (UNCED), helped put the environment on the WTO's agenda. Several member states of the European Free Trade Area (EFTA) requested EMIT's activation in order to debate the trade-related impacts of environmental measures.

10.3.2 WTO Bodies of Environmental Relevance

The major institutional manifestation of the WTO's environmental agenda is the Committee on Trade and Environment (CTE). Following the 1994 Ministerial Decision on Trade and Environment, the committee was established in January 1995 (i.e., at the very onset of the organization itself). The CTE has a standing agenda and includes all WTO members as well as several observers from intergovernmental organizations (but not from NGOs) which come together at least twice a year for formal meetings, plus further informal ones if necessary. Its chief mandate is to ensure a positive interaction between trade and environment measures inside and outside WTO law—and to recommend appropriate modifications to the latter where necessary. Subsequently, a major portion of its work addresses the relationship between WTO law and the trade-related rules and measures of multilateral environmental agreements (MEAs) [17]. Further items on the committee's agenda include concrete issues such as taxes, technical regulations, labeling, transparency and market access, as well as arrangements with NGOs.

The CTE is supported by one of the WTO Secretariat's divisions, the Trade and Environment Division. The division provides technical assistance to WTO members, reports to them about discussions in other intergovernmental organizations—including negotiations about trade-related measures in MEAs—and maintains contacts with non-governmental actors.*

Given these new bodies and their mandates, is it appropriate to speak of a proper WTO environmental *policy?* The answer to this question is clearly "no." The Trade and Environment Division is merely performing a service function while the WTO Secretariat has not been endowed with any power to set and exert its own environmental agenda. Likewise, the CTE is anything but proactive on ecological matters. The committee's mandate is *not* to tackle free trade's impact on the environment; instead, it is supposed to act under exactly reversed premises: to keep to the effects of environmental measures on trade policy [16]. Further, least common denominator outcomes will rather be the rule than the exception, since the CTE does not consist of independent agents, but of governmental representatives, its reports resting upon consensual decisions. As a result, though a good deal of promising modifications to WTO law has been discussed in the committee, the actual final reports on the matter frequently turned out rather vague. To set things right: this lack of environmental momentum from within the WTO was well intended by its creators, bearing justice to concerns voiced mostly by developing countries who feared a green conditionality for market access. During the Uruguay Round, members therefore agreed that "the WTO is not an environmental protection agency and that it does not aspire to become one. Its competence in the field of trade and environment is limited to trade policies and to

---

* Moreover, the division provides service to the Working Group on Technical Barriers to trade (WGTBT), if the TBT Committee so decides (http://www.wto.org/english/thewto_e/secre_e/div_e.htm [14 April 2006]).

the trade-related aspects of environmental policies which have a significant effect on trade."*

10.3.3 WTO Rules of Environmental Relevance

Before depicting some of the important WTO regulations of potential environmental impact, it is vital for the assessment of this impact to anticipate a key observation: the environmental agenda of the WTO is mostly set by its rules and their interpretation in the course of dispute settlement. Two peculiar aspects endorse this assessment. In the first place, as mentioned above, the WTO secretariat has no competency for its own environmental policy, hence rendering fairly impossible any *ex ante* coordination of regulatory activities in the fields of trade and environment [23]. Second, though WTO law presents no closed legal circuit, it implies an essential particularity as compared to other bodies of public international law: WTO obligations are *reciprocal* rules, that is, unlike MEA regulations (which are *integral* rules), they are not "immutable obligations to be respected at all times and as between all WTO members," but instead "can, at times, be supplemented or deviated from as between some or all WTO members, by other rules of international law" [24]. As a result, WTO rules, such as those presented in the remainder of this section, are not carved in stone or universally applicable; instead, their impact is comparably flexible, such that *ad hoc* decisions in the course of WTO dispute settlement present the *ultimo ratio* of the WTO's legal stance on ecological issues. One should therefore not mistake the following principles for an indisputable corroboration of arguments brought up by trade skeptics about the watering-down of environmental standards.

Two of the most noteworthy WTO principles which overlap with the trade provisions of some MEAs are included in the GATT and in the General Agreement on Trade in Services (GATS). According to the *most-favored-nation clause* (MFN) in Article I GATT (Article II GATS), parties have to grant any trade advantage (with regard to customs duties and charges of any kind) which they concede to any one country (no matter if or not this country is a party to the WTO) to all members. In the so called *national treatment principle* (NT), Article III GATT (Article XVII GATS) prohibits the discrimination of foreign goods (services) as compared to like domestic goods (services). The chief environmental implication of this principle stands and falls with the understanding of the term "like products". Taken at face value, GATT and GATS generally do not allow for the discrimination of goods and services on the basis of their origin, regardless of environmental or labor standards in the respective countries. However, as will be shown in the upcoming section, this

---

* http://www.wto.org/English/tratop_e/envir_e/envir_backgrnd_e/c1s3_e.htm (14 April 2006). Nonetheless and especially in the new millennium, several efforts have been made to provide the CTE with a more active role and to extend its mandate. Some of these attempts will be considered in Section 10.6.

understanding has been subject to changes across various reports of the GATT's and WTO's Dispute Settlement Body (DSB).*

Moreover, GATT and GATS include provisions which qualify the applicability of the MFN and NT principles. For instance, waivers can be granted for non-WTO environmental rules, on a case-by-case basis under Article 25(5) GATT. However, in order to take effect, this procedure would require the consent of a three-quarters majority of WTO members, which is a quite unlikely scenario. A more promising approach for suspending the non-discrimination principles is based on Article XX GATT (and Article XIV GATS, respectively) which grants "general exceptions" to the agreement's regulations. Eligible for such exceptions are measures "necessary to protect human, animal or plant life or health" (XX[b]) and measures "relating to the conservation of exhaustible natural resources if such measures are made effective in conjunction with restrictions on domestic production or consumption" (XX[g]).

The abstract phrasing of both formulas opens up considerable room for speculations—and hence leaves more concrete interpretations to the Dispute Settlement Body. Regarding clause XX(b), *inter alia*, controversies have arisen about the inclusion of measures to save not only domestic, but also extraterritorial human, animal or plant life (i.e., in the countries of origin). Likewise, debates addressed the scope of allowable measures under clause XX(g): does it only apply to restrictions of the trade in endangered natural resources, or also to import bans on goods whose process and production methods (PPMs) have endangered these very resources [25]? Furthermore, the term "exhaustible natural resources" itself needed clarification; in the decision on the so called Shrimp Turtle Case, "endangered species" were finally subsumed under that term (1998) [26].

The most remarkable difference in the conditionality of both clauses is the introduction of a so-called necessity test: the GATT only demands measures under clause XX(b) to be "necessary"; clause XX(g) contains no similar wording. This implies that the latter does not require eligible measures to be as little trade-restricting as possible; measures under clause XX(b), however, have to undergo a test which has to reveal that no measure less inconsistent with the GATT would have an equally positive effect for the protection of human, plant or animal life.†

---

* In addition to the MFN and NT clauses, another prominent anti-discrimination principle in WTO law is the prohibition of quantitative restrictions on imports and exports under Art XI GATT and Articles XVI + VI GATS, respectively.

† On the other hand, Art. XX(g) measures have to stand a so called "chapeau test" or "cap test" which, according to Chambers (ibid.), is perhaps the most difficult to apply: In this test, certain general provisions must be met, such as non-discrimination or non-arbitrariness, in order to strike a balance "between the right to invoke the exception and the rights of Members to the main provisions contained in the WTO". Such main provisions with an ecological bias can be found in the preamble of the Agreement Establishing the World Trade Organization (WTO Agreement) which thus presents another major source of environmentally relevant WTO law. The preamble's first paragraph explicitly names sustainable development as well as the protection and preservation of the environment as objectives of importance equal to economic growth. Regarding the efforts to be taken by WTO members in order to pursue these objectives, the preamble refers to the principle of common but differentiated responsibility, which has been established by Principle 7 of the 1992 Rio Declaration on Environment and Development.

Another WTO treaty with far-reaching environmental implications is the Agreement on Trade-related Aspects of Intellectual Property Rights (TRIPS)—and not only because it includes the non-discrimination principles such as MFN and NT. In fact, with its predominant goal to protect certain rights (instead of facilitating international trade which is the core goal of the bulk of WTO treaties), TRIPS takes a rather exceptional approach. The agreement's Part II on "Standards concerning the availability, scope and use of Intellectual Property Rights" touches upon the issues of biological diversity and genetic engineering. Article 27(3), states that "[m]embers shall provide for the protection of plant varieties either by patents or by an effective *sui generis* subsystem or by any combination thereof".* This promotion of individual patents can have ambiguous ecological consequences, while the protection of intellectual property rights of environmentally sound procedures and products might promote the dissemination of such technologies and goods, the privatization of hitherto openly accessible knowledge and publicly protected species can equally threaten biological diversity [25].

Finally, the Agreement on the Application of Sanitary and Phytosanitary Measures (SPS) and the Agreement on Technical Barriers to Trade (TBT) are WTO treaties with a potential environmental impact—especially, due to their treatment of PPMs: both agreements permit product labeling, if the production method has an effect on the final characteristics. In addition, the SPS permits safety measures up to import bans, however, these depend on scientific proof (to be provided by the importing party) of any health risks. This conditionality contradicts the genuine precautionary principle which puts the burden of proof on the exporting party. The SPS perspective might thus bear peculiar consequences for the trade in goods whose health implications can hardly be predicted (e.g., living modified organisms (LMOs)).

The above compilation of environmentally significant WTO law is far from being exhaustive, either with regard to the number of treaties or in terms of their various environmental implications.[†] Nonetheless, this synopsis of the most important regulations should serve as useful background information for the following sections: it is now time to consider these regulations in action, i.e., when applied or referred to in the course of actual conflicts with environmental law.

10.4 Conflicts between WTO Law and Domestic Environmental Law

Given the numerous domestic laws which rely on trade measures in order to enforce environmental protection, there is abundant potential for collisions

---

* Originally, deadlines for the introduction of such systems were 2000 and 2005, respectively, but at the Doha ministerial meeting, the deadline for least developed countries was extended until 2016.

[†] The WTO itself names the Agreement on Agriculture and the Agreement on Subsidies and Countervailing Measures (SCM) as further treaties with potential environmental impact (cf. http://www.wto.org/English/tratop_e/envir_e/envir_backgrnd_e/contents_e.htm [22 April 2006]).

between national environmental regulations and the free trade principles embedded in WTO law. Since the early 1990s, some of these latent legal frictions became manifested in the form of legal disputes brought before GATT/WTO institutions. The following will be a synopsis of some of the most influential rulings.*

10.4.1 Cases on Issues of Species Protection and Biological Diversity: Direct Import Restrictions

The first noteworthy judicially manifest conflict between domestic environmental law and international trade law was the Tuna Dolphin case, or *U.S.—Tuna I*. It was brought before the GATT Panel in 1991, more than three years before the establishment of the WTO. Mexico had complained about U.S. import bans on yellow fin tuna being harvested with purse seine driftnets by Mexican ships in the Eastern Pacific. The justification for these import bans was rooted in the 1972 U.S. Marine Mammal Protection Act, which ordered such restrictions towards countries which did not prescribe measures similar to U.S. standards for dolphin protection. The GATT Panel—whose report was never adopted due to an amicable settlement among the conflict parties—interpreted the import bans as a violation of Article XI GATT (prohibiting quantitative import or export restrictions), as well as of the national treatment principle under Article III GATT. As for the latter, the panel's decision was based on a very narrow understanding of the term "like products" with mere regard to their physical features. Only the end-uses, but not the process and production methods (PPMs) in the product's life cycle were taken into account. "Whether the production process of a final product entails a GHG [greenhouse gas]-emitting fossil-fuel-intensive method such as the burning of coal, or something as clean as wind or solar energy, is irrelevant to a WTO decision" [26]. Furthermore, the GATT Panel decided that parties could not refer to Article XX(g) to protect the global commons, but only to protect resources under their national jurisdiction [27,28].†

Three years later, in 1994, the European Community (EC) brought the issue back before another GATT Panel, *U.S.—Tuna II*, by complaining that the very same U.S. import bans kept it from exporting yellow fin tuna that were caught by

---

* The WTO Website lists nine environment-related disputes under GATT and the WTO Dispute Settlement Understanding. (cf. http://www.wto.org/english/tratop_e/envir_e/envir_-backgrnd_e/c8s1_e.htm [17 April 2006]). In the following, four of these cases will be given particular attention, plus one case (*EC—Hormones*) which is not listed on the website.

† This very restrictive and classically trade-promoting ruling against national environmental standards seems to bolster the arguments of green GATT and WTO critics. This assessment notwithstanding, the panel's decision featured two more characteristics with slightly opposite implications for environmental concerns. First, the panel did not forbid the voluntary labeling of tuna as dolphin proof; and second, the Panel remarked that the U.S.A. had not "exhausted all options reasonably available … in particular through the negotiation of international cooperative agreements." This ruling implies an aspect which was further elaborated in the Shrimp Turtle case, namely "that internationally adopted standards such as those pursuant to MEAs could be grounds for justifying an exception" (Chambers 2001: 94).

Mexican vessels, but processed in EC countries. Though the Panel followed its predecessor in rejecting the import restrictions as violations of Article IX GATT, there was a slight, but essential difference from the first decision: this time, the justification of import bans because of extraterritorial PPMs was not considered to be fundamentally at odds with WTO law, due to Article XX(g) GATT. In other words: the stretching of environmental standards towards the country of origin was no longer ruled out.*

Such minor concessions notwithstanding, a profound redefinition of the dispute settlement system's stance on environmental protection matters was slow in coming. In fact, it only took place on the occasion of the 1998 Shrimp Turtle decision, well after the WTO Dispute Settlement Understanding (DSU) had entered into force.† Again, the U.S. environmental law was the object of contention—this time challenged by India, Malaysia, Pakistan and Thailand. Washington had justified import bans on shrimp from these countries, since their fishing fleets did not use turtle excluder devices, as demanded by Section 609 of U.S. Public Law. At first glimpse, both Panel and Appellate Body (AB) appeared to continue the tradition of the aforementioned Tuna Dolphin rulings: they considered the import restrictions as a breach of WTO law. Yet, when taking a closer look at the AB report, it significantly upgraded the legal status of both domestic and multilateral environmental standards. For the first time, it comprehensively acknowledged the legitimacy of specific PPM demands voiced by an importing country in order to protect animal species outside its own territory [29]. Specifically, the AB ruled that such extraterritorial PPM requirements must not be decided unilaterally, but should be rooted in specific agreements adopted by the corresponding countries. Such an agreement could, *inter alia*, be an existing MEA, if applicable. As a reference for the *U.S.— Shrimp* case, the AB explicitly mentioned the Convention on Biological Diversity (CBD) and the Interamerican Convention for the Protection and Conservation of Sea Turtles. Alternatively to such

---

* However, the Panel's further interpretation of Article XX(g) turned out far more restrictive than in future cases of WTO dispute settlement, especially when denying the significance of MEAs as acceptable points of references for the conflict parties. More precisely, the Panel concluded that MEAs could not be accepted as a specification of WTO law (*lex specialis*) in the sense of Article 31(3) of the Vienna Convention on the Law of Treaties. This article states that "[t]here shall be taken into account, together with the context: (a) any subsequent agreement between the parties regarding the interpretation of the treaty or the application of its provisions; (b) any subsequent practice in the application of the treaty which establishes the agreement of the parties regarding its interpretation." A more integrative decision by the GATT Panel was nevertheless possible at the time (and would not have needed to take until the Shrimp Turtle decision): the GATT could have embraced the potential meaning of MEAs as "any relevant rules of international law applicable in the relations between the parties" under Article 31(3c) (Neumann 2002: 168).

† Nonetheless, the Shrimp Turtle decision was not the first environment-related report of the WTO Appellate Body: in *U.S.—Reformulated Gasoline* (U.S. vs. Venezuela and Brazil) of 1996, both the Panel and the AB had interpreted the diversity of verification methods for the composition of imported gasoline (under the U.S. Clean Air Act) as discriminatory, hence violating Article III GATT.

MEAs, the report conceded that import criteria could be developed on an *ad hoc*-basis in the course of negotiations with the potentially affected exporting countries—possibly flanked by financial support for the changeover of production methods in developing countries.* Unilateral action is hence only permitted if the potentially affected countries refuse to negotiate any such conditions at all.

To sum up the meaning of *U.S.—Shrimp* for the future practice of environmentally relevant WTO dispute settlement: it could be the starting point for a more extensive inclusion and consideration of non-WTO law. Apart from the enhanced relevance of MEA rules, this observation also concerns the general principle of common, but different, responsibility under Principle 7 of the Rio Declaration. This principle had already found its way into the preamble of the WTO Agreement; now, in its report, the AB picked it up as a point of reference, when requesting financial support for the adaptation of PPMs in exporting developing countries. When taking this request at face value, future tests of import restrictions by an industrialized country could involve examinations of financial fairness among the conflict parties—which again raises the question of the WTO's competency to fulfill such a task [25].

10.4.2 Cases on Human Health Issues: Risk Assessment, Prior Informed Consent, and Labeling Requirements

The *EC—Asbestos* report of April, 2001 is a good example of the Appellate Body's slowly emerging openness toward environmental law. In this report, the AB overruled the previous Panel decision about the essential similarity of asbestos products, regardless of their health effects. Canada, one of the world's biggest exporters of asbestos, had appealed to the WTO due to French import bans, induced by national working and consumption law, on asbestos fibers and asbestos-containing products. While examining the necessity of the French measure under Article XX(b) GATT, the AB renounced a strict testing and instead stressed the appropriateness of the import restriction in order to exclude any potential health risks [25]. Still, by referring to the SPS, the AB demanded a previous scientific assessment of these risks. However, it was willing to accept a qualitative assessment (i.e., an assessment about the mere existences of health risks, not about the dimensions of these risks), based on a scholarly minority opinion. In short: the eminent social importance of the import ban's objective considerably softened of the necessity test requirements. This ruling raises hopes for the prevalence of environmental law in

---

* The AB deducted this principle of financial equity and support from the preambular clause of Article XX GATT which states that exceptional measures shall not be "applied in a manner which would constitute a means of arbitrary or unjustifiable discrimination between countries where the same conditions prevail".

similar cases, at least as long as the corresponding trade-restricting measures aim at objectives which touch upon human health issues [30].*

Such a case, which stretches from the 1980s until present, is the European Economic Community (EEC)'s ban on the import of beef from animals treated with hormone growth promoters. Pointing at the potential risks of cancer, the EEC had reduced allowable quantities of such hormones in 1981 and finally abolished them altogether in 1986, leading to a first—though unsuccessful—GATT Panel appeal by Canada and the U.S. in 1987. After imposing trade sanctions against the EEC over the following years, both countries solicited the establishment of a WTO Panel in 1996. In its 1998 *EC—Hormones* report, the Appellate Body (which partially corrected some of the Panel's observations) ruled that national measures are not at odds with SPS regulations when relying on international health agreements. Only when exceeding the standards of such agreements does the importing country have to provide a timely assessment (again only a qualitative one) of the risk and the appropriateness of the measures taken. Hence, as in *U.S.—Shrimp* and *EC—Asbestos*, the WTO dispute settlement again bolstered the referential status of external law in order to define the leeway for environmental standards.

However, having so far read quite optimistic implications out of the judicial reports on health issues, it is time to qualify this view. Indeed, this is far from stating that these three reports mark the beginning of a green era in health-related AB rulings. First of all, clear limits have been set on the consultation of external agreements. This goes especially for the precautionary principle which, according to the *EC—Hormones* report, only prevails in its narrow SPS under-standing. The burden of proof is thus left with the importing countries, that is, with the consumers instead of the producers of a potentially harmful good. Second, the difficulties of sticking to deadlines for the qualitative proof of risk should not be underestimated [25]. In the aftermath of the AB's original ruling, this very problem of sufficient proof has been keeping the case from being closed, resulting in the establishment of two further WTO panels in early 2005.†

---

* These hopes were particularly nourished by two further cases of similar concern in the late 1990s, namely *Australia—Salmon* and *Japan—Varietals*. In the former case, the AB confirmed the legitimacy of Australian import bans on Pacific salmon and confirmed the sufficiency of qualitative assessments and scientific minority opinions about a potential animal epidemic. In the latter case, the AB decided on Japanese import restrictions serving as plant protection measures, again sufficing with qualitative tests. However, by strictly following the SPS, the AB set particular deadlines for the proof of health risks and formulated very precise conditions for such temporary measures (Neumann 2002: 217ff.).

† These panels were requested by the EU, which was convinced to have complied with the requirements of the 1998 decision, by basing its 2003 Hormones Directive on a full scientific risk assessment conducted over the years 1999–2002. On the other hand, Canada and the U.S. continued their sanctions against EU exports, complaining about the lack of any multilateral confirmation of the EU's risk evaluation. While continuously imposing their trade sanctions, both countries refused to challenge the new EU Hormones Directive before the WTO. As a matter of fact, they even blocked the EU's first request to establish respective panels in January 2005 (http://www.wto.org/english/news_e/news05_e/dsb_17feb05_e.htm [2 April 2006]). The final reports of these panels, which are expected in the first half of 2006, will elucidate to which extent previous rulings on risk assessment can be interpreted in a flexible and thus environmentally sound and health-oriented manner.

10.4.3 Conclusion: the WTO is Taking Over

Summarizing the major implications of the abovementioned and some further cases, three major sets of observations can be made. First, with regard to extent and quantity, the WTO has definitely been assuming considerable competency and power about numerous non-trade issues [31]. Through decisions on various environmental topics, from species protection via air pollution (namely in the *U.S.-Reformulated Gasoline* report) to consumer and health standards, the WTO Dispute Settlement Body has constantly broadened its ecological agenda. If this development continues apace, the WTO will also "colonize" other environmental domains, thereby ultimately deciding to what extent countries can unilaterally set trade restrictive standards in these issue areas. What is more, since neither the Panel nor the Appellate Body can issue reports on its own initiative, it is not the WTO as such which exerts this extensive influence across policy fields; after all, it is the member states who can invoke the DSB in order to block the implementation of other countries' ecological policies [32]. Hence, paradoxically, by using the instrument of WTO law, these parties do the very thing they are complaining about: they have a severe impact on extraterritorial standards. This observation appears to be a strong corroboration of the race-to-the-bottom argument brought up against the WTO.

Nonetheless, a second major trend—which goes hand-in-hand with the aforementioned formal extension of the WTO's agenda—qualifies this finding. In terms of substance and quality, there has been a tendency towards more flexible and integrative decisions by the WTO dispute settlement mechanism. This concerns both key types of contested environmental standards, namely the precautionary principle, as addressed in the asbestos and hormone cases, and the PPM-related provisions, as addressed in the tuna and shrimp cases. Whereas in the first Tuna Dolphin case, the GATT Panel had clearly refused to take into account the environmental or social relevance of the production cycle of a good, later reports by the WTO Appellate Body (who sometimes overruled a previous panel decision) stressed the strong interdependence between international trade and other policy issues. These non-trade preoccupations have eventually become positively integrated into the decisions—either through demands for multilateral negotiations and agreements in order to specify WTO law (as in the *U.S.—Shrimp* report) or through the intensified recognition of the actual objectives of the contested trade-restrictive measures (especially health issues as in the *EC—Asbestos* decision). However, given increasing protests by WTO members about the Appellate Body's flexible interpretation of the agreement [17], only time will tell to which extent this tendency towards more environmentally friendly rulings will prevail.

Third and most generally, the key object of contention in all cases was the WTO consistency of trade-related measures in national environmental law with WTO law. In this regard, three kinds of jurisdictional scope should be distinguished [25]. First, measures to protect the domestic environment are consistent with WTO law as long as they affect similar goods of all exporting countries in the same way. Second, measures aimed at safeguarding transboundary resources need to stand tests of appropriateness and necessity; furthermore, they have to be backed up by previous negotiations or agreements, and they need to be applied equitably across all exporting countries. Third, measures to protect the global commons, as they are promoted by MEAs, have so far been beyond concern: no Panel or AB report has dealt with the relationship between the WTO and such agreements in the first place. This notwithstanding, one should not conclude that overlaps or conflicts of WTO law and international environmental treaties do not exist or have no impact on the effectiveness of these treaties. The next section will therefore outline some of the most notable of these overlaps.

10.5 Conflicts between WTO Law and Multilateral Environmental Agreements

10.5.1 Increasing Institutional Overlap and Conflict among International Institutions

At first glance, one might wonder about the widespread existence of legal conflicts between international trade and environmental agreements, especially among those which have been negotiated and adopted by nearly identical parties. At second glance, however, the counterintuitive observation of international regime overlap or even regime conflict should not come as a total surprise—for particularly two reasons. First of all, since the end of World War II, international relations have been marked by a growing interdependence of widely disparate policy areas, entailing a corresponding increase in the number of international organizations and regimes. Further impetus has been given by the ending of the Cold War, principally for institutions with subject matters beyond the "classical" issues of international security and economic integration. As a result, observers are counting between 200 and over 700 MEAs at the time of writing—depending on the criteria applied for their definition (e.g., issues to be considered as environmental, minimum number of states parties, consideration of soft law, etc.).* Most of these rule systems have been developed independently of each other, do cover different geographic and substantial scopes, and are partly marked by very different patterns of codification, institutionalization and cohesion, including different compliance mechanisms and sanctioning capacities.

---

* The lower number represents the concise WTO understanding of the term (cf. http://www.wto.org/english/tratop_e/envir_e/cte01_e.htm [25 April 2006]). The higher number is derived from the *International Environmental Agreements Website*, by R.B. Mitchell, available at http://www.uoregon.edu/~iea/ (25 April 2006) (cf. Mitchell 2003).

Second, this fragmentation of international law is considerably advanced in the fields of trade and environment due to the cross-cutting nature of both issues.* On the one hand, whatever can be traded can fall under WTO jurisdiction, a fact which is well exemplified by the agenda of the international trade regime which has been steadily expanding [31]. Today, no less than 60 legal instruments under the auspices of the WTO cover a multitude of different policy fields, from agriculture to labor rights and from international finance to telecommunications. On the other hand, many issues regulated by MEAs such as biological diversity, climate change or ozone layer depletion touch upon such different fields as technology, lifestyle—and trade.

Already in 1996, the WTO Committee on Trade and Environment identified "about 20" multilateral environmental agreements containing trade provisions.[†] Clearly, overlap does not equal collision: not all of these provisions are incompatible with WTO law. But wherever MEA regulations come into conflict with international trade rules, they basically do so on the same grounds as domestic environmental regulations. They either collide over import restrictions due to particular PPMs and product qualities, or they clash because of flanking conditions such as precautionary risk assessment, prior informed consent procedures or product labeling.

10.5.2 The Basel Convention, Cites and the Montreal Protocol: Direct Import Restrictions

All three regimes include TREMS (trade-related environmental measures) which collide with the MFN principle "by banning the import of various substances on

---

* Roughly over the last ten years, the fragmentation of international environmental law has been attracting the attention of scholars from various disciplines, with many of them focusing on the overlaps with trade agreements (e.g., Bernauer and Ruloff 1999; Moltke 1996; Neumann 2002; Pauwelyn 2003; Stokke 2001; Young 1996). Two encompassing and comparative research projects about the interplay of international trade and environment institutions are: first, the Institutional Interaction Project (Oberthür and Gehring 2006a); and second, the ongoing Institutional Dimensions of Global Environmental Change (IDGEC) project (cf. King 1997; Young 2002, 2002a).

    Moreover, it is not only scientists which grow aware of the increasing overlap between trade and environmental agreements, but also the negotiators of these very agreements. Chambers (2001:85ff.) observes a tendency towards implicit or explicit recognition of such overlaps in the text of respective treaties, e.g., in MEAs such as the Convention on Biological Diversity (CBD, Article 22) and the United Nations Framework Convention on Climate Change (FCCC, Articles 3[5] and 4[2e]), but also in trade law, e.g., in NAFTA Article 104 (granting three MEAs prevalence in case of conflict), the preamble of the WTO Agreement or GATT Article XX on general exemptions.

† In two more recent documents, the CTE has narrowed its focus down to 14 agreements, namely: International Plant Protection Convention, ICCAT, CITES, CCAMLR, Montreal Protocol, Basel Convention, CBD, Cartagena Protocol on Biosafety, UNFCCC, Kyoto Protocol, International Tropical Timber Agreement, UN Fish Stocks Agreement, Rotterdam Convention, and Stockholm Convention on Persistent Organic Pollutants (Docs. WT/CTE/W/160/Rev.1, 14 June 2001, and WT/CTE/W/160/Rev.2, 25 April 2003).

the basis of the status of the country of origin (e.g., countries that are not Parties to the MEA, Parties to the MEA that fall into particular categories, and Parties not in compliance with the MEA)" [33].

In its Articles III, IV and V, the Convention on International Trade in Endangered Species (CITES) requires the "prior grant and presentation of an export permit" for the export of any specimen of a species included in the appendices of the convention, no matter whether the importing country is party or non-party.* Likewise, in its Article 7, the 1989 Basel Convention on the Control of Transboundary Movements of Hazardous Wastes and Their Disposal demands notification of importing countries, no matter if such wastes are traded from a party to a non-party or *vice versa*.† In addition, the 1995 Ban Amendment to the Basel Convention, which is one single ratification short of entering into force, prohibits exports from OECD to non-OECD countries for final deposit.‡

Of the three mentioned regimes, the Montreal Protocol to the 1985 Vienna Convention for the Protection of the Ozone Layer presents the most interesting case, since its negotiators explicitly anticipated a potential conflict with the GATT. Article 4 of the protocol deals with the "Control of trade with non-parties"; it obliges each party to ban the import and export of the controlled substances in the different annexes of the Protocol from or to "any State not party to this Protocol". These substances include ozone-depleting substances (ODS) and products containing ODS.¶ However, import bans were not extended to goods produced with the use of ODS into the Protocol, because such a rule seemed hardly applicable and might have deterred potential signatories. According to statements by some of the protocol's negotiators, this decision was not primarily motivated by the desire to avoid a legal collision with the GATT [33,23]. Nevertheless,

---

* More precisely, the three appendices differentiate between different levels of protection and subsequent measures, namely: permits for both import and export (Appendix I), only export permits (Appendix II), and permits by countries which have previously acknowledged the need to protect the corresponding species (Appendix III). CITES, which entered into force in July 1975, has been strongly supported by the U.S.A. which advocated the cooperation with the initiator, the World Conservation Union (then: International Union for Conservation of Nature [IUCN]). Despite its regulations, each year between $20 billion and $50 billion specimen are traded, about a quarter of them illegally.

† Originally, some African countries were against the convention, asking for more intensive restrictions, similar to those adopted two years later in the 1991 Bamako Convention, which nearly banned exports of hazardous wastes to Africa altogether. On the other hand, the U.S. (no member until present) had reservations concerning the ratio of municipal waste to hazardous waste. This criticism notwithstanding, the Basel Convention entered into force on 5 May 1992 (http://www.basel.int/ratif/frsetmain.php [8 May 2006]).

‡ By May 2006, the Ban Amendment had been ratified by 61 countries. The 1999 Liability Protocol to the Convention has been facing more lack of support (only 7 parties as of May 2006; ratification by 20 parties needed).

¶ Furthermore, it grants developing countries a special status (Article 5: "Special situation of developing countries"), entitling them "to delay for 10 years" the compliance with the control measures, i.e., standards and phase-out dates under Article 2.

compatibility with international trade law was a carefully-regarded issue when drafting the protocol: parties agreed on the establishment of an *Ad Hoc* Working Group of Legal and Technical Experts which should detect and prevent potential collisions with GATT rules. Surprisingly though, the working group did not see any need for immediate action such as modifications of the draft text [34].* Chambers [26] explains this finding with the fact that, at the time, the issue of compatibility in international environmental politics "was not the focus of as much concern as it is today". Indeed, the same question was interpreted quite differently a few years later, i.e., after the establishment of the WTO: the WTO Secretariat voiced clear opposition to the Montreal Protocol's trade restrictions, fearing they could serve as a role model for future MEAs. In this spirit, the CTE "opted not to welcome their replication in an emissions-trading scheme" [35].

A common property of the three named MEAs is the range of their jurisdiction, since they are all operating on a global level and display a nearly universal membership. This feature might well prevent these MEAs from being challenged before the WTO dispute settlement system, since party vs. non-party constellations should be rare. Comparably, regional environmental regimes with similar trade restrictions might be more prone to such a challenge. Such regional MEAs which collide with WTO law are the International Commission for the Conservation of Atlantic Tunas (ICCAT) and the Convention on the Conservation of Antarctic Marine Living Resources (CCAMLR). Both include import bans (based on PPMs) which—just like in the cases of CITES, the Basel Convention, and the Montreal Protocol—contradict the GATT's MFN principle [36].

10.5.3 The Climate Change Regime: Mix of Direct and Indirect Trade Restrictions

The climate change regime, i.e., the 1992 Framework Convention on Climate Change and its 1997 Kyoto Protocol, can collide with WTO law in a number of aspects. First of all and similar to the aforementioned agreements, the Kyoto Protocol confines the trade in particular products; but unlike other MEAs which affect *existing* goods, the Kyoto Protocol, in its Article 17, *introduces* the very products it regulates. These emissions or "Parts of Assigned Amounts" (PAAs) shall only be traded within certain limits ("caps") and between designated industrialized countries listed in Annex B of the protocol.

However, what can be traded is subject to WTO agreements, regardless of the difficult characterization of PAAs as either goods or services, hence either

---

* The Working Group considered the exceptions under Article XX GATT and the corresponding rules of the 1969 Vienna Convention on the Law of Treaties (VCLT) as sufficient in order to avoid conflicts.

falling under the GATT or the GATS.* A legal challenge of the global climate regime might only be a question of time: "In the absence of express rules limiting PAA-related issues to the UNFCCC, difficulties may arise because there is no legal barrier preventing a country from bringing the case before the WTO dispute settlement" [26,37].

With the Kyoto Protocol entering into force in February 2005, the compatibility issue of PAA-trading has not only become more virulent, but will also turn out more complex, since the parties have to decide on concrete procedures under Article 18 which asks "to approve appropriate and effective procedures and mechanisms to determine and to address cases of non-compliance". As a matter of fact, the first Meeting of Parties in December 2005 has already taken a major step in this direction, by adopting the Marrakesh Accords, including "the most elaborate compliance regime of any existing multilateral environmental agreement" [38]. If upcoming meetings decide to include trade-related sanctions into this compliance regime, the Kyoto Protocol might yet in another way collide with GATT or GATS.

Another type of provision, which could at least indirectly lead to a conflict with WTO law, involves the so-called PAMs under Article 2 of the Kyoto Protocol. Parties ought to apply these "policies and measures" in order to meet their quantified emission limitation and reduction commitments. Among these PAMs are "fiscal incentives, tax and duty exemptions and subsidies in all greenhouse gas emitting sectors" (Article 2[v])—in other words: steps "which are likely to affect the competitiveness of national industries" [26,39]. In particular, border cost adjustments have recently entered debates about appropriate measures [40]. These tools aim at balancing competitive disadvantages of domestic goods which face higher licensing costs under the Kyoto Protocol. However, in light of more trade-consistent alternatives, cost adjustments might

---

* Werksman (Will International Investment Rules Obstruct Climate Protection Policies? 2001: 155f.) denies this interpretation of emissions allowances as either goods or services. This notwithstanding, he agrees that Kyoto Protocol regulations can promote behavior which is at odds with GATT or GATS rules: "design choices regarding the *incidence of regulation* and *allocation of allowances* will probably affect the competitive relationship between products and services that are governed by WTO disciplines." In particular, Werksman predicts legal conflicts not so much for the primary market, i.e., trade in allowances by end-users, but rather for the secondary market, i.e., trade in derivative financial instruments based upon allowances: "If the ETS [Emissions Trading Scheme] rules allow financial-service providers to buy, own, and hold allowances, the EC and its Member States may be under a GATS obligation to extend MFN and national treatment to foreign services and service suppliers" (ibid.: 171). Depending on the design of the ETS, especially on the point of a carbon-based fuel cycle, at which allowances are required, the trading scheme could run counter to WTO provisions. This holds especially true for upstream allocations requested from energy producers, since, whenever exporting their energy to another ETS country, such allocations would be equal to import licenses to be held by these producers.

not stand tests of necessity and appropriateness under Article XX GATT, once being challenged and brought before the DSB.*

10.5.4 The Convention on Biological Diversity: Benefit-Sharing, Prior Informed Consent and Labeling Requirements

The importance of the above examples notwithstanding, it is another potential incompatibility between an MEA and WTO law which has been attracting the bulk of scholarly attention, namely the overlap among the Convention on Biological Diversity (CBD) and the TRIPS Agreement. Unlike the aforementioned cases, the CBD–TRIPS conflict involves less an incompatibility of particular rules than a general programmatic conflict. The CBD reaffirms "that states have sovereign rights over their own biological resources" (4th preambular) and advocates the equitable sharing of benefits from utilization of genetic resources (Article 1). On the other hand, Article 27 TRIPS seeks to strengthen and harmonize intellectual property rights systems and calls for patent legalization in all technical fields including biotechnology.[†]

Hence, with its general approach to intellectual property rights, TRIPS contradicts the CBD objective of an equitable distribution of benefits. Bound to this objective, the CBD has established a different type of property rights regime "where national sovereignty is introduced to counterbalance intellectual property rights" [41].[‡] Since patenting is a costly business, multinational corporations can take advantage of the TRIPS approach by securing monopolies over numerous varieties of genetic material, including those which have been developed over generations by indigenous and local communities.

---

* In light of the abovementioned *U.S.—Shrimp* report, one might argue that the negotiations on the global climate regime fulfill the WTO's demand for consultations among the affected parties prior to trade-restricting measures. Nevertheless, border cost adjustments are just one among several measures which were taken into consideration by the negotiators. In fact, during Conferences of the Parties to the UNFCCC, member states could not agree about whether trade restrictions were an appropriate tool at all (Werksman 2001:178ff.).

  In addition to the scenarios mentioned in the text, there are further possible collisions between the climate change regime and international trade law. Some observers argue that the climate regime, particular the Clean Development Mechanism which aims at stimulating investment flows, can also be considered as an investment regime. Since it conditions such investments, the CDM potentially gets into conflict with international investment rules, e.g., the OECD's Multilateral Agreement on Investment (cf. Werksman and Santoro 2001; Werksman, Baumert, and Dubash, 2003).

† Article 27(1) states that "patents shall be available for any inventions, whether products or processes, in all fields of technology, provided that they are new, involve an inventive step and are capable of industrial application".

‡ More precisely, the CBD advocates the transfer of environmentally safe technology, including biotechnology and technologies covered by intellectual property rights on "fair and most favorable terms" (Article 16 [2]). It also calls for the fair and equitable sharing of benefits arising from the utilization of knowledge (Article 8 and 12th preambular) from research and development (Article 15) and from biotechnologies (Article 19). Most remarkably, the CBD even explicitly refers to a potential regime conflict in its Article 16(5), stating that intellectual property rights systems should "not run counter to its [the convention's] objectives".

In fact, such behavior termed as *biopiracy* or *bioprospecting* has already taken place to a considerable extent: today, developing countries do not hold more than three per cent of all patents worldwide [42].

Apart from the issue of access and benefit sharing, there is a second potential conflict between CBD and TRIPS which takes place on the level of treaty implementation, namely with regard to the sustainable use of the plant varieties in question. In the long run, the TRIPS-induced property structure might threaten the chief objective of biological diversity itself: patent owners, i.e., mostly multinational corporations of industrialized countries will promote the cultivation of "their" varieties; subsequently, incentives for farmers in developing countries to conserve other species will clearly decrease [42].

As is the case with other MEA–WTO incompatibilities, the incoherence of CBD and TRIPS has so far not led to any legal disputes. Nonetheless, the overlap of both treaties and their subject matters became the subject of several controversies on the level of bureaucracies and negotiating parties. These controversies date back to the founding phases of both regimes which partially, in the early 1990s, took place at parallel timelines. Clearly, both processes of regime genesis exerted mutual impacts on each other, while developing and industrialized countries could score quite differently in the two arenas. Though the CBD had originally been advocated by several OECD countries (including the United States), eventually, its content became strongly influenced by developing countries. On the other hand, the genesis of the TRIPS Agreement in the course of the Uruguay Round was clearly dominated by Western European countries and the United States—with the latter explicitly complaining about the strategy of some developing countries to undermine TRIPS via the biodiversity convention [42,43].

Even after the original negotiations had ended and both documents had entered into force, these disputes have continued until this day within different settings and arenas, generally revolving around the question whether further institutional steps are desirable—either to enhance the robustness of one treaty or to instigate the mutual harmonization of both agreements. Roughly, four theatres of this ongoing conflict can be distinguished: First of all, controversies have taken place on a regime-internal level, that is, within the institutional architecture of both regimes (e.g., in the CBD's Ad Hoc Open-ended Working Group on Access and Benefit-sharing). On the WTO level, the United States— not being a party to the CBD—repeatedly voted against the CBD secretariat's request for observer status during TRIPS conventions [42]. Moreover, parties keep on debating a treaty change in order to include into the TRIPS Agreement a requirement for disclosure of the source of patent-relevant biological resources.*

---

* For instance, Brazil, India, and further countries with highly diverse biological resources keep pushing for an amendment of the TRIPS Agreement, which would clearly safeguard key CBD objectives. Accordingly the amendment shall allow members to ask patent applicants for disclosure of (a) the country of origin of biological resources or traditional knowledge used in inventions, (b) evidence of prior informed consent by the country of origin, and (c) evidence of fair and equitable appropriate benefit-sharing agreements with the country of origin (cf. Meier-Ewert 2005).

Second, disputes have taken the form of an "arms race" [42,44] of follow-up or side agreements. On the one hand, regional agreements on intellectual property rights (which partially run counter to TRIPS rules) have been adopted by the Andean Community (CAN) and by the Organization of African Unity (OAU) [45].* On the other hand, bilateral "TRIPS plus" agreements between the U.S. or EU and a developing country even exceed TRIPS demands on patent standards.

Third, and apart from such disputes within the extended architecture of both regimes, further negotiating forums have been established—for example, within the UN's Food and Agriculture Organization (FAO) and within the World Intellectual Property Organization (WIPO)—in order to deal with the issues of access to genetic resources, of prior informed consent and of benefit sharing.[†] Fourth and finally, the CBD's Cartagena Protocol on Biosafety (BSP) contains rules which collide with several WTO treaties—though in a rather indirect manner.[‡] For instance, the BSP protects the rights of importing states to be informed about the pending introduction of living modified organisms. On the other side, the GATT, SPS, and TBT safeguard the interests of exporters

---

* The CAN IPR-regime was established in the name of TRIPS, however, it asks for an amendment of the Agreement's Article 27(3b) in order to account for potential conditions of patentability such as prior informed consent. The OAU Model Law is even more straightforward in its opposition to TRIPS provisions and explicitly requires the permit and the prior informed consent of importing communities. Another type of CBD-endorsing follow-up treaties are bilateral agreements on bioprospecting; the CBD's Ad Hoc Working Group on Access and Benefit Sharing prepared the "Bonn Guidelines" in 2002 in order to include prior informed consent and other principles into such agreements (Rosendal 2003: 13ff.).

† These new forums and treaties include FAO's International Treaty on Plant Genetic Resources for Food and Agriculture and WIPO'S Intergovernmental Committee on Intellectual Property Rights and Genetic Resources, Traditional Knowledge and Folklore. This is not to state that FAO has only recently played a role in these issues. Quite on the contrary, had it not been for the pharmaceutical sector and its concern about emerging biotechnologies, the "gene wars" might have been left to the non-legally binding FAO documents (Rosendal 2003: 7). As early as 1983, the FAO International Undertaking on Plant Genetic Resources had declared all categories of such resources a common heritage of mankind. Moreover, the 2001 International Treaty on Plant Genetic Resources for food and agriculture explicitly prohibits patenting of material from gene banks in the public domain. However, this recent FAO agreement "will hardly block patenting altogether. Even slight modifications of the germplasm may qualify for patent protection and the isolation and description of any particular gene may still count as an invention" (ibid.:13),

‡ "Indirect" refers to the fact that there is no immediate contradiction between rules; instead, a regulation might be relatively vague about concrete measures to be taken, hence possibly inducing a behavior which could run counter o the provisions of other rules of international law. Whereas, for example, the Basel Convention (in the treaty text) or the ICCAT (in a follow-up resolution) explicitly name trade restrictions as sanctions for non-compliers (colliding with the GATT's MFN or NT principles), the BSP does not explicitly permit such measures. In fact, import bans could only be deducted from the protocol's rather indistinct policy recommendations.

through non-discriminatory regulations (e.g., with regard to labeling obligations) [36,16].*

10.5.5   Conclusion: No Dispute, No Problem?

All in all, what can be said about the impact of inter-regime conflicts? At first glance, there is good news for the involved MEAs: unlike the cases of incoherence among domestic environmental law and WTO law (presented in Section 10.3), none of these legal conflicts has so far become manifest in a legal controversy among (non-)member states of the respective treaties.† As possible explanations for this absence of WTO disputes, Werksman [46] names: (1) the "self-restraint" of parties, which prompts them to settle any differences within the context of the respective MEA; (2) the nearly universal membership of most of these MEAs (which rules out the problem of disputes of parties vs. non-parties); and (3) the potentially "narrow economic impacts" of most of the environmental agreements in question.

This is not the place to prove or rebut any of these reasons; nonetheless, in light of these observations, it is even more crucial to deny the merely theoretical

---

* A similar kind of incompatibility exists between the GATT and the Rotterdam Convention. The latter demands prior informed consent by the importing state as well as labeling by the exporting state for the introduction of certain hazardous chemicals and pesticides of the marine environment of the North–East Atlantic. But like the BSP, the Rotterdam Convention does not contain any obligatory trade bans, but instead leaves concrete measures to the states parties. Furthermore, the convention's preamble tackles this indirect incompatibility, by explicitly requesting mutual support between the convention and WTO agreements (Neumann 2002: 262).

† This observation might not meet general consent, depending on the definition of the terms "inter-regime" and "dispute" (i.e., based on the question to which extent the regimes need to be involved in the dispute). In fact, the 2000/01 *Chile—Swordfish* case between Chile and the European Community could be interpreted as a conflict between the GATT and the UN Convention on the Law of the Sea (UNCLOS). Chile had prohibited foreign and domestic vessels to unload swordfish harvested in the High Seas, referring to UNCLOS Articles 64, 118 and 119 which demand the cooperation of countries in order to guarantee the optimal use of fishery resources. Whereas Chile interpreted these UNCLOS rules as *lex specialis*, i.e., law specifying GATT provisions, the EC clearly objected any UNCLOS jurisdiction for the case and instead opted for WTO dispute settlement. These different interpretations notwithstanding, the controversy ended before any Panel report was filed, since both parties agreed on negotiating a particular multilateral agreement on swordfish (Neumann 2002: 198ff.). Even when—in the absence of an actual Panel or AB report—interpreting this dispute as a manifest inter-regime conflict, the question remains whether UNCLOS should be considered an *environmental* agreement, since it is rather a multi-issue agreement.

This notwithstanding, the *Chile—Swordfish* case points at another—so far only theoretical— nonetheless type of conflicts between MEAs and WTO law which might become highly relevant in the future, namely *jurisdictional conflicts*. These are meta-conflicts among regimes, not rooted in direct collisions of their rules, but instead circling around the question which regime should be entrusted with the settlement of conflicts between domestic environmental law and international trade law. As Neumann (ibid.: 513ff.) rightfully observes, the *U.S.—Shrimp* case, if taking place today, could as well fall under the jurisdiction of the International Tribunal on the Law of the Sea.

character of such inter-regime conflicts on two grounds. First, the lack of legal disputes simply is no indicator for the future absence of them; the majority of the respective MEAs have only been adopted within the last 15 years, and some of them (including agreements with considerable economic implications) have either not yet or only recently entered into force. For instance, the implementation of the Kyoto Protocol might well instigate cases for the WTO dispute settlement mechanism.* And if one day such a legal dispute about an MEA takes place, the consequences would be far more comprehensive than any of the challenges hitherto brought up against domestic environmental regulations: taken at face value, a decision against the MEA could lead to a "domino effect" which would extend well beyond the jurisdiction of the dispute parties. In the long run, such a decision could also undermine environmental standards in countries which were not involved in the actual legal dispute, supposing these standards have resulted from the implementation of the contested MEA rules.

Second, and even more importantly, the absence of WTO disputes should not at all be mistaken for an absence of impact of international trade law on the shape or effectiveness of these MEAs. In fact, the collisions of rules might provoke severe compliance problems for some environmental agreements in the long run. True, it is more than difficult (and a definite research lacuna) to roughly determine the extent by which the legal backup provided by WTO law has triggered non-compliance with MEA regulations.† One might wonder, for example, about the TRIPS Agreement's approximate share in the lack of motivation of the vast majority of CBD parties when it comes to enforcing prior informed consent procedures upon users of genetic resources [44]. But as speculative as such assumptions might sound at present, no convincing justification exists for the opposite claim (i.e., that there is no mutual influence at all on agreements' compliance rates.

Moreover, although there are no judicial controversies, there definitely are debates taking place within the architecture of the respective regimes, as was shown for the CBD–TRIPS case: thus, the shadow of WTO law and its strong dispute settlement system might provoke *anticipative conflicts*, for example, when negotiators of an MEA refrain from building in more ambitious trade-relevant measures, or when countries refuse to ratify an agreement or one of its protocols [24].‡ In short, unlike in the case of collisions of domestic

---

* As Werksman (2001: 156f.) himself observes, "no MEA has the potential to affect so many sectors of the economy, so many economic interests, and such high volumes of trade in products and services, as does the climate change regime."

† Currently, counter-factual studies—as developed by Mitchell (2004) or in the "Oslo-Potsdam solution" Hovi, Sprinz, and Underdal 2003, 2003a) present a promising approach to this research question. Sprinz (2003) suggests the application of such an extended counter-factual approach in order to determine the fictitious effectiveness of a regime in the absence of the regime(s) it collides with.

‡ Naturally, such anticipative conflicts can also take place with regard to domestic law. For instance, Austria took back its 1992 import restrictions on tropical timber after timber exporting countries such as Brazil, Malaysia, and Singapore had threatened to apply their own import restrictions to Austrian goods (Bernauer 1999a: 132f.).

environmental law and WTO law, inter-regime conflicts often take place in the corridors of international negotiations. This renders the environmental impacts of such conflicts rather subtle, but certainly anything but marginal. One hopes that further research by scholars of international relations, economics and law can open this peculiar black box of environmental impacts of world trade law. Regardless of such analyses and their prospective results, both policy-makers and academics have meanwhile come up with suggestions and concrete strategies to address the incoherence of WTO provisions and both domestic and multilateral environmental law. The next section will outline some of the most pivotal of these proposals.

10.6 Strategies and Proposals to Improve WTO Compatibility with Environmental Law

10.6.1 A Solution under the Legal Status Quo?

The creators of the WTO did not build any comprehensive and sustainable clause into the agreements in order to address specific multilateral or domestic environmental standards. Instead of such an *ex ante* approach, they relied on a strategy of case-by-case interpretation. With regard to potential collisions with domestic environmental law, such an interpretation should concretize generally phrased exceptions under Article XX GATT. And as for potential collisions with MEAs, negotiators hoped for sufficient backup by existing superordinate international law—in particular by the 1969 Vienna Convention on the Law of Treaties (VCLT). Strikingly, it is this very reliance upon the VCLT which can also be held responsible for the inclusion of trade-related measures into MEAs such as CITES or the Montreal Protocol.

Indeed, at first glance, the Vienna Convention hosts satisfying principles to determine the hierarchy among agreements in a given legal dispute. For instance, as laid out in Articles 30–32 VCLT, agreements prevail when containing more specific rules (*lex specialis*) or when being adopted later (*lex posterior*) than a rival treaty. However, in order for these principles to apply, the colliding treaties should feature identical parties, which is a rather hypothetical and obsolete request given today's fragmentation of international law.*

In sum, sole confidence in the VCLT's applicability is at best outdated and at worst, could backfiring at MEA objectives—in particular when leaving treaty coordination between MEA parties and non-parties to WTO dispute settlement organs. Hence, in order to reduce the potentially disruptive impact of the world

---

* This notwithstanding, some AB reports have referred to MEA rules, arguing that it is sufficient that the dispute parties are members of the respective MEA. Thus, in the *U.S.— Shrimp* case, the AB referred to the CBD and to the Convention on Migratory Species. This can be justified by the fact that WTO agreements, unlike MEAs, are bipolar contracts, implying that *inter se* modifications are possible, i.e., *ad hoc* modifications of WTO law which only apply to the conflict parties in a particular dispute (see Section 10.3.3; cf. Neumann 2002: 368ff.; Pauwelyn 2003: 52ff.).

trade regime on both domestic and multilateral environmental regulations, jurisdictional clarity via an explicit *ex ante* approach is desirable—for at least two obvious reasons: first, as long as no legal disputes take place, such clarity can help diminish the anticipative effect of the WTO "shadow" on environmental legislation both national and international, as outlined in the preceding Section 10.5.5; and second, if it comes to actual disputes, a respective approach could set limits to the current process of a self-expanding mandate of the WTO Dispute Settlement Body.

10.6.2 Initiatives from the Inside

With the ubiquitous applicability of the VCLT cast in doubt, the WTO started several initiatives in order to ensure a stronger coherence among international trade rules and environmental law. In accordance with its chief mandate, the CTE took on this matter from the very start: in its 1996 Report to the Singapore Ministerial Meeting, the committee recommended that disputing parties which are members in both the WTO and an MEA should first try to resolve their dispute through the MEA's mechanisms. As much as this appears a major concession to MEAs, the report remains "decidedly vague on disputes pursuant to an MEA arising between Parties and non-Parties" [26].

This indistinctness is the result of a second-rate compromise between strongly diverging proposals which some parties had brought up in the preparatory process of the Singapore meeting. The more daring of these proposals, voiced by the European Community and Switzerland, suggested the inclusion of provisions for a so called "environmental window" into WTO agreements, or even the adoption of a whole new "MEA agreement". Both of these tools intended to enduringly classify selected MEA rules as necessary measures, thus granting them a permanent waiver with regard to non-discriminatory WTO principles [47].* However, such proposals met considerable resistance by other parties, in particular by Association of Southeast Asian Nations (ASEAN) countries and India, who renounced any sort of treaty amendment and refused to grant any further environmental indulgence [25]. The poor outcome of this early intra-WTO debate exhibits the abovementioned key weakness of the CTE: resting upon the consensual decisions of governmental representatives, the committee cannot act as source of a self-contained WTO environmental policy. Subsequently and— as shall be shown—well until the time of writing, the structure and mandate of the committee have been perpetuating the failure of WTO parties during the Uruguay Round to come up with an appropriate *ex ante* treatment of environmental law.

A second initiative on the matter was sparked off in 1999, when then WTO Director-General Renato Ruggiero called for a regular framework in order to deal with MEAs in a coherent and effective manner [17]. That same year, the secretariats

---

* In June 2000, Switzerland made another proposal for a solution of the matter. This time, the Swiss representative suggested an authoritative interpretation of the WTO Agreement by the General Council about the relevance of MEAs for WTO law. The proposal was endorsed by the EC, Japan, Canada and members of the WTO Secretariat, however, it was turned down by the U. S., Australia, India, and Brazil (Neumann 2002: 341).

of the WTO and the UN Environment Programme (UNEP) signed a cooperation agreement which launched their regular exchange of information on legal issues. Such exchange should *inter alia* take place at the occasion of staff meetings which, where feasible, ought to include representatives from MEA secretariats.* Finally, this initiative resulted in an extensive consideration of environmental matters during the Qatar Ministerial Meeting in November, 2001 and the subsequent inclusion of a "trade and environment" section into the Doha Declaration. Article 31 of the declaration sets the goal of "enhancing the mutual supportiveness" of both policy fields. To this end, it requests further negotiations on "the relationship between existing WTO rules and specific trade obligations set out in multilateral environmental agreements (MEAs)" as well as "procedures for regular information exchange between MEA Secretariats and the relevant WTO committees".[†] Moreover, Article 32 extended the CTE's mandate towards "the effect of environmental measures on market access", the environmentally relevant provisions of the TRIPS Agreement and "labeling requirements for environmental purposes".

Pursuant to this explicit request for compatibility, a CTE Special Session (CTESS) was to discuss a number of models for harmonizing WTO law and the trade-related measures of MEAs. The number of formal proposals from all sides was considerable. MEAs willingly joined the process, not least out of concern about the growing number of WTO disputes on domestic environmental law: "the lack of clarity between WTO and MEA rules has lead to confusion in the negotiation of the MEA" [17].[‡] Another reason for the MEAs' increasing interest in an *ex ante* approach might have been the emerging influence of NGOs and academics who had briefed the secretariats on the potential implications of the

---

* UNEP hosted the first of these joint meetings of WTO and MEA secretariats in June 1999. Since then, the UNEP has been organizing further meetings, e.g., two key events in 2000: a high level panel discussion on WTO-MEA relations in New York and a Geneva meeting on Enhancing Synergies and Mutual Supportiveness, featuring both UNEP's Executive Director and the WTO Director General (cf. UNEP Report to the 45th Meeting of the CITES Standing Committee SC 45 Doc. 7.3, http://www.cites.org/eng/com/SC/45/E45-07-3.pdf [22 April 2006]).

† Besides, in Article 6, the declaration welcomes "the WTO's continued cooperation with UNEP and other inter-governmental environmental organizations". It also encouraged "efforts to promote cooperation between the WTO and relevant international environmental and developmental organizations, especially in the lead-up to the World Summit on Sustainable Development to be held in Johannesburg, South Africa, in September 2002." Interestingly though, a couple of months later, heavy debates evolved about the actual inclusion of a similar request for coherence into the final document of the World Summit. The Draft Plan of Implementation, which had been issued at the fourth PrepCom in Bali on 12 June 2002, still contained the heavily bracketed Paragraph 122c. This paragraph stated that the international community should "promote initiatives to ensure the coherence and mutual supportiveness between the rules of the multilateral trading systems and the rules of multilateral environmental agreements." It called for "further collaboration between on the one hand the WTO and on the other ILO, UNCTAD, UNDP, UNEP and other relevant agencies". This harmonization should be "consistent with the goals of sustainable development". However, none of these several formulas ever was included into the final plan.

‡ For instance, Switzerland argued that negotiations surrounding the Biosafety Protocol had turned out difficult because of the protocol's relationship to the WTO (ibid.).

current legal constellation [17,48]. Thus, in May, 2003, secretariats from UNEP and six trade-related MEAs participated in the CTESS.* However, the secretariats were not allowed to make interventions and had to leave the session before issues under Article 32 of the Doha Declaration were discussed. In the end, this meeting, as well as the follow-up meetings to this date, share one specific result—no matter if taking the form of further CTE sessions or of bilateral meetings among bureaucrats from the WTO and a particular MEA (e.g., CITES):[†] they have stimulated little agreement among WTO members on the further coordinative process [49].

If there is a success at all, it is an informal one: "These sessions have clearly facilitated a mutual understanding of the linkages between the multi-lateral environment and trade agendas, and built awareness of the use of trade-related measures in MEAs" [17]. Even this assessment only holds true for those MEAs which so far have been granted observer status in the CTE such as the CBD, CITES, and the UNFCCC, whereas requests by the Ozone Secretariat or the International Tropical Timber Organization (ITTO) are still pending.

On the other hand, the lack of substantive results of these meetings reveals a dangerous pitfall: besides its stagnation, the Doha-induced process might turn out as a one-way street on which MEAs eventually leave the initiative for harmonization to the WTO, but have little to gain, most definitely no comprehensive "safety net" [32]. From the side of the CTE, the predominant objective of the process is to diminish the negative impact of environmental measures on WTO law, not *vice versa*—an intention which should hardly surprise given the CTE's clear-cut mandate.[‡]

10.6.3 Suggestions from the Outside

In the absence of an accord within the CTE, "the question of whether and how environmental aspects should be integrated into the world trade regime has mainly been taken up outside the context of the world trade regime—above all, in academic and environmental institutes" [16]. Generally, three groups of proposals can be distinguished: a first one focusing on a reform of WTO law, a second one suggesting changes in the organizational structure,

---

* These MEAs included the Basel Convention, the CBD, CITES, the International Tropical Timber Organization (ITTO), the Montreal Protocol and the UNFCCC.
[†] Besides these inter-regime meetings, the WTO has been organizing internal consultations on the trade-environment nexus among experts of its various divisions, e.g., at the occasion of the WTO Symposium on Trade and Sustainable Development in Geneva in October 2005.
[‡] "Members at this stage are still attempting to define what constitutes an STO [specific trade obligation], which MEAs should be considered, and ultimately how to go about clarifying the WTO-MEA relationship.... [I]t was not clear that MEAs had anything to gain from devoting resources to the WTO-MEA endeavour" (ICSTD 2003). At the meeting, special emphasis was put on decisions taken at MEA Conferences of the Parties (COPs) which might bear trade-related implications, e.g., the Marrakesh Accords, resulting from UNFCCC COP7 in November 2001.

and a third one which, instead of "greening" the WTO, shifts the focus on the strengthening of MEAs.

As for the proponents of the first group, some of their suggestions follow those voiced by reform-oriented parties in the CTE who promote an "environmental window" or a "savings clause" for certain MEAs. More precisely, some observers call for an expansion of Article XX GATT, either by amending clauses XX(b) or XX(g) or by entering a new clause XX(k) [50,51]. Such proposals are not as unrealistic as they might sound at first glance; in fact, they can point at a prominent role model: Article 104 NAFTA contains a priority clause which confirms that in cases of inconsistency between NAFTA on the one hand, and CITES, the Montreal Protocol and the Basel Convention on the other hand, the obligations of the latter shall prevail.*

Hence, akin to the initiatives taken up within the WTO, a large number of scholarly suggestions also concentrate on legal exceptions to the benefit of multilateral environmental treaties. This might be the time to ask why certain principles inherent to *domestic* environmental rules are not considered in these proposals. The answer is that in fact these principles are not at all excluded from the debate. Quite on the contrary: what has been said in Section 10.5.5 about a potentially negative "domino effect" of legal challenges against MEA rules, in turn implies positive effects for domestic standards under reversed premises. An environmental window for MEAs would also open up for related national regulations, enhancing the robustness of the latter against legal challenges before the WTO. For instance, a savings clause for trade-related measures under the Montreal Protocol should equally provide a backup for national import bans on ODS from certain countries.

This interconnectedness among multilateral and national environmental law notwithstanding, there are also alternative reform proposals which propagate safeguards for specific green principles and standards. In particular, suggestions are dedicated to the precautionary principle. Environmental NGOs as well as the European Union advocated a change of the corresponding provisions in the SPS agreement, thereby reverting the burden of proof for health risks from importers back to exporters [16]. Drawing lessons from the Tuna Dolphin cases, other observers demand stronger consideration of processing and production methods (PPMs) when determining the alikeness of products. To this end, Helm [51] suggests the inclusion of PPMs into Article III GATT on national treatment.

No matter how adequate some of these ideas might appear, they will remain fruitless academic exercises as long as they only focus on the legal side of the problem. Clearly, in order to bear practical relevance, suggestions have to

---

* NAFTA is also more progressive than WTO law when it comes to general exceptions under Articles 904, 907, and 915 which expressively take into account factors like climate impact and scientific risk assessment. Apart from such explicit treaty modifications, treaty *changes* can also be made implicitly, e.g., through shifts in customary law (Neumann 2002: 343ff.).

equally address the political or institutional reasons for the WTO's inflexibility, namely the weak agenda-setting position of the CTE and the ongoing stalemate among its members. Therefore, a second group of proposals advises structural changes within the WTO. Environmental groups opt for the dissolution of the CTE and, instead prefer a mainstreaming of environmental issues across the other WTO committees and sub-committees. Gary Sampson [17], former director of the organization's Trade and Environment Division, strongly disagrees with this idea, warning that this move would even further dilute ecological interests: "resources by governments to questions relating to the environment are already spread thinly in WTO meetings."

Still, instead of abolishing the CTE altogether, it might make sense to occasionally circumvent the impasse of its meetings via complementary activities by other WTO organs. Besides further intensifying its ties with UNEP, the WTO secretariat could initiate bilateral agreements with specific MEAs, similar to those it already negotiated with WIPO or the IMF. For instance, Asselt, Gupta, and Biermann [52] recommend a Memorandum of Understanding between the WTO and the UNFCCC in order to allow for package deals on contentious issues.

Another approach to tackle the CTE's stalemate might be to enhance the influx of ecological data into the WTO's policy-making processes, and, by the same token, to alter the positions of some of the hitherto eco-skeptical developing countries. With the help of improved impact assessment methods, science could provide for more robust and more comprehensive evidence about the world trade regime's effects on the environment [53]. Depending on the outcome of such impact assessments, developing countries might be persuaded to deviate from a one-sided perception of green standards as merely protectionist measures. Santarius et al. [16] name two ways to integrate environmental impact assessment into the WTO's institutional structures: either by incorporating them into the WTO's Trade Policy Review Mechanism (*ex post* assessments) or by creating a new Strategic Impact Assessment Body within the organization (*ex ante* assessments). However, if not carried out by independent institutions, the initiatives for such assessments might be an easy prey for the very deadlock they want to overcome, since developing countries might resist the inclusion of environmental aspects into current evaluations from the beginning.*

Unlike the aforementioned ideas, a further group of proposals does calls neither for a legal reform of the WTO nor for a change in the organization's

---

* In fact, developing countries have already done so in a similar discussion, namely when debating the integration of labor standards into the annual Trade Policy Reviews (Santarius et al. 2004: 45). Moreover, there has already been a first WTO-internal debate about environmental impact assessment studies. Following an earlier proposal by the Commission on Sustainable Development (CSD), the EU, Canada and the United States announced in 1999 plans to perform environmental impact assessments. However, they could not convince further WTO parties to join in (ibid.: 36ff.).

institutional structure. In fact, they do not conceive of the WTO as the adequate arena at all for the strengthening of environmental interests. Rather, they argue that any further consideration or even inclusion of green rules and standards might prove counterproductive, since, this way, the WTO would keep expanding its jurisdiction and mandate at the expense of environmental regimes. For instance, via savings clauses for specific standards, the organization would assume the right to determine which regulations are trade restricting in the first place (only explicitly or also potentially trade-related measures); what is more, the WTO would also have the privilege to define which of these regulations are legitimate, and which ones are not [16].

As a counterweight to this "big brother" mentality, some observers suggest boosting the effectiveness of MEAs from within, i.e., independent from the mercy of the WTO and its parties. In this regard, it deems quintessential to strengthen the judicial side of MEAs, i.e., to come up with proper agencies for case-by-case decisions, thereby hampering further takeovers by the DSB. For instance, in light of prospective clashes with international trade regulations, Chambers [26] proposes the establishment of a strong dispute settlement system for the global climate regime. Likewise, Pfahl [32] makes a case for the International Court of Justice and the UN's International Law Commission as the most suitable institutions to decide upon disputes between WTO and MEAs.

Meanwhile, UNEP "should strengthen its technical role in order to influence the policy debate", e.g., through a clearinghouse "for identifying successful examples of MEA trade-measure implementation" [32]. A plethora of more audacious proposals propagates the establishment of a World Environment Organization or an even more ambitious World Environment and Development Organization [54]. The potential functions of the new organization might range from a UN specialized agency which harmonizes existing MEAs [55] to a direct competitor of other global institutions including the WTO [56].* Finally, some proposals focus less on the institutional design and more on the membership of MEAs, suggesting stronger efforts to integrate the global South. In this regard, regional environmental agreements could provide an effective stepping-stone; by dealing with ecological issues particularly relevant for countries in a certain area of the world, these agreements could help raise the environmental awareness in those nations [12].

10.7   Summary and Concluding Remarks

At the onset of this chapter, by listing six quite diverse hypotheses about the WTO's impact on the environment, I tried to sketch how broad the assumed

---

* For a comprehensive discussion of different proposals in favor or against a World Environment Organization, see Biermann and Bauer (A World Environment Organization: Solution or Threat for Effective International Environmental Governance? 2005).

scope of this impact can possibly be: it ranged from optimistic expectations of a raise in environmental awareness to deeply pessimistic predictions of an accelerated depletion of worldwide ecological assets. The variety of these predictions mirrors the diversity of ecological matters which are in one way or the other affected by the international trade regime, from biological diversity to ozone layer depletion, from global climate change to hazardous wastes. On the other hand, it is this complexity of overlaps of trade and several environmental issues which also renders unfeasible any waterproof examination of the assumptions it has inspired.

Apart from these methodological obstacles, it was also the apparent lack of evidence for some suppositions (e.g., the rather sluggish removal of un-ecological subsidies) which insinuated to single out one particular hypothesis for further examination. The choice was made for the prediction that the WTO will provoke a race to the bottom between domestic and multilateral environmental standards and policies. Still, this concentration on one particular type of environmental impact was far from an over-simplification: given the plethora of intersecting and partially conflicting agreements and rules, the focus on the WTO's role in this institutional mosaic should produce anything but one-dimensional results.

And indeed, when finally asking whether the assumption of a WTO-induced race to the bottom has stood the test, the answer is far from a simple yes or no. In fact, at the time of writing, this question seems more undecided than ever before. Things were different around the time of the WTO's establishment, when two observations clearly seemed to corroborate the watering-down assumption. First, from its very beginning, the environmental policy-making of the organization had been structurally doomed to meet the least common denominator of its member states. Neither the secretariat nor the CTE had been endowed with the competency to exert a proper WTO environmental policy [57]. Instead, the deadlock between industrialized and developing countries on ecological matters had been perpetuated from the Uruguay Round into the CTE, whose decisions tend to be taken consensually among governmental representatives. Second, the organ which was to fill up this environmental policy vacuum, namely the Dispute Settlement Body (DSB), inherited anything but a green legacy from the old GATT Panel which had issued reports clearly unfavorable to domestic environmental standards. Moreover, the DSB cannot set its agenda on its own behalf, but is dependent from WTO parties who have to appeal to it.

Paradoxically, the DSB—while not entitled to set the agenda—has well managed to constantly expand it via groundbreaking decisions; and by the same token, it has expanded its mandate on diverse ecological issues. Yet at the same time, it has also developed greater flexibility in its reports (e.g., when taking into account the life cycle of products, or when recognizing, in certain limits, the backup of national policies by previously agreed MEAs). In this spirit, both the CTE and the DSB acknowledged that conflicts about trade-related rules of an MEA should first be handled by the environmental agreement, supposed that both dispute parties are among its members. In fact, so far no MEA has ever been challenged before the WTO. And finally, the ongoing debate about the inclusion of an environmental window into WTO law nurtures further hopes for an undisturbed coexistence of key green standards and the international trade regime.

So given these pale green spots which have recently been covering the WTO's surface, can we call off the race to the bottom altogether? Such a level of optimism is unjustified. At best, the race might have slowed down in light of these concessions. But it could well regain pace, depending on some upcoming decisions which may serve as signposts for the further environmental course of the WTO. First of all, member states have increasingly questioned the legitimacy of the Appellate Body's recent flexibility towards domestic environmental regulations. The body's next reports on such provisions will show whether this criticism has made it review its practice. And second, the impasse of the debate about the WTO–MEA relationship needs to be broken—the sooner the better. The uncertainty of the *status quo* is definitely not in the interest of environmental conventions, no matter if or not a "hot" legal dispute about an MEA will take place soon. In the absence of clear priority rules for one regime or the other, the shadow of the WTO's stronger enforcement mechanism makes its members think twice before complying with trade-related measures of an MEA.

Suggestions to solve this dilemma either have focused on legal or institutional reform of the WTO or instead have concentrated on strengthening the judicial status of MEAs. The best approach might well be a reasonable mix of some of these measures, taking the shape of a multi-forum-approach. No doubt, MEAs are the better advocates of environmental concerns. It is hence imperative to make the best out of the current stagnation of the WTO's MEA-related initiatives. This means: using the time at hand and the undecidedness of the matter in order to piece by piece strengthen the position of MEAs vis-à-vis a double expansionism: first, in order to counterbalance the self-inflating jurisdiction and mandate of the DSB, and most of all to do so *before* the first MEA party vs. non-party dispute will have taken place; and second, in order to keep the CTE from having the final word about which environmental regulations are appropriate and which ones are not.

On the other hand, it is equally important neither to exclude the WTO from the environmental debate in general nor to give up on the CTE in particular. The anti-WTO attitude, as exposed by many protesters from Seattle to Cancún, keeps overlooking the very simple fact that the organization is the only forum which is to some extent capable of controlling trade on a global scale. In other words: no WTO would not mean no free trade, but instead more unregulated free trade—with potentially worse implications for the environment. Therefore, a two-track strategy inside and outside the WTO shows the best potential: enhancing the institutional design of MEAs, while at the same time promoting further WTO–MEA cooperation and attuning WTO law towards the creation of an environmental window. Such efforts across various forums should also be best suited for breaking the ongoing impasse among states parties, by allowing for issue-linkages and hence for a broad acceptance of negotiation results [58,59].* After all, there is enough substance for package deals: across the WTO and a number of MEAs, similar groups of countries are facing each other, but sometimes with reversed roles regarding ecological matters.† Moreover, the overlap of WTO law with international treaties of other issue areas such as labor rights, human rights or international finance [25], should open up further chances for more complex issue-linkages.

To sum up, there are currently several ambiguous tendencies in the relationship between WTO law and both domestic and international environmental regulations. With the outcome of these developments still uncertain and a considerable number of proposals at hand, we are well kept in suspense about the direction which the presumed race to the bottom might finally take. Having affirmed this enduring uncertainty, it is time to bring back to mind that this chapter's focus on legal overlaps presents but one portion of the highly complex mutual impact between free trade and the global environment. With the future findings of new comprehensive research approaches, especially environmental impact assessments, some of this uncertainty should be transformed into a deeper understanding of the trade-environment nexus. However, it remains to be seen if this increasing insight will ever be sufficient to justify statements as plain and as optimistic as the one by Pascal Lamy cited at the beginning of this chapter.

References

1. Lamy, P., Video address to the 8th Conference of the Parties of the Convention on Biological Diversity, Curitiba, Brazil, 28 March 2006. Available at http://www.wto.org/english/news_e/sppl_e/sppl22_e.htm. (accessed on April 21, 2006).
2. Meadows, D.H., Meadows, D.L., Randers, J., and Behrens, W.W.W. III, *The Limits to Growth: a Report for the Club of Rome's Project on the Predicament of Mankind*, Universe Books, New York, 1972.
3. Bernauer, T., Kompatibilitätsprobleme zwischen internationaler Handelsliberalisierung und Umweltschutz, in *Handel und Umwelt: zur Frage der Kompatibilität*

---

* The notion that issue-linkages and multiple forums alter the interests of member states and enhance cooperation is deeply rooted in the neo-institutionalist school of international relations theory. Unlike their neo-realist counterparts (who understand international institutions as the short-lived epiphenomena of power constellations among members [Mearsheimer, International Security, 1994]), neo-institutionalists like Keohane (After Hegemony: Cooperation and Discord in the World Political Economy 1984; International Institutions and State Power: Essays in International Relations Theory, 1989) believe that organizations and regimes can make a difference by connecting issues and by enhancing the continuity of political relationships over time (cf. Hasenclever, Mayer, and Rittberger 1997).

  However, as Raustiala and Victor (2004) further observe, multi-arena constellations can also be abused by member states through a practice of "forum shopping", i.e., actors seek out the forum most favorable to their interests. Thus, in order to create win–win effects for both objectives, issue-linkages always need to be flanked by a further strengthening of the involved institutions.

† For instance, in the WTO, the global climate regime or the ozone regime, the bulk of developing countries have been acting as environmental laggards; but when it comes to the issues of biological diversity and intellectual property rights, they have been playing an almost reversed role (cf. Biermann, Climate Policy 2005).

internationaler Regime, T. Bernauer and D. Ruloff, Eds., Westdeutscher Verlag, Opladen, 1999, 41–69.

4. Eckersley, R., *Environmentalism and Political Theory: Toward an Ecocentric Approach*, State University of New York Press, Albany, 1992.

5. Hardin, G., *Living Within Limit, Ecology, Economics, and Population Taboos*, Oxford University Press, Oxford, 1993.

6. Ophuls, W., *Ecology and the Politics of Scarcity Revisited: the Unraveling of the American Dream*, Freeman, New York, 1992.

7. Ophuls, W., *Requiem for Modern Politics: The Tragedy of the Enlightenment and the Challenge of the New Millennium*, Westview Press, Oxford, 1997.

8. Bhagwati, J. and Srinivasan, T.N., Trade and the environment: Does environmental diversity detract from the case for free trade? in *Fair Trade and Harmonization: Prerequisites for Free Trade. Volume 1: Economic Analysis*, J. Bhagwati and R. Hudec, Eds., MIT Press, Cambridge, 1996, 159–223.

9. Cairncross, F., *Costing the Earth: The Challenge for Governments, the Opportunities for Business*, The Economist Books, London, 1991.

10. Anderson, T.L. and Leal, D.R., *Free Market Environmentalism*, Westview Press, Oxford, 1991.

11. Anderson, T.L. and Leal, D.R., *Free Market Environmentalism Today*, Palgrave, New York, 2001.

12. Kulessa, M.A. and Schwaab, J.A., Konzepte zur, Ökologisierung' der internationalen Handels- und Wirtschaftspolitik, *Internationale Politik und Gesellschaft (International Politics and Society)*, 3, 2000, 254.

13. Barry, J., *Rethinking Green Politics. Nature, Virtue and Progress*, Sage, London, 1999.

14. Bartelmus, P., *Environment, Growth and Development: the Concepts and Strategies of Sustainability*, Routledge, London, 1994.

15. Rivera-Batiz, L.A. and Oliva, M.A., *International Trade: Theory, Strategies, and Evidence*, Oxford University Press, Oxford, 2004.

16. Santarius, T., Dalkmann, H., Steigenberger, M., and Vogelpohl, K., Balancing Trade and Environment: an Ecological Reform of the WTO as a Challenge in Sustainable Global Governance, Wuppertal Paper No. 133e, Wuppertal Institute for Climate, Environment and Energy, Wuppertal, Germany, 2004. Available at http://www.wupperinst.org/globalisierung/pdf_global/balancing_trade.pdf. (accessed on May 9, 2006).

17. Sampson, G.P., *World Trade Organization and Global Environmental Governance*, United Nations University Press, Tokyo, 2002.

18. Miles, E.L., *et al.*, *Environmental Regime Effectiveness: Confronting Theory with Evidence*, MIT Press, Cambridge, 2002.

19. Oberthür, S. and Gehring, T., Conceptual foundations and institutional interaction, in *Institutional Interaction in Global Environmental Governance: Synergy and Conflict among International and EU Policies*, S. Oberthür and T. Gehring, Eds., MIT Press, Cambridge, 2006, 19–52.

20. Underdal, A., Methodological challenges in the study of regime effectiveness, in *Regime Consequences: Methodological Challenges and Research Strategies*, A. Underdal and O.R. Young, Eds., Kluwer Academic, Dordrecht, 2004, 27–48.

21. WCED (World Commission on Environment and Development). *Our Common Future*, Oxford University Press, Oxford, UK, 1987.

22. Eglin, R., Trade and environment, in *The Uruguay Round and Beyond: Essays in Honour of Arthur Dunkel*, J. Bhagwati and M. Hirsch, Eds., Springer, Berlin, 1998, 251–263.

23. Bernauer, T., Handelsliberalisierung und Umweltschutzpolitik: Konflikte und Synergien, in *Handel und Umwelt: Zur Frage der Kompatibilität Internationaler Regime*, T. Bernauer and D. Ruloff, Eds., Westdeutscher Verlag, Opladen, 1999, 118–140.

24. Pauwelyn, J., *Conflict of Norms in Public International Law: How WTO Law Relates to Other Rules of International Law*, Cambridge University Press, Cambridge, 2003.

25. Moltke, K.v., Information exchange and observer status. The World Trade Organization and multilateral environmental agreements: paragraph 31 (ii) of the Doha Ministerial Declaration, 2003. Available at http://www.ecologic.de/download/verschiedenes/2003/documents/paper_moltke.pdf. (accessed on May 9, 2006).

26. Chambers, W.B., International trade law and the Kyoto Protocol: potential incompatibilities, in *Inter-linkages: The Kyoto Protocol and the International Trade and Investment Regimes*, W.B. Chambers, Ed., United Nations University Press, Tokyo, 2001, 87–118.

27. Housman, R.F. and Durwood, Zaelke D., The collision of the environment and trade: the GATT Tuna/Dolphin decision, *Environmental Law Reporter*, 22, 1992, 10268.

28. Zaelke, D., Housman, R.F., and Gary, S., Frictions between international trade agreements and environmental protections: the greening of world trade, in *Trade and the Environment: Law, Economics and Policy*, D. Zaelke, P. Orbuch, and R.F. Housman, Eds., Island Press, Washington, DC, 1993, 44–77.

29. Jackson, J.H., Comments on shrimp/turtle and the product/process distinction, *European Journal of International Law*, 11, 2000, 303.

30. Howse, R. and Tuerk, E., The WTO impact on internal regulations: a case study of the Canada-EC asbestos dispute, in *The EU and the WTO: Constitutional and Legal Aspects*, G.D. Burca and J. Scott, Eds., Hart Publishing, Oxford, 2001, 283–328.

31. Sampson, G.P., *WTO and Sustainable Development*, United Nations University Press, Tokyo, 2005.

32. Pfahl, S., Is the WTO the only way? Safeguarding multilateral environmental agreements from international trade rules and settling trade and environmental disputes outside the WTO, A briefing paper by Adelphi Consult, Friends of the Earth Europe, and Greenpeace, Greenpeace International, Amsterdam, 2005. Available at http://www.greenpeace.org/raw/content/international/press/reports/is-the-wto-the-only-way.pdf. (accessed on May 9, 2006).

33. Werksman, J., Greenhouse-gas emissions trading and the WTO, in *Inter-linkages: the Kyoto Protocol and the International Trade and Investment Regimes*, W.B. Chambers, Ed., United Nations University Press, Tokyo, 2001, 153–190.

34. Brack, D., *International Trade and the Montreal Protocol*, Royal Institute of International Affairs, London, 1996.

35. Zhang, Z.X., Greenhouse-gas emissions trading and the world trading system, in *Inter-linkages: the Kyoto Protocol and the International Trade and Investment Regimes*, W.B. Chambers, Ed., United Nations University Press, Tokyo, 2001, 119–151.

36. Palmer, A., Chaytor, B., and Werksman, J., Interactions between the World Trade Organization and international environmental regimes, in *Institutional Interaction in Global Environmental Governance: Synergy and Conflict among International and EU Policies*, S. Oberthür and T. Gehring, Eds., MIT Press, Cambridge, 2006, 181–204.

37. Brack, D., Grubb, M., and Windram, C., *International Trade and Climate Change Policies*, Earthscan, London, 2000.

38. IISD (International Institute for Sustainable Development), A brief analysis of COP 11 & COP/MOP 1, *Earth Negotiations Bulletin*, 12, no. 291, 2005, 18–20. Available at http://www.iisd.ca/climate/cop11/. (accessed on May 8, 2006).

39. Charnovitz, S., Trade and climate: potential conflicts and synergies, in *Beyond Kyoto: Advancing the International Effort against Climate Change*, Pew Center for Global Climate Change, Ed., Pew Center, Arlington, 2003, 141–170.

40. Biermann, F. and Brohm, R., Implementing the Kyoto Protocol without the United States: the strategic role of energy tax adjustments at the border, *Climate Policy*, 4, 2005, 289.

41. Rosendal, G.K., Impacts of overlapping international regimes: the case of biodiversity, *Global Governance*, 7, 2001, 95.
42. Rosendal, G.K., *The Convention on Biological Diversity and TRIPs: different approaches to property rights to genetic resources—cause for worry?* Institutional Interaction Project Deliverable No. D 5, Final Draft, 2003. Available at http://www.ecologic.de/download/projekte/850899/890/indepth/convention_on_biodiversity.pdf. (accessed on May 8, 2006).
43. Raustiala, K., Global biodiversity protection in the United Kingdom and the United States, in *The Internationalization of Environmental Protection*, M.A. Schreurs and E.C. Economy, Eds., Cambridge University Press, Cambridge, 1997, 42–73.
44. Rosendal, G.K., The Convention on Biological Diversity: tensions with the WTO TRIPS agreement over access to genetic resources and the sharing of benefits, in *Institutional Interaction in Global Environmental Governance: Synergy and Conflict among International and EU Policies*, S. Oberthür and T. Gehring, Eds., MIT Press, Cambridge, 2006, 79–102.
45. Raghavan, C., Andean pact's new IPR regime shaped in U.S. interests? Third World Network Briefing Paper, Penang, Malaysia, 2000. Available at http://www.twnside.org.sg/title/andean.htm. (accessed on May 8, 2005).
46. Werksman, J. and Santoro, C., Investing in sustainable development: the potential interaction between the Kyoto Protocol and the Multilateral Agreement on Investment, in *Inter-linkages: the Kyoto Protocol and the International Trade and Investment Regimes*, W.B. Chambers, Ed., United Nations University Press, Tokyo, 2001, 191–213.
47. Sampson, G.P., WTO rules and climate change: the need for policy coherence, in *Inter-linkages: the Kyoto Protocol and the International Trade and Investment Regimes*, W.B. Chambers, Ed., United Nations University Press, Tokyo, 2001, 69–85.
48. Moltke, K.v., *International Environmental Management, Trade Regimes and Sustainability* International Institute for Sustainable Development 1996.
49. Thomas, U.P., Trade and the environment: stuck in a political impasse at the WTO after the Doha and Cancun Ministerial Conferences, *Global Environmental Politics*, 4, 2004, 9.
50. Biermann, F., Internationale Umweltverträge im Welthandelsrecht, Discussion Paper FSII 99-403, Wissenschaftszentrum, Berlin, Germany, 1999. Available at http://skylla.wz-berlin.de/pdf/1999/ii99-403.pdf. (accessed on May 9, 2006).
51. Helm, C., *Sind Freihandel und Umweltschutz vereinbar? Ökologischer Reformbedarf des GATT/WTO-Regimes*, Edition Sigma, 1995.
52. Asselt, H.v., Biermann, F., and Gupta, J., Advancing the climate agenda: exploiting material and institutional linkages to develop a menu of policy options, *Review of European Community International Environmental Law*, 14, 2005, 255.
53. WWF (World Wildlife Fund), Balanced process, balanced results: sustainability assessments and trade, WWF Briefing Paper, 2001. Available at http://www.balancedtrade.panda.org/pdf/balpro.pdf. (accessed on May 9, 2006).
54. Biermann, Frank, and Simonis, U.E., Institutional reform of international environmental policy: advancing the debate on a World Environment Organization, Discussion Paper FSII 00-401, Wissenschaftszentrum, Berlin, 2000. Available at http://skylla.wz-berlin.de/pdf/2000/ii00-401.pdf. (accessed on May 9, 2006).
55. Biermann, F., The rationale for a World Environment Organization, in *A World Environment Organization: Solution or Threat for Effective International Environmental Governance?* F. Biermann and S. Bauer, Eds., Ashgate, Aldershot, 2005, 117–144.
56. Charnovitz, S., Toward a World Environment Organization: reflections upon a vital debate, in *A World Environment Organization: Solution or Threat for Effective International Environmental Governance?* F. Biermann and S. Bauer, Eds., Ashgate, Aldershot, 2005, 87–116.

57. Senti, R., Handel und Umweltschutz in der neuen Welthandelsordnung WTO, in *Handel und Umwelt: Zur Frage der Kompatibilität Internationaler Regime*, T. Bernauer and D. Ruloff, Eds., Westdeutscher Verlag, Oplanden, Germany, 1999, 97–116.

58. Raustiala, K. and Victor, D.G., The regime complex for plant genetic resources, *International Organization*, 32, 2004, 147.

59. Young, O.R., Institutional linkages in international society: Polar perspectives, *Global Governance*, 2, 1996, 1.

Chapter 11

United Nations Conferences and the Legitimization of Environmental NGOs

Kyle Farmbry and Aroon Manorahan
Rutgers University

11.1 Introduction

The rise of nongovernmental organizations (NGOs) as important actors in the international arena during the latter decades of the 20th century, particularly during the 1990s, has been of increasing interest in policy arenas [1,2]. Much of the growth can be contextualized within the framework of institutionalization theories that explore the emergence and evolution of these organizations. Through activities such as providing social services, engaging in advocacy and relief operations in international arenas, and implementing strategies for economic development, NGOs have increasingly found themselves in positions of legitimizing their institutional roles.

Paralleling much of the rise in the visibility and legitimacy of NGO activities has been a growing interest in environmental policies on domestic and international levels. Triggered by an awareness that has grown about environmental challenges over the past 40 years among citizens and governments—from an awareness of the impact of global warming, to concerns about the factors that are being felt due to pollutants in many communities, and rising awareness of many of the environmental challenges we face on an ongoing basis in many settings—environmental issues have increasingly fallen within a public discourse.

This chapter explores processes of NGO institutional legitimization vis-à-vis a global discourse on environmental issues. It uses the evolution of various nongovernmental activities as related to United Nations' (UN) conferences pertaining to the environment (the 1972 UN Conference on the Human Environment, the 1992 UN Conference on Environment and Development, and the 2002 Summit on Sustainable Development) to help shape the discourse on the emerging roles of NGOs in shaping environmental activities by governments and citizens around the world.

We begin our examination of NGO growth and development in the global environmental discourse with a brief examination of NGO emergence within a global civic and political context over the past several decades. In particular, the latter three decades of the 20th century were marked with both radical changes in the visibility and expectations associated with government as the primary deliverer of services and actions on behalf of the needs of a populous. People's expectations of government, as the primary agent for addressing their needs, have met with frequent disappointment as governments' abilities increasingly have fallen short of the expectations and desires of people in various settings. As a result, this is a period marked largely by the rapid evolution of roles of NGOs as non-state actors and their vital roles in the provision of societal needs.

We continue with our framework for examining the legitimization and institutional roles of NGOs in environmental issues. Specifically, we use an overview of the changing scope of activities of NGOs within an evolving UN environmental discourse that stretches between the UN Conference on the Human Environment, held in Stockholm in 1972, and the Summit on Sustainable Development, held in Johannesburg in 2002. Here we provide a general overview of key outcomes of the three summits and the roles of NGOs in the context of the meetings. Ultimately, as we attempt to demonstrate, NGOs have become more central to the evolving discourse related to environmental issues.

We close with a set of general observations and projections of the future of NGO activities vis-à-vis the global environmental movements, particularly as NGOs play a role in the growth of the environmental movement over the next several decades. In our conclusion, we examine potential scenarios that NGOs face as actors within the global environmental context in relation to shifting roles of non-state actors in policy discourse related to further legitimizing NGO roles.

11.2 Conceptualizing NGO Growth

The past 30 years have seen rapid growth in the activities and awareness of organizations in the nonprofit sector. The rise of these organizations reflects a shift during the 20th century of non-state actors and their roles within the global discourse. At the beginning of the 20th century, the relevance of nongovernmental agencies within global political and policy arenas is evidenced by the lack of mention of them in the League of Nation's charter. They simply were not thought of as institutions able to create or leverage change. Instead, governmental institutions were viewed as the agencies best positioned for making continual change in communities. By mid century, the lack of specific mention of NGOs in the charters of the World Bank and the International Monetary Fund, also suggest the limited role that these organizations had in official global political discourse. However, at the close of the century, they were depended upon by both state and interstate actors such as the World Bank, the UN, and the International Monetary Fund in vital areas related to developmental agenda implementation.

Salamon [1] referred to this rapid emergence of NGOs as important actors on a global scale during the latter years of the 20th century as the global NGO revolution. He argued that it was the result of four crises and two "revolutionary changes." The first of the crises he notes is one around the changing expectations vis-à-vis the welfare state. Government is no longer perceived by many to be able to respond to people's needs, particularly as people find themselves facing questions regarding their continued general well-being. As a result, the concept of the state as the general benefactor of the people is one that no longer exists in as regular a degree as before. The second crisis is one of development. The lack of economic progress in some regions of the world has led to a search for new institutional models to address needs in the areas of food concerns, sanitation, medical access, and other results of growing economic imbalances. The third is a crisis of the environment. Salamon notes that environmental degradation in both wealthy and economically marginalized nations has led to the need for the engagement of citizens in a number of voluntary efforts aimed at addressing environmental needs within their societies. The final crisis Salamon observes is one that confronted the legitimacy of Communist governments from the late 1970s to the late 1980s and ultimately led to a number of governmental transitions of the early 1990s.

In addition to the four crises, Salamon argues that the sector has developed at a rapid scale because of two revolutionary changes that have ultimately shaped the direction of the sector's emergence. The first focuses on advances in global communications. It is easier to communicate with one another, despite where the communicators are situated. In addition to advances in communications technology, increases in literacy rates and global commonalities have impacted communications processes.

The second revolutionary change relates to the economic growth of the 1960s and early 1970s. Ultimately this growth resulted in the creation of a middle-class to respond to many of the social conditions to which the nongovernmental sector might respond. It was ultimately this class that responded to the challenges of the late 1970s and 1980s, which underscored opportunities that were created during this time period and ultimately helped lead to the development of the sector.

Matthews [2] argues that the emergence of these nongovernmental actors is a vital reflection of the realignment of global power structures to a degree unseen since the Treaty of Westphalia and which shaped our current perspective of the state as the vital entity in the global political system. She argues that such a shift is largely the result of the end of the Cold War, and with it, both changing realities around security needs from a notion of security as defined by foreign relations and military perspectives to security as defined by the needs of daily life (i.e., food, safety, shelter). Matthews agrees with Salamon's notion that advances in communications have driven much of the shift in power from government to NGOs. Ultimately, hierarchies, established largely as a result of governmental controls of information flows, have been replaced by networks of nongovernmental networks that have more of a distributed flow of information linked into them.

If the growth and development of NGOs is a by-product of the failings of governments, as pointed out by both Matthews and Salamon, then there are a number of areas to explore on how these organizations have been involved with building a strategy of legitimacy vis-à-vis governmental processes and systems.

From our perspective, such an examination should assume both a descriptive and prescriptive stance. Descriptively, an examination of the evolution of the nonprofit sector should examine the emergence of various trends that impact the development of the sector. Prescriptively, there should be an emphasis on the potential steps that various stakeholders might assume to move forward with their agendas related to the development of the sector. Our exploration assumes a descriptive framework and offers a resulting set of prescriptive recommendations for advancing the abilities of organizations within the nongovernmental sector that are working on environmental development and reform. In the next section, we examine in depth the development of an infrastructure related to global NGO growth in relation to environmental needs. We use as a parallel framework for this examination, the development of the UN system on the environment, with an emphasis on the three major UN environmental meetings between 1972 and 2002. We follow this section with a set of prescriptive recommendations related to the evolution of the sector-with an emphasis on long-term sectoral development.

11.3 NGOs and Environment Discourse: between Stockholm and Johannesburg

Within an environmental context, the growth of NGOs has provided much of the momentum in activities and the emergence of policies and perspectives. The thirty-year period between the 1972 UN Conference on the Human Environment and the 2002 Summit on Sustainable Development represents the culminating recognition of many of the post-industrial environmental realities for many parts of the world. It also represents a time period when NGOs increasingly were able to move to a more central role in the articulation and advocacy of various environmental policies that ultimately placed environmental concerns at the center of many national and international discussions about the future of humankind. Finally, it represents a period during which a number of vital issues related to a North–South discourse within a development framework surfaced. Each of these shifts—the post-industrial, the changing make-up of the advocates, and the shifting North–South developmental discourse—have all had integrated within their frameworks a role for and by non–governmental organizations. The UN's environmental meetings serve as useful benchmarks for examining the evolving discourse on these issues. Our examination of the progression of these meetings vis-à-vis the various conferences aims to present a background on the conferences with a focus on key outcomes for each conference and implications for NGOs.

11.3.1 Stockholm (1972)

Increasingly during the 1960s, global environmental issues fell within the scope of various actors in international arenas. Growing populations and a resulting demand on natural resources, increasing awareness of the impact of greenhouse gases (GHG), and the impact of deforestation led to a more widespread awareness of the challenges faced in an environmental context for global issues, and the awareness of the environmental costs of many of our industrial advances.

In May of 1968, in recognition of the need for more global dialogue on environmental issues, Ambassador Sverker Astrom of Sweden raised a series of questions about the role of the UN system in relation to global environmental concerns [3]. In December of 1968, the General Assembly approved Resolution 2398 (XXIII), calling for a conference in 1972 to focus on matters pertaining to the environment. The resolution also asked the Secretary General to prepare a report on the problems of the human environment in consultation with UN bodies, governments, and NGOs.

The planning process for the 1972 meeting was coordinated within four meetings of a Preparatory Committee, which began in 1970 and continued for the next 2 years. Each meeting lasted for 10 days. Nongovernmental organizations were represented at the preparatory meetings in limited capacities, attending the sessions as observers and participants in the international working groups that developed draft recommendations to be presented at the conference. Some NGOs were involved as consultant agencies in the development of the Only One Earth report by the committee.

The actual UN Conference on the Human Environment was held in Stockholm from June 5-16, 1972. Official participants included representatives from 113 states. However, representatives from 255 international and national NGOs were also present. Nongovernmental organizations were marginally involved in the conference, and for the most part, had only specific conference representation through a handful of formal observers. They sent formal observers, who coordinated and participated in the Environmental Forum, which occurred outside of the conference.

This alternative forum, arranged by the UN Association of Sweden and the National Council of Swedish Youth, provided an outlet for the expression of views by almost 200 participating groups. Ultimately, it served as the vehicle for NGOs to have a presence in Stockholm at the same time as the UN Forum. More importantly, however, it established a model of establishing a locale for NGOs to articulate the concerns of their constituencies that was later replicated at the 1992 Rio Summit and the 2002 Johannesburg Summit.

Several major outcomes of the UN Conference on the Human Environment resulted from the global environmental discourse. The primary one was the December 15, 1972 approval by the UN General Assembly for the establishment of the UN Environmental Program (UNEP). UN Environmental Program's emergence was the culmination of a number of explorations of a potential institutional framework for the development of a mechanism to address environmental issues and concerns that surfaced within and outside of the UN framework. For example, the discussion of the idea for the development of an institutional framework surfaced in the writings of George Keenan, who proposed in 1970 an institution to monitor and work on the behalf of global environmental needs [4].

Second, as a result of Stockholm, over 100 nations established environmental ministries and agencies [5]. In the years since Stockholm, these organizations have played key roles in impacting environmental agendas within their nations from both a political and an administrative framework. These organizations have become the nation-based champions of the environment, as well as their repository for many programmatic, regulatory, and other strategies for addressing environmental concerns.

Third, Stockholm indirectly triggered the emergence and growth of nongovernmental agencies focused on environmental issues. Many of the organizations that participated in Stockholm ultimately grew as the momentum around environmental issues developed. As agencies that were among the few nongovernmental representatives at Stockholm, many were able to help with the growth and development of a larger environmental organizational network. A global discourse had officially begun on the environmental needs facing the planet, and with it emerged a set of questions related to the roles of governmental and nongovernmental entities in addressing these needs. Both the NGOs that had been at Stockholm and many of the ones that would later emerge were critical players in the dialogue.

11.3.2 Implications for NGOs

It should be noted that the institutional framework established as a result of the 1972 UN Conference on the Human Environment was framed largely from the perspective of governmental or intergovernmental institutions such as UNEP. The direct impact from or by NGOs was, however, limited. There was not a critical mass of organizations from the nonprofit sector to actively shape the evolution of the discourse among policy makers, and because the state (and its interstate institutions) was seen as the most legitimate actor at the time, the impact and role of the sector was limited.

Participating NGOs did find themselves engaged in a few ways to effect change, however. They were at the nexus of a flow of information between their global policymakers who were reviewing environmental concerns and a wide public, of which their constituents were a crucial part. They were able to share with their constituencies findings and conclusions related to the environment that surfaced from the meetings. In some cases, they were able to provide some of the necessary scientific expertise needed by UN or governmental representatives. The third way, though limited, was to lobby for specific programmatic efforts on governmental strategies related to addressing environmental concerns. While limited in their impact, these strategies did shape some of the efforts of NGOs that were involved in subsequent efforts.

11.4   United Nations Conference on Environment and Development, Rio de Janeiro, 1992

The years between 1972 and 1992 witnessed both a new institutional framework for enhancing NGO activities on global issues and critical changes in the global political environment that ultimately impacted the environmental discourse in several ways. The emergence of the institutional framework was the result of several phenomena. First, there was a growing awareness of further challenges related to environmental issues. Citizens of nations around the world were increasingly expressing interest and concern about the environment. Much of this interest began to surface in political discourse as elected and administrative officials framed agendas related to the environment that responded to citizens' interests, largely as articulated via citizen-driven nongovernmental institutions. The interests also began to surface in legal arenas as citizens in many nations, again often through the mechanisms of nongovernmental institutions, began to hold business and government accountable for environmental activity. Finally, the interests began to surface in economic arenas, as more and more consumers began to place expectations on business regarding the interaction between their activities and environmental needs.

Second, the world had experienced the end of the Cold War era discord and was moving to a post-Cold War period. With the shift, a number of new expectations of government roles, vis-à-vis the deliverance of societal issues, rose. In many cases, this opened up awareness to many of the environmental challenges that had impacted many of the nations of Central and Eastern Europe (former Soviet Bloc nations) during the Cold War era and several of the environmental realities that impacted them. Pollution was a by-product of much of the rapid industrialization that had taken place in many of the nations of Central and Eastern Europe during the era. Citizens of many of these nations were both becoming increasingly aware of environmental conditions that impacted their lives as a result of Eastern-bloc industrialization, and of citizen-driven strategies for addressing such challenges.

Finally, NGOs had increased in scope, size, and influence. The emergence of more organizations, often due to issues that Salamon, Matthews, and others observed, simply left more organizations for activity related to nongovernmental issues. More organizations and a greater preponderance of NGO-grounded strategies for addressing community challenges increased in value.

In 1989, largely as a result of increasing awareness and activity on issues pertaining to the environment, the UN General Assembly decided that in 1992, it would convene the UN Conference on Environment and Development in Rio. One of the overriding goals of the conference was to bring some unity to the various agendas of organizations that had surfaced in the activities of various nations since the Stockholm conference. There were a number of governmental, nongovernmental, and business-focused organizations that had been involved in the environmental discourse, and each of them brought a set of contributions to the discussion. There were, importantly, numerous issues surfacing between Northern and Southern nations that also had an impact on the shape of environmental discourse. Many of the nations from the global South that participated felt they needed to articulate the linkages between environmentalism and their economic development needs. Some participants expressed the view if matters of the environment were to be addressed effectively, matters of economic development would also have to be addressed, particularly as the link between environmental degradation and poverty were becoming increasingly recognized.

Following the example set by the preparatory process for the Stockholm meeting, the preliminary work of the UN Conference on the Environment and Development was done through the Preparatory Committee, which was held as an organizational meeting in March 1990 and in four subsequent sessions from August 1990 to April 1992. The most important of these was the final preparatory committee meeting, held in New York. It was during this session that the bulk of agreement was reached on the majority of the text for Agenda 21 and the Rio Declaration.

The actual UN Conference on Environment and Development was held from June 3-14, 1992 in Rio. In attendance were more than 150 nations, 1,400 NGOs and 8,000 journalists. Of the NGOs that participated, one third were from the lesser industrialized nations, whereas in comparison only 10% of the NGOs in attendance at Stockholm were from these nations. The Rio conference was the first time that NGOs were able to come together on a single platform, and this allowed the UN and the conference officials to bring out frameworks and agendas for sustained cooperation. The NGOs expressed their ideas and enthusiasm to be involved in many activities of the UN.

Rio, however, also provided a forum in which division between NGOs in the global South were able to surface vis-à-vis those in the global North. In particular, Southern NGO suspicion of their governments surfaced and appeared troublesome, in comparison to relations between NGOs in the North vis-à-vis their governments, with whom they often had a much longer relationship.

Again, as was the case in Stockholm, NGO representatives had an alternate forum through which they were able to participate in activities. Specifically, they were able to engage in a Global Forum, which occurred concurrently with the Earth Summit. The Global Forum provided an opportunity for NGOs to incorporate their various perspectives and agendas into a collaborative framework. It also provided an opportunity and an open forum for many organizations that might have previously been under such financial or political constraints within their own nations that they had felt the development and implementation of their agendas had been seriously hampered. Finally, it established a set of follow-up measures for NGOs to better coordinate their activities both within their countries and between nations, as well as to enhance the growth and development of an international agenda.

The most important outcomes of the Rio conference were Agenda 21 and the Rio Declaration. Both had significant implications for NGOs. Agenda 21 was a program of action that outlined various strategies for building the framework for engaging various segments of societies into dialogue and action on the environment. Three of the document's sections were particularly relevant for the activities of NGOs. First, Chapter 27 specifically outlined roles of NGOs as vital partners for sustainable development. Nongovernmental organizations were recognized as partners in enabling sustainable democratic processes and as vital actors in helping to ensure the activity of agencies engaged in grassroots movements. Chapter 27 also outlined mechanisms for the larger UN system to enhance the processes by which NGOs could contribute to policy design, development, and implementation [6,7].

Chapter 28 of Agenda 21 recognized the growing influence of local authorities and framed an agenda for their involvement in consultation processes. Specifically, it framed an argument for increasing involvement by these organizations throughout the 1990s, with a goal of local authorities having extensive consultation processes with both members of local populations and representative government agencies working with local populations [8].

Finally, Chapter 38 of Agenda 21 explored in detail the roles of various institutional arrangements. It created the Sustainable Development Commission, with responsibility to carry out the objectives that surfaced in the Rio Summit. The Commission was to be the main agency tasked with monitoring the implementation of Agenda 21. Most importantly from the perspective of NGOs, it was the agency that would identify and develop further mechanisms for engaging NGOs in activities that followed Rio [8].

Another outcome of the Rio conference was the Rio Declaration, which established a set of principles on environmental and economic action. This declaration laid the groundwork for involving communities and their representatives in decision-making processes on environmental issues. Relevant to NGOs was Principle 10 of the Rio Declaration, which acknowledged the role of citizen engagement in activity related to the environment. Principle 10 called for greater access to information pertaining to the environment. In addition, of relevance for NGOs was Principle 22, which called for the engagement of indigenous groups in decision making vis-à-vis the environment and established a framework for the agenda setting related to environmental issues [9].

11.5 Implications for NGOs

The Earth Summit set the stage for NGO involvement in environmental issues. The major documents that came out of the summit, The Rio Declaration and Agenda 21, established a legitimizing framework for activity related to the Summit. Each outlined specific ways that NGOs could work with actors from the public and private sectors to implement both a discourse process and actionable steps related to the environment.

The Rio Summit triggered a more visible presence of NGOs in the activities of the UNEP. In 1995, for example, a Governing Council resolution was passed, calling for the involvement of civil society, and in 1999, the Governing Council called for the establishment of a NGO Civil Society Unit. The years following the framework that emerged from the Rio Summit witnessed an increasing involvement of NGOs in the environmental activities of the UNEP. In 1999, the Civil Society and NGOs Unit of UNEP was formed in the Division of Policy Development and Law. This was a part of the restructuring of UNEP and was also followed by the creation of the Division of Early Warning and Assessment. This unit set upon its task quickly by organizing the Global Civil Society Forum (GCSF) in May 2000, before the start of the 6th Global Ministerial Environment Forum at Malmo, Sweden in the following year [10].

Towards the end of the 1990s, nations incorporated discussions of sustained economic growth in partnership with attention on the earth's economic resources. This notion became coined as "sustainable development" by the World Commission on Environment and Development and represents the combined effort of promoting development and protecting the environment.

The 1990s also witnessed growing concern over the level of GHG in the environment. During the Earth Summit at Rio, the UN Framework Convention on Climatic Change (UNFCCC) was developed and served as an international treaty reached by the participating nations on the issue of reducing their global emissions of the GHG. The issue of GHG was further put into the international agenda with the Kyoto conference and the resulting Kyoto Protocol in 1997.

Nongovernmental actors were, largely as a result of how they had been able to integrate themselves into the agendas of the 1992 Earth Summit and subsequent environmental meetings of the 1990s, actors that would play a vital role in the global environmental discourse. Whether or not they would retain the role they had been able to begin to shape for themselves in later decades of activity and other arenas, would be open to later exploration.

11.6 Summit on Sustainable Development, Johannesburg, 2002

In 1999, the UN General Assembly, recognizing the arriving tenth anniversary of the Earth Summit, called for a 2002 World Summit on Sustainable Development (WSSD), to enable countries to review and follow-up on many of the initiatives initially orchestrated in Rio 10 years earlier. The WSSD was to be an opportunity to see what progress had been made since Rio, and an opportunity to explore new directions that should be charted for global environmental activity.

In developing the designs for WSSD, the conference organizers provided for NGOs many more opportunities to interact with official delegations than occurred in Rio—thus, initiating a framework for even greater interaction and roles for NGOs than had been experienced before. Nongovernmental organization representatives were able to present their proposals during the preparatory meetings, attend some negotiations, and present some of their positions on the floor of the Johannesburg meeting. They were able to lobby WSSD authorities and government delegations in support of proposals that NGOs wanted to include in (or exclude from) the official plan for implementation, stage public and media events to put pressure on the official process regarding specific demands, and conduct broader campaigns to direct the attention of the public and media onto social issues. Much of this activity was a direct result of an acknowledgement, largely from the lessons of Rio, that NGOs were a growing force in environmental and other human development areas.

Following the models set for Stockholm and Rio, there was a 2 year run-up process that included national, regional, and thematic meetings and four international preparatory conferences. The run-up process to WSSD, however, ran behind schedule and was, in comparison to the run-up process for Stockholm and Rio, poorly organized. The UN secretariat was unable to gain support for its draft documentation, however, and by the time the delegations assembled in Johannesburg, the draft plan was full of bracketed text still being debated by participants. In one of the final preparatory meetings, held in Bali, several of the NGOs involved threatened to boycott the Johannesburg conference, due largely to much of the dissatisfaction they felt regarding progress toward any tangible resolution for the upcoming Johannesburg meetings.

In 2002, the WSSD was held in Johannesburg from August 26 to September 4. This event was a major milestone in terms of NGO participation, as measured by the number of NGOs that had representatives attend. The conference attracted a large number of NGOs—about 800 were accredited for attendance. However, many NGOs were not totally satisfied with the outcomes of the summit as they viewed it as a "ministerial conference," with little outcome other than wide ranging pronouncements by government officials who they feared would have minimal follow-up. They complained of being able to wield less influence on major issues and also being sidelined by business groups from the private sector. Much of this dissatisfaction was a spillover from the dissatisfaction from some of the preparatory conferences.

Much of the dissatisfaction also probably stemmed from the lack of general receptivity from many of the more powerful global forces to the conference. From its beginning, most participants in WSSD confronted difficult odds with the declining global economy, the lack of support of the Bush Administration for environmental issues, and an international political agenda that was dominated by issues revolving around terrorism.

Despite these obstacles, Johannesburg generated two key documents: the Johannesburg Declaration on Sustainable Development and the Plan of Implementation. The Johannesburg Declaration on Sustainable Development was similar to the Declarations of Stockholm and Rio in that it spelled out broad goals and challenges associated with sustainable development. It also specified a number of general commitments such as the promotion of women's empowerment and greater democratic participation in sustainable development policies.

The Plan of Implementation is a longer document that identified goals for the summit and its aftermath, such as eradicating poverty, challenging consumption and production patterns, and protecting the earth's natural resource base. Much of it revolved around priority areas of water, health, energy, biological diversity, and agriculture.

Johannesburg also established a mechanism for engagement on sustainable development known as Type II Partnerships. These partnerships initially were touted as the innovation that would bring about significant commitments by NGO stakeholders. They were structured largely as a mechanism to engage not only actors within the public and nongovernmental sectors, but also a mechanism for engaging actors within the private for-profit business communities in environmental discourse and action.

Interestingly, this engagement of business reflected two dynamics. First, a development of support for a potential role of business as a partner with NGOs on environmental issues emerged, as exemplified by relations between organizations, such as Greenpeace that began to work with such traditional adversaries as the World Business Council for Sustainable Development. It also reflected a movement of social responsibility within businesses, as expressed in their goals. It also, however, represented a point of concern, as some NGOs viewed such partnerships as mechanisms for government to merely absolve itself from various responsibilities it might face regarding environmental matters.

11.7 Implications for NGOs

While the Johannesburg Declaration established a set of goals and principles for continued activity related to sustainable development, the most direct impact on NGOs of the WSSD was the framework established by the Type II partnerships. This added to the initial legitimization process framed by organizations engaged in these structures.

For NGOs the perspective of WSSD was mixed. On the one hand, NGOs had to face the reality that they had gone into the conference with no clear central message. However, the framework established by the Type II partnerships provided NGOs with a framework for some activity, which they otherwise lacked. Type II partnerships also provided a means for NGOs to engage in mechanisms of involvement in communities.

Overall, the Johannesburg Summit did not enable NGOs to depart with a sense of overarching accomplishment, particularly in comparison to earlier summits, such as Rio and even Stockholm. In particular, the ability of NGOs to leverage a strong agenda was minimal in comparison to what NGOs were able to achieve in earlier summits. The failures of the Johannesburg Summit, particularly in relation to the roles of NGOs in the larger environmental discourse, provided, however, a framework for some of the more prescriptive adaptations and issues related to environmental activities that we will now explore.

11.8 Prescriptive Thoughts

Having provided a historical, descriptive framework for exploring the development and evolution of NGO involvement vis-à-vis environmental issues, particularly in relation to the involvement of strategies in relation to the evolving UN environmental conferences, we now turn to prescriptive frameworks for developing the sector.

Let us begin with an assertion that we are now at a critical juncture in both the development of the scope of roles of NGOs and the development of the scope of the activities of these organizations vis-à-vis environmental issues. In the mid 1990s the recognition of the roles of NGOs led to arguments by observers of this revolution of NGOs, such as Salamon and Matthews. However, as they and others examining the growth of the sector projected, the 1990s was a time devoted to understanding the further growth of the sector.

The confusion of the roles of NGOs at WSSD and the reemergence of models of business activity that has social grounding vis-à-vis the environment suggests that with WSSD, new models of NGOs as partners, not drivers of social change, may be emerging. It is in such a context that we offer our prescriptions.

First, the growth of an infrastructure for NGOs as they relate to the environment calls for several shifts in addressing the evolution and growth of the sector. We have witnessed rapid sectoral growth in multiple areas of activity. So, there are issues related to enhancing the infrastructure faced within these organizations and the networks of the organizations.

Second, there are issues related to the longer-term sustainability of such organizations as those in the nongovernmental sector. On the one hand, government and intragovernmental agencies have increasingly touted the power of NGOs. However, with an articulation of the value of the sector comes a series of questions on the degree of government support to the nongovernmental sector for the provision of services the government expects. In the 1980s, Salamon and Abramson [11] explored the roles and expectations placed on the sector. Ultimately, they argued that various expectations that government had of the sector were unmatched by actual fiscal support of the sector, particularly as devolutionary models of interaction among federal government, local government, and nonprofit organizations advanced. Such elements are vital considerations as the sector is increasingly viewed as the implementer of services for societies and one questions whether the government supports the NGO service deliverers at the rate expected for service delivery.

Third, are matters of institutionalization. If the trend continues, NGOs will continue to have significant roles to play in the development and implementation of environmental agendas. Their ability to implement such agendas will be dependent on the strength of each individual institution and networks between the various institutions. In the case of the evolution of NGO processes, the progress depicted partially through the UN system can be viewed as a process that paralleled mechanisms by which NGOs and their roles in the wider discourse were institutionalized. In reviewing the history of the past 20 years, we can see the development of UNEP and other intragovernmental institutions and raise certain questions: How might these play a role in advancing environmental agendas? What additional institutions are needed, and what agencies should assume a role in shaping them? Fukuyama [12] argues that institutional creation is one of the goals and strategies for administration today. The notion of institutional creation for environmental activity that emerged in Stockholm, as well as the other conferences, draws questions of institutional models that might emerge.

Fourth are matters related to national-level enabling factors for the development and response to environmental issues. Nongovernmental organizations can serve as partners and advocates for environmental issues. As partners, NGOs can function as the catalysts for the implementation of agendas that the state, for a number of reasons, might be hesitant to implement. In such a case, enabling strategies would entail ensuring the appropriate legal framework for the evolution of such entities, and helping to ensure an adequate financial infrastructure. As many nations in Central and Eastern Europe made transitions in the late 1980s, the emergence of a legal framework for nongovernmental institutions became a core element under the transitional processes. If not for an early focus on a legal enabling framework, many such institutions would not have come into existence and would not have been able to begin advancing environmental agendas.

It should be noted that developing NGOs' infrastructure and, ultimately, increasing their capacity to address concerns regarding the environment does not imply that government should be absolved of responsibility vis-à-vis environmental issues. This leads to an important set of discussions for continued NGO roles vis-à-vis environmental issues in order to make sure that the state is held to a degree of accountability for future actions. One concern that has emerged recently, particularly in the case of Type II partnerships, relates to how much are NGOs ultimately relieving the state of its responsibilities by engaging in problems such as those of the environment.

Fifth are areas concerning partnerships with business concerns. The Type II partnership that emerged from the Johannesburg conference provided a mechanism for such models to emerge, and provided a framework for intra-governmental support of such efforts. Business has begun to frame value propositions for involvement in environmental affairs, particularly over the past several years. Over time, such models of partnership have had potential impact on sectoral evolution and growth.

11.9 Conclusion

The global environmental movement has paralleled a changing level of legitimization of organizations working in the nongovernmental sector. From the late 1960s to the present, we have experienced a greater degree of engagement in several environmental issues and matters. The same time period has also witnessed an explosion of organizations working in the third or nongovernmental sector.

The activity related to the three UN summits examined provide a framework for examining the growing patterns and processes related to legitimacy vis-à-vis the nongovernmental sector. The Stockholm Summit occurred at a time when governmental actors were viewed as the most legitimate in terms of institutions positioned to respond to the needs of a society, including environmental issues within their society. Rio saw the emergence of NGOs as vital actors. Both at Rio and the years immediately following Rio, NGOs played vital roles in advancing the agendas in environmental as well as other areas.

Johannesburg occurred when the general environment facing NGOs that was prevalent during the 1990s had begun to shift. Whereas we realized in the early 1970s that government could not do it all by itself, and by the 1990s we had a discourse on action for engaging NGOs, we had begun to recognize by early

2000 there might be a route to engage business in partnerships with NGOs by the time of the Johannesburg conference.

The evolution of the discourse on the role of NGOs vis-à-vis the state, in particular in the "post-state" era, is evolving. As we have noted, some have argued that the emergence of NGOs in such an era, has led to the exploration of them as the institutions that might fill in several of the voids in addressing concerns of the environment as well as other needs facing the world in the future.

References

1. Salamon, L., The rise of the nonprofit sector, *Foreign Affairs*, 73, 4, 1994.
2. Matthews, J.T., Power shift, *Foreign Affairs*, 76, 50, 1997.
3. Cooper, A.F., *Tests of Global Governance*, United Nations University Press, Tokyo, 2004.
4. Kennan, G.F., To prevent a world wasteland, *Foreign Affairs*, 48, 401, 1970.
5. Rogers, A., *Taking Action: An Environmental Guide for You and Your Community*, UNEP, Nairobi, Kenya, 1995.
6. Johannesburg Summit, Agenda 21, 2002a., /http://www.johannesburgsummit.org/html/basic_info/agenda21.html/ (accessed on November, 2005).
7. Johannesburg Summit, UN Conference on Environment and Development/Rio Declaration, 2002b., /http://www.johannesburgsummit.org/html/basic_info/unced.html/ (accessed on November, 2005).
8. UNEP, State of the Environment and the Contribution of the United Nations Environment Programme to Addressing Substantive Environmental Challenges, 2004a., /http://www.unep.org/GC/GC23/documents/GC23-3-Add4.pdf (Nairobi)/ (accessed on November 2005).
9. UNEP, UNEP's Mandate and Civil Society Engagement, Global Civil Society Forum, 2004b., /http://www.unep.org/PDF/Natural_Allies_en/Natural_Allies_chapter1_eng.pdf./ (accessed on October 2005).
10. UNEP, Engaging Civil Society Engagement in the Work of the United Nations Environment Programme Strategy Paper: Division of Policy Development and Law, 2002. /http://www.unep.org/DPDL/civil_society/PDF_docs/Enhancing_Civil_Society_Engagement_In_UNEP.pdf/ (accessed on November 2005).
11. Abramson, A. and Salamon, L., *The Nonprofit Sector and the New Federal Budget*, The Urban Institute Press, Washington, DC, 1986.
12. Fukuyama, F., Why is there no science of public administration?, *Journal of International Affairs*, 58, 189, 2004.

Chapter 12

Global Academia: the State of Environmental Learning and Awareness

Brent S. Steel and Rebecca L. Warner
Oregon State University

12.1   Introduction

In his recent book, *Collapse: How Societies Choose to Fail or Succeed*, Jared Diamond poses the following question in the context of Australia's contemporary environmental problems [1]:

> On the one hand, the development of environmental problems in Australia, as in the whole world, is accelerating exponentially. On the other hand, development of public concern…is accelerating exponentially. Which horse will win the race?

Implicit in this quote is the notion that the expansion of knowledge and thus awareness of environmental issues may well lead people and policy-makers to pursue more sustainable types of behaviors and policies that will leave a smaller ecological footprint on the earth. Environmental education (EE) is almost universally seen as an important component of an effective policy framework for protecting and managing the world's natural resources and environment [2]. Some even suggest that we evaluate environmental and ecological research in terms of its capacity to shape the behaviors of the public and the decisions of policymakers [3].

Social scientists have long argued that knowledge "is essential if citizens are to discern their real interests and take effective advantage of the civic opportunities afforded them" [4]. They see a direct link between knowledge and behavior, with people who have higher levels of policy relevant knowledge being more likely to engage in behaviors consistent with that knowledge. While there is a substantial body of empirical literature identifying the link between environmental knowledge and pro-environmental attitudes [5–7], many argue that simply raising environmental awareness is insufficient to bring about change. Therefore, EE must also directly promote the need for personal and societal environmentally responsible behavior [8–10].

Because the entire human species shares a single, interconnected ecosystem, finding acceptable solutions for environmental and natural resource education and awareness efforts require a cross-cultural, multi-national and comparative perspective. As Sheldon Kamieniecki observes, "Regardless of where people reside, nearly everyone has experienced threats to the environment and his or her health. Often, these problems are transnational and require binational or even multinational cooperation to solve them" [11]. Therefore, this chapter employs an international and comparative approach—as opposed to an exclusively North American outlook—on contemporary national and international EE and awareness efforts.

However, while we understand that many environmental problems and their solutions are transnational, the United Nations (UN) Environment Programme suggests that how individual nations reach this awareness and develop concern for the environment will be influenced by other, more specific, development priorities [12]. It is not uncommon for developing nations to place greater emphasis on issues such as basic nutrition, disease, shelter needs, and clean drinking water.

Because these more immediate survival and infrastructure concerns are of such priority concern, government officials and public agencies in these countries may not accord much weight to environmental and natural resource issues in the course of their development work [11].

Therefore, different approaches to EE and awareness may be warranted. This is not to say that efforts for EE and awareness are not warranted in the advanced industrial countries. However, the more affluent countries tend to have addressed many of the foregoing problems rather well, and therefore place emphasis on health and well-being, protection of natural resources, and ozone destruction [12]. We also see an increased concern among many of these nations for biodiversity and endangered species. In addition, postindustrial societies have become increasingly concerned about environmental conditions in the developing world. According to Uday Desai, this growing concern is due in part to the realization that lifestyles in advanced industrial countries are affected by the environmental degradation taking place in the developing world. Desai also suggests that another reason for this concern is "the heightened recognition that the earth's natural resources are finite and that the existence of modern industrial societies depends on the continuing availability of these resources" [13].

In addition to addressing EE and awareness issues in developing and advanced industrial countries, it is important to examine the rather unique political and socio-economic situation present in the post-Communist nations. The state of the environment in the former Soviet Union and Communist Eastern/Central Europe was horrendous and helped lead to the collapse of the empire. As Barbara Jancar-Webster has stated: "The principal issue that became symbolic of the arbitrary and dictatorial nature of the Communist system was the environment. In every East European country and in republics of the Soviet Union the population rallied to demand the end of the regime which had brought them to the brink of environmental catastrophe" [14].

After the collapse of the Soviet Union, many observers and academics predicted better environmental conditions due to the demise of political and economic centralization and the growth of markets, which would encourage the more efficient use and allocation of natural resources. However, in reality the collapse of Soviet Communism "left behind a legacy of ecological destruction and declining health conditions in all the territories of the former Soviet Union" [15]. Given the poor economic and social conditions facing many post-Communist countries, not to mention continuing political instability and a relatively recent understanding of how to educate people about the relationship between society and nature [16], there is a patent danger of continued environmental destruction.

Again, we point out these regional variations as they reinforce the idea that a one-size-fits-all approach to increasing environmental knowledge and aware-ness will not be effective. A more informed strategy should include both a transnational as well as area-specific components in its design.

This chapter will examine these and other issues. We begin with a review of literature on why EE and awareness is considered important for adopting more sustainable behaviors and policies. Next, we turn our attention to the current state of global environmental awareness. Finally, we present various approaches that have been suggested to increase global environmental awareness and education in developing, post-Communist, and postindustrial countries. We conclude the chapter with a discussion of future prospects and trends concerning the state of global environmental learning.

12.2   Why is Environmental Learning Important?

In December 2002, the UN General Assembly adopted Resolution 57/254, establishing the UN Decade of Education for Sustainable Development (ESD), and designated UNESCO as the lead agency for the promotion of ESD. The purpose of ESD is to rally people, organizations, and governments to shift their thinking and behavior toward more sustainable lifestyles [17]. According to UNESCO [18]:

> ...education is the primary agent of transformation towards sustainable development, increasing people's capacities to transform their visions for society into reality...The international community now strongly believes that we need to foster—through education—the values, behavior and lifestyles required for a sustainable future.

Other recent reports by commissions examining the status of the world's oceans have come to the same conclusion. On April 20, 2004, the U.S. Commission on Oceans Policy issued a report detailing the deteriorating condition of the nation's coastal waters [19]. The Commission's report, along with the recently released Pew Oceans Commission report, *America's Living Oceans: Charting a Course for Sea Change* [20], argues for new approaches and actions to mitigate and correct these deteriorating conditions. First, these reports call for a new level of ocean literacy among the public that includes an understanding of how people are connected to the marine environment [20]. In order for people to become literate, it is imperative that they receive scientific information about ecosystems that is readily understood. It is assumed that once people gain this new appreciation for how they are connected to our fragile ecosystem, their interest will lead to greater involvement in sustainable activities and behaviors. It will take both interest and engagement to make progress on environmental protection and sustainable development [21].

Almost all governmental environmental agencies and ministries in the world, where they exist, have endorsed the need for public EE efforts. For example, the U.S. Environmental Protection Agency states [22]:

> Environmental education increases public awareness and knowledge of environmental issues and challenges. Through EE, people gain an understanding of how their individual actions affect the environment, acquire skills that they can use to weigh various sides of issues, and become better equipped to make informed decisions.

A more informed public can also play a vital role in helping governments design and implement effective environmental policies [5,23–25]. However, the critical gap between the need for policy-relevant knowledge and the generally poor level of public understanding of many public policy issues has led some commentators to proclaim the existence of a "legitimacy crisis" [26]. As Mondak points out,"…popular input into government will be vacuous if citizens fail to…comprehend the intricacies of policy debates" [27]. Therefore, EE can serve to inform the public and invite a more sophisticated conversation between the public and their government.

Because of this general consensus that knowledge is central to the policy-making process, many argue that improving the knowledge base of citizens should be the first step in establishing international efforts to protect the environment in developing, post-Communist and postindustrial countries alike. Eagly and Kulesa have argued, "…communications directed to the general public are important not only because they may influence public opinion, and therefore have an impact on public policy, but also because they are potentially effective in inducing individuals to engage in behavior that can lessen the destructive impact of humans on the environment" [28]. The lack of knowledge is often identified as a major reason for public non-involvement in environmental activities [29].

In summary, scholars and policymakers alike believe that increasing environmental knowledge through education will provide extensive contributions to sustainable development and a clean environment. It has also been argued that there will be a greater need for a scientifically literate workforce due to advances in technology requiring new skills and the ability to process and conceptualize new types of information [30]. However, there are various barriers to increasing environmental awareness that we should examine first before discussing the realm of approaches that can be used in developing, post-Communist and postindustrial countries alike.

12.2.1 Correlates and Sources of Environmental Knowledge and Awareness

As we have discussed, there is consensus among social and natural scientists, along with many policy makers, that knowledge enhances the ability of individuals to recognize and act on their values and self-interest—especially concerning environmental issues. Contemporary research concerning the distribution of public knowledge in various areas of public policy, however, has documented a "knowledge gap" that separates persons of lower and higher socioeconomic status (SES) [4,5]. Lower SES individuals typically have significantly lower levels of policy relevant knowledge when compared to those of higher SES [31,32]. And as Tichenor, Donohue and Olien argue, "...the infusion of mass media information into a social system increases, segments of the population with higher SES tend to acquire this information at a faster rate than lower status segments, so that the gap in knowledge between these segments tends to increase rather than decrease" [33]. Of course, citizens in the developing countries are relatively disadvantaged as poverty, lack of access to modern communication networks, and inadequate or non-existent formal educational institutions result in less access to scientifically-based environmental information [30].

Two theories have been proposed to explain the knowledge gap separating higher and lower SES citizens. The first theory focuses on "trans-situational" conditions associated with lower SES status, such as level of formal education, income, and occupation [34]. All three of these factors strongly correlate with environmental knowledge holding in the United States, Canada, Japan, and Russia [5,35,36]. Gender and age also have been found to be important correlates of knowledge, with youth and women exhibiting lower levels of policy relevant knowledge when compared to older cohorts and men [7,37]. However, recent research suggests that the gender gap in scientific and environmental knowledge may be declining among younger cohorts due to increased participation of women in higher education in postindustrial countries [6,10].

If low levels of knowledge concerning the environment is a product of trans-situational factors alone, the prospects for increasing knowledge levels with public information and media campaigns may be limited due to the relatively static nature of these factors [35]. However, if low levels of knowledge can be explained by a second theory of "situation-specific" factors, there is more hope that educational efforts may be successful. This second theory suggests that even when controlling for SES characteristics, situational indicators will exhibit independent effects on knowledge holding [36].

Situational factors are motivational in character in that their presence leads to the acquisition of information by citizens irrespective of their SES characteristics. According to this approach, knowledge-seeking and knowledge-holding is highest among individuals who see a particular stake in policy outcomes [7], among those who are strongly committed to their policy views [5], and among those who discuss such issues frequently [35]. For example, one might expect higher levels of knowledge concerning environmental issues among those individuals who are economically and culturally dependent on natural resources, such as forests, rivers, grasslands, the ocean, etc. [6]. Certainly this has been an argument by those who propose integrating "indigenous" knowledge into scientific or "Western" forms of knowledge [38,39].

Many in the last decade, including the UN and the World Bank, have considered indigenous knowledge, based on local grassroots experience, an important component of sustainable development. Dei has defined indigenous knowledge as resulting from "...direct experience of the workings of nature and its relationship with the social world" [40]. And as Warren has argued in a report for the World Bank: "Indigenous knowledge is an important resource that can facilitate the development process in cost-effective, participatory, and sustainable ways" [41]. More inclusive decision-making encourages greater buy-in by members of local communities and therefore encourages longer-term success of environmental programs.

Certainly indigenous forms of environmental knowledge resulting from situational experiences should be considered as an important factor in raising awareness and insight into environmental policy problems [39,42]. At the same time, there is widespread concern among the World Bank, the UN, and many academics that the developing world, while potentially rich in indigenous knowledge, is being left far behind in terms of ecological science literacy. Reasons for this include trans-situational factors such as poverty, lack of educational opportunities, lack of research and outreach funds [12,30], and even lack of concern among scientists, researchers and policymakers in the postindustrial countries [43]. The general consensus is that environmentally responsible and sustainable development "depends on the production of a scientifically literate populace capable of using their knowledge to improve the quality of daily life" [30].

12.2.1.1 Information Sources

Another important factor to consider in addition to the trans-situational and situation-specific correlates of environmental policy-relevant knowledge is how information reaches the public. Previous research in postindustrial countries has shown that citizens use many sources of policy-relevant information, and that the scope of sources tapped is dependent on a number of characteristics of individuals [36,44]. These include personal (e.g., education), cognitive (e.g., information base), and affective (e.g., ideological orientation) attributes of individuals and the substantive content of the particular policy area [5,45].

According to Brians and Wattenberg, "...the mass media are widely recognized as providing the primary sources of political information for most citizens" in the postindustrial countries and increasingly in many developing countries [46]. Television has been identified as the most used source for information—especially environmental information—even though most citizens and social scientists question the reliability of information provided [5,6]. While some researchers have found a negative correlation between television use and levels of environmental knowledge in Canada and the United States [6,45], others have found little relationship between watching national news programs and amount of knowledge in a variety of domains [37]. Reading newspapers, however, is positively correlated with levels of policy-relevant knowledge concerning the environment. This finding is consistent with most other research showing a positive relationship between newspaper readership and knowledge holding in general [37,46]. Of course, in many developing countries where literacy is very low, the availability and impact of newspapers would be negligible.

Additional information sources where people can learn about environmental issues include the Internet and radio. Concerning the Internet and its impact on knowledge holding, the results are mixed. The range of possible information sites is enormous; however, the quality of sites is varied at best [47]. While some Internet sites are highly informative and useful sources of policy-relevant information, others are unreliable [48,49]. Norris and Jones [50] argue that when the Internet is used for information and communication, it can have a very beneficial impact on citizens' roles in public affairs, whereas when it is used for entertainment and recreation, it may actually erode citizen participation in public affairs, much like television. Therefore, it would appear that the Internet is rather like all other information sources—it can either inform or misinform users. Because there are excellent sources of information on the Internet, however, it has been advocated as a potentially important source of such information for the developing world, especially when used in formal educational settings [2,51]. For example, the 1998 UNESCO World Education Report [52] states that the new technologies, particularly those providing access to the Internet and the World Wide Web, can transform traditional schooling and, consequently, be an important source of learning concerning the environment and sustainable development. However, the report also emphasizes the danger of a widening gap in access to the Internet between "information rich" postindustrial countries and the "information poor" developing countries.

As with the Internet, radio can be used for a diverse set of purposes ranging from the transmission of educational programming, such as that often featured on National Public Radio in the United States or the British Broadcasting Corporation in Europe and other parts of the world, to the airing of various "talk shows" catering to ideologues. Lee and Cappella have found when a radio audience is "exposed to an intense, one-sided message, their agreement with the positions advocated increases as exposure and reception increase" [53]. They also found that the public typically selects radio programs that are consistent with their own partisan predispositions, which then reinforces their existing political attitudes and beliefs. Research reported by Steger et al. [45] found that radio use is positively correlated with environmental knowledge in Canada, but in the American context it had a negative impact on knowledge holding. Research conducted by Delli Carpini and Keeter [4] found that radio use has a slightly positive effect on general political knowledge. Therefore, as with the Internet, the capacity of radio to increase knowledge concerning the environment is mixed.

12.2.1.2 Formal Environmental Education

One of the most important sources of environmental awareness and knowledge in the developing, post-Communist, and postindustrial worlds are formal educational systems—primarily for youth but often for adults as well [54,55]. As Bregman and Fisker state [2]:

> The education system can be an effective partner in promoting environmental awareness. School systems can teach students about the interactions between society and the environment, fostering an understanding of our dependence on the natural world.

While the influence "of EE is certainly not as dominant or successful as it ought to be" [54], most agree that the goal of including environmental awareness programs in formal education is a worthy one. In the United States alone, 30 of the 50 states now require EE in their public secondary schools [56]. It should be noted, though, that there are potentially enormous problems with such an approach in many developing and some post-Communist countries due to constrained budgets, poor infrastructure, and the general lack of trained teachers and appropriate curriculum [57].

12.3 State of Global Environmental Awareness

Just what is the extent of global environmental awareness? What level of EE is needed in developing, post-Communist and postindustrial countries? To begin this discussion of the extent of environmental awareness and knowledge in the world, there are those who argue from a "world society" or "world polity" perspective that environmental concern and action is a worldwide phenomenon with almost all nations and people embracing the need for environmental protection [58]. These observers argue that "contrary to the view that nation-states are autonomous actors shaped by internal preferences and interests…nation states are enactors of wider world cultural institutions" [59]. Therefore, implicit in this perspective is the notion that global environmental awareness and knowledge is widespread across different cultures, regions and levels of development. However, there are many social scientists who strongly disagree with this perspective and argue that there are distinct differences between countries—especially between the poorer developing and wealthy postindustrial countries [11,60]. For example, Frederick Buttel argues that many environmental policies in developing countries "have been imposed on developing countries against their will" and therefore are not properly implemented and do not reflect an environmentally informed and knowledgeable public and elite [60]. They also argue from a more common sense perspective, "Those persons who have traveled extensively in developing countries, most of which have planning ministries, will attest that there is uneven, and often minimal, development planning" in terms of protecting the environment [60].

Also contrary to the world society perspective, most academics have argued that the shift from an agricultural to an industrial society has been accompanied virtually everywhere in the world by a greater concern and awareness of environmental issues due to changing values, access to modern information technologies, and increasing levels of education and affluence [34,61–63]. This trend toward enhanced environmental awareness appears to be most prominent in the affluent postindustrial nations, although its presence can be seen worldwide in the thousands of environmentalist non-governmental organizations (NGOs) active in the former Communist countries and in the developing countries. Personal value structures among citizens (particularly younger, more highly educated cohorts) are developing in ways that involve what psychologist Abraham Maslow termed "higher order" needs (e.g., quality of life, connection to transcendent values), supplanting more fundamental subsistence needs (e.g., material acquisition) as the motivation for much individual and societal behavior [62]. Value changes entailing greater attention to post-materialist needs are thought to have brought about changes in many types of personal attitudes and public policy preferences, including those related to the environment [34,61].

Some careful observers of societal change suggest that the development of the environmental movement in virtually all industrialized nations around the world was a direct consequence of the profound social and economic changes that took place in postwar postindustrial societies [64–66]. The development of widespread environmental consciousness and knowledge among the citizenry and the advent of the global environmental movement have resulted in the questioning of many of the traditional political and economic institutions characteristic of modern society [67,68]. In time, these changing social and economic conditions led to an increase in environmental awareness and overall environment knowledge among individuals, groups, and elites.

More consistent with the world society perspective, public opinion research conducted by Riley Dunlap for the Gallup Poll organization in 24 nations suggests that environmental concern may be more global in its reach. While many citizens in postindustrial nations have expressed support for the environment, many citizens of developing nations have also expressed concern about the environment. Surprisingly, Dunlap's Gallup survey indicated that a majority of respondents in *both* developing and postindustrial nations give a higher priority to protecting the environment than to the pursuit of economic growth [69]. These findings led Dunlap and his associates to suggest "...residents of the poorer nations—which often suffer from poor water quality and high levels of urban air pollution—are much more likely to see their health as being negatively affected by environmental problems at the present" [69,70].

In a more comprehensive analysis of global public awareness using the 1990–1993 *World Values Surveys* involving respondents from 43 countries, Ronald Inglehart concludes that while public environmental concern tends to be high in countries that have severe environmental problems (such as high levels of air pollution and water pollution in the developing countries), citizens in the postindustrial countries are much more apt to give high priority to protecting the environment and are much more likely to be active members of environmental groups than citizens in the developing world [63]. Consequently, while objective environmental conditions, such as the presence of polluted air and water, can lead to environmental awareness, changing values resulting from broad socio-economic forces, including access to environmental information and education in the wealthy postindustrial countries, has created the conditions where concern and action is more pronounced. This perspective is consistent with the UN's World Youth Report 2003, which argues [56]:

> A look at the existing state of environmental awareness and education indicates that picture is at first glance positive, at least in the countries of the developed world. In developing countries, the picture is more mixed, though enviornmental education has made some inroads.

The most recent data available concerning world environmental awareness and concern comes from the 1999–2002 *World Values Surveys* and *European Values Surveys*. While these data, like the various studies cited above, do not measure actual environmental knowledge levels, they do provide us with responses to two questions that can reveal general views of environmental awareness or concern. The first question asks respondents to choose between the following two statements as more reflective of their views:

■ Protecting the environment should be given priority, even if it causes slower economic growth and some loss of jobs, or
■ Economic growth and creating jobs should be the top priority, even if the environment suffers to some extent.

The second question asks respondents to choose between one of the following two statements to more accurately reflect their values:

■ Human beings should master nature; or
■ Humans should coexist with nature.

The data presented in Table 12.1 for postindustrial, developing and former/current Communist countries indicate overall majority support for environmental protection as a higher priority when compared to economic growth. As suggested previously, the strongest level of support is found in the postindustrial countries. Results for the second question are presented in Table 12.2. There is strong support among citizens in postindustrial, developing, and former/current Communist countries for *coexisting* with nature in lieu of

Table 12.1   Citizen Orientations Toward Environmental-Economic Tradeoffs: Results from the World Values Surveys: 1999–2002

Question: Here are two statements people sometimes make when discussing the environment and economic growth. Which of them comes closer to your own point of view? (1) Protecting the environment should be given priority, even if it causes slower economic growth and some loss of jobs; (2) Economic growth and creating jobs should be the top priority, even if the environment suffers to some extent.

	Percent Choosing Environmental Protection (%)	*Percent Choosing the Economy (%)*
Postindustrial Nations [*n*=7397 citizens in 20 countries]	62	38
Current and Former Communist Countries [*n*=5246 citizens in 19 countries]	51	49
Developing Nations [*n*=31960 citizens in 23 countries]	52	48

Source: From Inglehart, R. et al. *World Values Surveys and European Values Surveys, 1999–2002* (ICPSR 3975). Inter-university Consortium for Political and Social Research, Ann Arbor, MI. With permission.

Table 12.2   Citizen Views Toward Nature: Results from the World Values Surveys: 1999–2002

Question: For each of the following pairs of statements, please tell me which one comes closer to your own views? Human beings should master nature; or humans should coexist with nature.

	Percent Choosing Humans Should Master Nature (%)	*Percent Choosing Humans Should Coexist with Nature (%)*
Postindustrial Nations [*n*=7397 citizens in 20 countries]	10	90
Current and Former Communist Countries [*n*=5246 citizens in 19 countries]	23	77
Developing Nations [*n*=31 960 citizens in 23 countries]	25	75

Source: From Inglehart, R. et al. *World Values Surveys and European Values Surveys, 1999–2002* (ICPSR 3975). Inter-university Consortium for Political and Social Research, Ann Arbor, MI. With permission.

mastering and controlling it. Again as might be expected, the level of support for coexisting with nature is the highest in postindustrial nations (90%). However, more than 75% of citizens in developing nations and 77% in former/current Communist nations also support this principle. In general, there appears to be widespread concern and awareness concerning the environment, which means there is potentially fertile ground for global EE efforts.

We now turn to actual approaches that have been used in postindustrial, developing and post-Communist countries to increase environmental literacy and awareness. While this will not be a comprehensive review, we will attempt to shed some light on approaches that have been successful from a comparative perspective. As discussed above, different countries have differing resources, cultures, educational systems, and information dissemination infrastructures to provide environmental learning.

12.4   Approaches to Increasing Environmental Awareness

The UN, the World Bank, national governments, various policymakers, and academics have all called for increasing environmental awareness and knowledge through education. It is seen as the cornerstone of any effort at sustainable development in all countries. However, the international contexts within which states must make environmental policy differ widely. Consequently, while there are international and regional environmental treaties to abide by as well as new desired international environmental outcomes (e.g., mitigating climate change), not all EE and outreach efforts are appropriate in all contexts. For example, Asia-Pacific Economic Cooperation (APEC) leaders have concluded that environmental issues in their region are typically and significantly different than those experienced in the postindustrial countries [71]. Consequently, we will address various approaches to environmental learning and education in developing, post-Communist, and postindustrial countries, beginning with a brief discussion of the context for EE in each location. To help frame this discussion we will begin by presenting what most experts consider to be critical elements of EE programs.

Most observers believe that effective EE programs—i.e., those programs that both inform and lead to more environmentally responsible behavior—should include at least four main components [72]. First, they must provide information on ecological concepts such as populations, food chains, carrying capacity, etc. Second, they should bring about conceptual awareness where individuals are made cognizant of the ways individual and group behaviors influence the quality of the environment. Third, effective programs need to provide opportunities for investigating, and then evaluating, solutions for environmental protection. Finally, programs need to offer skills for implementing such solutions. EE experts in both developing and postindustrial countries have argued that sustainable environmental actions tend to increase when people have actually learned and used their investigative and evaluation skills in seeking solutions to real and salient environmental problems—i.e., a "hands on" approach to a salient environmental issue [72].

Efforts to increase environmental knowledge, and thus more responsible environmental behaviors, generally fit into one of two strategies—formal and non-formal [22]. Formal approaches typically take place through elementary and secondary schools, colleges, universities and technical institutes. Non-formal approaches, on the other hand, include a wide array of techniques and delivery methods (magazines, newspapers, Internet, etc.) and can involve NGOs, industry, foundations, etc. Formal and non-formal approaches also can be used simultaneously such as collaborative efforts between local environmental centers and schools.

12.4.1 Developing Countries

Environmental issues compete with many other policy issues for the finite attention of political leaders in all countries. They are increasingly at the center of political debate in postindustrial countries, and many people in these countries tend to be sympathetic to them. However, the salience of these issues to citizens and elites in postindustrial societies often takes a back seat compared to other "bread and butter issues" such as crime, unemployment, inflation, and level of taxation. For example, while the overwhelming majority of Americans would use the term "environmentalist" to describe their own orientation on environmental issues, only a small percentage of these people are inclined to identify environmental issues as the most important problems facing the nation. If the significance of such issues is low compared to other issues, such as crime and the state of the economy in affluent postindustrial nations, how much importance would EE be given in less economically developed nations wherein people face a myriad of economic, social, and political problems? With nearly half of the world's population (approximately 3 billion people in developing countries) living on less than two U.S. dollars a day and one billion unable to read or write, promoting EE in the developing world can be daunting.

Those working on EE programs in developing countries lament the fact that there is very little if any such content in the curricula of school systems, and that formal education is woefully under-funded and often unavailable. This is also the case with non-formal approaches, which are also virtually non-existent in many developing countries. However, the World Bank's report on *Science and Environment Education: Views from Developing Countries* [30] does offer some examples of successful EE programs in developing countries. Many of the programs discussed would agree with Forsyth's [73] argument that both formal and non-formal approaches should follow a "hybridity" approach whereby EE should combine both scientific and indigenous knowledge to make it more salient to the public. Forsyth [73] conducted a pilot project in the Himalayan Mountains to examine problems associated with deforestation. He found that adults learned more when they were given both knowledge from indigenous sources as well as that coming from formal scientific research.

Similarly, Pande [74] describes an effective EE course in India's central Himalayans, which followed a hybrid approach as well. Curricula were developed by teachers and NGO volunteers that were holistic in their approach, and were integrated into either focused short-term and long-term programs, or as part of regular secondary school curriculum. The courses were viewed as very successful because they were participatory and had students actively engaged in environmental experimentation. The program designers also found the use of abstract concepts and computer modeling to be less effective in this context. More "hands on" research in local communities with local issues led to greater success in learning. Similar results have been found in educational research in the country of Lesotho [75].

Another strategy proposed for certain developing counties is a "Young Masters Program" [17]. This is an international EE course that connects students through the Internet to teachers and other students, ages 15–18, in a variety of other countries. Evaluations of the program in Egypt and China have showed positive outcomes in student environmental literacy. Similarly, Berenfeld [51] and Bregman and Fisker [2] argue for the increased use of Internet resources, both in formal and non-formal approaches, because it is cost effective and allows for rapid and broad transmission of environmental information as well as the ability for students to interact with other students, teachers and citizens in other countries.

One major problem with formal approaches in the developing world, according to Ware [30], is that successful EE programs and curricula require major reforms in order to achieve their objectives. In most contemporary developing countries, the teacher is seen as an authority figure basically following an elitist style of top-down teaching. The teacher has all of the answers and the students are considered naïve and passive receivers of information. This approach to education does not do well in preparing "self-directed" learners. As with most successful formal EE programs discussed in the literature, an entirely different approach is required—one that replaces this top down approach with one that utilizes collaborative study groups who engage in "inquiry" based participatory research projects. While the use of top-down "expert" approaches is not unique to developing countries, they are considered a particular problem in EE because future teachers and decision-makers need to be nurtured with the very limited resources available.

In summary, most research concerning developing countries advocate: the inclusion of EE in formal education settings where they exist; the use of the Internet to access environmental information for students, teachers, and NGOs; the use of "hands on" research in local communities with local environmental issues; and, the use of "hybrid" information, which integrates both science and local indigenous knowledge. These multi-faceted strategies target people of all ages and have the potential to make environmental consciousness a priority by connecting scientific knowledge to local contexts.

12.4.2 *Postcommunist Countries*

"No other industrial civilization so systematically and so long poisoned its land, air, and people" [15]. While this assessment of the environmental history of the former Soviet Union by Murray Feshbach is stark, it is nonetheless an accurate picture of what gave rise to the horrible environmental situation that now confronts Russia and other post-Communist countries. During the period of Soviet control, there was no opportunity for citizens or NGOs to oppose or protest environmental degradation and the resulting negative consequences for human health [76]. Citizens were routinely denied access to environmental information about pollution levels and the information that was available was generally limited to highly selective media coverage and propaganda [77].

Environmentalists and environmental NGOs were typically labeled right wing or even counterrevolutionary, or anti-socialist/anti-Communist, because they were considered a threat to the socialist dream by imposing costly demands on the government [78]. Many observers have argued that the application of Marxist–Leninist ideology and its anthropocentric view of the world led to environmental devastation in all Communist countries [79].

The legacy of the Soviet Union is still highly apparent in the values and orientations of many citizens in many post-Communist societies. While citizens tend to express high levels of concern for environmental issues, there has been reluctance on the part of these citizens to participate in efforts to shape environmental policy, to join environmental NGOs, or to participate in environ-mental-oriented political parties [78]. Even NGOs exhibit a basic mistrust toward the political process and have not fully participated in the governmental policy process. This creates enormous problems for EE efforts.

In one of the first and most thorough analyses of EE in the former Communist countries, Boh and Kornhouser [80] found that while most countries had well-organized science education programs in primary, secondary and university schools, there was little specialized information concerning the environment included in the curriculum, and many teachers lacked training in EE. The main obstacle to increasing environmental content in curricula, as well as the training of teachers, is economic. Like developing countries, many post-Communist countries have many social, economic and political problems that compete with environmental needs and education. However, unlike developing countries, the level of literacy is very high and formal educational structures are in place with very high levels of participation. Notwithstanding the financial constraints, Boh and Kornhauser and other contributors to the study do identify several EE programs that work well in these countries. These include the use of mass media to reach all citizens, which has a well-developed infrastructure and level of coverage. They also argue for the use of youth research projects and camps whereby students on with environmental problems with their own hands.

Observers of EE in post-Communist countries typically focus on formal approaches because of the lack of a well-developed civil society with active and vibrant environmental NGOs. For example, in 1995 only 12 Russian Federation universities had environmental science training. By 2003 that number had increased to 129 [16]. And while the economy is still having problems, progress in EE has proceeded through the formal education process. According to Kasimov et al. [16], the most effective curriculum involves the use of issues facing Russia using Russian generated science and information. They argue this helps to make environmental issues more salient and therefore interesting to students. They also advocate for an integrated approach to EE using five levels of schools including pre-school, primary and secondary schools, university undergraduates, graduate programs at universities, and retraining programs for natural resource managers. In conclusion, Kasimov et al. [16] suggest that while EE in Russia still falls short of many postindustrial countries, progress has been made through formal integrated education efforts utilizing specifically Russian science and Russian case studies.

In the few post-Communist countries with developed civil societies, the ability to use non-formal and collaborative formal/non-formal approaches is more readily apparent. For example, Caha [81] argues that successful EE approaches in the Czech Republic involve collaboration among schools, local EE centers, environmental NGOs, and local governments. The use of non-formal approaches and organizations allows for a greater pooling of resources that can significantly improve environmental literacy levels. However, Caha also argues that economic constraints for these approaches hamper the overall effect of such education efforts.

In conclusion, because of the presence and high participation rate in formal education, the availability and broad coverage of mass media, and the high level of literacy, many argue for formal approaches through schools in post-Communist countries. In addition, these formal educational approaches should strive for holistic, integrated approaches that utilize local and country specific issues of interest to students. In those few post-Communist countries with well-developed civil societies, environmental NGOs, local environmental centers, and other relevant organizations can be used in conjunction with the formal education approaches.

12.4.3 Postindustrial Countries

Environmental concerns have played a central role in the political processes of many postindustrial countries in recent decades. Issues such as acid rain, nuclear waste, pollution of all kinds, loss of biodiversity, climate change, and global warming have all found their way to the front pages of newspapers. However, while survey data indicate the increasing presence of environmental concern and awareness among the public in these countries, it remains the case that a culture of consumerism continues to dominate the lives of most citizens. Carl Boggs describes life in postindustrial societies as "an unprecedented resort to personal consumption, which finds ready expression through the countless images circulated in the spheres of advertising, mass media, popular culture, sports and fashion" [82]. According to this view, postindustrial nations are well on their way to ecological catastrophe through an insatiable desire for such material items as electronics, cosmetics, multiple cars, etc. To fulfill all these material wants, huge amounts of natural resources are required and the associated production processes pour pollutants into the environment. Therefore, the key to EE in many postindustrial countries is to move citizens from environmental awareness to more sustainable behaviors consistent with that awareness.

There is an enormous amount of literature on formal and non-formal approaches to EE in postindustrial countries as well as the attitude-behavior quandary. Much of the literature suggests that effective education does not "trickle down" from scientists through textbooks and the media; it must be translated into a format that "our families, neighbors and communities can understand" [8].

In regard to formal approaches to education, Pfirman et al. [83] studied successful environmental programs at 11 liberal arts colleges in the United States and found that they had the following characteristics: programs must be interdisciplinary and involve interdisciplinary research projects; coursework and student research projects should focus on local environmental issues; service learning and internships are required outside of the classroom; and there are opportunities to organize and build campus communities to organize environmental events, etc.

Other successful programs involve sending students or volunteers out in the field—either domestically or internationally—to work on solving environmental problems or assisting in environmental research. Brewer [84] has identified a very successful U.S. college student program in Costa Rica concerning the Sea Turtle Education Program. The program first developed background knowledge in a typical academic setting followed by the development of mini-projects through collaborative research teams. Students then left for their field experience (i.e., combing the beach for leatherback sea turtles) in organized research teams. As with other successful programs in other areas of the world, this project stresses the need to work with local communities in collaborative field research experiences. As Brewer argues: "Thoughtfully constructed programs focused on local conservation issues help participants enjoy and engage in science learning because they can recognize the effects and context of their learning" [84]. In fact, Hancock and others almost universally argue that successful EE programs include: self-directed learning components in the field; multidisciplinary approaches to science; reflection and documentation on the internship learning experience; and collaborative/teamwork based projects [85].

In terms of non-formal education, advocates of "free-choice" (i.e., outside of school) learning view people as "life long" learners who get their information from means such as trips to libraries, museums, aquariums, zoos, reading books, watching certain television programs, the Internet, NGO activities and participation, among other activities. Research by Falk has found that most people participate in free-choice learning typically to satisfy a personal sense of identity or to fulfill personal intellectual and emotional needs [86]. He argues that successful free-choice learning must be engaging and meaningful to citizens and take into account the variety of interests, emotions, and learning capacities of the public. He further argues that the more learning overlaps with specific spheres of life—such as family, work, school, etc.—the more likely it is that people will become successful lifelong environmental learners.

There are literally hundreds, maybe thousands, of successful EE programs we could discuss in postindustrial countries, but there is not space to review them all, and the studies presented above identify some common themes of these programs. They typically involve domestic or international field research or outreach activities, internships, interesting and engaging topics, use of both formal and non-formal sources of information, and making connections between one's personal environmental values and behavior.

12.5   Conclusion

In the beginning of this chapter, we cited a passage from Jared Diamond's recent book *Collapse: How Societies Choose to Fail or Succeed* [1] concerning the massive increase in global environmental awareness at the same time we are facing massive global environmental problems. This poses the question on the utility of environmental awareness and learning if it does not lead to sustainable behaviors and lifestyles. Similarly, the UN World Youth Report 2003 states that [56]:

> Environmental education has grown steadily in recent years. However, questions remain concerning its impact. During the past three decades there has been massive growth in environmental awareness in many countries…but has humanity come any closer to achieving a sustainable society?

As discussed throughout this chapter, EE is seen almost universally as an important component in our quest for a sustainable world. Because everyday citizens and other non-expert stakeholders are either directly or indirectly involved in behaviors that affect the environment, increasing levels of environmental literacy and thus awareness is the first step in changing behaviors and developing support for public policies that promote sustainability. However, as the quote above indicates, EE itself is not sufficient. It must eventually lead to change in behavior and policies.

Even if people and policymakers are provided with the best available scientific knowledge concerning environmental issues, it does not mean that action will follow. While it was once assumed that there was a linear relationship between scientific knowledge and environmental policy—i.e., improved environmental decisions with more and better inputs of scientific knowledge—the actual relationship has been more complicated as science has become "politicized" [87,88]. By the 1990s, scientists were producing enormous amounts of environmental knowledge, discovering and publicizing global warming, atmospheric ozone depletion, declining biodiversity, etc. However, some policymakers, citizens and other interests questioned the validity of this information (primarily for political and economic reasons) and argued that we should wait for "better" science in order to stall action or ignore the problem [88].

Arguably, this could complicate efforts at EE because it raises uncertainty about the content and substance of environmental curricula.

While most of the information and data presented in this chapter indicates that global environmental awareness and concern is relatively widespread across different cultures, regions, and levels of development, there are still many additional challenges as well. In much of the developing world there are problems with both formal and informal EE due to poverty, low levels of literacy, under-developed school systems, lack of trained teachers, limited mass media infra-structure, and generally poor economic conditions. In many post-Communist countries there have been some laudable efforts in the formal education sector.

However, poor economic conditions, political instability in some countries, a lack of trained teachers, and an under-developed civil society sector with few NGOs constrain EE efforts. In the postindustrial countries, there is widespread environmental awareness and very sophisticated and innovative formal and non-formal education efforts in place. However, as discussed above, despite widespread public concern for the environment and enormous efforts at EE in most postindustrial countries, the connection to the adoption of environmen-tally sound behaviors remains weak. While there have been major policy initiatives alleviating many types of pollution and the adoption of many sustainable practices, such as recycling, citizens in the postindustrial world are still the largest consumers of natural resources and energy in the world. Certainly, there needs to be additional EE efforts aimed at narrowing this attitude-behavior gap.

References

1. Diamond, J., *Collapse: How Societies Choose to Fail or Succeed*, Viking, New York, 2005, 416.
2. Bregman, J. and Fisker, M., Environmental education: The millennium challenge, in *Science and Environment Education: The Millennium Challenge*, S. Ware, Ed., The World Bank, Washington, DC, 1999, 235–247.
3. Robertson, D. and Hull, R.B., Beyond biology: Toward a more public ecology for conservation, *Conservation Biology*, 15, 970, 2001.
4. Delli Carpini, M. and Keeter, S., *What Americans Know About Politics and Why it Matters*, Yale University Press, New Haven, CT, 1996, 3.
5. Pierce, J.C., Steger, M.A., Steel, B.S., and Lovrich, N.P., *Citizens, Political Communi-cation, and Interest Groups: Environmental Organizations in Canada and the United States*, Praeger Publishers, New York, 1992.
6. Steel, B.S., Smith, C., Opsommer, L., Curiel, S., and Warner-Steel, R., Public ocean literacy in the United States, *Ocean and Coastal Management*, 48, 97, 2005.
7. Steel, B.S., Soden, D., and Warner, R.L., The impact of knowledge and values on perceptions of environmental risk to the Great Lakes, *Society and Natural Resources*, 3, 331, 1990.
8. Brewer, C., Cultivating conservation literacy: Trickle-down education is not enough, *Conservation Biology*, 15, 1203, 2001.
9. Ballantyne, R. and Packer, J., Promoting environmentally sustainable attitudes and behaviour through free-choice learning experiences: What is the state of the game? *Environmental Education Research*, 11, 281, 2005.

10. Steel, B.S., Thinking globally and acting locally? Environmental attitudes, behavior and activism, *Journal of Environmental Management*, 47, 27, 1996.

11. Kamieniecki, S., *Environmental Politics and Policy in the International Arena*, SUNY Press, Albany, NY, 1993, 3.

12. United Nations Environment Programme, Global environment outlook-1997. United Nations Environment Programme's Report on the Environment, Oxford University Press, New York, 1997.

13. Desai, U., Environment, economic growth, and governance in developing countries, in *Ecological Policy and Politics in Developing Countries: Economic Growth, Democracy, and Environment*, U. Desai, Ed., SUNY Press, Albany, NY, 1998, 1.

14. Jancar-Webster, B., *Environmental Action in Eastern Europe: Responses to Crisis*, M.E. Sharpe, Armonk, NY, 1993, 1.

15. Feshbach, M., *Ecological Disaster: Cleaning up the Hidden Legacy of the Soviet Regime*, The Twentieth Century Fund Press, New York, 1995, 3.

16. Kasimov, N.S., Malkhazova, S.M., and Romanova, E.P., Environmental education for sustainable development in Russia, *Journal of Geography in Higher Education*, 29, 49, 2005.

17. McCormick, K., Muhlhauser, E., Norden, B., Hansson, L., Fong, C., Arnfalk, P., Karlsson, M., and Pigretti, D., Education for sustainable development and the young masters program, *Journal for Cleaner Production*, 13, 1107, 2005.

18. UNESCO, *Education for Sustainable Development* website, Available at: www.gdrc. org/sustdev/un-desd/ (accessed on November 7, 2005).

19. U.S. Commission on Ocean Policy, *Preliminary Report of the U.S. Commission on Ocean Policy Governor's Draft*, Washington, DC, 2004.

20. Pew Oceans Commission. *America's Living Oceans: Charting a Course for Sea Change*, Pew Oceans Commission, Arlington, VA, 2003.

21. Daigle, D., Involving the public in coastal conservation, in *Values at Sea*, D. Dallmeyer, Ed., University of Georgia Press, Athens, GA, 2003, 230–238.

22. U.S. Environmental Protection Agency. *Report Assessing Environmental Education in the United States and the Implementation of the National Environmental Education Act of 1990*, Environmental Protection Agency, Washington, DC, 1996, i.

23. Beierle, T. and Cayford, J., *Democracy in Practice: Public Participation in Environmental Decisions*, Resources for the Future, Washington, DC, 2002.

24. McAvoy, G., *Controlling Technocracy: Citizen Rationality and the NIMBY Syndrome*, Georgetown Press, Washington, DC, 1999.

25. Janicke, M., The political system's capacity for environmental policy, in *National Environmental Policies: A Comparative Study of Capacity-Building*, M. Janicke and H. Weidner, Eds., Springer, New York, 1997.

26. Dahl, R., *Controlling Nuclear Weapons: Democracy Versus Guardianship*, Syracuse University Press, Syracuse, NY, 1985.

27. Mondak, J., Newspapers and political awareness, *American Journal of Political Science*, 39, 513, 1995.

28. Eagly, A. and Kulesa, P., Attitudes, attitude structure and resistance to change implications for persuasion on environmental issues, in *Environmental Ethics and Behavior: The Psychology of Environmental Valuation and Degradation*, M.H. Bazerman, D.M. Messick, A.E. Tenbrunsel, and K.A. Wadebenzoni, Eds., The New Lexington Press, San Francisco, CA, 1997, 122–153.

29. McKenzie-Mohr, D., Nemiroff, L.S., Beers, L., and Desmarais, S., Determinants of responsible environmental behavior, *Journal of Social Issues*, 51, 139, 1995.

30. Ware, S., Ed, *Science and Environment Education: The Millennium Challenge*, The World Bank, Washington, DC, 1999, 1.

31. Gaziano, E. and Gaziano, C., Social control, social change, and the knowledge gap hypothesis, in *Mass Media, Social Control, and Social Change: A Macrosocial*

Perspective, D.P. Demers and K. Viswanath, Eds., Iowa State University Press, Ames, IA, 1999, 117–136.

32. Genova, B.K. and Greenberg, B.S., Interest in the news and the knowledge gap, *Public Opinion Quarterly*, 43, 79, 1979.

33. Tichenor, P.J., Donohue, G., and Olien, C., Mass media flow and differential growth in knowledge, *Public Opinion Quarterly*, 34, 159, 1970.

34. Lovrich, N.P. and Pierce, J.C., Situation-specific and trans-situational factors affecting "knowledge gap" phenomena, *Communication Research*, 11, 415, 1984.

35. Milner, H., *Civic Literacy: How Informed Citizens Make Democracy Work*, University Press of New England, Hanover, NH, 2002.

36. Pierce, J.C., Lovrich, N.P., and Dalton, R., If the truth hurts, consider the source: Public trust of environmental information about nuclear facilities in Russia and the United States, in *Handbook of Global Environmental Policy and Administration*, D.L. Soden and B.S. Steel, Eds., Marcell Dekker, New York, 1999, 433–452.

37. Jamieson, K.H., *Everything You Think You Know About Politics …and Why You're Wrong*, Basic Books, New York, 2000.

38. Agrawal, A., Dismantling the divide between indigenous and scientific knowledge, *Development and Change*, 26, 413, 1995.

39. Martello, M.L., A paradox of virtue?: Other knowledges and environment-development politics, *Global Environmental Politics*, 3, 114, 2001.

40. Dei, G., Sustainable development in the African context: Revisiting some theoretical and methodological issues, *African Development*, 18, 97, 1993.

41. Warren, D.M., Using indigenous knowledge in agricultural development, World Bank Discussion Paper 127, World Bank, Washington, DC, 1991.

42. Brokensha, D., Warren, D., and Werner, O., Eds., *Indigenous Knowledge Systems and Development*, University Press in America, Lanham, MD, 1980.

43. Gibbs, W., Lost science in the third world, *Scientific American*, 273, 92, 1995.

44. Steel, B.S., Lovrich, N.P., and Pierce, J.C., Trust in natural resource information sources and post-materialist values: A comparative study of U.S. and Canadian citizens in the Great Lakes area, *Journal of Environmental Systems*, 22, 123, 1992.

45. Steger, M.A., Pierce, J.C., Steel, B.S., and Lovrich, N.P., Information source reliance and knowledge acquisition: Canadian/U.S. comparisons regarding acid rain, *Western Political Quarterly*, 41, 747, 1988.

46. Brians, C. and Wattenberg, M., Campaign issue knowledge and salience: Comparing reception from TV commercials, TV news, and newspapers, *American Journal of Political Science*, 40, 172, 1996.

47. Uslaner, E., Trust, civic engagement, and the internet, *Political Communication*, 21, 223, 2004.

48. Bimber, B., The internet and political transformation: Populism, community, and accelerated pluralism, *Polity*, 31, 133, 1998.

49. Lupia, A. and Baird, Z., Can web sites change citizens?: Implications of web white and blue 2000, *Political Science and Politics*, 37, 77, 2003.

50. Norris, P. and Jones, P., Virtual democracy, *Harvard International Journal of Press/Politics*, 3, 1, 1998.

51. Berenfeld, B., The internet in our classrooms: Teaching tomorrow's skills for tomorrow's world, in *Science and Environment Education: The Millennium Challenge*, S. Ware, Ed., The World Bank, Washington, DC, 1999, 215–234.

52. UNESCO, *World Education Report: Teachers and Teaching in a Changing World*, Paris, 1998.

53. Lee, G. and Cappella, J., The effects of political talk radio on political attitude formation: Exposure versus knowledge, *Political Communication*, 18, 369, 2001.

54. Palmer, J., *Environmental Education in the 21st Century: Theory, Practice, Progress and Promise*, Routledge, London, 1998, 135.

55. Glasgow, J., Environmental education in the formal system: The training of teachers, in *A Sourcebook for Environmental Education*, W.L. Filho, Z. Murphy, and K. O'Loan, Eds., The Parthenon Publishing Group, London, 1996, 72–91.

56. United Nations, *World Youth Report 2003: The Global Situation of Young People*, United Nations Publications, New York, 2004, 139.

57. Feiter, L. and Ncube, K., Toward a comprehensive strategy for science curriculum reform and teacher development in Southern Africa, in *Science and Environment Education: The Millennium Challenge*, S. Ware, Ed., The World Bank, Washington, DC, 1999, 177–198.

58. Haas, P., Global environmental governance, *Issues in Global Governance, Commission on Global Governance*, Kluwer Law International, London, 1995.

59. Frank, D., Hironaka, A., and Schofer, E., The nation-state and the natural environment over the twentieth century, *American Sociological Review*, 65, 96, 2000.

60. Buttel, F., World society, the nation-state, and environmental protection: Comment on Frank, Hironaka, and Schofer, *American Sociological Review*, 65, 117, 2000.

61. Catton, W. and Dunlap, R., A new ecological paradigm for post-exuberant sociology, *American Behavioral Scientist*, 24, 15, 1980.

62. Inglehart, R., *Modernization and Postmodernization: Cultural, Economic, and Political Change in 43 Societies*, Princeton University Press, Princeton, NJ, 1997.

63. Inglehart, R., Public support for environmental protection: Objective problems and subjective values in 43 societies, *PS: Political Science and Politics*, 28, 57, 1995.

64. Caldwell, L., Globalizing environmentalism: Threshold of a new phase in international relations, in *American Environmentalism*, R. Dunlap and A. Mertig, Eds., Taylor and Francis, Philadelphia, PA, 1992, 63.

65. Milbrath, L., The world is relearning its story about how the world works, in *Environmental Politics and Policy in the International Arena*, S. Kamieniecki, Ed., SUNY Press, Albany, NY, 1993, 21.

66. Van Liere, K. and Dunlap, R., The social bases of environmental concern: A review of hypotheses, explanations and empirical evidence, *Public Opinion Quarterly*, 44, 181, 1980.

67. Habermas, J., New social movements, *Telos*, 49, 33, 1981.

68. Offe, C., New social movements: Challenging the boundaries of institutional politics, *Social Research*, 52, 817, 1985.

69. Dunlap, R., Gallup, G. Jr., and Gallup, A., Of global concern: Results of the health of the planet survey, *Environment*, 35, 6–15, 1993, (see also 33–39).

70. Brechin, S., Objective problems, subjective values, and global environ-mentalism: Evaluating the postmaterialist argument and challenging a new explanation, *Social Science Quarterly*, 80, 793, 1999.

71. Le Grew, D., Links, not boundaries: An Asian-Pacific environmental education network, in *Integrated Environmental Management*, Y., Itakura, J.S. Eades, and F. D'Iltri, Eds., CRC Press, Boca Raton, FL, 1999, 241–252.

72. Hungerford, H., Peyton, R.B., and Wilke, R.J., Goals for curriculum development in environmental education, *Journal of Environmental Education*, 11, 42, 1980.

73. Forsyth, T., Science, myth and knowledge: Testing Himalayan environmental degradation in Thailand, *Geoforum*, 27, 375, 1996.

74. Pande, A., Environmental education in rural central Himalayan schools, *The Journal of Environmental Education*, 32, 47, 2001.

75. Nthunya, E., Environmental issues in the educational system of Lesotho, *Convergence*, 35, 71, 2002.

76. Weidner, H. and Janicke, M., Environmental capacity building in a converging world, in *Capacity Building in National Environmental Policy. A Comparative Study of 17 Countries*, H. Weidner and M. Janicke, Eds., Springer, Berlin, 2002, 409–443.

77. Ziegler, C.E., *Environmental Policy in the USSR*, University of Massachusetts Press, Amherst, MA, 1987.

78. Axelrod, R., Democracy and nuclear power in the Czech Republic, in *The Global Environment: Institutions, Law, and Policy*, N. Vig and R. Axelrod, Eds., CQ Press, Washington, DC, 1999, 279–299.

79. Jehlicka, P. and Kara, J., Ups and downs of Czech environmental awareness and policy: Identifying trends and influences, in *Protecting the Periphery: Environmental Policy in Peripheral Regions of the European Union*, S. Baker, K. Milton, and S. Yearly, Eds., Frank Cass, London, 1994, 153–170.

80. Boh, B. and Kornhauser, A., *Environmental Education in the Central and Eastern European Countries, International Centre for Chemical Studies*, Slovenia, 1992.

81. Caha, M., Understanding environmental issues in central and eastern Europe, REC Paper Series, Number 3, Regional Environmental Center for Central and Eastern Europe, Hungary, 2000.

82. Boggs, C., *The End of Politics: Corporate Power and the Decline of the Public Sphere*, Guilford Press, New York, 2000, 80.

83. Pfirman, S., Hall, S., and Tietenberg, T., Environmental programs: Liberal arts colleges and interdisciplinary education, *Environmental Science and Technology*, 15, 221, 2005.

84. Brewer, C., Outreach and partnership programs for conservation education where endangered species conservation and research occur, *Conservation Biology*, 16, 4, 2002.

85. Hancock, C., Storey, A., Downing, J., and Szewczak, S.M., Interagency resource teams: A model for collaborative approaches to environmental education, *Conservation Biology*, 15, 596, 2001.

86. Falk, J., Free-choice environmental learning: Framing the discussion, *Environmental Education Research*, 11, 265, 2005.

87. Harrison, N. and Bryner, G., in *Toward theory, in Science and Politics in the International Environment*, N. Harrison and G. Bryner, Eds., Rowman and Littlefield, Boulder, CO, 2004, 469–502.

88. Jasanoff, S. and Martello, M.L., Conclusion: Knowledge and governance, in *Earthly Politics: Local and Global in Environmental Governance*, S. Jasanoff and M.L. Martello, Eds., MIT Press, London, 2004, 335–350.

ENVIRONMENTAL MANAGEMENT AND ACCOUNTABILITY

Chapter 13

Government Green Procurement in the U.S.: an Approach to Meeting Global Environmental Challenges

Jerrell D. Coggburn and Dianne Rahm
The University of Texas at San Antonio

13.1 Introduction: Global Environmental Challenges

A number of environmental challenges confront our world. Past are the days when the only worry was how nations might provide clean air and water to their own citizens. Clean air and water remain important matters, but environmental concerns now include such problems as acid precipitation, depletion of the ozone layer, greenhouse gas emissions and global climate change. These problems span national borders (thus defying any single-country solution) and are deeply complex. For several of these problems, acid rain and global climate change in particular, the link to fossil fuel use is well established.

As the volume and scope of environmental problems becomes more generally understood and popularly recognized, a new way of thinking about the world's environmental challenges is emerging. This altered way of thinking is moving away from the practice of use and disposal and toward the notions of reuse, recycling, conservation, and sustainable consumption. The idea of using raw materials for the production of products that are disposed of when no longer wanted is gradually losing support. The newer way of thinking focuses on minimizing environmental impacts by reducing raw material extraction, reducing energy use, increasing recycled content of products, increasing product reuse potential, and eliminating or reducing toxic discharges or side effects.

An obvious fact, but one well worth restating, is that those who consume more have the greatest impact on use and disposal or reuse, recycling, conservation, and sustainable consumption. With the total value of goods and services produced valued at $10.2 trillion in 2001, the U.S. economy is by far the largest in the world. While 72% of that economy operates solely in the private sector, government spending accounts for 28. This simple fact means that U.S. federal, state, and local government spending—for good or for bad—has a huge environmental impact. Reforming the way governments in the U.S. spend money (consume resources) will not, in and of itself, solve the world's environmental challenges. It is, though, a very good place to start.

13.2   The U.S. Environmental Framework

The U.S. environmental movement is most often depicted as beginning in the 1970s. By that decade, the environmental legacy of urbanization and industrialization was widely understood: landfills were jammed with solid waste, many lakes and streams were becoming unable to support aquatic life, the state of the oceans was coming into question, urban air was choked with smog, and the negative impacts of chemicals in prominent use since the 1950s were becoming alarmingly clear. The U.S. public and the press often date the start of the environmental movement with the first Earth Day Celebration of April 1970. In fact, in the decades preceding the first Earth Day, many environmental groups formed and pressed for a change of national policy that would elevate environmental concerns to the highest priority. The decade of the 1970s marked the success of their early efforts and a major transition in the environmental movement [1].

Prior to the 1970s, the federal environmental regulations that did exist were largely limited to voluntary approaches. With the growing concern over environmental degradation that emerged in the 1970s, however, federal regulations became mandatory. In the years that followed the first Earth Day, a series of strong federal laws was passed regulating emissions into the air and discharges to water and land. The U.S. Environmental Protection Agency (EPA) was established and rapidly became the federal government's largest regulatory agency. For its first several decades, EPA's mode of engagement was typified by "end-of-pipe command and control," in that most of the agency's activities involved issuing mandatory regulations and enforcing compliance. Emphasis was placed on setting regulatory limits on the quantity and content of permitted emissions to air and discharges to water or land.

Discontent with command and control regulatory efforts began to emerge by the 1980s. Both opponents and proponents of environmental regulation expressed concern over the lack of effectiveness of such mechanisms. This discontent resulted in a national discussion regarding the use of alternative policy instruments that could move the country toward its policy goals without all the cumbersome aspects of command and control regulation. By the 1990s, the policy debate shifted to focus more closely on pollution reduction efforts. The notion was that a policy constructed to reduce pollution at the source would improve traditional end-of-pipe command and control regulatory approaches by reducing the amounts of pollution that had to be regulated. Finding ways to reduce sources of potential pollutants, rather than regulating them after they were created, became a critical activity [2]. New policy tools emerged to encourage procedures and products that reduced the quantity of potential pollutants. "Green," or environmentally preferred, procurement was one of these new policy tools.

13.3   What is "Green" Procurement?

Before discussing "green" procurement, a brief discussion of procurement itself is in order. Procurement is the activity of government whereby it specified and purchases the goods and services it needs to run the government and to provide for government services. This is a sizeable operation involving local, state, and federal governments. Government can approach procurement and provision of service in two ways. The unit of government can buy the materials it needs from a vendor and then use its own personnel to provide the service, or the unit of government can enter into a contract with a second party provider for the needed service. The second party might be another unit of government, a nonprofit organization, or a for-profit firm that will provide both the materials and the service.

The more than sixty federal government agencies, employing more than 1.7 million civilian workers, acquire most of their goods and services through contracts. For instance, in 2001 the federal government spent more than $235 billion in goods and services contracts or nearly one-quarter of its discretionary resources [3]. State and local governments independently spent another $385 billion for contracted goods and services in 2000 [4,5]. All units of government considered together, therefore, spend more than a half a trillion dollars annually on procurement. The amount of money spent by the government on goods and services has been increasing rapidly. The amount spent in 2001 showed an 11% increase from 5 years earlier [3]. The downsizing of the federal government has been accompanied by an increase in the number of service contracts and an growing number of high-dollar procurement actions [6]. These trends make scrutiny of procurement practices of high importance.

Green procurement generally refers to including "environmentally friendly" practices into government purchasing processes. When governments buy products from vendors or when governments use second party providers to deliver services, adherence to environmentally preferable procurement practices would suggest spending taxpayer dollars in an eco-friendly way. The large government expenditure on goods and services provides a unique policy tool, if government units decide to use their purchasing power to achieve policy ends [7,8]. In the case of green procurement, these policy ends are a cleaner environment. Reaching this goal requires that units of government target their spending so that strong markets are created for products that are recycled, use reduced raw materials, are energy efficient, and are non-toxic. The power of half a trillion purchasing dollars annually can have enormous impact on market creation and strength. The federal, state, and local governments in this country purchase everything from automobiles to zucchini. Governments could use this purchasing power to support a growing green industry sector within the U.S. economy [9]. As this suggests, green procurement holds great promise as a policy tool for creating a cleaner environment.

Purchasing goods and services in a way that does not harm the environment, however, is no easy task. Deciding what precise characteristics a product or service must possess to be considered "environmentally preferable" is a complex activity. Green procurement may refer to the purchase of products that use a lower content of raw or virgin materials in their production. Paper or plastic products, for instance, containing some recycled content would conform to this criterion. Products could also be categorized as environmentally preferable based upon other features such as absence of harmful or toxic chemicals. Biodegradable products, or those shipped using low volumes of packaging materials so that disposal is facilitated, are eco-friendly. Products manufactured, transported, or used with reduced energy requirements are normally considered appropriate for green procurement. Green procurement might also consider a life-cycle assessment (LSA). LSA is a process for evaluating the environmental impacts tied to a product, process, or activity that captures the entire burden placed on the environment, including extracting and processing the raw materials, manufacturing, transport, use, reuse, maintenance, recycling, and final disposition [10]. Energy-efficient items and products that conserve water are usually considered environmentally preferable, as are products that are lead-free, ozone-safe, and those that put off no volatile organic compounds (VOCs). If services are acquired, green procurement considerations might include the commissioning of services from organizations that engage in environmentally sound practices.

Green procurement must also confront the conflict between purchasing green and following other dictates of procurement logic. The two most critical of these are performance and cost. Green products must compete on the basis of performance and cost to be in the running for selection. For the criterion of cost, unfortunately, this is sometimes not the case because of a chicken-or-egg sort of dilemma. Some green products tend to be more expensive because they are not yet widely enough demanded to increase volume and drive down the cost. Another barrier to use may also exist. Even when green products are cost-effective (for example, park benches made from recycled plastic "lumber" that last for 50 years), their initial costs may be high and the payback period on initial investment long.

13.4 Evolution of Green Procurement in Federal Government

The Carter Administration ushered in the green government procurement movement with the passage of the 1976 Resource Conservation and Recovery

Act (RCRA). RCRA mandated that all paper purchased by the government contain 30% recycled content. It took quite a while for agencies to comply with this requirement, but by the end of the Clinton Administration, use of paper with recycled content was widespread [9].

Shortly after coming into office in the early 1990s, the Clinton administration began what would become a series of federal efforts to reform government procurement. Beginning with Executive Order (EO) 12873, entitled *Federal Acquisition, Recycling and Waste Prevention*, the federal government turned its attention to green procurement [11]. Through this executive order, the position of the Federal Environmental Executive was created within the Environmental Protection Agency (EPA). The role of the Federal Environmental Executive is [CaMS1] to encourage improved federal environmental stewardship through the creation of environmental management systems within federal agencies and through the incorporation of environmental concerns in daily operations of federal agencies. To assist the Federal Environmental Executive with responsibilities, four full time staff persons were drawn from the Department of Defense (DOD), General Services Administration (GSA), EPA, and one other agency [CaMS1]. The Federal Environmental Executive's main tasks were to develop a plan to encourage the use of recycled and environmentally preferable products across the federal government, to develop a plan for implementing "an economically efficient federal waste prevention, energy and water efficiency programs, and recycling programs" within each federal agency [11].

EO 12873 instructed agencies to consider a variety of factors before planning for, designing, or acquiring any products or services. These factors include the "elimination of virgin material requirements; use of recovered materials; reuse of product; life cycle cost; recyclability; use of environmentally preferable products; waste prevention…; and ultimate disposal…." [11]. The order instructed agencies to consider these matters for all procurement and in the evaluation of contracts.

EO 12873 extended provisions of Section 6002 of the (RCRA), which required EPA to create guidelines for procuring agencies so that their procurement practices would maximize energy and resource recovery. Section 6002 of RCRA referred to all procurement agencies but restricted purchasing items to those exceeding $10,000. RCRA required that those agencies develop an "affirmative procurement program" (or APP), which was to ensure that items composed of recovered materials were purchased to the maximum extent practicable. RCRA established guidelines for "paper and paper products, vehicular products, construction products, transportation products, park and recreation products, landscaping products, and non-paper office products" [12]. EO 12873 expanded the function of affirmative procurement programs by requiring for all agencies that 100% of purchased products meet or exceed the EPA guidelines for resource recovery. Failing this, the procuring agency was required to provide a written justification that such a product was not available at a competitive price or in a timely fashion. EO 12873 also instructed agencies whenever possible to rely on electronic documents, double-sided printed documents, and use of recycled paper. The executive order also instructed agencies to review and revise federal and military specifications and standards to enhance procurement of products made from environmentally preferable or recovered material [11].

Under EO 12873, agencies were required to report their compliance annually to the Federal Environmental Executive and through that office to the Office of Management and Budget (OMB). To speed the adoption of affirmative procurement programs, EPA was instructed to produce guidance on designated items that are or can be made with recovered materials and what constitutes an environmentally preferable product. Agencies were also required to set goals for waste reduction and procurement of recycled and environmentally preferable products. EO 12873 specified that all future contractors must comply with the order and that current contracts should be modified to allow compliance where feasible [11].

On September 29, 1995 the EPA published *Proposed Guidance on Acquisition of Environmentally Preferable Products and Services* (60 FR 189). This guidance, developed as called for by EO 12873, suggested seven guiding principles:

- Principle #1 (Pollution Prevention): Consideration of environmental preferability should begin early in the acquisition process.
- Principle #2 (Multiple Attributes): Environmental preferability is a function of multiple attributes.
- Principle #3 (Life-cycle Perspective): Environmental preferability should reflect life-cycle considerations to the extent feasible.
- Principle #4 (Magnitude of Impact): Environmental preferability should consider the scale (global versus local) and temporal aspects (reversibility) of the impacts.
- Principle #5 (Local Conditions): Environmental preferability should be tailored to local conditions where appropriate.
- Principle #6 (Competition): Environmental attributes should be important factors in competition among vendors.
- Principle #7 (Product Attribute Claims): Agencies should examine product attribute claims carefully [13].

EPA proposed several pilot programs to test the adequacy of these principles. The first of these was the three-year collaborative effort with the General Services Administration (GSA) to identify environmentally preferable cleaning products. The pilot began before the executive order in 1993, with the goal of identifying cleaning products with reduced human health and safety impacts for use in federal buildings. After the issuance of EO 12873, the pilot was modified to test the guidance issued under the executive order [10].

The cleaning products pilot revealed a great number of complexities associated with selection of environmentally preferable products. One of the issues that emerged was whether EPA should issue a list of products that it approved. The cleaning products pilot showed that an "approved products list" was not always the best way to go about selection, since the importance of specific attributes can vary based upon local circumstance. In the cleaning products pilot, for instance, it became clear that communities with adequate water treatment plants might be more concerned with air emissions from cleaning products, while communities with inadequate water treatment plants might be far more concerned with impacts on water quality from cleaning product use. To accommodate a variety of local priorities, the pilot adopted a compromise approach. Products that met certain threshold levels for lack of toxicity would be identified by a "green dot" on a list of all products. Each product was further described by a product attribute matrix. The matrix allowed assessment of product performance on specific criteria, including skin irritation, bio-concentration properties, air pollution potential, containing fragrance or dyes, reduced/recyclable packaging, and minimization of exposure to concentrated product. The matrix allowed users to pick among features that met their community's needs best, while the "green dot" approach provided for ease of selection [10].

The method eventually adopted and incorporated by GSA in its Commercial Cleaning Supplies catalog incorporates both approaches tested in the pilot. GSA identifies products that meet toxicity and biodegradability standards separately under the heading GSA's Biodegradable Cleaners/Degreasers. Manufacturers of the products provide specific information for the matrix of product attributes. This two-pronged approach allows users to select the product that most effectively meets their needs [10].

In September of 1998, the Clinton Administration again issued an executive order addressing the issue of green procurement. EO 13101, entitled *Greening the Government through Waste Prevention, Recycling, and Federal Acquisition* strengthened and expanded EO 12873. EO 13101 required that each executive agency incorporate recycling and waste prevention into its daily activities. Perhaps one of the more important aspects of this executive order was the recognition of the need to expand the market for recycled products to make them cost-effective. This executive order instructed agencies to create a market for such products by becoming consumers themselves. The order stated:

> It is the national policy to prefer pollution prevention, whenever feasible. Pollution that cannot be prevented should be recycled; pollution that cannot be prevented or recycled should be treated in an environmentally safe manner. Disposal should be employed only as a last resort [14].

All of these activities, however, were premised by the phrase, "Consistent with the demands of efficiency and cost effectiveness" [14] which appears at odds with recognition of market forces at work with recycled products.

EO 13101 established a Steering Committee on Greening the Government through Waste Prevention and Recycling. The committee was to be composed of the Chair of the Council on Environmental Quality (CEQ), the Federal Environmental Executive, and the Administrator of the Office of Federal Procurement Policy. In addition, the executive order required that every federal government agency designate an Agency Environmental Executive (AEE).

Working together, the AEEs and the Federal Environmental Executive were directed to produce a Government-wide Waste Prevention and Recycling Strategic Plan and a biennial report to the president on the actions taken by agencies to comply with the order. The Federal Environmental Executive was also instructed to work in coordination with the Office of Federal Procurement Policy, the EPA, the Department of Agriculture (USDA), and the GSA to convene a group of procurement managers and state and local governmental environmental managers to work with state and local governments to improve state and local procurement practices. EO 13101 directed EPA to issue final guidance to agencies drawn from the earlier proposed guidance [14]. The document was issued in final form in August of 1999.

The final guidance issued took into account several changes in federal purchasing practices put in place between 1995 and 1999. The first was the acquisition streamlining that resulted as a consequence of passage of the National Technology Transfer Act of 1995. That Act required the federal government to utilize industry standards rather than setting separate government standards. The second was the 1997 revisions to the Federal Acquisition Regulations that incorporated policies mandating the acquisition of environmentally preferable and energy efficient products and services. These changes to the Federal Acquisition Regulations put in place requirements to include environmental considerations in all aspects of acquisition planning, market surveying, describing agencies' needs, evaluating and selecting vendors, and contract administration. The acquisition streamlining that resulted from reforms initiated in the 1990s included the decentralization of purchasing. The extension of the use of credit cards by federal agency personnel (from 10,000 in use in 1989 to 250,000 in 1996) made the statement of clear guidance necessary. No longer were central purchasing offices the only ones with the need to understand the requirements of environmentally preferable purchasing [15].

The proposed guidance issued in 1995 was modified largely as a result of the pilot programs initiated to test its soundness. The changes resulted in the merging of several guiding principles and the addition of one. The final guidance includes five rather than seven principles. A new principle on product safety was added and is now the first principle. This was made the first principle in large part because of comments regarding the fact that the proposed guidance did not fully address traditional purchasing factors. Making this the first principle of the guidance clearly indicated EPAs willingness to balance environmental concerns with traditional purchasing values of safety, price, performance, and availability. Other changes were also made. The proposed guidance principles on life cycle and multiple attributes were combined into one principle. The guiding principles on impacts and local conditions were combined into one to remove the perception of any conflict between the two. Finally, the proposed principles on competition and product attributes were combined and revised to emphasize the importance of having relative environmental information. The final guidance principles, issued in 1999, read:

- Principle #1 (Environment + Price + Performance = Environmentally Preferable Purchasing): Environmental Considerations should become part of normal purchasing practice, consistent with such traditional factors as product safety, price, performance, and availability.
- Principle #2 (Pollution Prevention): Consideration of environmental preferability should begin early in the acquisition process and be rooted in the ethic of pollution prevention, which strives to eliminate or reduce up-front, potential risks to human health and the environment.
- Principle #3 (Life-cycle Perspective/Multiple Attributes): A product's of service's environmental preferability is a function of multiple attributes from a life cycle perspective.
- Principle #4 (Comparison of Environmental Impacts): Determining environmental preferability might involve comparing environmental impacts. Federal agencies should consider: the reversibility and geographic scale of the environmental impacts, the degree of difference among competing products or services, and the overriding importance of protecting human health.
- Principle #5 (Environmental Performance Information): Comprehensive, accurate and meaningful information about the environmental performance of products or services is necessary in order to determine environmental preferability [15].

Section 503 of EO 13101 encouraged agencies to establish pilot programs to test and evaluate the principles in EPA's guidance. The executive order required agencies to set up demonstration programs to show how they could incorporate environmentally preferable products into their agencies. Agencies were encouraged to draw on the examples set by prior pilots in developing their demonstration projects. The extensive cleaning products pilot was followed by a series of other pilots. These included a Department of Defense (DOD) pilot to apply green procurement techniques to the letting of parking lot repair and maintenance contracts, an EPA pilot to use green building techniques in the construction of the Ronald Reagan Building and the Research Triangle Park Office Complex, and a DOD pilot using green approaches to the Maintenance of the Pentagon and other DOD facilities [15]. Each of these pilots was useful in providing models for agencies to use in establishing their demonstration programs.

In April of 2000, the Clinton Administration issued EO 13123 emphasizing the importance of reducing the use of energy in the more than 500,000 federal buildings. Energy efficient improvement goals were set by the square foot for federal buildings and agencies were ordered to reduce their energy consumption 30% by 2005 and 35% by 2010. Section 403 of the order encouraged agencies to meet Energy Star criteria where they were cost effective for energy performance and indoor air pollution standards. The order also mandated the use of Energy Star performance ratings for federal buildings. Agencies were required to evaluate their buildings' energy performance and to use the rating to plan building updates and maintenance. The Department of Energy's Federal Energy Management Program (FEMP) was assigned the task of working with agencies to insure their compliance [16].

Late in the Clinton Administration, three additional executive orders were implemented, each dealing with some aspect of green procurement. EO 13148 sought to improve federal government environmental leadership by ensuring that the head of each federal agency was directly responsible for taking all actions necessary to fully integrate environmental accountability within the agency [17]. EO 13149 specifically sought to ensure that federal government leadership act to reduce petroleum consumption [18], while EO 13150 allowed federal workers to exclude from taxable wages funds spent to commute using mass transit [19].

To date, the Bush Administration has issued only one additional executive order regarding environmentally preferable procurement. EO 13221 ordered executive agencies, when purchasing commercially available off-the-shelf products that use external standby power devices, to ensure that these devices use the lowest possible standby power wattage [20].

The Bush administration has continued the use of the Federal Environmental Executive (originally established by President Clinton's executive order), most recently appointing Edwin Pinero to the post. Under Pinero and his predecessors, John Howard (Bush appointee) and Fran McPoland (Clinton appointee), the Office of the Federal Environmental Executive (OFEE) works to promote better environmental stewardship across all agencies in the federal government. In particular, the OFEE coordinates and tracks green procurement, waste reduction, and recycling efforts within the executive branch of government. The OFEE works with the OMB and CEQ to promote environmentally sound procurement practices. The OFEE also works with the Department of Agriculture through the "Buy Bio" program to encourage the use of biomass and other renewable sources.

13.5   Green Procurement in U.S. State and Local Governments

The federal government has not acted alone, nor necessarily as the leader, in environmentally friendly procurement in the U.S. It is actually America's subnational governments that have led the way in green procurement development, thus living up to their reputation as "laboratories of democracy" in policy innovation. Beginning in the late 1980s and early 1990s, subnational governments initiated a number of pioneering efforts in green procurement. These early "pioneers" [5] included, among others, the states of Massachusetts and Minnesota, and the local governments of Santa Monica, California; Seattle, Washington; and King County, Washington.

Among the states, Massachusetts has been a bellwether. Under Governor William Weld in 1993, Massachusetts began an aggressive green procurement program. From its inception, the state's program has focused on purchasing recycled goods. Today, these purchases include recycled paper and office supplies, plastic lumber benches and tables, recycled motor oil, and recycled traffic cones. Massachusetts also owns 37 zero-emission electric vehicles and

87 natural gas vehicles. The state has adopted eco-friendly standards for cleaning projects and acts to reduce the use of pesticides [9]. In 2001 alone, Massachusetts purchased $68 million worth of products with recycled contents [21]. The state also publishes the *Recycled and Environmentally Preferable Products and Services Guide for Commonwealth of Massachusetts State Contracts*. This guide includes information not only about recycled content products but also about low-toxicity cleaning products, energy efficient lighting, bio-based lubricants, and swimming pool ionization systems that reduce chlorine substantially [5]. And, since the state's contracts can be used not only by state agencies, but also by municipalities, schools, public colleges and universities, public hospitals, certain nonprofits, and even other states, Massachusetts makes it relatively easy for many government units to identify and purchase environmentally preferable products.

For its part, Minnesota has emphasized offering environmentally preferable products through the state's central purchasing stores. In 1992, for example, the state offered only 122 recycled content items. By 2001, that number had soared to over 2200 [22]. In March 2001, the state signed its first hazardous waste disposal contract for computers and other electronic components [22]. As for state vehicles, Minnesota has a large fleet (over 600 vehicles) of "flexible fuel vehicles" powered by E85, a clean-burning blend of 85% ethanol and 15% gasoline. The state also has an extensive cooperative purchasing program called the Cooperative Purchasing Venture (CPV). For an annual fee of $350, members of the cooperative can purchase goods and services from the state's contracts. In addition to the cost savings that accrue through contract purchases, cooperative members save time and money by not having to develop their own environmentally preferable product specifications. As of December 2000, 446 public entities are participating in Minnesota's program [23].

Local governments also have been green procurement leaders in the U.S. King County, an early adopter of green procurement, stands as a perfect example. King County began its environmentally preferable purchasing program in 1989. Initially, the program encouraged agencies to buy recycled content goods "whenever practicable." In 1995, the policy was expanded beyond recycled content products to include other environmentally preferable materials and processes [24]. Today, the county's green purchases include not only recycled paper (which accounts for over 97% of the county's paper purchases), but remanufactured toner cartridges, re-refined antifreeze and motor oil (both of which are used by all county fleets, including 1200 buses), plastic lumber, retread tires, and plastic lumber. The county also purchases energy efficient lighting and low-toxicity cleaning products, and has developed a green building program. Altogether, the county estimates that it purchased $4 million in environmentally preferable products in 2002 alone, *saving* over half a million dollars in doing so. Importantly, the savings accrued to the county through green procurement demonstrate that the approach *can* produce savings in both the short term (in initial cost savings) and long term (over the life cycle of the good or product).

Finally, the city of Santa Monica stands as another particularly effective model of local government green procurement. The city council voted in 1994 to make Santa Monica a "sustainable city." The city has replaced toxic cleaning products with safe alternatives and in the process reduced its spending on these products by five% [25]. The city estimates that implementing the safe cleaning products program eliminated approximately 3200 pounds of hazardous products purchased annually. The city has converted 75% of its 500-vehicle fleet to alternative fuels, and it uses recycled motor oil and less toxic antifreeze in those vehicles. Santa Monica is also involved in efforts to change procurement practices themselves by replacing the lowest price purchasing model with one that looks at life cycle costs and factors them into the purchasing equation [9] and by developing pass/fail standards for environmentally preferable cleaning products.

These examples are, of course, only a sampling of government green procurement efforts underway at the subnational level. North Carolina's "Sustainable North Carolina," Vermont's "Clean State," and California's "State Agency Buy Recycled Campaign" are examples of other leading state green procurement initiatives. At the local level, Seattle, Washington, San Diego, California, and more recently Phoenix, Arizona, have each implemented noteworthy green procurement programs [5]. Together, these efforts attest to the diffusion of green procurement as a policy tool for environmental sustainability.

13.6 Adopting and Implementing Green Procurement

13.6.1 Green Procurement Policies: Mandatory versus Voluntary

Given the success of green procurement in a number of government settings and its potential as an effective tool for environmental sustainability, questions naturally arise over how to establish a green procurement program. In practice, green procurement programs fall into two categories, mandatory and voluntary. Mandatory efforts *require* environmentally preferable purchasing. Depending on the level of government involved, a mandatory program may come in the form of a state or federal statute, local ordinance, executive order, or administrative rule. Voluntary efforts, on the other hand, range from individual purchasing agents exercising their discretion to buy green products, to more formal policy directives encouraging—but not requiring—environmentally preferable purchasing. Opinion is split as to which approach is more efficacious. On the one hand, unless green procurement is mandated, those with purchasing authority may not feel that they "have to" purchase green and, therefore, simply will not do so. This would suggest the importance of formally mandated green procurement requirements. On the other hand, some of the most successful green procurement programs are found in governments that have adopted voluntary policies [5].

Whether the program is mandatory or voluntary, governments wishing to pursue environmental sustainability through procurement should adopt a green procurement policy or amend their existing procurement policy to incorporate green language. There are several advantages to adopting a specific green procurement policy, including generating greater momentum for the effort and sending strong signals to government personnel and potential vendors that the jurisdiction is serious about making green procurement a part of its routine administrative practices [26]. Several pioneers mentioned in the previous section (e.g., Minnesota, King County) offer model green procurement policies on their websites. These model policies are meant to serve as general guides to jurisdictions looking to adopt their own green procurement policies. Appendix A presents King County's model policy. As the model policy demonstrates, the central procurement agency (or "lead agency") typically plays a primary role in identifying green products and services, establishing environmentally preferable specifications, educating end-users about green procurement and its benefits, and raising awareness about the green procurement program. On the other hand, the other agencies and departments are integral to implementation, as they are usually responsible for identifying specific opportunities to use environmentally preferable products and making sure that their contracts and purchases incorporate green characteristics. The model policy also shows that the list of available environmentally preferable products and services is long, and it will only grow longer in future years as the market responds to government demand.

13.6.2 *Integrating Green Procurement*

As is the case with all public policies and programs, merely adopting a policy is insufficient for success. Indeed, the success or failure of green procurement is determined by implementation. At the most basic level, successful green procurement—just like any other strategic initiative [27]—requires active commitment from policy leaders, strong advocates, and integration within a jurisdiction's overall management system. Visible support from high-level officials (e.g., city council, city manager, governor, legislators) provides the stamp of legitimacy to green procurement, thus increasing its likelihood of success [25,28]. Similarly, an advocate can serve as an effective champion of the program, thus creating useful momentum and enthusiasm for implementation [5].

Assuming the program has legitimacy and active support, governments can further increase the chances of success for their green procurement efforts by taking steps to align them with broader governmental objectives. For example, in a study of both public and private sector green procurement programs, New, Green and Morton [29] found the most successful effort belonged to a local government that integrated its green procurement program into overall missions regarding environmental protection and economic development. The researchers contend that this integration gave the program a measure of validation because of its association with broader government objectives. While environmental sustainability is certainly an appropriate broad government objective (e.g., Santa Monica's "Sustainable City"), it might be that "improving quality of life" represents an even broader (hence, potentially better) objective for framing green procurement. Since governments have elevated quality of life to the top of their agendas in recent years [30], such an approach could be used to tie green procurement into existing momentum. Regardless, the point is that aligning green procurement with overarching and widely supported objectives can help ensure its success.

An example of an attempt to integrate environment-friendly values into an agency's (as opposed to government's) overarching purpose comes from the city of Seattle, Washington. Specifically, Seattle's Division of Purchasing Services has adopted the following mission and vision statements [31]:

> *Mission*: "The Purchasing Services Division provides departments with quality contracts and tools that incorporate City values, meet departmental needs, support the vendor community, and procure goods and services in a cost effective and timely manner."
> *Vision*: "Purchasing Services has a reputation for excellence both nationally and within the City. We are committed to providing resources and experience to assist departments in successfully meeting their procurement and warehousing needs. We are committed to an enterprise-wide approach to leverage City buying power and to incorporate City values such as sustainability and inclusion of small, women and minority owned businesses. Our commitment to a safe and respectful workplace is shown in high morale and job satisfaction."

As both the mission and vision statements show, the city's purchasing division has made a clear statement that it incorporates the city's values—including environmental sustainability—into its operations. Meeting departmental needs, supporting the vendor community, and achieving cost-effectiveness are important, but so are promoting environmental sustainability and a safe working environment. In other words, these statements send the message to internal (e.g., city employees, purchasing agents, other departments) and external (e.g., vendors, other governments, the public) audiences about the emphasis Purchasing Services places on environmental stewardship: their performance cannot be deemed successful unless it incorporates and achieves environmental objectives.*

13.6.3 Strategies for Green Procurement Implementation

At the operational level, a number of specific strategies exist for implementing green procurement. These strategies include setting price preferences for recycled content and other environmentally preferable products or services, developing environmentally preferable product and service specifications, using "best value" and life cycle cost criteria, setting specific goals for levels of green procurement to be achieved, raising awareness about green procurement through vendor fairs, training, and educational outreach, establishing project-based "green teams," and developing and adopting cooperative purchasing. Each of these strategies will be considered briefly.

---

* It is worth noting that Section 6002 of RCRA and EO 13101 attempt to incorporate environmental concerns into federal agency procurement planning and management by requiring agencies to prepare Affirmative Procurement Plans (APP). The White House Task Force on Recycling has created a model APP that can be downloaded from the Office of the Federal Environmental Executive at: http://www.ofee.gov/eo/app.pdf. (accessed July 16, 2003).

13.6.3.1 Price Preferences

When governments initially created green procurement programs in the early 1990s, the most popular policy approach was to adopt purchasing preferences favoring environmentally preferable products. A typical policy would allow the purchasing agent to select a bidder offering an environmentally preferable product or service, as long as the product or service met the performance requirements announced in the bid specifications and as long as the price was within a certain percentage (e.g., 5, 10, or even 15%) of its non-green counterparts. The rationale behind price preferences was simple: initially, environmentally preferable products were more expensive due to limited suppliers and limited production, so paying a small increment more for these products to meet green procurement objectives made sense [26]. The pervasiveness of this approach was demonstrated in a recent survey by the National Association of State Procurement Officials [32]. NASPO found that 37 of the 43 states (or 86%) responding to the survey had price preference policies in place, with sizes ranging from 5 to 15%.

More recently, cost-conscious observers have begun to consider the unanticipated effects price preferences may have on vendor behavior. Specifically, some question whether vendors' knowledge about the availability of price preferences induces them to offer their environmentally preferable products at inflated prices [33]. As the EPA [5] notes, "Sellers of environmentally preferable products could be very price competitive, theoretically, but might lack any incentive because they can earn more as long as price preferences exist." Given such concerns, governments may find it advantageous to pursue a second green procurement strategy: including specific environmentally preferable language such as "recycled only" requirements in procurement specifications.

13.6.3.2 Green Specifications

Specifications describe the good or service being sought by government (e.g., general product or service descriptions, the number of units needed, the purpose to be served by the product or service) and indicate any standards or requirements that the product or service must meet (e.g., performance characteristics, materials composition, appearance and finishes, etc.). To incorporate environmentally preferable language into procurement policies and specifications, governments need to do two things. First, governments need to review existing contracts and product and service specifications to ensure that green products and services are not precluded. For example, if a government has solicited bids for printing and photocopying paper and specified "virgin paper" in its bid announcement, that would, by definition, exclude recycled content paper. Such language should be removed so as to eliminate barriers to procuring environmentally preferable goods.

Second, governments need to add language to their procurement polices and specifications that encourages vendors to offer environmentally preferable products. Continuing with the paper example, if a government unit wanted to consider recycled content paper and virgin paper, it might specify that virgin and recycled content paper would be considered but that a price preference would be given to bids offering recycled content paper. For reasons mentioned above, however, a better approach might be to include language in the specifications *requiring*, say, "50% recycled content paper." Thus, only bidders offering the environmentally preferable product would be considered. The cost and performance of the virgin paper is immaterial, as the government's procurement need for a recycled product has been clearly specified. This general "make it clear" logic is captured by an official form King County [5]:

> "If the price and performance of low-toxicity cleaning products meets your needs, then the price of the traditional cleaning product is irrelevant. You're not trying to buy a traditional cleaning product. You're trying to buy low toxicity. If you want to buy oranges, it doesn't matter how expensive apples are."

As this suggests, language can easily be included in specifications requiring certain energy-efficiency standards, minimum recycled content requirements, toxic-free materials, or other environmentally preferable characteristics. Detailed guidance on writing environmentally preferable specifications is available from a number of sources. One good example is the state of Minnesota's [34] publication, *The Environmentally Preferable Purchasing Guide*. As shown in Appendix B, the guide recommends several ways to put environmental attributes "in writing."

13.6.3.3 "Best Value" Approach and Life Cycle Analysis

When it comes to evaluating bids, the traditional procurement approach is to award a contract to the "lowest responsible bidder." In other words, the vendor submitting the lowest priced bid that meets stated specifications is awarded the contract. The "best value" approach, in comparison, expands the number of factors considered in evaluating a product or service. For example, a purchaser employing the best value approach might consider the actual performance of a product or service provider (for example, during a required testing phase), the maintenance and operating costs of a product, and the environmental impacts of the good or service over its life cycle. The life cycle analysis aspect has generated particular interest among green procurement proponents. As mentioned earlier, such analyses might include not only the initial acquisition costs but also the costs of extracting the raw materials used in producing the product, the costs of producing a product, the costs associated with packaging and transporting the product, the costs of operating and maintaining the product over its functional lifespan, and the costs of disposing or recycling the product. A traditional product may have a lower upfront cost, but the cost of the good over its full life cycle may be much higher in comparison to an environmentally preferable alternative. When this is the case, government officials have a sound basis for procuring environmentally preferable products. EPA funded an effort by the National Institute of Standards and Technology (NIST) to develop a tool to help governments make life cycle-based decisions. Free software for the NIST's decision-enabling tool, Building for Economic and Environmental Sustainability (or "BEES" for short), is available for free download at the EPA's website (see http://www.epa.gov/oppt/epp/tools/bees.htm; Accessed on July 22, 2003).

13.6.3.4 Setting Green Procurement Goals

A fourth strategy for successful green procurement implementation is adopting annual goals for environmentally preferable purchases.* The goal-setting approach could work with price preferences, green-only specifications, best value analysis, or any other green procurement strategy. That is to say that specific green procurement goals can be articulated and the means to their achievement can vary according to what a particular government's procurement practices and capacity allow. As for the scope of the goals, experience suggests that governments may want to start small with, for example, a recycled content program, then gradually expand environmental preferences to other products and service areas. This focused goal approach was utilized successfully by both Massachusetts and Santa Monica [26]. Finally, green procurement goals are more likely to be met if they are measurable, include clear timetables for attainment, are periodically reviewed, and hold agencies accountable for their performance [28]. An example might be, "The Department of Transportation will increase by 50% its use of recycled content asphalt for road resurfacing projects during the upcoming fiscal year."

Green procurement goals are required at the federal level where agencies must submit specific goals as part of their Affirmative Procurement Plans (APP). The little evidence that exists for other levels of government suggests that governments have not fully embraced the goal setting approach. Specifically, a recent survey by the National Institute of Governmental Purchasing (NIGP) [35] found that only 5.4% of respondents reported that their agencies set green procurement goals for 2000, only 6.0% did so in 2001, and only 6.5% planned to so for 2002. Despite this lackluster evidence, setting goals is a recommended strategy for assuring green procurement success [36,28].

13.6.3.5 Raising Awareness about Green Procurement

Green procurement efforts suffer if end-users and purchasers are unaware of a government's preference for environmentally preferable products and services, or if they are unfamiliar with or misinformed about available green products and services that could meet their procurement needs. To overcome this, governments may pursue efforts to raise awareness of green procurement programs, products, and services and the benefits of "buying green." Two specific examples of this are vendor fairs and training and educational outreach programs. Vendor fairs provide a forum for bringing together vendors of various green products and services and government purchasers. This allows purchasers

---

* A related approach to goal setting is the use of green procurement set-asides. Set-asides require that a certain percentage of a government's purchases be environmentally preferable. For example, a government might adopt a policy that 50% of all paper products purchased annually contain recycled content.

to see firsthand the products and services that are available and provides the opportunity to ask vendors directly about the performance, price, and availability of their products and services. Vendor Fairs have been used successfully by the likes of Santa Monica [25], Kansas City, Portland, and Massachusetts [26].

A second awareness-raising strategy is to offer training and educational outreach to government purchasers and end-users. Such efforts might entail staff from the central procurement agency or an environmental purchasing project team (if such a team exits) educating purchasers and end-users on the availability and benefits of environmentally preferable products and services. It might also include offering technical training to purchasers on how to use existing procurement processes (e.g., state contracts, central supply stores, requests for bids) to purchase green products and services. A good example is the state of Minnesota. The state's Materials Management Division (MMD) offers extensive training on environmental purchasing as a segment of its required state purchasing certification classes. The training focuses on helping purchasers request and review environmental considerations in their bids and proposals. Also, the state's Resource Recovery Office has prepared environmental purchasing information that is included in a purchasing training notebook provided by MMD to all state purchasers. The EPA [26] reports that Connecticut focuses its training on end-users (as opposed to purchasers) in an attempt to create demand for environmentally preferable products. Further, EPA's Environmentally Preferable Purchasing (EPP) program offers a variety of training tools through its web-based module, the EPP Training Tool (see http://www.epa.gov/oppt/tools.html). Generally, these awareness-raising efforts can go a long way toward dispelling misconceptions about the performance and availability of green products and services and can generate momentum for green procurement.

13.6.3.6 "Green Teams"

A team-based approach to green procurement recognizes the benefits of cross-functional teams whose members possess different perspectives and insights about government's purchasing needs and constraints [28]. Ideally, these teams would include purchasers, end-users, staff from the central procurement agency, and individuals with environmental expertise [26]. These so-called "green teams" may be responsible for a variety of tasks, including formulating a green procurement policy, reviewing purchasing practices and tendencies to identify areas where environmentally preferable products could have an impact, formulating green procurement goals, publicizing the green procurement program, and monitoring progress.

One variant of the team-based approach is to organize commodity teams that focus on specific product or service areas. An excellent example of the commodity team approach comes from Seattle. The city's "Copernicus Project" consists of 18 separate commodity teams, including teams for building materials, printing, communication equipment, furniture, hazardous materials, and janitorial supplies, among others [31]. In each instance, the commodity teams seek ways to improve the efficiency and effectiveness of procurement in their respective commodity areas while simultaneously incorporating environmentally preferable benefits. The city's efforts have not gone unnoticed in the professional procurement community: In 2000, the Copernicus Project received the "Best Practices in Public Procurement Award" from NIGP.

13.6.3.7 Cooperative Green Procurement Efforts

The final strategy to be considered here is cooperative green procurement. The cooperative approach applies to the development of green procurement programs and to the actual purchase goods and services. Excellent illustrations of the former are collaborative efforts for developing specifications and standards for environmentally preferable products. Developing these specifications is difficult, time-consuming, and expensive. The costs are multiplied when governments replicate the work of other governments. Cooperative approaches avoid this by bringing together several governments to develop and adopt uniform standards and specifications. In one such effort, Massachusetts, Minnesota, King County, Santa Monica, and several other governments developed a national standard for environmentally friendly cleaning products [37]. In another case, the Coalition of Northeastern Governors' (CONEG) Source Reduction Task Force developed model specifications for six separate compost products [38]. In both of these cases, the goal was to create consensus criteria for environmentally preferably products so as to encourage vendors to invest in and market green products acceptable to a large number of government purchasers.

The second form of cooperative green procurement focuses on purchasing. The strategy, in a nutshell, is for public agencies to combine their purchasing power through a cooperative purchasing arrangement. The benefits of these arrangements include lowering unit costs, lowering administrative costs, increasing the volume of green products and services purchased, and establishing common standards and specifications for vendors to follow [36]. Minnesota's Cooperative Purchasing Venture (CPV) is illustrative. As mentioned above, the CPV allows public entity members to purchase goods and services from the state's contracts. The state estimates that members may be able to enjoy cost savings as high as 75%; plus, members have access to over 2200 environmentally preferable products. And, since the state devised the green product specifications, solicited the bids, and awarded the contracts, CPV members save additional time and resources. Vendors of green products likewise benefit as their products are required to meet only one set of specifications that are nonetheless acceptable to hundreds of public entities. Obviously, cooperative strategies have much to offer green procurement.

13.7   Challenges Facing Green Procurement

As is the case with every government policy, green procurement faces a number of challenges to successful implementation. Given the partisan dynamics that surround any governmental program, green procurement will always face political challenges. In certain political circles, the mere word "green" can conjure up images of environmental extremism. In the case of green procurement, such images would seem to be unwarranted. Indeed, there is some evidence that green procurement has become a bipartisan commitment in the U.S. [39]. Still, some elected officials, and their governments, will be more "environmentally friendly" than others. For example, Santa Monica's high-profile green procurement program hinges in part on a liberal interpretation of the "lowest responsible bidder" clause: the Environmental Programs Division uses the "responsible bidder" language as a gateway to considering environmental criteria. For some time now, the city council has accepted this broad interpretation, but that does not mean it will always be the case [25]. Even where green procurement is explicitly mandated, implementation can be affected by the priorities and enthusiasm of the administration: if an administration places a low priority on green procurement and does not enthusiastically endorse it, then implementation will be uneven at best. The challenge for green procurement proponents is to garner the support of political leaders, which often requires educating them on the benefits of green procurement and the costs—both pecuniary and environmental—of doing nothing. Still, the vagaries of the political system will always have an effect on the success of government green procurement.

Of course politics is not the only challenge to green procurement: A number of practical problems must also be addressed. For example, in the aforementioned NIGP survey [35], respondents were asked to "indicate any challenges/barriers that have limited your efforts in purchasing green goods and/or services." The items indicated most often were inadequate awareness (46.1%), conflicting priorities (44%), decentralization of decision making/purchasing (37.6%), and inadequate guidance (35.5%). Findings like these suggest the importance of raising the awareness of green procurement and its benefits among purchasers and end-users, clarifying the priorities and values to be achieved through public procurement, and dealing effectively with the realities of a decentralized world of administrative decision making.

First, to be successful the practical problems of raising awareness of green procurement and its benefits and correcting misinformation and misconceptions must be addressed. These challenges have not gone unnoticed. The White House Task Force on Recycling, for example, recently identified several common green procurement myths and offered responses that attempted to debunk them [36]:

- Myth #1 (Performance): The first myth is that recycled products are inferior. Most recycled products meet the same technical and quality specifications as their virgin material counterparts and may actually provide superior characteristics.
- Myth #2 (Price): It is untrue that recycled products cost more. At one time, before there were ample numbers of suppliers and products, recycled items may have cost more. Today, however, recycled products such as paper may actually be cheaper than their virgin counterparts. In most cases, recycled products are at least competitively priced.

■ Myth #3 (Availability): The third myth is that recycled products are not readily available. American industry has responded to government and industry demand for recycled products. More and more products are being made available in greater quantities every day.

Importantly, myths like these do not exist solely in the minds of end-users and casual observers. Indeed, green procurement must work to overcome skepticism *within* the public procurement community. For example, NASPO still pejoratively refers to environmentally preferable purchasing policies as one of several "restraints on competition" [28]. Their position on environmentally preferable purchasing and other procurement preferences (e.g., in-state, minority-owned, or small business preferences) aimed at achieving socio-economic goals is clear: "Despite nearly two decades of experience with these programs, there is no substantial body of data to indicate whether their often laudable goals are being met and, thus, worth the cost of government of maintaining them, included losses due to restricted competition" [28].

Debunking myths, ameliorating skepticism, and raising awareness requires constant effort on the part of agencies and green product users to tout the successes they enjoy through their green procurement programs. One obvious approach is to produce and publicize green procurement success stories. Fortunately, there is a growing body of evidence suggesting that green procurement can provide products and services government needs and that it can actually save money in both the short term (through lower product costs, such as with recycled paper) and the long term (through lower life cycle costs). Federal agencies are required by EO 13101 to promote their programs, both internally and externally, so as to spread the word about green procurement's benefits and successes. Strategies mentioned above like vendor fairs and educational outreach also hold promise for raising awareness about green procurement.

Conflicting procurement priorities and values present a second broad challenge to green procurement. In making procurement decisions, policy makers and procurement officials often struggle to balance traditional "procurement goals" (e.g., efficiency, economy, performance, fairness) with "non-procurement goals" (e.g., environmental preferences) [7]. The challenge can be daunting:

> "… [P]urchasing agents are increasingly called upon to balance the dynamic tension between competing socioeconomic objectives, provide a consistence [sic] agency face to suppliers of goods and services, satisfy the requirements of fairness, equity and transparency, and at the same time, maintain an overarching focus on maximizing competition while maintaining economy and efficiency" [8].

Unfortunately, there are no easy answers to this challenge. The appropriate weight afforded environmental factors relative to other procurement factors will depend upon jurisdictions' priorities and political climate. Ideally, procurement officials could show that environmental goals do not necessarily detract from traditional procurement goals. For example, using life cycle cost assessments, it may be possible to show that environmentally preferable products meet government's procurement needs while maximizing economy, especially over the long run. Some help also may be provided in this regard as governments and third-party nonprofits like Green Seal develop product standards and specifications and technical tools that clarify the tradeoffs associated between green and traditional products. Green Seal, for example, has initiated a "Greening Your Government Program" that includes specific recommendations on environmentally preferable products based upon performance criteria and life-cycle costs assessments. Another tool, developed jointly by the White House Task Force on Recycling, the U.S. Postal Service, EPA, and Environmental Defense, is the "Paper Calculator." The calculator allows users to compare the life cycle environmental impacts of paper made with different levels of post-consumer recycled content. The calculator can be accessed at the OFEE's website: http://www.ofee.gov/recycled/calculat.htm. Yet another tool, as mentioned previously, is NIST's "BEES" software for determining life cycle costs of various products. Finally, the EPA has developed several cleaning product "decision wizards" which are designed to help users select environmentally preferable products based upon attributes selected and weighted by the user (see http://www.epa.gov/opptintr/epp/cleaners/select/matrix.htm). When combined with clearer guidance by procurement officials and policy makers on the values to be maximized in procurement decisions, the continued development of decision making tools such as these hold promise for the meeting the challenge of multiple and, at times, conflicting procurement priorities.

The third and perhaps biggest, practical challenge to successful green procurement is associated with public administration's current emphasis on decentralization. Decentralization of decision-making is a defining feature of the so-called "new public management" (NPM) that has spread across the globe over roughly the last 15 years. The challenge is in ensuring that lower-level governmental actors empowered with procurement authority are aware of green procurement policies and the benefits of green products and services. These newly empowered purchasers may not know about existing green procurement programs and obligations and/or they may subscribe to common green procurement myths. Either way, decentralization can potentially undermine green procurement success.

The problems associated with decentralization are exacerbated by other procurement reform efforts that streamline purchasing processes. Recognizing the administrative costs associated with formal procurement processes, many jurisdictions have raised their dollar thresholds for purchases requiring formal bidding. Concomitantly, a growing number of governments have adopted purchasing cards ("p-cards," for short). P-cards are used in much the same way as a credit card, thereby facilitating efficient procurement transactions. When coupled with decentralization, these changes mean that growing numbers of government employees have discretion to make substantial purchases using methods designed to facilitate the purchasing process.

To ensure that this discretion is exercised responsibly and in accordance with green procurement objectives, central procurement agencies, green procurement project teams, and/or green procurement advocates must undertake concerted efforts to educate purchasers. An advisable approach is to require formal training—including training on environmental preferences—for all individuals who have purchasing authority. Governments may also wish to create web-based tools that can be accessed as needed. The EPA, for example, has created a web-based training tool designed to introduce green procurement principles and to teach purchasing agents how to apply them (see http://www. epa.gov/oppt/epp/tools.html). For its part, the OFEE has published specific guidance to federal employees on using p-cards to buy green products (see http://www.ofee.gov/whats/greenprod.pdf). Another approach would be to require purchasers to use the government's central purchasing stores or contracts. If these central sources stock and publicize the availability of green products, then the likelihood that individual purchasers will use them increases. Whatever the specific method, the point is that contemporary administrative approaches have decentralized and streamlined government procurement, thereby necessitating training and education if green procurement's objectives are to be realized.

Finally, a chapter in a *Handbook of Globalization and the Environment* would be incomplete if it did not mention the challenge green procurement faces in an increasingly global environment. In particular, certain policies of the World Trade Organization (WTO) may pose a direct challenge to government green procurement efforts. In particular, the WTO's Government Procurement Agreement (GPA) prohibits obstacles to international trade that stem from government purchasing polices [9]. As Motavalli and Harkinson [9] argue, "If interpreted strictly, the agreement could dismantle almost all government progress on green purchasing and effectively ban procurement of many environmentally preferable goods." This possibility stems from GPA language that forbids purchasers from considering how products were manufactured when making their purchasing decisions. Meeting this global challenge could require efforts to "green" WTO's policies or, more radically, to limit the organization's role altogether. Since environmental sustainability is a global concern, it may make the most sense to utilize global mechanisms like the WTO and its GPA to incorporate widely shared preferences for green procurement. For this to occur, WTO members must work cooperatively, recognizing their collective responsibility for ensuring environmental sustainability. That said, recent research suggests that major trade agreements like the GPA may not create the serious barriers to green procurement that were originally feared [39].

13.8 Conclusion: Assessing Government's Green Procurement Efforts

This chapter has considered green procurement as a policy tool for meeting global environmental challenges. Using examples from the U.S. federal and subnational governments, the chapter demonstrates that there is cause for both concern and optimism regarding green procurement. On the one hand, there have been numerous laws and orders promoting green procurement, but efforts to harness the purchasing power of the federal government to create and support green markets have been less than successful. Part of the reason for this is the lackluster manner in which EPA has gone about promoting green procurement. In all fairness to the overly stressed agency, this may be more a capacity issue than a commitment problem. Part of the problem is also the chicken-and-egg dilemma mentioned earlier: to purchase green products they must be cost and performance competitive, but for them to become cost and performance competitive a strong private sector market first needs to be developed. While there was at least lip service paid under the National Performance Review years of the Clinton Administration, efforts under the Bush Administration have been uninspiring.

On the other hand, things at the state and local levels are not so grim. As demonstrated, several states and localities have made substantial progress in green procurement. Led by Santa Monica, King County, Seattle, Minnesota, and Massachusetts, state and local governments have advanced knowledge of green procurement and the characteristics that make these programs successful. A spirit of cooperation is also evident among subnational governments. Collective efforts to devise uniform product specifications and to harness the power of government purchasing through cooperative purchasing programs underscore the seriousness and intensity of effort shared by many state and local governments. This would seem to lend credence to Bergeson's [40] observation that "state and local initiatives will continue to eclipse federal procurement initiatives." Perhaps these efforts will allow green procurement to become more fully integrated into government's procurement function. If so, then Eun-Sook Goidel's observation as director of the EPA's EPP program may prove to be prescient: "In 5–10 years this whole concept [green procurement] will become yet another part of what people do on an everyday basis as part of their decision making process" [41]. In other words, the distinction between "traditional procurement" and "green procurement" could one day disappear.

Appendix A Example Green Procurement Policy

A Policy establishing procedures and programs to encourage and increase the procurement of recycled and other environmentally preferable products by (City) agencies and contractors

Purpose

This policy shall be known as the "(City) Environmentally Preferable Procurement Policy." Its purpose is to support markets for recycled and other environmentally preferable products by encouraging (City) agencies and contractors to buy such products whenever practicable

Definitions

The following terms shall have the assigned definitions for all purposes under this policy:

  A. "Agency" means... [insert definition for City agency]

(continued)

Appendix A Example Green Procurement Policy *(Continued)*

B. "Compost Products" means mulch, soil amendments, ground cover, or other landscaping material derived from the biological or mechanical conversion of cellulose-containing waste materials

C. "Environmentally preferable products" means products that have a lesser or reduced effect on human health and the environment when compared with competing products that serve the same purpose. This comparison may consider raw materials acquisition, production, manufacturing, packaging, distribution, reuse, operation, maintenance, or disposal of the product

D. "Post-consumer recycled material" means only those products generated by a business or consumer which have served their intended end uses, and which have been separated or diverted from the solid waste stream for the purposes of collection, recycling, and disposition

E. "Practicable" means sufficient in performance and available at a reasonable price. Final determination of the practicability of any given product must lie with the users of the product, since it is they who understand their performance and budgetary requirements. Evaluation should consider life-cycle and replacement costs

F. "Price Preference" means a percentage by which offered prices for recycled products are reduced for purposes of bid evaluation. *For example, under a 10% price-preference, if a bid of $1.00 per unit is received for a recycled product meeting specifications, the bid price will be reduced by $0.10 (10%) and evaluated as though it had been $0.90. If this bid results in a contract award, the price actually contracted will be the bid price of $1.00 per unit*

G. "Recyclable product" means a product which, after its intended end use, can demonstrably be diverted from (City)'s solid waste stream for use as a raw material in the manufacture of another product

H. "Recycled material" means material and byproducts that have been recovered or diverted from solid waste and that can be utilized in place of raw or virgin material in manufacturing a product. It is derived from post-consumer recycled material, manufacturing waste, industrial scrap, agricultural waste, and other waste material, but does not include material or byproducts generated from, and commonly reused within, an original manufacturing process

I. "Recycled product" means a product containing recycled material

Responsibilities of (Lead) Agency

The (Lead) Agency shall:

A. Develop and maintain information about environmentally preferable products and recycled products containing the maximum practicable amount of recycled materials, to be purchased by agencies whenever possible. Initially, these shall include the products designated in section five of this policy. The (Lead) agency may modify this list as needed;

B. Inform agencies of their responsibilities under this policy and provide implementation assistance;

C. Disseminate information on recycled and environmentally preferable product procurement opportunities, specifications, and performance, to agencies;

D. Communicate with agencies to review policy requirements and new procurement opportunities, and to monitor the status of policy implementation product research results;

(continued)

Appendix A Example Green Procurement Policy *(Continued)*

E. Publicize the progress of policy implementation; and

F. Submit an annual report to the (City) Council reflecting the implementation status of the procurement program, including:

1. A compilation of procurement data collected from all agencies and other parties charged with implementation responsibility under this policy;

2. An account of the current status of product evaluations conducted by agencies;

3. An assessment of procurement program effectiveness, an evaluation of program goals, and projections of future procurement opportunities; and

4. Recommendations for changes in procurement policy

Responsibilities of all (City) Agencies

Each (City) Agency shall:

A. Evaluate each recycled or environmentally preferable product designated by the (lead) agency to determine the extent to which the product may be practicably used by the agency and its contractors;

B. Purchase recycled products with the maximum amount of recycled material practicable;

C. Ensure that contracts issued by the agency require recycled and environmentally preferable products wherever practicable

D. Ensure that contracts issued by the agency for recycled products require the maximum practicable amount of recycled material and that contractors provide certification of this content and report amounts used;

E. Ensure that all printing by (City) agencies uses recycled paper and bears the chasing arrow logo or other imprint identifying it as such;

F. Use both sides of paper sheets whenever practicable in printing and copying;

G. Ensure that requests for bids and proposals issued by (City) require that, whenever practicable, contractors and consultants use recycled paper and both sides of paper sheets;

H. Report the progress of policy implementation by the agency to the (Lead) agency, including the status of product evaluations conducted by the agency and types of environmentally preferable products purchased by the agency and its contractors; and

I. Report total purchases of environmentally preferable, recycled, and non-recycled products by the agency and its contractors annually to the (Lead) agency

Environmentally Preferable Products

A. Paper and paper products;

B. Compost products;

C. Horticultural mulch made with recycled land clearing and other wood debris;

D. Construction aggregates made with recycled cement concrete, glass, or asphalt;

E. Cement and asphalt concrete containing glass cullet, recycled fiber or plastic, tire rubber, or fly ash;

F. Lubricating oil and hydraulic oil with re-refined oil content;

G. Antifreeze;

H. Recycled plastic products;

I. Remanufactured tires and products made from recycled tire rubber, including rubber mats and playfield surfaces;

(continued)

Appendix A Example Green Procurement Policy *(Continued)*

J. Insulation products;

K. Paint;

L. Remanufactured laser printer toner cartridges;

M. Other products as designated by the (Lead) agency

Exemptions

A. Nothing contained in this policy shall preclude user agencies from requiring recycled material content as a bid specification

B. Nothing in this policy shall be construed as requiring an agency or contractor to procure products that do not perform adequately for their intended use or are not available at a reasonable price in a reasonable period of time

Source: Model Recycled Product Procurement Policy for Environmentally Preferable Products. King County, Washington, Environmental Purchasing Program Implementation Guide (Revised: March, 1997). Available at http://www.metrokc.gov/procure/green/mdpolicy.htm (accessed July 16, 2003).

Appendix B Incorporating Green Language into Procurement Specifications

"Put it in writing"

Consider including environmental attributes as specifications in your bid solicitations or proposal requests. Here are some strategies other public agencies have used

Avoid using language that prohibits the purchase of environmentally preferable products

Example: Avoid specifications that require new equipment so that vendors are able to offer remanufactured items, such as auto parts, office furniture, and toner cartridges.

Require recycled content if adequate competition exists for a product that is readily available with recycled content

Example: Require 30% post-consumer recycled-content copy paper

If you are uncertain about the availability of a particular recycled-content product, you could instead give a preference to bids offering recycled content, or award additional points based on the level of recycled content offered in the bid or proposal

Example: You could award zero points for bids offering computer forms with no recycled content, five points for 10% recycled content, and 10 points for 30% recycled content

Eliminate over-specification without compromising performance. Allow alternatives that satisfy the end use. Specify product qualities that are critical to performance and leave other options open

Example: Avoid specifying clear plastic trash bags. Otherwise, you may eliminate recycled-content trash bags that are often darker or opaque in color, but perform just as well.

Include environmental criteria—such as post-consumer recycled content, mercury-free, or Energy Star® compliance—for the product you want to purchase

Example: Specify the federal standard of 25% post-consumer recycled content in a solicitation for re-refined oil. Similar standards exist for most of the products listed in this Guide, and are ready for you to use in your bid solicitations

(continued)

Appendix B Incorporating Green Language into Procurement
Specifications *(Continued)*

Take into account the life-cycle costs of products, such as savings on maintenance, replacement, and disposal costs, which are not factored into the initial unit price

Example: Your evaluation criteria for bids offering plastic benches and tables could include price, durability, manufacture warranty, required maintenance, recycled content, testing of product samples, and references

If packaging or containers are necessary, specify types that are refillable, returnable, or recyclable. Otherwise, specify that no packaging or container be provided.

Require vendors to report your environmental purchases on a quarterly or annual basis so that your organization can track its progress, such as amount of recycled-content copy paper and file folders purchased

Source: *The Environmentally Preferable Purchasing Guide*. 2002. Produced by the state of Minnesota's Solid Waste Management Coordinating Board. The guide is Available at http://www.swmcb.org/eppg/default.asp. The selection is from Section 2.3: Writing Specifications (see http://www.swmcb.org/eppg/2_3.asp) (accessed July 16, 2003).

References

1. Hays, S.P., *A History of Environmental Politics Since 1945*, University of Pittsburgh Press, Pittsburgh, 2000.
2. Rosenbaum, W.A., *Environmental Politics and Policy*, 5th ed., CQ Press, Washington, DC, 2002.
3. U.S. General Accounting Office, *Federal Procurement: Spending and Workforce Trends*, GAO-03-443, U.S. General Accounting Office, Washington, DC, 2003.
4. Cooper, P., *Governing by Contract: Challenges and Opportunities for Public Managers*, CQ Press, Washington, DC, 2003.
5. U.S. Environmental Protection Agency, State and Local Government Pioneers: How State and Local Governments are Implementing Environmentally Preferable Purchasing Programs, EPA742-R-00-004, U.S. Environmental Protection Agency, Washington, DC, 2000.
6. U.S. Government Accounting Office, *Contract Management: Comments on Proposed Serves Acquisition Reform Act*, GAO-03-716T, U.S. General Accounting Office, Washington, DC, 2003.
7. Thai, K.V., Public procurement re-examined, *Journal of Public Procurement*, 1, 2001, 9.
8. McCue, C.P. and Gianakis, G.A., Public purchasing: Who's minding the store? *Journal of Pub Procurement*, 1, 71, 2001.
9. Motavalli, J. and Harkinson, J., Buying green: Harnessing the incredible procurement power of governments, hospitals, colleges and America's biggest corporations to protect the environment, *The Environmental. Magnazine.*, 13, 26, 2002.
10. U.S. Environmental Protection Agency, *Environmentally Preferable Purchasing Program: Cleaning Products Pilot Project*, EPA742-R-97-002, U.S. Environmental Protection Agency, Washington, DC, 1997.
11. Clinton, W.J., *Federal Acquisition, Recycling and Waste Prevention*, Executive Order 12873, 1993.

12. U.S. Environmental Protection Agency, *RCRA, Superfund & EPCRA Hotline Training Module: RCRA Statutory Overview*, EPA530-R-99-063 PB2000-101 903, U.S. Environmental Protection Agency, Washington, DC, 2000.

13. U.S. Environmental Protection Agency, *Summary of Comments at the Public Meeting on Proposed Guidance on Acquisition of Environmentally Preferable Products and Services*, EPA742-R-96-005, U.S. Environmental Protection Agency, Washington, DC, 1996.

14. Clinton, W.J., *Greening the Government through Waste Prevention, Recycling, and Federal Acquisition*, Executive Order 13101, 1998.

15. EPA Final guidance on environmentally preferable purchasing for executive agencies, *Federal Register*, 64, 45810, 1999.

16. Clinton, W.J., *Greening the Government through Efficient Energy Management*, Executive Order 13123, 1999.

17. Clinton, W.J., *Greening the Government through Leadership in Environmental Management*, Executive Order 13148. 2000.

18. Clinton, W.J., *Greening the Government through Federal Fleet and Transportation Efficiency*, Executive Order 13149, 2000.

19. Clinton, W.J., *Federal Workforce Transportation*, Executive Order 13150, 2000.

20. Bush, G.W., *Energy Efficient Standby Power Devices*, Executive Order 13221, 2001.

21. Commonwealth of Massachusetts, How to do Business with the Commonwealth of Massachusetts: A Guide for Manufacturers and Suppliers of Environmentally Preferable Products, The Chelsea Center for Recycling and Economic Development and the Commonwealth of Massachusetts Operational Services Division, Boston, 2002.

22. State of Minnesota, Department of Administration, Materials Management Division, Green Government—What is the State of Minnesota Doing, and What More Should be Done?, Department of Administration, St. Paul, 2002. Available at http://www.mmd.admin.state.mn.us/pdf/MNGreenGovernmentActions.pdf (accessed on July 18, 2003).

23. State of Minnesota, Department of Administration, State Resource Recovery Program, Fiscal Years 1999–2000, Department of Administration, St. Paul, 2000.

24. King County, Washington, Environmental Purchasing Program 2002 Annual Report, King County Environmental Purchasing Program, Seattle, 2002.

25. U.S. Environmental Protection Agency, *The City of Santa Monica's Environmental Purchasing: A Case Study*, EPA742-R-98-001, U.S. Environmental Protection Agency, Washington, DC, 1998.

26. U.S. Environmental Protection Agency, *Waste Wise Update: Environmentally Preferable Purchasing*, EPA530-N-01-002, U.S. Environmental Protection Agency, Washington, DC, 2001.

27. Bryson, J.M., *Strategic Planning for Public and Nonprofit Organizations: A Guide to Strengthening and Sustaining Organizational Achievement*, Jossey-Bass Publishers, San Francisco CA, 1995.

28. National Association of State Procurement Officials (NASPO). *State and Local Government Purchasing Principles & Practices*, NASPO, Lexington, 2001.

29. New, S., Green, K., and Morton, B., An analysis of private versus public sector responses to the environmental challenges of the supply chain, *Journal of Public Procurement*, 2, 2002, 93.

30. Barrett, K. and Greene, R., The government performance project. Grading the cities: A management report card, *Governing*, 13, 2000, 22.

31. Seattle, City of, Purchasing Services Division, Annual Report 2001, Purchasing Services Division, Seattle, 2001. Available at http://www.cityofseattle.net/purchasing/docs/2001psdreport.pdf (accessed on July 16, 2003).

32. National Association of State Procurement Officials (NASPO). *2001 Survey of State and Local Government Purchasing Practices*, NASPO, Lexington, 2001.
33. Raymond, M., It's not easy buying green, *Governing*, 10, 1997, 49.
34. State of Minnesota, Solid Waste Management Coordinating Board, The Environmentally Preferable Purchasing Guide, Department of Administration, St. Paul, 2002. Available at http://www.swmcb.org/eppg/default.asp (accessed on July 16, 2003).
35. National Institute of Governmental Purchasing (NIGP). *NIGP Survey of Green Procurement Initiatives*, NIGP, Herndon, 2001.
36. White House Task Force on Recycling, Greening the Government: A Guide to Implementing Executive Order 13101, White House Task Force on Recycling, Washington, DC, 2001. Available at www.ofee.gov/eo/greening.pdf (accessed on July 16, 2003).
37. Case, S., Environmentally preferable purchasing—Moving beyond "buy recycled", *Government. Procurement*, Oct, 8, 2002.
38. Farrell, M., Source separated procurement specifications, *BioCycle*, 37, 1996, 48.
39. Earley, J., Green Procurement in Trade Policy, The Commission for Environmental Cooperation, Montreal, 2003. Available at http://www.cec.org/files/pdf/ECONOMY/green-procurement-in-trade%20Policy_en.pdf (accessed on May 15, 2006).
40. Bergeson, L.L., Green buy programs: An important procurement factor, *Pollution Engineering*, 34, 30, 2002.
41. Maxwell, A., Green government: The move toward environmentally friendly federal purchasing practices is blossoming, *Government Execution*, 29, 37, 1997.

Chapter 14

Environmental Management

Laura E. Pasquale*

Florida Department of Environmental Protection

14.1 Introduction

In this chapter, system science constructs are used to gain a deeper understanding of the forces and issues involved in environmental management. The first section covers U.S. environmental regulation, including legislative milestones and the current range of pollution prevention approaches, both voluntary and mandatory, being used to promote better environmental quality. It highlights the recognition among the regulatory community that, in order to improve environmental quality, we need to view the environment, and the cultures within it, as complex systems. In the second section, the environmental management system (EMS) is presented as one option to address that complexity, beginning with a description of its system-based strengths. The chapter concludes with recommendations for future research on sustaining participation in EMSs.

14.2 U.S. Environmental Regulation

14.2.1 Introduction

Along with diplomatic, economic, health, and social issues, many in the U.S. view the condition of our environment as a primary concern. Stories of local, regional, national, and global impacts of human activity, including the contamination of our food and water supplies, degradation of our air and soil, and the increased prevalence of environmentally influenced diseases, such as asthma, are in the

---

* Currently affiliated with the Say brook Graduate School and Research Center, San Francisco, CA.

news daily. Despite a long history of regulation in the U.S., including federal air and water legislation, environmental problems persist. These affect the quality of life of our citizens and drain money from our national coffers. The U.S. Congress found that, "The United States of America annually produces millions of tons of pollution and spends tens of billions of dollars per year controlling this pollution." Despite this reality, we know relatively little about how and why pollution prevention initiatives work. To begin to bridge that knowledge gap, this chapter surveys the history of regulation, including significant legal and intellectual milestones and their impact on regulation, and follows with a review of current approaches to pollution prevention.

14.2.1.1 Legislative History

The original federal laws governing air, waste, and water—three primary regulated media—have lengthy legislative histories. The laws regarding water regulation, for example, go back as far as 1899, and current standards for safe drinking water were derived from laws enacted in 1974 and 1976 [1]. Some experts consider the Air Pollution Prevention and Control Act of 1970 to be the trigger for our current improved air quality [2], even though the Clean Air Act of 1990 now receives more official attention [3]. Following the public regulation of media came the regulation of toxic substances. In 1947, Congress passed the Federal Insecticide, Fungicide, and Rodenticide Act (FIFRA), and later passed the 1976 Toxic Substances Act [4]. Continuing this type of regulation, lobbyists and regulators are now championing new laws to govern—or to ban entirely—the use of toxic substances such mercury [5,6].

While these laws were created to address the effects of modern chemicals, they often used the same "silo" approach to regulation as those older laws governing media. These laws also reflect the reductionism that colored the industrial worldview [7]; existing statutes (usually) are media specific, differ in goals and approaches, and define key terms differently. The same compartmentalized foundations exist in the regulatory mechanisms for air and waste. Government agencies built on statutory authority are likewise structured along such functional lines and categories [8,9]. The U.S. Environmental Protection Agency (EPA), its regional offices, and its state enforcement agencies are examples, with departments established largely to monitor and enforce media-based codes and regulations [10–12].

While the current regulatory structure is a predictable result of media-specific legislation, it has several shortcomings. First, the judicial branch often carries out regulatory enforcement, through a legal model meant to limit abuse by regulators. Due to competing pressures from environmental groups and corporations, gridlock is a frequent result [13,14]. Second, the environmental impact of this legislation has been mixed. While regulators and others have made progress in improving the quality of air and decreasing the use of pesticides, other goals remain elusive. Water pollution persists, as reported by Center for Disease Control. Their data indicate that 44 states have issued warnings about the significant risks of eating locally-caught fish [5]. Mercury is the key obstacle in some areas, but in others the factors are harder to identify [15,16]. This is tied to the third shortcoming of "silo" regulation: its inherent inability to address mobile or non-point source pollution. These types of pollution result not from the activities of regulated polluters, such as manufacturing or power plants, but from those of millions of individuals and businesses not referenced under law. The nature of non-point source pollution is often difficult to clearly determine and/or impossible to monitor directly, making its cumulative impacts difficult to control. A fourth, related limitation of the current U.S. regulatory structure is the inability of traditional regulation to address the environmental impact of over-consumption and unchecked population growth [17]. Finally, piecemeal laws and regulatory approaches often serve only to shift the pollution rather than to eliminate it, thereby creating geographic and socio-economic disparities in environmental quality [17–19].

14.2.1.2 Pollution Prevention

In an attempt to address the limitations of media-specific laws and statutes, the U.S. Congress passed the 1990 Pollution Prevention Act [20,21]. This act defines pollution prevention as "source reduction" of pollution, and includes any practice which, (a) reduces the amount of any hazardous substance, pollutant, or contaminant entering any waste stream or otherwise released into the environment (including fugitive emissions) prior to recycling, treatment, or disposal; and (b) reduces the hazards to public health and the environment associated with the release of such substances, pollutants, or contaminants.

These practices include both increasing efficiency in resource use and/or conservation [10], with the intent of eliminating pollution altogether, rather than simply regulating its production. By allowing flexibility in adopted practices, the Act also takes regulation beyond the traditional "command and control" approaches, which establish both standards of performance and the means of achieving them [4].

14.2.1.3 Current Regulatory Options

Over 30 years after the creation of the U.S. EPA and passage of the Air Pollution Prevention and Control Act [22] and the Safe Drinking Water Act [23], the regulatory issues are complex, with economic, ethical, and social implications. Therefore, to protect the complex environmental system, regulators and other concerned parties are developing a greater range of options [24–26]. The broad option categories include consumer-directed choices and decisions (e.g., social marketing); financial incentives, such as sales taxes and eco-zoning; integrative regulation (such as the establishment of total maximum daily loads for water pollution); limiting or removing a quantifiable threat to health; long-term structural, and/or societal approaches (i.e., sustainability projects) [11]; traditional regulation and enforcement (i.e., "command and control" approaches that set targets and the means to reach them); pollution prevention (e.g. recycling); promotion of new technologies, including industrial processes and managerial approaches; public announcements regarding environmental performance; and self-certification (e.g., dry cleaning programs).

With these options in mind, how should agencies determine which approaches to apply? According to Allenby [2], they must first decide which hazards most urgently require attention by conducting a Comprehensive Risk Assessment (CRA). The key steps are: (1) identify the hazard, (2) determine the "delivered dose" of the hazard, (3) assess the probability of an undesirable effect of the dose, (4) determine the exposed population, and (5) characterize the risk in measurable terms. In addition, Allenby [2] suggests that other risks should be included in a comprehensive assessment of risk, including trade-offs among environmental impacts (or environmental and other impacts); the need to address multiple endpoints, rather than the most feared or the one for which most data can be gathered; and the inherent ambiguities of complex environmental and economic systems within which risky activities occur.

In deciding which regulatory approach to select, regulators may then develop a Comprehensive Policy Support Assessment (CPSA) using all the risks identified. To be comprehensive, the approach should allocate at least some resources to alternatives that address complex systems and interactions and support the goal of sustainability. These may have a higher risk of failure, but also higher rates of return. Allenby [2] proposes four steps in the CPSA: (1) possible responses to the risk are identified; (2) a CRA is developed for each option; (3) each CRA is "monitarized" to the extent possible; and (4) once monitarized, the CRA should be integrated into the cost/benefit analysis for each approach.

While this model is helpful, it has limitations. For instance, the literature supports the public perception that some things have a value beyond measure (e.g., human life, biodiversity), and that the public may react strongly against an attempt to "monitarize" these [14]. In addition, as Nordhaus [27] indicates, an accurate measure of the costs of specific types of environmental damage is often unavailable. Further, the operations of multinational corporations make it difficult or impossible for geographically-bounded governments to exact payment for damage [13]. In these situations, any "end of pipe" strategy may be undesirable, and a more proactive strategy may be needed. Finally, experts estimate that of the 65,000 individual chemicals in use, only 1% have full toxicology data, and 80% have not even been tested [28,29]. Under these conditions, even the first step in Allenby's model—hazard identification—is often impossible.

14.2.2 Systems Analysis

14.2.2.1 System Characteristics and Policy Implications

In addition to a desire to expand the range of regulatory options, the Pollution Prevention Act (see above) also signaled a changing mindset. Metaphors for our environment have reflected our mindsets, varying greatly over time, ranging from divine creation, to living being, to machine [7,30]. As compared with early reductionist programs, recent regulation initiatives are more consistent with the view of the environment as a complex system [2]. Churchman's [31] description of simple and complex systems may be summarized as follows:

14.2.2.1.1 Simple System

This type of system demonstrates a clear, linear connection between input and output, with clear cause-and-effect relationships. It uses static processes that move consistently toward the same endpoint and contain a hierarchical structure, thus creating predictable behavior toward an ideal state. Most regulatory systems are built on this model, with hierarchical authority structures, inspections, and monitoring that encourage gradual, linear progress toward a particular target. Their incentives and disincentives are aimed at shaping behavior.

14.2.2.1.2 Complex System

This type of system demonstrates discontinuous, non-linear and/or unclear connections between input and output, mediated by "feedback loops" within the system itself. These feedback loops allow for self-regulation and even rejuvenation within the system. A complex system also uses processes that react to the internal and external environment, so that the evolving process itself is the only constant. The system's behavior changes qualitatively as it evolves, with many possible outcomes.

Systems theory would indicate that the U.S. environmental regulatory structure is nestled within the larger natural and human-made systems. Systems principles also dictate that the process of organizational development must be studied at all levels. Without this depth of understanding, it is difficult to direct the system's energy effectively. The constant and unpredictable interactions of individuals and groups, plants and animals, and local and global ecosystems reveal our environment to be a complex system. This existence of complex environmental characteristics is also supported by cross-media data reports, which demonstrate the interaction between one environmental impact and another, as well as the impact of regulation on ecosystems [8,15,32]. Clearly, a mismatch exists between the simple structure of most regulatory agencies and programs and the complex ecosystems they are set up to protect [33].

14.2.2.2 Context

As Ostrom [34] points out, institutional analysis must take place within the prevailing cultural and physical context. Therefore, now that the particulars of the U.S. environmental regulatory structure have been examined, it is helpful to review the system in which this structure is based.

14.2.2.2.1 Political

First, there exists at the federal level a unique set of political circumstances in which government, in conjunction with the court system, attempts to enforce externally imposed policies on regulated entities and individuals. Several actors, including non-profit organizations, influence the development of these policies in the democratic legislative process. A further complication in the federal regulatory model is the role of states. In the absence of a unified national vision [35], some states have taken a lead role on issues such as auto emissions, often emboldening other states to do the same [29,36–38].

The resulting overall U.S. regulatory model is far from perfect. While many actors may influence environmental policy, the legislative process and resulting legal documents are sometimes too arcane and complex for those outside the regulatory arena to understand [39]. In addition, even if solid background information on environmental hazards exists, it is possible that decision-makers will not act to remove the hazards [31,40,41].

In contrast to the U.S. regulatory system, other cultural, economic, and physical factors in other countries have produced very different national responses to regulation. In Japan, for example, non-profits do not have the same status as those in the U.S., and the application process for these organizations is prohibitively expensive. These factors make non-profits less common and often less influential than those in the U.S. Japan has also taken a more collaborative stance toward industry. Where this approach has been successful, Japanese corporations have become self-regulating, cleaning up their environmental damage and factoring costs into daily operations [42,43]. A different approach also arose in Germany, where environmental issues became the Green Party's focus in Germany's multiparty system. As that party fares, so fares environmental policy. While this arrangement allows direct access to the political process, it contains the inherent geographic and temporal limitations of the political system [43]. In addition, environmental initiatives may become stalled if the Green Party is not united or in power.

14.2.2.2.2   Geographic

A second factor in resource conservation and protection is geographic limitation. Both in the U.S. and other countries, many international and/or common-pool resource (CPR) challenges are not addressed by formal or informal agreements [44,45]. While the design principles and theory of CPR agreements are slowly becoming clearer [45–47], the challenges to implementation persist, including scientific disagreements, bureaucracy, lack of resources, and legal traps [48,49].

14.2.2.2.3   Intellectual

Third, in the intellectual arena, human "exceptionalism" assumes that humans are above the natural laws that maintain our planet. This notion permeates Western life [50], including U.S. thought, appearing in disciplines such as environmental sociology, which presumes that human social and behavioral intervention can eradicate environmental problems [51]. In reality, the environmental interventions of human beings are imperfect. For example, Spath [29] estimates that less than 1% of pesticides actually reach the pests they are designed to eradicate In addition, human interventions sometimes result in problems as great as those they attempt to solve (e.g., the case of drug-resistant bacteria) [52–55].

In contrast, rather than using social re-engineering, Mol [56] proposes extracting ecological values and setting them apart, then embedding them in other, existing economic and scientific institutions. Thus, Mol's environmental rationality theory predicts that all institutions would be internally directed by these embedded values toward beneficial environmental goals. The resulting structure might resemble that of Japan, where industrial institutions contain many of their own environmental controls [42,57].

Both the human exceptionalism and environmental modernization views allow for the reversal of the environmental impact of human activity, including pollution, after the fact. In contrast, the Gaia theory [58] states that the earth is a self-regulating organism, and that mutual influence and interaction occurs between humans and the planet. Further, due to the complexity of the earth organism and its self-regulating mechanisms, Gaia theory predicts that the ultimate, comprehensive impact of human activity cannot be accurately or absolutely known. This uncertainty is compounded by the use of flawed analytical tools to determine impact [47,56]. To address these limitations, academicians and non-governmental organizations (NGOs) have derived the "precautionary principle." Rather than assuming the capacity to contain or reverse environmental damage, this principle dictates a conservative approach to human activity, including avoiding the use of non-renewable resources and synthetic chemicals in the first place [59,60].

Finally, at the individual level, research indicates that intellectual predispositions affect our ability to adapt. Lewin [61], for example, found that rigid mental models lead to a reduced ability to deal with complexity. As mentioned earlier, the environmental challenges we face today are nothing if not complex. In addition, Adams [17] states that short-term or long-term perspectives have different impacts on our day-to-day decision-making. Specifically, short-term thinkers tend to miss the impact of their choices in a rush to act as quickly as possible—a finding supported by Lewin [61]. Long-term thinking is a key skill for leaders, including those who champion environmental and/or organizational change efforts. These findings are important in the environmental arena, since individual behavior is the foundation for any larger organizational and social change [17,62,63].

14.2.2.2.4 Economic

Finally, the U.S. and its regulatory structure evolved through interdependence with a capitalist economic system. Like all human systems, capitalism contains unique dynamics. One is the treadmill of production, or TOP [42,57], which drives industry to reduce prices and profit margins, expand markets, and increase output. Some predict that the TOP will inevitably overtax the supply of natural resources [42]. A similar dynamic is reflected in the "IPAT" equation: Impact = Population size + Affluence + Technology [29]. According to this formula, each factor can contribute to, or can ameliorate, the overall impact. Developed nations like the U.S., for example, might experience few problems with population growth due to the availability of family planning options. However, greater affluence may cause developed nations to consume too many goods and resources, thereby increasing their overall environmental impact. Unlike the TOP theory, the IPAT equation allows for mitigation of impact through the use of technology to develop less environmentally harmful means of production [28,29].

Corporate rights are a second key aspect of the U.S. economic system. While the corporation began as a vehicle sanctioned by law to encourage group investment, it has now assumed a status beyond a simple financial collective. Corporate status now entitles organizations to relief from taxation [64] and from legal liability [66]. Further, the scale of corporate activity and interest has grown, extending outside the jurisdiction of the legal entities that recognize them. This unchecked growth makes legal regulation of such entities extremely difficult, if not impossible, at a municipal, state, or national level [65] and has led to questions about whether the corporate status and rights in their current form are supported by the U.S. Constitution [66]. In the U.S., corporate legal and tax status continue to hamper government and individual efforts in environmental regulation [64,66–68].

Third, the functioning of any capitalist system hinges on the free market. Some see this market as having the power to transform the economy to a force for environmental good through informed consumer choice [13]. However, that effect is mitigated by: (1) the small percentage of products that are eco-friendly; (2) an infrastructure that doesn't always support "green" choices (e.g., city planning without public transit arrangements); (3) "green-washing" of products that have harmful effects on the environment, and (4) the disparity between individual attitudes/values and behavior [57,69]. Further, other experts argue that the so-called free market is a myth. Young [70] stated that while the U.S. government owns 1/3 of the land, 1/2 of the softwood, and regulates oil and gas exploration, it cannot present itself as a disinterested or uninvolved actor. Snidal [71] argues that, ideally, a centralized authority should involve itself by codifying helpful practices, providing useful information, and facilitating the smooth operation of the resulting conventions. This picture is quite different from the current environmental regulatory structure's role of monitoring and enforcement. To summarize, leaning on market forces alone seems an inadequate strategy for addressing current environmental concerns.

While unchecked economic expansion is a danger, even operating in our current mode is problematic [29], because the unchecked use of limited and of environmentally damaging materials has the potential to create a crisis of some sort [17,28]. As Hawken, Lovins, and Lovins [13] state, the environment is not a factor in production; *it is the envelope that contains the entire economy.* Therefore, whether capitalist, communist, or socialist, the means of production must utilize renewable, non-toxic resources in order to keep the environment— and itself—healthy and the financial infrastructure economically viable. According to McDonough and Braumgart [29], the challenge is to transform capital economic investment from a negative to a positive environmental force, focusing on economic development and diversification rather than unbalanced, unchecked expansion [72]. However, as Adams notes, the inertia and investment present in a corporate economic infrastructure (such as the oil industry's installed base of gas stations, refineries, pipelines and distribution vehicles) can work against interventions at that level [73]. This next section of this chapter presents the use of EMSs as a possible vehicle for transformation of the U.S. regulatory approach.

14.3   Environmental Management Systems

14.3.1   *Background*

In order to protect our environment and ourselves from further damage, municipalities, states, and the federal government are pursuing creative approaches to environmental regulation. Some involve the reapplication of traditional "command and control" programs, which spell out specific goals and technological requirements, or the use of an assessment of environmental risk to determine the appropriate regulatory response. Still others focus not on reducing pollution, but on clean-up or recycling of waste. Finally, unregulated entities, such as small businesses and households, are being encouraged by institutions to control pollution and waste voluntarily.

Because the control of pollution, particularly hazardous substances (such as petrochemicals or nuclear waste) is sometimes insufficient to protect the public, other approaches seek to eliminate pollution at the source of production.

In addition to the potential for reducing environmental risk, new pollution prevention options are gaining attention, both because they are becoming more common and because of the potential cost savings to taxpayers [2,74,75]. One such organizationally-directed strategy is the environmental management system, or EMS [74,76–80] which state and local agencies have recently hailed as an important and useful component in their environmental approaches. An EMS is… "a formal set of procedures and policies that define—sometimes in great detail—how an organization will manage its potential impacts on the natural world and on the health and welfare of its workers and nearby citizens" [77].

The U.S. EPA definition adds that an EMS is "a continual cycle of planning, implementing, reviewing, and improving the processes and actions that an organization undertakes to meet its business and environmental goals." The North Carolina Division of the Pollution Prevention and Environmental Assistance [81] states that an EMS serves as a tool to improve environmental performance; provide a systematic way of managing an organization's environmental affairs; give order and consistency to address environmental concerns through the allocation of resources, assignment of responsibility and ongoing evaluation of practices, procedures, and processes; and focus on continued improvement of the system.

At its core, an EMS is a formal set of procedures and policies that that are created by individual organizations. The organization implements these procedures to manage potential environmental impact through changes in daily operations and self-monitoring. This is quite different from traditional "command-and-control" regulation, in that the organizations that might otherwise pollute design their own EMS, rather than external regulators imposing their own systems. Further, the organization implements controls prior to, during, and at the point of production, rather than after pollutants have been generated. Finally, each organization determines the acceptable evidence of impact, resulting in greater variety in external reporting. In some cases, regulators consider the existence of an EMS alone as an end point, regardless of the particulars of its external reports.

It is this focus on continual improvement of the entire business process, rather than just one aspect of it, that sets EMSs apart from other self-regulated approaches. For example, one state's compliance certification program for dry cleaners—known as the Massachusetts Environmental Results Program (ERP)—focuses only on controlling the discharge of the hazardous substance tetrachloroethylene, known as "PERC." Used in many dry cleaning facilities, this substance is highly toxic and a known carcinogen [82]. A shortcoming of the traditional approach is that it cannot find and monitor all dry cleaners, and is especially ineffective in regulating small operations, which make up a large percentage of U.S. dry cleaners. Many view the self-certification process, which enlists owner and employee assistance in self-regulation, as an improvement over traditional regulation, which requires onsite inspection and monitoring of large polluters by regulatory staff. In contrast to both the self-certification and traditional approaches, an EMS would require dry cleaners to focus on all aspects of the business, including materials and services from their providers, as well as PERC used on site, to realize greater environmental performance.

First adopted by manufacturing industries, EMSs are now being used throughout the private sector, and increasingly, by public agencies. The U.S. EPA itself has developed a management policy for its own facilities to meet environmental goals [83]. Massachusetts has adopted EMSs as part of its State Sustainability Program [78,84]. In addition, several state agencies are participating in the development of the National Database on EMSs (NDEMS), including: Arizona, California, Illinois, Indiana, New Hampshire, North Carolina, Oregon, Pennsylvania, Vermont, and Wisconsin [85].

Three key assumptions underlie the EMS approach. First, like many continuous improvement processes, bottom-up implementation is viewed as more effective. Therefore, management of environmental controls is often shifted to those on the shop floor. Second, proactive interventions are assumed to produce better environmental impacts than "end of pipe" approaches, by promoting cost control through prevention and internal waste management, rather than clean-up. Finally, regulators often see adoption of an EMS as a sign that the organization will fulfill its "social contract" through self-regulation. Faith in the ability and willingness of organizations to do so is sometimes based on their past performance [81]. In other cases, judges frequently order EMSs for injunctive relief [86]. Injunctive relief is defined as a court-ordered act or prohibition against an act or condition requested via petition to the court. Such an act by the court usually employs a hearing rather than a trial and is not a judgment for money. Instead, organizations are ordered to implement and to document the use of an EMS [87]. In such cases, the decision is not made based on faith in the organization, but on a desire for a cost-effective and expedient solution to a regulatory problem.

In the U.S., the most common EMS structure is the International Organization for Standardization's ISO 14000-certification framework, developed through consultation with business, governmental, and NGO representatives in response to the Earth Summit [57,88]. In the European Union, the parallel Eco-Management and Audit Scheme (EMAS) is the favored model [89]. Some organizations are attempting to surpass even these standards, moving toward development of common elements for a sustainability management system, or SMS [74]. While there are data to indicate that external certification per se does not determine the success of a pollution control system [89], industry still considers the ISO 14000 EMS the gold standard, in part for its use of external third-party verification and standard development. This model is also increasingly prevalent internationally: in 1998, there were 1542 ISO EMSs in Japan, 1100 in Germany, and 210 in the U.S. [43].

14.3.2   Systems Analysis

A systems framework (applied above to the environment as a complex system) can also be applied to better understand the potential advantages of using the EMS approach.

14.3.2.1   Better Alignment

Systems theory posits that alignment of function and structure, or syntony, should be considered a system's strength [90]. The EMS approach achieves alignment within smaller units of the larger system, focusing on one regulated entity at a time. Taking a multi-media and a "cradle-to-cradle" approach, products are manufactured and services delivered with a minimum of waste and resource consumption, as well as a focus on eco-friendly materials. Thus, the actions of the worker at the lowest operational levels mesh with the environmental vision of leadership [34]. Such a shared vision in itself has been observed to be a powerful vehicle for positive organizational change in general [91]. Further, EMSs may facilitate alignment of values between the economic and political sectors toward a more unified environmental focus [57].

14.3.2.2   Decreased Resistance

Systems interventions are most successful when the energy in the system is harnessed, rather than suppressed [92,93]. By tapping into production at the source, an EMS modifies the behavior of the economic system in important two ways. First, it redirects the treadmill of production that drives the capitalist economy, moving it to reduce toxicity and waste and to focus, instead, on using renewable resources. Second, by making more eco-friendly products available, it provides an infrastructure for green consumerism, thereby harnessing the power of the free market.

14.3.2.3   Enhanced Use of Information

By improving information flows and links, the content and timing of data reports, and by shortening feedback loops, systems' responsiveness can be enhanced [28,93]. Moving both the source and the use of data in-house makes data more readily available to decision-makers, and helps to allay concerns or suspicions about data validity [56,94,95]. Further, by internalizing the costs of pollution cleanup and prevention into the cost of business, both producers and consumers of goods can calculate more accurate, valid information about the real environmental cost of their choices [29]. The resulting price tag might then inform and regulate consumer behavior.

14.3.2.4   Increased Range of Response

Ashby's Law of Requisite Variety dictates that systems thrive when they have more, and more varied, response options [96,97]. As described above, statutes and arcane, complex political processes often constrain the U.S. regulatory system, including federal, state, and local branches. Shifting the locus of system control to smaller, individual entities allows more rapid and more innovative responses. Including public stakeholders in designing and implementing an EMS can also increase the availability of new ideas and perspectives. The result might resemble what Spath [29] calls the "Jazz scenario," in which all environmental actors improvise but play from the same sheet of music: "complex, not complicated" [98].

14.3.2.5   Stronger Foundation

"Endosymbiosis" is the evolution of organisms from simple to complex, such that the simpler organisms become linked and/or absorbed to form a new organism [99]. Systems theorists also recognize this natural development process in organizations [7,31]. A uniform EMS model—such as ISO 14000—provides diverse regulated entities with a common map that spans geographic boundaries, media, and processes. As Becker and Ostrom [44] have observed in their research, such design principles are often more important than specific institutional solutions. A common map could also provide greater cohesion for regulated and non-regulated entities than currently exists within a silo-based regulatory system.

14.3.2.6   Tighter Feedback Loops

The responsiveness of a system to changing conditions is determined by feedback loops, which translate incoming data and influence the system's response. If a signal, or the system's response to it, is delayed, damage can occur in the interim. In regards to the environment, technology sometimes exacerbates these delays by producing substitutes for non-renewable resources, thereby giving the impression that scarcity is not an issue. But ultimately, substitutability does not replace sustainability [13,44]. Spath [29] notes that local action tightens the feedback loops considerably, lending some credibility to the trend toward decentralized prevention and regulation of pollution, such as that found in EMSs.

14.3.3 Research Data

While there is considerable interest in the EMS approach, both in the U.S. and abroad, formal research is still in its infancy, particularly within the broader context of contemporary organizational development theory.

14.3.3.1 Systems Research

It is ironic that while systems theory has been applied to both the environment and to organizational development, its principles have not been consistently applied to the development of organization-based environmental initiatives. Entrepreneurs, engineers, mathematicians, and social scientists have long applied systems theory to study and solve complex problems. More recently, professionals and others have employed these principles to help understand our environment, including the impact of human activity.

Systems theory dictates that dynamics at all levels are important to overall understanding, thus bringing the importance of individuals within systems to the fore. In recent years, the understanding and use of individual participation in decision-making and governance approaches has gained prominence. This practice is now evident in business, in NGOs programs, and in municipal, state, national, international and global communities and governments [63,100–107]. One decision that organizations must make when implementing an EMS is how to involve stakeholders.

14.3.3.2 Stakeholder Participation

There are numerous definitions of the terms "stakeholder" and "participation" in the literature, with foundations in the corporate [108,109], information technology [100], legal [111], government [109] and social science arenas [94,95,104,110]. In order to avoid prematurely limiting their scope, the most basic definitions of both terms are used here. Thus, a "stakeholder" is defined as "one who has a share or an interest, as in an enterprise" [111]; and "participation" is defined as "the act of taking part in an activity" [112]. "Participation" is used rather than "engagement," as the latter implies that one individual or entity is has the authority or obligation to convene the group [113]. "Inclusion," "identification," and "involvement" were not chosen, as they do not always imply that an individual has actively taken part in an initiative [107].

Both government agencies and NGOs have recognized that stakeholder participation is critical to successful initiatives, issuing guidance about how to identify and appropriately involve stakeholders [107,114]. In that arena, the stakeholder relationship may pivot around environmental crisis management or be part of a proactive environmental strategy. Guidelines recommend communicating with internal and external stakeholders with financial, geographic, topical, and legal ties to the project, as well as their inclusion in the design and implementation phases.

The University of North Carolina at Chapel Hill (UNC) and the Environmental Law Institute (ELI) developed the NDEMS as a 5-year project. Their project summary report indicates that 43 participating facilities included interested parties in their EMS implementation [77], and that 28 organizations provided more specific information to NDEMS about the nature of that involvement. According to the project findings, industry has used a variety of means to date, both in the design and management processes, to incorporate input from internal and/or external stakeholder groups [77].

The role of individuals has been given little attention compared with other facets of EMSs, such as environmental performance or cost/benefit ratios. Primarily quantitative EMS data has been collected, analyzed, and presented by individuals external to the change process, such as academic researchers, corporations, consultants, government officials, and others, each with different assumptions and perspectives. Overall, the experiences and perspectives of individuals inside the environmental system are usually unseen.

Despite the reality of increased public reliance on EMSs and the growing prevalence of stakeholder involvement in corporate operations, including pollution prevention [115], there is little data available as to the specifics of stakeholder involvement, and whether stakeholder involvement increases the ability of an EMS to reach its goals and targets. Moreover, understanding at multiple levels and from many perspectives is not always achieved. In 2002, Gallagher presented her typology of stakeholder involvement, which provides a qualitative synopsis of organizational approaches to environmental impact management. However, neither it nor the larger NDEMS summary report [77] provided a detailed qualitative analysis of involvement, or a quantitative analysis of the relationship between the level or type of stakeholder involvement and environmental performance. In addition, my pilot research revealed that varying types of stakeholder involvement were clustered together for coding in the NDEMS summary report, making conclusions regarding specific mechanisms of involvement problematic [117].

Because EMSs require organization-wide change, such involvement is critical to success [62]. However, the ISO 14000 standards provide few specifics regarding this involvement [74]. The certifiers' lack of standardization and guidance regarding stakeholder involvement is surprising for several reasons. First, data indicate a positive relationship between greater employee and stakeholder involvement and successful EMS implementation [116,118–120]. Second, leveraged stakeholder involvement is common and integral to other types of pollution prevention programs [121]. Third, EMS parallels total quality management (TQM), another highly participatory endeavor [122]. Finally, in her review of 33 published studies, Hillary [123] concluded that a lack of human resources is ultimately even more problematic than a lack of financial resources for small and medium sized businesses seeking ISO certification. This last finding in particular heightens the importance of identifying EMS factors with a high cost-benefit ratio and with measurable environmental performance enhancements.

Kitazawa and Sarkis [124], for example, studied employee participation in three case study firms, concluding that employees' empowerment, their willingness to suggest improvements, and management's efforts to include employees in decision-making were critical to managing ISO 14000 continuous source reduction programs. This was true despite the numerous cultural differences between the firms. Delmas [119] mailed surveys to 152 individuals responsible for EMS implementation, who then reported on external stakeholder involvement. Delmas concluded that their involvement is critical to credibility, and, therefore, to organizational competitiveness.

14.3.3.3 Future Research

In its evaluation summary of 30 agency-led stakeholder collaborations, the U.S. EPA [107] recommended that future studies address several questions, including:

- What were the stakeholder perceptions regarding their ability to participate in the process?
- To what degree were those expectations met?
- What was the level of effort required by stakeholders to participate?
- Were the goals and steps of the process clearly explained?
- To what extent did the effort meet those goals?
- What major factors contributed to the success or shortcomings of the stakeholder involvement/public participation effort?
- How could the stakeholder/public involvement effort have been designed differently to work more effectively?

It remains to be seen whether the stakeholder model developed by business, government, the social sciences, or some hybrid will be most applicable to environmental initiatives, or whether a new model will be needed. It may be that an initiative focused on one corporation—whether enforced or voluntary—is better guided using a business-based model, with the organization as primary leader and organizer. Community-based initiatives, especially those that center on capacity building, are proactive, and are not time sensitive, might be better handled using a social science fieldwork model. Finally, use of the term "stakeholder" itself may be counterproductive or inaccurate, as it connotes a formal contractual or legal basis for participation [113]. For example, the author interviewed twelve (12) participants from across the U.S. about their experiences in pollution prevention or sustainability projects. Many of the participants interviewed were involved in initiatives without any contractual or legal basis. Further, they were largely unfamiliar with the term "stakeholder" and did not use it to refer to themselves.

In any case, a useful model must include not only the system-level details of implementation, but also the roles of individuals, as they describe them [92,94,125–129]. Further, while research links successful organization performance to both participation and to environmental initiatives, research on the link between the types of participation and the success of the environmental initiatives themselves is not conclusive.

Due to the complex nature of our environment, it is necessary to check the effects of our actions to determine if the result is what we intended, or if the risk is worth the return. Intuitive predictions about system behavior are frequently wrong, based on untested assumptions or incomplete information [14,69,130]. Therefore, research on such models should examine the functional, systemic aspects of successful initiatives, as well as the subjective experiences of participants.

More important than whether ISO certification is achieved, for example, is whether the applicant organization is able to meet its ultimate environmental goals via the EMS. In other words, are positive environmental outcomes evident? This question is urgent, as tight budgets have forced some public regulators to scale back on their activities and to rely more heavily on private, internally driven environmental monitoring approaches such as EMSs [11,26].

References

1. U.S. Environmental Protection Agency, Basic laws related to water, 2002 Available. at: http://www.epa.gov/win/law.html (accessed on December 19, 2003).
2. Allenby, B.R., *Industrial Ecology: Policy Framework and Implementation*, Prentice Hall, Upper Saddle River, NJ, 1999.
3. U.S. Environmental Protection Agency, Toxics release inventory (TRI) program: Background on the stakeholder dialogue, 2002, Available at: http://www.epa.gov/tri/programs/stakeholders/background.htm (accessed on December 26, 2003).
4. Goldstein, E.S., *Economics and the Environment*, Prentice Hall, Englewood Cliffs, NJ, 1995.
5. Mines and Communities Organization, nd, Mercury legislation rising in 24 states as pollution exposure concerns grow, say advocates, Available at: http://www.minesandcommunities.org/Action/press25.htm (accessed on December 19, 2003).
6. State Environmental Resource Center, Bill text, 2003, Available at: http://www.serconline.org/mercury/legislation.html (accessed on December 19, 2003).
7. Wheatley, M.J., *Leadership and the New Science: Discovering Order in a Chaotic World*, Berrett-Koehler, San Francisco, CA, 1999.
8. Helms, S.C., Report card, *The Environmental Forum*, 16, 20, 1999.
9. National Academy of Public Administration. *Resolving the Paradox of Environmental Protection: An Agenda for Congress, EPA, and the States*, National Academy of Public Administration, Washington, DC, 1997.
10. Florida Department of Environmental Protection, Pollution prevention (P2), 2003, Available at: http://www.dep.state.fl.us/air/programs/p2.htm (accessed on December 19, 2003).
11. U.S. Environmental Protection Agency, *Pollution Prevention: Framework*, 2003, Available at: http://www.epa.gov/p2/p2policy/framework.htm (accessed on December 19, 2003).
12. U.S. Environmental Protection Agency, Region 4, Home Page, 2003, Available at: http://www.epa.gov/region4/ (accessed on December 19, 2003).
13. Hawken, P., Lovins, A., and Lovins, L.H., *Natural Capitalism: Creating the Next Industrial Revolution*, Little Brown, Boston, MA, 1999.

14. Prugh, T., *Natural Capital and Human Economic Survival*, ISEE Press, Solomons, MD, 1995.
15. Chesapeake Bay Project, Watershed Profiles, 2004, Available at: http://www.chesapeakebay.net/wspv31/(rh41dg4502qw3iem0zwbfw45)/WspAbout.aspx?basno= 1&topic=5 (accessed November 9, 2004).
16. Florida Department of Environmental Protection, Florida Hospitals for a Healthy Environment—Florida Pollution Prevention Program and Hazardous Waste Management, 2003, Available at: http://www.dep.state.fl.us./waste/categories/p2/pages/ H2E.htm (accessed on December 19, 2003).
17. Adams, J.D., *Thinking Today as if Tomorrow Mattered: The Rise of a Sustainable Consciousness*, Eartheart Enterprises, San Francisco, CA, 2000.
18. Diaz-Veizades, J., Beans and Rice, A poster session presented at the Saybrook Graduate School Residential Conference, Santa Rosa, 2003.
19. U.S. Environmental Protection Agency, Region 5, nd. Pollution Prevention Act, Available at: http://www.epa.gov/region5/defs/html/ppa.htm (accessed on December 22, 2003).
20. Legal Information Institute, Title 42, Chapter 133: Pollution Prevention, nd, Available at: http://www4.law.cornell.edu/uscode/42/ch133.html (accessed on December 19, 2003).
21. U.S. Congress, Title 42, Chapter 133: Pollution Prevention, nd, Available at: http:// www4.law.cornell.edu/uscode/42/ch133.html (accessed on December 19, 2003).
22. U.S. Congress, Title 42, Chapter 85: Air Pollution Prevention and Control Act, nd, Available at: http://www4.law.cornell.edu/uscode/42/ch85.html (accessed on December 19, 2003).
23. U.S. House of Representatives, Title 42: Safe Drinking Water Act, 1974, Available at: http://uscode.house.gov/title_42.htm (accessed on December 15, 2003).
24. Arrandale, T., A growth industry, *Governing*, 17, 53, 2003.
25. Arrandale, T., Guide to managing water: Making the most of a rainy day, *Governing*, 17, 52, 2003.
26. Sostek, A., Managing performance: People power, *Governing*, 16, 54, 2003.
27. Nordhaus, W.D. The ecology of markets, *Proceedings of the National Academy of Sciences*, 89, 843, 1992.
28. Meadows, D.H., Meadows, D.L., and Randers, J., *Beyond the Limits*, Chelsea Green, Post Hills, 1992.
29. Spath, J.G., *Red Sky at Morning: America and the Crisis of the Global Environment*, Yale University Press, New Haven, CT, 2004.
30. Cohen, A. (Producer) and Capra, F. (Director), *Mindwalk* [Motion picture], 1991. (Available from The Video Den collection at Rare Video.com, P.O. Box 36, Vestal, NY 13851-0036).
31. Churchman, C.W., *The Systems Approach*, Dell, New York, 1968.
32. Pasquale, L.E., Evaluating systems of care, A poster session presented at the Southeastern Evaluation Association 2004 Annual Conference, Tallahassee, 2004.
33. Ritchie, B., *State Waterways Still Polluted*, 2004, Available at: http://www.tallahassee. com/mld/tallahassee/news/8133358.htm (accessed on March 9, 2004).
34. Ostrom, E., Institutional analysis, design principles, and threats to sustainable community governance and management of commons, in *Law and the Governance of Renewable Resources: Studies from Northern Europe and Africa*, E. Berge and N.C. Stenseth, Eds., ICS Press, Oakland, 1998, 27–53.
35. Clark, W.C. and Dickson, N.M., Civil science: America's encounter with global environmental risks, in *Learning to Manage Global Environmental Risks, Vol. 1: A Comparative History of Social Responses to Climate Change, Ozone Depletion, and Acid Rain*, P.M. Hass, S. Jasanoff, and G. Rochim, Eds., MIT Press, Cambridge, 2001, 259–282.

36. Amburn, B., Building with a green thumb, *Governing*, 17, 54, 2004.

37. Ehrenhalt, A., Spreading out the clout, *Governing*, 17, 6, 2004.

38. Sostek, A., Air pollution effort gains steam, *Governing*, 17, 60, 2004.

39. Deterding, B., personal communication, March 2004.

40. Bousquet, Steve, Fee Hikes Would Fund Cleanup of Gun Ranges, 2004, Available at: http://www.sptimes.com/2004/03/03/State/Fee_hikes_would_fund_.shtml (accessed on March 3, 2004).

41. Young, O.R., The effectiveness of international institutions: Hard cases and critical variables, in *The Library of International Political Economy, Vol. I: The International Political Economy and International Institutions*, H. Milner and R.O. Keohane, Series Eds., and O. Young, Vol. Ed., Edward Alger Publishing Company, Brookfield, 1996, 151–185.

42. Broadbent, J., *Theories of Transition to Sustainability: Lessons from Japan*, Unpublished manuscript, University of Minnesota, Minnesota, MN, 2003.

43. Scheurs, M.A., *Environmental Politics in Japan, Germany, and the United States*, Cambridge University Press, New York, 2002.

44. Becker, C.D. and Ostrom, E., Human ecology and resource sustainability: The importance of institutional diversity, *Annual Review of Ecology and Systematics*, 26, 113, 1995.

45. Gardner, R., Ostrom, E., and Walker, J.M., The nature of common-pool resource problems, in *Rationality and Society*, D.D. Heckathorn, Ed., Sage, Newbury Park, CA, 1990, 335–358.

46. McGinnis, M. and Ostrom, E., Design principles for local and global commons, in *The Library of International Political Economy, Vol. II: The International Political Economy and International Institutions*, H. Milner and R.O. Keohane, Series Eds., and O. Young, Ed., Edward Alger Publishing Company, Brookfield, 1996, 464–493.

47. Young, O.R., *The Institutional Dimensions of Environmental Change: Fit, Interplay, and Scale*, MIT Press, Cambridge, 2002.

48. Haas, P.M. and McCabe, D., Amplifiers or dampeners: International institutions and social learning in the management of global environmental risks, in *Learning to Manage Global Environmental Risks, Vol. 1: A Comparative History, of Social Responses to Climate Change, Ozone Depletion, and Acid Rain*, P.M. Hass, S. Jasanoff, and G. Rochim, Eds., MIT Press, Cambridge, 2001, 323–348.

49. Schreurs, M.A., Clark, W.C., Dickson, N.M., and Jager, J., Issue attention, framing, and actors: An analysis of patterns across arenas, in *Learning to Manage Global Environmental Risks, Vol. 1: A Comparative History of Social Responses to Climate Change, Ozone Depletion, and Acid Rain*, P.M. Hass, S. Jasanoff, and G. Rochim, Eds., MIT Press, Cambridge, 2001, 349.

50. Catton, W.R. and Dunlap, R.E., Environmental sociology: A new paradigm, *The American Sociologist*, 13, 41, 1978.

51. Dunlap, R.E. and Catton, W.R., Struggling with human exceptionalism: The rise, decline, and revitalization of environmental sociology, *The American Sociologist*, 25, 5, 1994.

52. Arrandale, T., Trading for clean water, *Governing*, 17, 32, 2004.

53. Antibiotics and breast cancer, *Better Nutrition*, 66, 20, 2004.

54. Lovins, A.B., *Negawatts: Twelve Transitions, Eight Improvements, and One Distraction*, 1996, Available at: http://www.rmi.org/images/other/Energy/U96-11_Negawa tts.12-8-1.pdf (accessed on November 2, 2004).

55. How subsidies destroy the land, *The Economist*, 345, 21, 1997.

56. Mol, A., Ecological modernization and institutional reflexivity: environmental reform in the late modern age, *Environmental Politics*, 5, 302, 1996.

57. Humphrey, C.R., Lewis, T.L., and Buttel, F.H., *Environment, Energy, and Society*, Wadsworth, Belmont, 2002.

58. Lovelock, J., *Introductory: Gaia: A New Look at Life on Earth*, 1979, 1, Available at: http://www.maxists.org/reference/sugject/ohilosphy/works/us/gaia/htm (accessed on November 12, 2004).

59. BE SAFE, BE SAFE Platform, 2003, Available at: http://www.bessafenet.com/platform.html (accessed on October 7, 2003).

60. Young, O.R., *The Institutional Dimensions of Environmental Change: Fit, Interplay, and Scale*, MIT Press, Cambridge, 2004.

61. Barker, R., Dembo, T. and Lewin, K., *Extract from Frustration and Regression: An Experiment with Young Children*, 1941, Available at: http://gestalttheory.net/archive/lewin41.html (accessed on June 7, 2005).

62. Adams, J.D., Successful change: Paying attention to the intangibles, *OD Practitioner*, 35, 3, 2003.

63. McKenzie-Mohr, D., *Quick Reference: Community-Based Social Marketing*, 2003, Available at: http://www.cbsm.com/Reports/CBSM.pdf (accessed on January 5, 2004).

64. Petersen, J.E., Tax avoidance inc, *Governing*, 17, 58, 2004.

65. Moyers, B., *Trading Democracy*, 2002, Available at: http://www.pbs.org/now/transcript/transcript_tdfull.html (accessed on April 29, 2004).

66. Grossman, R., Linzey, T., Esq. and Brannen, D.E., Jr., Esq., *Model Amici Curiae Brief to Eliminate Corporate Rights*, 2003, Available at: http://www.ratical.org/corporations/demoBrief.html (accessed on April 28, 2004).

67. Associated Press, EU Orders Microsoft to Pay $613 Million Fine, 2004, Available at: http://www.msnbc.msn.com/id/4591561/ (accessed on March 24, 2004).

68. Privatization Will Precipitate Water Crisis, 2003, Available at: http://www.thehindu.com/2003/12/19/stories/2003121903161300.htm (accessed on October 22, 2004).

69. McKenzie-Mohr, D. and Smith, W., *Fostering Sustainable Behavior: An Introduction to Community-Based Social Marketing*, New Society, Gabriola Island, 1999.

70. Young, O.R., *Natural Resources and the State: The Political Economy of Resource Management*, University of California Press, London, 1981.

71. Snidal, D., Coordination versus prisoners' dilemma: Implications for international cooperation and regimes, in *The Library of International Political Economy, Vol. I: The International Political Economy and International Institutions*, H. Milner and R.O. Keohane, Series Eds., and O. Young, Vol. Ed., Edward Alger Publishing Company, Brookfield, 1996, 233.

72. Kiuchi, T. and Shireman, B., *What We Learned in the Rainforest*, Berrett-Koehler, San Francisco, CA, 2002.

73. Adams, J., personal communication, 2005.

74. Quevedo, E., California firms to use new management system to achieve sustainability: "Next generation" unveiled for performance-driven results, in *International Environmental Systems Update*, WSP Environmental, San Francisco, CA, 2002, 9.

75. Pahl, D. and Norland, E., Evaluation of federal environmental research: Extending the focus from outputs to outcomes, in *Managing for Results in Environmental Initiatives*, S. Montague, Ed., Performance Management Network, Ottawa, 2002, 1.

76. Hester, L., *EPA Press Advisory: EPA Promotes Environmental Management Systems*, Environmental Protection Agency, Washington, DC, 2002.

77. University of North Carolina at Chapel Hill and Environmental Law Institute, National Database on Environmental Management Systems: The Effects of Environmental Management Systems on the Environmental and Economic Performance of Facilities, 2003, Available at: http://www.ndems.cas.unc.edu/document/NDEMS 2001compendium.pdf (accessed on January 7, 2003).

78. Swift, J.M., Commonwealth of Massachusetts Executive Order No. 438: State Sustainability Program, Commonwealth of Massachusetts, Springfield, 2002.

79. U.S. Environmental Protection Agency, EPA's Strategy for Determining the Role of Environmental Management Systems in Regulatory Programs, Draft Paper Presented at the Quarterly Meeting of the Multi-State Working Group, Golden, CO, 2004.

80. U.S. Environmental Protection Agency, *The Plain English Guide to the Clean Air Act*, 2002, Available at: http://www.epa.gov/oar/oaqps/peg_caa/pegcaain.html (accessed on December 19, 2003).

81. Gallagher, D.R., Darnell, N., and Andrews, R., *Drivers, Designs, and Consequences of Environmental Management Systems: Research Findings to Date from the National Database on Environmental Management Systems*, University of North Carolina at Chapel Hill and the Environmental Law Institute in cooperation with the United States Environmental Protection Agency, and the Multi-State Working Group on Environmental Management Systems, Chapel Hill, 2001.

82. Agency for Toxic Substances and Disease Registry (ATSDR), ToxFAQS for Tetrachloroethylene (PERC), 2003, Available at: http://www.atsdr.cdc.gov/tfacts18.html (accessed on December 14, 2003).

83. U.S. Environmental Protection Agency, *Executive Order 13148: The Greening of Government through Leadership in Environment Management*, 2000, Available at: http://www.epa.gov/ems/federal/eo13148.htm#part1 (accessed on December 15, 2003).

84. Locke, G., State of Washington Executive Order 02-02: Sustainable Practices by State Agencies, State of Washington, Olympia, 2002.

85. University of North Carolina at Chapel Hill and Environmental Law Institute, National Database on Environmental Management Systems: The Effects of Environmental Management Systems on the Environmental and Economic Performance of Facilities, 2003, Available at: http://ndems.cas.unc.edu/document/NDEMS2001compendium.pdf (accessed on January 7, 2003).

86. Suarez, J.P., *Guidance on the Use of Environmental Management Systems in Enforcement Settlements as Injunctive Relief and Supplemental Environmental Projects*, Environmental Protection Agency, Washington, DC, 2003.

87. Law.com, Injunctive Relief, 2000, Available at: http://dictionary.law.com/definition2.asp?selected=963&bold= (accessed on February 4, 2004).

88. International Organization for Standardization, ISO 14000 Standards, 2002, Available at: http://www.iso.ch/iso/eu/prods-services/otherpubs/iso14000/environment.pdf (accessed on January 7, 2003).

89. Environmental Agency, *Environmental Management Systems and Operator Performance at Sites Regulated Under Integrated Pollution Control* (R&D technical report #P6-017/2/TR), Author, Bristol, 2002.

90. Lazlo, K., Evolutionary Systems Design, A poster session presented at the Saybrook Graduate School and Research Center Residential Conference, San Mateo, CA, 2004.

91. Cooperrider, D.L., Positive image, positive action: The affirmative basis of organizing, in *Appreciative Inquiry: An Emerging Direction for Organization Development*, D.L. Cooperrider, P.F., Jr. Sorensen, T.F. Yaeger, and D. Whitney, Eds., Stipes, Chicago, 2000, 29.

92. Head, T., Appreciative inquiry as a team development intervention for newly formed heterogeneous groups, *OD Practitioner*, 32, 59, 2000.

93. Senge, P.M., *The Fifth Discipline: The Art and Practice of the Learning Organization*, Currency Doubleday, New York, 1990.

94. Schein, E.H., in *The Clinical Perspective in Fieldwork*, J. Van Maanen, P.K. Manning, and M.L. Miller, Eds. in *Qualitative Research Methods Series*, Vol. 5, Sage, Thousand Oaks, CA, 1987, 1.

95. Whtye, W.F., *Learning from the Field: A Guide from Experience*, Sage, Newbury Park, CA, 1984.

96. Metcalf, G., Developments in Organizational Systems Thinking, Presented at the

Saybrook Graduate School and Research Center Residential Conference, San Mateo, CA, 2004.

97. Stalinski, C., Developments in Systems Thinking, Paper presented at the Saybrook Graduate School and Research Center Residential Conference, San Mateo, CA, 2004.

98. Walton, D., Introduction to Social Systems Design, Paper presented at the Saybrook Graduate School and Research Center Residential Conference, San Mateo, CA, 2004.

99. Benyus, J., *Biomimicry: Innovations Inspired by Nature*, William Morrow, New York, 1997.

100. Ambler, S.W., *Active Stakeholder Participation*, 2001, Available at: http://www.agile modeling.com/essays/activeStakeholderParticipation.htm (accessed on December 26, 2003).

101. Andriof, J. and Waddock, S., Unfolding stakeholder engagement, in *Unfolding Stakeholder Thinking*, J. Andriof, S. Waddock, B. Husted, and S.S. Rahman, Eds., 2002, 19–42, Available at: http://www.greenleaf-publishing.com/pdfs/ustanwad.pdf (accessed on December 26, 2003).

102. Cleveland, H., The future is uncentralized, *Public Administration Review*, 60, 293, 2000.

103. Gardiner, R., *Earth Summit 2002 Explained*, 2002, Available at: http://www.earth-summit2002.org/ES2002.pdf (accessed on December 26, 2003).

104. Hemmati, M., *Multi-Stakeholder Processes for Governance and Sustainability: Beyond Deadlock and Conflict*, Earthscan, Sterling, 2002.

105. The Malcolm Baldrige National Quality Improvement Act of 1987: Public Law 100–107, Available at: http://www.quality.nist.gov/Improvement_Act.htm (accessed on December 26, 2003).

106. Texas Natural Resource Conservation Commission, Texas Environmental Management System (EMS) Program, 2003, Available at: http://www.tnrcc/state.tx.us/exec/sbea/ems/index/html (accessed on December 26, 2003).

107. U.S. Environmental Protection Agency, *Stakeholder Involvement and Public Participation at the U.S. EPA: Lessons Learned, Barriers, and Innovative Approaches* (Report # EPS-100-R-00-040), Author, Washington, DC, 2001.

108. Kluzick, R.S., *Stakeholder Analysis*, 1999, Available at: http://www.kulzick.com/Stakehr1.htm (accessed on December 26, 2003).

109. Rahman, S.S., Waddock, S., Andriof, J., and Husted, B., Introduction, in *Unfolding stakeholder thinking 2*, 2003, Available at: http://www.greenleafpublishing.com/catalogue/unfold2.htm (accessed on December 26, 2003).

110. Schein, E.H., *Organizational Culture and Leadership*, 2nd ed., Jossey-Bass, San Francisco, CA, 1992.

111. Stakeholder, *The American Heritage Dictionary of the English language*, 4th ed., nd, Available at: http://education.yahoo.com/reference/dictionary/entries/76/s0697600.html (accessed on December 26, 2003).

112. Participation, *Encarta World English Dictionary, North American Ed., Microsoft Corporation*, 2004, Available at: http://encarta.msn.com/dictionary_/participation.html (accessed on January 5, 2004).

113. Andriof, J., Waddock, S., Husted, B., and Rahman, S.S., Introduction, in *Unfolding Stakeholder Thinking*, J. Andriof, S. Waddock, B. Husted, and S.S. Rahman, Eds., 2002, Available at: http://www.greenleaf-publishing.com/pdfs/ustintro.pdf (accessed on December 26, 2003), 9–16.

114. Carter, M., personal communication, 2004.

115. McIntosh, M., Leipziger, D., Jones, K., and Coleman, G. *Corporate Citizenship: Successful Strategies for Responsible Companies*, Financial Times Professional Limited, London, 1998.

116. Gallagher, D., From coercion to cooperation: Influences on environmental management systems, *Dissertation Abstracts International*, 63, 195, 2002.

117. Pasquale, L.E., *Participation in Environmental Management Systems: The Relationship of Stakeholder Involvement to Environmental Targets*, Unpublished Manuscript, Saybrook Graduate School and Research Center, San Francisco, CA, 2003.

118. Brio, J.A., Fernandez, E., Beatriz, J., and Vazquez, C.J., Motivations for adopting the ISO 14001 standard: A study of Spanish industrial companies, *Environmental Quality Management*, 10, 13, 2001.

119. Delmas, M., Stakeholders and competitive advantage: The case of ISO 14001, *Production and Operations Management*, 10, 343, 2001.

120. Rondinelli, D. Panacea, common sense, or just a label?: The value of ISO 14001 environmental management system, *European Management Journal*, 18, 499, 2002.

121. Koelsh, R., Rosenthal, S., and Steward, C., Pollution Prevention Strategies, Poster session presented at the regional meeting of the Multi-State Working Group (MSWG), Omaha, NE, 2002.

122. Hanna, M., Newman, R., and Johnson, P. Linking operational and environmental improvement through employee involvement, *International Journal of Operations and Production Management*, 20, 148, 2000.

123. Hillary, R., *Evaluation of Study Reports on the Barriers, Opportunities, and Drivers for Small and Medium Sized Enterprises in the Adoption of Environmental Management Systems*, Network for Management and Auditing, London, 1999.

124. Kitazawa, S. and Sarkis, J., The relationship between ISO 14001 and continuous source reduction programs, *International Journal of Operations and Production Management*, 20, 225, 2000.

125. Allen, W., Bosch, O., Kilvington, M., Oliver, J., and Gilbert, M., Benefits of collaborative learning for environmental management: Applying the integrated systems for knowledge management approach to support animal pest control, *Environmental Management*, 27, 215, 2001.

126. Argyris, C., Putnam, R. and Smith, D., Part one: Designing a science of human action, in *Action Science*, Jossey-Bass, San Francisco, CA, 1985, 4.

127. Bernstein, R.J., *Beyond Objectivism and Relativism: Science, Hermeneutics, and Praxis*, University of Pennsylvania Press, Philadelphia, PA, 1983.

128. Jick, T.D., Mixing qualitative and quantitative methods: Triangulation in action, *Administrative Science Quarterly*, 24, 602, 1979.

129. Nichols, F., *The Accountability Scorecard: A Stakeholder-Based Approach to Keeping Score*, 2000, Available at: http://home.att.net/~nickols/scorecard.htm (accessed on December 26, 2003).

130. Dahlstrom, K., Howes, C., Leinster, P., and Skea, J., Environmental management systems and company performance: Assessing the case for extending risk-based evaluation, *European Environment*, 13, 187, 2003.

Chapter 15

Sustainable Waterfront Development in the Great Lakes Basin

Wendy A. Kellogg and Erica M. Matheny
Cleveland State University

15.1 Introduction

Globalization has changed the economic role of cities, as each has become part of an international network [1]. The resulting structural shift to a "post"-industrial economy in North America has had great significance for cities in the Great Lakes region. The Great Lakes of North America are the largest system of freshwater lakes on Earth, covering 94,000 square miles, and contain roughly 18% of the world's fresh water. The lake system consists of five lakes (Superior, Michigan, Huron, Erie, and Ontario) and spans 750 miles (1200 kilometers) in the heart of the North American continent, forming the eastern border between Canada and the United States. These vast "freshwater seas" drain west to east, one lake "emptying" into the next, finally reaching the North Atlantic through the St. Lawrence River. The lakes and the St. Lawrence River form a large basin that includes two Canadian provinces (Ontario and Quebec) and eight states in the United States (New York, Pennsylvania, Ohio, Indiana, Illinois, Michigan, Wisconsin, and Minnesota [2] (Figure 15.1).

During this economic shift, many cities in both Canada and the United States witnessed a decline in their industrial base and a loss of population and

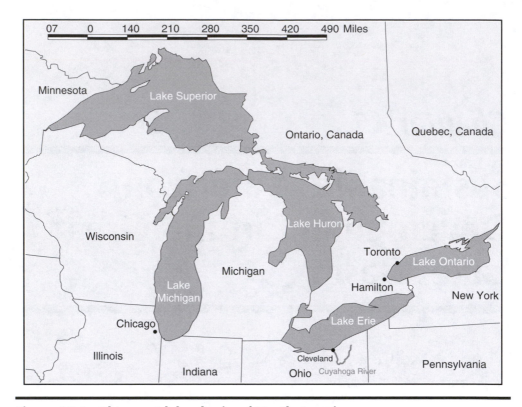

Figure 15.1   The great lakes basin of North America.

investment to suburban areas or to developing economies overseas. In the last several decades, many cities have sought to revitalize and bring their urban cores, and waterfronts, into the 21st century. For some, this has meant a reinvestment in industry. Others have focused on quality of life amenities and ecological restoration. These efforts have been based on partnerships among public and private stakeholders, and many have involved input to planning processes from the general public. The most inspirational cities have attempted to integrate these aspects under an umbrella of "urban sustainability."

Waterfronts today are the mechanism through which many cities are redefining themselves and responding to a changing world. This chapter describes efforts in four cities in the Great Lakes basin to redevelop their waterfronts as a centerpiece for the city. The chapter first describes the importance of waterfronts for cities and the recent history of waterfront regeneration as a focus for city planning and development. It then presents key attributes that have formed the basis of urban sustainability. Four case studies are based on a review of key planning documents, presentations by the planners who led development of the plans, and follow-up telephone interviews with these planners. The cases are then compared as to the themes and practices by which these communities articulated the meaning of sustainability in their waterfront regeneration processes.

15.2 Waterfront Growth, Decline and Redevelopment in the Great Lakes Basin

The urban waterfront, be it on an ocean, lake or river, is often the symbolic "door" of the city, the place of entry for new citizens and the place of exit for goods that are traded through shipping. The relationship between a city and its waterfront or riverfront is shaped by the unique location and history of the city, and in this sense, each urban waterfront has its own idiosyncratic story [3]. Each waterfront is also influenced by broader economic, political, and social forces at the national or global level [4]. The waterfront is a local articulation or response to broader macro-economic trends such as globalization or technological change.

The story of the North American Great Lakes waterfront is a narrative about land use and the relationship of the waterside area to the rest of the city. This relationship can be explained by a set of factors that shape all settlements, no matter their location: proximity to life-sustaining natural resources; the use and exploitation of resources for trade and other economic purposes; changes in production, transportation and communication technology; changes in a variety of connections to the rest of continent and to the globe; and changes in how the people think about natural resources.

The location of early settlements, whether established by the First Americans living on the continent over 500 generations prior to European intrusion [5–8] or as part of European exploration and dominance of the continent [9], was determined in large part by the physical characteristics of the landscape and the water's edge. Settlements were located on safe harbors, among abundant natural resources (including extensive marshes and estuaries rich with animals and vegetation), or at critical junctures of rivers and lakes for enhanced transport. Many settlements were atop coastal dunes, which had for generations been used for pedestrian travel.

European settlements in the Great Lakes basin, which began to flourish during the 18th century, brought a story of water diversion, land creation, and an overall hardening of the edge between the shoreline and the settlement. As settlements grew in population, each needed to grow in territorial size. Typically the first extension of territory to meet expanded port and land needs was to drain and fill marshes and estuaries along the shoreline. Such land reclamation has been an experience typical to cities on the shoreline and allowed urban centers and ports to expand [10]. In the 19th century, settlements associated with shipping agricultural and forest products on the lakes grew dramatically, as a vast network of canals built across the basin connected the lakes to the Mississippi River, the Ohio River, and the eastern seaboard of the United States, and thereby to Europe. These cities, located where the lakes and rivers met canals and railroads, grew as "break of bulk" centers, where raw natural resources and agricultural products were transferred into smaller boats or railroad cars or processed into products for easier shipping (from trees to lumber, from wheat to flour, etc.). The processing and storage facilities drew workers and businesses, creating public and private resources that financed new infrastructure and transportation systems [11,12]. Eventually, railroads followed the canals in the later 19th and early 20th centuries, and the need for additional docking space and railroad yards required further shoreline stabilization, anchorage improvements, and land creation. The spoils of harbor dredging and the garbage of the city were often used for land reclamation [3,10,12,13]. These new transportation facilities and the commercial buildings they required expanded into the settlement, often blocking access to the port area from other parts of the city.

The Great Lakes region became the manufacturing heartland of both Canada and United States in the late 19th and early 20th century. Steel, shipping, automobile, paint, and other industries succeeded in the basin, and the cities that developed these industries grew large. These included Chicago, Detroit, Cleveland, Buffalo, and Milwaukee in the United States, and Hamilton, Windsor, and Toronto in Canada. By the mid-20th century these cities and their metropolitan regions were home to more than 30,000,000 people. The rise of the automobile and trucking industry resulted in expanded access to the waterfront areas by highways. Many cities in the Great Lakes basin built elevated highways along the waterfront to relieve traffic congestion and speed truck transport, further separating the city and the water.

Dominance of these cities lasted well into the mid-20th century, but structural changes in the manufacturing sector, largely a result of globalization of industrial capacity, resulted in dramatic shifts for Great Lakes cities. Two great waves of plant closings occurred in the southern Great Lakes basin between 1969 and 1984, washing away millions of jobs. From 1979 to 1984, a 40% reduction in steel jobs occurred in the United States. Between 1978 and 1982, 300,000 autoworkers lost their jobs. In some areas entire industries disappeared [14].

These changes were often felt most dramatically in the ports and on the waterfronts. As industry declined, the need for port facilities did as well. Jobs left for warmer climates and cheaper wages, leaving large tracts of land abandoned or vacant [15]. Solvents, heavy metals, and other chemicals used for manufacturing and shipping contaminated much of this land. Adjacent neighborhoods, once vibrant centers for port and riverfront workers and their families suffered a loss of population, investment and activity.

During the 1980s, cities began urban redevelopment efforts. Eventually these efforts turned to reinvigorating waterfronts and riverfronts, which came to be seen as opportunities to provide quality of life benefits and new economic opportunities for cities in a post-industrial economy. Several trends can explain the renewed interest in waterfront redevelopment, illustrating the tensions that inhere in land use and function in waterfront areas. Movement of industry to suburban areas resulted in vacant land along the waterfront [16] as port and industrial activities declined, raising the opportunity for redevelopment. "Just in time" delivery and containerization required less land for warehousing [3,17]. More strict environmental regulations for dredging and fill slowed or restricted creation of new land for port activities [3]. Cleaner water, a result of environmental regulations and an advanced cooperative effort between Canada and the United States to restore the Great Lakes, created opportunities for alternative types of activities along the shoreline, including recreation, housing, boating, and "ecological" tourism. The historic preservation movement has spurred the adaptive reuse of existing buildings as locations of cultural tourism [16]. Renewed interest in the private sector for water-oriented, high-end development has spurred construction of new mixed-use complexes [3,18]. People's attitudes toward coastal areas (they want them protected) and urban waterfronts (they want access to them) have changed as well [17]. Increased citizen activism seeking public spaces such as parks and boardwalks has also fueled competition for land. The urban center, and therefore the waterfront, is increasingly seen as a regional asset, a key part of regional economic success [19–21]. All these trends have increased the competition for waterside land between traditional port and trade functions and urban or ecological tourism, which bid up the demand on land, making it more profitable for redevelopment by urban entrepreneurs [3,22].

In light of all these trends, many city governments have recognized the need for plans to guide the transformation of the urban waterfront. While waterfronts have typically been a product of intelligent transformative work [23], waterfronts have not historically been carefully or coherently planned. Growth and change has been disjointed and incremental [3], shaped by the interests and actions of local entrepreneurs who form coalitions with other actors and government agencies through planning processes as part of the urban "growth machine" [22]. This coalition is central to urban waterfront redevelopment today and typically focuses on promoting land development to attract regional, national, and international tourism and business [3]. Its goals often directly conflict with the interests of urban residents, who typically envision a waterfront with public open space, free access to the water, moderately priced housing, and authentic places to be used by urban residents.

Urban development in North America, perhaps more than any other continent, has been influenced by port activities, and was in many ways the birthplace of contemporary waterfront revitalization [24]. The largest and most well known efforts have been in San Francisco, Baltimore, Boston, Vancouver, and New York over several "generations" of waterfront redevelopment [25]. With each succeeding "generation," waterfront redevelopment has moved toward a more human scale, preserving existing building assets when possible, and responding to tighter financial markets [18,25].

The land-water interface in the Great Lakes basin differs from waterfronts on the oceans in several important aspects. Ecologically, there are no lunar tides, so weather is a more important determinant of water flow. The water is fresh, although wetlands play the same role as in a marine environment, to protect the shoreline form harsh weather. While most Great Lakes waterfronts grew as a result of a combination of shipping and transport, they have been more influenced by industry than marine waterfronts. Waterfronts in the basin did not experience the dramatic changes resulting from containerization and intermodal transport of the 1970s and 1980s, because the large ships that pushed this change could not pass into the Great Lakes system through locks on the St. Lawrence River, which were built in the 1950s. As a consequence most waterfronts in the basin, even in the largest cities, are smaller than marine waterfronts and the separation from the city as time goes forward has been more a consequence of automobiles and highways than changes in water transport technologies.

15.3 Urban Sustainability as a Framework for Waterfront Regeneration

By 2010, more than 50% of the world's population and more than 75% of the population in the more developed economies will live in cities. The future of the planet rests on remaking urban settlements to be ecologically, economically, and socially sustainable. Urban sustainability is both an overall goal and a framework to guide decision-making. It asserts that urban areas can be healthy and viable for current populations while still maintaining resources and capital to provide for future generations. This concept integrates ecological, economic, and cultural/social considerations that affect current and future urbanites. Both the goals and the process for urban sustainability must be flexible to accommodate the changing requirements of urban areas [26], including the long-term duration and regeneration of growing metropolises to provide a decent quality of life for urban residents [27].

Urban sustainability is created by a self-reinforcing feedback loop of reciprocity [28]. The choices made by a community shape its ecological, economic, and social environment, which in turn restricts or supports the future choices the community can make. Ecological resources in the city include land development, water quantity and quality, air quality, and extractable natural resources. As cities develop and modernize, their environmental impact gradually shifts from local to regional or global. Initially, a city may use local resources for its citizens, find local ways to deal with issues of waste, and creates pollution on a local scale. As a city grows it begins to import resources to sustain its burgeoning population, looks for places to store its growing wastes, and creates pollution that is no longer local.

In many respects, transportation choices have the greatest effect on ecological sustainability [29]. The development of extensive highways and reliance on personal automobiles for the majority of transportation during the second half of the 20th century in North America has increased air pollution and changed the built form to accommodate cars, not people [19]. As cities have grown into vast metropolitan regions, pollution generated by automobiles moving urbanites and suburbanites to and from work, stores, and recreational amenities constitutes one of the largest sources of pollution contributing to climate change, illustrating the expanding influence of cities as they grow [29].

Urban sustainability is also essential from an economic perspective. For a city to maintain itself in a viable way, businesses with "staying power" and some attachment to place must be present. The sustainable city needs to attract and maintain business that will stay for the long term and will not harm the ecological sustainability of the city, and that will contribute to its economic vitality. Cities have sought to redevelop areas in which business can locate, and to draw residents and visitors to the heart of the city [22]. In parallel, the development of growth boundaries can be an important aspect of sustainable city planning, as it can help to maintain a city on an efficient territorial scale [28].

Finally, the social capacity of the city has an undeniable impact on its sustainability. The presence of trust, safety, and community amongst citizens of a metropolis influences their decision to stay there. A sense of history, a sense of place, and quality of life amenities all also play an important role in this process. Public participation in decision-making processes is a key component for building social and political capacity in the sustainable city [28].

In short, planning the sustainable city requires finding the synergies between global forces and local preferences and needs, between different types of economic uses (that require different configurations spatially), and between the hard edge of the built form and the softer edge of ecological systems at the interstices of land and water. A sustainable development framework is appropriate given the significance of urban waterfronts and riverfronts to Great Lakes cities. In many Great Lakes cities, active and degenerate port facilities sit next to abandoned, yet naturalizing brownfields, which are next to areas slated for redevelopment as housing, recreational amenities or tourist attractions. Waterfronts in the Great Lakes basin are increasingly recognized for their economic development potential, for their potential as areas offering quality of life amenities for the "new" economy, and for their enduring capacity in providing habitat and ecosystem services.

How can these competing uses, sometimes even competing value systems, be reconciled? In many Great Lakes cities, the conflicts among land uses have been negotiated through involvement of stakeholders and citizens. As cities struggle to reconcile the contested terrain of their waterfronts, to define for each the dominant type or the mix of types of uses, plans must address the inherent urban complexity that waterfronts embody. Waterfront plans must allow for a plurality of function, link to the rest of the city, and provide for both public and private spaces [23,30]. Increasingly waterfronts are being used to redefine the identity of the city, to market the city to the world in a globalizing economy [31]. Indeed, the task for the planning and design professions is to create memorable places that serve the needs of residents while using waterfront revitalization to achieve economic development goals identified for the city as a whole, recognizing that redevelopment of the urban waterfront is not a panacea for the economic and physical problems of the entire city [30].

15.4   Case Studies

15.4.1   *Selection of Cases*

The cities discussed in this chapter were among those featured at a conference on Great Lakes cities and their waterfronts held at the Levin College of Urban Affairs at Cleveland State University [32]. The cities share a common history of settlement and development as part of the vast land and water territory of the Great Lakes basin. They also all share a history of transport and industrial growth and decline. The two larger cities, Chicago and Toronto, are centers of trade and financial markets, and not only are the primary cities of their large regions, but important international centers. The smaller cities, Hamilton and Cleveland, are the centers of smaller regional economies and still maintain strong connections to manufacturing. The cities also contrast in their political culture, with two in Canada and two in the United States, helping us to understand the influence of different planning contexts. The waterfront redevelopment processes in these cities are in various stages from mature and ongoing to early implementation, allowing us to examine the role of institutional capacity that accrues over time.

15.4.2 Waterfront Redevelopment Cases

15.4.2.1 Toronto, Ontario, Canada

The city of Toronto is located in the core of a large metropolitan region of nearly 4 million people on the north shore of Lake Ontario. Several large rivers rise in rural areas to the north of the city and flow southward across an increasingly urbanized landscape to the Lake Ontario shoreline across the Toronto region. Political jurisdictions in Canada are controlled at the provincial level, in this case the Province of Ontario, and over the last several decades the City of Toronto and its major suburbs have been consolidated into regional special districts (such as one featured in this case study, the Toronto and Region Conservation Authority) and Metro Toronto, a general purpose government. Eventually, the province created one unified planning area known as the Greater Toronto Area (GTA) in the mid-1990s, to address the regional scale of urbanization and public services. The waterfront area of the city and the region is large, running 155 miles (250 kilometers) along the Lake Ontario shoreline. It includes urbanized river mouths, a few remaining wetlands, suburban shorelines, the central district and port area of Toronto, and a set of islands that form the Toronto inner harbor area [33–35].

The city and region of Toronto in their various forms have engaged in a series of planning exercises focused on the lakeside areas for forty years. In the early 1960s, the Metropolitan Toronto Planning Board identified the need for a comprehensive waterfront plan to coordinate public and private development rather than risk haphazard growth. In 1970, the Toronto and Region Conservation Authority (TRCA) was designated the implementing agency for the 1967 Waterfront Plan for the Metropolitan Toronto Planning Area. The TRCA reviews and comments on land use plans at the municipal and regional level, and carries out its own planning for natural areas and watersheds. In 1981, TRCA's Lake Ontario Waterfront Development Program identified a goal to create "...a handsome waterfront, balanced in its land uses, complementary to adjacent areas, readily accessible and fully cognizant of the features which nature has provided" [36]. Another layer of planning resulted after creation of The Royal Commission on the Future of the Toronto Waterfront in 1988. Through the Royal Commission, Canada's federal government asserted its "interest" in the waterfront, in part, to reconcile the many water-related plans of different agencies and levels of government. The Royal Commission established the Waterfront Regeneration Trust, which exists today as the Toronto Waterfront Revitalization Corporation (TWRC), an organization seeking to facilitate investment in the waterfront area.

Beyond coordinating the multiple jurisdictions with interest, the ongoing major challenge to adopting a comprehensive waterfront plan in Toronto is private waterfront property ownership: "Development in Metropolitan Toronto historically commenced along the waterfront and then northward… [resulting in sections of] waterfront [property that] are privately owned or [prohibit]… public access to the water's edge…" [36].

Over the years, the change from these uses to park space and public access required a paradigm shift among the decision makers to allow the new uses to prosper. Adoption of an urban sustainability framework for the Toronto waterfront has been an additive process across the plans of different agencies and planning processes. The Metro Toronto Remedial Action Plan process, which focused on water quality issues, brought a heightened awareness of ecological sustainability to the waterfront during the late 1980s and early 1990s [37]. Building on these efforts and growing awareness of the connect of the city's vitality to the overall health of the Great Lakes, the Royal Commission developed principles for waterfront development which included the need to apply an "ecosystem approach" addressing the overlapping spheres of environment, economy and community [33]. This emphasis defined a holistic view of waterfront development in the Toronto region. As the Commissions final report suggested: "…waterfront-related strategies, plans, and programs to improve the quality of the environment, encourage community development or foster appropriate economic activities cannot be implemented in isolation: they must be undertaken in a regional context that recognizes the interdependence of the region and its waterfront, as well as the special qualities and characteristics of the waterfront itself" [33]. The present-day TWRC's Sustainability Framework of 2005 guides plans and investment "to ensure that sustainability principles are integrated into all facets of TWRC management, operations and decision-making… to create vibrant sustainable communities on the Toronto waterfront" [38].

The key meaning of sustainability guiding today's plans by the Toronto and Region Conservation Authority was derived from the 1987 Brundtland Commission's definition of sustainability as "development which meets the needs of the present without compromising the ability of future generations to meet their own needs" and builds on previous articulations: "The sustainability goals for Toronto's waterfront were derived from a variety of sources and pro-active planning for the future. The overall inclusion of sustainability goals within waterfront planning was something that evolved over time… over a period of approximately 40 years to eventually incorporate the concept of sustainability" [36].

Recently the TRCA adopted the Living City Vision to define a community that integrates human settlement requirements with environmental protection [39]. The TRCA worked with regional partners to ensure that the Living City is built upon a natural foundation of healthy rivers and shorelines, regional biodiversity, sustainable communities, and business excellence. Building on the earlier work of the Royal Commission, the TRCA's Toronto Waterfront Aquatic Habitat Restoration Strategy uses an ecosystem approach as a planning framework to create a more sustainable waterfront. The program seeks to increase ecological integrity, to provide suitable conditions for the maintenance of self-sustaining aquatic communities, and to improve ecological connectivity [36].

Adoption of a sustainability framework has led to a set of key principles for the TRCA: accessibility for the enjoyment and use of future generations, ecological integrity (as it is an integral part of its resource conservation and management role), and community engagement in project planning and implementation. For example, the TRCA incorporated extensive public and stakeholder consultation in the planning and implementing stages in waterfront development. Some mechanisms utilized include public meetings, open houses, workshops, questionnaires, newsletters, and website information. Working groups and implementation groups involved key community association leaders, Councilors, Members of Provincial Parliament, Members of Parliament, and key agency technical staff [36].

Demonstrating the degree to which a sustainable planning framework has been adopted in Toronto, plans for the city of Toronto as a whole have been changed by the development of a sustainable waterfront plan, in part due to the work of the TRCA. Because Toronto's waterfront is directly linked to the ten watersheds within TRCA's jurisdiction in the region, it has become obvious that waterfront health depends directly on the health of the region as a whole.

15.4.2.2   Chicago–Calumet, Illinois, United States

The city of Chicago was founded on Lake Michigan in 1837 on the site of an older trading fort at the mouth of the Chicago River. The name Chicago is said to derive from the Ojibwa (a First American nation) word for wild onions, which covered the low-lying areas along the riverbank [11]. Chicago grew dramatically in the late 19th century as a result of a network of canals and railroads, becoming the gateway to the upper Great Plains for settlement and trade. It survived a disastrous fire in 1871 (that destroyed $200 million worth of property) and grew to be the third largest city in the United States, today with a population of nearly 3 million. The greater Chicago waterfront spans 20 miles along the shore of Lake Michigan [40].

While the lakefront park area of Chicago is famous for its public open space that forms the core of the urban waterfront, more recent redevelopment initiatives focus on the Lake Calumet area, a 5,000-plus acre area with both large tracts of vacant industrial land that were created by filling in large parts of the original lake, and a sizeable area of rare wetlands located south along the Lake Michigan shoreline from downtown Chicago [41]. Several historical attempts to redevelop the Calumet (pronounced with the "t") area between 1909 and 1990 were never fully realized. Two recent planning processes led to the development of the current land use plan: *CitySpace: An Open Space Plan for Chicago;* and the *Calumet Area Implementation/Action Plan*. The City of Chicago, the Chicago Park District, and the Forest Preserve District of Cook County, with the Chicago Department of Planning and Development (DPD) as lead agency, developed these projects collaboratively. The projects addressed the significance of the land ecologically and the importance of the area to industry and the local economy.

In 1999, the Calumet Area Land Use Plan was developed in cooperation with the DPD in order to maximize the potential industrial and environmental benefits of this land adjacent to the Calumet River. The Southeast Chicago Development Commission, Openlands Project, and the Calumet Area Industrial Commission were also involved in the planning process. A U.S. Environmental Protection Agency Sustainable Development Challenge Grant and a grant from the Forest Service/U.S. Department of Agriculture funded the project. In addition to this, industrial Tax Increment Financing (TIF) was implemented for the region to encourage industry to relocate in the Lake Calumet area.

To develop realistic and salient sustainability goals for the Calumet plan, the public was involved in the planning process in several ways. Smaller focus groups of community representatives were set up to present and obtain feedback on the principal elements of the Calumet Project, including parks and open space, industry, transportation, and natural areas. These meetings with local community groups and citizens created a shared vision in which all stakeholders were vested. The City of Chicago entered into intergovernmental agreements with the two majority stakeholders, the State of Illinois, and the Forest Preserve District of Cook County, which established the shared vision and delegation of responsibilities for implementation of the Calumet Open Space Reserve.

Sustainability was articulated in the Calumet Area Land Use Plan as attaining "balanced growth for both industry and nature." The main goal of the plan was "to alter the decades long entrenched viewpoint of nature and industry as diametric opposites, and replace it with a vision that 'nature is good for business,' and that 'business is good for nature'" [42]. The objectives of the plan include addressing quality of life issues through the economic opportunity needs of local residents, environmental protection, including preservation of endangered species and natural areas, and retention and growth of existing industry while stimulating the development of new businesses in the area.

The planning process focused primarily on ecological and economic sustainability through a long-term view towards land development to integrate and balance the needs of area residents and stakeholders today with the projected needs of the future. The land use plan incorporates a variety of uses, including industrial facilities, public open space, habitat open space, recreational open space, and reclaimed landfill/waste management open space. The plan calls for preservation and development of connected green space within the Calumet Open Space Reserve and development of a heavy truck transportation route to industrial sites.

An important result of the planning process was changing the mindset of the parties involved to incorporate environmental principles into development and land use planning. "The land use plan established the goal that 'nature is good for business', and that 'business is good for nature'" [42], a key synergy possible through a sustainability framework. Political leadership played an important role in developing this new understanding of sustainable development, and the sustainability goals for the Lake Calumet area were a result of the leadership of "the Mayor of Chicago and the Governor of Illinois... work[ing] together and provid[ing] the financial resources and tools to develop a sustainable plan" [42].

One of the best examples of Chicago's effort to incorporate sustainability in the Calumet Area Land Use Plan involved the development of a facility that minimizes waste by using manufacturing processes that do not require long-term storage of parts and associated wasted resources. The Ford Motor Company Chicago Manufacturing Campus is a 155-acre/1.5 million square foot facility that houses eleven suppliers and employs 1400 people. Located a quarter mile away from the existing Ford Torrence Avenue Assembly Plant, is an example of "just in time" manufacturing to provide materials on demand, as opposed to the traditional stockpiling of materials. This site, funded in part by both the City and the State, was constructed on a former brownfield site, and also included numerous public benefits including new road infrastructure, remediation of contaminated soils, integration of stormwater BMPs, and restoration of 2000 ft. of a channelized stream to wetlands and riverine habitat. As a staff planner noted, "This project epitomizes the goal of the Calumet Project for public/private partnerships to rehabilitate and reinvest business in a sustainable manner protective of the environment" [42].

Overall, the Calumet plan has influenced the planning goals for the City of Chicago in a positive way towards equilibrium between the environment and the economy. "Regardless of viewpoint, the residential community, environmental advocates, and business community all want the Calumet area to improve. Decades have past, and the disinvestment in the area is the immediate concern. Sustainability for the local community [right now means]… jobs and economy" [42].

15.4.2.3   Hamilton, Ontario, Canada

Hamilton sits at the extreme western tip of Lake Ontario on Hamilton Harbour, which is separated from the lake by a sand bar that was cut by a shipping canal in the mid-19th century. Today Hamilton is a city of several hundred thousand, and has the largest single concentration of steel mills in Canada. The commercial and industrial legacy of the city resulted in Hamilton Harbour's designation as an Area of Concern (AOC) by the International Joint Commission in the mid-1980s. The promotion of a healthy Hamilton Harbour by using an ecosystem approach has been important since the implementation of the Hamilton Harbour Remedial Action Plan (RAP) in the early 1990s. Since then, the province, city and region, surrounding conservation authorities and local stakeholders have worked to deal with contaminated sediments in the harbor and to revive some of the marshes that once dominated the end of the lake.

Significant progress to regenerate shoreline areas have been made in the area known as West Harbour, located adjacent to the downtown core. The City of Hamilton adopted a policy for the West Harbour area in 1980 that envisioned this area of the City as the "people's waterfront." In recent decades, much of the industry in the area had departed, leaving behind large parcels of vacant, underused and contaminated land. The vision for the West Harbour area emphasized neighborhood redevelopment to preserve and enhance its diverse and historic character and the more effective employment of underutilized resources. The goals of the West Harbour plan were to create a "swimable" waterway through storm water management and water conservation; to improve aquatic and shoreline habitat; to manage potentially harmful sub-surface materials in the land through statutory policy; to protect scenic vistas from the neighborhoods to the harbor; to improve public access to the harbor; and to increase public awareness of benefits of the harbor as a natural resource [43].

Three public planning processes, each more detailed, shaped the redevelopment of the shoreline and its adjacent neighborhoods in the West Harbour area. In 1992, the city developed *"Putting People First: the New Land Use Plan for Downtown Hamilton"* as part of its *Vision 2020 Plan,* Hamilton's overall strategy for sustainability [44]. These plans identified the West Harbour area as an important focal point to connect the overall redevelopment of Hamilton to its waterfront, which industry and transportation corridors had separated for generations.

Setting Sail [45], which followed the downtown plan, presented a comprehensive plan for West Harbour area, including the Waterfront, the several neighborhoods adjacent to the harbor, and adjacent former industrial lands. The plan also focused on strategic redevelopment and streetscape improvements to strengthen the economic vitality of the street corridors and provide additional amenities to adjacent neighborhoods such as improvement of local parks and commercial areas, historic property preservation, contaminated site clean-up, relocation of heavy industrial land use, and the creation of necessary community services, such as schools, health care, libraries, and emergency services.

A key outcome of these plans was creation of Bayfront Park, Pier 4 Park and the Waterfront Trail, which opened vast stretches of the waterfront for public enjoyment. The increase in public access to the waterfront through these parks was important for "providing not just more water's edge experiences but also a greater variety of passive and active experiences," including the maintenance of boating access in the area and a year-round waterfront ...with additional cultural, commercial, and institutional attractions [46]. Finally, a West Harbour Secondary Plan was developed to guide detailed planning, zoning, and development decisions and to identify the city's priorities for publicly funded initiatives (Figure 15.2).

The plans created for the West Harbour area integrate the ecological, economic and social aspects of urban sustainability. These aspects include the long-term aesthetic and environmental appeal of the area, removal of physical barriers to the waterfront, enhancement of waterfront open space and public space, development and promotion of a balanced network of both public and private transportation means and the promotion and use of "best practice" building design to create a unique, memorable, and energy efficient West Harbour.

The land use plan for the West Harbour area recognizes that the City's long-term prosperity and sustainability will rely on a central core and a waterfront that are attractive, diverse, vibrant, and healthy. The land use plan was guided by

Figure 15.2   West Harbour Waterfront, Hamilton, Ontario.

eight core principles that emerged from extensive public consultation in the early stages of the study. The principles reflect and build upon many of the City's VISION 2020 goals for creating a healthy and sustainable city.

One of the greatest challenges faced was the translation of the sustainability goals into land use and infrastructure (e.g., transportation routes) decisions. Like the land use plan, the West Harbour Transportation Master Plan (TMP) reflects the eight core principles and encourages a balanced transportation network made up of automobiles, transit, pedestrians, and cyclists [46]. While many people supported creation of continuous public access to the water as a broad goal of sustainability (it was one of the original goals of the Remedial Action Plan for Hamilton Harbour), the translation of that goal into reality caused the biggest controversy in the project. Changes to the shoreline included in the plan would allow greater access through the neighborhoods by residents from across the region. Promoting a healthy harbor will likely include enhancing fish habitat through shoreline restoration, harbor bed vegetation, and removal of contaminated material at the water's edge and could impede boating club operations and marina operations or might reduce the number of slips available. As a result, local residents and boating clubs strongly opposed some aspects of the plan.

The waterfront plan influenced the plan or goals for the city as a whole. The City-wide growth management strategy for the City of Hamilton incorporated many of the objectives identified through the waterfront plan. These included: the encouragement of a compatible mix of uses in neighborhoods; concentration of new development within existing built-up areas having a firm urban boundary; expansion of transportation options to encourage travel by foot, bike and transit and enhance efficient inter-regional transportation connections; maximized use of existing buildings, infrastructure and vacant or abandoned land; protection of ecological systems and improved air, land, and water quality; maintenance and creation of attractive public and private spaces and respect for the unique character of existing buildings, neighborhoods and settlements; and improved waterfront access.

Despite the controversies that sometimes were generated, public consultation was a key part of these planning processes. The strategy was to reach landowners, tenants, community organizations, businesses, elected officials (locally, provincially, and federally) and residents of the project area. A key challenge was to ensure that the broader public interest in the waterfront was represented and balanced with local community interests. As one planner suggested, "We felt very strongly that there needed to be discussion, debate, issue identification, and resolution throughout the entire process. At each step of the way, we needed to check in with the community to ensure we were incorporating ideas, issues, and feedback. We would not move from one milestone until we were sure we had consulted stakeholders, identified issues, and ensured that these were incorporated into the milestone decision. We wanted to ensure that this was a truly iterative process with the community, the stakeholders, the businesses, residents, and those participating in the study" [46].

15.4.2.4 Cleveland, Ohio, United States

Founded in 1796, Cleveland is located on the southern shore of Lake Erie at the mouth of the Cuyahoga River. Both the lakefront and river valley were developed for commercial and later industrial enterprise. During the mid- and late 19th century, railroad and port facilities dotted the shoreline, as Cleveland's steel, chemical, and other heavy industries came to dominate [13,47]. Planning for Cleveland's waterfront has been, for the most part, piecemeal, narrowly focused, uncoordinated across jurisdictions, and driven by real estate and commercial interests in the city. Today, land use along the 18 miles (29 kilometers) of greater Cleveland's shoreline is still dominated by traffic arteries, industrial facilities, and other private land uses. Pedestrian and local access, lakefront parks and recreation and public land uses are secondary [48]. During the 1990s, the city developed an inner harbor area focused on tourism that includes the Great Lakes Science Center and the Rock and Roll Hall of Fame (Figure 15.3). Despite this success, the city struggles with the legacy of development decisions made over the past 100 years and has been unable to identify and forge a shared vision of how the entire lakefront should be used.

In April 2002, then-Mayor Jane Campbell launched "Connecting Cleveland: The Lakefront Plan" to develop a community consensus for the future of Cleveland's lakefront. The goal of the comprehensive planning effort was to create a long-range plan for the eight miles of lakefront in the City of Cleveland [49]. Two local foundations agreed to fund development of a

Figure 15.3 Central Waterfront, Cleveland, Ohio.

lakefront plan, but required formation of the Lakefront Partners to oversee development of the plan. The Lakefront Partners included the City of Cleveland, Cleveland Tomorrow (leaders in the business community), the Growth Association (the chamber of commerce), Cleveland Neighborhood Development Corporation (representing community development corporations and neighborhood groups), and Project BLUE (an ad hoc organization representing a coalition of citizen and environmental organizations). Through this partnership the foundations sought a planning process and outcome that would represent the major stakeholders in the community, including the business community.

A team of planning consultants with years of experience on waterfront development (although from outside northeast Ohio) was hired by the partners to oversee the lakefront plan development. The planning process had three phases. Phase 1, in 2002, focused on improved access between Cleveland's neighborhoods and its waterfronts, as well as the changes Clevelanders wanted to the lakefront. Phase 2, in 2003, took feedback from the community on the consultants' concepts in nearly 20 meetings in neighborhoods along the lakefront, and investigated constraints and opportunities for transforming Cleveland's lakefront. The resulting framework, known as the *Waterfront District Plan*, was approved in August 2003 by the City Planning Commission and was used to guide the preparation of more detailed development plans for six specific lakefront areas during Phase 3. The final lakefront plan was presented to the public in the fall of 2004 as a comprehensive, long-term plan that connects Cleveland's neighborhoods with its lakefront.

The plan was developed with an unprecedented (for Cleveland) level of public involvement that included the meetings in different lakefront neighborhoods and collaboration with the Levin College of Urban Affairs at Cleveland State University on a waterways/lakefront-focused series of public educational forums [50]. In an editorial, the *Plain Dealer,* the regional newspaper, celebrated the high level of public involvement with the planning process: "Anyone whose voice hasn't been heard since Mayor Jane Campbell initiated the conversation in April 2002 hasn't tried to be heard…. And they (the city planning director and staff) listened. As this plan has evolved, the public's impact has been evident" [51].

The plan was developed by first identifying a vision ("to shape the lakefront as the most vital element in the transformation of Cleveland as a place to live, work and play") and five planning parameters: integrate neighborhoods to the shoreline; capitalize on topography and natural features as assets; improve the three existing parks on the lakefront; transform a limited-access shoreway into a lakefront scenic byway; and develop accessible and connected public spaces. Planners developed the comprehensive plan by integrating five systems of study (access and connections, water-related improvements, parks and open space, neighborhood development, and sustainability) [49]. Each of these systems set parameters for design and planning decisions, and was developed into a planning agenda that provided action steps for implementation of the plan. The "sustainability" system in the plan "represents the underlying framework which defines the plan's values and strategy to create a sustainable urban environment." The planning agenda for each system stresses the lakefront as a special place, with a "unique combination of physical, cultural, social, and perhaps spiritual characteristics" that may "inspire people to care for and invest in their community" [49].

Key action areas under the sustainability system include buildings, energy, stormwater/water quality, transportation, materials, education and policy, landscape, and the ecological environment. Although the Waterfront District Plan is relatively new, several key steps have been taken to implement various aspects of the five systems and their action agendas to include sustainable practices. For future buildings, the city adopted guidelines for green building standards and will encourage developers to use them. For energy, the city has partnered with an energy-focused non-profit organization and a regional entrepreneur to assess the feasibility for creating a wind-turbine facility offshore along the lakefront. A windmill has been placed atop the city's drinking water intake crib some three miles into the lake that is measuring wind speed and consistency for the next six months [52]. The goal will be to incorporate energy from the windmills into current city-owned energy generation capacity.

Improving stormwater and overall water quality is a significant challenge that will be addressed over several years. The Waterfront District is home to several large combined sewer overflow fall out pipes that introduce sewage and non-point source pollutants into the lakefront beaches and docksides each time the city receives a significant rain. The regional sewer district and the city secured monies to construct a series of underground storage vaults that will contain stormwater and gradually release it to the sewage treatment plant, avoiding the outfall along the beaches. Once these are completed, the waterfront district will have significantly improved water quality.

Two transportation projects are moving forward. The existing waterfront light rail, which has not received much use since it was built in mid-1990s, will be connected to the downtown core and a high-speed bus system that will soon link the waterfront to other key cultural and employment centers in the city. Secondly, on the western portion of the Waterfront District, a limited access highway that has separated the water from several neighborhoods will be converted to a boulevard. This will allow for at-grade street connections from the lakeshore area to the neighborhoods, and will allow for development of what will become prime real estate along the lakefront boulevard to provide much-needed income and property tax revenues to the city. Less project-oriented progress has been made in terms of materials, education and policy, landscape, and the ecological environment.

Despite the successful completion of the plan and the start of implementation, it should be noted that the entire lakefront planning process was characterized by some degree of controversy. The mayor often heard criticism from many in the city's political leadership that the city should be focused on jobs and schools, not planning for the next 50 years on the lakefront. Many commuters and in-town residents rallied against conversion of the shoreline highway, expressing a preference for the "quick trip" downtown over the boulevard approach. The lakefront planning process stimulated the traditional political/economic coalitions in the city to organize a successful opposition to the mayor's re-election in 2005. It remains to be seen how deeply the sustainability principles and actions identified in the lakefront plan will be implemented by the new administration, which may not accept the need for a dramatic makeover of the lakefront as a long-term economic development strategy for the city.

15.5 Discussion

What can we learn from the experiences of these cities on the Great Lakes? Several themes emerge from these cases of waterfront planning and redevelopment.

15.5.1 Shared Historic Experiences

In all the water and riverfront areas we have featured, historic growth of the city had resulted in extensive infill of shoreline areas for industry and port activities. These changes allowed the city to expand its economy, but destroyed most of the natural shoreline's ecological function. Likewise, transportation infrastructure, primarily railroads and then highways, separated the water from the city in all cases. In all cases, decline of industry opened up land for redevelopment, but the existing infrastructure along the shoreline is proving to be a significant challenge to changes in land uses. And, as was seen consistently, restoration of the urban waterfront relies on restoration of water quality in the

Great Lakes that has occurred over the last 30 years through stronger environmental regulation and investment of billions of dollars for improved water treatment.

15.5.2 Land

Land reclamation is still an important part of the changing waterfront. This process is now less a result of the need for port expansion than an effort to restore existing contaminated lands along the shoreline for alternative uses. Land decontamination is a first step toward restoration of a more natural land/water interface at ecologically significant areas in Hamilton and Lake Calumet. In Cleveland's case, new land will be created out of dredged river sediments, which will fill a containment dike over the next 25 years and be used for an urban park.

Land use tensions are ever present in all of our cases as the cities transition certain areas from working ports or industrial areas to recreation and ecological uses. These tensions are often between redevelopment for use value of the waterfront versus redevelopment for exchange value and between public and private spaces. That is, will the waterfront be redeveloped for the people of the city to use, or to attract tourists or other businesses from outside the region as part of an economic development strategy? Will the waterfront space be open to all, or controlled by private owners?

All the featured cities have needed to address these tensions. In Hamilton, the plan for the West Harbour area explicitly designated the waterfront as a place for people, and connects it to recreational and ecological areas around the entire harbor. Even this generated controversy, as conflict arose between different types of use, and between public access for residents versus private marina areas. In Cleveland, certain areas on the waterfront are designed for city residents (the outlying parks and boulevards), while the central district plan builds on existing tourist attractions. The conflict between public space and access and private marinas and plans for waterfront housing also arose during the planning process. In Toronto, the central district has long been managed to attract tourists, but the waterfront development work along the more suburban metropolitan areas has focused on recreational access to trails and natural areas for residents. The Lake Calumet area offers an interesting juxtaposition—industrial redevelopment for jobs and restoration of natural areas—both oriented to residents. Of course, as these cities have learned, high quality amenities for urban residents often enhance the appeal of the city for tourists from around the region and for businesses seeking attractive communities for their employees.

15.5.3 Political System

Our cases demonstrate that the political system that frames the planning process matters. Differences in the political system and planning function between Canada and the United States have shaped the overall planning and redevelopment procedure. In Canada, authority flows from the federal government to the provinces to the region, and to the locality. This means that official plans adopted at the provincial and regional level exert influence in determining local land use and development. The presence of multi-purpose regional governments in Canada introduces planning at a regional scale as an official context for waterfront development. The influence of the regional conservation authorities, which have a legal role in land use plans at the regional scale, should not be underestimated. In both Toronto and Hamilton, the conservation authorities have been successful in their efforts to ensure that recreational open space and habitat areas were preserved and restored as part of waterfront redevelopment plans. No comparable governmental influence, either in terms of regional government or regional conservation authority, exists in the United States, and as a result local governments in our two featured cities guide waterfront redevelopment. In these cases, commercial real estate and nongovernmental advocacy organizations compete to influence the process in the absence of a strong regional influence.

15.5.4　The Timeframe of Planning

It takes time to articulate the meaning of urban sustainability that fits each city. The longer the process goes on, the more citizens and decision-makers recognize the need to tailor the waterfront to their needs and their city. In these cases, sustainability becomes part of the basis of place making, which is fundamentally linked to a restored ecosystem, development of social capital, and a shared sense of community.

15.5.5　Sustainability as a Waterfront Planning Framework

In all cities, a "systems approach" to guide planning and redevelopment has evolved over the years. Planners and decision-makers exhibited an increasingly more sophisticated view of all the components that make up a waterfront as an asset to the city and region. This systemic framework has been explicitly articulated in terms of sustainability, as these cities attempt to enhance economic, ecological, and social capital through changes to the built form. For example, in all the cases, cities are planning for not just the central waterfront, but have expanded their planning to consider the lake and river shoreline, integrating with tributary streams that flow into the waterfront. The plans call for not only rebuilding a hard edge, but also integrating the built form with open space recreation and ecological restoration to provide both hard and soft edges between the land and water. Plans suggest building places that will attract economic investment while preserving the inherent cultural and historic amenities of the city. In some aspects, sustainability folded in values and objectives that have long been part of exemplary urban planning practice, such as public recreation, neighborhood quality, and transportation efficiency. It is significant, however that in all of the cities, these aspects were tied explicitly to environmental quality in a way that exceeds traditional regulatory compliance. These plans acknowledge that ecological stewardship can serve as a foundation for a healthy, sustainable economy as well as protect the physical health of urban residents. While each plan does not embody all aspects of sustainability equally, each incorporates a mix of economic, ecological quality, and social engagement goals that will guide waterfront redevelopment efforts into the twenty-first century.

Acknowledgments

The authors thank the practitioners in Hamilton, Cleveland, Toronto and Chicago who participated in the Great Lakes Cities conference and who assisted in document retrieval and interviews for this chapter.

References

1. Sassen, S., *Cities in a World Economy*, 2nd ed., Pine Forge Press/Sage, Thousand Oaks, 2000.
2. USEPA/Environment Canada, *The Great Lakes: An Environmental Atlas and Resource Book*, 3rd Ed., Great Lakes Program Office/United States Environmental Protection Agency, Chicago, USEPA Document # 905-B-95-001, 1995.
3. ULI-The Urban Land Institute, *Remaking the Urban Waterfront*, ULI, Washington, D.C., 2004.
4. Riley, R. and Shurmer-Smith, L., Global imperatives, local forces and waterfront redevelopment, in *Revitalising the Waterfront: International Dimensions of Dockland Development*, B.S. Hoyle, D.A. Pinder, and M.S. Husain, Eds., Belhaven Press, London, 1988, 38–51.
5. Dennis, J., *The Living Great Lakes: Searching for the Heart of the Inland Seas*, St. Martin's Press, New York, 2003.
6. Sjonger, R. and Kalman, B., *Nations of the Eastern Great Lakes*, Crabtree Publishing, New York, 2005.
7. Smithyman, K. and Kalman, B., *Nations of the Western Great Lakes*, Crabtree Publishing, New York, 2003.
8. Kallen, S., *Native Americans of the Great Lakes*, Lucente Books, San Diego, CA, 2000.
9. Goetzmann, W. and Williams, G. *The Atlas of North American Exploration*, Prentice, New York, 1992.
10. Hudson, B., *Cities on the Shore: The Urban Littoral Frontier*, Pinter, London, 1996.
11. Cronon, W., *Nature's Metropolis*, W.W. Norton, New York, 1991.
12. Kellogg, W., Nature's neighborhood: Urban environmental history and neighborhood planning, *Journal of the American Planning Association*, 68, 356, 2002.
13. Keating, W., Krumholz, N., and Wieland, A., A century of planning of Cleveland's lakefront, Paper in the Association of Collegiate Schools of Planning Annual Conference, Baltimore, MD, 2002.
14. High, S., *Industrial Sunset: The Making of North America's Rust Belt, 1969–1984*, University of Toronto Press, Toronto, 2003.
15. Environment Canada/USEPA, *Land Use Background Paper, State of the Lakes Ecosystem Conference*, EPA 905-D-96-001e, USEPA, Washington, D.C., 1996.
16. Breen, A., and Rigby, D., *The New Waterfront: A Worldwide Urban Success Story*, McGraw-Hill, New York, 1996.
17. Hayuty, Y., Changes on the waterfront: A model-based approach, in *Revitalising the Waterfront: International Dimensions of Dockland Development*, B.S. Hoyle, D.A. Pinder, and M.S. Husain, Eds., Belhaven Press, London, 1988, 52–64.

18. Iannacci, A., *Revitalizing the Waterfront*, l'Arca, Milano, Italy, 1997.
19. Calthorpe, P. and Fulton, W., *The Regional City*, Island Press, Washington, D.C., 2001.
20. Ledebur, L. and Barnes, W., Cities and suburbs working together, in *The Inner City: A Handbook for Renewal*, R. Kemp, Ed., McFarland, Jefferson, N.C., 2001, 327–333.
21. Downs, A., *New Visions for Metropolitan America*, The Brookings Institution/Lincoln Institute of Land Policy, Washington, DC/Cambridge, MA, 1994.
22. Logan, J. and Molotch, H., The city as a growth machine, in *Urban Fortunes: The Political Economy of Place*, University of California Press/Regents of the University of California, Berkeley, CA, 1987, 50–98.
23. Bruttomesso, R., Complexity on the urban waterfront, in *Waterfronts in Post-Industrial Cities*, R. Marshall, Ed., Spon Press, London, 2001, 39–51.
24. Tunbridge, J., Policy convergence on the waterfront? A comparative assessment of North American revitalisation strategies, in *Revitalising the Waterfront: International Dimensions of Dockland Development*, B.S. Hoyle, D.A. Pinder, and M.S. Husain, Eds., Belhaven Press, London, 1988, 67–89.
25. Shaw, B., History at the water's edge in *Waterfronts in Post-Industrial Cities*, R. Marshall, Ed., Spon Press, London, 2001, 160–172.
26. World Commission on Environment and Development. *Our Common Future*, Oxford University Press, Oxford, 1987.
27. Moomaw, W.R., A sustainability postscript, *Environmental Impact Assessment Review*, 16, 425, 1996.
28. Maser, C., Beaton, R., and Smith, K., *Setting the Stage for Sustainability: A Citizen's Handbook*, Lewis Publishers, Boca Raton, FL, 1998.
29. Kenworthy, J.R. and Laube, F.B., Automobile dependence in cities: An international comparison of urban transport and land use patterns with implications for sustainability, *Environmental Impact Assessment Review*, 16, 279, 1996.
30. Marshall, R., Contemporary urban space making at the water's edge, in *Waterfronts in Post-Industrial Cities*, R. Marshall, Ed., Spon Press, London, 2001, 3–15.
31. Iwata, N. and del Rio, V., The image of the waterfront in Rio de Janeiro: Urbanism and social representation of reality, *Journal of Planning Education and Research*, 24, 171, 2004.
32. Levin College of Urban Affairs, Forum Program, *Great Lakes Cities Symposium*, 2003. Available at: http://urban.csuohio.edu/forum/waterways/great_lakes_cities/ (accessed on December 2005).
33. Royal Commission on the Future of the Toronto Waterfront. *Regeneration: Toronto's Waterfront and the Sustainable City: Final Report*, Minister of Supply and Services, Canada, 1992.
34. City of Toronto, *Waterfront Plan*, Available at: http://www.toronto.ca/waterfront/index.htm (accessed on December 2005).
35. City of Toronto, *Waterfront Trail Map*, Available at: http://www.waterfronttrail.org/maps/wt-2_11.pdf (accessed December 2005).
36. Phillips, A., personal communication, 2005.
37. Environment Canada, Environmental Ontario, Ministry of Natural Resources, and Metropolitan Toronto and Region Conservation Authority, *Metro Toronto Remedial Action Plan: Environmental Conditions and Problem Definition*, Author, Toronto, 1988.
38. Toronto Waterfront Revitalization Corporation, *Sustainability Framework 2005*, Available at: http://www.towaterfront.ca/dbdocs/4394549db60f1.pdf (accessed on August 2005).
39. Toronto and Region Conservation Authority, *The Living City*, Available at: http://www.trca.on.ca/living_city/ (accessed on December 2005).
40. The Columbia Encyclopedia, 6th ed. 2001–2004. Chicago. Columbia University Press, New York, Available at: www.bartleby.com/65/ (accessed on December 2005).

41. City of Chicago, *Lake Calumet Initiative Lake Calumet Land Use Plan*, 1999. Available at: http://egov.cityofchicago.org/webportal/COCWebPortal/COC_ATTACH/CalumetAreaLandUse Plan (accessed on December 2005).

42. Cheung, N., personal communication, 2005.

43. City of Hamilton, Ontario, *West Harbour Planning Area Map*, Available at: http://www.myhamilton.ca/NR/rdonlyres/ABA5447F-4AFE-4A16-A0CD-50CDF6428D24/0/SettingSailM2.pdf (accessed December 2005).

44. City of Hamilton, Ontario, *Vision 2020*, 2004. Available at: http://www.vision2020.hamilton.ca/default.asp (accessed on December 2005).

45. City of Hamilton, Ontario, *Setting Sail*, Available at: http://www.myhamilton.ca/NR/rdonlyres/80002DC2-37A4-47D3-8C5D-2FA838E25D0A/0/SSSecondaryPlan.pdf (accessed on December 2005).

46. Tanner, M., personal communication, 2005.

47. Rose, W., *Cleveland, The Making of a City*, World Publishing, New York, 1950.

48. Cuyahoga County Planning Commission, *Lakefront Landuse Map*, Cuyahoga County Planning Commission, Cleveland, 2002.

49. City of Cleveland, *Connecting Cleveland: The Waterfront District Plan*, 2004, Available at: http://planning.city.cleveland.oh.us/lakefront/cpc.html (accessed on December 2005).

50. Levin College of Urban Affairs, Forum Program, *Waterways Forum*, Available at URL: http://urban.csuohio.edu/forum/waterways/index.htm (accessed on December 2005).

51. *The Cleveland Plain Dealer*, editorial, "Finally, a plan," November 14, 2004.

52. Green Energy Ohio, *Cleveland Crib Wind Monitoring*, Available at: http://www.greenenergyohio.org/page.cfm?pageID=700 (accessed on December 2005).

Chapter 16

Getting Agricultural Productivity and Environmental Sustainability at the Same Time: What Matters, What Doesn't?

Edward P. Weber
Washington State University

Madina Khalmirzaeva
Tashkent Institute for Irrigation and Melioration

Mark Stephan and Tetyana Lysak
Washington State University

Ilhom Esanov
Tashkent Institute for Irrigation and Melioration

16.1   Introduction

Developing and developed countries across the globe are struggling with the same policy conundrum—how to improve agricultural productivity and maintain, or even enhance environmental sustainability simultaneously [1–3]. Conventional wisdom has tended to focus almost entirely on technical fixes (e.g., more effective water delivery infrastructure, land leveling, more machinery, etc.), the availability of resources, the role of economic incentives, the proper design of decision-making institutions, and top-down control by central authorities as preferred solutions to the conundrum [3,4]. There is no doubt that in many, perhaps even most cases, these types of measures can be quite effective. Recently, however, it has become clear that conventional approaches do not work well for significant numbers of natural resource problems as well as other key public problems.

Indeed, there is a growing consensus that a more refined understanding of institutional and social dynamics is needed if the variations in outcomes associated with institutions, especially locally based, collaborative institutions, are to be to understood such that we improve our ability to develop effective short- and long-term problem solving capacity [1,5–11]. As part of this, there is mounting evidence of the value of inclusive and educative problem-solving approaches, or new rules of civic engagement, to effective policy programs. According to this view, communities seeking to achieve environmental sustainability, or other policy goals, will benefit to the extent that there is substantive citizen participation in policy processes, the use of collaborative decision processes, and the discretion to make many of the decisions in the areas directly affecting their communities and livelihoods. This approach reflects the belief that long-term policy success necessarily must involve citizens and community leaders from diverse social roles ultimately taking on the responsibility for translating policies into on-the-ground results in their own respective communities [12–18]. And increasingly, countries are taking these ideas to heart. In recent years, the national governments of as many as sixty developing countries have launched reforms to decentralize the governance of natural resources [19,20].

This research focuses on Uzbekistan in Central Asia, a country that faces many challenges as it attempts to move toward economic development and environmental sustainability [1,21]. Historically, Uzbekistan and other Central Asian countries, as is the case with many Western democracies, have approached environmental and agricultural policy problems by assuming that knowledge accumulated in the physical and natural sciences is the key to managing their policy problems wisely. Yet, in 2000, the national government of Uzbekistan passed legislation that created a new set of institutions to govern water resources at the local level. The aim of the reform is to devolve more authority over water resources and farming decisions to locally developed, collaborative Water User Associations (WUAs). The Uzbek reforms are predicated on the expectation that the creation of collaborative institutions embracing the basic tenets of the civic engagement model of decision-making will lead to positive policy outcomes for agricultural production (improved productivity, defined as higher yields, more efficiently produced) and environmental sustainability [21]. In this chapter, we focus our attention on seven WUAs spread throughout five regions of Uzbekistan—Fergana Valley, the Tashkent region, Karakalpakstan, Jizzhak, and Syr Darya—and primarily on the major crops of cotton and wheat. We ask two main questions. The first question is basic: Are the new institutions producing the intended results? The short answer is that the results are generally positive, yet mixed, with three cases reporting improvements in both crop productivity and environmental sustainability, and four cases reporting some drop in productivity coupled with environmental improvement.

The second question seeks to understand the variation in policy outcomes. What explains the overall policy performance of these seven WUAs, with policy performance defined as the ability to achieve (or not) the dual goals of agricultural (crop) productivity and improvements in environmental sustainability? In order to get at this, we test three alternative explanations— the presence (or absence) of formal institutions, physical wealth, or informal institutions. The short answer is that the policy performance of the Uzbek WUAs supports the informal institutions thesis, which does a markedly better job of explaining outcomes in these seven cases than the physical wealth framework, and a better job than the formal institutions approach.

The analysis proceeds with a methods section and a reporting of the crop productivity and environmental sustainability "outcomes" for each WUA before turning to the three alternative frameworks and their results.

16.2   Research Methods

The research group, consisting of both U.S. and Uzbek scientists and graduate students, hand-administered 378 member surveys and 7 Chairman surveys in the seven cases during November and December 2004. Taking from lessons learned by the USAID-sponsored NRMP project in Central Asia, we employed a stratified random sample method for data collection. First, all farmer/members listed on WUA membership logs were split into three groups, based on member location within their WUA irrigation/water supply system—head of ditch, middle, or tail. Head, middle and tail were decided by the amount of land under irrigation, with every attempt made to split the three areas as evenly as possible in terms of acreage/hectares (e.g., in a 1500 hectare WUA, an optimal split would be 500 hectare for each strata). Second, within each stratum, members to be surveyed were then randomly selected. Third, the number of respondents for any one stratum was limited to 25 in order to ensure similar size groups (equal representation of views) as much as possible and to capture a high percentage of the membership of virtually every WUA included in the study. If additional WUA members existed for a particular strata and case, an alternates list, also randomly generated, was developed all the way through the 40th member. With this size of sample, we were able to target the full WUA membership for 3 of the 7 cases, more than 60% of the total membership for two other cases, and more than 50% of the membership in two final cases. Response rates* for

---

* In cases of non-response, the team attempted face-to-face contact three times over two days. If unsuccessful after two days and three contact attempts, the researchers moved to the next name, if available, in the randomly generated list of WUA members for the particular strata at issue (i.e., head, middle or tail of canal). Enumerators kept track of all non-respondents using individual tracking sheets showing dates and times contacted, and whether a survey was actually administered or a person ended up in the non-respondent category.

Table 16.1   Survey Response Rates for Uzbek Water User Associations

WUA Name	Total Number of Members	Members Contacted vs. Responses	Survey Response Rates (%)
Aganay	159	62/68	91.2
Amir Temur	49	48/49	97.9
Berdakh	39	34/39	87.2
Dnepr Kama	113	75/89	84.3
Jambul	113	56/56	100
Oq Oltin	143	75/75	100
Tulkun	28	28/28	100

WUA members in all cases were extraordinarily high, ranging from a low of 84.3%–100% in three cases (see Table 16.1). We attribute the high response rates to the focus groups and socializing (dancing girls and vodka) that accompanied the focus groups with the WUA Chairmen in Tashkent, Uzbekistan. We had the opportunity to explain the research and its importance, and were able to enlist their help in tracking down and mobilizing survey respondents once we drew our random samples. In every case, instead of having to make hundreds of time-consuming treks from farm-to-farm in remote rural areas, hoping that a farmer was home and willing to be interviewed, the WUA Chairs succeeded in persuading almost every single farmer/member to come to a central location, usually the WUA offices, to conduct their interviews on the days we were in town.

We selected the seven WUAs (cases) based on the following criteria. First, we selected only WUAs with at least two years of operation (started operations in either 2002 or 2003), figuring that this gave local farmers time to organize and structure their WUAs, as well as to have ample experiences with the new institutions (in whatever form they developed). Second, in order to assure variation across cases, we selected a range of WUAs from strong institutional functionality to weak, and from high physical wealth to poor, based on expert advice from in-country government, academic, and NGO officials well versed in Uzbek agricultural practices and the WUA reforms. The lack of data on social capital and informal institutional dynamics meant that we were unable to select for variation on this count; we simply assumed that the complexity of social dynamics being what they are, we likely would see variation across cases (Table 16.2).

16.3   Performance Outcomes

The WUA reforms in Uzbekistan are an attempt to use local, collaborative institutions to improve both crop productivity and environmental sustainability. To get at policy performance for crops, we used 2001, a year prior to the establishment of any of the WUA institutions, and compared it to 2004, the latest year for which data was available on crop outputs, number of hectare planted, and the costs of crop production. The research team focused primarily on the

Table 16.2   Sources of Data for Framework Variables

Institutional "Functionality" variable

Degree of structure	WUA Chairman surveys/focus group, cross-checked against WUA member surveys
WUA meetings frequency	WUA Chairman surveys/focus group, cross-checked against WUA member surveys
Involve membership in decision-making?	Participation index from WUA member surveys
Make and implement "major" decisions?	WUA Chairman and WUA Member surveys

Physical wealth-

Land/soil resources	Expert estimates from TIIM/WUA Chairman surveys/focus group

Water resources, availability of

Volume/precipitation	Expert estimates from TIIM/WUA Chairman surveys/focus group
Access—location on canal	WUA Chairman surveys/focus group

Economics

Wealth of surrounding area	Expert estimates from TIIM/WUA Chairman surveys/focus group
Access to "outside" resource	WUA member surveys

Social Capital/Democratization

Social capital—Three trust indexes	WUA member surveys
Egalitarian decision-making index	WUA member surveys
Accountability index	WUA member surveys

two major crops in Uzbekistan, cotton and wheat, with attention given to corn (maize) in two cases. The crop productivity function is developed by first taking the rate of productivity (in centners per hectare)* for 2004 and dividing that rate by the rate of productivity for 2001. This gives a measure of how much crop production increased or decreased on a centner/hectare basis. Second, the cost measure is developed in the same way. The costs of crop production for 2004 are calculated on a cost per centner basis, and this cost function is then compared to 2001's, using division (2004 cost function divided by the 2001 cost function). Third, the increases (or decreases) in crop productivity are then divided by the increases (or decreases) in the cost of production function to arrive at the cumulative productivity measure. Ratings above "one" indicate that a WUA has met the goals of the WUA policy reform for agricultural productivity across all the crops in the survey. Ratings below one signal a decline in productivity. Finally, the cumulative productivity scores are weighted to reflect the dominance

---

* Centners are the basic measure of weight used in Central Asian agriculture, much like bushels in the U.S.

Table 16.3   Crop Productivity by WUA

WUA Name	RANK	Cumulative Productivity[a]	Cotton	Wheat	Maize
Aganay	4th	0.86	0.845[c]	0.874[c]	N/A
Amir Temur	3rd	1.72	2.477[b]	1.186[c]	0.672[b]
Berdakh	1st	2.49	2.064[c]	2.914[c]	N/A
Dnepr Kama	5th	0.77	0.853[b]	0.647[b]	N/A
Jambul	6th	0.62	N/A	0.618[c]	N/A
Oq Oltin	7th	0.60	0.752[c]	0.442[c]	N/A
Tulkun	2nd	1.91	1.289[b]	2.563[b]	1.769[b]

[a] Inflation for 2002 (7.6%) and 2003 (2.8%) is factored into these figures. Source for inflation data is the National Bank of Uzbekistan.
[b] Sole source of crop planting, production and cost data are the individual WUA farmer /member surveys.
[c] Crop planting, production and cost data are derived from both the individual WUA farmer/member surveys and the examination of WUA records.

of cotton and wheat.* (See Appendix A for all planting, harvest, and cost data for each crop and each WUA.)

When it comes to cumulative crop agricultural productivity, three WUAs show strong gains—Berdakh with a score of 2.49, Tulkun with a score of 1.91, and Amir Temur, which scores a 1.72 (see Table 16.3). Yet the other four WUAs suffer productivity declines, with Aganay, in the Tashkent region, showing a slight decline all the way down to Oq Oltin, in the Fergana Valley, where the decline is significant, particularly for wheat.

To understand the picture better requires digging into some of the specifics of each case. For example, many of the cases showed large to massive increases of hectares planted, even to the point of quintupling the planting area for cotton in Aganay, Amir Temur, Berdakh, and two other cases (see Appendix I). This suggests that the WUA reforms were responsible, at least in part, for unleashing latent farming demand in which additional opportunities for planting crops afforded by the reforms were fully embraced by Uzbek farmers. Thus, while productivity declined in some WUAs, overall WUA farmers were in a better position because the added increases in planted areas more than made up for the losses in per hectare production rates. A generous reading of such an outcome might claim that what appears to be a lack of success in meeting the WUA reform "productivity" goal, i.e., less efficiency, simply masks the larger picture, which is that of more economically successful WUA farming enterprises. At the same time, in the case of Jambul, Tashkent region, the original wheat production rate was high (relative to other Uzbek WUAs) and increased by 25% from 2001 to 2004. The overall cumulative productivity number, however, showed a decline because these farmers, much more so than others, experienced trouble keeping their

---

* Cotton and wheat are factored together at 90% of total crop production for each WUA. Added crops, if any, are weighted at 10% of total production. If there are no other crops than cotton and wheat, then their combined weighted score equals 100%.

production costs under control. Their costs for producing the wheat more than doubled. Further, the Aganay case started with high levels of productivity for both cotton and wheat relative to other WUAs, and while suffering a slight productivity decline (0.86), still maintained levels of production per hectare that were second only to Amir Temur in cotton production and much higher than other WUAs for wheat (the next closest WUA produced at a rate fully 18% less). The Fergana Valley WUA, Oq Oltin was in a similar situation—the WUA farmers were already quite productive in 2001 and so, while their productivity did slide significantly due to increasing costs, they were still producing more crops/hectare for both wheat and cotton in 2004 than the base year of 2001, and more crops/hectare than four of the seven surveyed WUAs in 2004. The Aganay and Oq Oltin outcomes may suggest that high performing agricultural areas prior to the reforms had the least to gain from any institutional changes, especially in the case of Oq Oltin, where the farming tradition extends back several thousand years. They know how to farm, regardless of whatever institution is organizing their efforts (Table 16.3).

WUA performance in the area of environmental sustainability is the other public policy outcome of interest to the Uzbek government and to this research. Farmer/members were asked a series of questions after being read the following statement: "My next questions concern environmental sustainability. As you no doubt know, the idea of environmental sustainability is that decisions taken today will maintain or promote a healthy natural environment both now and into the future." By asking three questions specific to environmental quality in the areas of the overall natural environment, the quality of water resources, and the quality of land resources, we established that the perceived overall trend in environmental conditions for all seven WUAs was positive from 2001 to 2004. Each question asked the farmer/members whether each particular item had (a) improved a great deal, (b) improved a little bit, (c) stayed the same, (d) become a little bit worse, or (e) become a lot worse.* The composite scores for these three questions showed that even in the weakest scoring WUA, Dnepr Kama, over half (55.5%) of the respondents perceived positive improvements (improved a great deal or improved a little bit) for environmental sustainability, while the strongest score of 72% came from the Oq Oltin WUA. This means that, generally speaking, the environmental goals of the legislation are being met in these seven cases.

Yet these results are not necessarily tied to the formation and practices of the WUAs. The more important policy question is whether, from the perspective of the farmer/members, the new WUAs are either promoting or deterring environmental sustainability. We assessed the effects of the WUAs using the following question and response set:

---

* We asked these questions for the purpose of establishing overall trends and to give us a better perspective for interpreting the results from the "WUA formation and practices" question. For example, we wanted to make sure that if the farmer/members believed strongly that WUAs were contributing to an improved ability to achieve environmental sustainability, yet the local environment in a particular case was getting much worse, then we would know that any positive effects of the new WUAs would be largely meaningless from the perspective of overall environmental sustainability.

Table 16.4   WUA Environmental Sustainability Scores

	Rank	Environmental Sustainability Score	Positive	Negative	No Effect	Don't Know
Aganay	5	0.592	43.2	4.1	25.7	27.0
Amir Temur	7	0.364	26.1	2.2	43.5	28.3
Berdakh	2	0.875	56.8	2.7	5.4	35.1
Dnepr Kama	3	0.691	50.7	0.0	22.7	26.7
Jambul	4	0.689	55.4	5.4	19.6	19.6
Oq Oltin (Fergana)	1	0.939	43.8	0.0	2.7	53.4
Tulkun	6	0.411	25.9	0.0	37.0	37.0

Q82. What has been the effect of the formation and practices of the WUA on environmental sustainability in your area? Would you say a...

☐ Positive effect or a
☐ Negative effect
☐ No effect (volunteered)
☐ Don't know

Table 16.4 shows that three of the seven WUAs—Berdakh, Jambul, and Dnepr Kama—had more than an absolute majority of respondents giving the WUAs a "positive effects" score, while *only four WUAs scored any negative responses*, with all such scores at extremely low levels (from 2.2 to 5.4%). We extrapolated from these results to develop an "environmental sustainability" score and rank for each WUAs by focusing on only those farmer/members able to make an active assessment—members who felt they knew enough to respond—of the impact of their WUA on environmental sustainability (i.e., we excluded those who responded "Don't Know"). The outcome scores reflect the number, or percentage, of respondents crediting their WUA with a "positive effect" in relation to the total number, or percentage, of "active" respondents scoring their WUAs as having a "positive," "negative," or "no effect" on sustainability. For example, 56.8% of all respondents in Berdakh gave their WUA a positive score, out of a total of 64.9% of active respondents. This translates into an environmental sustainability score of 87.5%, the second strongest sustainability score among the seven cases (Table 16.4).

In order to set up the comparative analysis between the institutional functionality, physical wealth, and informal institutional frameworks, we combined the agricultural productivity and environmental sustainability scores into a single measure giving each score equal weight.* (See Table 16.5.) The single measure is comprised of the sustainability scores in their present form (a 0–1 scale) and the productivity scores after being standardized to the

---

* Others may think that the two measures deserve different weightings. We chose equal weighting given that the Uzbek legislation was intent on achieving both outcomes simultaneously.

Table 16.5   WUA Policy Performance Scores and Ranks

	Agricultural Productivity Score	Environmental Sustainability Score	Total Score	Final Rank
Aganay	0.324	0.592	0.916	7th
Amir Temur	0.647	0.364	1.011	4th
Berdakh	0.939	0.875	1.814	1st
Dnepr Kama	0.291	0.690	0.981	5th
Jambul	0.233	0.689	0.922	6th
Oq Oltin	0.225	0.940	1.165	2nd
Tulkun	0.720	0.411	1.132	3rd

same zero to one scale.* The two scores were then added for the final combined measure and ranking (see Table 16.5). Unsurprisingly, Berdakh ranked first overall given strong scores for both the environment and crop productivity (1.814 out of a possible 2), and Aganay, with relatively weak scores on both counts, especially for crop productivity, ranked last among the seven WUAs. Oq Oltin in the Fergana Valley ended up in second place given their extremely strong environmental sustainability score and despite productivity scores that actually reflected declining productivity from 2001 to 2004. Tulkun, with a third place rank, reversed the Oq Oltin situation, scoring well for productivity, yet with a relatively low environmental score—reflecting the fact that the most Tulkun farmer/members do not believe the WUA is having a positive effect on environmental sustainability.

16.4   Explaining the Policy Performance of the Uzbek WUAs

How are we to explain the varying policy performance of these seven WUAs? Is it simply a matter of each group of farmer/members developing the formal institutional structure and mechanics of a local, collaborative decision-making institution? Does the availability of, and access to, physical wealth matter? Or, do the informal institutional dynamics associated with social relationships and WUA operations improve our ability to understand policy outcomes in these cases?

16.4.1   Formal Institutions: form and Function

The formal institutions framework focuses on the degree to which formal institutions are present. The expectation of this thesis, which accords with the

---

* In converting the productivity numbers to the new scale, we assigned the highest score (2.489 for Berdakh) the same weighting of 93.9% as the highest scoring WUA on the environmental sustainability scale. This meant our nominal scale ranged from a high of 2.65 down to zero. WUA productivity scores were divided by the 2.65 high score to produce the percentage scores seen in Table 16.5.

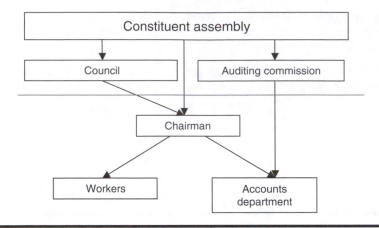

Figure 16.1 The structure of water user association, Uzbekistan.

expectations of the Uzbek national government when it created WUAs, is that the presence or absence of formal structures and operational mechanics equates with policy success. If the formal institutions framework is right, we should find noticeable policy performance differences among WUAs according to how much or how little institutional form and function are present. Formal institutions are operationalized using several criteria.

First, how much of a formal governance structure exists? Figure 16.1 shows the full structure of an Uzbek WUA. There is a Constituent Assembly consisting of all WUA members. The Assembly elects a Chairman, a WUA Council of seven to ten members, and an Auditing Commission, usually of three to four members. The elected Chairman is responsible for hiring and managing the Accounts Department and the workers (irrigators, technicians, pump regulators, etc.). The governance structure component was scored from one to three according to the degree of structure established in a WUA. One point represents a minimal structure—at least a Chairman, but little else.* Three points are awarded if all elements of the formal structure are present, while two points are awarded if some structure is in place at more than the minimal level (see Table 16.6).

Second, the formal functioning, or operation, of the WUA is defined in terms of three items: the frequency of WUA Constituent Assembly meetings on an annual basis, the degree to which WUA members are involved in decision-making, and whether a WUA is making and implementing major decisions (see Table 16.6). Frequency of Assembly meetings was scored on a one to six point scale, with higher numbers indicating greater frequency of meetings.[†]

---

* The optimal WUA "structure" discussed in the text, and taken from the WUA reform legislation, did not always occur in practice. In a number of cases throughout Uzbekistan, Chairmen were appointed, rather than elected, by government officials at either the oblast (state) or national level. In such cases, a Constituent Assembly, or the Auditing Committee, might not always exist.

[†] Weekly=6 points; Biweekly=5 points; Monthly=4 points; Quarterly=3 points; Biannually=2 points; Annually=1 point.

Table 16.6 Formal Institutions Scores and Predicted Rank

	Governance Structure	Frequency of Assembly Meetings	Member Participation (ParAware Scores)	Major Decisions: Yes or No	Total Formal Institutions Score (14 Possible Points)	Predicted Rank
Aganay	Some structure (2)	Biannually (2)	Solid (2)	Yes (2)	8	4th (tie)
Amir Temur	Some structure (2)	Quarterly (3)	Solid (2)	No (0)	7	7th
Berdakh	Full structure (3)	Monthly (4)	High (3)	Yes (2)	12	1st
Dnepr Kama	Some structure (2)	Quarterly (3)	Solid (2)	Yes (2)	9	3rd
Jambul	Weak structure (1)	Every 4 months (2.5)	Solid (2)	Yes (2)	7.5	6th
Oq Oltin	Some structure (2)	Every 4 months (2.5)	High (3)	Yes (2)	9.5	2nd
Tulkun	Some structure (2)	Biannually (2)	Solid (2)	Yes (2)	8	4th (tie)

The member involvement, or participation, in WUA proceedings and decisions, is scored using a Participation Index (ParAware) created from survey responses and represents farmer/member perceptions of their level of participation and sharing of decision-making responsibilities with the Chair and Council. Participation Index scores, scaled from zero to five, are then categorized according to whether there is zero/low participation, a situation where the Chair and Council make most or all of the decisions (ParAware score of less than one), solid participation, in which there is a good deal of sharing of decision-making responsibilities between rank-and-file members (ParAware scores between one and four), and high participation, a case in which farmer/members are relatively equal partners in decision-making with their leadership (Par Aware scores above four). Zero/low participation is given a score of one for the purposes of ranking, solid participation is scored as a two, and high participation a three (see Appendix B for the ParAware cross tab results).

The final element of formal institutional "functioning" is whether a WUA is making and implementing major decisions. Data were derived from Chairman surveys and a focus group involving all the WUA Chairmen in Tashkent, Uzbekistan, and checked against WUA member surveys for accuracy. We allowed WUA chairs and members to self-define major decisions and then asked for specific examples to support their claim. As we sorted through the examples offered by WUA Chairmen and farmer/members, it became clear that major decisions are those in excess of 500,000 soum in cost (roughly U.S. $500) and/or those allocating and rationing scarce resources among WUA members. Examples include the purchases of new farming and/or storage equipment (such as tractors, earth movers, irrigation equipment, grain bins/elevators, trucks, and ditch diggers), the spending of WUA budget moneys on outside consultants to assist with farm practices and management assessment, and the allocation of WUA money to irrigation and drainage improvement projects on specific parts of the larger irrigation system.

Table 16.6 lists the results of the formal institutions' form and function scores across the WUAs. Berdakh, with strong scores across the four criteria, is predicted to be in the best position among the seven cases to achieve the WUA policy goals, while Oq Oltin in the Fergana Valley ranks second. Jambul, on the other hand, with a weak governance structure, relatively infrequent Assembly meetings, a solid participation score, and a "yes" on major decisions, is expected to achieve the lowest levels of policy performance, with Tulkun and Aganay close behind in a tie for 5th place.

16.4.2 The Physical Wealth Framework

Framework two focuses on the availability of, and access to, physical wealth. Physical wealth is defined as a combination of natural conditions, natural resources, and economics (see Table 16.7). The first component involves land resources and focuses on the richness of the area's soil and general agricultural conditions. Component two includes the availability of water

Table 16.7 Physical Wealth Framework and Scoring System

Physical Wealth Component	5 Points Possible Per Each Component/25 Possible Points
Land Resources	Rich–Above Average–Middle–Below Average–Poor
Water Resources/Volume	Plentiful/wet–Above Average–Middle–Below Average–Scarce/arid
Water Resources/Access (location)	Strong/first in line–Above Average–Middle–Below Average–Weak/end of canal
Economics/Wealth of surrounding area	Rich–Above Average–Middle–Below Average–Poor
Economics/Access to outside resources	Rich–Above Average–Middle–Below Average–Poor

resources, both in terms of volume (plentiful/wet to scarce/arid) and access. With respect to access, the focus is on the location of a WUA within the larger irrigation/canal system. The strongest position is first in line, or closest to the original point of water diversion, while those at the tail end of a distribution system are in the weakest position. The third component of physical wealth—economics—is measured by the general wealth of the surrounding area vis-à-vis the rest of Uzbekistan (more is better) and access of the WUA to "outside" resources (government assistance, non-governmental assistance, etc.) (see Appendix C for the survey questions and formatting used to derive "outside" resource scores). The hypothesis is that greater physical wealth translates into policy performance success because WUAs will have the necessary resources to achieve the goals of crop productivity and environmental sustainability [1,2]. Each component is scored according to the 5-point scales found in Table 16.7.

Table 16.8 displays the predicted policy performance rankings of the Uzbek WUAs associated with the physical wealth framework. The predicted results are far different from the formal institutions framework, with only two of the five cases—Jambul and Dnepr Kama—keeping their same predicted rank.

16.4.3 Informal Institutions: the Social Side of the Street

The third and final explanatory framework involves a series of informal institutional elements focused on the civil society and engagement dynamics within WUAs and the farming communities themselves [22–24]. To capture this dynamic, we measure social capital and the degree of democratization of WUAs, as measured by egalitarian and accountability indexes. This framework posits that a collaborative WUA will more likely achieve the two policy goals of improved crop productivity and improved environmental sustainability to the extent that a community possesses strong social capital combined with a belief by WUA members that they have "ownership," or

Table 16.8 Physical Wealth Scores and Predicted Rank

	Land Resources	Water Resources (Volume)	Water Resources (Access)	Economics (Surrounding Area)	Economics (Access to Outside Resources)	Total Physical Wealth Score (25 Possible Points)	Predicted Rank
Aganay	Middle (3)	Middle (3)	Strong (5)	Above Average (4)	Below Average (2)	17	2nd
Amir Temur	Middle (3)	Scarce/arid (1)	Weak (1)	Middle (3)	Poor (1)	9	6th
Berdakh	Poor (1)	Scarce/arid (1)	Middle (3)	Poor (1)	Rich (5)	11	5th
Dnepr Kama	Middle (3)	Above average (4)	Middle (3)	Middle (3)	Poor (1)	14	3rd
Jambul	Below average (2)	Scarce/arid (1)	Weak (1)	Below average (2)	Below average (2)	8	7th
Oq Oltin	Rich (5)	Plentiful/wet (5)	Middle (3)	Above average (4)	Below average (2)	19	1st
Tulkun	Middle (3)	Middle (3)	Below average (2)	Middle (3)	Poor (1)	12	4th

Table 16.9 Trust Index Scores and Rankings of WUAs

	Trust Index #1 Occupation	Trust Index #2 Ethnic/Cultural	Trust Index #3 Community Cohesion	Cumulative Score	Predicted Rank
Aganay	−0.3095	−0.5093	−0.5407	−1.36	7th
Amir Temur	0.2816	−0.0201	−0.3983	−0.137	5th
Berdakh	0.392	0.3084	0.8542	1.555	2nd
Dnepr Kama	0.0957	−0.3859	−0.5798	−0.87	6th
Jambul	−0.0523	0.1952	0.1225	0.265	4th
Oq Oltin	0.7087	−0.5758	0.4143	0.547	3rd
Tulkun	1.6899	0.6355	0.2765	2.602	1st

a real stake in, and influence over, WUA decisions and the way the institution works.*

Social capital is defined as the extent to which a community develops a web of horizontal, cooperative relationships built on trust. To explore social capital, we employed a battery of questions from the Social Capital Survey of the World Bank that are designed for use by researchers in developing countries around the globe [25]. From our survey data, we constructed three indexes of trust, and then combined them into a single measure. Trust Index 1 focuses on how much trust WUA members have for different types of people in terms of their occupation,† while Trust Index 2 elaborates on the amount of trust WUA members have for people of different cultures and ethnicities, and Trust Index 3 elucidates the amount of community trust/social cohesion found in each WUA "community" of members (see Appendix D for the cross tab results). Table 16.9 displays the trust scores.

Democratization is defined as the extent to which the WUA has set up informal means by which its membership (and even those outside of the organization) can participate in decision-making and expect that those in leadership positions will be responsive. To explore democratization, we created a number of questions related to how the WUA operates in terms of leader and member interaction, the nature and extent of participation of members, and the informal mechanisms by which WUA members have their voices heard and their concerns addressed. From our survey data we created two key indexes. The first, our Egalitarian Index, pulls together thirteen

---

* [9,29–31], among others, find that high levels of social capital (trust) and/or ownership are important for effective environmental protection, natural resource governance, and sustainability. [10,28,32], among others, find that the central component of social capital, trust, is critical to economic development, with higher levels of trust associated with improved efficiency and economic development.

† For pragmatic and security reasons as regards the research effort, we dropped the World Bank instrument's references to trust in "police" and "national government."

Table 16.10   Combined Trust, Egalitarian and Accountability Index Scores

	Trust Score (standardized)	Egalitarian Score (standardized)	Accountability Score (standardized)	Informal Institutions Cumulative Score	Predicted Rank
	(5 to −5)	(5 to −5)	(5 to −5)		
Aganay	−4.9	−4.67	−3.62	−13.19	7th
Amir Temur	−1.85	−4.92	−4.58	−11.35	6th
Berdakh	2.375	4.99	1.44	8.81	1st
Dnepr Kama	−3.675	−2.18	−0.95	−6.81	5th
Jambul	−0.825	0.57	0.70	0.45	3rd
Oq Oltin	−0.125	2.14	3.89	5.91	2nd
Tulkun	5.0	−3.46	−3.36	−1.82	4th

questions related to the participatory nature of the WUAs. For example, are most decisions left to those in leadership or are there opportunities for wider participation? Does the member-based Assembly meet often or infrequently? Who gets to choose the Chairman for the WUA?* The second index, our Accountability Index, brings together questions related to the ability of members to influence the actions of the leadership. Can WUA members replace the Chairman if needed? Can members replace Council members? Are all decision-making records open to the membership for their review? Combined with the summary "trust" score, these two indexes allow us to better understand the extent to which decision-making is hierarchical within each of the WUAs. Table 16.10 displays the scores along with the Trust Index scores and a combined score for the three social capital and democratization indexes.

16.4.4   The Three Frameworks and the Policy Results: How Do They Measure Up?

If we want to understand WUA performance in terms of the two major goals of the Uzbek national reforms, it is clear that the Social Capital and Democratization (informal institutions) Framework is markedly better in explaining why some communities are doing well with the collaborative decision-making reforms, while others are not (see Table 16.11). In four of the seven cases—Aganay, Berdakh, Dnepr Kama, and Oq Oltin—Informal Institutions does a better job of predicting the performance rankings of WUAs than Physical Wealth, while in two other cases—Amir Temur and Tulkun—the explanatory power is exactly the same. Informal Institutions also scores better than the

---

* The only questions that might merit the "formal" institution designation, as opposed to informal, are two questions that ask about the specific decision rule by which Chairmen and Council members are selected. We asked whether these positions were appointed or elected.

Table 16.11 Comparing Frameworks and Policy Performance Outcomes

WUA Name	Formal Institutions Predictions Rank	Physical Wealth Predictions Rank	Social Capital & Democratization (Informal Institutions) Predictions Rank	Actual Productivity & Environmental Sustainability Outcomes Rank
Aganay	4th (tie)	2nd	7th	7th
Amir Temur	7th	6th	6th	4th
Berdakh	1st	5th	1st	1st
Dnepr Kama	3rd	3rd	5th	5th
Jambul	6th	7th	3rd	6th
Oq Oltin (Fergana)	2nd	1st	2nd	2nd
Tulkun	4th (tie)	4th	4th	3rd

Formal Institutions thesis upon which the Uzbek law was based by better predictions in three cases—Aganay, Amir Temur, and Dnepr Kama—while sharing the same explanatory power in three other cases—Berdakh, Oq Oltin, and Tulkun. In only a single case, the same case of Jambul, did the Formal Institutions and Physical Wealth frameworks do a better job of prediction. Moreover, the Informal Institutions framework correctly predicted the policy performance rankings among the seven WUAs in four cases—Berdakh (1st), Oq Oltin (2nd), Dnepr Kama (5th), and Aganay (7th)—while closely predicting a fifth case (Tulkun) by predicting its placement only one rank away from the actual performance ranking. This compares to the Wealth framework, which predicted zero cases successfully, three cases closely, and four quite poorly. The Formal Institutions predictions fared better with three cases predicted successfully, one closely, and three poorly.

16.5   Conclusion

Contrary to the expansive multi-variate model inclusive of both physical wealth and social items developed by Pretty [4], and in support of Pretty [9], in which he suggests that social capital is critical to understanding the performance success of WUAs/local irrigation governance mechanisms, the social side of things appears to matter more than either the trappings of formal institutions or physical wealth itself. We say "appears" because of the fact that we have a small number of cases (seven), which places obvious limits on our ability to claim causation and to generalize from these results. Nonetheless, the clear difference in the ability of the informal institutions framework to predict the policy performance of the WUA collaboratives in relationship to each other, especially versus the physical wealth hypothesis, provides additional support for the conclusion that resolving the conundrum of achieving both agricultural productivity and environmental sustainability requires close attention to social dynamics and relationships. Put differently, constructing a decision-making institution on poor social, or community "soil," i.e., without the right kind of supporting social infrastructure, is less likely to bring policy success. This appears to be especially true with a collaboratively based institution; more so than top-down institutions, it demands high levels of social trust and the kinds of informal, unwritten types of social rules and relationships able to foster the positive, constructive and productive discussions and cooperative processes required to move decision-making processes forward to successful conclusions [18,26].

The strong support for the informal institutions thesis further suggests that policymakers, whether in Uzbekistan or elsewhere, need either to approach locally based institutional reforms armed with a robust array of alternative institutions, each suited to a particular community, or to foster social capital and positive social interaction within decision-making institutions in those communities which lack these antecedent conditions. On this latter point, and contrary to some social capital research [10,27], building trust may not be an impossibility. Mutz [28], in an experimental design grounded in a national survey on trust and economic development, finds that "levels of social trust are malleable" and therefore subject to alteration "by what [people] see, hear, and read." In any case, both the "community selectiveness" and "building social capital" approaches will require more scientific information than is currently available in the literature on communities in most every country—developed or developing—and will require financial support for research from a variety of sources, including research funding agencies, non-governmental organizations, and governments interested in improving policy performance. Before taking any of these suggested steps, however, the findings reported here on the agricultural productivity, environmental sustainability, and collaborative institutions puzzle should be subjected to further and more extensive testing on a large number (exceeding 100) of WUAs in Uzbekistan and elsewhere to see if the findings hold. If done in Uzbekistan, the larger research agenda should include numerous Fergana Valley cases in order to separate out the potential effects of over 1000 years of farming tradition from the institutional, physical wealth, and social/informal institutions effects. Another improvement would be to incorporate a series of "hard" sustainability indicators in addition to, or, if they are robust enough, in lieu of, farmers' perceptions of sustainability. While offering a clear improvement on the current research design, such "hard" indicators may not always be available, as we found in the Uzbek situation. Finally, in a perfect world, researchers would be able to collect social capital and other community-based data both before and after WUA development. Given that we could not accomplish the *pre-WUA* collection of data, it is not clear whether the social capital was strong or weak prior to the WUA formation, and whether or how much the WUA formation contributed to the trust scores. We did find, however, that in every single community except one that trust among community members had improved significantly over the past several years.

Appendix A Crop Productivity Data

		Cotton				Wheat				Maize			
		Planted	Harvest	Cost (w/inflation)	Cumulative Score	Planted	Harvest	Cost (w/inflation)	Cumulative Score	Planted	Harvest	Cost (w/inflation)	Cumulative Score
Aganay	2004	6.14	26.58	10037.7		6	47.5	2903		N/A	N/A	N/A	
	2001	1.14	24.13	7700		1.59	43.04	2300					
			1.101533361	1.303597403	0.844995057		1.103624535	1.262173913	0.87438389				
Amir Timur	2004	17.46	46.14	8971		3.72	20.5	4220		1.64	18.05	806	
	2001	2.19	20.29	9770.25		0.95	22	5369		0.3	15	450	
			2.274026614	0.918195543	2.47662563		0.931818182	0.785993667	1.185528867		1.203333333	1.791111111	0.671836228
Berdakh	2004	22.74	21.33	20,495		5.55	26	2075		N/A	N/A	N/A	
	2001	3.04	12.83	25,450		0.82	11	2559					
			1.66250 9743	0.805304519	2.064448546		2.363636364	0.810863619	2.914961665				
Dnepr Kama	2004	23.27	13.25	20,784		22.29	18.85	8375		N/A	N/A	N/A	
	2001	7.23	15.12	20219.88		5.42	19.62	5637.62					
			0.876322751	1.027899275	0.852537571		0.960754332	1.485555962	0.646730488				
Jambul Ota	2004	2.56	N/A	19,877		9.74	39.88	4656		N/A	N/A	N/A	
	2001	0	N/A	7700		1.73	31.88	2300					
			N/A	2.581428571	N/A		1.250941029	2.024347826	0.617947673				
Oq Oltin	2004	9.42	25.66	10,575		7.28	36.95	5774		N/A	N/A	N/A	
	2001	4.76	24.45	7575		4.24	32.71	2260					
			1.049488753	1.396039604	0.751761447		1.129623968	2.554867257	0.442145855				
Tulkun	2004	34.22	22	10,135		6.56	29.004	5335		0.74	43.19	7932	
	2001	0.37	16	9500		0	23.128	10,906		0.51	36.792	11,951	
			1.375	1.066842105	1.288850518		1.254064338	0.489180268	2.563603686		1.173896499	0.66371015	1.768688485

Inflation figures are from National Bank of Uzbekistan—2002 = 7.6%; 2003 = 3.8%.

Appendix B Participation and Awareness Index

Taken from Question 58 through Question 66, and 67 of the Uzbekistan Washington State University/Tashkent Institute for Irrigation and Melioration WUAs Research Survey.

	N	Mean	Standard Deviation	Standard Error	95% CI for Mean	
					Lower Bound	Upper Bound
Aganay	74	2.7973	1.70398	0.19808	2.4025	3.1921
Amir Temur	48	2.8750	1.74582	0.25199	2.3681	3.3819
Berdakh	38	4.4474	0.97807	0.15866	4.1259	4.7689
Dnepr Kama	75	3.3333	1.78078	0.20563	2.9236	3.7431
Jambul	56	3.8750	1.34924	0.18030	3.5137	4.2363
Oq Oltin	75	4.4000	0.97260	0.11231	4.1762	4.6238
Tulkun	27	3.0000	1.83973	0.35406	2.2722	3.7278
Total	393	3.6609	3.6609	1.59868	3.5144	3.8073

Appendix C Levels and Sources of Outside Help

All WUA farmer/members were asked Question 91 of the Uzbekistan Washington State University/Tashkent Institute for Irrigation and Melioration WUAs Research Survey. In cases where outside help occurred, respondents were then "skipped" to a more specific question such as Question 92 below in order to elicit the significance of each source of outside help. As indicated by the Q91 skip patterns, Questions 93 through 98 covered the listed sources of outside help. The subsequent questions were presented in the same exact format as seen in Question 92 below.

Q91. What sources of outside help have you had in getting your WUA up and running/functioning? (Please check all that apply.)
☐ Non-governmental Organizations (NGOs) →SKIP TO Q92
☐ National government →SKIP TO Q93
☐ Oblast government →SKIP TO Q94
☐ Regional/Rayon government →SKIP TO Q95
☐ Local government →SKIP TO Q96
☐ Private businesses →SKIP TO Q97
☐ Other (describe) _____ →SKIP TO Q98
☐ Don't Know →SKIP TO Q99

Q92. What type of help did you receive from Non-governmental organizations? Would you say that there was significant help, some help, or only minimal help?

Type of Help	Level of Help		
(Check all that Apply)	Significant	Some	Minimal
	▽	▽	▽
☐ Financial	1	2	3
☐ Technical help (science)	1	2	3
☐ Technology (tractors, etc.)	1	2	3
☐ Personnel/workers	1	2	3
☐ Other_____	1	2	3

WUA, Outside Support Crosstabulation Results

■ A score of zero represents no support, while the highest registered score of 22 represents significant outside help across "sources" and "types" of help.

	0–4 (%)	5–9 (%)	10–13 (%)	14–18 (%)	19–22 (%)
Aganay	73.0	21.7	5.5	0.0	0.0
Amir Temur	91.7	4.2	4.2	0.0	0.0
Berdakh	10.5	7.9	76.4	2.6	2.6
Dnepr Kama	90.7	6.6	2.6	0.0	0.0
Jambul	60.8	37.4	1.8	0.0	0.0
Oq Oltin	74.6	20.1	1.3	0.0	4.0
Tulkun	96.3	3.7	0.0	0.0	0.0

Appendix D   Egalitarian and Accountability Indexes

Egalitarian Decision-Making Index

Taken from Questions 40, 41, 42, 43, 45, 46, 50, 57, 62, 64, 65, 72, and 74 of the Uzbekistan Washington State University/Tashkent Institute for Irrigation and Melioration WUAs Research Survey.

					95% CI for Mean	
	N	Mean	Standard Deviation	Standard Error	Lower Bound	Upper Bound
Aganay	74	−4.3827	6.06230	0.70473	−6.2373	−3.4382
Amir Temur	48	−5.1114	7.85317	1.13351	−7.3917	−2.8310
Berdakh	38	5.9938	3.88977	0.631	4.7152	7.2723
Dnepr Kama	75	−2.0422	7.98697	0.92226	−3.8799	−0.2046
Jambul	56	1.0388	6.17627	0.82534	−0.6153	2.6928
Oq Oltin	75	2.7988	4.06630	0.46954	1.8632	3.7344
Tulkun	27	−3.4795	8.31942	1.60107	−6.7705	−0.1884
Total	393	0.0000	7.38080	0.34413	−0.6763	−0.6763

Accountability Index

Taken from Questions 49, 56, 60, 77, 78 of the Uzbekistan Washington State University/Tashkent Institute for Irrigation and Melioration WUAs Research Survey.

	N	Mean	Standard Deviation	Standard Error	95% CI for Mean	
					Lower Bound	Upper Bound
Aganay	74	−2.1715	2.92030	0.33948	−2.8481	−1.4949
Amir Temur	48	−2.7454	2.74666	0.39645	−3.5430	−1.9479
Berdakh	38	0.8615	2.4716	0.40091	0.0492	1.6738
Dnepr Kama	75	−0.5680	3.40501	0.39318	−1.3514	0.2154
Jambul	56	0.4171	2.90994	0.38886	−0.3622	1.1963
Oq Oltin	75	2.3356	2.69646	0.31136	1.7152	2.9560
Tulkun	27	−2.0169	3.66460	0.70525	−3.4666	−0.5672
Total	393	0.0000	3.45875	0.16127	−0.3169	0.3169

Acknowledgments

The authors thank the U.S. State Department's Newly Independent States and Countries University Partnership Program (NISCUPP) for the financial support that made this research possible. The U.S. researchers would also like to extend their gratitude to our research colleagues and students at the Tashkent Institute for Irrigation and Mechanization (TIIM) in Uzbekistan who are not named as authors for this chapter. Their assistance in general research design, survey implementation, and data entry was critical to our success. Particular thanks goes to Vice Rector and Dean Abdulhakim Salokhiddinov, Mansur Amanov, Furkat Olimov, Masud Ismailov, Ahmad Hamidov, and Svetlana Madraimova. Yu-Sheng Lin of Washington State University also assisted in the data analysis for this chapter.

References

1. Kindler, J., Invited feature, freshwater systems: Linking ecological and development objectives: Trade-offs and imperatives, *Ecological Applications*, 8, 591, 1998.
2. Lichtenberg, E., Some hard truths about agriculture and the environment, *Agricultural and Resource Economics Review*, April, 251, 2004.
3. MacDonnell, L.J., *From Reclamation to Sustainability: Water, Agriculture, and the Environment in the American West*, University of Colorado Press, Boulder, 1999.
4. Pretty, J., Can sustainable agriculture feed Africa? New evidence on progress and processes, *Environment, Development and Sustainability*, 1, 3, 1999.
5. Bagadion, B.U. Sr., The role of water user associations for sustainable irrigation management, *Organizational Change for Participatory Irrigation Management APO*, 7, 1, 2002.
6. Hayward, B.M., Effective citizen engagement and social learning in environmental policy: The New Zealand experience, Paper presented at the 101st Annual Meeting

of the American Political Science Association, Washington, DC, (September 1–4), 2005.

7. Pfirman, S., *National Science Foundation, Complex Environmental Systems: Synthesis for Earth, Life, and Society in the 21st Century, A 10-Year Outlook for the National Science Foundation*, NSF Advisory Committee for Environmental Research and Education, National Science Foundation, Washington, DC, (January), 2003, 1–69.

8. Ostrom, E., Collective action and the evolution of social norms, *Journal of Economic Perspectives*, 14, 137, 2000.

9. Pretty, J., Social capital and the collective management of resources, *Science*, 302, 1912, 2003.

10. Putnam, R.D., *Making Democracy Work: Civic Traditions in Modern Italy*, Princeton University Press, Princeton, 1993.

11. Weber, E.P., *Bringing Society Back In: Grassroots Ecosystem Management, Accountability, and Sustainable Communities*, MIT Press, Cambridge, MA, 2003.

12. Evans, B. and Theobald, K., Local Agenda 21 and the shift to soft governance, in *Local Environmental Sustainability*, S. Buckingham and K. Theobald, Eds., Woodhead Publishing, Cambridge, UK, 2003, 91–113.

13. Karkkainen, B., Fung, A., and Sabel, C., After backyard environmentalism, *American Behavioral Scientist*, 44, 690, 2000.

14. Mazmanian, D.A. and Kraft, M.E., Eds., *Toward Sustainable Communities: Transition and Transformations in Environmental Policy*, MIT Press, Cambridge, MA, 1999, 113–151.

15. O'Leary, R., Durant, R.F., Fiorino, D.J., and Weiland, P.S., *Managing for the Environment: Understanding the Legal, Organizational, and Policy Challenges*, Jossey-Bass, San Francisco, CA, 1999.

16. Pharr, S.J. and Putnam, R.D., Eds., *Disaffected Democracies: What's Troubling the Trilateral Democracies?* Princeton University Press, Princeton, 2000, 31–51.

17. Ribot, J., *Democratic Decentralization of Natural Resources: Institutionalizing Popular Participation*, World Resources Institute, Washington, DC, 2002.

18. Weber, E.P., Lovrich, N.P., and Gaffney, M., Collaboration, enforcement, and endangered species: A framework for assessing collaborative problem solving capacity, *Society and Natural Resources*, 18, 1, 2005.

19. Agrawal, A., The regulatory community: Decentralization and the environment in the Van Panchayats (forest councils) of Kumaon, *Mountain Research and Development*, 21, 208, 2001.

20. World Resources Institute. Decentralization and local voice, in *World Resources 2002–2004—Decisions for the Earth: Balance, Voice and Power*, World Resources Institute, Washington, DC, 2003, 20–33.

21. Khasankhanova, G., Public participation to improve water resource management in Uzbekistan, In *Public Awareness/Education, Diffuse Pollution Conference Proceedings*, Dublin, Vol. 11, 2003, 1.

22. Ensminger, J., Culture and property rights, in *Rights to Nature: Ecological, Economic, Cultural, and Political Principles of Institutions for the Environment*, S. Hanna, C. Folke, and K.G. Maler, Eds., Island Press, Washington, DC, 1996, 179–204.

23. North, D.C., *Institutions, Institutional Change, and Economic Performance*, Cambridge University Press, Cambridge, MA, 1990.

24. Young, O.R., Rights, rules, and resources in world affairs, in *Global Governance: Drawing Insights from the Environmental Experience*, O.R. Young, Ed., The MIT Press, Cambridge, MA, 1997, 1–23.

25. Grootaert, C., Narayan, D., Jones, V.N., and Woolcock, M., *Measuring Social Capital: An Integrated Questionnaire*, Working Paper No.18, World Bank, Washington, DC, 2004, 153.

26. Schusler, R., Decker, B., and Pfeffer, J., Social learning for collaborative natural resource management, *Society and Natural Resources*, 16, 309, 2003.
27. Jackman, R.W. and Miller, R.A. Social capital and politics, *Annual Review of Political Science*, 1, 47, 1998.
28. Mutz, D.C., Social trust and e-commerce: Experimental evidence for the effects of social trust on individuals' economic behavior, *Public Opinion Quarterly*, 69, 393, 2005.
29. Fiorino, D.J. and Kirtz, C., Breaking down walls: Negotiated rulemaking at EPA, *Temple Environmental Law and Technology Journal*, 4, 29, 1985.
30. Lachapelle, P.R. and McCool, S.F., Exploring the concept of "ownership" in natural resource planning, *Society and Natural Resources*, 18, 279, 2005.
31. Weber, E.P., *Pluralism by the Rules: Conflict and Cooperation in Environmental Regulation*, Georgetown University Press, Washington, DC, 1998.
32. Miller, G.J., *Managerial Dilemmas: The Political Economy of Hierarchy*, Cambridge University Press, Cambridge, MA, 1992.

Chapter 17

Sustainability Issues in Public Procurement

Brian Pangrle
Lee & Hays PLLC

17.1 Introduction

17.1.1 Government Spending

Executive Order 13101, issued by President Clinton in 1998, carried the title "Greening the Government through Waste Prevention, Recycling, and Federal Acquisition" [1]. Senate Bill 3271, entitled "the Greening the Government Act of 2000," was submitted in response to Executive Order 13101 and recognized that the Federal government has a tremendous opportunity to use its more that $200 billion in annual purchasing power to improve the environment [2]. More perplexing is how to make more than 30 million procurement actions or decisions in a manner that achieves this goal [3].

17.1.2 Sustainable or Green Procurement?

Without a doubt, governments are big spenders and hence have a profound effect on people and the environment. Like most governments, the U.S. federal government has adopted various procurement codes which aim to ensure interested parties access, fairness and value while also providing guidance and redress. However, to date, few procurement codes account for the environmental impact of government procurement. Those codes that do account for environmental impact are often referred to as "green" procurement codes. Rarer still are "sustainable" procurement codes. As discussed below, some important distinctions exist between "green" and "sustainable". For example, the City of Austin, Texas, provides the following definition of "sustainability":

> Sustainability has been defined as meeting current generations' needs without compromising future generations' ability to meet their needs. Thus, the goal of sustainability requires that we seek to improve the quality of life in our communities without depleting the many resources—social, economic, and environmental—on which all human activity depends [4].

In theory, sustainable procurement codes aim to promote practices that try to avert all paths to an environmental and/or social disaster while green procurement codes or green practices merely make an effort to be cognizant of the environment. Unfortunately, objective standards have yet to emerge to determine *what* is sustainable or to determine *if* a practice is sustainable. In contrast, the practice of recycling aluminum cans or newspapers may be considered "green". Thus, at the onset, some hurdles exist in moving from green to sustainable.

Metric or philosophical concepts such as Life Cycle Analysis (LCA), ecological management, cradle-to-grave and cradle-to-cradle all have merit in their attempts to address system or global consequences related to production and consumption. These concepts may lead to an objective standard for sustainability and, in turn, pave the way for sustainable procurement codes.

In the United States, the concept of ecological management was introduced at the federal level around 1920, at least in part by Aldo Leopold. Leopold examined individual ethics that prompted cooperation in human communities and then redefined community to include "soils, waters, plants, and animals, or collectively: the land". This is the "Land Ethic," which Leopold articulated in *The Sand County Almanac*, published in 1948 [5].

17.1.3 Implementation through a Procurement Code

The fact that many governments are now pondering sustainability issues may demonstrate that a shift has occurred in the traditional human-centric definition of community. While the shift may arguably embrace Leopold's philosophy or other environmental philosophies, some explanations may simply point to common sense, fairness, hard economics, etc. For most governments, a thread may be established leading from a core reason to a present desire for sustainable practices and even sustainable procurement codes. In the United States, Leopold's philosophy undoubtedly lies near the core. More pointedly, with respect to the prospect of arriving at a model procurement code that embraces sustainable practices and the adoption of such a code by every state, an examination of other model codes and the Land Ethic suggest, whether optimistically or pessimistically, that the question is a matter not of if, but when.

Thus, as outlined below, a two-pronged approach may chart issues that will arise in arriving at a model procurement code that embraces sustainable practices, and in adoption of such a code at various levels of government. The first prong addresses practical sustainability issues faced by governments in implementation of concepts such as the Land Ethic, and whether local efforts can succeed without global harmonization; the second prong addresses practical issues faced in making objective determinations as to sustainability. Finally, an analysis of the Model Procurement Code is presented that points to various articles therein that may be subject to amendment, should one wish to transform it into a sustainable procurement code [6].

17.2   Brief Background

As already explained, this chapter aims to uncover issues that may arise in development of a model procurement code that promotes sustainable practices. While the American Bar Association's (ABA) Model Procurement Code is discussed in more detail below, attention should be drawn to the work of John B. Miller [7,8] circa 1997. Mr. Miller and Margaret E. McConnell served as the two reporters responsible for completion of the ABA's 2000 Model Procurement Code for State and Local Governments. Mr. Miller's work is perhaps the first in the U.S. to address issues of sustainability in relationship to a harmonized procurement code. Of further note, the field of sustainable procurement is expanding at a rapid pace. Thus, practices by governments and other organizations need to be monitored constantly for updates.

17.3   What is "Sustainable"?

17.3.1   Experience of U.S. Forest Service

Aldo Leopold was involved heavily with the U.S. Forest Service, now an agency of the U.S. Department of Agriculture; thus, it is not surprising that a current management goal of the U.S. National Forests is to achieve ecological sustainability. At a 1999 conference entitled "Building on Leopold's Legacy," Douglas MacCleery of the U.S. Forest Service delivered a speech that was later published in *Forest History Today* under the title: "Aldo Leopold's Land Ethic: Is it only half a loaf unless a consumption ethic accompanies it? Or is the shift to 'ecological sustainability' on U.S. Public Lands merely a sophisticated "NIMBYISM" masquerading as a 'paradigm shift'?" [9].

MacCleery's article points to a flaw in the U.S. government's implementation of ecological sustainability practices. According to MacCleery, the U.S. government's program cannot succeed unless the public makes a corresponding shift in commodity consumption habits. The validity of MacCleery's claim rests on the U.S. government's notion of success and its definition of "ecological sustainability". Indeed, if success is defined as preserving the forests *and* the scope of the "land" does not extend beyond national borders, then MacCleery may be wrong. However, Leopold put no limits on the land, i.e., the land did not end at government-designated national boundaries. Thus, MacCleery's claim appears to have some merit.

MacCleery's proposed solution is to limit public consumption; however, as discussed below, another solution may exist, namely international cooperation (i.e., global harmonization). Yet further, a combination of international co-operation and limitation on public consumption may provide the optimal result. Regarding the latter, a recent article states that "[a]t the level of high environmental politics, the Organization for Economic Cooperation and Development (OECD), the United Nations Commission on Sustainable Development (UNCSD), and the United Nations Environment Program (UNEP) have played key roles in reframing environmental deterioration as a consumption problem, rather than a production problem" [10]. Thus, at the international level, some organizations appear to be addressing the relationship between consumption and sustainability.

In arriving at his reduced consumption solution, MacCleery recognizes that "the dirty little secret" about the shift to ecological sustainability is a corresponding shift of burden and impact to non-managed ecosystems. MacCleery gives two examples of non-managed ecosystems: private lands in the U.S. and lands in other countries. MacCleery's solution, a reduction in consumption, has potential to at least partially address impact to these ecosystems. For example, a cut in consumption by the U.S. public may reduce resource demands on private lands. However, if the decrease in demand in the U.S. causes private land owners to export resources, then the reduction in public consumption in the U.S. is not a global solution. Similarly, while a reduction in public consumption in the U.S. may result in a drop in imported resources from foreign lands, there is no guarantee that owners of foreign lands will not decrease prices to compensate for such reductions and/or find other foreign markets with at least equal demand for the resources. While international cooperation in ecological sustainability management will impact foreign government lands, it may have little impact on private lands in the U.S. Thus, it appears that the U.S. Forest Service's current approach to ecological sustainability will fail unless something changes, such as greater public and international cooperation.

A primary question of the first prong inquiry is "do analogous issues exist for sustainable government procurement?" In particular, is there a way for a government to embrace sustainable procurement practices that can achieve meaningful results? Or, will such practices suffer the same ills of the U.S. Forestry Service's program?

Differences in purpose exist between public land management and government procurement. For example, in the former, government is primarily tasked with managing a natural resource for the public, whereas, in the latter, government is primarily tasked with managing public monies to purchase resources, whether goods or services. With respect to MacCleery's solution of cutting public consumption, this solution may apply equally to government because a cut in government consumption will certainly decrease demands placed on natural resources and the environment. But, this solution may be contrary to one of the goals of sustainable procurement, i.e., to act as an economic leader to drive industries toward sustainable practices. Thus, to apply the teachings of the U.S. Forestry Service to government procurement, goals of sustainable government procurement may be elucidated. Goals may be discerned by examining various definitions for "sustainable procurement," which are often tied closely with the term "sustainable development".

17.3.2 Sustainability at Various Levels

At the level of global intergovernmental organizations, the United Nations has set up several departments tasked to address sustainable development and sustainable procurement. The U.N.'s Environment Programme (UNEP) includes a sustainable procurement component. The following definition for sustainable procurement is provided by the UNEP:

> Sustainable Procurement Schemes: Sustainable procurement is the process in which organizations buy supplies or services by taking into account, the best value for money considerations such as, price, quality, availability, functionality, etc., environmental aspects, the lifecycle of products, and the social aspects such as poverty eradication, international equity in the distribution of resources, labour conditions, and human rights [11].

UNEP mentions that the inclusion of sustainable development principles in procurement practices is already a reality in a number of countries, such as Canada, the Netherlands, Norway, the United States and South Africa.

Another U.N. department, the United Nations' Department of Economic and Social Affairs (UNESA) maintains the Commission on Sustainable Development (CSD). The website for this division of the U.N. provides a link to national information related to sustainable procurement [12]. In 2004, a website for UNESA CSD provided various specific links to national and international organizations involved in sustainable procurement. By 2005, as mentioned above, the website for the UNESA CSD was more sophisticated, with many more links to national information, indexed both by country and by organization [13].

Using the "National Information" page of the UNESA CSD website [12] and selection of "United States," links are provided for the U.S. Government Sustainable Development Partnerships, which includes additional links to various programs. For example, the U.S. Environmental Protection Agency (EPA) has an Environmentally Preferable Purchasing Program (EPP) and Comprehensive Procurement Guidelines (CPG) Program; the U.S. Department of Energy (DOE) has a Federal Energy Management Program; the Energy Star Program is a government-backed program (e.g., EPA and DOE); and the U.S. executive branch has the Office of the Federal Environmental Executive (OFEE). These programs address various aspects of sustainable development.

In brief, the EPA's CPG program aims to promote the use of materials recovered from solid waste whereby the EPA is required to designate products that are or can be made with recovered materials, and to recommend practices for buying these products. The EPA's EPP is a federal-wide program that encourages and assists Executive agencies in the purchasing of environmentally preferable products and services. The EPA's website offers definitions for the EPP terms and concepts, and provides a number of tools and case studies to help make environmentally preferable purchasing more tangible [14].

An examination of the U.S. OFEE's website provides some indication of how the U.S. government views green purchasing:

> Green purchasing includes the acquisition of recycled content products, environmentally preferable products and services, biobased products, energy- and water-efficient products, alternate fuel vehicles, products using renewable energy, and alternatives to hazardous or toxic chemicals. The White House Task Force on Waste Prevention and Recycling, in conjunction with the Environmental Protection Agency (EPA) and the U.S. Department of Agriculture (USDA), assists Federal agencies to promote the acquisition of recycled content, environmentally preferable, and biobased products; non-ozone depleting substances; and products containing alternatives to certain priority chemicals. The U.S. Department of Energy (DOE) and EPA assist agencies to implement the energy-related purchasing requirements, including the purchase of alternative fuel vehicles and alternative fuels. The General Services Administration and the Defense Logistics Agency, as central sources of supply, are key to making the Federal green purchasing program successful [15].

Note that this definition of "green purchasing" does not address squarely "sustainability". Indeed, in 2004, the OFEE's website link for "sustainability" merely stated "Under Construction". However, now the term "Sustainable Environmental Stewardship" appears, as does an explanation of "sustainable development":

> What is "sustainable environmental stewardship" and how does it relate to sustainable development? First, sustainable development is a concept with many definitions that vary not only across national borders, but also over time. Suffice to say that at its core, most definitions concur that the essence of sustainable development includes the advancement of societies in a way that balances the social, economic, and environmental needs of current and future generations.
>
> We define sustainable environmental stewardship to include those concepts, strategies, tools, practices, and approaches that lead to environmental improvement in a manner that is sustainable over time, considers the long term effects as well as the shorter term, more immediate effects, and that contributes positively, even if indirectly, to the social and economic condition [16].

An organization known as the Government Purchasing Project (GPP) claims to be "dedicated to protecting the environment and human health through market-based strategies" and purports to work "to encourage the government to use its immense purchasing power to promote safe, cost-effective, energy-efficient, and environmentally-sound products" [17].

The GPP website includes links to "Federal Government Environmentally Preferable Purchasing Policies," to Canada's "Green Procurement" policy, to various "State Government Environmentally Preferable Purchasing Policies"

(CA, DE, GA, HI, IN, MA, MN, NJ, NC, OH, OR, PA, TX, VT and WI) and to various "Local Government Environmentally Preferable Purchasing Policies". Under this latter heading, the GPP website lists seven cities or counties; however, only two use the word "sustainable" in their policy title: the City of Austin, Texas ("Sustainable Purchasing") and the City of Santa Monica, California ("Sustainable Purchasing"). Others do include "sustainable" in subheadings.

The North American Commission for Environmental Cooperation website provides a listing of governments and organizations having "green procurement" initiatives [18]. This listing includes the states of California, Georgia, Massachusetts, Michigan, Minnesota, New Jersey, North Carolina, Ohio, Pennsylvania and Vermont, the cities of Austin, Phoenix, Santa Monica and Seattle and the county of King in Washington State. Considering the distinction between "green" and "sustainable," one can expect that the listing of "sustainable procurement" initiatives would be smaller.

17.3.3 Summary of Programs

Thus far, various programs have been identified from an international level to a local level; ultimately, however, all, action is taken locally. An examination of this hierarchy of programs, policies, etc., may help understand how efforts by local municipalities to achieve sustainability can be carried out while keeping global realties and global efforts in mind. In particular, can sustainability be achieved in a piecemeal fashion from bottom–up, or is top–down implementation (i.e., from global to local) an inherent requirement? The type of approach touches on the aforementioned "half-a-loaf" analysis of MacCleery.

In the introduction, the City of Austin's definition for "sustainability" was given, however, it does not include definitions for "sustainable procurement" or "sustainable purchasing". On this point, another municipality, the City of Santa Monica, provides some guidance:

> sustainable can mean slightly different things depending on the context in which it is used. For the purpose of this document, the following definitions are used:

- sustainable (in reference to resource use): a method of harvesting or using a resource so that resource is not depleted or permanently damaged.
- sustainable business: for the purpose of this document, sustainable business refers to a business that provides goods and services, and/or has incorporated into its daily operations practices that result in cleaner air and water, less waste and pollution, conservation of energy and natural resources, less traffic, improved quality of life for residents and workers, and contribute to a strong and viable local economy.
- sustainable community/city: a community or city that meets its present needs without sacrificing the ability of future generations to meet their own needs. More specifically, a sustainable community is one that improves and enhances its natural, social and economic resources in ways that allow current and future members of the community to lead healthy, productive and satisfying lives.

- sustainable modes of transportation/travel: same as alternative modes of transportation above
- sustainable procurement: procurement of environmentally preferable goods and services in a way that also takes into consideration social responsibility and
- sustainable economic development issues in the manufacture, transportation, sale and use of those goods and services [19].

While the City of Austin recognizes social aspects of sustainability in general, the City of Santa Monica goes a step further and defines sustainable procurement as having consideration of social responsibility. A more in-depth analysis of the City of Santa Monica's program is included in a report by Curkendall [20]. This report also discusses programs of the City of Seattle and King County, in an effort to develop recommendations for the City of Portland's and Multnomah County's sustainable procurement policies.

Turning outside the U.S. for an example of a program implemented below the national level, the government of New South Wales, Australia appears to have made a sincere effort at defining "sustainable procurement," in particular, with respect to "sustainable development":

> Sustainable Development is integrating the economic, social and environmental objectives of society, in order to maximise human well-being in the present without compromising the ability of future generations to meet their needs. Sustainable procurement builds on that concept. Sustainable procurement is becoming an increasingly important issue for government and is a focus in the Total Asset Management strategy (TAM), Government Procurement Policy and Construct NSW, among other whole of government initiatives [21].

As another example below the national level, in a similar vein, the Scottish government (The Scottish Executive) also defines sustainable procurement with respect to sustainable development:

> Sustainable procurement is the application of sustainable development principles to procurement and is a key activity in helping to ensure that the world remains habitable and that people have a decent quality of life. There is a wide range of approaches to sustainable procurement, which can be applied at all stages in the procurement process [22].

Thus, governments in the U.S. may consider definitions for sustainable procurement developed by foreign governments as well as those developed by grass root communities in the U.S.

17.4 Implementation in the U.S.: National and Local

From the foregoing non-exhaustive sampling of intergovernmental, national and local efforts, a question arises as to whether the U.S. government or local governments in the U.S. are ready and willing to embrace "sustainable procurement" as opposed to green purchasing practices that relate solely to ecological friendliness of products. As described below, some governments appear to be following a top-down approach from the level of the U.N. to the national government.

17.4.1   U.N. to National Level

17.4.1.1   U.N. to U.K. and Concerning EU

In November 2001, the United Kingdom established an interdepartmental Sustainable Procurement Group (SPG) [23], arguably in response to developments at the intergovernmental level such as the U.N. Commission on Sustainable Development's (CSD10) 2002 World Summit on Sustainable Development. The 2002 World Summit on Sustainable Development stated that relevant authorities at all levels should: "promote public procurement policies that encourage development and diffusion of environmentally sound goods and services" [24]. Between the U.K. government and the U.N. is the European Union. The U.K. government's "Framework for Sustainable Development on the Government Estate" addresses sustainable procurement in relationship to the European Union. In particular, the U.K. government's sustainable procurement policy aims for consistency with "value for money principles, Government Accounting rules, public expenditure constraints and EC rules" [25]. Thus, the U.K. government's approach may be viewed as multilevel and a combination of top–down and bottom–up.

17.4.1.2   U.S. Involvement in the U.N.: Millennium Challenge Account

The 2002 summit resulted in a "Plan of Implementation" that included the following chapters: Poverty eradication, Changing unsustainable patterns of consumption and production, Protecting and managing the natural resource base of economic and social development, Sustainable development in a globalizing world, Health and sustainable development, Sustainable development of small island developing States, Sustainable development for Africa, Means of implementation and Institutional framework for sustainable development [26]. While the U.N. Secretary-General's High-Level Advisory Panel for the 2002 summit did not include any members from the United States, President G.W. Bush selected Secretary of State Colin Powell to lead a delegation from the United States that included Environmental Protection Agency Administrator Christie Todd Whitman, Chairman of the Council on Environmental Quality James Connaughton, U.S. Agency for International Development Administrator Andrew Natsios, and Under Secretary of State Paula Dobriansky.

From all accounts, the United States appeared to consider the Millennium Challenge Account (announced March 14, 2002) as an official policy that would benefit sustainable development, as addressed by the 2002 World Summit.

Indeed, on June 5, 2002, Administrator Natsios stated "the United States is once again launching a major new foreign assistance initiative, one whose significance may one day rival the Marshall Plan. I am speaking of the Millennium Challenge Account—or MCA—that President Bush launched on March 14 in a speech at the Inter-American Development Bank." Further, in a speech on February 14, 2002 delivered to the National Oceanic and Atmospheric and Agency, President Bush announced a policy that aimed to assure the world that the United States was doing its part to address environmental concerns: "Today, I'm confident that the environmental path that I announce will benefit the entire world. This new approach is based on this common-sense idea: that economic growth is key to environmental progress, because it is growth that provides the resources for investment in clean technologies". Secretary Powell acknowledged in a speech of July 12, 2002, regarding the 2002 World Summit, that sustainability could benefit the United States noting: "And as rich as we are, as powerful as we are as a nation, we still have pockets of poverty, pockets of people who are living in despair and wondering whether or not their nation cares about them. We have to deal with that".

However, these measures announced prior to the 2002 World Summit may show some weakening. For example, the President's proposed federal budget for 2005 included $2.5 billion for the Millennium Challenge Account, which fell short of the $3.4 billion officials had said the program would disburse in 2005. For 2005, Congress appropriated $1.5 billion. The President's budget for 2006 requested $3 billion.

The U.S. government's approach to the 2002 World Summit recognized that "sustainable" means more than "green" and that participation from wealthy countries could contribute greatly to global sustainability. Perhaps the 2002 summit indicated that global sustainability can be achieved only by full participation of all countries—the lesson learned in implementation of the Land Ethic? If sustainability can only be achieved through international cooperation and any significant degree of such cooperation is unlikely, then what can be achieved at the local, regional or national level? Can local sustainability initiatives operate without shifting burdens elsewhere? Can varying levels of "sustainability" be addressed in public procurement?

17.4.2 U.S. National Level to Local Level

In *Cradle-to-Cradle*, McDonough and Braungart state "all sustainability is local" [27]. At face value, this statement seems to contradict MacCleary's analysis of the government's effort to achieve ecological sustainability. But McDonough and Braungart explain further, "[I]f we import a material from a distant place, we honor what happened there as a local event" [27]. McDonough and Braungart cite the Hannover Principles, in particular: "Recognize interdependence. The elements of human design are entwined with and depend upon the natural world, with broad and diverse implications at every scale. Expand design considerations and recognize distant effects." The nine Hannover Principles were prepared for EXPO 2000, The World's Fair, Hannover, Germany. If McDonough, Braungart and MacCleary are correct, can this type of thinking be put into practice? Further, is this really necessary to achieve local sustainability?

17.5 Objective Definitions for "Sustainable" in a Procurement Code

Given the aforementioned efforts at local and global levels, arriving at an objective definition for "sustainable" appears to be a daunting task. Further, the development of metrics is confounded by the lack of such an objective definition. Without a doubt, a sustainable procurement code should include a definition of sustainability and an explanation of how the code promotes and achieves sustainability. For example, sustainability may be applied to the need for procuring particular goods or services. Sustainability may also be applied to the actual physical good or service. Yet further, sustainability may be applied to broader aspects of the provider (labor, pay, family leave, taxes, etc.).

Where sustainability applies to the need for procuring goods or services, the focus should be on the government addressing needs of the public. For example, if new furniture is not necessary and possibly considered a luxury, a decision not to purchase new furniture will inherently be a sustainable decision, at least until the furniture no longer functions properly. On the other hand, if a local company has designed sustainable furniture, then the government may choose to accelerate the decision to purchase new furniture if, over the long run, this results in a higher degree of sustainability.

With respect to sustainable goods or products, an article in the *Wall Street Journal*, "Is Your Grocery List Politically Correct? Food World's New Buzzword Is 'Sustainable' Products" addressed several issues surrounding the definition of a sustainable product [28]. The article quotes Jerry DeWitt, spokesman for the Sustainable Agriculture Network program of the U.S. Department of Agriculture: "[T]here are probably over 600 definitions of 'sustainable'"; it then states that the most widely accepted definition is three-pronged: products that are made in a way that is (i) profitable, (ii) environmentally sound, and (iii) beneficial for local communities. The article also asks the question "How Local is Local?"

17.5.1 Example: the Mirra™ Chain and Aluminum

McDonough and Braungart present an argument for using "local" materials for sustainable design wherein they state that use of local materials opens the doors to profitable local enterprise and avoids problems of bioinvasion, citing the Herman Miller factory as an example [29]. However, when it comes to shippable sustainable products, Herman Miller's Mirra™ chair serves as an example. The Mirra™ chair is designed to accommodate 95% of the world's population and to be up to 96% recycled. The chair represents Herman Miller's vision of "sustainable capitalism—using benign, closed-loop materials and processes that protect and enhance the natural environment for future generations" [30]. In essence, products made from already existing plastics or already extracted metals,

Table 17.1   Material Content and Recyclability for Mirra™ Chair

	Material-Type Recycled Content (%)	Percent PIR of Total Weight	Percent PCR of Total Weight	Percent of Total Product Weight	Percent of Total Product Recyclable
Aluminum Total	100	6	6	2	100
Foam Total	0	0	0	2	100
Plastic Total	0	0	0	29	89
Steel Total	53	5	25	56	100
Textile Total	0	0	0	0	0
	42	11	31	100	96

PIR is post industrial recycled; PCR is post consumer recycled.

alloys, etc., may be deemed sustainable, as most of the Mirra™ chair's materials may be sourced and formed from already existing stock.

Herman Miller provides a document entitled "Mirra™ Seating Material Content and Recyclability" (Table 17.1). This document outlines several elements of the McDonough Braungart Design Chemistry (MBCD) Cradle to Cradle Design Protocol:

■ Material Chemistry and Safety of Inputs—what chemicals are in the materials we specify, and are they the safest available?
■ Disassembly—can we take products apart at the end of their useful life to recycle their materials?
■ Recyclability—do the materials contain recycled content, and more importantly, can the materials be recycled at the end of the product's useful life?

With respect to aluminum, a commodity material, the Mirra™ chair includes 100% recycled aluminum. Thus, at some level, production of the Mirra™ chair impacts the aluminum industry. According to the U.S. Geological Survey, in 2003, 7 companies operated 15 primary aluminum reduction plants and 6 smelters were temporarily idled [31]. Further, in 2003, the U.S. aluminum production industry employed about 60,000 (about one-third at primary smelters) while imports for aluminum consumption continued to increase, primarily from Canada. World production also continued to increase as capacity expansions, most notably those in China, India, Mozambique, and Norway, were brought on-stream. These statistics demonstrates the far- reaching consequences of using aluminum in a product. This simple Mirra™ chair example also demonstrates that a sustainability analysis requires a web approach—where each step from the product outward appears to require more information from more entities.

To make the point more clearly, consider efforts taken by the aluminum producer Alcoa. Alcoa recognizes that recycling aluminum is much less costly than mining bauxite ore and extracting aluminum, an extremely power intensive process—typically subsidized by the construction of hydroelectric dams.

One may speculate that at some point in the future all of the aluminum needs of the world will be met by recycling. Does a sustainable policy account for retraining workers in the bauxite mining and processing industries, redirecting the power from the dams or even removing the dams?

Alcoa recognizes that "Sustainability requires environmental excellence, economic success and social responsibility." Alcoa has developed a vision where: "All wastes have been eliminated; products are designed for the environment; the environment is fully integrated into manufacturing; the workplace is free of injuries, spills and leaks, and Alcoa is recognized as a leader and partner in every community where it has operations" [32].

Alcoa also participates in the Green Power Group, which was convened by the World Resources Institute and Business for Social Responsibility in 2000. Again, the aluminum industry is one of the most power intensive industries on earth. The Green Power Group's goal is to create 1000 megawatts of new cost-competitive green power for corporate markets by 2010. Members of the Green Power Group include Cargill Dow LLC, Delphi Corporation, The Dow Chemical Company, DuPont, General Motors, IBM, Interface, Johnson & Johnson, Kinko's, Pitney Bowes, and Staples. Thus, Alcoa appears to have a glimpse of the future and to be taking steps toward sustainability to ensure its continued existence. Further, in early 2004, another aluminum company, Alcan Inc., created a $1 million annual prize to recognize outstanding contributions from the not-for-profit sector to the goal of sustainability. Alcan made the announcement at the 2004 Annual Meeting of the World Economic Forum in Davos, Switzerland [33].

Certain aspects of the aluminum industry are at the forefront of sustainability rhetoric due to the success of aluminum can recycling on behalf of consumers. For example, in 2002, about 53% of all aluminum cans shipped were collected for recycling. Incredibly, this number is down from a high of about 67% in 1997 [34]. However, when compared to statistics for some foreign countries, it is apparent that the U.S. is not at the forefront. For example, in an article from *American Metal Market*, "Specialty alloys, zinc spur Imco Recycling's earnings," an official from Imco Recycling, Inc. stated that "the sinking proportion of cans recycled in the United States had cut the availability of can scrap by 400 million pounds annually" [35]. He added that "[T]his trend must be reversed in our industry or legislative action by state and federal governments may become necessary," while other Imco executives noted that Brazil and Japan recycled more than 80% of their aluminum cans. Thus, in terms of a global sustainability, would it be best for Herman Miller to acquire its recycled aluminum from countries other than the U.S.? Would a sustainable procurement code provide measures to account for such subtleties?

17.5.2 Example: Sustainable Buildings

While government procurement of sustainable chairs may certainly make a positive impact, sustainability efforts in building construction may cause the most profound change. X percent of government procurement relates to construction of buildings. Further, with an average life-time of Y years, the government has an interest in ensuring proper maintenance at a reasonable cost. The building industry has responded to this need through the U.S. Green Building Council (USGBC), which is a coalition of leaders from across the building industry. These leaders are working to promote buildings that are environmentally responsible, profitable and healthy places to live and work.

The cornerstone of the USGBC is the Leadership in Energy and Environmental Design project, known as LEED™. According to the USGBC, the LEED™ program's mission aims to "encourage and accelerate global adoption of sustainable green building and development practices through the creation and implementation of universally understood and accepted standards, tools and performance criteria" [36]. However, while the term "sustainable" appears in the mission statement, "sustainable" or "sustainability" appear in the Policy Manual only as follows:

- The buildings that we live in work from and enjoy during our leisure activities represent the largest contributions to anthropogenic environmental impacts and resource depletion and threaten our *environmental, economic and social sustainability* either directly or indirectly;
- The USGBC is the foremost advocate of *transforming the building and real estate market towards sustainability* while promoting human health, environmental restoration, economic prosperity and social welfare and equity;
- LEED™ must also grow and adapt as we *learn more about sustainability* and to keep promoting change within its target markets;
- LEED™…is a design guideline to move building construction and operation toward sustainability;
- LEED™ operates on sound business principles and practices: Generates its own sustainable revenues for administration, customer support, training and ongoing program development;
- The LEED™ standard is the heart of the LEED™ System… [I]t covers environmental actions in: Sustainable Sites;
- In addition, future systems [of LEED™] may weight credits to better reflect their relative *impacts on sustainability*; and
- The USGBC recognizes the *importance of local conditions in promoting sustainability* and the need for LEED to be flexible to accommodate these conditions.

[Emphasis added]

Thus, it appears that the LEED™ program has yet to embrace "sustainable" and, instead, opted for "green," which appears about 40 times in the Policy Manual.

17.6 Harmonization of Procurement Codes and Sustainable Codes

Sustainable procurement stands to benefit from harmonization. In the U.S., a history exists of "uniform laws" and "model codes" that have been adopted throughout the states. Harmonization through such efforts can lead to significant efficiencies. While states may choose not to adopt uniform laws or model codes as promulgated, uniform laws and model codes often provide guidance and prompt discussion of important issues.

For example, in the 1950s, a model probate code was promulgated that aimed to facilitate estate planning, administration, and adjudication. In 1969, the Uniform Probate Code followed. Since 1969, the Uniform Probate Code has been adopted in whole by about 15 states, in part by other states and has influenced probate reform in yet other states. Other uniform or model codes include the Uniform Commercial Code, the Model Penal Code and the Model Procurement Code, which has been adopted by about 20 states.

Just as penal laws responded to technological advances in genetics, procurement laws should also adapt to technological advances. Recent revisions to the Model Procurement Code [37] were sponsored by the American Bar Association's Section of Public Contract Law and its Section of State and Local Government Law. Revisions aimed to reduce transaction costs for all governmental entities at the state and local levels; reduce transaction costs to private sector suppliers of goods and services; substantially increase available levels and ranges of competition through modern methods of electronic communications; and encourage the competitive use of new technologies, new methods of performing, and new forms of project delivery in public procurement, particularly in the construction area.

Caretakers of the MPC recognized that technology changed dramatically since the 1979 MPC was formulated (e.g., personal computers, email, the Internet, widespread use of fax machines, etc.). Technological advances have arguably reduced risk, facilitated risk assessment, increased the number of bidders and lowered procurement transaction costs to both government and private sector suppliers. Advances in computing have transformed aspects of the construction industry leading to processes such as Design-Build, Design-Build-Operate, and Design-Build-Finance-Operate. However, in turn, a need for procurement of significant computing resources arose including procurement of single-source proprietary technology.

The MPC includes twelve articles that serve as a framework for highlighting potential issues in sustainable public procurement. Article 1 of the MPC sets forth purposes and various definitions; thus, a sustainable procurement code may include purposes and definitions for sustainable procurement as general provisions.

Part A of Article 2 is entitled "Procurement Policy Office" and includes an option for an outside board. Early on, sustainable metrics may require an outside board with expertise in life-cycle analysis and other aspects of sustainability. For example, environmentalists, sociologists and economists cognizant of sustainability metrics may be needed until a cadre of competent sustainability experts becomes readily available.

Part E of Article 2, entitled "Coordination, Training, and Education," provides for an advisory council and a procurement institute. An advisory board may substitute for the aforementioned option of an outside board of experts, while a procurement institute may provide training of sustainability experts.

Part F of Article 2 elaborates duties of the state's attorney general. Attorneys general often render opinions on procurement issues. Thus, competency at the level of the attorney general office or equivalent legal office should be provided prior to implementation of a sustainable procurement code.

Article 3 includes Parts A–G which provide definitions, methods of source selection, cancellations of invitations/requests, qualifications and duties, types of contracts, inspection of plant and audit of records, and determinations and reports. While various provisions in Article 3 may include terms related to sustainability, particular attention should focus on provisions that can support government controls that promote sustainability. For example, a procurement code may include evaluation factors that promote sustainability.

MPC 3-203(5) pertains to "Evaluation Factors" and says "The Request for Proposals shall state the relative importance of price and other factors and subfactors, if any." The commentary for 3-203(5) recognizes that factors other than price may be used to evaluate a proposal or award a contract. However, the commentary does not explicitly mention sustainability; instead, it refers to a notice function such that the jurisdiction may obtain the optimum benefits of the competitive solicitation based on well-prepared proposals. Further, the commentary does not recommend extending this notice to any emphasis of the mental process of the evaluators in formulating their scores.

Ideally, a procurement code that promotes sustainability would choose to explicitly state that the evaluation factors are integral to a life-cycle analysis, a land ethic or other analytical philosophy that promotes sustainability. The concept of life-cycle appears in various places in the MPC, for example, in 3-202(5): "Those criteria that will affect the bid price and be considered in evaluation for award shall be objectively measurable, such as discounts, transportation costs, and total or life cycle costs". Further in R3-202.12.4 (determination of lowest bidder):

> Only objectively measurable criteria which are set forth in the Invitation for Bids shall be applied in determining the lowest bidder. Examples of such criteria include, but are not limited to, transportation cost, and ownership or life cycle cost formulas. Evaluation factors need not be precise predictors of actual future costs, but to the extent possible such evaluation factors shall:

> (a) be reasonable estimates based upon information the [State] has available concerning future use; and (b) treat all bids equitably.

Yet further, the commentary for 3-202(5) states: "The bid evaluation may take into account not only acquisition costs of supplies, but the cost of their ownership which relates to the quality of the product, including life cycle factors such as maintainability and reliability."

Due to the complex nature of sustainability determinations, a sustainable procurement code may include provisions for prequalification of suppliers such that competitors understand goals and metrics prior to bidding. MPC 3-402 pertains to prequalification of suppliers. The commentary states that "prequalification is only of limited utility if a procurement cannot be limited to prequalified suppliers" and that "regulations should establish that unless an emergency exists or the contract is for a small purchase, a competition may not be limited to pre-qualified offerors unless public notice of the procurement was given in sufficient time for any interested firms to prepare necessary submissions and become prequalified". A sustainable procurement code may choose a different approach that places the onus on the prospective bidders to conform to sustainable practices or to otherwise refrain from competition. If a state awards a contract to a bidder that uses sustainable practices instead of a bidder that has no knowledge of such practices, the result would be close to ideal. First, the contract promotes sustainability and second, those that use sustainable practices are rewarded, which is an incentive for all bidders to comply with sustainability criteria for prequalification.

Sustainable prequalification criteria may be general, i.e., not bid-specific. A state, national or multinational organization may set forth such criteria for adoption. A base level of prequalification may be met with higher levels attained upon successful performance of awarded contracts or through meeting stricter criteria.

Part F of Article 3 pertains to inspection of plant and audit of records. In particular, 3-601 states that, at reasonable times, an agency may inspect the part of the plant or place of business of a contractor or any subcontractor which is related to the performance of any contract awarded or to be awarded by the agency. This right to inspect should extend to sustainability practices, especially where such practices touch on the evaluation factors that are sustainability metrics.

Article 4 of the MPC pertains to specifications, i.e., "any description of the physical or functional characteristics, or of the nature of a supply, service, or construction item". A sustainable procurement code should provide for specifications that promote sustainable practices. For example, recycled or recyclable content may be an important specification (e.g., the Herman Miller Mirra™ office chair). Regulation 4-201 suggests a preference for commercially available products and that "unique requirements shall be avoided, to the extent practicable". Unfortunately, until sustainable practices take hold, the agency may prefer unique requirements that promote sustainability. Again, public agencies are in a position to drive sustainability due to purchasing power.

Code provision 4-205 pertains to maximum practicable competition and states that "all specifications shall seek to promote overall economy for the purposes intended and encourage competition in satisfying the [State's] needs, and shall not be unduly restrictive". The promotion of sustainable practices may at the onset exist in an environment where competition is weak. However, market forces will generally increase competition over time. Further, if a company produces a pen for $3 using sustainable practices and another company produces a pen for $1 in upfront costs but $2.50 in environmental damage, then the $3 pen represents the optimal choice. While such an example may seem extreme, consideration of Superfund cleanup and health costs may provide needed perspective.

Article 5 of the MPC addresses procurement of infrastructure facilities and services. Commentary to Part A (Definitions) states reasons for an updated definition of architectural and engineering services: "Current nationwide efforts to improve overall Infrastructure Asset Management techniques and strategies reflects a growing need for public owners to assess the effects of alternative designs, technologies, projects, schedules, and finance methods on initial and life-cycle quality, cost, and time of delivery of entire collections of infrastructure facilities". Thus, the concept of life-cycle is indirectly part of the MPC's definitions. The commentary further states that "public owners need to structure long-term strategies for the design, construction, operation, and maintenance of collections of infrastructure facilities". In particular, a long-term strategy is an important component of sustainability. The MPC's inclusion of design-build-finance-operate-maintain also represents a step toward sustainability (5-201(1)(e)). Article 5 even mentions environmental concerns in addition to life-cycle (see, e.g., R5-203.01.4 -Lease, Buy, or Build).

Article 8 of the MPC addresses supply management and establishes requirements for control over the life cycle of supplies procured and establishes criteria for management, transfer and disposal of surplus property. Again, the concept of life-cycle is introduced.

Article 10 of the MPC pertains to intergovernmental relations and includes provisions covering cooperative purchasing. For example, 10-201 authorizes cooperation between public procurement units.

Article 11 of the MPC covers assistance to small and disadvantaged businesses. A disadvantaged business is a small business which is owned or controlled by a majority of persons who have been deprived of the opportunity to develop and maintain a competitive position in the economy because of social disadvantages (11-101(1)). A small business is a United States business which is independently owned and which is not dominant in its field of operation or an affiliate or subsidiary of a business dominant in its field of operation (11-101(2)). The corresponding commentary recognizes that problems of small and disadvantaged businesses are widespread and may be addressed more broadly than solely through the public procurement process. A sustainable procurement code inherently accounts for disadvantaged people or communities, especially where unsustainable practices cause or maintain such disadvantage.

This brief overview on code harmonization and the MPC may provide some guidance along the path to a sustainable procurement code. Certainly, issues will arise such as those presented herein and others.

17.7   Conclusion

Significant difficulties often hinder the development of a sustainable procurement code. In particular, issues exist with respect to definitions of sustainable, objective measures of sustainability, and harmonization. Reflecting on the experiences of the U.S. Forestry Service, one may argue that sustainability requires, inherently, a global approach. The path to global harmonization may start with local government efforts aimed at green procurement and industry efforts to survive or progress (e.g., aluminum industry and building industry). Lastly, in the U.S. at least, while harmonization among the states has taken place for various legal codes, the Model Procurement Code has an arduous path to travel. At some point, however, we may expect that the Model Procurement Code will indeed be a sustainable procurement code and adopted by a majority of the states, following the path of other model codes.

References

1. Executive Order 13101, Greening the Government through Waste Prevention, Recycling, and Federal Acquisition, September 14, 1998.
2. Senate Bill 3271, The Greening the Government Act of 2000, November 14, 2000.
3. Drabkin, D., Thai, K.V., U.S. Federal Government Procurement: Structure, Process and Current Issues, International Purchasing and Supply Education and Research Association's Comparative Public Procurement Cases Workshop, Budapest, Hungary, April 2003, 10–12.
4. City of Austin, Texas Website. Available at http://www.ci.austin.tx.us/sustainable/purchasing.htm, (accessed on December 30, 2005).
5. Leopold, A., *A Sand County Almanac*, Oxford University Press, New York, 1948.
6. American Bar Association, The 2000 Model Procurement Code for State and Local Governments.
7. Miller, J.B., Procurement Strategies Which Encourage Innovation: The Fundamental Element of Sustainable Public Infrastructure Systems. International Council for Building Research Studies and Documentation (CIB), 1997 Symposium of Working Commission W92, "Procurement—A Key to Innovation," University of Montreal, May 19–23, 1997; Publication. 203 ISBN 0-9682215-0-5
8. Miller, J.B., The Fundamental Elements of Sustainable Procurement Strategies for Public Infrastructure; First International Conference on Construction Industry Development, Conference Proceedings, National University of Singapore, December 9–11, 1997, Singapore.
9. MacCleery, D.W., Aldo Leopold's Land Ethic: Is it only half a loaf unless a consumption ethic accompanies it? *Forest History Today*, Spring, 2000, 39–41.
10. Cohen, M.J., Sustainable consumption in national context: an introduction to the symposium, *Sustainability: Science, Practice, & Policy*, 1(1), 2005, 22–28, Available at http://ejournal.nbii.org/archives/vol1iss1/0410-008.cohen.html (accessed on December 31, 2005).
11. Cleaner Production Status Reports 2004, Appendix 3: Description of Terms. Available at http://www.uneptie.org/pc/cp/library/catalogue/regional_reports.htm (accessed on December 30, 2005).
12. U.N. Department of Economic and Social Affairs, Division for Sustainable Development, Commission on Sustainable Development. Available at http://www.un.org/esa/sustdev/csd/csd.htm, (accessed on December 30, 2005).
13. U.N. Department of Economic and Social Affairs, Division for Sustainable Development, Commission on Sustainable Development. Available at http://www.un.org/esa/sustdev/sdissues/consumption/spp_web_info.htm (accessed on December, 2004).

14. U.S. Environmental Protection Agency, Environmentally Preferable Purchasing Website. Available at http://www.epa.gov/opptintr/epp/ (accessed on December 30, 2005).

15. U.S. Office of the Federal Environmental Executive, Green Purchasing Website. Available at http://www.ofee.gov/gp/gp.htm (accessed on December 30, 2005).

16. U.S. Office of the Federal Environmental Executive, Sustainable Environmental Stewardship Website. Available at http://www.ofee.gov/sustain/sustainability.htm (accessed on December 30, 2005).

17. Government Purchasing Program Website. Available at http://www.gpp.org/index.html (accessed on December 30, 2005).

18. The North American Commission for Environmental Cooperation Website. Available at http://www.cec.org/files/PDF/ECONOMY/Green-Procurement_Initiatives_en.pdf (accessed on January 1, 2006).

19. Santa Monica Sustainable City Plan, Update Adopted February 11, 2003. Available at http://santamonica.org/epd/scp/pdf/SCP_2003_Adopted_Plan.pdf (accessed on December 30, 2005).

20. Curkendall, J.A., An Evaluation of the Task Force Process Used to Develop the City of Portland's and Multnomah County's Sustainable Procurement Policies, May 2003. Available at http://irtest.uoregon.edu/dspace/bitstream/1794/44/1/susprocur.pdf, (accessed on December 31, 2005).

21. Government of New South Wales, Australia, Smart Buying for Government Website. Available at http://www.smarterbuying.nsw.gov.au/sustainable_proc.shtm (accessed on December 30, 2005).

22. Government of Scotland, The Canny Buyer Website. Available at http://www.canny-buyer.com/susproc.shtml (accessed on December 30, 2005).

23. U.K. Government, Framework for sustainable development on the Government estate, Website. Available at http://www.sustainable-development.gov.uk/delivery/integrating/estate/estate.htm (accessed on January 1, 2006).

24. UNESA, Division for Sustainable Development, Johannesburg Plan of Implementation, Ch. III. Changing unsustainable patterns of consumption and production. Available at http://www.un.org/esa/sustdev/documents/WSSD_POI_PD/English/POIChapter3.htm (accessed on December 30, 2005).

25. U.K. Government, Framework for sustainable development on the Government estate, Part F, Procurement, Website. Available at http://www.sustainabledevelopment.gov.uk/delivery/integrating/estate/documents/ProcurementPDF.pdf (accessed on January 1, 2006).

26. UNESA, Division for Sustainable Development, Johannesburg Plan of Implementation of the World Summit on Sustainable Development. Available at http://www.un.org/esa/sustdev/documents/WSSD_POI_PD/English/WSSD_PlanImpl.pdf (accessed on December 30, 2005).

27. McDonough, W. and Braungart, M., *Cradle to Cradle: Remaking the Way We Make Things*, North Point Press, New York, 2002, 123

28. *Wall Street Journal*, Is Your Grocery List Politically Correct? Food World's New Buzzword Is "Sustainable" Products February 17, 2004, D1.

29. McDonough, W. and Braungart, M., *Cradle to Cradle: Remaking the Way We Make Things*, North Point Press, New York, 2002.

30. Herman Miller Introduces the Mirra Work Chair, News Release, Herman Miller, June 11, 2003.

31. U.S. Geological Survey, Mineral Commodity Summary, 2004. Available at http://minerals.usgs.gov/minerals/pubs/mcs/2004/mcs2004.pdf (accessed on December 30, 2005).

32. Alcoa Urges Aluminum Association to Adopt Ambitious Approach to Sustainable Development, News Release, Alcoa, October 1, 2002.

33. News Release, Alcan, January 22, 2004.
34. Aluminum Beverage Can Continues to be Most Recycled Consumer Beverage Package, News Release, The Aluminum Association, April 11, 2003.
35. American Metal Market, Specialty alloys, zinc spur Imco Recycling's earnings, August 1, 2002.
36. LEED™ Policy Manual, Spring 2003.
37. American Bar Association, The 2000 Model Procurement Code for State and Local Governments.

Chapter 18

Managing Nuclear Waste

Catherine Horiuchi
University of San Francisco

We need to ensure a strong and diversified energy mix to fuel our nation's economy, and nuclear power is an important component of that mix. In order to expand our nuclear generating capacity, we need a safe, permanent, geologic repository for spent nuclear fuel at Yucca Mountain.

Samuel W. Bodman, U.S. Secretary of Energy [1]

18.1 Introduction

At the beginning of the nuclear age, beyond the novelty of glow-in-the-dark watch faces, government scientists engaged in developing new weaponry unleashed incredible quantities of energy through the collapsing of atomic-level bonds. Since then, nation-states have used this technology for civilian and military purposes. But the by-products of these uses cannot be managed conventionally. This chapter explores how post-consumption radioactive material and corollary waste is managed, using the approved U.S. permanent repository Yucca Mountain Project as an example.

Nuclear waste is not monolithic, so this account begins by classifying it by type and source, continuing on to issues in establishing accountability and public oversight of waste management. Certain attributes of nuclear waste—radioactivity, toxicity, longevity, and criticality—differentiate it from other trash and increase governmental interest in managing the waste stream. Beyond these general difficulties, spent nuclear fuel can be reprocessed for use in nuclear and radiological weapons, and so nuclear waste must be guarded securely. The plethora of disjointed governing and regulatory bodies further complicates managing this waste amid its trans-national diffusion.

Regulatory oversight agencies manage differing aspects of the nuclear waste stream from authorization of its creation to its ultimate disposition. Governments have also established relationships with other governments and private firms to enable the storage and transportation of spent nuclear fuel. These institutions and relationships are described as encountered.

The Yucca Mountain Project, the approved long-term waste repository in the Nevada desert, lies approximately 100 miles northwest of Las Vegas, at the ridge known as Yucca Mountain. It anchors this chapter as an example of the issues associated with nuclear waste management. The story of the U.S. strategy for permanent spent fuel storage is a tale of organizational and political expediency, geographic stability, and questioned capacity. With the facility sited far from the bulk of nuclear facilities in the sparsely populated Western desert, opponents include the state of Nevada and many local governments, in addition to environmentalists and anti-nuclear organizations. Protests have ranged from demonstrations near the site to art exhibitions underscoring the difficulty of warning people away millennia into the future. Appendix I illustrates several conceptual models for long-term warnings.

One man's trash is another man's treasure, goes the saying. The rationale for reprocessing as an alternative to storage is explored, especially in response to multi-national agreements to reduce dependence on fossil fuels and emissions from their combustion. France is committed to a reprocessing strategy at Beaumont-Hague. The U.S. has at least one major exploratory project underway; the Bush Administration after 9/11 shifted away from the country's longstanding policy against reprocessing, despite its risk of increasing the proliferation of nuclear materials.

The chapter closes by suggesting areas for further research in managing long lasting nuclear waste within an unstable geopolitical context.

18.2 How is Nuclear Waste Categorized?

Radiation is the output of a natural and spontaneous process. Radioactivity is the term describing how unstable atomic nuclei degrade. A moderate amount of radiation is part of everyday life. The exposure considered the average background or ambient radiation is quite low, about 300 millirems or 0.3 rems per year [2]. Through nuclear engineering, we create commercial and military radiological material in quantity for consumption in a controlled nuclear fission process. The development of manmade nuclear material has the collateral effect of increasing the overall amount of irradiated trash needing to be managed once the fuel is spent.

Nuclear waste is the general term for the by-products of processes associated with humanly constructed uses for radioactive materials. Some elements decay naturally over a short period of time, while others must be avoided for tens of thousands of years. Limited mitigation and storage options exist, targeted to specific types of post-consumption trash. Both the nuclear energy industry and the nuclear weapons complex create high-level waste, in the form of spent nuclear fuel [2]. The controlled nuclear reaction in a reactor vessel consumes the usable fuel in approximately one-quarter to one-third of the fuel rods each year. These rods are replaced with new ones, and the spent fuel rods are placed in temporary storage, pending availability of a permanent repository, such as the one in the U.S. required under the 1982 Nuclear Waste Policy Act (NWPA) [3]. Safety in storage is paramount.

> I know that the American people share my deep belief that if a danger exists in the world, it is a danger shared by all; and equally, that if hope exists in the mind of one nation, that hope should be shared by all.
>
> President Dwight D. Eisenhower [4]

The most stringent management controls in the nuclear waste stream relate to high-level radioactive material, but a second general type of post-consumption waste exists. Low-level waste either contains very small quantities of radioactive material, or is created through contamination by proximity to or contact with radioactive material. The luminescent watch dials common in the first half of the 20th century are classified as low-level waste. The clothes, gloves, and cleaning materials worn or used by workers in the immediate vicinity of nuclear reactors, residues from treatment of reactor water, and laboratory materials employed in nuclear medicine are also considered low-level waste. Ordinary waste that is discarded with contaminated waste becomes contaminated thereby. Low-level waste varies in risk, depending on the radioactive nature of the particles.

In addition to the basic categories of high- and low-level waste, several other types of waste describe radioactive materials, based on their origin. These included transuranic waste, mill tailings, mixed waste, orphaned waste, and accelerator-produced radioactive or technologically enhanced naturally occurring material (APRM or TENORM). Defense-related research and weaponry results in transuranic waste, often referenced more generally as high-level waste. Mill tailings are uranium mining residuals. Mixed waste contains radiological and hazardous chemical waste. Orphaned waste is the term used for discarded, unlabeled drums found in scrap yards that are determined to be radioactive. Particle accelerators produce APRM or TENORM [5].

The total waste stream can only be estimated, since there exist both overt and covert sources of irradiated trash. The Treaty on the Non-Proliferation of Nuclear Weapons (NPT, adopted June 12, 1968, entered into force March 5, 1970, and reviewed at conferences in 1995 and 2000) hoped "to prevent the spread of nuclear weapons and weapons technology, to foster the peaceful uses of nuclear energy, and to further the goal of achieving general and complete disarmament" [6]. The first goal has been moderately successful, with the number of nation-states known to possess nuclear weapons remaining low. However, other states desire mastery over nuclear technology, as do stateless actors who might be regarded as terrorists, insurgents, or participants in tribal, civil, or global war, depending on the ideology of the observer. North Korea and Iran are two nations openly and actively engaged in nuclear development despite international pressure to cease. And while the International Atomic Energy Agency (IAEA) monitors and inspects nuclear facilities, it does not monitor military installations in the U.S. or other acknowledged nuclear states. Though the stockpile of weapons has been reduced, the third goal of complete disarmament may be unattainable.

We have some, if limited, information about the quantity and location of nuclear waste. For instance, the U.S. Department of Energy (DOE) reported in 2006 that over 50,000 metric tons are stored at more than 100 above-ground sites in 39 states with an additional 2000 metric tons produced each year [7]. In its 2004 report to Congress, the Office of Civilian Radioactive Waste Management (the agency responsible for the Yucca Mountain Project) mapped the temporary storage sites for the 50,000 metric tons from commercial reactors, and also noted requirements for 2500 metric tons from nuclear weapons production and 50 metric tons of extra plutonium no longer required in the post-Soviet era [8].

Military installations worldwide produce substantial quantities of nuclear waste, with little civilian control or public oversight. While security clearance within any given military complex allows a certain degree of knowledge, this does not authorize the release of information to the public. Even if a researcher or a member of the public were to somehow gain security clearance, it does not resolve the information asymmetry, as whatever understanding is developed cannot be brought into public discourse. Nor does one nation's clearance ensure access to other military complexes of allies or opponents. So it is not a simple thing to accurately and completely discern the type and quantity of irradiated materials. As one example of the complexity of the relationship between intelligence and decision making, consider the invasion of Iraq in 2003. The Bush Administration became convinced that Saddam Hussein's government was operating a credible nuclear program, based in part on internal intelligence, despite contrary reports from IAEA inspectors who had not found evidence of recent activity [9]. It has also been demonstrated through examination of government-operated facilities such as Hanford in Washington state [10] or the Savannah River Site (where 11 of 16 tanks leaked) [11,12], that within military systems, environmental management of hazardous material is of lower priority than security controls; prevention of site contamination is peripheral to primary weapon development or research interests [13].

Since 2003, the U.S. Department of Defense (DOD) has sought release from environmental rules, claiming that these regulations and the existing process for specific instance exception interfere with training and readiness. It has received an interim exemption from the Migratory Bird Treaty Act, and a broad exemption from the Marine Mammal Protection Act and from portions of the Endangered Species Act. Exemptions from the Clean Air Act and the Solid Waste Disposal Act that have been sought have not yet been approved by Congress, though DOD argues that existing federal regulation considers used munitions solid waste only after DOD removes them from where they land. While not specific to radiological waste, this exemplifies the potential amount of hidden contaminated waste that is dispersed [14].

In the post-Soviet era of small-scale warfare in theaters around the world, some complaints have focused on an emerging and controversial dispersal of minimally radioactive material in the form of depleted uranium (DU) ordnance [15]. Using uranium alloys or DU in bullets makes them heavier and thereby more powerful; since this spent ammunition is left in place at the end of the battle, area populations are concerned about possible long term negative effects [16,17]. The U.S. government, for one, remains unconvinced that DU constitutes a hazard to civilians, and limits its hazard assessment to military personnel injured with DU shrapnel [18].

18.3   Distinguishing Attributes of Nuclear Material

Radioactive waste resembles no ordinary trash. Four issues related to the nature of the material are described here: contamination, toxicity, duration, and criticality. That these properties can be contained in a very small package also makes the material attractive to thieves. This idea is developed below.

Containment and contamination concerns arise from emission of radioactive particles. Radioactive decay affects objects in the immediate vicinity of the radioactive material, resulting in site contamination. While other waste products also cause some dispersion of pollution, mitigation can be achieved by removal of the material through washing, steaming, or chemical modifications. For example, if a site is polluted with post-industrial fuel distillates, the material might seep through soil, enlarging the trash site. However, the contamination can be remedied by removing the distillates from the wider area, leaving clean soil. Radioactive contamination involves emissions that irradiate the ground, which must be removed along with the radioactive particles. The simple existence of high-level nuclear waste thus substantially enlarges the area that is polluted. As a result, the first task of nuclear waste management is the construction of containers to shield humans and the immediate environment from the radioactive particles. Common shielding materials include water, concrete, lead, steel, even DU. Pending the opening of a permanent storage facility, most spent fuel is stored at individual nuclear plants, covered by a minimum 20 feet of water.

Nuclear waste is highly toxic, and exposure leads to unconventional poisoning with limited treatment options. In order to prevent radiation sickness, exposure is carefully monitored in the nuclear industry. The intensity of the exposure drops geometrically over distance, so exposure is measured by reference to distance and time as well as the quantity of material. The response to even a small accident with high-level waste is managed within minutes of exposure, to prevent immediate injury or death. The amount of radioactivity in fuel rods is immense. For instance, if a person were to stand one meter away from a spent fuel assembly, the exposure would exceed over 20,000 rems per hour (compare this to baseline background radiation, measured in rems per year.) At accidental industrial exposure rates, 15 min of exposure is deadly.

A long time must pass to reduce radiation through natural decay of uranium, thorium, and plutonium. High-level spent nuclear fuel in the form of fuel rods remains toxic for eons. Plutonium-239, for instance, has a half-life of 24,000 years;

plutonium-240 seems almost benign by contrast, with a half-life of 6800 years. Although irradiated material decays over time, human beings do not live long, compared to the half lives of nuclear materials.

Finally, unlike most waste, any more than a small amount of nuclear material will reach critical mass and initiate a self-sustaining nuclear reaction, releasing orders of magnitude greater heat and radioactivity.

To the four natural attributes must be added security issues related to terrorism, insurgency, tribal warfare or civil war. A small amount of stolen high-level radioactive material magnifies the effect of many violent acts. A conventional car bomb, such as those that explode nearly every day somewhere in the world, would be two or three orders of magnitude more dangerous if irradiated materials were used in a densely populated urban area. A so-called dirty bomb can be constructed using a few pounds of radiological waste, without the technical sophistication of a nuclear device. While such a bomb might not cause the immediate wide-scale damage of a conventional nuclear device, it would require the complete evacuation of a population for an extended period of time.

Due to these four natural properties, along with the human factor, nuclear waste requires governmental, institutional management. A patchwork of agencies fulfills elements of this management role.

18.4 The Regulatory Framework

The management of the nuclear industry and weapons complex involves national agencies such as the Nuclear Regulatory Commission (NRC), the DOE, and the Department of Transportation (DOT). International agencies such as the IAEA are essential for non-proliferation. Private firms such as Envirocare and Bechtel/SAIC have become increasingly important in the medium- to long-range storage of nuclear waste, part of a general trend in U.S. government toward privatization. Multinational corporations own an increasing number of nuclear plants; the loss of local or national management has become a concern in several countries as they work to manage energy according to their national interests. The distribution of interests is fluid, as international mergers and acquisitions routinely alter relationships. For example, in February 2002 Toshiba bought Westinghouse for $5.4 billion. While Westinghouse might be most familiar for consumer appliances and Toshiba for personal computers, each firm manufactures nuclear reactors and the combined company holds 28% of the world market; this acquisition produced the number one nuclear power company in the world [19]. A globalized firm can use fiscal and other controls to manage its far-flung enterprises. No government has this reach and power, which complicates nuclear waste management.

Russia has sought to be more closely involved with the Chinese government in providing some of the thirty nuclear plants the Chinese plan to build over the next 13 years [20]. The short list of bidders for the first four plants, valued between one and two billion dollars each, includes Westinghouse and France's state-owned Areva. While China originally favored Westinghouse, the merger has dampened Chinese enthusiasm, as the state is concerned about Japanese control of sensitive technologies. The multiple international agencies, such as the IAEA, cannot alleviate Chinese political concerns, since they have limited political influence and serve more as technical or monitoring resources. Similar to the problems in France, members of the European Union are also skeptical about trans-national mergers of energy companies.

18.5   Yucca Mountain

> This will always be a controversial program. It always will be. Even after it's done.
>
> > Paul Golan, Acting Director,
> > U.S. Office of Civilian Radioactive Waste Management [21]

Long ago, each city or village managed its own energy sources and its own waste stream, since all consumption and pollution was local. The modern era post-consumption waste stream has changed dramatically. In a pre-industrial society, trash degrades rapidly. Modern and ancient society equally share a propensity to move waste beyond sight and smell and tend to discount long term effects. This dynamic has changed as the world has grown more populous and our waste more dangerous, and the lasting negative consequences of the latter become more evident.

> People understood taking our own waste [but we] couldn't accept becoming the trash can for the world.
>
> > Beaumont-Hague representative for
> > Greenpeace Yannick Rousselet [22]

Eisenhower's "Atoms for Peace" speech at the United Nations in 1953 signaled the beginning of the industrialized world's efforts to harness for benign use the seemingly clean (e.g., no smokestack emissions) and unlimited power of atomic energy. Research, generation, and nuclear medicine require the sharing of some nuclear technology and the creation of waste. While much U.S. waste is stored in situ pending transfer to the national repository, 41 countries are shipping spent fuel back to the U.S. regardless of available permanent storage. The first shipment transported by train to Idaho National Engineering and Environmental Laboratory was received at the Concord Naval Weapons Station, California, in 1998. This transport occurred despite a legislative resolution calling on DOE to stop shipments pending due notice, safety and environmental reviews. City councils, boards of supervisors, and other elected officials opposed the shipments [23]. East Coast arrivals are received in Charleston, South Carolina and transported to Savannah River [24]. Of 20 metric tons to be returned, 19 will arrive on the East Coast; a portion of this waste will be transported cross country to the Idaho facility.

Countries using nuclear power share a problem beyond managing spent fuel and other waste; the generation facilities also deteriorate over time, and ultimately will be decommissioned (taken out of use.) Of 438 commercial reactors operating in 31 countries, 100 are at least 40 years old. The common strategy of managing waste onsite in spent fuel pools cannot be continued when the plant itself, also contaminated, becomes part of the waste stream. So every decommissioning strategy must include waste management of entire facilities [25]. A handful of U.S. commercial nuclear units have closed, among them San Onofre-I, Yankee, Trojan, Shoreham and Rancho Seco, principally because ongoing operations and maintenance expenses make the electricity uncompetitive with fossil fuel generation. The NRC is responsible for decommissioning activities, and these cannot be complete until spent fuel is removed to Yucca Mountain.

A site, when decommissioned and delicensed, also disposes of all facilities at the location. In the case of Rancho Seco, management contracted for removal and long term storage of contaminated facilities with a private firm, Envirocare of Utah, which operates a storage site near a railroad siding named Clive, 80 miles west of Salt Lake City [26]. Envirocare is a privately-held firm originally established to store naturally occurring radioactive waste from a Superfund site—the Vitro tailings alongside I-15 in Salt Lake City. It upgraded its license to accept several thousand railcars of radium-contaminated soil from a Denver Superfund site and obtained a Resource Conservation and Recovery Act (RCRA) Part B permit to receive mixed waste. The firm was sold in 2005, at which point it gave up its RCRA Part B Permit and withdrew its application for class B and C waste. It retains a Class A low-level permit.

The government of France has developed an energy strategy to reduce dependence on imported fossil fuels. This has resulted in increasing dependence on nuclear power for electric generation. The nation meets more than three-quarters of its electric needs through nuclear generation, though this still comprises only about 20% of its total energy supply, due to dependence on oil for transportation. To limit the amount of long-term storage required for spent fuel, France reprocesses it, at substantial cost, at Beaumont-Hague for its own industry. The nation reduces its direct subsidy for this task by offering to reprocess spent fuel for other nations, particularly Germany and Japan [26].

The Yucca Mountain repository has yet to be constructed, though it will develop as an extension to the Exploratory Studies Facility (ESF) tunnel. More than two decades after Congress tasked DOE to provide a permanent geologic repository, the site consists of a 5 mile, U-shaped tunnel, 25 feet in diameter, adjacent to the repository block and associated surface structures. Basically level, the tunnel is bored into the side of the ridge whose top rises to approximately 1000 feet above the geologic layer of dense volcanic tuff where smaller tunnels will be drilled to contain the spent fuel. Experiments have been done in thirteen alcoves and niches (smaller, unventilated alcoves) of varying depth below the ridge, to investigate geologic and hydrologic properties of the rock. A second, smaller tunnel, called the Cross Drift, crosses the repository block. This tunnel allowed researchers to investigate faulting at the block's margins and to perform thermal simulations of spent fuel decay. Based on these studies, the DOE's Office of Civilian Radioactive Waste Management (OCRWM) is preparing an application with the NRC to license the block's operation. The application may be submitted by 2008, with an anticipated date for opening the repository for shipments of 2020 [21]. This would be 22 years later than the original target date, with all existing waste stored elsewhere in the meantime.

While the Yucca Mountain Project is being completed, interim storage must be arranged. Onsite storage at U.S. power plants is near or at capacity, and the managers of these facilities have sued the DOE to develop interim options. In September 2005, the Nuclear Regulatory Commission approved for temporary use a site in Utah at the Goshute Reservation/Skull Valley; it serves as a warehouse for as much as 44 thousand tons in mobile containers [27]. However, an enlargement of the Cedar Mountains Wilderness Area signed into law as part of a defense bill in January 2006 may block the development of this site.

If and when the Yucca Mountain repository is licensed to receive shipments, the process will be slow. It will take 108,000 truck shipments or 3000 train trips to deliver all the waste to Yucca Mountain, and these shipments are expected to take over 20 years [27,28].

The logistics of moving well over 100,000 tons of material to Yucca Mountain opens the question of whether the longstanding U.S. policy against reprocessing of nuclear fuel might be revisited. The only approved permanent storage facility in the U.S. has a designed capacity of 70,000 metric tons. In 2002, The NRC estimated that 45,000 metric tons of high-level waste was in temporary storage, mainly onsite at power plants and national research laboratories. This has grown to some 55,000 metric tons, with an annual growth rate of 2000 metric tons per year. Existing nuclear facilities will completely fill Yucca Mountain with the current and future spent fuel, based on the estimated life of the plants.

> What is the point of creating a storage site that will be filled to capacity before it even opens?
>
> Senator Dianne Feinstein [28]

Three solutions have been suggested to resolve the Yucca Mountain capacity problem: increasing its storage capacity, reprocessing spent fuel to reduce the volume of material that must be permanently placed in secure storage, or storing material at one or many secondary sites yet to be determined. On April 4, 2006, in an administrative sleight of hand, the U.S. Department of Energy announced it would support restating Yucca Mountain's ability to manage spent fuel to its "true technical [unstated] capacity," estimated at more than twice the statutory quantity. This action appears directly linked to the nuclear industry's expressed "wish list" for legislative action, made public weeks earlier [29]. The industry is unhappy that decades of payments to the Federal government to establish the repository have yet to result in any available storage, requiring individual firms to construct expensive and sophisticated temporary storage facilities. Additionally, if there is to be any augmentation in nuclear energy, there must be a collateral increase in available permanent storage.

> They [DOE] have our money, we have their fuel; it's time to close the deal.
>
> Nuclear Energy Institute Director of Used
> Fuel Management Steve Kraft [29]

The issue of confirmed storage space for the nuclear industry is called waste confidence, because it represents confidence in the Department of Energy to create and manage a permanent waste repository. Over $750 million is collected each year through rate surcharges to fund the permanent repository (tentatively Yucca Mountain) and DOE is contractually obligated to receive commercial nuclear waste. The original 1998 target date and subsequent dates have not been achieved.

In addition to spent nuclear fuel, some defense waste is also tentatively scheduled for Yucca Mountain. In 2002, the Department of Energy changed its plans for the management of a quantity of surplus weapons-grade plutonium. Rather than "immobilize" half of it in casks for long term storage, DOE decided to reprocess all 34 tons into mixed-oxide fuel, at a plant to be constructed specifically for this purpose at Savannah River. The reprocessed material will be fuel for Duke Power's nuclear generators from 2008 to 2021 [30]. In Hanford, 55 million gallons of mixed radioactive waste water will be processed into vitrified pellets, stable enough for transport from Washington to Yucca Mountain. The project to build the vitrification plant, however, has tripled in estimated cost and its completion date has been extended an estimated 6 years, to 2017 [31]. The Government Accountability Office (GAO) April, 2006 report attributes some portion of the problem to a "design/build" project orientation that allows for construction prior to full specification.

The Yucca Mountain Project continues to experience management problems that seem resistant to correction. A March 2006 GAO report highlights the inability of DOE to establish essential credibility with the NRC. Persistent quality assurance problems must appear resolved prior to submitting a credible license application as required to construct and open the Yucca Mountain facility. Project leadership has been unstable, with 9 of 17 key management positions turning over between 2001 and 2006, under three different directors. Over 14 million e-mails are being reviewed, following the disclosure in some e-mails from the period from 1998 to 2000 that suggest possible falsification of records [32].

> Science by peer pressure is dangerous but sometime [SIC] it is necessary.
> You don't really need to do an analysis just say this is the data I used.
> Maybe that would work.
> P.S. please destroy this memo.
>
> Excerpts from U.S. Geological Survey e-mails
> on the Yucca Mountain Project [33]

The e-mail messages under Congressional review call into question the reliability of computer models confirming that the Yucca Mountain area is geologically suitable. These models were created after an earthquake of magnitude 5.6 damaged a nearby DOE field office in 1992, undermining earlier assertions that the site is adequately distant from seismic zones. Nevada, the nation's third most seismically active state, displays a "basin and range" geology consisting of many small, roughly north/south fault lines pushing up rocky ridges with flat, dry basins between. At Yucca Mountain, two fault lines are involved in the repository layer. For long term nuclear waste storage, site suitability derives from the presumption that the storage can be deep and dry. Near the repository site, the water table is several hundred feet lower than in surrounding areas, as it is geologically linked to Death Valley, the lowest place in the U.S. The depth of the repository, hundreds of feet underground by virtue of the ridge directly above, is also several hundred feet above this water table; however it is lower in places than the neighboring water table. Hypothetically, if an earthquake were to fracture the rock separating these two areas, the repository could be flooded, potentially resulting in wide dispersion of radioactivity [34]. Computer modeling and testing onsite suggest this will not happen.

18.6 Policy Modifications Resulting from the "Global War on Terror"

In the years prior to the attacks at the World Trade Center and the Pentagon on September 11, 2001, an ideologically motivated stateless organization, Al Qaeda, initiated an escalating if unconventional series of attacks. The U.S. responded to the attacks by invading Afghanistan and overthrowing the Taliban government that sponsored Al Qaeda leader Osama Bin Laden. While Bin Laden has not been captured, his network has been damaged. Attention has therefore shifted to states not signatories to the non-proliferation treaty that have been openly pursuing nuclear weapon capacity, principally Iran and North Korea. Pakistan's nuclear chief was implicated in the sale of nuclear technologies, though the state of Pakistan remains allied with the U.S. interests in the region. In the U.S., nuclear facilities are more closely guarded as a result.

The DOE, and the NRC to a lesser degree, has a vested interest in maintaining a status quo assessment of Yucca Mountain's suitability as a repository [35]. This results most strikingly in a DOE that, according to critics, understates the potential for a major transportation accident or deliberate sabotage. Some argue that local autonomy is most responsive to public interests, but local control in the case of a national repository would result in the rejection of Yucca Mountain. Nevada Senator Harry Reid, through his leadership role in Congress, has created numerous roadblocks to the project but has been unable to effect absolute rejection of the site. The fear of weapons of mass destruction (WMD) that require nuclear composite elements has greatly increased the cost of guarding the hundreds of nuclear facilities, a cost not shared by coal or natural gas plants in a market for electrons that are identical as product. Yucca

Mountain Repository is essential for a viable nuclear industry, an important national goal at a time when dependence on foreign oil from unfriendly states is a national security concern.

Creating a nuclear weapon or a less-sophisticated radiological device requires a quantity of a controlled radiological substance. The IAEA maintains its Illicit Trafficking Database (ITDB) as a log of deliberate and inadvertent incidents reported by its members and other parties. These incidents include the unauthorized actual or attempted acquisition, possession, transfer or disposal of nuclear materials [36]. The IAEA interprets incidents involving minute quantities of weapons grade material (uranium and plutonium) as samples for what might be available in higher amounts. This database added 121 incidents in 2004 alone, possibly due to improved accounting; most of these concerned inadvertent rather than criminal acts. Since 1999, incidents have occurred in the former Soviet state of Georgia (3 of 6 reported instances since 2000), Bulgaria, Germany, Greece, and France. In the early years after the collapse of the Soviet Union and reconstitution of its nuclear weapon complex in several states, the quantities of nuclear material in some cases were substantial—2–3 kilograms. The reported incident in 2003 involved 170 g, and most are only a few grams. Of 664 confirmed incidents since the database's initiation, 220 have involved nuclear material, mostly fuel pellets, natural uranium, and depleted elements. These indicate issues in control and security systems, rather than immediate threats. Its September, 2005 report suggests criminal actions derive from perception of a black market interest in any sort of radioactive material [37].

18.7 Effect of the Kyoto Protocol

A global problem of the highest order has captured public interest and catapulted nuclear power (a worldwide pariah following the accidents at Three Mile Island in 1979 and Chernobyl in 1986) to the first rank of electricity generation sources. Scientific evidence implicates combustion gases emitted by fossil fuel power plants in global warming (the "greenhouse" effect). This warming due to increased carbon in the atmosphere cannot be corrected by any known technology. Effects of higher surface and ocean temperatures endanger the well-being of billions of people who live in already marginal tropical climates or in coastal areas that will be submerged as polar ice melts. Further, it threatens species, such as cold water fish, that provide most of the protein consumed by certain populations.

The Kyoto Protocol [38], signed by President Clinton but never ratified (and later rescinded by the Bush administration) is a plan to reduce fossil fuel emissions to limit global warming as understood with near universal agreement by scientists and researchers worldwide. Kyoto has resulted in four interlocking responses, even in the U.S. Cities, states, and nations are modifying or creating policies to encourage the development of renewable energy sources, favoring natural gas over coal in new fossil fuel plants, revisiting energy conservation to limit growth of fossil fuel consumption, and commissioning additional nuclear power plants as alternatives for the non-intermittent, high-density energy available from fossil fuel combustion. Emissions trading is a market response that also offers international potential.

Efforts to replace fossil fuels by sources considered renewable, mainly hydroelectric, wind, and solar, have not been as successful as hoped. Despite substantial growth in the total amount of renewable energy, there have been similarly large increases in fossil fuel consumption [39].

Production of electricity from nuclear power avoids emission of carbon-based greenhouse gases. For instance, electric generation from coal produced 83% of the industry's CO_2 emissions from 1990 to 2004 [40]. Contributions from natural gas rose from 10% to 13% over the same period, reflecting the increased preference for natural gas plants. From 1980 through the mid-1990's, when decline flattened, the use of nuclear power constituted the primary reason for a decline in carbon intensity in the U.S. energy supply [40].

When reduction of greenhouse gas emissions becomes a monolithic policy goal, and the substitution of nuclear energy products becomes a featured solution, the collateral effect of increasing nuclear waste is in the main ignored in public policy discussions. Similarly unmeasured are externalities from other production alternatives, such as the collateral effects of "mining" water to grow corn to produce methanol as a substitute for fossil fuel. The complexity of energy use, rich with geo-political interests, business and government subsidies, and environmental concerns, becomes a hurdle to reasoned public deliberation.

18.8 Conclusion

Nuclear waste has become a singular impediment to the mid-twentieth century promise of cheap, emission-free electricity to transform the world. While several nations ship radioactive waste to others for reprocessing, concern over loss of control over the waste products from this secondary processing led the U.S. toward a decision to establish a permanent and secure repository. The construction of the repository has been excruciatingly slow, due to technical problems, political opposition, and a measure of questionable work performance.

It is not unreasonable to assume that for the life of post-consumption nuclear waste, human nature will remain more or less unchanged. Therefore, we can expect most of these problems to persist into the far future. If this is so, what type of knowledge might contribute to the most positive outcomes? The newly developing field of complexity studies, the study of informatics, and new models of decision making each offers relevant public policy enhancements that can be recommended from a public management perspective.

On the technical side, capacity, environmental hazards, and safety-in-transportation questions remain. The capacity issue is directly linked to energy consumption and conservation, topics that historically seem particularly subject to whims of policy fashion and the price of fossil fuels. Perhaps persistent high prices, combined with the bugaboo of global warming, will keep this perennially on the table. Some argue that spent fuel cask construction trumps the environmental hazard question—that is, an impermeable cask reduces the need for an impermeable site. This is the Pandora's Box model, and let us hope no one ever opens the box. The third topic, transportation, struggles with competing forces regarding primary use, capacity, inter-sector and intergovernmental oversight, and encroachment on right-of-way.

Perhaps there are more questions than answers when we reflect on the issue of managing nuclear waste. Some of these time and money may address, while others may be outright unanswerable. However, the industrialized world continues, hour by hour, to produce this waste. So long as current processes do not result in massive loss of life or widespread ecological calamity, this appears to be acceptable.

Appendix A   Warnings across Millennia

Suggested site warnings from the U.S. Department of Energy's Office of Civilian Radioactive Waste Management

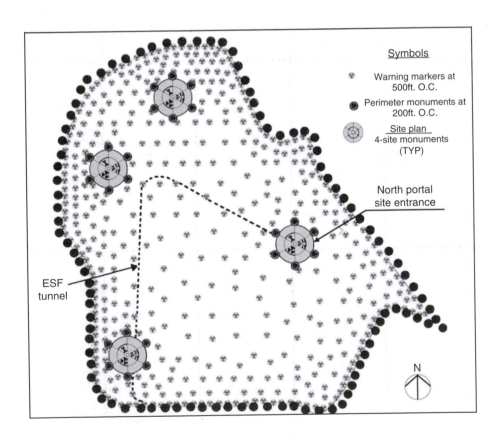

Artist's conception of one of the large warning monuments that also serve as information centers on the crest of Yucca Mountain after permanent closure of the proposed geologic repository.

Joshua Abbey
Desert Space Foundation

Appendix B

Table 18.1   Estimated Storage Requirement from the Office of Civilian Radioactive Waste Management's 2004 Report to Congress

Source	Amount	Type	Current Location	Comment
Commercial nuclear power generation	50, 000 metric tons	Spend fuel	72 reactor sites in 33 states	
Production of nuclear weapons	2500 metric tons	Spend fuel and high-level waste	Sites in 3 states	High-level waste created from chemical separation of uranium and plutonium
Disposal of surplus plutonium	50 metric tons	Weapons grade plutonium		34 metric tons will be transformed prior to storage. 16 metric tons has no disposition
Operation of naval nuclear vessels (40% of fleet)	Not specified	Spent fuel	"Surface facilities" in U.S.	
Research reactors	Not specified	Spent fuel	39 sites in 24 states and DOE sites	Include returns from foreign reactors and laboratories

References

1. U.S. Department of Energy, DOE to send proposed Yucca Mountain legislation to Congress, U.S. Department of Energy, Office of Public Affairs, Washington DC, 2006. Available at http://www.energy.gov/print/3428.htm, accessed on April 4, 2006.
2. U.S. Nuclear Regulatory Commission, Radioactive waste: Production, storage, disposal, (NUREG/BR-0216. Rev. 2), 2002, 16, Available at http://www.nrc.gov/reading-rm/doc-collections/nuregs/brochures/br0216/r2/index.html (accessed on April 4, 2006).
3. U.S. Department of Energy, Nuclear Waste Policy Act, as amended, Office of Civilian Radioactive Waste Management, Washington DC, 2004. Available at www.ocrwm.doe.gov/documents/nwpa/css/nwpa_2004.pdf, (accessed on April 4, 2006).

4. Eisenhower, D.D., Atoms for Peace, Address by Mr. Dwight D. Eisenhower, President of the United States of America, to the 470th Plenary Meeting of the United Nations General Assembly, 1953. Available at http://www.iaea.org/About/history_speech. html (accessed on April 4, 2006).

5. National Safety Council, Understanding radiation in our world, nd.

6. United Nations, Treaty on the Non-Proliferation of Nuclear Weapons (NPT), 1968, Available at http://www.iaea.org/Publications/Documents/Treaties/npt.html (accessed on May 23, 2006).

7. U.S. Department of Energy, DOE to send proposed Yucca Mountain legislation to Congress, U.S. Department of Energy, Office of Public Affairs, Washington DC, 2006, Available at http://www.energy.gov/print/3428.htm (accessed on April 4, 2006).

8. Office of Civilian Radioactive Waste Management, Annual Report to Congress December 2004, (DOE/RW-0569), U.S. Department of Energy, Energy Information Administration, Washington DC, 2004, 6–7.

9. Pillar, P.R., Intelligence, Policy, and the War in Iraq, Foreign Affairs, March/April, 2006, Available at http://www.foreignaffairs.org/20060301faessay85202/paul-r-pillar/inte lligence-policy-and-the-war-in-iraq.html, accessed on April 3, 2006.

10. Washington State Department of Ecology, Hanford Frequently Asked Questions, nd. Available at http://www.ecy.wa.gov/features/hanford/hanfordFAQ.html, accessed on April 5, 2006.

11. Subramanian, K.H. and Wiersma, B.J., Functions and Requirements for the Leak Mitigation System of the Savannah River Site Double Shell High-Level Waste Tanks (WSRC-TR-2001-00438, Rev. 1), Westinghouse Savannah River Company, 2002. Available at http://sti.srs.gov/fulltext/tr2001438r1/tr2001438r1.html (accessed on April 4, 2006).

12. Savannah River nuclear-waste tanks have cracked, rusted or leaked, Detroit Free Press, Available at http://www.freep.com/news/latestnews/pm20601_20040710.htm (accessed on November 1, 2005).

13. Dianne, Rahm, Ed, in *Toxic Waste and Environmental Policy in the 21st Century*, McFarland, Jefferson, 2002, 37–58.

14. Bearden, D.M., Exemptions from Environmental Law for the Department of Defense: An Overview of Congressional Action, CRS Report for Congress, Order Code RS22149, Congressional Research Service, 2005.

15. World Health Organization, Fact Sheet No. 257: Depleted uranium, 2003, Available at http://www.who.int/mediacentre/factsheets/fs257/en/ (accessed on April 4, 2006).

16. United Nations Environmental Program, Depleted Uranium Awareness, United Nations Environmental Program, Post-Conflict Assessment Unit, 2003, Available at http://postconflict.unep.ch/publications/DUflyer.pdf (accessed on April 6, 2006).

17. United Nations Environmental Program, Depleted uranium in Bosnia and Herzego- vina. Revised Edition, 2003.

18. Veterans Health Administration, Depleted uranium follow-up program, Veterans Health Administration, Office of Public Health & Environmental Hazards, 2004, Available at http://www.vethealth.cio.med.va.gov/DUProgram.htm (accessed on April 5, 2006).

19. Yageyama, Yuri, Toshiba faces hurdles to buy Westinghouse, Associated Press, 2006, Available at http://biz.yahoo.com/ap/060221/japan_buying_westinghouse. html (accessed on April 5, 2006).

20. Oster, S., Moscow courts Beijing over nuclear power, *Wall Street Journal*, A6.

21. Werner, E., Yucca Mountain chief predicts application in 2008, dump by 2020, Las Vegas Sun, 2006, Available at http://www.lasvegassun.com/sunbin/stories/nevada/2006/ mar/31/033110451.html (accessed on April 1, 2006).

22. Ball, J., With a Big Nuclear Push, France Transforms Its Energy Equation, *Wall Street Journal*, A1.

23. California Energy Commission, Fact sheet on the U.S. Department of Energy shipments of foreign research reactor spent nuclear fuel via the Concord Naval Weapons Station, 1998. Available at http://www.energy.ca.gov/nuclear/foreign_factsheet.html (accessed on April 5, 2006).

24. Eureka County Yucca Mountain Information Office, Foreign Research Reactor Fuel Shipped through Nevada, 2003. Available at http://www.yuccamountain.org/newslet5. htm (accessed on April 5, 2006).

25. IEE, *Nuclear Decommissioning Factfile*, 2nd ed., Institution of Electrical Engineers, London, 2003, 17–18.

26. U.S. Regulatory Nuclear Commission, Rancho Seco, 2005. Available at http://www. nrc.gov/info-finder/decommissioning/power-reactor/rancho-seco-nuclear-gener- ating-station.html, accessed on April 5, 2006.

27. Silverstein, K., Yucca Mountain: Long Row to Hoe, EnergyBizInsider, 2005. Available at http://www.energycentral.com/site/newsletters/ebi.cfm?id=36 (accessed on October 3, 2005).

28. Feinstein, Dianne, Statement of Senator Dianne Feinstein in opposition to a resolution making Yucca Mountain the national repository for nuclear waste, 2002, Available at http://www.senate.gov/~feinstein/Releases02/yucca07.htm (accessed on April 5, 2006).

29. Platts, Industry's legislative wish list seeks Yucca Mt. revamping, 2006. Available at http://www.platts.com/Nuclear/News/7299425.xml (accessed on April 4, 2006).

30. Powers, M.B., DOE opts to recycle plutonium, scraps immobilization, *ENR: Engin- eering News Review*, 14.

31. GAO, Hanford Waste Treatment Plant: Contractor and DOE Management Problems Have Led to Higher Costs, Construction Delays, and Safety Concerns, (GAO-06-602T), General Accountability Office, Washington DC, 2006. Available at http://www.gao. gov/new.items/d06602t.pdf (accessed on May 15, 2006).

32. GAO, Yucca Mountain: Quality assurance at DOE's planned nuclear waste repository needs increased management attention, (GAO-06-313), General Accountability Office, Washington DC, 2006. Available at http://www.gao.gov/new.items/d06313. pdf (accessed on March 30, 2006).

33. Committee on Government Reform, Chairman Jon Porter's Initial Probe into Allegations that Federal Scientists Falsified Data Used to Establish the Safety of the Yucca Mountain Nuclear Waste Repository Reveals Disturbing Results, Committee on Government Reform, Subcommittee on the Federal Workforce and Agency Organization, 2005. Available at http://www.state.nv.us/nucwaste/news2005/pdf/porter050401p- robe.pdf (accessed on April 4, 2006).

34. State of Nevada Nuclear Waste Product Office, Earthquakes in the Vicinity of Yucca Mountain, nd. Available at http://www.state.nv.us/nucwaste/yucca/seismoo01.htm (accessed on April 5, 2006).

35. Ballard, J.D. and Mullendore, K., Weapons of mass victimization, radioactive waste shipments, and environmental laws, *The American Behavioral Scientist*, 46, 2003, 766.

36. International Atomic Energy Agency, Illicit Nuclear Trafficking Facts & Figures, nd. Available at http://www.iaea.org/NewsCenter/Features/RadSources/Fact_Figures. html (accessed on April 4, 2006).

37. International Atomic Energy Agency, Press Release 2005/15: Nuclear Trafficking Latest Statistics Released, 2005. Available at http://www.iaea.org/NewsCenter/PressReleases/ 2005/prn200515.html (accessed on April 4, 2006).

38. Kyoto Protocol, nd. Available at http://unfccc.int/resource/convkp.html (accessed on April 15, 2006).

39. Lorenzini, P., A second look at nuclear power, *Issues in Science and Technology*, 21, 2005, 31.
40. U.S. Department of Energy, Emissions of Greenhouse Gases in the United States 2004, (DOE/EIA-0573(2004)), U.S. Department of Energy, Energy Information Administration, Washington DC, 32, 2005.

Chapter 19

Inter-Agency Collaborative Approaches to Endangered Species Act Compliance and Salmon Recovery in the Pacific Northwest

Nicholas P. Lovrich and Edward P. Weber
Washington State University

Michael J. Gaffney
Vrije University

R. Michael Bireley and Bruce Bjork
The University of Texas at San Antonio

Dayna R. Matthews
Old Dominion University

19.1   Introduction

Beginning in the 1960s, federal and state agencies in a variety of regulatory policy areas have adopted what some have called a strict-compliance/deterrence or penal/punitive style of enforcement [1–5]. This approach is characterized by "a reliance on formal, precise, and specific rules; the literal interpretation of the rules; the (primary) reliance on the advice of legal technicians (attorneys); the quest for uniformity; and the distrust of and an adversarial orientation towards the regulated" [6].

While the strict-compliance/deterrence approach has dominated enforcement efforts, substantial scholarly evidence has been assembled that calls this approach into question with respect to both deterrence and goal achievement. Effective regulatory enforcement requires an approach that is grounded in collaboration, negotiation, flexibility, and a focus on achievable outcomes. Such a nuanced and "responsive" approach to regulation matches the enforcement style with the task or problem at issue [7–11]. In recent years, responsive enforcement and collaborative, negotiated policy implementation has been used in many policy areas, including education [12], taxation [13], rural development [14,15], employment training [16], and human health [17]. This trend has been prominent in the fields of environmental and natural resource policy and in local community law enforcement.*

Within the field of environmental policy, the *Endangered Species Act* (ESA) has long been at the center of controversy between landowners, natural resource users, environmentalists and wildlife habitat advocates. Viewed from an enforcement perspective, protecting endangered species is difficult work. Not only is it often hard to apprehend ESA violators, but local support for the law is weak in rural areas where most enforcement efforts occur. It is safe to say that not only does the general public possess scant knowledge of the legal requirements of the ESA, but there is little understanding regarding what actually constitutes an illegal take or violation under this law.

Because of the enforcement problems encountered in implementing the ESA, and due to the lessons learned from work with collaborative enforcement in community policing, in 1998 the National Oceanic and Atmospheric Administration (NOAA) Fisheries Office for Law Enforcement (OLE; better known as the National Marine Fisheries Service (NMFS)) and the Washington State Department of Fish and Wildlife (WDFW) Enforcement Program decided to test a collaborative model for ESA enforcement. Agency decision makers came to share an expectation that the application of a proactive, negotiation-oriented enforcement philosophy—which was designated *Resource-Oriented Enforcement* (ROE) [18]—would enhance the effectiveness of their respective enforcement efforts.

---

* For environmental/natural resource policy, see Born and Genskow (1999) [34], Brick, Snow and van De Wetering (2001) [35], John (1994) [36], Kemmis (2001) [37], Lubell, Schneider, Scholz, and Mete (2002) [38], Weber (1998, 2000) [39,40], and Wondollek and Yaffee (2000) [41]. See also Hunter and Waterman's (1996) [42] empirical study of federal Clean Water Act enforcement that finds that the enforcement style *in practice* is often different than conventional wisdom suggests (i.e., they find a pragmatic enforcement style instead of the expected and often reported coercive, punitive style). Their conclusions also suggest that practitioners, or regulators in the field, can and do vary their enforcement style in response to real world situations and changing contexts. For community policing, see Anderson, Bjork, and Powell (1995) [31], Bayley (1994 and 1998) [23,43], Sparrow (1994) [13], and Alport and Piquero (1997) [44].

This approach held the potential of both preventing the take of listed fish species (Steelhead, Salmon, and Bull Trout), and promoting trust and co-operation between regulatory agencies and the parties they regulate. Agency leaders felt that ROE would contribute to a restoration of public trust in the agencies responsible for ESA implementation. Fundamental to this approach was the belief that rural, nature-dependent communities *and* protected species can often prosper simultaneously if a collaborative, problem solving process is facilitated by locally-based and widely known WDFW officers and staff.

This chapter reviews outcomes observed in the first two cases in which NOAA Fisheries OLE and the WDFW Enforcement Program attempted to implement the ROE approach—the Methow Valley and the Walla Walla River Basin in eastern Washington. How the ROE *plan* translated into *programs* in the two watersheds provides valuable insight into how well a collaborative approach can adapt to natural resource enforcement.

19.2 Legal and Physical Setting

19.2.1 Background

In the fall of 1997, Steelhead were listed as endangered in the Upper Columbia River Evolutionarily Significant Unit (ESU). The listing was the 6th anadromous fish listing to occur in the Northwest Region in the previous 7 years, with 10 other stocks then still under review. In the period 1991–1997, fish protection enforcement activities had focused on addressing take* actions through traditional means (e.g., close monitoring of recreational and commercial fishing in the Snake and Columbia Rivers), and on federal projects in the region.

These traditional enforcement efforts, coupled with a lack of enforcement focus on take resulting from habitat destruction, made it difficult for NOAA Fisheries OLE to respond to allegations of lax enforcement. NOAA Fisheries OLE knew that various stakeholders felt that the ESA was a "paper tiger" statute [19,20]. This common perception had a negative effect on the willingness of some parties to pursue the timely development of proactive Habitat Conservation Plans (HCP)† that can minimize adverse effects on listed species [21]. Parties to these planning efforts would often pose the question: "Why should we seek potentially expensive take protection coverage through an HCP if, in fact, we are not at risk of an enforcement action on a take of listed fish?"

---

* As defined in the ESA, *take* means to harass, harm, pursue, hunt, shoot, wound, kill, trap, capture, or collect, or to attempt to engage in any such conduct. Harm is further defined to kill or injure a listed species, and "may include significant habitat modification" by significantly impairing essential behavioral patterns, including breeding, spawning, rearing, migrating, feeding, and sheltering.

† Upon voluntary application and completion of an HCP, the Secretary may permit, under terms and conditions, any taking otherwise prohibited if such taking is incidental to, and not the purpose of, the carrying out of an otherwise lawful activity.

19.2.2   The NOAA Response

The NOAA Fisheries OLE responded by analyzing options and developing a *Plan for Protection of West Coast ESA-Listed Anadromous Fish and Their Habitats* [22]. This plan proposed a combination of traditional and non-traditional enforcement measures to be carried out by OLE in two regions of the West Coast covering California, Idaho, Oregon, and Washington. The plan called for an interregional coordinator, a mid-level regional policy/planning team, and a field team featuring locally-based federal agents, biologists and a regional enforcement attorney.

In crafting its plan the OLE referred to the NOAA Fisheries Strategic Plan for guidance. Two specific agency objectives supported a focus on ESA-listed anadromous fish stock and fish habitat protection activities:

1. Recover Protected Species
   ■ Recover and maintain protected species populations.
   ■ Reduce conflicts that involve protected species.
2. Sustain Healthy Living Marine Resource Habitat
   ■ Protect, conserve, and restore living marine resource habitat and bio-diversity.

The stated performance measures of the plan directed NOAA Fisheries OLE to:

☐ Diligently enforce, with impartiality and equity, existing and future ESA laws, regulations, rules, and/or permit and contract conditions.

☐ Help evaluate and assist in solving societal problems regarding the listing of anadromous fish using a Community Oriented Policing and Problem Solving (COPPS) approach.

☐ Promote NOAA Fisheries objectives by developing partnerships with state, federal, tribal and local agencies, stakeholders and the public.

☐ Increase the use of non-traditional, preventative enforcement practices and improve the means for measuring the effectiveness of enforcement efforts.

For the OLE, achieving these objectives would require the development of new skills, strategies and resources, as well as the redirection of staff priorities. It would also require a coast-wide strategy featuring a deft combination of both traditional and nontraditional law enforcement with consistent emphasis being placed on preventing habitat loss. Sustained effort to develop close partnerships with state, tribal, and local natural resource management agencies, other stakeholders, and the public was also required. This new non-traditional approach to law enforcement is commonly referred to as *COPPS*.*

---

* Herman Goldstein, in his *Policing a Free Society* (1977) [45], discusses how American policing was revolutionized by realizing that the role of police was not just to respond to a criminal incident, but rather to solve the underlying problem leading to criminal activity. Goldstein identified a "problem" as a series of incidents (or a cluster) so similar, related, or recurring that it constitutes a substantive community concern and a significant unit of police business.

The philosophy underlying COPPS is based on the premise that local law enforcement agencies can be most effective when traditional activities are coupled with collaborative, community-involving efforts that identify and address the causal factors underlying problems. The widespread adoption of community-oriented policing strategies in the U.S. tends to confirm this premise. Significant positive impacts on crime rates, fear of crime, and community quality of life have resulted from the adoption of proactive, partnership-oriented collaborative efforts across the country [23].

It is the belief that this premise is also applicable to natural resource law enforcement agencies that served as the basis for the development of the collaborative, community-oriented component of the strategic planning processes. Once this approach was conceptualized, the OLE spent the spring and summer months of 1998 developing the requisite operational infrastructure to field-test the new approach. After review, a final plan was adopted in June of 1998.

19.2.3 The WDFW Response

At roughly the same time that OLE was planning its approach, the WDFW Enforcement Program was developing a strategic plan of its own, partly in response to a call from the Governor to prepare a *Salmon Recovery Strategy Framework*. At a July, 1998, Joint Natural Resources Cabinet Policy Retreat, a decision package was developed which included the following key provisions:

■ Existing state agency enforcement to protect salmon habitat needs to be enhanced.
■ Enhancement will include more effective enforcement of existing state laws and obtaining new authority to enforce if necessary.
■ Enforcement should be targeted toward priority areas for salmon recovery.
■ Interagency coordination is needed for enforcement. The possibility of cross-training and sharing enforcement staff should be explored.
■ The state should engage local citizens in developing its enforcement strategy.

The Strategic Plan prepared by WDFW for Fiscal Years 1999–2004 included two sections in direct response to the Governor's *Salmon Strategy Framework*: the ROE Program and ESA. The Strategic Plan contains this key provision [24]:

> The WDFW Enforcement Program believes fish and wildlife can best be served by full implementation of ROE. ROE is commonly referred to as community policing within the state and nation. ROE is working in partnership with communities sharing common concerns and common responsibilities, and influencing community decisions affecting fish and wildlife. The growing awareness of the limitations of the traditional role of the enforcement officer through strict regulation enforcement has caused us to look at alternative approaches to generate public support for fish and wildlife and increased voluntary compliance. The Fish and Wildlife Officer must become a facilitator of community problem

identification and problem solving. The switch from "me to we" and to teams and partnerships is the core of ROE.

The concept of ROE is not a unique program, but a philosophy that directs how an enforcement program does business. As it translates to fish and wildlife, ROE is the active collaboration between the Department's Enforcement Program and the community that identifies and solves community natural resource problems, i.e., habitat protection, illegal fish and wildlife harvest, unsafe or disorderly harvest, landowner relations, road management, problem wildlife resolution, and improved responses to customer service. ROE is the commitment by local officers to place an emphasis on customer service. It is the commitment to serve and interact with all members of the community, rather than just those in violation. The officer is the focal point for agency programs in the community because of geographic dispersed duty stations. ROE focuses on prevention as well as on apprehension.

19.2.4 Strategy for Implementation

The OLE hosted an ESA enforcement workshop in the state capital in September of 1998. That workshop promoted networking among policy and enforcement staff, biologists, and outreach specialists in the formulation of a coast-wide enforcement strategy for the protection of ESA-listed anadromous fish. NOAA Fisheries OLE staff from the Protected Resources and Habitat Conservation Divisions, as well as NOAA General Counsel and Department of Justice personnel attended, along with representatives from the WDFW, the Oregon State Police Fish and Wildlife Division, the California Fish and Game Enforcement Division, and several other state and private organizations.

In developing a common strategy, participants were asked to determine:

- What would desirable outcomes be for a West Coast enforcement strategy for ESA-listed anadromous fish?
- What enforcement priorities should NOAA Fisheries and the states pursue to achieve such outcomes?
- What actions should be undertaken, and by whom, to achieve these outcomes as stated?

Desired outcomes would be: (not listed in priority)

- Salmonid recovery, both in terms of habitat conditions and population.
- Compliance with existing resource protection laws and regulations.
- Stakeholders and communities possessing the knowledge and understanding of the biological needs of listed species.
- Stakeholders and communities possessing the knowledge and understanding of resource protection laws and regulations.
- Public support of program strategies.
- An ongoing plan for sustainability.

The next step in the application of the collaborative ESA enforcement program effort called for implementing this strategy in areas where pressing resource enforcement issues existed.

19.3   The Methow Valley

19.3.1   *Background*

The Upper Columbia River ESU featured endangered Steelhead and spring-run Chinook. As of September 1999, the Central Valley of California and the Upper Columbia were the only West Coast basins to contain two listed salmonid species. With regard to enforcement challenges, the Methow Valley in Okanogan County was one of only two areas within the Northwest Region where the taking of listed fish was strictly prohibited* [25,26].

In the summer of 1998, OLE began meeting with WDFW counterparts to address ESA-listed fish protection concerns in the Upper Columbia River ESU. By late fall of 1998, the two enforcement programs had identified a total of 56 gravity-fed irrigation ditches in the valley that either: (1) lacked properly functioning fish screens meeting jointly adopted WDFW and OLE juvenile fish protection criteria; and/or (2) blocked fish passage to historic spawning habitats. Both situations were violations of state law and could be considered a take under the ESA. Many (23) of these known diversions were in a tributary of the Methow River (Beaver Creek). Although the diversions in Beaver Creek were clearly not in compliance with state fish screening laws, they were not considered immediate potential take violations because a Washington State Department of Transportation (WSDOT) highway culvert blocked fish passage near the entrance to the stream. The remaining 33 stream diversions were located throughout the Twisp and Methow River drainages of the Methow Valley. These 33 ditches and the WSDOT Beaver Creek culvert became the focus for the OLE and the WDFW enforcement program within the Upper Columbia River ESU.

Fish protection in the Upper Columbia River ESU entails dealing with difficult water-related issues involving a triad of concerns, including fish screens, fish passage, and in-stream flow levels. The issue of in-stream flows had been a contentious subject in the Methow Valley for over a decade prior to the ESA listings. In the late 1980s a collaborative process referred to as the *Chelan Agreement* questioned the established pattern of having irrigators operating in the Methow, an area where water right claims had not yet been perfected through the process termed *adjudication*. Referring to these alleged wasteful practices, the Colville Confederated Tribes and Yakama Indian Nation filed suit in 1991 against the largest water diverter in the Methow basin, the Methow Valley Irrigation District (MVID), asserting that the district's water distribution practices were having a detrimental effect on anadromous Salmon and Steelhead

---

* The prohibition on take is immediate when a species is listed as endangered. When an animal is listed as threatened, the Secretary shall issue such regulations, as he or she deems necessary and advisable to provide for the conservation of such species.

populations. It was asserted that the MVID was infringing on tribal treaty fishing rights by its irrigation practices. In settling this lawsuit, the MVID agreed to seek an alternative water source.

By 1997, an alternative water source and new delivery system (a series of wells, pumps, and pressurized pipes) had been developed for MVID use. The Environmental Impact Statement (EIS) had been completed, and funding (in excess of $6 million) had been secured for the project through the Bonneville Power Administration (BPA), the Washington Department of Ecology (WDOE), and the WDFW. In the final hour, however, a special election conducted by MVID stakeholders recalled the MVID Commissioners who had brokered this deal and a new Commission was seated. In February 1999, the newly elected Commission withdrew the previous commitment and announced its intention to retain the status quo system utilizing gravity-fed ditches to deliver water to its customers.

It was against this general backdrop of contentious water allocation history, lack of compliance with state fish screening and passage laws, and new regulatory burdens under the ESA that OLE and the WDFW staff began meeting in the spring of 1999. These agency law enforcement officials sought to formulate an action plan specifically to address state and federal compliance objectives for the protection of ESA-listed fish in the Methow Valley. The guideposts available for use by staff at those meetings were the goals of the OLE Protection Plan and the WDFW ROE initiative.

From February to April 1999, WDFW and OLE and policy staff labored in various workshops to formulate an *Okanagon County Action Plan*. Field level staff representing multiple disciplines—including enforcement, biologists, and educators from multiple agencies including the WDOE, U.S. Forest Service (USFS), U.S. First and Wildlife Service (USFWS), and county governments—met and developed an *Interagency Action Plan for Okanogan County and the Methow Valley*. Using a 9-step Action Team process, the Okanogan County Action Plan consisted of two primary components. The first entailed the monitoring of conditions placed upon Special Use Permits issued by the USFS for conveyance of water by irrigation ditches, while the second required addressing the passage and screening compliance issues identified in the Beaver Creek tributary to the Methow River. Bridging these two components would require active monitoring to address potential take violations. The 4-step compliance plan for addressing ESA-related enforcement issues in Okanogan County consisted of a process designed to:

1. Seek Voluntary Compliance by Affected Parties
2. Initiate Follow Up Contacts with Holdouts
3. Issue Written Warnings and Establish Deadlines for Action
4. Achieve Final Accountability through Court Action if Necessary

In order to initiate the plan, local WDFW Officers were assigned the task of contacting all surface water users within the Methow Basin to:

■ Identify issues and problems
■ Use a District Team to develop solutions and funding proposals

- Present funding options to users where possible
- Monitor for take, permitting violations, and compliance
- Determine schedule for Biological Opinion completions

19.3.2 Okanogan County Memorandum of Understanding

The ongoing Section 19.7 regulatory consultations and enforcement efforts in the Methow Valley were intended to support a larger policy effort. NOAA Fisheries policy staff representing the Regional Administrator, along with WDFW Regional staff and WDOE staff representing their respective Directors and the Governor's Office, were involved in negotiating a MOU with the Okanogan Board of County Commissioners. An MOU is typically viewed as a precursor to the development of negotiated HCP.

Under the ESA, mechanisms for protection against take liability are not provided for until after an HCP is negotiated and legally in effect. Negotiations related to HCPs can and often do take years to complete, while in the interim liability for the taking of endangered species continues in force. Whereas fish screening and passage issues can often be addressed through engineered designs that can usually be implemented in a relatively short period of time, addressing take caused by inadequate flows frequently requires substantial study and complicated, long-term multi-party policy negotiations. The MOU in the Okanogan County scenario was intended to provide some assurances to local water districts, including an understanding about prosecutorial discretion in certain circumstances while an HCP was being negotiated.

19.3.3 Compliance in the Methow Valley

By the fall of 1999, 32 of the 33 ditches identified as being in violation had achieved compliance with state fish screening and passage laws. Of these, 14 were issued *Special Use Permits* from the Forest Service and received incidental take statements from NOAA Fisheries enabling them to continue operation. These compliance measures did not come without considerable sacrifice or cost to the local area. For example, plans to build a destination vacation resort in the valley were abandoned. In addition, a well-established Bed and Breakfast Inn was forced into bankruptcy, while many other businesses incurred financial hardship.

In its first year, the Okanogan County Action Plan had achieved a commitment that ultimately lead to the replacement of the WSDOT culvert at Beaver Creek, and was instrumental in 32 of the 33 ditches alleged to be in violation of state screening and passage laws achieving compliance without further enforcement activity, thus substantially reducing or eliminating their take liability under the ESA. Of the 33 non-compliant ditches identified within the basin, the MVID was the only entity that chose to continue to operate in open violation of state and federal law during the 1999 irrigation season. Hundreds of salmonids were stranded when the district ceased operation in the fall of 1999 and drained their 34-mile long irrigation ditch. The subsequent investigation led to the issuance of two Notices of Violation Assessment (NOVA), as well as a court injunction and consent decree issued by the Federal District Court in April of 2000.

19.3.4 MOU Negotiations Fail

Following two years of negotiation, attempts to craft an MOU were terminated by the Okanogan Board of County Commissioners in December of 2000. As a result, many water consumers in the area were left with potential take liability resulting from inadequate flows caused by their water diversions. The negotiations associated with the MOU had been contentious; from the outset many local citizens advocated adopting a position of refusing to negotiate with the "Feds," based on a belief that the ESA represents an unwarranted federal intrusion upon individual and state rights. Accordingly, litigation, rather than serious negotiation, became the course of action taken on ESA issues [27].

19.4 The Walla Walla River Basin

19.4.1 Background

Historically, the Walla Walla River Basin supported healthy populations of spring Chinook Salmon, Steelhead and Bull Trout. With the arrival of early settlers in the 1800s and the ensuing development of agricultural based communities, irrigation withdrawals, dams and diversions took a heavy toll on each of these species.

The general economy of the Walla Walla Basin is supported primarily through agriculture, which represents 58% of the watershed, with forestland and range land covering 25 and 17% of the basin, respectively. Over the course of the past century, management of agricultural lands has been a significant factor in the decline of salmonid habitat, due in large part to practices such as farming to the edge of streams, removal of riparian vegetation, filling off-channel areas, diking, channelization and extensive irrigation. In some locations in the area, irrigation practices have reduced stream flows to a trickle and, in other locations, totally de-watered streams [28].

19.4.2 A Take Occurs in the Walla Walla Basin

On June 13, 1997 a proposed rule to list the Columbia River distinct population segment of Bull Trout as a threatened species, including populations within the Walla Walla River Basin, was published in the *Federal Register*. A final rule listing these Bull Trout populations as threatened under the ESA was published in the *Federal Register* on June 10, 1998, and became effective on July 10, 1998. Upon the effective date, 50 C.F.R. Section 17.31(a), which prohibited the take of Bull Trout, enabled federal agencies to initiate enforcement actions within the Walla Walla watershed and other affected areas.

For a period of roughly the past 100 years, the 2.5–5-mile portion (depending on seasonal weather conditions) of the Walla Walla River located in Oregon a short distance upstream of the Washington-Oregon state line, known as the Tumalum, had experienced documented annual dewatering events. During the occurrence of such a dewatering event in the summer of 1999 on this portion of the Walla Walla River, substantial numbers of Bull Trout (108) and Steelhead (6482)* as well as other species of fish, were recovered during salvage operations undertaken by the Oregon Department of Fish and Wildlife, with assistance from the WDFW and the Confederated Tribes of the Umatillas, as well as several local groups and the USFWS. Through these salvage and recovery efforts, many listed Bull Trout were documented as an illegal take and became a catalyst for regulatory compliance measures that followed. Although threatened Steelhead were also imperiled as a result of these de-watering events, take prohibitions on this species were not yet in place. The promulgated "4d" rule prohibiting take of listed Steelhead was proposed and published in the *Federal Register* in the summer of 2000, and became effective and enforceable through finalization on September 9, 2000.[†]

Upon invitation, and in response to local concerns, OLE and USFWS met with representatives of the Walla Walla Watershed Council and various community leaders in Milton-Freewater, Oregon in December of 1999 for the purpose of discussing the merits of developing an HCP and the potential liability for take of listed species which confronted irrigators in the basin. During the meeting, the Watershed Council representatives discussed with the federal agency staff the unique cross-state boundary adjudication of water between Oregon and Washington.

19.4.3 Compliance Issues in the Walla Walla River Basin

In response to the documented take of Bull Trout in the summer of 1999, the USFWS initiated an official investigation. While this investigation was developing, a number of other Salmon recovery-related activities and events were beginning to unfold within the basin that would affect how major actors would approach key issues of ESA compliance in the Walla Walla Basin. During discussions among several of the parties, policy staff from NOAA Fisheries and USFWS clarified the top priorities for recovery efforts of listed species under ESA for the Walla Walla River Basin, with the priority being flow regimes and fish screens. In Washington, regulatory authority for screening was the responsibility of WDFW, while authority to regulate flow regimes and water right compliance was the responsibility of the WDOE. Various perspectives on how to address these priorities were discussed, and two schools of thought emerged. Some officials advocated a traditional approach to compliance that would necessitate direct enforcement by federal and/or state agencies. Others favored a

---

* Data on Bull Trout and Steelhead salvage efforts derived from Michelle Eames, a biologist with the USFWS, Spokane, WA. 2002.

† The *4d rule* prohibiting take of Steelhead in the Snake River ESU was finalized in the summer of 2000 and became enforceable on 9/1/00.

collaborative process focusing on proactive problem solving. There was no clear consensus as to how the ESA issues of flow and screening should be addressed.

In February and March of 2000, the USFWS contacted the three irrigation districts to inform them that the U.S. Solicitor General was prepared to issue a NOVA charging them with liability for the take of Bull Trout under the ESA, stemming from the de-watering event of 1999. USFWS and NOAA Fisheries policy staff subsequently met to discuss the NOVA and determine its potential implications for future HCP negotiations. It was from these meetings that negotiations ensued regarding a Civil Penalty Settlement Agreement between the USFWS and the three designated irrigation districts. The decision by the three affected irrigation districts to engage in civil penalty settlement negotiations rather than pursue a protracted legal battle was pivotal in determining how subsequent events would unfold within the basin.

As an extension of these negotiations, representatives of the three districts and the Walla Walla Basin Watershed Council began discussions with local government officials in Oregon and Washington regarding the desirability of developing an HCP for the basin as a whole in an effort to achieve ESA liability relief. It was through these particular lengthy discussions that the Walla Walla Board of County Commissioners opted to begin reviewing the requirements and taking the steps necessary to begin the HCP process. It is noteworthy to consider the circumstances under which this decision was made, and take note of the long-term implications it posed for the community. At the time the decision was made to initiate an HCP process, local government leaders and stakeholder groups, especially those associated with agricultural and water interests, were well aware that similar issues were being addressed in the Methow Valley. Both public and private interest groups in watershed basins throughout the state were becoming alarmed because of reports detailing highly contentious decisions linked to ESA enforcement and Salmon recovery. Nonetheless, the Walla Walla County Board of Commissioners chose to pursue a proactive, collaborative approach. The Commissioners succeeded in getting two adjoining counties to take part in HCP discussions. This initiative served to influence events within the Walla Walla Basin in ways that were positive and non-polarizing.

19.4.4 *The Environmental Advocacy Component*

As in the Methow Valley, issues involving significant threats to threatened or endangered species are often subjected to close scrutiny by potential third party litigants. In early 2000, as developments were unfolding as part of settlement negotiations and HCP discussions, a consortium of seven environmental groups met with representatives of the three irrigation districts to discuss flow regime issues in the Walla Walla River Basin.

Officials from three of these environmental groups (Oregon Water Watch, The Center for Environmental Law and Policy (CELP) and Trout Unlimited), along with representatives of the Confederated Tribes of the Umatilla Indian Reservation and the three irrigation districts, met to discuss mutual concerns. At the time it was widely believed that the objective of the environmental groups was to initiate a "60-day Notice of Intent to Sue" under ESA third party provisions. However, based on the outcome of the meeting and encouraging indications that considerable potential existed for progress to be achieved through settlement negotiations between USFWS and the three irrigation districts, the environmental groups chose not to litigate, dependent upon a favorable outcome of the negotiations. This decision, in conjunction with the efforts of the Irrigation Districts and County Commissioners, proved pivotal in maintaining an atmosphere of collaboration [29].

19.4.5   Compliance in the Walla Walla Basin-Cooperation Rather than Confrontation

In January 1999, the WDFW Enforcement Program began evaluating the issue of compliance with state fish screening laws within the Washington portion of the basin. Preliminary information indicated that little to no enforcement activity involving fish screens had occurred over the course of several decades. Records regarding the number and type of surface water diversions, and ownership and compliance rates were virtually non-existent. Although existing diversions were required to operate with permits issued by WDFW and within established water rights regulated by the WDOE, neither agency had a monitoring record. Walla Walla WDFW enforcement staff conferred with their counterparts in the Methow Valley to learn how such issues had been addressed there.

It was during this consultation process that Walla Walla WDFW enforcement staff learned of the four-step Voluntary Compliance Plan. It became apparent that implementation of the voluntary compliance plan in the Methow Valley had met with limited success, at best. Although a plan existed to achieve voluntary compliance, it lacked provisions to help citizens come into compliance [30]. As a result, state and federal officials faced the need to rely heavily on traditional enforcement measures. To avoid this, the WDFW Enforcement Program began to develop a Voluntary Compliance Plan similar to the Methow Valley experience. This program was predicated on the belief that the goal of assisting landowners in achieving compliance could best be accomplished through a process structured to be *cooperative* (i.e., featuring partnerships and collaborative problem solving) rather than *voluntary*.

19.4.6   The Cooperative Compliance Initiative

In the spring of 2000, WDFW Enforcement staff in the Walla Walla Basin began adapting the four-step Methow Valley voluntary compliance plan to the Walla Walla setting. They designed an agency initiative characterized as the *Cooperative Compliance Review Program*. Early on, the Walla Walla WDFW Enforcement staff conferred with the County Prosecuting Attorney to discuss the merits of pursuing compliance with state screening laws by utilizing approaches other than prosecution. The WDFW reasoned that citizen compliance could best be achieved through cooperative, incentive-based measures taken as an *initial approach*, with a clearly articulated assurance that compliance would be commanded through prosecution and court action if and when such confrontational steps became necessary.

Key incentive elements to the new program that offered participants: (1) reduced risk from prosecution under state law; (2) technical assistance in designing and acquiring new screens; (3) financial cost-sharing assistance (to the degree it could be obtained) (4) clarification of landowner water rights; and (5) assistance in obtaining all necessary permits to operate their surface water diversions in compliance with state and federal laws. This new approach stressed cooperative participation by landowners, as a matter of choice, with a stated commitment to follow through with the steps necessary to achieve full compliance. The WDFW communicated publicly that while *participation in the Cooperative Compliance Program was optional, ultimate compliance with state screening and passage laws in the Walla Walla River Basin was mandatory.* During the spring and early summer of 2000, Enforcement staff in the Walla Walla initiated a variety of contacts, forums, and workshops involving local farmers, private landowners, legislative leaders, agricultural organizations and multiple state and federal regulatory resource. The purpose was to identify and develop key elements of the program.

The major newspaper in the area, the *Union-Bulletin*, provided front-page coverage of ESA issues and the WDFW's Cooperative Compliance Program in its August 13, 2000 edition. An Editorial column, which followed roughly a week later, counseled local landowners to be proactive in dealing with ESA issues emerging in the community; the newspaper specifically encouraged them to take advantage of the opportunity to participate in the Cooperative Compliance Program being offered by WDFW. Over the next six months more than 300 individuals in the Washington portion of the basin applied to participate in the program, bringing more than 450 existing surface water diversions into compliance with state fish screening and fish passage laws.

Based on such a favorable response, the WDFW was able to establish partnerships with a variety of agencies and organizations involved in Salmon recovery-related efforts. Highly effective working relationships were established with key local entities such as the Walla Walla County Conservation District and the Walla Walla Community College's Irrigation Technology Program. Within the space of a year, the Cooperative Compliance Program in the Walla Walla watershed obtained funding in excess of $4,000,000 from several sources to assist with implementation and monitoring.

19.4.7   Interim Outcomes in the Walla Walla

In the month of June of 2000, negotiations between the three irrigation districts in Oregon and Washington and the USFWS resulted in a Civil Penalty Settlement Agreement that insured a minimum instream water flow of 13 cfs^{-1} (1 cfs equals roughly 450 gallons) in the Walla Walla River immediately below the Nursery Bridge diversion, with provisions for 10 cfs to be maintained through the Burlingame Diversion operated by the Gardena Farms Irrigation District #13. As a result of this agreement, in the summer of 2000 not only did the Tumalum portion of the Walla Walla River remain watered throughout the irrigation season for the first time in modern memory, it did so during the worst drought conditions experienced within the Walla Walla basin in nearly three decades. In June of 2001, a final settlement agreement between these same parties resulted in minimum instream flows of 18 cfs below the Nursery Bridge in 2001, and a guarantee of 25 cfs during 2002 and every year thereafter. Minimum flows at the Burlingame Diversion were set at 14 cfs in 2001 and at 18 cfs in 2002 and beyond.

In the Washington portion of the basin, efforts are underway to complete the upgrade of hundreds of surface water diversions identified through the Cooperative Compliance Program. As of October 2003, program staff and partnering agencies have successfully installed new fish screens on over 200 previously non-compliant sites. WDFW Enforcement staff in the Walla Walla Basin are engaged in an on-going process to identify all remaining diversions in pursuit of their stated goal of achieving 100% compliance with state fish screening and passage laws within the basin.

The Walla Walla Board of County Commissioners has continued its efforts to prepare a basin-wide HCP by engaging the private firm Economic and Engineering Services (EES) to facilitate the planning process. Planning efforts continue to move forward with regards to both federal HCP and legislatively prescribed Watershed Basin Planning programs related to salmon recovery.

19.5   Methods

19.5.1   Defining Success

The OLE and WDFW Enforcement Program could point to the fish protection measures and to compliance statistics emerging from the Methow Valley and from the Walla Walla Basin to affirm a high degree of success in achieving their goals. However, to do so would be quite misleading. Simply reporting outcomes does not reveal whether an agency was effective in solving the underlying problem, nor whether the stated goals of collaboration (e.g., building support among the public for natural resource protective activities, building good will for future issues to be addressed, etc.) were achieved.

19.5.2   The Need to Measure Outcomes

In collaboration with the OLE, and with the Enforcement Program of the WDFW, we developed an outcome measurement approach to assess whether the performance goals of the COPPS efforts were achieved. Adapted from the work of Anderson, Bjork, and Powell [31], the performance measurement tool involved the use of citizen surveys and structured personal interviews to measure the long- and short-term impacts of COPPS. The process we developed was used to accomplish the following goals: (1) to document public perceptions of collaborative problem solving; identify lessons from interagency partnerships and collaborative outreach efforts; and (2) to spell out how the results of this research could be used to enhance natural resource protection efforts in future ESA enforcement.

Our findings were derived from a three-part process consisting of mail-out surveys of citizens, mail-out surveys of agency personnel, and personal interviews of key participants in the ROE processes. The purpose of the two citizen surveys was to measure the degree to which the collaborative processes affected the general population, assess citizen perceptions of the processes and the agencies, and collect data on contextual variables including demographics and general attitudes which might account for any differences between the cases. The agency staff involved in the two basins from NOAA Fisheries and the WDFW received similar survey instruments. In addition to these surveys, the "triangulation" process included a substantial number of personal interviews conducted with key actors (federal, state, local agency personnel, and local stakeholders) to determine if the survey results could be verified by direct observation, and to obtain more detailed and richly nuanced information.

The parallel surveys of citizens in the two areas were conducted by the application of a modified "Dillman total design" [32] methodology that entails making multiple wave mailings to households selected at random. Samples of approximately 1800 household addresses in each area were purchased from Survey Sampling, Inc., and non-respondents were contacted by two follow-up mailings. The Methow Valley citizen survey produced a total of 801 completed questionnaires, with a response rate of 48%. The Walla Walla Basin survey produced a total of 946 completed questionnaires, and a response rate of 60%. The content of the two citizen surveys was designed to be very similar so as to permit direct comparisons. The content of the survey instruments featured "measures of trust" in government agencies and groups, assessments of respondents' perceptions of the extent of "good faith" efforts, indicators of support for the ESA, degree of support for the collaborative process, personal background traits, environmental attitudes, and ideological predispositions. Respondents were also asked numerous open-ended questions, and were provided the opportunity to comment at length. Many citizens wrote lengthy and detailed comments on the ESA-related activities they had witnessed.

The strong response rates attained, along with respondent and area demographics, provide considerable confidence that the survey returns gathered were fairly representative of the two areas. There is, however, a skew toward educated older males. Both sets of respondents were over 70% male (the survey was mailed to heads of households), with average ages of 58 (Methow) and 59 (Walla Walla). More than 40% of the respondents in each area reported holding a bachelors degree or higher. The household income and race/ethnicity distributions of survey respondents closely conformed to the demographics documented in the 2000 Census for the two areas.

The survey administered to NOAA Fisheries and WDFW agency personnel yielded 19 responses (representing almost all personnel who received a survey) from the Methow Valley case. In the Walla Walla Basin case, ten agency personnel responded (representing nearly all the involved personnel). Finally, a total of twenty-five key actors were interviewed either face-to-face or over the telephone in each of the two watersheds. Virtually all major figures representing significant interests affected by the ESA enforcement actions were interviewed in the two settings under study.

Transcription and careful analysis of those interviews provided very useful context and insight for in-depth analysis of the citizen survey data and citizen comments collected in the mail survey. The personal interviews conducted with major actors were analyzed for key themes and issues, and standard methods of content analysis were employed to identify key themes in both watersheds. The key themes were used as reference points to assist us in interpreting the results of the mail-out surveys and in understanding more fully the nature of the comments and observations recorded in citizen comments.

19.6   Findings

19.6.1   Demographic Factors

The following five tables document the demographic similarities among respondents to the citizen surveys in the two cases (Table 19.1 through Table 19.5).

Table 19.1   Gender

	Methow Valley (%)	Walla Walla Basin (%)
Female	25	22
Male	75	78

Table 19.2   Age Groups

Year of Birth	Methow Valley (%)	Walla Walla Basin (%)
Pre 1940	38	44
1940–1949	28	20
1950	34	35

Table 19.3   Education Levels

Educational Level	Methow Valley (%)	Walla Walla Basin (%)
Some grade school	1	1
Completed grade school	2	1
Some high school	3	3
Completed high school	17	14
Some college/trade school	36	39
Completed 4-year degree	15	17
Some graduate work	8	8
Hold an advanced degree	18	18

Table 19.4   Family Income Levels

	Methow Valley (%)	Walla Walla Basin (%)
Less than $4000	2	2
4000–6999	4	2
7000–9999	2	2
10,000–14,999	6	4
15,000–19,999	4	4
20,000–24,999	8	5
25,000–29,999	10	11
30,000–49,999	28	27
50,000–69,999	18	23
70,000+	19	21

Approximate Family Income (before taxes in 1999).

19.6.2   Environmental and Political Values

Respondents' environmental attitudes were documented using responses to four statements taken from the *Dunlap New Environmental Paradigm Scale* [33]. This multi-item attitude scale, which has been used in numerous studies over the years, asks survey respondents to agree or to disagree with the following four controversial value statements concerning the environment:

- Plants and animals are primarily for human use.
- Mankind was created to rule over nature.
- Humans have an ethical obligation to protect plants and animals.
- The Earth should have far fewer people on it.

On the first two scale items, a positive response indicates support for a human-centered perspective on environmental values. What is remarkable in the tables setting forth citizen survey findings is how little difference there is in the patterns of responses from the two watersheds under study. Almost 39% of the Methow Valley respondents and 38% of the Walla Walla Basin respondents

Table 19.5   Occupation

	Methow Valley (%)	Walla Walla River Basin (%)
Farmer/rancher	16	12
Professional	13	9
Business owner	25	21
Blue collar worker	20	17
Office worker	9	9
Office manager	9	9
Homemaker	5	5
Student	1	2
Unemployed	2	2

either agree or strongly agree that "plants and animals are primarily for human use," while about 45% of those surveyed in the Methow Valley and almost 43% of those responding to the survey in the Walla Walla Basin either agree or strongly agree that "mankind was created to rule over nature." The last two statements, in contrast to the first two, indicate the degree of support for a decidedly environmentally sensitive viewpoint on environmental protection. Again, as on the first two items, on these two "pro environment" value statements there is strong agreement between the two communities, especially on the statement "the earth should have far fewer people on it." 43% of respondents in the Methow Valley and 40% of the respondents in the Walla Walla Basin either agree or strongly agree with this particular statement. With respect to the ethical obligation of humans to protect plants and animals, Walla Walla Basin respondents display extremely strong support for this proposition (74% either agreeing or strongly agreeing), and Methow Valley residents also register strong (62%) agreement (either agree or strongly agree).

Value Statement 1: Plants and Animals are Primarily for Human Use

	Methow Valley (%)	Walla Walla Basin (%)
Strongly agree	20	18
Agree	19	20
Neutral	19	24
Disagree	19	17
Strongly disagree	23	18

Value Statement 2: Mankind was Created to Rule Over Nature

	Methow Valley (%)	Walla Walla Basin (%)
Strongly agree	28	26
Agree	17	17
Neutral	16	19
Disagree	16	13
Strongly disagree	23	25

Value Statement 3: Humans have an Ethical Obligation to Protect Plans and Animals

	Methow Valley (%)	WallaWalla Basin (%)
Strongly disagree	7	4
Disagree	10	7
Neutral	21	15
Agree	32	33
Strongly agree	30	42

Value Statement 4: The Earth Should have Far Fewer People on it

	Methow Valley (%)	Walla Walla Basin (%)
Strongly disagree	16	16
Disagree	12	11
Neutral	29	33
Agree	16	16
Strongly agree	27	24

With respect to partisan affiliation and fiscal and social policy preferences, the same picture of high similarity of the two study sites emerges. The two areas are strongly Republican (see Table 19.6), and are represented in the state legislature nearly exclusively by Republican legislators. In addition, both areas are quite conservative, both in terms of fiscal policy and in terms of social policy (see Table 19.7).

These demographic, environmental and policy preference comparisons clearly indicate that the Methow Valley and Walla Walla Basin respondents hold very similar attitudes. This observation holds true across all indicators, with the *exception* of one very important aspect: social capital. Two measures related to social capital stand out as dramatically different in these two areas. These indicators are derived from answers given to the question "How would you describe your general outlook on life with regards to people being trustworthy and honest?" The answers from the two scales contained in this compound question reveal a stark contrast between respondents in the two areas (Table 19.8).

These citizen survey responses have the effect of complicating the analysis of the impact of agency approaches somewhat, making the effort to distinguish between the impact of social capital and the impact of agency activities at once more problematic, but also more important. The salience of social capital for collaborative processes is likely considerable, but the degree to which that

Table 19.6 Political Party Preferences

	Methow Valley (%)	Walla Walla Basin (%)
1—Strong republican	7	7
2	16	18
3	16	16
4—Moderate/independent	40	38
5	9	9
6	9	8
7—Strong democrat	4	4

1, Strong Republican; 4, Moderate/Independent; 7, Strong Democrat.

Table 19.7 Fiscal and Social Policy Preferences

	Methow Valley (%)	Walla Walla Basin (%)
Fiscal Policy (e.g., taxes and government spending)		
1—Very conservative	11	16
2	19	17
3	20	15
4—Moderate	34	27
5	11	13
6	4	9
7—Very liberal	1	4
Social Policy (e.g., women's rights, assisted suicide)		
1—Very conservative	17	16
2	15	17
3	11	15
4—Moderate	22	27
5	13	13
6	15	9
7—Very liberal	8	4

salience is determinative of favorable outcomes is a matter for further study in the context of multiple cases and multiple jurisdictions. Additional key elements evaluated through the survey included:

- Levels of Trust of Key Actors
- Support for ESA
- Perceptions of Good Faith Bargaining

Table 19.8 General Outlook on Life (Test of Social Capital)

	Methow Valley (%)	Walla Walla Basin (%)
Trust		
Most people are honest		
1. Agree	25	57
2. Uncertain	17	20
3. Disagree	58	23
Honesty		
Most people are honest		
1. Agree	16	59
2. Uncertain	22	25
3. Disagree	63	16

Table 19.9 Methow Valley: Trust in Major Actors

	% High	% Uncertain	% Low
Local irrigators	62	23	15
County commissioners	53	25	22
Local Washington state department of fish and wildlife (WDFW) officers	43	33	24
Methow planning unit	34	43	23
USFS	27	34	39
WDFW	22	29	49
USFWS	15	29	56
Environmental groups	12	16	72
WA. department of ecology	11	25	64
National marine fisheries service (NMFS)	10	18	72

Trust in major actors listed in descending order.

19.6.3   Level of Trust in Key Actors

The first question in this battery, which reveals key differences in outcome between the Methow Valley and Walla Walla Basin, asks: "How much trust do you have in the information provided by the major actors involved in the process of developing an agreement for salmon recovery under the ESA?" (see Table 19.9).

In the Methow Valley case there exists a distinct insider/outsider perspective, with resource agencies seen as "interfering" outsiders. The regulatory approach adopted here seems to have significantly exacerbated this dynamic and the underlying issues present became highly polarized. Unlike the Walla Walla Basin, in the Methow Valley there is virtually no uncertainty on these issues;

Table 19.10 Walla Walla: Trust in Major Actors

	High (%)	Uncertain (%)	Low (%)
Washington state department of fish and wildlife (WDFW)	44	33	23
Local WDFW officers	44	37	19
USFWS	38	35	27
Bonneville power administration (BPA)	35	43	22
Local irrigators	34	40	26
National marine fisheries service (NMFS)	29	41	30
County commissioners	28	42	30
WA. department of ecology	27	37	36
Watershed council	25	56	19
Environmental groups	14	30	56

Trust in major actors listed in descending order.

people have taken sides in the dispute. However, local WDFW officers living within the community are considered to be "insiders." One key to understanding the Methow Valley case is that locally-based state Fish and Wildlife officers can become highly effective conduits for the development and implementation of community-oriented problem solving strategies.

In clear contrast with the observations from the Methow Valley, a state resource agency WDFW and its field officers located in the area held the highest level of trust among the major actors involved in multi-agency negotiations in the Walla Walla case, followed by a federal regulatory agency, the USFWS. (See Table 19.10).

Rather than polarizing the population, the issues and method by which they were addressed seem to have left a large percentage of the population without clearly formed opinions. Those who have formed such opinions view the regulatory agencies and their agents in a much more favorable light than was evident in the Methow Valley case.

19.6.4 Support for the ESA

Survey respondents were asked to articulate in what way their observations of the collaborative approach to ESA compliance relative to Salmon recovery efforts affected their perception of the ESA as a resource protection tool. The responses suggest that citizens in the Methow Valley were far less supportive of the ESA as an effective means to protect natural resources in a rural community setting than were their counterparts in the Walla Walla River Basin (Table 19.11).

Although compliance with federal and state environmental regulations and ESA-listed fish protection measures was achieved in both the Methow Valley and Walla Walla River Basin cases alike, this accomplishment resulted in a substantial long-term loss of public support in the Methow Valley, but *not* in the Walla Walla area. Responses to questions on "good faith bargaining" and the achievement of "acceptable outcomes" demonstrate this point rather dramatically (see Table 19.12).

Table 19.11 Support for the Endangered Species Act (ESA)

Question: "How has the Experience of the (Methow Valley) (Walla Walla River Basin) Fish Habitat Protection Effort Affected Your Views of the Endangered Species Act?"

	Methow Valley (%)	WallaWalla (%)
I am *more supportive* for ESA	3	10
Level of *support did not change*	24	56
I am *less supportive* of ESA	73	34

Impacts on support for the ESA ascribed to the multi-agency negotiations taking place in the Methow Valley and the Walla Walla River Basin.

Table 19.12 Public Perceptions of Good Faith Bargaining in the Methow Valley Trust in Major Actors

	High (%)	Uncertain (%)	Low (%)
County commissioners	55	29	16
Local Washington state department of fish and wildlife (WDFW) officers	31	46	23
WDFW	16	42	42
USFWS	12	35	53
WA. department of ecology	9	33	58
National marine fisheries service (NMFS)	6	23	71

Public Perceptions of good faith bargaining in the Methow Valley Case. Major actors listed in order of descending trust.

19.6.5 Citizen Perceptions of Good Faith Bargaining

Each survey participant was asked to provide answers to the question: "What is your impression of the 'Good Faith Bargaining' exhibited by the major actors involved in the salmon recovery process?" The responses to this question illustrate the major differences in public perceptions between the Methow Valley watershed and Walla Walla River Basin.

Important to note in connection from the Methow Valley case, especially as compared to the Walla Walla case, are three significant observations: First, relatively few survey respondents were "undecided" on the issue of good faith bargaining. Second, there is a clear preference for local actors in the Methow Valley, with local commissioners and local WDFW officers receiving the most favorable rankings. Third, for everyone *except* the County Commissioners there are disturbingly low perceptions of good faith bargaining.

The findings reported in Table 19.13 illustrate the remarkable differences between the two cases. In the Walla Walla Basin, a majority of respondents are undecided on the question of good faith bargaining. Clearly, this was not a

Table 19.13 Public Perceptions of Good Faith Bargaining in the Walla Walla River Basin Trust in Major Actors

	High (%)	Uncertain (%)	Low (%)
Local Washington state department of fish and wildlife (WDFW) officers	34	55	11
WDFW	33	49	18
USFWS	29	51	20
County commissioners	27	59	14
National marine fisheries service (NMFS)	21	56	23
WA. department of Ecology	19	53	28

Public Perceptions of good faith bargaining in the Methow Valley Case. Major actors listed in order of descending trust.

polarizing issue in that area. This perception is confirmed by the different rank-ordering observed. While local WDFW officers ranked highest, two *agencies* received the next most favorable rankings. Finally, there is a clear increase in perceptions of good faith (and concomitant reduction in perceptions of bad faith) evident toward all of the participants, as compared to the Methow Valley (excluding the Methow Valley commissioners) on this question. Very clearly, the perceptions generated are much more favorable toward the process and agency participants in the Walla Walla River Basin than was the case in the Methow Valley.

Following the administration of the citizen surveys, face-to-face and telephone interviews were conducted with key actors from both watersheds. The results supported the finding from the citizen surveys. Although federal and state agencies and agency personnel, with the exception of locally-based WDFW Officers, were not trusted actors in the Methow Valley; they were accorded substantial trust in the Walla Walla Basin.

19.7 Discussion

Locally resident representatives of public agencies fared much better on "perceived trustworthiness" in both jurisdictions—confirming the importance of long-term personal relationships to the collaborative process. A critical component in the success of collaborative processes is the interpersonal element, those contacts necessary to initiate, conduct, and sustain collaborative decision-making. In the Methow Valley and Walla Walla Basin cases, the vital importance of the "agency agents" was evident from the citizen surveys and personal interviews. Consistency, reliability, and predictability on the part of agency representatives had a significant effect on the success of the negotiations. Both the surveys and the interviews demonstrated that while neither *agency* conduct nor *agent* behavior is *sufficient* to achieve trust and cooperation; they are both *necessary* elements of the process. Only when the both are consistent, reliable, and supportive of the collaborative model will the process have the potential to lead to successful outcomes.

Beyond this general observation, a number of factors combined to make it likely that a collaborative approach would be more successful in the Walla Walla Basin than in the Methow Valley. The existence of a federal nexus in the Methow Valley militated against achieving a successful federally-led enforcement effort. The lack of such a federal nexus in the Walla Walla Basin facilitated emergence of a state-led joint effort. The existence of an "endangered" listing in the Methow Valley somewhat restricted agency options in terms of response—a situation that did not exist to the same degree in the Walla Walla Basin where the listing was for "threatened" species only. Walla Walla Basin had a local history of community engagement in civic projects; no similar history was noted by the interviewees in the Methow Valley.

The history of relations between agency personnel and local actors was also much different in the two cases. More onerous regulatory and enforcement activity had taken place and/or been threatened in the Methow Valley before the collaborative approach was engaged, and threats of "more of the same" had been raised during the collaborative process. Although an enforcement action had occurred recently in the Walla Walla Basin, the negotiated outcome of that action was deemed fair, effectively reducing any perception of overt threat.

The most critical of the differences between the two watersheds, however, were those that describe the relationships (actual, potential or perceived) between individuals and agencies. *Trust* is probably the most appropriate one-word descriptive of the dynamic of these relationships, and most likely to account for the differences. In the Walla Walla Basin the actors trusted each other for the most part. Survey and interview results suggest that local residents tended to trust the federal and state agencies and their respective agents. Factors such as history, personality, and consistency of approach all negatively affected these levels of trust in the Methow Valley.

Simply put, for a relationship of trust to exist each party must be both trusting and trustworthy. Thus, the potential relationship is one of innate expectations and perception or observed conduct. Our experience suggests that social capital may offer significant explanation for the capacity or willingness of citizens in a local community to trust others from outside. The qualities of consistency, predictability, and reliability likewise have a critical influence on community perceptions of an agency's trustworthiness. In the Methow Valley case, according to the interviews with key actors and confirmed by citizen survey results, the capacity to trust outside actors was quite low. This lack of capacity was confirmed or exacerbated by agency failure to act with consistency and predictability, thus reducing reliability and hence trustworthiness. In the Walla Walla River Basin case, in stark contrast, social capital and the willingness and capacity to trust were quite high, as evidenced by both survey findings and the personal interviews conducted. This potential was expanded and reinforced by a consistent, predictable and reliable multi-agency approach adhered to over time, thus ensuring that the collaborative approach was deemed more attractive than non-collaboration. It would seem that *the concerted effort on the part of agencies to provide their locally-based and locally assigned agents working on collaborative processes with the skills, tools, and exposure to positive examples is necessary for the successful accomplishment of such activities.*

19.8 Conclusion

In the short term, the Methow Valley and Walla Walla Basin experiences proved highly successful in achieving legal compliance and protection for the targeted species. Both reflected attempts to use a collaborative approach. In the Methow Valley case very little support was generated for the ESA. Issues became highly polarized politically with low social capital (trust) representing a negative factor. High compliance rates were achieved, but at a high social cost. In contrast, the collaborative approach was more successful in the Walla Walla Basin. Significant public support was generated for the ESA. Issues never became polarized locally, and a high social capital (trust) setting was used as a positive factor in promoting collaboration. Compliance was achieved on a major scale, and the prospect of future cooperative compliance is quite strong for further work needed on water scarcity.

This study offers some support for the intertwined propositions that collaborative problem solving is the best long-term approach, but that in the absence of collaboration, interest-based negotiations can yield positive results even if conducted between intense adversaries. Resolving the conflicts is more likely when the process and the conduct of the participants provide a degree of certainty that the outcome of negotiations can be preferable to a formal regulatory outcome.

This study illustrates the critical need to develop alternative enforcement approaches, thereby enhancing the range of natural resource enforcement tools employed to promote compliance with resource protective laws and agency regulations. Traditional natural resource agency enforcement has typically reflected a reactive model of enforcement that relies on catching people in the act or after the fact. This approach requires a known and unsympathetic offender—such as a poacher or a thief. But in the world of scarce and endangered natural resources the threat is often not from such an offender, but rather an entire community attempting to co-exist with the endangered species. In this situation, the challenge becomes one of practicing purposeful cooperation rather than threatening confrontation.

To address this new paradigm in natural resource protection, natural resource policy and enforcement organizations need to adopt new strategies and embrace nontraditional methods to achieve compliance and resource protection. They must begin a process of transitioning from *reactive* to *proactive* enforcement when applicable—while maintaining the capacity to conduct traditional enforcement when required. Agency leaders must ensure that their personnel are prepared, empowered, and adequately trained in proactive enforcement.

The results of our study demonstrate that the ROE and its evolving hybrid *Community Oriented Resource Enforcement* can play a significant and vital role in achieving future long-term compliance and resource protection in the Pacific Northwest. The experiment in collaborative, multi-party environmental negotiations in the Methow Valley and in the Walla Walla Basin carried out by OLE and the WDFW is highly instructive. These agencies succeeded in protecting natural resources in both cases, but in one case the potential for cooperative compliance was realized while in the other a legacy of distrust and alienation was the long-term byproduct of successful enforcement activity. In the more successful case, the seeds for further progress toward resource protection have been sown; in the less successful case, a future of heightened conflict and citizen animosity is a virtual certainty.

References

1. Claybrook, J., *Retreat from Safety*, Pantheon Books, New York, 1984.
2. Council on Environmental Quality, *23rd Annual Report of the Council on Environmental Quality Together with the President's Message to Congress*, U.S. Government Printing Office, Washington, DC, 1993.

3. Freeman, A. and Haveman, R., Clean rhetoric and dirty water, *Public Interest*, 28, 51, 1972.

4. Hawkins, K., *Environment and Enforcement: Regulation and the Social Definition of Pollution*, Clarendon Press, Oxford, 1984.

5. Viscusi, W. and Zeckhauser, R., Optimal standards with incomplete enforcement, *Public Policy*, 27, 437, 1979.

6. Shover, N., Clelland, D., and Lynxwiler, J., *Enforcement or Negotiation: Constructing a Regulatory Bureaucracy*, SUNY Press, Albany, 1986.

7. Ayres, I. and Braithwait, J., *Responsive Regulation: Transcending the De-regulation Debate*, Oxford University Press, New York, 1992.

8. Hawkins, K. and Thomas, J., The enforcement process in regulatory bureaucracies, in *Enforcing Regulation*, K. Hawkins and J.M. Thomas, Eds., Kluwer Nijhoff Publishing, Boston, MA, 1984, 3–22.

9. Scholz, J., Cooperative regulatory enforcement and the politics of administrative effectiveness, *American Political Science Review*, 85, 115, 1991.

10. Scholz, J., Cooperation, deterrence, and the ecology of regulatory enforcement, *Law and Society Review*, 18, 601, 1984.

11. Vogel, D., *National Styles of Regulation: Environmental Policy in Great Britain and the United States*, Cornell University Press, Ithaca/London, 1986.

12. Matthews, D., *Is There a Public for Public Schools?* The Kettering Foundation, Cleveland, 1996.

13. Sparrow, M., *Imposing Duties: Government's Changing Approach to Compliance*, Praeger, Westport, 1994.

14. Radin, Beryl A., Agranoff, Robert, Bowman, Ann O'M., Gregory Buntz, C., Steven Ott, J., Romzek, Barbara, S., Wilson, and Robert, H., *New Governance for Rural America: Creating Inter-Governmental Partnerships*, The University Press of Kansas, Lawrence, 1996.

15. Radin, B. and Romzek, B., Accountability expectations in an inter-governmental arena, *Publius*, 26, 59, 1996.

16. Bardach, E. and Lesser, C., Accountability in human services collaboratives—for what? and to whom? *Journal of Public Administration Research and Theory*, 6, 197, 1996.

17. Walters, J., *Measuring Up: Governing's Guide for Performance Measurement*, Governing Books, Washington, DC, 1997.

18. NOAA: National Marine Fisheries Service, Office for Law Enforcement and Washington Department of Fish and Wildlife, *Statement of Work for Evaluation of NOAA Fisheries Office for Law Enforcement (OLE) and Washington Department of Fish and Wildlife (WDFW) Interagency ESA/ ROE Program*, Olympia, 2000.

19. Mann, C. and Plummer, M., *Noah's Choice: The Future of Endangered Species*, Alfred Knopf, New York, 1995.

20. Campbell, J., *Evaluation of the Program for Enhanced Harvest and Habitat Law Enforcement and Public Awareness for Anadromous Salmonids and Resident Fish in the Columbia River Basin: Balancing Problem Solving Strategies with Traditional Law Enforcement Approaches*, Campbell-DeLong Resources Inc., Portland, 1997.

21. Bean, M., *Reconciling Conflicts Under the Endangered Species Act: The Habitat Conservation Planning Experience*, World Wildlife Fund, New York, 1991.

22. NOAA: National Marine Fisheries Service, Office for Law Enforcement, Northwest and Southwest Enforcement Divisions, *Plan for Protection of West Coast ESA-Listed Anadromous Fish and Their Habitats*, [Contact Person: Dayna Matthews, Olympia, Washington], 1998.

23. Bayley, D., *Police for the Future*, Oxford University Press, New York, 1994.

24. Washington State, Department of Fish and Wildlife Enforcement Program, *Strategic Plan: Fiscal Years 1999–2004*, WDFW, Olympia, 1998.

25. Tu, J., Farmers rail against plan for ditches, *Wall Street Journal*, May 5, NW1, 1999.

26. Tu, J., Local farmers want to ditch fed's fishy proposal on irrigation, *Wall Street Journal*, December 8, NW4, 1999.

27. Hansen, D., Okanogan county irrigation threatened ruling: Agencies can limit ditches to protect species, *The Spokesman-Review*, March 20, B1–B8, 2002.

28. Kuttle, M., *Salmonid Habitat Limiting Factors, Water Resource Inventory Area 32, Walla Walla Watershed*, Washington State Conservation Commission, Olympia, 2001.

29. Weber, E., Lovrich, N., and Gaffney, M., A New Way of Doing Business: Natural Resource Agencies, Endangered Species, and Collaborative Enforcement, presented at the 60th Annual Meeting of the Midwest Political Science Association, Chicago, 2002.

30. *High Country News*, Western roundup: Farmers asked to ante up for salmon, 26, 4, 2001.

31. Anderson, J., Bjork, B., and Powell, A., *Performance Measures for Community Policing*, The Evergreen State College, Olympia, 1995.

32. Dillman, D., *Mail and Telephone Surveys: The Total Design Method*, Wiley-Interscience Publishing, New York, 1978.

33. Dunlap, R. and Van Liere, K., The new environmental paradigm, *Journal of Environmental Education*, 9–10, 1978.

34. Born, S. and Genskow, K., *Exploring the Watershed Approach: Critical Dimensions of State-Local Partnerships*, River Network, Portland, 1999.

35. Brick, P., Snow, D., and van de Wetering, S., Eds., in *Across the Great Divide: Explorations in Collaborative Conservation and the American West*, Island Press, Washington, DC, 2001, 163–171.

36. John, D., *Civic Environmentalism: Alternatives to Regulation in States and Communities*, Congressional Quarterly Press, Washington, DC, 1994.

37. Kemmis, D., *This Sovereign Land: A New Vision for Governing the West*, Island Press, Washington, DC, 2001.

38. Lubell, M., Schneider, M., Scholz, J., and Mete, M., Watershed partnerships and the emergence of collective action institutions, *American Journal of Political Science*, 46, 148, 2002.

39. Weber, E., *Pluralism by the Rules: Conflict and Cooperation in Environmental Regulation*, Georgetown University Press, Washington, DC, 1998.

40. Weber, E., A new vanguard for the environment: Grass-roots ecosystem management as a new environmental movement, *Society and Natural Resources*, 13, 237, 2000.

41. Wondollek, J. and Yaffee, S., *Making Collaboration Work: Lessons from Innovation in Natural Resource Management*, Island Press, Washington, DC, 2000.

42. Hunter, S. and Waterman, R., *Enforcing the Law: The Case of the Clean Water Acts*, M.E. Sharpe, Armonk, 1996.

43. Bayley, D., *What Works in Policing*, Oxford University Press, New York, 1998.

44. Alpert, G. and Piquero, A., Eds., in *Community Policing: Contemporary Readings*, Waveland Press, Prospect Heights, 1997, 45–62.

45. Goldstein, H., *Policing a Free Society*, Ballinger, Cambridge, MA, 1977.

CONTROVERSIES IN GLOBALIZATION AND THE ENVIRONMENT

IV

Chapter 20

Eco-Terrorism: a Natural Reaction of Violence?

Michael J. Mortimer
Virginia Polytechnic Institute and State University

20.1   Introduction to a Cause

The behavior of militant, radical environmentalists has recently drawn unprecedented attention, both from the media and from law enforcement authorities. The flamboyancy, economic impact and countercultural bravado of their actions have provided material for books, regular media coverage, and even congressional hearings in the United States. While the movement is certainly not new, arguably arising during the late 1970s and early 1980s, the heightened international emphasis and awareness of terrorist activities since the international terror attacks in the United States in 2001 has cast the efforts of these individuals and groups in a new light. The advance of globalization, regardless of the particular international setting, may also be providing new rallying points or *causa belli* for the expansion of aggressive direct action environmentalism.

This collection of activists is defined largely by the causes they champion, particularly animal rights and environmental preservation [1]. Tactics used to oppose what they perceive as undesirable progress or developments commonly include arson, sabotage, animal liberations, and miscellaneous vandalism [2]. Targets are often public and private research facilities, housing developments under construction, fur shops, meat processing facilities, recreational facilities located in objectionable places, and more recently, automobile dealerships [3–5]. While property is currently the preferred target in the U.S., tactics in Europe reflect more of a willingness to target individuals [6]. The U.S. Federal Bureau of

Investigation reports over 600 incidents of domestic eco-terror in the six-year period from 1996 to 2002, with damages exceeding $60 million dollars [7],* while other estimates suggest well over 500 incidents of illegal animal rights actions alone worldwide, with attacks occurring in 17 different countries between 1981 and 2004 [8]. According to the Animal Liberation Front (ALF), more than 137 illegal actions occurred in North America in 2001 alone, resulting in $17.3 million in damages [9].

Few scholarly writings exist on the subject, and even fewer studies of the participants in violent direct action environmentalism have been conducted. The ephemeral nature of the organizations and individuals involved makes such research naturally difficult to accomplish. Nonetheless, it is important to recognize that the recent law enforcement and legislative emphases on the tactics of these groups in the United States and Europe represents a heightened awareness of the role played by militant direct action environmentalism, and interest in the goals or causes espoused by its advocates.

Globalization, or perhaps the manifestations of globalism, has begun serving as targets for direct action campaigns of varying intensities—for political, economic, environmental, and broader philosophical rationales. This global bricolage, as Taylor describes it [10], reflects a variety of interests whose attraction to direct action environmentalism is based upon an array of complementary if not entirely mutual beliefs. Taylor identifies these beliefs as the common perception that environmental deterioration is threatening both the planet and human life; that elite control of land and resources is driving the relentless advance of globalism; and that resources and power must be taken from the abusers and given to those with the wisdom and knowledge to better manage the planet [10]. Regardless of these commonalities, it would be unfair and inaccurate to uniformly categorize all direct action environmentalists. While sharing core beliefs, differing contexts, tactics, and goals distinguish the groups and individuals from one another to varying degrees. Likewise, the propensity for violence, the nature of potential targets, and the threat of escalation cannot be generalized. For example, the attacks on individuals attributed to Stop Huntingdon Animal Cruelty (SHAC) in the U.K. differ from the primarily property-focused attacks of the ALF in the U.S., though both groups have similar animal rights agendas.

It stands to reason that violent direct action environmentalism has the potential to play a greater role in opposition to the various facets of globalization [11]. To lend resolution to the role that direct action activists currently play and may play in the future, the history, propensity for violence, and the motivations of the movement must be examined in the context of the globalism debates. It takes only the most cursory review to discover that the eco-terror question is far from simple, that causal consensus is lacking, and that information useful to predict the prevalence of violence in response to the forces of globalism is rare. It is difficult, for instance, to equate the vandalism of a McDonald's restaurant in the U.S. to indigenous resistance to international industrial consortiums in

---

* This estimate likely under-represents the total damages. The 2003 arson of a housing development in California attributed to the Earth Liberation Front (ELF) purportedly caused $50 million in damages.

developing nations. Nonetheless, it is worthwhile to consider what we do know of this violent reaction, if not to accurately forecast future violence, then at least to heighten awareness of the causes of the current movement, and the potential for unforeseen triggers for expansion of this natural [CaMS1] cult of violence.

20.2 Definitions, Semantics, and a Common Syntax

Every discussion of eco-terrorism faces the recurrent difficulty of defining precisely what is being described. Terms such as "eco-terrorism," "environmental terrorism," and "ecotage," are used almost interchangeably, generating confusion and misunderstanding, and sub-definitions such as "impact eco-terror" and "ideological eco-terror" [12] further complicate the lexicon. An excellent example of this confusion is found within the Encyclopedia Britannica, where ecological terrorism and environmental terrorism are lumped together, with a definition that includes both terroristic crimes utilizing or targeting environmental resources, and the use of terror for the sake of protecting the environment [13]. Additionally, the terms environmental terror and eco-terror are often used interchangeably [14], though they represent very different practices. Effort must be made to distinguish exactly which actions of concern are being addressed [15].

While the term "eco-terrorism" has been well-recognized in a number of arenas [1,16], it nonetheless may be most accurate to use "violent, radical, direct action environmentalism" to describe the behaviors in question. The unwieldiness of that descriptor, however, calls for a shorter label. For the purposes of brevity and consistency, we shall use the term "eco-terrorism" to refer to: "the use or threatened use of violence of a criminal nature against innocent victims or property by an environmentally oriented, subnational group for environmental-political reasons, or aimed as an audience beyond the target, often of a symbolic nature" [1].

Even within the confines of this term and definition, however, we must face several related and ongoing issues, including (1) recognizing that the term "terrorist" is laden with connotations that have the risk of being inappropriately applied to the broader non-violent environmental movement; (2) discerning who in fact qualifies as an eco-terrorist; and (3) determining the nature or role of violence in the definition of eco-terror. Each merits a brief discussion before moving on to consider eco-terror and globalism.

The observation that the mere term "terrorism" carries with it social and legal connotations certainly gives pause to any careless application of the term [17]. The illegitimacy or criminal presumption that attaches to the term may taint those to whom the term is applied, regardless of the actual activities they undertake. This concern is particularly important in considering the chilling effect that labeling otherwise legitimate forms of social protest as eco-terrorism might cause. A uniform definition of eco-terrorism is therefore highly desirable to minimize any inappropriate usages, and to prevent inadvertent or intentional corruption of the term. The definition provided by the Federal Bureau of Investigation in the U.S. [1] is certainly open to semantic or philosophical debate. It does, however, provide a consistent reference for discussing the subject, and by virtue of its adoption by federal law enforcement, it provides an official meaning for both opponents and apologists of eco-terroristic behavior.

Eco-terror in a broader anti-globalism context clearly implies more than a single definition of terrorism, and in a number of nations, eco-terrorism is not specially defined [18]. There is, of course, no pressing need for a globally accepted definition of eco-terror, provided each country has addressed the issue in some manner. It is more important that official definitions be developed, and that these respective national legal definitions are well-articulated and consistently applied. Anything less risks enveloping broader environmental activism within the specific, criminalized confines of eco-terror [19]. For illustration, while the European Union has taken note of the threat posed by eco-terror [20], the depth of that attention does not reflect the priority that law enforcement in the United States has placed on this crime, nor the problems inherent in defining eco-terroristic actions.

Related to the matter of eco-terror definitions is the question of what behavior qualifies one as an eco-terrorist. While any definition, such as the federal definition in the U.S., may imply what actions are terroristic, the articulation of the crime does not specifically suggest what is being prohibited. For example, in 1999 the FBI noted that it has become "increasingly difficult to differentiate acts of terrorism from acts of vandalism" [3]. The FBI's narrow interpretation of the definition of terrorism under existing federal law allowed, in the agency's opinion, a number of crimes that might well have been committed by eco-terrorists to instead be classified as extremist vandalism. The FBI notes that it does not serve as the lead investigative body for such vandalism cases [3]. The difference between this depiction in 1999 and the statements made before the U.S. Congress in 2002 on behalf of the agency [1] signal that the FBI has broadened its approach. The definition expressed in 2002 is, not surprisingly, similar to the definition of domestic terrorism espoused in the 2001 Patriot Act.*
In any anti-globalism setting, therefore, it is important to understand the limitations of existing laws and policies. Regardless of the criminality or social undesirability of certain acts, law enforcement agencies may lack the specific authority to effectively investigate and prosecute these crimes.

Somewhat tangential from the relationship between the definition of an act of eco-terror and law enforcement efforts, is a more philosophical debate over who is committing acts of terror, or who actually qualifies as an eco-terrorist. On one hand, Arnold [5] suggests that the anti-globalist and anarchist ranting of Theodore Kaczynski (the Unabomber), along with his familiarity with "green" activism, categorizes him as an eco-terrorist. With his string of deadly targeted mail bombs, Kaczynski was certainly a terrorist, but what additional criteria might be necessary to label him an eco-terrorist? Even with the federal definition in the U.S., it is necessary to delve into the motives of the Unabomber before one can proclaim him an eco-terrorist. At the other end of the spectrum are those that would argue that the various environmental policies of the U.S. government [21]

---

* Public Law No. 107-56, 2001

or the actions of corporate animal researchers [22] would qualify as eco-terroristic. Embedded within this semantic exercise is a fundamental moral question: is the violence intended to harm or terrorize a populace, or is it merely incidental to another activity? In other words, can the criminal efforts of the Unabomber in any way be likened to the activities of an animal researcher? If an easy distinction between the two is apparent, then arguing that researchers are eco-terrorists becomes more difficult. Certainly, public perceptions of differences in the two have led to the prevailing legal structure and standards, wherein the former is a crime, and the latter, practiced within bounds, is not.

Finally, the concept of violence is a recurring problem in defining eco-terror. Direct action environmentalism has a long relationship with various forms of violence. When Edward Abbey's character Doc objects to some of the proposed actions of the Monkey Wrench Gang: "'All this violence,' Doc said. 'We are a law-abiding people,'" he is chastised by Hayduke: "'What's more American than violence?'" Hayduke wanted to know. "'Violence, it's as American as pizza pie.'" [23]. While Abbey's Hayduke may have had little difficulty with his version of violence, there exists an apparent intellectual, though not legal, distinction between violence directed towards inanimate objects such as property and violence directed at persons. This distinction forms the foundation upon which direct action environmentalism maintains its claims to non-violence. The perceived difference is premised upon the assertion that so long as persons are neither targeted nor harmed, the related direct actions are not "violent." Actions such as arson, tree-spiking, vandalism of machinery or buildings, and other property-focused crimes would be considered non-violent under this paradigm, whereas mail bombs, letters containing razor blades, and the direct assault on an individual would qualify as violent. Direct action environmentalists, in many cases, claim to eschew the latter while embracing the former [2]. Interestingly, property crimes do not necessarily enjoy any particular relief under criminal law. For example, in the United States, arson is categorized as severely as the offenses of rape, assault, and manslaughter [24]. Kumar [25] notes that "there is no real distinction between violence to people and violence to property." It is a very thin line indeed, relying upon a distinction between the targets, rather than the acts themselves. It is important to recognize that the concept of violence may be interpreted far more broadly than direct action environmentalists may foresee or desire. As one commenter notes: "Violence in any form can inspire terror in its victims and in those indirectly affected by the violence" [18].

It is further troubling that violence against property targets has been recognized as a potential precursor to escalated violence such as kidnappings and murder [17,26], and that we may indeed expect an increase in environmentally-motivated attacks against specific individuals [27]. With individuals reporting attacks against their properties and harassment of their families [28–30], and with the attempted use of toxic compounds during protests [2], direct action environmentalism may indeed be precariously poised to escalate.

The violence dichotomy can become further confused by its role in anti-globalism direct actions. In protests such as Seattle's World Trade Organization (WTO) in 1999, the ensuing street violence resulted in arrests, curfews, and deployment of National Guard troops to restore order [31]. While the protesters did not directly assault individuals, and while the majority of the protesters may not have engaged in the most destructive acts [4,32], it is nonetheless difficult to excuse the chaos caused as non-violent, particularly when juxtaposed with the tradition of non-violent, civil disobedience displayed by such causes as the civil rights movement in the U.S. Some would argue that the violence inherent in such anti-globalist protests is merely a convenient excuse for public rioting [33]. The "Battle in Seattle" nonetheless continues to stir debate as a prime example demonstrating the boundary between non-violent and violent protests in the name of anti-globalism.

20.3 Direct Action in a Contemporary Context

One of the most interesting aspects of eco-terror is the choice of direct action tactics. While arson is typically preferred, certainly due to its destructive effect and anonymity, others tactics include property-based crimes (e.g. sabotage to equipment, vehicles, buildings, laboratories), animal liberations (e.g. from research facilities, farms), intimidation campaigns (e.g. harassing letters, telephone calls, vandalism), and direct physical violence (e.g. assault). In the wake of the September 11, 2001 attacks in the United States, widespread concerns have arisen over the potential for terrorist use of weapons of mass destruction (WMD). This heightened concern has had implications for whether the actions of eco-terrorists might present a more serious threat, and if such activists might consider use of WMDs for indiscriminate attacks. While the likelihood of such an occurrence remains debatable [19,27], the potential for such an attack has not gone unnoticed by anti-terrorism authorities [34]. The increased attention being paid to domestic eco-terrorists has been reflected in the increases in law enforcement efforts [3] and in direct Congressional oversight of those efforts [1].

Available resources suggest that attacks carried out in opposition to globalism are relatively rare, representing perhaps 3% of the Earth Liberation Front's (ELF) targets in the five-year period between 1996 and 2001 [2], and perhaps 4% of the ALF's attacks in 2001 [9]. It appears that very few recent eco-terror attacks are premised upon anti-globalistic motives, though it certainly becomes more difficult to discern the motive of the attacks when they are examined in detail. For example, attacks on McDonald's fast food restaurants have been separately reported by the ALF as both attacks on the meat industry and as anti-globalism protests [9].

As the McDonald's attacks suggest, the eco-terrorist rationale for attacks may at once diverge and overlap. The central underlying motivation for eco-terror attacks by one of the prominent groups in the U.S. was succinctly captured by Ackerman [27]: "The ELF's outlook is an apocalyptic vision of a natural world imperiled by corporate greed and a corrupt system, with ELF members being the only true defenders of the living earth." It is perhaps unfortunate that broader, non-criminal efforts to prevent ecologic decline have been addressed in equally bellicose terms [35]. Such metaphors illustrate the militancy that can creep into preservationist ideology.

While applicable to the ELF, the themes of a despoiled planet and of corporate abuses of natural systems are commonly integrated with an over-arching message of social justice into the mission of the ALF [9]. In reality, the ELF and the ALF share far more in common than they differ. With multiple and overlapping ways to categorize the actions of these groups, analysis of the groups' tactical motivations in any particular case becomes somewhat arbitrary. Certainly, anti-globalist direct actions are easily categorized in more than one way. It is more useful, perhaps, to recognize that strategically, the groups share very similar agendas, and that tactically, reliance upon well-demonstrated methods such as arson will likely continue to prevail.

Because eco-terrorists may share a common vision of the problems they seek to address, they also tend to share the same notions of suitable targets. Leader and Probt's [2] typology of targets is, for example, representative of both ELF and ALF:

- Logging/related
- Government
- Corporate
- Global economy/Anti-Globalism
- Urban sprawl/development
- Genetic engineering/biotech
- Animal research/containment facilities

As noted earlier, relatively few attacks have specifically occurred within the Global economy/Anti-Globalism category.

Violence occurring in conjunction with anti-globalism protests is somewhat more difficult to classify, as the participants in these events are quite hetero-geneous [4,32]. For example, John Zerzan and the Black Bloc are often identified as primary contributors to the violent components of protests at Seattle's WTO meeting in 1999 [4,32,36]. Zerzan and the Black Bloc, however, are better described as anarchists, not eco-terrorists. While the preferred anti-globalism targets of Black Bloc and eco-terrorists do overlap, there appears to be little evidence suggesting that recognized eco-terror groups were directly involved in the anti-globalism violence in Seattle. Eco-terrorists appear to prefer the opportunistic use of anonymous arson directed at globalist targets, rather than direct confrontation with law enforcement.

20.4 Causal Factors: Self-Defense, Environmental Preservation, and Anti-Global Rhetoric

The motivations driving eco-terrorist activity are diverse. While concern for preventing environmental degradation is often at the core of such actions, the philosophy of Deep Ecology plays no small role in forming an intellectual framework from which eco-terrorists may justify their actions. This biocentric view is a hallmark of splinter activists, including eco-terrorists [2,37], and can

440 <Handbook of Globalization and the Environment

explain much of the opposition to industrialization, an emphasis on preserving the natural order, and the seeming disregard for human institutions such as private property. It is not difficult to understand particular activists embracing violence as a means for actualizing their philosophical beliefs, any more than it is hard to understand how fundamentalist terrorists the world over regularly rely upon a violent interpretation of their respective creeds to justify their actions.

The tenets of Deep Ecology provide a backdrop well-suited for the opposition to timber harvesting, itself a cornerstone of eco-terrorist activity since its inception. Tree-spiking and "monkey wrenching" logging equipment have been mainstays of eco-terrorist efforts. The safety hazards associated with tree-spiking reached the federal level in the U.S., with Congress acting in 1988 to make tree-spiking a federal offense.* Changes in forest management over the last several decades, both on private and public lands in the U.S., may have led to a corresponding shift in eco-terror emphasis. Drastic reductions in the amount of timber being harvested from national forests during the early 1990s, and a shift in commercial production to plantations on private lands have drained much of the urgency from the forest preservation cause. Appeals and litigation by main-stream environmental groups have proven far more effective as tools to challenge forest management decisions than could any sporadic protests or acts of violence [38,39]. Forest-related actions have instead focused more upon research laboratories, particularly where genetic tree improvement research is being conducted. Arson attacks on a Forest Service research facility in Pennsylvania in 2002 and on the University of Washington's Center for Urban Horticulture in 2005 are prime examples of this change in emphasis. There remains, however, a substantial direct action environmental presence in forest management debates, with a recent paper reporting Earth First! active on 75% of the national forests studied [40].

More notable have been actions against a wide array of commercial endeavors, ranging from ski resorts and car dealerships, to partially constructed housing developments. While an environmental component may exist to each of these actions, it is becoming more evident that attacks have an anti-development, anti-corporate, and perhaps, anti-global flavor to them. To illustrate, while less than 20% of direct actions attributed to the ELF were *logging/related* from 1996–2001, the *corporate, global economy/anti-globalism* or *urban sprawl/development* categories accounted for 62% of actions in that time period [2]. This trend has raised concern that there may be a growing relationship between eco-terrorists and anti-globalism activists [11].

There are, however, other motivations that may spur eco-terrorism. Related to environmental concerns is the perception that the environment needs defenders or champions willing to take the steps necessary to protect the natural world. This obligation is compounded by a reactionary perception that direct action environmentalists are being persecuted. Beltran presents the interesting argument that eco-terror in the U.S. is a response to violent repression of environmental interests in the 1980 and 1990s, coupled with a general

---

* Public Law 100–690 (1988).

disenfranchisement of the mainstream environmental movement from the political and legal systems [41]. While it is far from certain that mainstream environmental groups have been co-opted or otherwise excluded from the governing process, the impression Beltran provides of eco-terror as a manifestation of other anti-environmentalist violence and perceived injustices suffered by the environmental community suggests a self-defense motivation for the movement. Beltran goes on to suggest that as policies are developed to sanction environmental groups not actually engaged in eco-terror, they will spur even greater responses from the eco-terrorists. This concept, that eco-terrorists are the defenders of the Earth and of the larger environmental movement, is demonstrated in the actions of groups such as the Sea Shepherd Conservation Society (SSCS). The organization acts as a self-appointed enforcer of natural laws on the world's seas [33], taking those steps that governments and other environmental groups cannot or refuse to take. A claim of self-defense is a potent excuse for violence, certainly under the law in the use of violence to protect oneself, and apparently in the use of violence by eco-terrorists [27].

What these observations suggest is that the eco-terror movement, though often sharing common goals and tactics, relies upon an array of rationales supporting decisions to adopt direct action, rationales that typically set it apart from the mainstream environmental movement. Eagan [17] captures this distinction: "On one hand are the mainstream environmental groups, which articulate legal, nonviolent, and democratic actions. On the other hand are the antidemocratic fringe, almost all of which are advocates of Deep Ecology and are willing to take direct action in order to achieve that goal." The relationship between these groups can also be paradoxical, with eco-terrorists serving as the militant defenders of the mainstream environmental movement [41], but also at odds with the mainstream's perceived lethargy and moderation [17]. There are few generalizations that can be made regarding the eco-terrorist movement, let alone individual eco-terrorists. It is safe to acknowledge, however, that the motivations of the groups are often complex, elements of which tend to overlap with the motivations of the anti-globalization movement.

20.5   Defining Anti-Globalism

Anti-globalists are largely defined by their opposition to capitalism, modern civilization, technology, and what they perceive as the resultant despoliation of cultures, the environment, and imperilment of human survival [11]. Sometimes described as green anarchists, this movement also tends to be defined by its tactic of direct action, including public protests and demonstrations, violence, and sabotage. Anti-globalists are not necessarily active only in developed nations. The Zapatista uprising in Mexico, for example, suggests that the movement is both geographically and demographically broad, and that the issues it represents are equally diverse [32]. There are, in fact, dramatic differences between the actions and targets of green anarchist violence in the U.S. and the popular anti-globalist movements among indigenous peoples. In contrast with such issues as opposition to the construction of dams, illegal logging, or oil development [42], the actions of violent green anarchists in the U.S. seem trivial by comparison. Consider that the attacks on Seattle storefronts by Black Bloc in 1999 targeted "rapers of Northwest forests" (Old Navy, Banana Republic and the GAP), makers of "overpriced" sweatshop products (Nike), "slave-wage fast food peddlers,"(McDonald's) "peddlers of an addictive substance" (Starbucks), and "Planet Hollywood for being Planet Hollywood" [36]. It becomes difficult to envision how such violent protests can effectively address any of the primary drivers of environmental degradation [43].

But these political protests can illustrate the movement's overall heterogeneity. While protests surrounding the recent WTO meeting in Hong Kong reflect primarily a discontent with agricultural policies and practices (not with the environmental polices that might attract "greener" activists) [44], the "Battle in Seattle" attracted a:

> …spectacular panorama of protesters. There were women's groups, and students from universities around the country. There were animal rights groups and small business associations. There were Marxists and anarchists, Democrats and Republicans, internationalists and bioregionalists, liberals and conservatives, white-collar and blue-collar, gays and straights. There were people from rich countries and poor countries around the world [31].

These disparate activists do not uniformly practice the violence that has sporadically occurred among anti-globalist demonstrations. There is, in fact, evidence to suggest that violence is not tolerated among the majority of anti-globalists [19,31,32]. The violence/non-violence dichotomy has been used to break the anti-globalism movement into two groups: one that will oppose globalism in all its forms, and one that recognizes that globalism has and will continue to occur and hope to steer it in a sustainable direction [31]. Juma [45] described the tension that exists between these two philosophies: "Environmentalism is driven by a sense of urgency that is not quenched by calls for time and adjustment, while international trade is driven by age-old dynamics and patterns that do not change overnight." It is this "urgency," however, that may beckon the direct action tactics of eco-terrorists into a more intimate partnership with their anti-globalist comrades.

20.6   Implications for the Future

A modern concern exists that the overlapping ideologies and tactics found among anti-globalists willing to embrace violence and those of eco-terrorists may combine to create a new, more violent version of the anti-globalist movement. This concern is a blend of two perceptions: one, that violence among eco-terrorists is on the rise, both in frequency and in intensity [3,8,46–51]; and two, that the anti-globalist ideology and movement are becoming increasingly intertwined with the eco-terror agenda, particularly in their common desire to disassemble the capitalist system. This amalgam can be manifested both in the expansion of the eco-terrorist perspective from its traditional targets to include those that would be more traditionally considered globalist [2]; and from the green anarchist perspective, it might herald new tactics that go well beyond street violence.

Specifically worrisome is the potential for eco-terror attacks to shift their targets from property to individuals. Recent attacks have become more personal, and analysis of terrorist predispositions suggests that intentional bodily harm is probable, at least from members of the ELF [27]. Should such attacks materialize, they would signal a new chapter in direct action environmentalism in the United States. While isolated instances such as the Unabomber's postal terror campaign targeting specific individuals are far from typical, there appears to be a trend towards an increasing number of attacks on individuals, rather than the traditional government or business interest targets [52]. This personalization of attacks is the most troubling element of eco-terror, as the focus of violence drifts slowly away from anonymous property destruction to singling out individual "ecological offenders." Law enforcement responses to a shift in targets will most certainly include enhanced investigation resources, thus increasing pressure on eco-terror groups and the non-terrorist groups that allegedly fund eco-terrorists activities. Of course, if Beltran [41] is correct, such increased law enforcement efforts may spark reprisals from the eco-terrorists in the form of increased attacks, forming a classic vicious cycle. Michael Crichton's fictional portrayal [53] of the struggle between eco-terrorists and government anti-terror agents demonstrates a level of violence that, though dramatically suited for a novel, may also reinforce Beltran's notion of the actions and reactions common to both terrorist and anti-terrorist tactics.

The second modern perception, that the increasing camaraderie between green anarchists and eco-terrorists may lead to a more virulent strain of anti-globalist activism, has been repeatedly supported [11,34,51]. While distinctions between the two movements certainly exist, that distinction may be shrinking, with the potential outcome being a unified ecological/anti-globalist ideology [11]. As noted earlier, the shift in eco-terror targets toward the symbols of capitalism and globalism suggests that an accompanying ideological shift is also occurring. How this metamorphosis will ultimately settle remains speculative, though the potential for violence is arguably higher among the green anarchist movement [19]. Should the violent elements of the anarchist movement and the eco-terrorist movement blend into a new variant of green anarchism, the new entity's direct actions might well include generic street violence, a continuation of the current arson and sabotage campaigns, as well as an increase in attacks on individuals.

20.7   Remedies

Solutions to eco-terrorist actions have largely been premised upon traditional law enforcement tactics: investigation, infiltration, arrest, and prosecution. In the U.S., the FBI has testified that increased anti-terror resources and emphasis have led to successful arrests of eco-terrorists [54]. The agency attributed its successes to its analysis experience, intelligence capabilities, and partnerships with state and local law enforcement. Notable successes include the recent arrest of six persons related to the multi-million dollar arson attacks on the University of Washington's Center for Urban Horticulture and a poplar farm [55]. The suspects face federal charges and incarceration from 20 years to life, depending upon the specific charge. Certainly, the weight of the penalties for these types of actions can act as deterrent. Consider that a high school student in Virginia was sentenced to three years in federal prison for his role in arson attacks on a car dealership [56]. The severity of penalties for eco-terror attacks is also embedded in the symbolic need to ensure that potential activists are aware of the risks and costs:

> Prosecutors must send a clear message to eco-terrorists that their violent behavior will not be tolerated. Eco-terrorists need to know that when the line between legitimate protest and a criminal act is crossed, even if only misdemeanor, the prosecutors of America will react. You do not need an exotic anti-terror law to charge a terrorist; eco-terrorists can be punished within the parameters of any existing laws, such as arson or destruction of property. The environment needs to be protected, but so does society [57].

There does nonetheless appear to be a trend occurring in the U.S. with "exotic" or tailored anti-terror statutes. At the federal level, the 1992 Animal Enterprise Protection Act* was enacted to prosecute those that carried out sabotage actions against the various types of commercial and research animal facilities, including zoos and aquariums. The 2001 Patriot Act,[†] while resulting from the tragedies of September 11, 2001, provided a powerful array of tools that may have applicability to the activities of eco-terrorists [58]. At the state level, at least seven states have embarked on the process of adopting versions of the Animal and Ecological Terrorism Act, a model law developed by the American Legislative Exchange Council [59].

More traditional legal tools have also been suggested. The use of the federal Racketeer Influenced and Corrupt Organizations (RICO) statute has been offered as a means to address the actions of an array of eco-terrorists [60,61]. Equipped with both civil and criminal components, the RICO could potentially cover a great breadth of environmental direct actions, including prosecution of groups that lend financial support to eco-terrorists. It also has the added advantage of providing a remedy to the individual harmed by the actions of eco-terrorists separate and apart from any criminal prosecution:

> The RICO remedies are an appropriate deterrent to protest that crosses the line from legitimate speech to prohibited conduct. If the conduct

---

* 18 U.S.C. §43 (2001)
† Pub. L No. 107-56 (2001)

meets the requirements of RICO, then RICO's broad remedies should provide the same protection to the victims of environmental terrorism that has been provided to the victims of abortion violence [61].

Its use for this purpose, however, has largely remained hypothetical.

Finally, it has been suggested that anti-eco-terror efforts take a lesson from anti-terror efforts in other national contexts. Italy's successful elimination of its Red Brigade terror cells has been offered as a template for dealing with groups such as the ELF [26]. Use of the Italian *pentiti* incentive, it is suggested, might lead to a greater number of eco-terrorists surrendering themselves, thus potentially providing greater information on those that choose to remain at-large. This incentive system, however, is predicated upon sufficiently severe penalties should the activist not wish to accept the state's offer of lenient prosecution. It is possible that the Patriot Act may provide that set of penalties, though the U.S. has yet to adopt anything even close the Italian model of formalized clemency incentives.

Any of these legal approaches that have potential to deter eco-violence are also suited to addressing anti-global violence. To the extent that the two movements are converging, and to the degree that resultant violence escalates, it may be time to consider the full range of anti-terror legal mechanisms.

20.8   Conclusions

Conceptually and pragmatically, eco-terror is a challenging subject. The various and diverse actors make generalizations difficult and analysis elusive. When juxtaposed with the actions and ideologies of anti-globalists, it becomes ever more difficult to reach a consensus of opinion on the effects and futures of these movements. We can, however, judiciously set forth the following:

- Eco-terrorism, regardless of its semantic challenges, is a pattern of violent actions carried out by individuals embracing a fluctuating, but cohesive view of how the ecological world is and should be in the future;
- Anti-globalists or green anarchists, to the extent they overlap, represent a broad dissatisfaction with international policies and practices that are at once prevalent and difficult to alter;
- While the violent actions of individual groups or memberships will vary considerably, there appears to be an observable increase in the scope and intensity of that violence when viewed collectively;
- There is early evidence that the ideologies of the eco-terror movement and the anti-global movements are beginning to merge. While it is difficult to say which group will influence the other the most, it appears likely that eco-terror attacks on globalism-type targets will maintain current levels or increase, while attacks on more traditional targets will decline;
- Increased law enforcement efforts and anti-terror legislative initiatives will continue to be offered in an effort to stem this form of illegal activism. Care is warranted to avoid sanctioning otherwise legal forms of civic protest.

References

1. U.S. Congress, House. Committee on Resources. Subcommittee on Forests and Forest Health *The Threat of Ecoterrorism*: Hearings before the Subcommittee on Forests and Forest Health, 107th Cong, 2002 (testimony of James F. Jarboe).
2. Leader, S.H. and Probst, P., The earth liberation front and environmental terrorism, *Terrorism and Political Violence*, 15, 37, 2003.
3. Federal Bureau of Investigation, *Terrorism in the United States 1999*, U.S. Department of Justice, Washington, DC, 2000, 21.
4. Long, D., *Ecoterrorism*, Facts on File, Inc., New York, 2004.
5. Arnold, R., *Ecoterror: The Violent Agenda to Save Nature*, Free Enterprise Press, Bellevue, 1997.
6. U.S. Congress, Senate. Committee on Environment and Public Works, *Eco-terrorism*, 109th Cong, 2005 (testimony of John Lewis).
7. U.S. Congress, House. Subcommittee on Forests and Forest Health, *The Threat of Ecoterrorism*, 107th Cong, 2002 (testimony of James F. Jarboe).
8. Foundation for Biomedical Research, Illegal incidents report, 2004. Available at http://www.fbresearch.org/animal-activsm/vioence.htm (accessed on December 5, 2005).
9. North American Animal Liberation Front, 2001 Year-end direct action report, North American Animal Liberation Front Press Office, Courtenay, BC, Canada, 2002.
10. Taylor, B., Diggers, wolves, ants, elves, and expanding universes: global bricolage and the question of violence within the subcultures of radical environmentalism, in *The Cultic Milieu: Oppositional Subcultures in an Age of Globalization*, J. Kaplan and H. Lööw, Eds., AltaMira Press, Walnut Creek, Lanham, MD, 2002.
11. Chalk, P., Hottman, B., Reville, R., and Kasupski, A.-B., *Trends in Terrorism: Threats to the United States and the Future of the Terrorism Risk Insurance Act*, Rand Center for Terrorism Risk Management Policy, Santa Monica, CA, 2005.
12. U.S. Congress, Senate. Environment and Public Works Committee, *Oversight on eco-terrorism specifically examining the Earth Liberation Front ("ELF") and the Animal Liberation Front ("ALF")*, 109th Cong, 2005 (testimony of Bradley Campbell).
13. Ecoterrorism, *Encyclopedia Britannica*. Available at Encyclopedia Britannica Premium Service http://www.Britannica.com/eb/article-9384368 (accessed on August 25, 2005).
14. Alexander, G.A., Ecoterrorism and nontraditional military threats, *Military Medicine*, 165, 1, 2000.
15. Chalecki, E.L., A new vigilance: identifying and reducing the risks of environmental terrorism, *Global Environmental Politics*, 2, 46, 2002.
16. Kushner, H.W., *Encyclopedia of Terrorism*, Sage Publications, Thousand Oaks, CA, 2003.
17. Eagan, S.P., From spikes to bombs: the rise of eco-terrorism, *Studies in Conflict and Terrorism*, 19, 1, 1996.
18. Tiefenbrun, S., A semiotic approach to a legal definition of terrorism, *ILSA Journal of International and Comparative Law*, 9, 357, 2003.
19. Taylor, B., Threat assessment and radical environmentalism, *Terrorism and Political Violence*, 15, 173, 2003.
20. Council of the European Union, *Situation in the terrorist activity in the European Union: situations and trends*, Document No. 5759/02, Brussels, 2002.
21. U.S. Congress, House. Committee on Resources. Subcommittee on Forests and Forest Health, *The Threat of Ecoterrorism*, 107th Cong, 2002 (testimony of Craig Rosebraugh).
22. Phillips, T., Who is the legally defined terrorist: HLS or SHAC?, *Animal Liberation Philosophy and Policy Journal*, 2, 1, 2004.

23. Abbey, E., *The Monkey Wrench Gang*. 1st Perennial Classics Edition HarperCollins Publishers Inc., New York, 1975, 176.
24. American Law Institute, Uniform Model Penal Code, §§210, 211, 220 Philadelphia, 2004.
25. Kumar, S. and Bowers, J., Can the use of violetnce ever be justified in the environmental struggle? *The Ecologist*, 30, 20, 2000.
26. Dunham, M.E., Eliminating the domestic terrorist threat in the United States: a case study on the eradication of the Red Brigades, *Dickinson Law Review*, 107, 151, 2002.
27. Ackerman, G.A., Beyond arson: a threat assessment of the Earth Liberation Front, *Terrorism and Political Violence*, 15, 143, 2003.
28. Richardson, J., Plum Creek vandalism sparks shock, outrage, Portland Press Herald, 2005.
29. U.S. Congress, Senate. Committee on Environment and Public Works, *Eco-terrorism*, 109th Cong, 2005 (testimony of Mark Bibi).
30. U.S. Congress, Senate. Committee on Environment and Public Works, *Eco-terrorism*, 109th Cong, 2005 (testimony of Skip Boruchin).
31. Warden, A., A brief history of the anti-globalization movement, *University of Miami International and Comparative Law Review*, 12, 237, 2004.
32. Steger, M.B., *Globalism: Market Ideology Meets Terrorism*, Rowman & Littlefield Publishers, Lanham, MD, 2005.
33. Hrab, N., Direct action, The tactics of radical activism: Part I, Capital Research Center Organization Trends Newsletters, 2004. Available at http://www.capitalresearch.org/pubs/pubs.asp?ID=168 (accessed on February 11, 2004).
34. Advisory Panel to Assess Domestic Response Capabilities for Terrorism Involving WMD, Fourth Annual Report to the President and the Congress, Congress, Washington, DC, 2002.
35. Woodbridge, R., *The Next World War: Tribes, Cities, Nations, and Ecological Decline*, University of Toronto Press, Toronto, Ont., Canada, 2004, 221.
36. Acme Collective, N30 Black Bloc Communiqué, 1999. Available at http://www.infoshop.org/octo/wto_blackbloc.html (accessed on December 14, 2005).
37. Kamieniecki, S., Coleman, S.D., and Vos, R.O., The effectiveness of radical environmentalists, in *Ecological Resistance Movements: The Global Emergence of Radical and Popular Environmentalism*, B.R. Taylor, Ed., State University of New York Press, Albany, NY, 1995.
38. Malmsheimer, R.W., Keele, D., and Floyd, D.W., National forest litigation in the US Courts of Appeals, *Journal of Forestry*, 102, 20, 2004.
39. Mortimer, M.J., The delegation of law-making authority to the United States Forest Service: implications in the struggle for national forest management, *Administrative Law Review*, 54, 907, 2002.
40. Chavez, D.J. and Tynon, J.F., Triage law enforcement: societal impacts on national forests in the West, *Environmental Management*, 26, 403, 2000.
41. Beltran, X., Applying RICO to eco-activism: fanning the radical flames of eco-terror, *Boston College Environmental Affairs Law Review*, 29, 281, 2002.
42. Geddicks, A., International native resistance to the new resource wars, in *Ecological Resistance Movements: The Global Emergence of Radical and Popular Environmentalism*, B.R. Taylor, Ed., State University of New York Press, Albany, NY, 1995.
43. Speth, J.G., *Red Sky at Morning: America and the Crisis of the Global Environment*, Yale University Press, New Haven, CT, 2004.
44. Associated Press, Clashes on Opening Day of WTO Meeting, 2005.
45. Juma, C., International trade and environment: towards integrative responsibility, in *Globalization, Globalism, Environments, and Environmentalism*, S. Vertovec and D. Posey, Eds., Oxford University Press, Oxford, 2003.

46. Southern Poverty Law Center, *Eco-Violence: fringe eco-radicals growing more violent*, Intelligence Report, 2003. Available at http://www.splcenter.org/intel/intelreport/ (accessed on December 2, 2005).

47. Mobley, M., The new wave of radical environmentalism: America's inaction and reaction to domestic ecoterrorism, *Appalachian Journal of Law*, 1, 19, 2002.

48. Journo, E., The mounting threat of homegrown terrorism, Capitalism Magazine, 2003. Available at http://capmag.com/articel.asp?ID=3129 (accessed on December 14, 2005).

49. Federal Bureau of Investigation. *Terrorism 2000–2001,*. Publication #0308, U.S. Department of Justice, Washington, DC, 2002.

50. California Department of Justice, *Organized Crime in California: 2003 Annual Report to the Legislature*, Sacramento, 2004.

51. Anti-Defamation League, *Ecoterrorism: extremism in the animal rights and environmental movements*, 2004. Available at http://www.adl.org/Extremism/ (accessed on December 2, 2005).

52. Southern Poverty Law Center, *Eco-Violence: The Record, 2003*. Available at https:// secure.splcenter.org/intel/intelreport/article.jsp?sid=29 (accessed on December 14, 2005).

53. Crichton, M., *State of Fear*, HarperCollins Publishers Inc, New York, 2004.

54. U.S. Congress, Senate. Committee on Environment and Public Works, *Oversight on eco-terrorism specifically examining the Earth Liberation Front ("ELF") and the Animal Liberation Front ("ALF")*, 109th Cong, 2005 (testimony of John Lewis).

55. Associated Press, *Feds Announce Arrests in Ecoterrorism Attacks*, 2005.

56. Campbell, T., *Teen reflects on damage 'radical activism' caused*, Richmond Times-Dispatch, 2004.

57. Marquis, J.K. and Weiss, D.M., Eco-terror: special interest terrorism, *Prosecutor*, 39, 30, 2005.

58. Case, D.R., The USA Patriot Act: adding bite to the fight against animal rights terrorism? *Rutgers Law of Journal*, 34, 187, 2002.

59. Bourne, S.L. and McNabb, M., Eds., in *Animal and Ecological Terrorism in America*, American Legislative Exchange Council, Washington, DC, 2003.

60. Correll, D. E., No peace for the greens: the criminal prosecution of environmental activists and the threat of organizational liability, *Rutgers Law of Journal*, 24, 773, 1993.

61. Cason, W.W., Spiking the spikers: the use of civil RICO against environmental terrorists, *Houston Law Review*, 32, 745, 1995.

Chapter 21

Globalization, Environmental Challenges and North–South Issues

Joyeeta Gupta
Vrije University

21.1   Introduction

Globalization is not a new phenomenon. However, it may be that it comes in waves. The first major wave of globalization was the phenomenon of colonization that began in the 16th century and lasted for more than 300 years. This wave of globalization was spurred on by mercantilism, which aimed to achieve economic and political stability. European states encouraged their nationals to develop agriculture and industries and to export more than they imported. An important feature of mercantilism was to have sea power and control overseas markets. States encouraged colonization as a means to acquire raw materials and find markets for goods that were resulting from the industrial revolution taking place in Europe. Mercantilism led to the large-scale development of trade routes and the establishment of trading companies in different parts of the world; the world was thus divided in terms of colonies and colonizers. Economic and political order was spread through the export of the laws and policies of the colonizers.

In the 20th century, the decolonization process began in the wake of the world wars and the new idealism of the period led to the birth of the United Nations in 1945. The United Nations Charter [1] sought "To maintain international peace and security, and to that end: to take effective collective measures for the prevention and removal of threats to the peace"… "in conformity with the principles of justice and international law"; "To develop friendly relations among nations based on respect for the principle of equal rights and self-determination of peoples"; and "To achieve international co-operation in solving international problems of an economic, social, cultural or humanitarian character." The establishment of the UN system implied a new central forum for global and regional policy and law making. At around the same period, the Bretton Woods Institutions were established. These organizations became the center for policy-making in the area of monetary policy and investment.

In the 1990s the rapid evolution of transport and communication technology, combined with the end of the Cold War, has led to a revolution in the processes of societal development. Globalization today encapsulates a number of different trends, ranging from changes in the way war is fought to the way investments are made. Some elements of globalization are possibly orchestrated and planned, some are debated within the formal portals of UN institutions and some on the streets outside, and many of the trends are autonomous—i.e., the results of a range of different activities by different social actors that together lead to major, seemingly irreversible changes in society. In the meanwhile, industrialization world-wide has had impacts on the global environment, impacts that may be also harmful to society.

This chapter examines globalization and its impacts on the environment from a north–south perspective. It focuses on the following question: Does globalization exacerbate the existing tense north–south relations with respect to the already complicated relationship between environmental and developmental issues? In order to address this intricate question, this chapter will first focus on globalization (Section 21.2), discuss the complicated relationship between environmental and developmental issues (Section 21.3) before moving on to elaborate on north–south relations (Section 21.4). It then discusses some of the challenges in the area of environmental governance (Section 21.5) before integrating the discussion in the conclusions.

21.2 Globalization

21.2.1 Introduction

This section briefly reviews globalization in terms of whether globalization seeks to modernize or re-colonize (Section 2.2), whether globalization enriches or impoverishes countries (Section 2.3), whether managed globalization is anarchic or rule based (Section 2.4), whether "spontaneous" globalization is autonomous or orchestrated (Section 2.5) before drawing the different ideas together in integrated inferences (Section 2.6).

21.2.2 Theories on Globalization: Modernization versus Re-colonization

Theories on globalization focus either on its modernizing ideology or its re-colonization ideology. Much has been written on globalization, and without attempting a comprehensive literature review, one could nonetheless submit that four different although possibly complementary theories on globalization exist. World system theory [2] sees globalization as a process through which capitalism spreads throughout the world, more rapidly with the end of the Cold War. Although the origin of globalization can be traced back to European political economy thinking, there is no political core and globalization flourishes through a number of different political systems in different parts of the world. Those countries that have highly skilled labor and capital intensive production are in the center and other countries are in the periphery of the system.

World polity theory focuses on how globalization leads to a sharing of a common culture with its roots in Christianity. This common culture creates rules and models within which society functions. Rules are not dictated by a body or country, but emerge from the globally shared values of sovereign states and the system that they set up. Over time, states adopt similar norms, constitutions, principles, rules, and structures, and increasingly civil society and non-state actors play a role in defining these rules and structures [3,4].

World culture theory [5] puts emphasis on global interaction and the development of global consciousness. Globalization implies changes for states, the system of states, individuals and humankind and goes hand-in-hand with modernity. In this system each unit shapes itself relative to others (relativization), each unit emulates the characteristics of other cultures that it respects (emulation), each interprets the norms in distinctively local and cultural styles (globalization), universalism and particularism are closely related (inter-penetration), and the elements of globalization are contested and debated in different contexts.

At the other end of the world, from the school of the Third World Approaches to International Law, B.S. Chimni [6], argues that globalization is not an autonomous process but a process that is orchestrated and promoted by the Western countries; that a combination of institutional constraints and freedoms is created to facilitate eleven types of influences: the internationalization of democracy, property rights, conditions for the exchange of commodities, internationalization of currencies, human rights, labor market deregulation, digital capitalism, the proliferation of tribunals, the participation of non-state actors, the tendency to gradually stop differentiating between rich and poor countries, and the reconstitution of the relationship between states and the UN with the entry of the corporate sector. Chimni puts forward the notion that globalization is perhaps in many ways a new type of colonization.

The theories focus on different aspects of the same phenomenon and highlight different elements. But while for some the process of globalization is a conscious project that is pushed by key actors who are ideologically motivated, for others globalization is an inevitable process that moves in mysterious ways. Each theory in its own way contributes to understanding globalization, and these are not necessarily contradictory. One can conclude that a key element, although not the only element, of globalization is the capitalist ideology that finds its roots in Western culture. Another element of globalization is the rise of common values which may be either linked to capitalist ideology or to the need for the rule of law and the respect for human rights, or both. This, too, finds its links in Western culture. The third element of globalization is that although there is a common surface flow of ideals and norms, this dominant flow will give rise to opposition and the development of alternative schools of thought, and further that when these ideas, values, norms and rules are interpreted in a local context, they will get a truly local flavor and the outcomes may not always be those that were predicted in advance.

21.2.3 Impacts of Globalization: Enrichment versus Impoverishment

From the above discussion, it is clear that there will typically be two divergent discourses on globalization. The main discourse is that globalization will lead to increased wealth and welfare for all countries and that this will trickle down to the poorest of the poor. Those who support globalization argue that reducing tariff barriers and opening national economies reduces the costs of goods and services while increasing the range of products and services available to local communities. Opening up national economies potentially brings in foreign resources and investments and leads to greater investments in countries. It also leads to increased access to technology and advances learning in general. This discourse is based on the theory of capitalism. Its supporters cite evidence of reduced inequalities in income and show how China and India are rapidly developing. They also focus on how the communication revolution has led to the development of Internet cafes and mobile telephones, which will empower the local people all over the world. This will improve the opportunities for participating in the market, leapfrogging into modern systems of technology and opening up opportunities for tourism. It will also allow for outsourcing and the creation of jobs in other parts of the world, thereby bringing prosperity to people with low incomes. Not only do Western theorists make this argument, but Asian experts also claim that globalization is a powerful tool for economic growth and countries have to seek to identify ways to unleash its potential [7]. Das [8] makes the point that liberalization will ensure that these economies will be released from the constraints that they have imposed on themselves. In the political arena, the G-8 [9] argues that: "We are determined to make globalization work for all our citizens and especially the world's poor. Drawing the poorest countries into the global economy is the surest way to address their fundamental aspirations. …The most effective poverty reduction strategy is to maintain a strong, dynamic, open and growing global economy…. We shall help developing countries promote: accountability and transparency in the public sector; legal frameworks and corporate governance regimes to fight corruption; safeguards against the misappropriation of public funds and their diversion into non-productive uses; access to legal systems for all citizens, independence of the judiciary, and legal provisions enabling private sector activity, active involvement of civil society and Non Governmental Organisations' (NGOs) freedom of economic activities."

The alternative discourse is that globalization will empower some at the cost of others. The anti-globalists show that the number of people living below $1 a day is steady and those below $2 a day is increasing. They point out that the gap between the richest and the poorest in the world is also increasing. They argue further that even though the Internet may empower some, the great Internet divide will still remain. Furthermore, countries that have greater resources can monopolize the information that is circulated via the Internet and hence can create a new divide between the English speaking universe and that outside it, leading to cultural imperialism. Khor [10] points to the fear that globalization will benefit the top layers of society but the benefits will not trickle down to the poor. De Rivero [11] submits that the development model, and the liberalization theory that it is encapsulated in, will export models that are not viable for most countries in the world. In the political arena, the G-77 [12] argues: "We note with concern that the countries of the south have not been able to share in the benefits of globalization on an equal footing with the developed countries and have been excluded from the benefits of this process. Asymmetries and imbalances have intensified in international economic relations, particularly with regard to international cooperation, even further widening the gap between the developing countries and the industrialised countries."

In many ways, Bhagwati and Mahathir Mohammed argue the same point although they emphasize different aspects. Mahathir [13] argues: "The fact that globalization has come does not mean we should just sit by and watch as the predators destroy us." Mahathir's key argument is that there is some inevitability about globalization, and that globalization can have benefits for Asian countries like Malaysia. However, he goes on to argue that the system of explicit and implicit rules that accompanies globalization is often crafted by a few countries and is designed in their favor. He argues that it is the power politics in the system that is the most frightening part of globalization. Bhagwati [7] argues that economic globalization calls for a transition in most countries. The key, in his view, is to time the transition in a manner that is appropriate to the country and the context. For those who see globalization as an expression of capitalism, only those countries that have skilled labor and capital intensive production on a large scale will succeed in this process. It is also those countries who are not vulnerable to currency speculation that may survive. It is thus those countries who can already cope with the impacts of global change that will be sustainable.

One may be tempted to conclude that those who are skeptical of the globalization process are also those who are more afraid of the potential impacts of global change in destabilizing countries, either through its direct environmental impacts or through a political process that will impose rules and regulations on these countries, constraining their economic growth [10,14]. They are afraid that globalization with its message of consuming more and more, exploiting more and more resources, and reducing subsidies and costs as far as possible, will lead to the externalization of environmental and social impacts to such an extent that the resource base and the poor people will be harmed beyond repair. The other school of thought focuses less on the negative impacts of global change and is convinced that globalization and human ingenuity will solve most problems for humans.

21.2.4 Managed Governance: Anarchy versus Rule-Based Order

Globalization is a word that encapsulates a number of different processes. Although the literature includes a vast number of definitions for the term [15,16], I prefer to refer to two pathways of globalization [17]. One is governed or managed globalization. This includes the processes of international policy and law making at the global level, or what some refer to as institutional change. The other is the process of "spontaneous" globalization. This includes the spread of the Internet and the World Wide Web, the rise of the global media, market forces and the ascension of multinationals in a world of increasing international economic integration, rapid technological progress, the knowledge economy, the spread of logistics and transport and cultural shifts.

Assuming that governance incorporates "managed" governance and "spontaneous" governance, this managed governance includes the rule-making processes within the UN. In the last few decades, the global community has seen a criss-crossing of global legislation on trade and environmental issues at bilateral through to multilateral levels. These laws increasingly provide a grid of rules and regulations that countries need to abide by.

There are two major schools of thought at the international level on the role and significance of international law and policy. According to one, we live in a global anarchy and the rules at the international level have minimal or no real significant influence on life. Realists and neo-realists are of the opinion that each country focuses on its own population and will use its power at the international level to seek conditions that are most favorable to it. They argue that international rules are at best epiphenomenal and that multilateralism is a poor tool. This is the view also of the dominant political leaders in the United States. The U.S. sees itself as the hub of the world, with spokes leading out to other countries [18]. As a result, the U.S. is declining to participate in a number of international environmental treaties, even though it is fairly active within the World Trade Organization and the Bretton Woods Institutions. The former is seen as promoting its economic interests, and in the latter the U.S. has a major say in policy making through the double majority voting systems that play a role, for instance in the World Bank. In contrast, the Europeans are moving towards a rule-based international order as a means to minimize global anarchy and as a route to achieve the Kantian dream. So these countries are not only developing a rule-based order that has extended from a handful of countries to more than 25 within the European Union, but have also moved towards pushing for international norms and rules [19].

Perhaps the difference in perspective can explain the fact that we do not have "good governance" at the international level. Good governance is participatory and democratic in nature, transparent, accountable, fair, efficient and effective, responsive and observant of the rule of law [20–25]. The rule of law includes clear and non-retroactive rules, but may also be stretched to include equity and democracy; where the former focuses on protecting the status quo, while the latter seeks to promote fairness [26–32]. It normally includes ideas like generality, publicity, non-retroactivity, clarity, consistency in design and application, stability and certainty, equity, and an independent judiciary. While increasingly the literature focuses on how most domestic problems can be attributed to poor domestic governance [33,34], at the international level, we are complacent about accepting a lack of good governance as a corollary of the fact that we live in a global anarchy. While scholars from the developing countries and sometimes Europe promote good governance at the international level [35–40] and the UN sees it as an unfinished project many other scholars argue that good governance and the rule of law are not possible because of global power politics, and because any attempt at promoting global equity will imply structural change—something Western countries are not necessarily willing to accept [36,41–43]. The legalization process, while in theory useful for developing countries as it limits the ability of the developed countries to work in an ad hoc manner, also creates problems for the developing countries, because it often not only reflects mostly the developed countries' positions as a result of power politics, but also because of the major problems faced by developing countries in the negotiating process [44].

The implication of the above is that, on the one hand, managed global governance has moved forward incrementally developing a network of rules to guide and constrain state behavior, while on the other hand the superpowers disagree about such questions as whether these rules amount to anything serious, whether multilateralism is important and whether the rule of law and good governance is necessary at international level.

21.2.5 Spontaneous Globalization: Autonomous versus Orchestrated

Apart from the forces of managed globalization, there is "spontaneous" globalization: globalization that occurs through market forces, technological advances and the rise of civil (and uncivil) society. One could argue that the so-called autonomous globalization may have both negative and positive effects. On the negative side, one can identify possibly three trends. The first is what I refer to as the tragedy of free trade. The second is the rise of vertically integrated markets and the third is a focus on some instruments promoted by civil society—namely eco and sustainability labelling [45]. There are several other trends in media, the World Wide Web and cultural shifts, but this chapter restricts itself to the first three.

While at the heart of capitalist globalization is the concept of free trade, a major challenge for the developing countries is that as long as they focus on resources such as food products there is a problem. As the quantity of food products increases, the price will fall, often to levels below what is sustainable to the farmer. Sometimes, because the price of these products is so low, the developed countries protect themselves with subsidies and tariffs in order to support their own domestic agricultural sector (e.g., the Common Agricultural Policy of the European Union). Sometimes the more differentiated food products which can command higher prices at the international market face different challenges when companies patent these crops in other countries and farmers and governments have to engage in dispute resolution in foreign courts (e.g., the disputes regarding Basmati rice in the U.S. courts). This implies that these companies have to diversify continuously and focus more on other types of products and services if they wish to compete successfully. In a previous paper I argued that hunger, a major developing country problem, is also partly the result of the "tragedies" in global governance in the areas of food aid, over-production, structural adjustment programs, free-trade, the EU's Common Agricultural Policy and the global fishing regime, intellectual property rights, and green and gene technology [45].

A related challenge is that in the international arena only the large companies with huge economies of scale are able to provide products at competitive prices. This has led to a vertical integration of markets such that the bulk of coffee, cocoa and banana crops are concentrated in the hands of a few companies. The vertical integration often implies that these big companies dictate to farmers what seeds, pesticides and herbicides they may use, and thus may increase the costs to the farmers while providing themselves low prices, since the farmer has no alternative market to sell his products to. There is increasingly less and less space for small farmers and companies to compete in a globalizing world.

Finally, in an attempt to control these companies, well-meaning civil society and non-governmental organizations are forcing these companies to adopt socially conscious practices. This is leading to a rise in voluntary codes and eco and sustainability labelling schemes as well as fair trade schemes. These are all voluntary and are developed by individual companies (and sometimes) countries. They may under limited conditions violate WTO rules, but there are ways to ensure that they don't. Nevertheless, the multiplicity of these schemes means that producers in developing countries have to meet different conditions to sell to different countries and often the conditions are either not known, or do not take the local circumstances into account. This can have a potentially devastating effect on those who wish to export to other countries [46].

One can also identify three positive trends. The comedy of technology is that jobs can move to other parts of the world without involving any physical movement of labor. Thus, outsourcing has become a major source of income in some parts of the developing world, leading, however, to a loss of income and jobs in the developed world, although no doubt the Western companies capitalize on the profits. Besides outsourcing, jobs are simply moving overseas where labor markets are much cheaper. The lack of restrictions on capital also implies that southern capital can be invested in Western land, labor, infrastructure, and technology. More recently, the attempt by Dubai, Inc. to purchase American ports raised a major debate in the U.S. about how safe this was in the post-9/11 world. The rise of the global media both Western (CNN and BBC) and also southern (Al-Jazeera), and the rise of the Internet as a source of information provide alternative perspectives on what is happening globally.

In the world of spontaneous globalization, there are problems with the lack of transparency in currency trade where speculators often wreak havoc on the economies of countries. Global media can often become the mouthpiece of a few powerful governments and spread propaganda, especially at times of security crises. This leads Herman [6,47] to argue that spontaneous globalization is engineered by corporate elites and is an attack on democracy. He argues that the project of globalization has been pushed by the rich and has been carried out behind closed doors and this has weakened democracy both directly and indirectly, since it is not a process that has been deliberated, discussed and voted on.

21.2.6   Inferences

A look at globalization from the north–south perspective shows that while some see it as an inevitable part of modernization, others perceive it as an orchestrated process to gain greater access to and control over resources; while some view it as playing an undeniable role in bringing wealth to all corners of the globe, others maintain that globalization will only benefit the few at the cost of others and will lead to relative impoverishment; while some see managed governance positively in terms of a gradual incremental process towards rule-based order globally with common but differentiated responsibilities, others see these rules as part of an anarchic process where one accepts the rules that suits one and avoids those that are not in one's interests; where so-called autonomous developments may be part of a larger plan which can both work in favor of developing countries' interests and against their interests. At this point, the picture is mixed. It would appear that globalization has both positive and negative features from a north–south perspective.

21.3   Are Resources and Environmental Space Limited?

21.3.1   Introduction

Part of the problem associated with globalization and environmental issues is the lack of clear scientific understanding about some of the key issues, especially in a north–south context. This section focuses on the development discourse and whether environmental pollution can be decoupled from economic growth and whether leap-frogging is a serious option for developing countries, the question of whether resources are limited, and how environmental space is to be shared between countries. The last section tries to integrate the key messages from this section.

21.3.2   The Goal: Development versus Sustainable Development

All countries share the goal of seeking to develop further. And yet development has become a complicated term. Are "development" and "sustainable development" in conflict with each other?

The South Commission [48] defines development as: "...growing self-reliance, both individual and collective. The base for a nation's development must be its own resources, both human and material, fully used to meet its own needs.... True development has to be people centered. It has to be directed at the fulfilment of human potential and the improvement of the social and economic well-being of the people." Others argue that the goal of development is so deeply embedded in the "sub-conscious of the political class" that they overlook the fact that "the technological revolution is making anachronistic the only two comparative advantages their countries possess, to wit abundant unskilled labor and natural resources" [11].

For some, the solution to this problem is the search for sustainable development, or development that can be sustained over a long period of time (this has then been further elaborated into a set of legal principles that can provide guidance to countries), while others see sustainable development as an overarching goal to reach for. In the north–south context, the question is does sustainable development attempt to meet the needs of all present generations before attempting to ensure that the future generations are able to meet their own needs, or does it attempt to meet future needs at the cost of current needs of those in the south?

One way to achieve sustainable development is to decouple environmental impacts from development. Dematerialization and decarbonization are the key words. The Environment Kuznet Curve theory postulates that as countries develop, they use more and more resources and they pollute more. Beyond a critical point, they may be successful in reducing their environmental impact while their economic growth continues. This results from an increased ability to invest in the environment and in environmental technology, because of a shift in society from heavy industry towards services and because of other structural changes.

At the same time, we have increasing evidence that while the Environment Kuznet's Curve does hold for certain types of local pollutants with high health impacts, where the pollutants are of a global nature (e.g., greenhouse gas emissions) there is less likelihood that countries will be willing to invest heavily to reduce these emissions because of the uncertain nature of the problem, the likelihood that the impacts will be spatially dislocated from the causes and because of the possibility of free-riders. Besides, researchers argue that Environment Kuznets Curve does not seem to exist for the total resource throughput in a society [49].

From the 1950s onward, development studies have postulated that it should be possible for developing countries to gain from the lessons learned by developed countries and to leap-frog their way to development. Leap-frogging suggests that developing countries can skip certain phases of their development process by adopting the most modern technologies and thereby avoid the pollution associated with the development process [50,51]. Leap-frogging is one of the key advantages of the late-comer to development, since it can benefit from the lessons already learned from society. Development studies over the last fifty years have suggested that technology transfer can help developing countries catch up with the West. However, the literature has also shown how difficult if not impossible it is to translate this into practice. The problems with leap-frogging are that the technologies associated are often too expensive and hence unaffordable to the poorer countries, the technologies may require a different weather, context or social environment in which they can function, and clearly there is also reluctance to transfer the latest knowledge to the south. A problem more clearly associated with the northern countries is the challenge of path dependency. The choice of a specific technology may imply a specific infrastructure. Everyone who wishes to sell something associated with this technology joins the bandwagon and the technology becomes part of the social structure. Changing such a technology once it is in place is often extremely difficult.

21.3.3 The Resource Base: Limited or Unlimited?

Resources are seen as necessary for development. Here, too, one can distinguish between two schools of thought. There is an increasing realization worldwide among certain individuals and groups that resources are limited and that there will not be enough for everyone's greed, to paraphrase Mahatma Gandhi. There is also an increasing perception that there is a limit to how much one can dispose wastes into the atmosphere and hydrosphere without having negative environmental, social and economic impacts. From Malthus [52] who projected that there would not be enough food for the growing populations, through Meadows [53] who argued that there are limits to growth, to the more recent publications of the Intergovernmental Panel on Climate Change that signal the need for action to reduce emissions of greenhouse gases and the Millennium Ecosystem Assessment that call for caution in dealing with our ecosystems, there are many who are nervous about the global and globally recurring impacts of uncontrolled extractions from the environment and unlimited waste streams that are dumped into the environment. All these, they argue, will lead to interlocking crises where environmental crises (e.g., climate change) will exacerbate other environmental crises (e.g., desertification and loss of biodiversity) and will eventually have tremendous impacts on the human economy [48]. This amounts to an increasing consciousness that we share one earth [54] with common global and globally recurring problems [55]. These include the challenge of climate change, loss of biodiversity, the hole in the ozone layer, deforestation, desertification, and many others, as well as the realizations that global society shares one hydrological and one bio-geosphere, and that our earth is not insured [56].

On the other hand, there are an equally large number of people who focus on the positive side of the equation. They argue that technologies and developments in society will ensure that there are enough natural resources for all. They argue that human ingenuity will find solutions for all the key challenges, which are not so much doom scenarios as signals that need to be taken into account. They argue that despite the litany of arguments made by the green movement, in fact, society has become much richer and more people live better and more enriching lives today than ever before [57,58]. The alternative discourse thus focuses on the fact that the science is uncertain, statistics are open to multiple interpretations and doom scenarios are unwarranted. They argue that global change will not be the main threat to humankind.

There are thus two major schools of thought—one focusing on the major negative environmental impacts on the globe and, hence, the need for action to deal with that; the other on the positive impacts of modernization and, hence, the need to cherish that and not to constrain it unduly. Both often rely on the same science and trends to make their different arguments. In layman's terms, they see the glass as, respectively, half-empty or half-full.

21.3.4 Environmental Space: Property or Human rights?

Let us then turn to the notion of global environmental space. This refers to the total amount of pollution that is possible without risking a particular common sink and implies that this space has to somehow be shared by countries, now and into the future. If we see access to resources and pollution of resources in terms of property rights, then those who access the resources first or who pollute the resources first will be the ones to have the property rights to the space. If, however, we see sharing the environmental space as something that has to be undertaken equitably and in accordance with the principles of human rights, the situation is different.

In different environmental regimes, different approaches have been taken. The regime on the depletion of the Ozone Layer, the 1986 Vienna Convention on the Protection of the Ozone Layer and the 1987 Montreal Protocol to the Vienna Convention divide responsibilities between countries by calling on all developed countries to phase out their emissions equally against a base year; and give developed countries a grace period before doing the same. When we discuss international fresh water regimes, we see that the 1997 UN Law on the non-Navigational Uses of International Watercourses, while recognizing the historical rights of countries in terms of water use (recognized in international water law as prior appropriation), still requests countries to take future needs into account and to equitably share the water resources. Under the climate change regime, we find that the adoption of the emissions trading regime in many ways legitimizes the property rights approach based on prior levels of emissions as opposed to per capita rights, thereby meeting the demands of the developed countries at the cost of the developing countries.

21.3.5 Inferences

An examination of the above section shows that from a north–south perspective there are often competing visions to be found in the literature with respect to development. While some argue that development is a prerequisite for engaging in sustainable development, others argue that unrestricted development may lead to complete destruction of the resource base. While some see resources as only being limited by human ingenuity, others argue that there is a physical limit to the resources available to humans. While some argue that environmental space is owned by those who have accessed it already, others submit that environmental space must be equitably shared between first- and late-comers. While some are highly optimistic about the potential for technological leap-frogging for developing countries, others see development as path-dependent and see this potential as quite limited.

21.4 A Brief History of North–South Issues

21.4.1 Introduction

From the discussion of development-environmental issues, we now move to north–south politics. The north–south paradigm is a creation of colonization politics. The north is a non-politically charged word for the Western countries, and the south refers to the developing countries of Asia, Africa and Latin America. Although, technically speaking, the U.S. and Australia were colonized, their historical experiences were so different from the rest of the colonized, that they are seen as part of the north. The South Commission [59] defines the developing countries of the south as: "Largely bypassed by the benefits of prosperity and progress, they exist on the periphery of the developed countries of the north. While most of the people of the north are affluent, most of the people of the south are poor; while the economies of the north are generally strong and resilient, those of the south are mostly weak and defenceless; while the countries in the north are, by and large, in control of their destinies, those of the south are very vulnerable to external factors and lacking in functional sovereignty."

21.4.2 North–South: Moot or Passé?

Before moving ahead, it may be useful to reflect on whether north–south issues are passé. While many argue that these divisions are out of date [60–62], there are many others who submit that efforts to dismantle the concept in scientific and political fields are part of the strategy to undermine the legitimate efforts of the vast majority of developing countries to get a level playing field (irrespective of whether a few of these countries can climb out of the poverty gap) [55,59,61,63–65]. For many of these authors, efforts to delegitimize the concept of the south/third world would imply that the UN "is absolved from its task of challenge, dissent and leadership, and like the Bretton Woods institutions, acts or should act in defence of the global *status quo*" [63]. In this context, Chimni [6] makes the point that globalization through its impacts on international law and institutions may in fact lead to a new process of recolonization where, through a regime of property rights, the developed countries gain control over resources and through the argument that most domestic problems in developing countries are attributed to poor governance, they gain the right to interfere in domestic politics. He thus calls for a Third World Approach to International Law (and Relations) to promote transparency of international institutions, accountability of transnational corporations, the sovereignty of peoples (not states), the effective use of the language of rights, the interests of peoples, monetary sovereignty, sustainable development and equity, and the mobility of humans. In the meantime, developing countries waver between two competing strategies—the realpolitik strategy, which argues that since the developing countries have less power than the developed countries, each should try and get as much out of the system as it can, and the counter-realpolitik strategy, which is to work together for a better and more equitable future [66].

21.4.3   UN Politics: Development versus Environment

With the establishment of the United Nations and the common expressed goal of the international community to foster economic and social prosperity world-wide, it became necessary to help the developing countries engage more effectively in the UN discussions, especially given the wide disparity in the interests of the developed and developing countries. This led to the establishment of the G-77 and China in 1964 as a caucus to help developing countries negotiate at international level. The G-77 has grown from its original 77 members to more than 130 members today. Their initial goal was to promote the New International Economic Order (NIEO), based on their shared vision of developmental problems and their common position on how trade should take place and also because they believed that "The injustice and neglect of centuries need to be redressed" [67]. Although the NIEO instruments were successfully negotiated at the international level, these were never implemented, and it is argued today that development issues have been neglected in the international arena compared to other issues such as environmental problems [68–71]. The G-77 [12] submits that "international cooperation for development has been downplayed on the agenda of the international community." As Hurrell [72] puts it: "First, the centrality and complexity of the normative dimension has been neglected or downplayed; above all in terms of the importance of a shared sense of community in understanding how the cooperative enterprise can get off the ground, and in terms of reviewing ethics as intrinsic to the process by which order is produced."

For many in the G-77, the last forty-two years have been a struggle for equitable treatment at the international level [63,66,73] especially since the gap between developed and developing countries has increased and globalization is perceived to exacerbate the gap between the rich and the poor, even as some benefits of globalization may trickle down to the poorest of the poor.

21.4.4   G-77 Power: Ebb and Flow

The north–south struggle is most evident in the fields of international trade, investment, and environmental issues. The south shares a common colonial history (barring some countries), a shared geography, clustered mostly south of the north (with the exception of Australia and New Zealand), deeply rooted cultural traditions, unstable political structures and weak institutional frame-works; its nations have not yet resolved the basic needs of their people, are mostly not on the cutting edge with respect to science and technology, and are frequently rich in biodiversity but at the same time often short of access to food and water. However, one can argue that the power of the G-77 has changed over time. Possibly three historical phases can be distinguished [74]. In the first phase of tripartite politics (1945–1990), we had three worlds—the first, second and third world. Since there was intense competition between the first and second world for control over the third world, the developing countries could occasionally play one world against the other. In the second phase of north–south politics (1990–2001), the second world dissolved, with some of its members being invited to join the first world and the rest by default becoming part of the third world. The developing countries could no longer play one group against the other and in fact had strong competition for foreign funding from the former Eastern Bloc countries. In the third phase (2001-) we have one superpower that often makes its own decisions irrespective of the multilateral politics promoted by the UN. This creates a much more confusing world order for the developing countries to function in. One could postulate that given the current economic prosperity in China and India, the next phase of global politics will take a much more complicated turn. We may move into a new world of superpowers, but with a major difference.

21.4.5 The Emerging Powers: Friend or Foe

Since the year 2000, there has been rapid economic growth in China and India. If this rate of growth continues, then these countries may have more economic and military power than many countries of the developed world, even while large proportions of their population still live in poverty. By their productive and consumptive power they will become a major force in environmental politics, and this too is a critical reason to be careful about how policies should develop in the future. Where major powers today try to evade the multilateral arena and seek to join global policymaking processes on an ad hoc basis, this might send a message to these countries that it is also legitimate for them to opportunistically participate in global policymaking, when it suits their needs. If indeed such a message is going out, as I suspect, and if indeed such a message is being received by the new emerging powers, environmental problems are unlikely to be urgently addressed in the coming years.

21.4.6 Inferences

I have argued that the north–south paradigm is a creation of colonization politics, and the ideological reaction to colonization shapes and colors much of the thinking from a north–south perspective. I have submitted that some argue that the differences between the developing countries are so great that the north–south classification is out of date, while others contend that whatever the internal differences may be and despite the fact that some developing countries have escaped the poverty trap, much of the experiences are shared and in many ways the south continues to exist by virtue of a much better defined north. The section shows that the power of the south has gone down since the end of the Cold War, and that this influences its ability to engage effectively in the international process. What the South Commission [59] stated in 1990 is still valid today: "The issue for the south is not whether to cut its links with the north, but how to transform them. The relationship must be changed from exploitation to shared benefit, from subordination to partnership." Although there are few powerful southern countries, it is still not clear whether these countries will be friend or foe in the effort to move towards sustainable global governance.

21.5   North–South Problems in Global Governance

21.5.1   Introduction

Within the context of globalization, juxtaposed against the history of north–south relations and the competing visions on how sustainable development is to be achieved by the countries of the world, this section looks at some of the north–south challenges with respect to environmental governance. It first examines the question of which issues are scaled up and what the implications of that are for north–south relations; next, it examines the dilemmas facing both developed and developing countries with respect to environmental issues; then it looks at the negotiation challenges faced, in particular, by the developing countries; finally, it briefly analyzes some of the negotiation outcomes of international negotiations.

21.5.2   Problem Definition: Scaling Up to Gain Control; Scaling Down to Avoid Responsibility

How a problem is defined is critical for ensuring that it is addressed. While some would be tempted to argue that there are scientific justifications for arguing that noise is a local problem, desertification a regional problem and climate change a global problem [75,76], others may reject this out of hand by arguing that if one were to develop a set of criteria for assessing whether a problem is local or global, and systematically apply these criteria to different environmental problems, one can see that in most cases the scale of the problem is socially constructed [55]. Following the determination by the United Nations Conference on Environment and Development that there were 40 areas of work for the international community, the decision of the Global Environment Facility to work on only four global areas led to a major reaction in the developing world; there, it was argued that only when problems were relevant to the developed world, were they defined as global [71,77].

A literature review reveals that negotiators and scientists are motivated to scale up an issue because they can take account of the externalities or indirect causes of a problem, want to focus attention on local health and welfare problems, wish to avoid a race to the bottom, wish to make domestic policies more cost-effective (or prevent the loss of competitiveness of domestic industry),or wish to create a level playing field, politically speaking, in order to enhance the power of less powerful countries. However, there may also be less benign reasons for scaling up a problem: it helps to postpone decision making, might help to pressure other national entities in the home country; or may help to gain access to resources in another part of the world (even though it might imply a loss of control over natural resources). A problem may be scaled down to enhance effectiveness, on the one hand, and to divide and rule on the other hand. To try to actually identify the appropriate scale of a problem and, hence, its solution, appears to be a scientifically challenging task [78].

21.5.3   Dilemmas: To Do or Not to Do

In the area of environment and development, developing and developed countries are aware of the problems, but they face a number of dilemmas [79]. Southern dilemmas include how to modernize without westernizing, where they want to emulate the West and at the same time see the Western lifestyle as a source of most environmental problems. This dilemma is most visible in UN discussions. A second dilemma is the challenge of surviving without squandering resources: cutting down the last tree, mining in forested areas, or "allowing" species to be traded in an effort to survive. This influences developing country positions in treaties on trade in endangered species and hazardous wastes. A third dilemma is begging for help without mortgaging resources, where countries seek financial assistance from the north but may through such assistance lose control over their land and natural resources. Such may be the case where private sector participation or foreign banks and agencies are invited in the natural resource sector as a result of international negotiation. A fourth dilemma is finding how best to empower the private sector to address public problems. One of the dominant internationally promoted solutions to the problem of lack of government funding in developing countries is to encourage the private sector to invest. While the private sector has the money, it will only engage where there are returns on the investment. But if there were returns on the investment, the government could have itself raised funding. Leaving aside for a moment the issue of corruption, the problem is that much of government work in developing countries focuses on services to the poor and cash strapped. Will the private sector be willing to take on this task? A fifth dilemma for these countries is how one can demand equity at the international level, when increasingly domestic equity discussions are heading nowhere. A sixth dilemma is how does one meet short-term economic interests without compromising long-term interests. A seventh dilemma is how does one unite the G-77 without falling to the highest of the lowest common positions? These dilemmas make it very difficult for these countries to effectively develop a good substantive position.

However, there are no easy solutions in the north. It, too, has dilemmas [80]. The first dilemma is whether it should act now or later, especially on issues like climate change where postponing decisions may seem like a cheaper and politically more feasible option in the short-term. A second dilemma is how does one transform society without sacrificing growth. While the theory of the inverted U curve and the potential for decarbonization and dematerialization exist on paper, the fear is whether restructuring society towards these goals is possible partly because of the path-dependency of many technologies in society and partly because of the huge costs restructuring will bring with it for vested interests. A third dilemma is how to spend resources without squandering them. Phasing out technologies and infrastructures (e.g., fossil fuel plants) that are still within their useful life-span is an unnecessary waste of resources. A fourth dilemma for the developed countries is how they should assist the developing countries without being seen to be compensating the latter and while still being accountable to national parliaments and their equivalent. A fifth dilemma is how Western governments can enhance the role of the private sector while still having some vestige of control over it and being able to influence the direction in which the private sector moves society [72]. A final dilemma is how to both solve problems at the international level without giving up on national interests. This, in fact, is a critical issue. Most developed countries are indeed motivated to solve problems and that is why they scale these up to the global level in the first place. And yet having done so, their hands are tied in the negotiations, as the room for negotiating is limited to national interests. For example, instead of focusing on when climate change becomes dangerous for the earth, countries are motivated to identify when climate change becomes a risk for them [81].

21.5.4   Negotiation Challenges

Apart from the dilemmas discussed above, countries face very specific challenges in the negotiating arenas. Although I will present primarily the challenges that face developing countries, clearly some of the poorer of the more developed countries have similar problems. In a number of environmental areas where negotiations have been stimulated by Western countries, developing countries have a hollow negotiating mandate at the national level—because of relatively low relevant scientific input, because the issue has not been extensively debated by domestic actors at the national level, and because ministers are unable to prioritize the issue. Because of the problems of coordinating with other countries as a result of limited resources (including often inadequate computer and Internet connections), developing a good common negotiating position between negotiating sessions becomes difficult. This often leads to a threadbare rhetorical common negotiating position. Then within the negotiating arena, since complex negotiations are often split into several negotiating groups where the UN translation rules do not operate, it becomes very difficult for the two-member team from an average developing country to participate effectively in these negotiations; especially as the preparatory processes for some treaties (e.g., climate change) can take up more than 100 days in a year. These difficulties compound the existing imbalance in power between the north and south.

21.5.5   Negotiation Outcomes

It is then not surprising that negotiation outcomes are both seen to favor the south as well as to marginalize its interests. Those who point to how the negotiations favor the south focus on the lack of quantitative restrictions on the south (e.g., on climate change) or the implementation of common but differentiated responsibilities which give room to the south to grow, or to the fact that the very inability of the south to come to a common position implies that no responsibilities can be carved out for them. Others argue that negotiation outcomes have not benefited the south, either because of the way an item was included in a treaty text or because of the way it was defined.

21.5.6 Inferences

The above section has argued that within the context of a globalizing world, where there is considerable difference of opinion in the scientific community, power politics operates through four mechanisms to frame issues in favor of the developed countries. The first is through the way problems are scaled up and down, the second is by virtue of the dilemmas that exist in both developed and developing countries, the third involves the practical difficulties in engaging effectively in the negotiations, and the fourth is because of the outcome of the negotiations.

21.6 Conclusion

This chapter has examined globalization, environmental challenges and north–south issues. It dealt with each of these concepts separately and attempted to link the different ideas together. Historically, there have been reasons for north–south friction arising from a colonial past. Although only a few of the Northern countries are the former colonizers, the colonization discourse has spread to affect much of north–south relations today. The centuries of colonization have cast a long shadow over the future, especially as in the post-World War II world the south has repeatedly pushed the development agenda, while the north has avoided this agenda and instead pushed the environment agenda. Against this background, this chapter has argued that although there are efforts in the theoretical and political world to see the north–south division as residing in the past, in the south, this division is seen as a very vital challenge, one that has to be confronted if global problems are to be addressed. As the power of the south continues to decline in a post-Perestroika world, the south seeks to reorganize itself as much as possible.

It is in this context that the environment and development issues become so complex. For some, development is absolutely essential before sustainable development becomes possible, while for others, the whole development concept is flawed and does not allow countries to think out of the box, while for still others, sustainable development itself is an illusion. Where the discussion is simplified into a technical discussion about whether one can decouple environmental problems from economic growth, there is increasing evidence that this may be the case where the pollutants and their impacts are local. But where the pollutants are local but the impacts dislocated from the original source, such decoupling is not easy or automatic; and every decoupling is followed by coupling as human demands increase. This chapter has also argued that there are two ideal typical schools of thought on the resource base; while one argues that in the ultimate analysis resources are limited, the other contends that the only limits that exist are those of human ingenuity. Finally, the environment versus development discussion was presented in the context of the environmental space discussion—whether such space should be shared according to existing use or "property rights" gained from appropriation, or whether such space should be shared according to human rights and equity principles. Clearly, the south would argue in favor of development before sustainable development (with a few intellectual dissenters), of the right to exploit its resource base and for equitable access to environmental space—and therein lies the north–south struggle. Introduce into this scenario the rapid process of globalization set in motion in the last decade or two and we can see the proponents of globalization see both the official processes and the autonomous processes as promoting the single surviving ideology after the end of history—capitalism and liberalism—to the world as the only way of enriching the globe, reducing the disparities between north and south while others see globalization in both its formal and informal forms as modifying but not reducing the divide, as a reincarnation of the processes of colonialism, as a process by which development in the south will be blocked through environmental legislation while doors will be opened for foreign investors to enter into the country. That this itself may imply an unintended contradiction has yet to be seen.

When one then moves to the governance arena, we see that the way problems are defined in order to put them on the international agenda are politically constructed. Once these items reach the global agenda, countries, whether rich or poor, face a number of dilemmas as to how they should deal with the inherent complexity of the environment and development debate. These dilemmas make the international negotiating process even more complicated, adding to the existing difficulties of multilateral negotiations involving more than 190 countries and the reluctant participation of one superpower. Add to that the nitty–gritty challenges facing the negotiators, in particular those from developing countries, and it is no wonder that developing country negotiators often feel extremely dissatisfied with the negotiation outcomes at the UN arena. Given that they have very little control over the autonomous process of globalization, it is no surprise that the G-77 is skeptical of the whole process and its ability to deliver in achieving solutions for the global development and environmental problems. In the years to come, the surprise factor will involve China and India and how they will perceive their role in a world of changing economic power.

Acknowledgments

This paper has been written in the context of the project—the VIDI project on Inter-governmental and private environmental regimes and compatibility with good governance, rule of law and sustainable development—financed by the Netherlands Scientific Organisation.

References

1. UN Charter, Charter of the United Nations, (San Francisco) 26 June 1945, and amended on 17 December 1963, 20 December 1965 and 20 December 1971, ICJ Acts and Documents No. 4, 1945.
2. Wallerstein, I., *Utopistics: Or, Historical Choices of the Twenty-First Century*, The New Press, New York, 1998.

3. Meyer, J.W., The World Polity and the Authority of the Nation-State, in *Studies of the Modern World-System*, A. Bergesen, Ed., Academic Press, New York, 1980, 109–137.
4. Meyer, J.W., Boli, J., Thomas, G.M., and Ramirez, F.O., World society and the nation-state, *American Journal of Sociology*, 103, 144, 1997.
5. Robertson, R., *Globalization: Social Theory and Global Culture*, Sage, London, 1992.
6. Chimni, B.S., Third world approaches to international law: A manifesto, in *The Third World and International Order: Law, Politics and Globalisation*, A. Anghie, B.S. Chimni, K. Nickelson, and O. Okafor, Eds., Koninklijke Brill nv, Leiden, 2003, 47–73.
7. Bhagwati, J., *In Defense of Globalization*, Oxford University Press, Oxford, 2004.
8. Das, G. *India Unbound the Social and Economic Revolution from Independence to the Global Information Age*, Anchor Books, New York, 2002.
9. G-8, The Final Official Notice, G-8, Genoa, 2001.
10. Khor, M., *Rethinking Globalization: Critical Issues and Policy Choices*, Zed Books, New York, 2001.
11. De Rivero, O., *The Myth of Development*, Zed Books, New York, 2001.
12. G-77, 2000, *Declaration of the South Summit*, Available at: http://www.g77.org/Docs/Declaration_G77summit.htm.
13. Mohammed, M., *Globalisation and the New Realities*, Pelanduk Publications, Selangor Darul Ehsan, 2002.
14. Alvis, A de, Sri Lanka: Its Industry and Challenges in the Face of Climate Change, in *Climate Change: Five Years After Kyoto*, V.I. Grover, Ed., Science Publishers, Plymouth, 2004, 377–396.
15. Junne, G., International Organisations in a Period of Globalisation: New (Problems of) Legitimacy, in *The Legitimacy of International Organizations*, J-M Coicaud and V. Heiskanen, Eds., United Nations University Press, Tokyo, 2001.
16. Nijkamp, P. and Verbruggen, H., Global trends and climate change policies, in *Issues in International Climate Policy: Theory and Policy*, E. Van Ierland, J. Gupta, and M. Kok, Eds., Edward Elgar Publishers, Cheltenham, 2003, 59–74.
17. Gupta, J., The Role of Non-State Actors in International Environmental Affairs, *Heidelberg Journal of International Law*, 63, 459, 2003.
18. Payne, A., Globalisation and modes of regionalist governance, in *Transformation Reader: An Introduction to the Globalization Debate*, D. Held and A. McGrew, Eds., Polity Press, Cambridge, MA, 2000, 217–219.
19. Kagan, R., *Of Paradise and Power: America and Europe in the New World Order*, Vintage Books, New York, 2004.
20. Doornbos, M., Good governance: The rise and decline of a policy metaphor?, *The Journal of Development Studies*, 37, 93, 2001.
21. Seif El-Dawla, A., Good Governance after September 11th 2001: A new dimension for international development cooperation, *Griffin's View*, 3, 15, 2002.
22. Botchway, F.N., Good Governance: the old, the new, the principle, and the elements, *Florida Journal of International Law*, 13, 159, 2001.
23. UNDP, Governance for Sustainable Human Development, 1997, Available at: http://magnet.undp.org/policy/chapter1.htm (accessed on May 18, 2006).
24. Ginther, K. and De Waart, P.J.I.M., Sustainable development as a matter of good governance: An Introductory View, in *Sustainable Development and Good Governance*, K. Ginther, E. Denters, and P.J.I.M. De Waart, Eds., Kluwer Academic Publishers, Dordrecht, 1995, 1–14.
25. Woods, N., Good governance in international organizations, *Global Governance*, 5, 39, 1999
26. Craig, P., Formal and substantive conceptions of the rule of law: An analytical framework, *Public Law*, 467, 1997.
27. Hager, B., *The Rule of Law, A Lexicon for Policy Makers*, The Mamsfield Center for Pacific Affairs, Mamsfield, 2000.

28. Fuller, L.L., *Morality of Law*, Yale University Press, New Haven, CT, 1964.
29. Esquith, S.L., Toward a democratic rule of law: East and west, *Political Theory*, 27, 334, 1999.
30. Neumann, F.L., The change in the function of law in modern society, in *The Rule of Law Under Siege*, W.E. Scheuerman, Ed., University of California Press, Berkley, 1996.
31. Reynolds, N.B., Grounding the rule of law, *En Ratio Iuris*, 2, 1, 1989.
32. Dworkin, R., *A Matter of Principle*, Harvard University Press, Cambridge, MA, 1985.
33. Santiso, C., Good governance and aid effectiveness: The world bank and conditionality, *The Georgetown Public Policy Review*, 7, 1, 2001.
34. Carothers, T., The rule of law revival, *Foreign Affairs*, 77, 95, 1998.
35. Kwaka, E., The rule of law and global governance in the twenty-first century, in *Proceedings of the 6th Annual Conference of the African Society of Internationa And Comparative Law*, Kampala, Ed., 1994, 3.
36. Watts, A., The international rule of law, *German Yearbook of International Law*, 36, 15, 1993.
37. Tsagourias, N., Globalization, order and the rule of law, *Finnish Yearbook of International Law*, Kluwer Law International, New York, 2002, 247.
38. Henkin, L., International organization and the rule of law, *International Organization*, 23, 656, 1969.
39. Correll, H., The visible college of international law: Towards the rule of law in international relations, *American Society of International Law, Proceedings*, 95, 262, 2001.
40. Kohona, P., The international rule of law and the role of the United Nations, *The International Lawyer*, 36, 1131, 2002.
41. Baum, R., Modernization and legal reform in post-Mao China: The re-birth of socialist legality, *Studies in Comparative Communism*, 14, 69, 1986.
42. Koskenniemi, M., The politics of international law, *European Journal of International Law*, 11, 4, 1990.
43. Franck, T.M., *Fairness in International Law and Institutions*, Oxford University Press, Oxford, 1995.
44. Gupta, J., The climate convention: Can a divided world unite?, in *Managing the Earth: The Eleventh Linacre Lectures*, J. Briden and E.D. Thomas, Eds., Oxford University Press, Oxford, 2002, 129–156.
45. Gupta, J., Global sustainable food governance and hunger: Traps and tragedies, *British Food Journal*, 5, 406, 2004.
46. Campins-Eritja, M. and Gupta, J., Non-State actors and sustainability labelling schemes: Implications for international law, *Non-State Actors and International Law*, 2, 213, 2002.
47. Herman, E.S., The Threat of Globalization, *New Politics*, 1999, 7, 1999.
48. World Commission on Environment and Development, *Our Common Future, The World Commission on Environment and Development*, Oxford University Press, Oxford, 1987.
49. Spangenberg, J.H., The environment Kuznets curve: A methodological artefact, *Population and Environment*, 23, 175, 2001.
50. SWCC, Scientific Declaration of the Second World Climate Conference, Geneva, 1990.
51. Goldemberg, J., Leapfrog energy technologies, *Energy Policy*, 26, 729, 2000. Goldemberg, J., Group of 77 South Summit, Declaration of the South Summit, Havana, 10–14 April 2000.
52. Malthus, T.R., An essay on the principle of population: or A view of its past and present effects on human happiness: with an inquiry into our prospects respecting the future removal or mitigation of the evils which it occasions, Cambridge University Press, Cambridge, MA, 1994.

53. Meadows, D.L., *The Limits to Growth, Report to the Club of Rome*, Spectrum, Utrecht, 1972.

54. FOE. *Only One Earth, an Introduction to the Politics of Survival*, Earth Island Limited, London, 1972.

55. Commission on Developing Countries and Global Change, *For Earth's Sake: A Report from the Commission on Developing Countries and Global Change*, International Development Research Centre, Ottawa, 1992.

56. Vellinga, P., *De aarde is niet verzekerd, Inaugural Lecture*, Vrije Universiteit Amsterdam, 1992.

57. Herrera, A.O., Chichilnisky, G., Gallopin, G.C., Hardoy, J.E., Mosovich, D., Oteiza, E., de Romero Brest, G.L., Scolnik, H.D., Suárez, C.E., and Talavera, L., *The Bariloche Report for the Club of Rome*, Utrecht University Press, Spectrum, 1978.

58. Lomborg, B., *Sceptical Environmentalist: Measuring the Real State of the Environment*, Cambridge University Press, Cambridge, MA, 2001.

59. South Commission, *The Challenge to the South: The Report of the South Commission*, Oxford University Press, Oxford, 1990.

60. UN Secretary General's Report 1998.

61. Toye, J., Is the third world still there? in *The developing World: An Introduction to Development Studies Through Selected Readings*, A. Farmar, Ed., Development Education Support Centre, Dublin, 1988.

62. Benedick, R.E., Perspectives of a negotiation practioner, in *International Environment Negotiation*, G. Sjostedt, Ed., IIASA, Austria, 1993, 219–243.

63. South Centre, A Commentary on 'Renewing the United Nations: A Programme for Reform, A Policy Brief Prepared by the South Centre at the Request of the Group of 77, 1999, Available at: http://www.g77.org/Docs/policy%20brief.htm (accessed on May 18, 2006).

64. Ramphal, S., South–south: Parameters and pre-conditions, in *South–South Strategy*, G. Atlaf, Ed., Third World Foundation, London, 1983, 17–23.

65. Minowitz, P.I., Machiavellianism come of age? Leo strauss on modernity and economics, *Political Science Reviewer*, XXII, 157, 1993.

66. Gupta, J., *The Climate Change Convention and Developing Countries—from Conflict to Consensus?* Environment and Policy Series, Kluwer Academic Publishers, Dordrecht, 1997, 256.

67. G-77, Joint Declaration of the Seventy-Seven Developing Countries Made at the Conclusion of the United Nations Conference on Trade and Development in 1964, Available at: http://www.g77.org/Docs/Joint%Declaration.html (May 18, 2006).

68. Fuentes, X., International law-making in the field of sustainable development: The unequal competition between development and the environment, *International Environmental Agreements: Politics, Law and Economics*, 2, 109, 2002.

69. Garcia-Amador, F.V., *International Law of Development: A New Dimension of International Economic Law*, Oceana Publications, New York, 1990.

70. Roberts, A. and Kingsbury, B., Introduction: The UN's roles in international society since 1945, in *United Nations, Divided World: The UN in International Relations*, A. Roberts and B. Kingsbury, Eds., Clarendon Press, Oxford, 1993, 1–63.

71. Chatterjee, P. and Finger, M., *The Earth Brokers*, Routledge, London, 1994.

72. Hurrell, A., International society and the study of regimes: A reflective approach, in *International Rules: Approaches from International Law and International Relations*, R.J. Beck, A.C. Arends, and R.D.V. Lugt, Eds., Oxford University Press, Oxford, 1996, 206–226.

73. G-77, Ministerial Declaration, Declaration of the Twenty-Sixth Annual Ministerial Meeting of the G-77, 2002, Available at: http://www.g77.org/Docs/Decl2002.html (accessed on May 18, 2006).

74. Gupta, J., Engaging developing countries in climate change: KISS and make-up, in *Climate Policy for the 21st Century: Meeting the Long-Term Challenge of Global Warming*, M. David, Ed., in *Centre for Transatlantic Relations*, Johns Hopkins University, Washington, DC, 2003, 233–264.

75. RIVM. *Concern for Tomorrow: A National Environmental Survey 1985–2010*, RIVM, Bilthoven, 1990.

76. GEF, *GEF Brochure*, World Bank, UNDP and UNEP, GEF Secretariat, Washington, DC, 1991.

77. Gupta, J., The global environment facility in its north–south context, *Environmental Politics*, 4, 19, 1995.

78. Gupta, J. and Huitema, D., Eds., *The theory of Scale in Multi-level Environmental Governance*, as one of the three books expected from the IHDP/IDGEC project.

79. Gupta, J., Environment and development: Towards a fair distribution of burdens and benefits, in *Ontwikkelingsproblematiek: The Winner Takes It All?* J.J.F. Heins and G.D. Thijs, Eds. in *Verdelings Vraagstukken in de Wereld, Themabundel Ontwikkelingsproblematiek Nr. 12*, Vrije Universiteit Amsterdam Press, Amsterdam, 2002, 35–50.

80. Gupta, J. and Tol, R., Why reduce greenhouse gas emissions? reasons, issue-linkages and dilemmas, in *Issues in International Climate Policy: Theory and Policy*, E. Ierland, J. Gupta, and M. Kok, Eds., Edward Elgar Publishers, Cheltenham Glos, 2003, 17–38.

81. Gupta, J. and van Asselt, H., Helping Operationalise Article 2: A Transdiciplinary methodological tool for evaluating when climate change is dangerous, *Global Environmental Change*, 16, 83, 2006, Available at: http://authors.elsevier.com/sd/article/S0959378005000762 (accessed on May 18, 2006).

Chapter 22

Environmental Justice: a Global Perspective

Celeste Murphy-Greene
Old Dominion University

22.1   Introduction

The environmental justice movement began in earnest in the United States (U.S.) in the 1980s. This movement began as a grassroots effort to address the issue of toxic waste disposal in poor and minority communities. The environmental justice movement shares aspects of both the social justice and environmental movements [1]. Often the term environmental justice is used interchangeably with the terms environmental racism and environmental equity. Although these terms sound alike, each has its own specific meaning. Environmental racism refers to any policy, proactive or directive, intentional or not, that differentially affects the environment of individuals, groups or communities based on their race [1,2]. The term environmental equity holds that all populations should bear a proportionate share of environmental pollution and health risks. Environmental justice is a broader term that encompasses both of these concepts and implies that laws must be applied with fairness and impartiality regardless of socio-economic differences, race, income, or geographic location. Therefore, environmental justice is defined as the achievement of equal protection from environmental and health hazards for all people regardless of race, income, culture, or social class.

Environmental justice refers to the distribution of environmental risks across population groups, as well as the policy responses to these distributions. The four main areas of environmental justice focus upon: (1) the distribution of environmental hazards; (2) the distribution of the effects of environmental problems; (3) the policy making process; and (4) the administration of environmental protection programs. By focusing on these four areas, one can more easily examine and understand the issue of environmental justice, and as a result, develop strategic methods for addressing the issue. At the federal level, the U.S. Environmental Protection Agency (EPA) has taken the lead in the environmental justice movement by developing formal goals. These goals are:

> No segment of the population, regardless of race, color, national origin, or income, as a result of EPA's policies, programs, and activities, suffers disproportionately from adverse human health or environmental effects, and all people live in clean, healthy, and sustainable communities.
> Those who live with environmental decisions—community residents, State, Tribal, and local governments, environmental groups, businesses—must have every opportunity for public participation in the making of those decisions. An informed and involved community is a necessary and integral part of the process to protect the environment [3].

While the majority of the literature on environmental justice focuses on issues in the U.S., recently more attention has been given to environmental justice issues around the world. The focus of this chapter is environmental justice from a global perspective. First, a chronological history of the development of the environmental justice movement will be provided. Next, a review of the recent environmental justice literature will be presented. The chapter will then focus specifically on global environmental justice issues.

22.2 Literature Review

22.2.1 Chronological History of the Environmental Justice Movement in the United States

The first concerns about environmental justice were raised in 1971 when the Council on Environmental Quality published its annual report acknowledging that racial discrimination adversely affects urban poor and the quality of their environment [4]. This was one year after the EPA was created, the National Environmental Policy Act was passed by Congress, and the first Earth Day had been celebrated [5].

The next major event in the environmental justice movement was Bullard's 1979 study of an affluent African American community's attempt to block the siting of a sanitary landfill [4]. In 1982, the environmental justice movement truly gained recognition when the residents of predominantly black Warren County, North Carolina protested against the siting of a polychlorinated biphenyl landfill in their county [4–7]. The protest in Warren County set off a chain of protests in the community, similar to the demonstrations of the 1960s Civil Rights Movement. These protests led to an investigation by the General Accounting Office of the socioeconomic and racial composition of communities surrounding the four major hazardous landfills in the southern region (U.S. EPA Region 4) of the U.S., which included the states of Mississippi, Alabama, Georgia, South Carolina, North Carolina, Kentucky and Florida [8]. The authors of the GAO study found that in 1983 three of the four landfills were located in predominantly black neighborhoods.

In 1987, the United Church of Christ followed the Warren County protests with a study in which patterns associated with commercial hazardous waste facilities and uncontrolled toxic waste sites were examined [9–12]. The study found that when examining the demographic characteristics of communities with commercial hazardous waste facilities:

> Race proved to be the most significant among variables tested in association with the location of commercial hazardous waste facilities. This represented a consistent national pattern;
>
> Communities with the greatest number of commercial hazardous waste facilities had the highest composition of racial and ethnic residents. In communities with two or more facilities or one of the nation's five largest landfills, the average minority percentage of the population was more than three times that of communities without facilities (38 % vs. 12 %);
>
> In communities with one commercial hazardous waste facility, the average minority percentage of the population was twice the average minority percentage of the population in communities without such facilities (24 % vs. 12 %) [12].

In addition to the above findings, the report illustrated that three out of the five largest commercial hazardous waste landfills in the U.S. were located in predominantly black or Hispanic communities. These three landfills accounted for 40% of the total estimated commercial landfill capacity in the nation [12]. It was concluded that the distribution of commercial hazardous waste facilities located in minority communities fits the pattern found in the South. In addition, in the study it was found that race was the single best predictor of where commercial hazardous waste facilities were located, even when other socio-economic characteristics such as average household income were taken into account.

22.2.2 *Environmental Justice Received National Recognition*

Following the report by the United Church of Christ, three other major events in the environmental justice movement took place in 1990. First, Bullard published his book, *Dumping in Dixie* [13], considered by many as the first textbook on environmental justice. In his book, Bullard chastised the federal government for the "urban apartheid" which exists in the U.S. Bullard blamed all levels of government for institutional racism and discriminatory land-use policies and practices due to their influence on the creation and perpetuation of racially separate and unequal residential areas for blacks and whites. He also asserted that the push for environmental justice was an extension of the Civil Rights Movement of the 1960s. Two other important arguments of Bullard's book revealed that environmental discrimination is easier to document empirically than to prove in a court of law, and that Florida was one of the three states in the U.S. known for not having strong pollution prevention and environmental programs.

Also in 1990, the University of Michigan School of Natural Resources hosted a working conference of national scope called the Conference on Race and the Incidence of Environmental Hazards. The conference focused on the identification of further research towards understanding the environmental risks faced by minority and low-income communities and pointed out that the data on environmental injustices had been available for over two decades [14]. The recommendations of the conference were summarized in a report and are as follows: (1) racial and socioeconomic equity considerations must be included in Regulatory Impact Assessments; (2) the ability of historically black colleges and universities and other minority institutions must be enhanced to encourage participation and contribution in the development of environmental equity; (3) an effort must be made to appoint special assistants for environmental equity at decision-making levels within the EPA; and (4) a policy statement on environmental equity must be developed.

As a result of the Michigan conference, then EPA Administrator William Reilly created the Environmental Equity Workgroup in March of 1990. The Workgroup focused on three tasks which were to: (1) review and evaluate the evidence that racial minority and low-income people bear a disproportionate risk and burden of environmental pollution and hazards; (2) review current EPA programs to identify factors that might give rise to different risk reduction and develop approaches to correct such problems; and (3) review institutional relationships, including outreach to and consultation with racial minority and low-income organizations, to assure that the EPA was fulfilling its mission with respect to these populations.

In 1992, the EPA released the report titled *Environmental Equity: Reducing Risk for All Communities* [6]. The term environmental equity was the former term used by the EPA to describe environmental justice. This report highlighted how the issue of environmental equity may be approached from several different perspectives, examining factors such as region, ethnic/racial group, type of pollutant and type of illness caused as a result of exposure to pollutants.

The next major event in the environmental justice movement was the publication of a 1992 *National Law Journal* article which demonstrated that there were major inequities in the way the U.S. EPA enforced its laws [11,15]. The authors argued that there was a racial divide in the way the U.S. government cleaned up toxic waste sites and punished polluters. The authors stated that white communities see faster action, better results, and stiffer penalties than communities where blacks, Hispanics, and other minorities live [15]. Due to the heightened publicity the environmental justice movement received, from the aforementioned publications, the Office of Environmental Equity was established at the EPA in 1992 [3,16]. The name was later changed to the Office of Environmental Justice (OEJ).

The establishment of the OEJ by the U.S. EPA gave the environmental justice movement increased credibility and legitimacy. Because of the creation of the OEJ in EPA, the Agency Administrator, Carol Browner, made environmental justice an agency priority in 1993 [3]. In addition to the establishment of the OEJ in 1993, the EPA also established the National Environmental Justice Advisory Council (NEJAC). The NEJAC is a federal advisory committee that was established by charter on September 30, 1993, to provide independent advice, consultation, and recommendations to the Administrator of the U.S. EPA on matters related to environmental justice [17].

22.2.3 President Clinton Formally Addressed Environmental Justice

President Clinton issued Executive Order 12898, titled *Federal Actions to Address Environmental Justice in Minority Populations and Low-Income Populations*, on February 11, 1994 [18]. The Executive Order designated eleven federal agencies to be accountable for environmental justice. The Executive Order stated that as part of the National Performance Review (a federal agency reorganization plan), each federal agency will make achieving environmental justice a part of its mission. Agencies will accomplish this by identifying and addressing, as appropriate, disproportionately high and adverse human health or environmental effects of their programs, policies and activities on minority populations and low-income populations in the U.S. and its territories and possessions, the District of Columbia, the Commonwealth of Puerto Rico, and the Commonwealth of the Mariana Islands. Additionally, Executive Order 12898 created the Interagency Working Group on Environmental Justice which is comprised of eighteen executive agencies and offices. The group's members are the Department of Defense, Department of Health and Human Services, Department of Housing and Urban Development, Department of Labor, Department of Agriculture, Department of Transportation, Department of Justice, Department of the Interior, Department of Commerce, Department of Energy, Environmental Protection Agency, Office of Management and Budget, Office of Science and Technology Policy, Office of the Assistant to the President for Domestic Policy, National Economic Council, Council of Economic Advisers, and such other government officials as the President may designate. The Working Group's main goals, as laid out in the Executive Order, are to: (1) provide guidance to federal agencies on criteria for identifying disproportionately high and adverse human health or environmental effects on minority populations, (2) assist in coordinating data collection, (3) examine existing data and studies on environmental justice, and (4) develop interagency model projects on environmental justice that show evidence of cooperation among federal agencies. After reviewing Executive Order 12898, it is evident that the primary focus of the order was on the federal level. Because of this federal emphasis, one of the criticisms of the order points to the need to devote more attention and resources to the local and state level, where administrators of environmental programs have a better understanding of their communities' needs.

Following the signing of the Executive Order, EPA Administrator Browner emphasized her support for environmental justice issues in her 1994 testimony before the House Appropriations Committee [19]. In her testimony, the

Administrator expressed the EPA's support for a new generation of environmental protection which invests in several strategic approaches to the issue
including, among other things, environmental justice. In identifying how the
agency will integrate environmental justice throughout its programs, the
Administrator stated the agency will examine permitting, grants, data collection
and analysis, and enforcement.

After the signing of the Executive Order, several other events occurred to
impact the environmental justice movement. In 1994, a report was issued by the
United Church of Christ titled *Toxic Waste and Race Revisited* [3]. This report
strengthened the association between race and the location of waste facilities. In
1995 the first Interagency Public Meeting on Environmental Justice was held at
Clark Atlanta University in Atlanta, Georgia. The purpose of the meeting was to
provide an opportunity for the public to share concerns and recommend
changes in the federal agencies' environmental justice strategies. In 1997 the
OEJ released the *Environmental Justice Implementation Plan*. This plan outlined
specifically how the agency would implement the rules identified in Executive
Order 12898.

From the late 1990s until the present, the U.S. EPA has worked to meet the
needs of communities in the U.S. most impacted by environmental justice issues.
The agency has held outreach activities and workshops in addition to providing
funds directly to impacted communities via grants. These include the Small
Grants Program and the Community University Partnership Grant Program.
Through the Small Grants Program, EPA awarded communities across the U.S.
thousands of dollars to address their specific needs. In Region 9 alone, which
includes California, Arizona and Hawaii, the Agency awarded 15 Small Grants to
support community-based efforts. These efforts included a $20,000 award to the
Haulapai Tribe's Used Oil Recycling Project in Peach Springs, AZ and another
$20,000 to the Toxic Free Barrio Logan Campaign in National City, CA. These
grants provided much needed funding to educate community members about
environmental hazards and to help clean up toxic pollution. This community-
based approach has enabled representatives from the U.S. EPA to see firsthand
the people and communities most impacted by environmental justice issues.
Additionally, the U.S. EPA has received valuable input from NEJAC which has
held yearly meetings around the U.S. The ongoing dialog between the members
of NEJAC and the U.S. EPA has enabled the Agency to receive valuable input
from members of the academic and non-profit sector.

22.2.4 Analysis of Recent Environmental Justice Literature

Thus far, a basic overview of the major factors that contributed to the
advancement of the environmental justice movement has been the focus of
this chapter. The next part of this chapter provides an in-depth review of the
recent literature on environmental justice.

The majority of the literature written on the issue of environmental justice
appeared in the 1990s. Edwards [20] focused his argument for social and
environmental justice on the issue of sustainable development in the U.S. The

author made three major points relevant to the environmental justice movement: (1) there can be no sustainable development in the U.S. without a sustained commitment to social justice; (2) ecologically sound and socially equitable development require a transformation of the current operating paradigm, which juxtaposes economic development against environmental protection; and (3) sustainable development in the U.S. must uniformly occur. The author drew the attention to three different but related issues which may be applied to the environmental justice movement. Thus, Edwards argued, in order to have sustainable development minority communities must become integral players in the development process.

When examining environmental justice, the issue of risk plays an important role. It is difficult to measure environmental risk to all groups in society [2]. However, the Republican majority in Congress sought to make risk assessment the foundation for a major reevaluation of federal environmental policy [21]. Environmental justice examines the risk exposure of minorities and low-income groups. Finkel and Golding [22] promoted the use of a refined comparative risk assessment (CRA) in order to achieve sensible priorities. The more refined approach would firm up the scientific underpinnings and/or soften them by actively involving laypeople in the ranking exercises. The two main goals of CRA are risk reduction and risk assessment. However, environmental justice scholar Robert Bullard, as noted by Finkel and Golding, argued that risk-based priority setting does not always work in favor of minority populations. Bullard argued that risk-based priority setting may perpetuate the failure to tackle the true hot spot. Instead of CRA, Bullard argued for an environmental approach which puts priority on all of the obvious geographic areas where minorities and low-income populations faced multiple risks from many sources.

Aside from CRA and the multiple risk approach, Burns et al. [23] found that perceptions of risk and social responses were more strongly related to exposure to risk than to the magnitude of exposure. The authors argued that what human beings perceived as threats to their well-being was influenced by their values, attitudes, social influences, and cultural identity. The authors discussed the framework of social amplification of risk, which integrated the technical assessment and the social experience of risk.

When examining the possible reasons why minority communities were often overlooked in the risk assessment process, these authors argued that due to the socialization of individuals, minority groups are socialized to accept a certain level of environmental risk as normal, whereas middle to upper-class, non-minority communities saw the same level of environmental risk as much more severe, thus calling greater media and government attention to these perceived risks. The outcome of this type of risk assessment was faster resolution of environmental problems in non-minority and non-poor communities. This type of risk assessment process was identified as one of the leading factors contributing to environmental racism that appeared in the literature.

Bullard [24] argued that minority communities were not more accepting of environmental hazards than non-minority communities. Instead, Bullard argued for example, that minorities' lack of social power was the main determinant of where hazardous waste sites were located. Bullard [25] also asserted that environmental racism exists within local zoning boards, as well as the U.S. Environmental Protection Agency and nongovernmental organizations such as mainstream national environmental and conservation groups.

Corroborating Bullard's argument that race is the single most significant determinant of a population's level of exposure to environmental pollution, Goldman [9] empirically demonstrated that both people of color and those with lower incomes faced disproportionate environmental impacts in the U.S. However, Goldman argued that racial disparities were more frequently linked to higher-than-normal levels of environmental pollution than income disparities. Goldman cited a study conducted by the National Wildlife Federation which examined 40,000 five-digit ZIP code areas in the U.S. Five different environmental concerns were examined in the study: (1) locations of industrial facilities, (2) human exposure to toxic substances, (3) ambient concentrations of conventional air pollutants, (4) regulatory costs or benefits, and (5) health effects. The study demonstrated that in 87% of the tests racial disparity was evident when examining each of the above five criteria, compared with 74% of the tests of income disparity. Thus, according to the study, race, rather than income was a more significant determinant of environmental pollution.

Some of the reasons for this racial disparity were explained through a historical perspective [26]. Lord and Shutkin argued the legal system had perpetuated environmental injustice by misreading or disregarding minority communities' history. The authors asserted that a flawed or careless approach to history was often a root cause of environmental injustice. The authors argued that the idea of history as it applied to law ought to be enriched, to be viewed as embodying past injustices and aspirations of communities. The authors used the cases of *Byda* v. *Board of Appeal of Boston* and *State of Vermont* v. *Elliott* to emphasize the importance of decision makers not only reckoning with history, but that communities fighting for environmental justice must articulate and advance a particular approach to history. The authors identified the relationships between different groups in society and said that the exclusion and subordination of one group by another ought to be a part of any responsible public history. They argued it is only when the issues of exclusion and subordination become a part of public history, and decision makers begin to adequately address the question of justice, will past injustices be corrected. They asserted historical treatment of a group may be a pivotal issue in determining present and future distribution of environmental burdens and benefits. The authors argued that these sorts of issues would challenge the status quo and lead to social change.

Environmental Protection Agency employee Deeohn Ferris also noted the impacts of past discriminatory practices affecting environmental policies [27]. Ferris argued that past discriminatory state and local sitings and land use practices appeared to guide existing and future land use decisions. Ferris argued that due to these past discriminatory patterns, Latinos were 32% more likely to live among multiple hazards, blacks were 35% more likely, and Asian Americans were up to three times more likely to live with combinations of hazards [27]. Ferris also argued that unequal environmental protection was a nationally significant issue and race was the predominant indicator of who was exposed. In order to correct the current situation, Ferris argued that Congress must correct existing statutory and programmatic deficiencies that failed to equally protect everyone.

Austin and Schill [28] argued the method which could be used to correct past discriminatory practices was to include more minorities in the decision-making process. Several authors argued that the lack of participation of minorities in decision making enhanced the tendency for the Not In My Back Yard (NIMBY) Syndrome [7,28,29]. The NIMBY Syndrome resulted when residents of a given community perceived a project as an environmental threat. This perceived environmental threat resulted in the rapid mobilization of local residents and their outside supporters against the industry in question [29].

22.3 Global Environmental Justice Issues

Thus far this chapter has concentrated on the environmental justice movement in the U.S. Now the focus will shift to examining environmental justice from a global perspective. During the 1980s and first part of the 1990s, the environmental justice movement was building strength and recognition in the U.S., moving from a local grassroots movement to a national issue. Now that environmental justice is well established as an issue of national importance, the U.S. EPA and scholars are addressing the issue from a global perspective.

One scholar, Schlosberg, [30] argues that achieving global environmental justice must involve three things: (1) equity in the distribution of risk; (2) recognition of the diversity of those impacted by environmental pollution; and (3) participation in the environmental policymaking process. The author notes in the U.S. the issue of distribution is consistently a key issue with environmental justice, but it is always linked with recognition and political participation. The same can be said for the global environmental justice movement. According to Schlosberg, the unequal distribution of environmental pollution on a global level is tied to the inequity of socio-economic and cultural status. These impacted communities are generally not politically connected. Schlosberg notes the recent actions by protesters against the most visible institutions of the new global economy—the World Trade Organization (WTO), the International Monetary Fund (IMF), and the World Bank—involve themes of environmental justice. When examining the issue of environmental justice from a global perspective Schlosberg states:

> A singular focus on justice as distribution…is not only limited in theory, but it cannot encompass the broad and diverse demands for justice made by the global environmental justice movement. Demands for recognition of cultural identity and for full democratic rights are integral for justice as well…[30].

Schlosberg also indicates how the global environmental justice movement demonstrates unity without uniformity by highlighting the plurality of the movement towards a unified goal. This is similar to the development of the movement in the U.S.

22.3.1 Environmental Pollution in Developing Nations

When examining the issue of environmental justice from a global perspective Adeola [31] presents three theoretical frameworks: dependency theory, the internal colonialism perspective, and the global environmental justice perspective. Each of these three perspectives will now be discussed.

Dependency theorists contend dependence is a condition in which the economy of certain countries, such as Third World countries, is influenced by the development and expansion of the economy of other countries, such as industrialized nations [32]. In this situation, the less developed nations are dependent upon the industrialized nations for their economic livelihood. The dependency theory focuses on industrialized nations shifting environmental burdens disproportionately to developing nations [31,33,34].

The internal colonialism perspective is another theory related to global environmental justice issues. According to Blauner [35], internal colonialism, unlike classic colonialism, is a condition where the dominant group and the subordinate groups coexist and are indigenous within the same culture. The dominant group represents a majority, as is the situation with the Ogoni minority and the dominant ethnic groups in Nigeria (which will be discussed later in this chapter). The three classic elements of internal colonialism in Nigeria include: (1) an ethnic-centered leadership, controlling and exploiting the natural resources of oil-rich minority communities for the benefit of the dominant ethnic groups; (2) the union between core ethnic groups such as the military, multinational corporations (MNCs), political elites and other state enterprises that represses the minorities; and (3) widespread damaging ecological disruption followed by the destruction of the basic modes of subsistence of the minority population.

The third theory offered by Adeola is the global environmental justice perspective. This perspective focuses on the pattern of the distribution of hazardous waste and toxic agents, including substances banned in the U.S., following the path of least resistance from developed nations in the North to developing nations in the South. Adeola contends that developing nations in the South are becoming reservoirs of garbage, toxic waste, DDT, and other hazardous products produced in industrialized nations. "Annually, approximately 50% of the officially acknowledged volume of exported hazardous waste is channeled to less developed nations. The number of countries involved in export and import schemes, volume of trade, and properties of materials involved are often difficult to establish due to the covert and criminal nature of the transactions" [31]. In the 1980s the number of Third World countries accepting hazardous waste increased when these countries faced difficult economic times.

Adeola argues that those most responsible for industrial pollution are the ones with the wealth and power. According to Adeola MNCs strip developing countries of their natural resources such as timber and minerals, as well as hydroelectric and other mega-industrial projects. In these developing countries, the indigenous people and other poor and marginalized groups bear the brunt of the negative environmental disruption caused by resource extraction.

The dumping of toxic waste is another problem faced by developing nations. Adeola argues that the disproportionate environmental burden these developing countries bear constitutes a violation of basic human rights: "Because human rights involve the assurance of people's means of livelihood, any threats to environmental bases of livelihood could be considered a violation of basic human rights" [31]. Adeola contends there are several factors contributing to the environmental injustices taking place in developing nations. One is the fact that most developing nations do not have rigorous national environmental laws and sanctions against polluters, thus leaving the vulnerable people little means of achieving legal action. Second, most developing nations are desperate to accept pollution for economic gain, making these countries attractive to MNCs for the disposal of their toxic waste dumping. According the Baram [36] and Moyers, [37] MNCs' operations in underdeveloped countries involve the use of hazardous products, the extraction of natural resources, and the spread of toxic substances, all of which pose immediate and long-term health risks to the indigenous people.

22.3.2 *Corporate Transnational Environmental Crime*

According to Simon [38] corporate environmental crime has a negative impact on developing nations. Simon argues large U.S.-based corporations often engage in the illegal dumping of toxic waste, both in the U.S. and abroad. The industries noted for being responsible for 60% of all corporate offenses prosecuted by the Department of Defense between 1974 and 1976 are petrochemicals, pharmaceuticals, and automobile manufacturing [39]. The advanced nations generate 400 million tons of toxic waste annually, 60% of which comes from the U.S. [40].

There is a high cost associated with disposing of waste in the U.S. The U.S. EPA requires companies to provide onsite disposal facilities for toxic waste, which costs approximately $30 million and takes years to construct. Therefore, it is appealing to these companies to export their waste to Third World nations where the toxic waste may be disposed of for as little as $20 a ton [38]. Simon [38] contends bribes are taken by Third World government officials to establish toxic waste dumps in their countries.

In response to the growing problem of developing nations being the depositories of hazardous waste, representatives of 117 nations gathered in Basel, Switzerland in 1989 to develop a treaty addressing the issue of toxic waste exportation. The Basel Convention calls for signing nations to accurately label all international waste shipments, in order to stop waste shipments to nations that have banned the toxic substance. However, there are several loopholes. One is that the treaty does not address waste shipments intended for recycling [37]. Therefore, thousands of tons of waste are disguised as recyclable waste and shipped across several international borders.

When examining the issue of toxic waste dumping from a cost/benefit perspective, some argue that it makes economic sense for developed nations to pay developing nations to deposit their hazardous waste. It has even been stated by Lawrence Summers, a World Bank official, that the lives of those in

Third World countries are considered of less value than those of the First World [41]. To suggest that the lives of those in the Third World are of less value than those in the First World is an extremely racist perspective. This type of rhetoric by high level government officials is not only damaging to international relations, it benefits no one. Both of these arguments make little sense from a human rights or economic standpoint. Not only does the mass influx of hazardous waste to developing nations pose immediate and long-term health problems to local people, these toxic waste products harm the very environment from which MNCs are interested in extracting resources. Additionally, developing nations have less technological capacity to safely store and/or dispose of toxic waste products. Therefore it is even more harmful for developing nations to accept toxic waste than it is for developed nations to dispose of the material.

22.4   Cases of Global Environmental Injustice

There are numerous countries throughout the world facing environmental justice issues. Now several examples of global environmental injustices will be presented. The regions to be highlighted are Nigeria, South Africa, and the U.S.-Mexican Border Region.

22.4.1   Nigeria's Ogoniland: a Region of Contrasts

In the African country of Nigeria, the Ogoni people have struggled for control of their land since the colonial period [32]. In the late 19th century the Ogoni people staged a strong armed resistance against colonial occupation of their territory until 1908 when the region was secured by the colonial power [42]. Ogoni is an area of half a million people in the Niger Delta [43]. The Delta region produces 90% of the country's foreign earnings, making Nigeria the seventh largest producer in OPEC. Ogoniland is the home of Nigeria's major fertilizer plant, two oil refineries, a large petrochemical plant and other oil-servicing businesses. By 1972 there were six oil fields producing a combined daily output of more than 200,000 barrels of oil. In the mid 1990s, in response to the Ogoni people's peaceful protests, the ruling military dictatorship imposed direct military rule. During these years more than 3000 people died.

Ogoniland is a region of contrasts—rich in natural resources, yet the Ogoni people remain living in poverty, in an ecologically devastated region, lacking basic infrastructure and plagued by environmentally induced health problems. According to the Sierra Club [44], Multi National Oil Companies (MNOCs) such as Royal Dutch Shell and others such as Chevron Corporation, have taken more than $30 billion from Ogoniland, leaving behind ecological devastation, poverty, environmentally caused illnesses, and a shorter life expectancy among the people. While major oil corporations have successfully withdrawn billions of gallons of oil from Ogoniland, the region still lacks basic infrastructure such as good roads, electricity, pipe-borne water, hospitals and schools [45]. While the MNCOs and the military are reaping the benefits of the oil drilling and the refinery activities, the landscape of Ogoniland has been completely devastated by oil spills, hazardous waste dumping, and toxic gas emissions. These destructive activities of the MNCOs have left the soil, water, and air of Ogoniland highly contaminated. For a group of people who are subsistence farmers, the negative environmental impacts of the MNCOs have had severe consequences for the Ogoni people. The farm fields are crisscrossed with pipes for the oil, making it difficult to farm the land and dangerous for the elderly farmers who try to climb over the pipes. The government does not require the MNCOs to conduct environmental impact statements for the region to determine the effects of the oil-related activities. Thus, the rights of the Ogoni people to a safe, clean, and healthy environment continue to be violated. Naanen [42] describes the plight of the Ogoni people as a case of genocide by the MNCOs against the local citizens, under the leadership of the military government in Nigeria.

In response to the problems of the Ogoni people, Movement for the Survival of the Ogoni People (MOSOP) was formed in 1990. Under the leadership of MOSOP president Kenule Saro-Wiwa, MOSOP drafted the Ogoni Bill of Rights (OBR). This bill seeks to: (1) provide the Ogoni people a reasonable share of the oil revenue from Ogoniland; (2) reduce the environmental degradation by oil producing MNCOs; and (3) provide the people of Ogoniland greater political autonomy to participate in the affairs of the republic as a distinct and separate entity [31]. The cause of the Ogoni people has also received the attention of several global organizations. In 1992 the case was presented before the United Nations Commission on Human Rights in Geneva and in 1993 Ogoni became a registered member of the Unrepresented Nations and Peoples Organization based in The Hague. Additionally, the New York- based International Federation for the Rights of Ethnic, Linguistic, Religious, and Other Minorities has become interested in the Ogoni case, as have several other non-governmental organizations (NGOs).

While the case of the Ogoni people has received worldwide attention, it has suffered several setbacks as well [31]. In 1995 founding president of MOSOP, Kenule Saro-Wiwa, was jailed along with 15 other members of MOSOP for engaging in protests against the MNCOs and the military government. He was tried by a military tribunal and executed. The execution of Kenule Saro-Wiwa highlights the adversarial relationship between the Ogoni people and the military government. Despite the execution of their founding president, MOSOP continues to gain world wide support and attention. The organization has developed a website (www.mosop.org) where people around the world can learn about the struggle of the Ogoni people.

22.4.2 Post-Apartheid South Africa

Within the African continent, the issue of environmental justice is not restricted to the country of Nigeria. On August 27, 2002 in Johannesburg, South Africa more than three hundred environmental justice leaders from around the world gathered for the Environmental Justice Forum [46]. This forum was sponsored by the South African-based Environmental Justice Networking Forum (EJNF) and served as the pre-summit opener of the World Summit on Sustainable Development (WSSD) and the Global People's Forum, a meeting of nongovernmental organizations that coincides with the official government meeting. The forum addressed the many issues post-apartheid South Africans face such as lack of access to energy, poor sanitation infrastructure, and lack of access to clean water.

South African human rights activist Dennis Brutus was critical of the government's slow pace of getting basic services to the people. He noted, "Almost 15 million Black South Africans out of a total population of 43.5 million are without electricity and live on less than $2 per day" [46]. The lack of access to affordable electricity is one of several issues contributing to health problems in South Africa.

The issue of overcrowding in substandard housing is another issue that contributes to health problems. The apartheid government herded approximately 87% of the black population into 13% of the country's land. Dr. Mildred McClain of Citizens for Environmental Justice based in Savannah, Georgia stated, "The land redistribution movement in South Africa is analogous to the reparations movement in the U.S.A. Both movements have recognized that the path to sustainable development can be achieved by ensuring that the most marginalized have access to the primary tools of economic development—land" [46]. Land redistribution is a core environmental, economic, and political issue.

Another important issue in South Africa is inadequate sanitation, which accounts for over 43,000 child deaths each year. More than 10 million South Africans had their water cut off. This is not an issue unique to South Africa. More than 1.4 billion people around the world lack access to safe water. The lack of access to clean water is one of the world's deadliest problems.

Contributing to the environmental and health problems of the people of post-Apartheid South Africa are polluting industries such as the Impala Platinum Mine, the Rostenburg Quarries, and Chevron Oil. These industries cause pollution problems such as mining waste, water contamination, and land destruction.

22.4.3 United States–Mexican Border Region

The issue of water pollution is also a problem for the people who live along the border of the U.S. and Mexico, referred to as the bi-national region (BNR). The BNR stretches 3141 km (1952 miles) from the Pacific Ocean to the Gulf of Mexico, crossing the four states of California, Arizona, New Mexico, and Texas [47]. The BNR is a 200 kilometer zone that extends for 100 kilometers (62.5 miles) on either side of the border. The BNR is one of the fastest growing regions in North America, especially in some of its sister cities such as the San Diego-Tijuana Metropolitan Area (SDTMA).

The SDTMA is a microcosm for the challenges faced by the entire border region. Both San Diego and Tijuana have experienced rapid growth in the last several decades, particularly since 1980. This rapidly increasing population has put particular strains on the ecosystem in Tijuana. As the population continues to increase, there is a lack of infrastructure in place to handle the growing population [48]. In Tijuana a significant portion of the population live in "self built" structures along the hillsides, creating what are called *colonias*. These are villages generally without access to clean water, sewage systems, or dependable and safe electricity. As the population continues to increase in this area, the amount of untreated sewage spilling into the Tijuana River increases. This untreated sewage flows to the Pacific Ocean and migrates up the California coast, negatively impacting the beach communities of San Diego.

These villages also lack paved roads, making the rainy season a dangerous time, often with several severe mudslides. The rest of the year, a lack of paved roads in the arid climate creates a dusty atmosphere with a high volume of particulate matter in the air. This problem has caused the people living in the *colonias* to suffer from a heightened number of cases of asthma and other respiratory illnesses [48].

Another contributor to the health problems of the people in Tijuana is the impacts of the *maquiladoras*. The term refers to foreign-built and -owned factories in Mexico. There is a high concentration of *maquiladoras* in Tijuana. These factories generally produce harmful air pollution. Due to the shared mixed of residential and industrial zones, people living in close proximity to the *maquiladoras* suffer from poor health. The problem is compounded by the lack of aggressive enforcement of environmental laws by the Mexican government. Additionally, there is a lack of scientific data to document negative environmental impacts.

In order to address the many problems that plague the BNR, the U.S. EPA has launched several multi-year programs. Border 2012 is a 10 year, bi-national, results-oriented environmental program for the BNR [49]. The Border 2012 Program is the latest multi-year program implemented under the La Paz Agreement and succeeds Border XXI, a five-year program that ended in 2000. The Border 2012 program focuses on border issues such as air quality and land contamination. On June 9, 2005, the Instituo Nacional de Ecologia (a division within the Secretaria de Medio Ambiente y Resursos Naturales, SEMARNAT) unveiled the first air emissions inventory for the six northern states of Mexico bordering the U.S. With the continued efforts of the Border 2012 Program, the many environmental problems of the BNR may finally be addressed.

22.5 Conclusion

This chapter has provided an overview of the history of the environmental justice movement. The recent literature on environmental justice has also been reviewed, and global environmental justice issues have been presented. When examining global environmental justice issues, it is evident from the cases presented that a wide variety of ecological problems impact communities throughout the world. The issue of corporate environmental crime creates an entire set of problems for developing nations. At the same time, countries such as Nigeria legalize the destruction of their land for the sake of oil production. The government of post-Apartheid South Africa is struggling with meeting the needs of its citizens after years of Apartheid rule. Additionally, the U.S. Mexican border region faces the challenge of coordinating efforts between the U.S. and Mexican governments to address the many issues facing the residents who live along the nearly 2000 mile stretch of land between the Pacific Ocean and the Gulf of Mexico.

While some foreign governments, such as Mexico, are working to address the unjust environmental problems facing their citizens, other states are not as responsive, and are even taking actions to exacerbate the problems. Theoretically, the only international court with jurisdiction over environmental issues is the International Court of Justice (ICJ) in The Hague [50]. However, no environmental disputes have been resolved by the ICJ in over 40 years. One of the problems with the ICJ is the fact that its jurisdiction is strictly limited to disputes submitted by state parties, with no standing provided to individuals, corporations, or other nongovernmental organizations. Aside from the ICJ, the European Court of Justice (ECJ), the European Court of Human Rights, and the Council of Europe have been progressive in defining and implementing international environmental norms that can be adjudicated at the regional and/or municipal level. However, McCallion and Sharma [50] believe the only true way for the wide variety of international environmental issues throughout the world to be properly addressed is through the establishment of an International Environmental Court (IEC). An IEC would be an impartial body established to provide a centralized database for all national, regional, and international environmental laws and regulations.

The right to a clean, healthy environment for everyone on earth should be acknowledged and supported by all governments. Human rights and environmental rights are closely tied issues on the international level, particularly in developing countries. This author supports the concept of an IEC as an impartial international body for citizens to have their cases fairly heard and adjudicated. If foreign governments are non-responsive to the human rights and environmental needs of their citizens, then an IEC would provide citizens around the world impacted by unjust environmental conditions a means of having their cases heard by an impartial body and resolved in a fair manner.

Environmental justice is an issue of both civil rights and environmental rights. Achieving environmental justice for all nations around the world is a challenging task, especially if countries do not support their citizens' civil rights. Therefore, it is important for global organizations such as the United Nations, the World Bank, and the IMF to push for environmental justice and hold governments accountable. The environmental justice movement in the U.S. took decades to achieve national recognition and to prompt action by the federal government. The global environmental justice movement is even more challenging, due to the variety of government structures existing in affected countries. Continued education and outreach is imperative if global environmental justice is ever to be achieved.

Acknowledgments

I dedicate this book chapter to my dear cousin Kelsey.

References

1. National Conference of State Legislatures, Environmental justice: a matter of perspective, Washington DC, 1995.
2. Kraft, M. and Scheberle, D., Environmental justice and the allocation of risk: the case of lead and public health, *Policy Stud. J.*, 23, 113, 1995.
3. U.S. Environmental Protection Agency, Environmental justice strategy: Executive Order. 12898, 1, 1995.
4. U.S. Environmental Protection Agency, Environmental justice 1994 annual report, back of cover page, 1995.
5. Bryant, B. and Mohai, P., Race, poverty, and the environment, *EPA J.*, 18, 8, 1992.
6. U.S. Environmental Protection Agency, Environmental equity, reducing risk for all communities, Volume 1: Workgroup Report to the Administrator: EPA report, May, 1992.
7. Callahan, P., Environmental racism: when civil rights are used to protect more than individual liberty, *Omni*, 16, 88, 1994.
8. U.S. General Accounting Office., 1980 Data for census area where EPA Region IV hazardous waste landfills are located, Table 4, 1983.
9. Goldman, B., *Not Just Prosperity: Achieving Sustainability with Environmental Justice*, National Wildlife Federation Corporate Conservation Council, Washington, DC, 1994.
10. Keeva, S., A breath of justice, *ABA J.*, 80, 90, 1994.
11. Rosen, R., Who gets polluted, *Dissent*, 41, 223, 1994.
12. United Church of Christ, Toxic waste and race in the U.S. The Commission for Racial Justice, 1987, xiii.
13. Bullard, R., *Dumping in Dixie: Race, Class, and Environmental Quality*, Westview Press, Boulder, CO, 1990.
14. Bryant, B. and Mohai, P., The Michigan conference: a turning point, *EPA J.*, 18, 10, 1992.
15. Coyle, M. and Lavelle, M., Unequal protection, *Nat. Law J.*, 15, S1, 1992.
16. Ember, L., EPA giving increased priority to environmental issues, *Chem. Eng. News*, 72, 22, 1994.
17. National Environmental Justice Advisory Council (NEJAC), Proceedings of the National Environmental Justice Advisory Council and Subcommittees: A Federal Advisory Committee Washington DC, 1, 1994, 2.
18. Clinton, W., Executive Order 12898, Federal actions to address environmental justice in minority populations and low-income populations, *Fed. Regist.*, 59, 1, 1994.
19. U.S. Congress. House of Representatives. Committee on Appropriations. Statement of Carol Browner, administrator, U.S. Environmental Protection Agency 1994.
20. Edwards, M.D., Sustainability and people of color, *EPA J.*, 18, 50, 1992.
21. Kris, M., Risky business, *Natl J.*, 27, 417, 1995.
22. Finkel, A. and Golding, D., Alternative paradigms: comparative risk is not the only model, *EPA J.*, 19, 50, 1993.
23. Burns, W., Kasperson, J., Kasperson, R., Renn, O., and Slovic, P., The social amplification of risk: theoretical foundations and empirical applications, *J. Soc. Issues*, 48, 137, 1992.
24. Bullard, R., *Confronting Environmental Racism: Voices from the Grassroots*, South End Press, Boston, 1993, 188.
25. Bullard, R., The threat of environmental racism, *Nat. Resour. Environ.*, 7(3), 23, 1993.
26. Lord, C. and Shutkin, W., Environmental justice and the use of history, *Environ. Aff.*, 22, 15, 1994.
27. U.S. Congress. House of Representatives. Committee on Government Operations. Subcommittee on Environment, Energy and Natural Resources. Prepared testimony of Deeohn Ferris. 1994.

28. Austin, R. and Schill, M., Black, brown, red and poisoned, *Humanist*, 54, 9, 1994.
29. Smith, D., Walsh, E., and Warland, R., Backyards, NIMBYs, and incinerator sitings: implications for social movement theory, *Soc. Probl.*, 40, 25, 1993.
30. Schlosberg, D., Reconcieving environmental justice: global movements and political theories, *Environ. Polit.*, 13, 517, 2004.
31. Adeola, F., Cross-national environmental injustice and human rights issues: a review of evidence in the developing world, *Am. Behav. Sci.*, 43, 686, 2000.
32. Dos Santos, T., The structure of dependency, *Am. Econ. R.*, 60, 231, 1970.
33. Bunker, S., *Under developing the Amazon: Extraction, unequal exchange, and the failure of the modern state*, University of Illinois, Urbana, 1985.
34. Buttel, E., New directions in environmental sociology, *A.R. Sociol.*, 13, 465, 1987.
35. Blauner, R., *Racial Oppression in America*, Harper & Row, New York, 1972.
36. Baram, M., Multinational corporations, private codes, and technology transfer for sustainable development, *Environ. Law*, 24, 33, 1994.
37. Moyers, B., *Global dumping ground: The international traffic in hazardous waste*, Seven Locks, Washington DC, 1990.
38. Simon, D., Corporate environmental crimes and social inequality: new directions for environmental justice research, *Am. Behav. Sci.*, 43, 633, 2000.
39. Clinard, M.B., Corporate crime, *Congressional Q.*, 549, 1998.
40. Cass, V., The international waste trade: who gets left holding the toxic trash bag?, Paper presented at the 1994 meeting of the American Society of Criminology, 1994.
41. Foster, J.B., The global policies of the U.S. are environmentally unjust, *in Environmental Justice*, B. Leone, S. Barbour, and J.S. Petrikin, Eds., Greenhaven, San Diego, 1995, 100.
42. Naanen, B., Oil-producing minorities and the restructuring of Nigerian federalism: the case of the Ogoni people, *J. Commonw. Comp. Polit.*, 33, 46, 1995.
43. MOSOP, Movement for the survival of the Ogoni people. Available at http://www.mosop.org/main/index.php?option=com_contact&trmind=3, (accessed on December 18, 2005).
44. Sierra Club, Sierra Club rebukes Nigerian death sentence (press release), October 31, 1995.
45. Welch, C.E., *Protecting Human Rights in Africa: Roles and Strategies of Non-Governmental Organizations*, University of Pennsylvania Press, Philadelphia, 1995.
46. Bullard, R., Blacks Call for Environmental Reparations at World Summit. Available at http://www.ejcr.cau/envreparationwssd.html (accessed on December 2, 2005), 1, 3.
47. Murphy-Greene, C. and Blair, J., Binational vital signs: a quality of life indicator program for the San Diego-Tijuana metropolitan region, *R. Policy Res.*, 21, 681, 2004.
48. Gaylord, C., Lecture at San Diego State University, 2002.
49. U.S. Environmental Protection Agency. U.S.-Mexico border environmental program: Border 2012. Available at http://www.epa.gov/usmexicoborder/index.htm, (accessed on December 2, 2005).
50. McCallion, K. and Rajan Sharma, H., Environmental justice without borders: the need for an international court of the environment to protect fundamental environmental rights, *G.W. J. Int. Law Econ.*, 32, 351, 2000.

Chapter 23

Globalization and Growth of Developing Countries

Dang Tran
California State University

23.1   The Globalization Process

Globalization is the process whereby the world and its economic and socio-cultural systems are made more uniform, integrated, and interdependent. Recent technological advancements—the Internet, communications, and transportation—reduce the distances between countries and make the world smaller. The combination of technological and geopolitical forces renders previously closed social and political systems more open and susceptible to change.

A crucial factor in promoting globalization is the reduction in transport and communications costs. The cost of sea freight has dropped by an annual average of 0.4% over the past 40 years, passenger air transport by 2.5% and trans-Atlantic telephone calls by 6.7% [1]. Revolution in telecommunications through fiber optics and satellites allows the development of worldwide networks connecting ten thousands of universities, government agencies, and research institutes with huge databases of computer programs and all kinds of information. Personal computers connected to these networks can access, communicate, and exchange information instantaneously with one another at little or no cost. Information as a part of capital becomes easily accessible and can be used to substitute for workers. Business firms now can move information instead of people across borders to where they can be used cheaply to serve the needs of consumers worldwide.*

Culture is increasingly globalized in the sense that beliefs are increasingly shared, alien social forms adopted and material products more uniform. Culture is defined as a body of customary beliefs such as religion, social forms such as language, and material goods such as food, clothing, and shelter. Globalization of culture is based on the diffusion of lifestyles and products from more developed countries, especially the U.S., via the instruments of worldwide television, music and consumption patterns.

The economy is increasingly globalized by way of globalization of finance, operations by multinational corporations (MNCs), foreign direct investment (FDI), global specialization in the location of production, globalization of the tertiary sector of the economy, globalization of the office function, and global tourism.

Telecommunication advances allow the establishment of a single global capital market. Computers can now monitor and trade in stocks, bonds, national currencies, and other financial instruments listed anywhere in the world instantaneously. Dealers and brokers with offices in New York, Tokyo, and London can trade practically 24 h a day. Communications and fast transportation allow international firms to move money, materials, products, and economic assets around the world in seconds. Economic activities around the world can be directed and monitored from a single location. Firms can outsource or subcontract certain activities, such as banking, credit and customer services, to a low-cost country. For instance, India has become a subcontractor for software programming and customer services for many U.S. software companies. The Internet provides opportunity for firms in developing countries to announce their presence and participation in the world market. The web has truly transformed nationally or regionally segregated markets into a one-world market.

Cheaper and faster transportation and communication open access to new markets, inputs, suppliers and contractors, with whom the buyers and international investors may not otherwise be able to establish relationships, allowing narrower forms of specialization in discrete ("fragmented") production processes. A low-wage developing country may provide only the production or assembly phase of a product. Consider the case of a toy licensed by an U.S. company to a Canadian firm, which together designed the toy. The Canadian firm looked for a cheap subcontractor in Southern China to produce the toy. The labor cost of the Chinese firm was $2 a day. The products were shipped to Hong Kong and other parts of China for inspection by chain stores such as Wal-Mart, K-Mart or Toy-"R"-Us. The Canadian company's subsidiary in Hong Kong arranged the delivery of the finished products to the U.S. by ship. The toy was sold at retail stores for $8, which covered the cost of licensing, production,

---

* Political power is also increasingly being shaped by taking advantage of the information structure rather than merely by the possession of money, as demonstrated by Governor Howard Dean, one of the Democratic hopefuls, in his campaign for President in the United States in 2003.

materials, shipping, and marketing, and of which the Chinese wage cost was only a tiny portion [2].

Foreign direct investment is instrumental in bringing the developing countries into the globalization process. Foreign direct investment has grown faster than world trade and four times faster than total world output. Although 80% of total FDI originates from the United States, Europe, and Japan, contrary to popular belief, most of FDI goes to developed regions. The United States and Canada alone absorbed 30% of FDI and the U.S. was the largest recipient of FDI from other countries. Of the $119.4 billion of FDI that went to less developed countries (LDCs) in 1997, 75% went to China, Brazil, Argentina, Mexico, South Korea, Chile, Poland, and Thailand; the remaining portion was divided among all other LDCs.

Multinational corporations play a vital role in globalization of the economy by establishing subsidiaries and plants where they find it most profitable. There are over 60,000 MNCs which produced, as of 1998, 25% of global output. In 1997, the top one hundred MNCs controlled 16% of the world's productive assets, and the top three hundred controlled 25% [3]. Many top MNCs are larger than most national economies. Sales of any four of the top 10 MNCs are greater than ghoss domestic product (GDP) of India. Each of the four top MNCs is larger than the economy of Indonesia. Around two-thirds of world trade is handled by MNCs in which one-third is within these companies (i.e., trading and transfers of resources, products, and technology among their subsidiaries and branches across national boundaries). In 1997, they employed 100 million people directly, which accounted for 4% of employment in the developed countries and 12% of total employment in developing countries. Multinational corporations are able to compete on a worldwide scale effectively since they can operate with greater information efficiency, sharing information with their subsidiaries and branches via the Internet, satellites and fiber-optic communication systems. They have an advantage on information over competing national firms since they know the worldwide markets, products, consumer preferences, characteristics of national labor forces, and business opportunities. In addition, MNCs possess a huge amount of capital, great technological capability, highly effective managerial skills, and overall economies of scale, and play a major role in innovation and technology transfer between the more developed countries (MDCs) and LDCs. Multinational corporations play a leading role in forming tightly-knit global value chains in which they establish specific procurement and distribution systems that include certain sourcing countries of their choice. This raises the minimum entry level and makes it difficult for many new aspiring industrializing countries to participate in the production chains.

Multinational corporations assess the economic value of each regional location in the world economy. Availability of natural resources no longer forms an important basis for comparative advantage and specialization. Substitutes for many raw materials (called transmaterialization) have been developed. For instance, metallic elements are being replaced by advanced engineering nonmetallic materials such as composites. Examples include graphite or glass embedded in plastic, and ceramics made of clay and silicon. Transmaterialization changes the nature of resources. The nature of the finished products is being changed as fewer material components and more intelligent components are being used in new products. This is called the dematerialization process. Examples include computers, telephones, videotape digital recorders, plasma television sets, flat screen high definition television and other smart products such as robotic vacuum cleaners. Furthermore, new man-made materials are being developed due to recent advances in materials science and engineering. These new materials are generated by new industrial processes and new industries such as super polymers, composites, fiber optics, and fine ceramics. The result is a decrease in investment of natural resources and an increase in investment of manufacturing and services by private investors. Today, of the estimated stock of FDI, petroleum and mining accounts for only 40% while manufacturing and services make up more than 50%.

In combination with the development of new materials is a new production process which is based on multipurpose, reprogrammable equipment and systems. The process is called the computer-integrated manufacturing system (CIM) using robotics, automated transfer, industrial lasers, new techniques for precision forming and shaping, and flexible manufacturing systems (FMS). It provides opportunity for much greater flexibility, small lot production, minimal inventories, rapid market response, and product adaptation, while maintaining or even enhancing economies of scale in the use of plants or equipment.

With brain power replacing mechanical power in products, improvement in transportation and communications, and the creation of new man-made materials, there is less need for firms to be located at the source of raw materials. As a result, more final goods are being produced at the point of consumption. This explains why in 1998, 75% of FDI went to developed countries. Multi-national corporations decide where to locate an operation or a factory in response to characteristics of the labor force, skill level, prevailing wage, attitude toward unions, government environment for business, tariffs, and transportation rates. This decision is made within the context of an overall optimal allocation of resources according to comparative advantage of each activity in each location. Thus, an MNC might close some factories in a high cost country and move them to locations in a low cost country if this enhances its competitive edge.

The path of economic development as seen in terms of output and employment structure is normally from agriculture to manufacturing to services. As FMS are increasingly adopted, new products are opened and new markets for quite different target groups of consumers are developed. Computer-integrated manufacturing system and FMS require a new management technology based on worker and customer participation in the production process. Since customers demand quality products, only they can evaluate them. Thus management technology must be customer-driven instead of product-driven. This calls for a new system of customer-integrating services called integrated process management (IPM). With the creation of the Internet, a global customer integrating service for even a specialty product can be easily implemented. Consequently, the service sector is growing fast in all countries.

Services account for a greater proportion of employment and output than manufacturing and agriculture in industrialized countries. Trade in business services grows at a much faster rate than production of manufacturing or primary commodities. In 1995, services trade amounted to over 1.5 trillion dollars. When MNCs operate overseas they utilize legal counsel, insurance, accounting, business consulting, advertising, medical care, licensing, designs, and computer services. The U.S. is the leading exporter of services. U.S. service exports are more than three times as much as automobile exports, at $200 billion in 1996. The major services exported by the U.S. are entertainment (movies, music, television programs), education, particularly university education, medical and legal services, business management, business consulting, banking services, accounting, insurance, computer software development, real estate development, stock and commodity brokerage. However, many large American entertainment firms, such as MGM/UA, Universal Studios, 20th Century Fox, and Walt Disney, are owned by foreign investors.

One of the most notable effects of globalization is expanding tourism across the globe. Many developing countries rely on tourism as a major export and foreign exchange-earning industry. Among these are China, Mexico, Thailand, and Turkey, to cite a few. In these countries, tourism grows much faster than the manufacturing industry and its share in their GDP has steadily increased over time. For instance, tourism accounted for 10% of the GDP of Thailand in 1995. Due to improvement in communications, transportation, and information technology, tourism has become the largest global industry, with world travelers spending about $15 trillion in gross output in 1995. It employed 250 million people and produced 14% of world GDP [2].

23.2   Effects of Globalization on LDCs

Rapid technological advance, which drives the globalization process, pushes the production structure toward more technology-intensive products and activities. This requires countries to invest more in human capital formation so as to raise the skill level and access and absorb constantly evolving technology. The new technology will fast become old technology, shortening product life cycles. This, together with the building up of technological capability by LDCs, leads to "desophistication" of products, which eventually benefits all LDCs.

The result is that sophisticated manufacturing activities have gained relative to resource-based and low technology industries, as the former grew at around 7% during 1980–2000 compared to about 4% for the latter. In LDCs over the same period, the five fastest-growing activities were electrical machinery (8% per year), industrial chemicals (over 6%), instruments (near 6%), transportation equipments (5.6%), and other chemicals (5%), and the five slowest were furniture (slightly above 2%), apparel (about 2%), textiles (1.5%), footwear (over 1%), and wood products (1%). Similar patterns are also observed in MDCs: the five fastest growing manufacturing activities are other chemicals (3.7%), tobacco (3.4%), electrical machinery (3.2%), printing and publications (3.1%), and plastic products (about 3%); the two slowest are pottery and china (0.2%), iron and steel (0.1%); and the last three contracting are textiles (-0.1%), apparel (-0.9%), and footwear (-1.9%).

With new markets and input sources being opened, there has been an inherent, either internal or external, pressure to open up the economies previously closed or protected, leading to economic liberalization around the world. This liberalization intensifies international competition, with the result that only the most efficient can stay ahead. Less developed countries, being propelled by rising technological capability, are growing faster than MDCs in all manufacturing categories, especially high-technology products. The LDCs' share in the overall global manufacturing exports doubled from 13.5% in 1981 to 27% in 2000, with the share in high-technology exports more than tripling from 10 to 33%. This bodes well for the LDCs, since their share of high- technology in total global exports was steadily rising from 8% in 1976 to 23% in 2000, while the shares of resource-based and low-technology exports have been on the decline slightly, with medium technology remaining stable. Unfortunately, the export performance is uneven among LDCs. The share of world manufacturing value added (MVA) by the East Asian countries increased the greatest from 4% in 1980 to 14% in 2000, while the second most competitive group, the Latin American and Caribbean countries (LAC), saw their share down from 6.5 to 5%. The share of South Asia and Middle East and North Africa (MENA) increased from 1 to 2% and from 1.8 to 2.2%, respectively, while that of Sub-Saharan countries and South Africa (SSA) decreased slightly. Similar patterns are also seen in global exports. The share of world manufactured exports of East Asia (excluding China) doubled from 6% in 1981 to 12% in 2000, while that of Latin American countries (excluding Mexico) actually decreased from 2.5 to about 2%. China gained the greatest, from 1 to above 6%, and Mexico the second, from 0.5 to 3%. The shares of MENA and SSA fell slightly from 2 to 1.9% and from 0.6 to 0.5%, respectively. Besides East Asia, South Asia is the only other region which raised its share in world manufactured exports, from 0.5 to 1.1%. East Asia dominated the developing world exports in all categories except primary. It controlled 85% of total LDCs high technology exports, 58% medium technology, 68% low technology, and 46% of resource based. The second most successful region is LAC including Mexico with 12, 25, 11, and 24% shares in high technology, medium technology, low technology, and resource based exports, respectively. Primary exports were distributed among MENA with 37%, LAC (including Mexico) 29%, East Asia 20%, SSA 12% and South Asia 2% [4].

So far we have been concerned mostly with industrial progress among LDCs. Development experience during the last 50 years shows that development is more than mere economic growth. The latter, however, is a prerequisite for development. Today, focus has been set on development of people rather than on things. It might be seen as a process of expansion of human capabilities or freedom that people enjoy [5]. Human capabilities can range from basic freedom from hunger, disease, and lack of adequate housing, to freedom to travel, participate in communal life, and create institutions to express political, social, and religious choices.

Modern economic development requires economic growth as the basis for promoting human development. For most countries, economic growth implies industrialization. In this paper, we look at how LDCs can promote growth through globalization.

Agricultural development, of course, is a prerequisite for growth since it not only supplies food for the industrial sector but also provides demand for the industrial goods in the pre-take-off stage.* It is important for agricultural productivity to increase to create the purchasing power and growing markets for industry's output. However, domestic income by itself cannot hope to rise to a level that allows a country to achieve its noblest objectives. This is because while expansion in industry can perpetuate itself by generating increasing returns through division of labor, complementaries, and linkages, agricultural expansion is limited by a fixed factor: land. To raise income beyond that which can be provided domestically, export industries need to be developed.

During the last 25 years we have observed that the fastest-growing countries are those whose share of industry in GDP is rising most rapidly. Examples include newly industrialized countries (NICs) such as Korea, Taiwan, Hong Kong (China), Singapore, Thailand, and Malaysia. The growth in manufacturing output is crucial to the growth of productivity in manufacturing as a result of static and dynamic returns to scale [6–13]. Static returns refer to the size and scale of the production units and are characteristic largely of manufacturing where, for instance, doubling of the equipment and complementary factors will lead to tripling of production.† Dynamic economies relate to increasing returns brought about by "induced" technological progress, learning by doing, external economies in production, and so on.

The terms of trade between industry and agriculture govern how the two dependent sectors grow. Agriculture acts as both a supply and demand sector with respect to industry. Too high an agricultural price relative to industrial price will constrain industrial growth. But too low an agricultural price will leave the agricultural sector insufficient purchasing power to buy industrial goods. Thus, balanced terms of trade must be established to promote the maximum growth for the economy.

Over time, however, the importance of the agricultural sector diminishes and export growth becomes critical in fostering economic growth through the growth of the manufacturing sector. Competitiveness among labor-intensive and less sophisticated products depends, among other things, on unit labor cost which can be brought down by rapid growth in labor productivity. But productivity growth depends on output growth. For most countries with small domestic markets, output growth requires expanding exports. Ultimately, export growth depends on the growth of world income. Even if domestic markets are large, import of machinery and technology is still needed in the industrialization process. Imports of capital goods and intermediate inputs are a vehicle for technology transfer which can have spillover effects on output. Thus, fast export growth permits fast GDP growth through technology transfer via imports and FDI without balance of current accounts difficulty.

There is another reason for the urgent need to industrialize. For most LDCs, their major exports are still primary products. For instance, Indonesia's export of

---

* There are exceptions, of course, such as the cases of Belgium and Netherlands.
† Large countries tend to have a lower ratio of export to GDP than smaller countries, because of the former's market size.

petroleum accounts for 49% of merchandise exports, which in turn account for 26% of GDP. Major primary products exported by LDCs are petroleum, copper, iron ore, tin, zinc, lead, silver, aluminum, bauxite, rice, rubber, tea, cotton, sugar, jute, coconuts, coffee, cocoa, tapioca, ground nuts, palm oil, wood, hides, and phosphates. But the net barter term of trade (NBTT) has been decreasing by 30% for the last 50 years. Worse yet, the rate of terms of trade deterioration has been substantially greater since 1980. In their trade with the European Union (EU) the commodities/manufactures terms of trade of developing countries deteriorated by an average 4.2% a year.

In addition, the 2.0% a year expansion in the volume of imports of commodities by the EU from developing countries means that the income terms of trade of developing countries (or the purchasing power of their total revenues from commodity exports in terms of manufactures imports) deteriorated by an average of 2.2% a year over the period to 1994. More generally, relating a unit value index of commodity exports from all developing countries to the United Nations index of the unit value of manufactures exported by developed countries shows a deterioration in the commodity/manufactures terms of trade of developing countries of 3.4% a year.

The deterioration varies according to the level of technology, barriers to entry, and market structure. The most technological advanced—South and East Asia—have experienced the smallest annual rate of deterioration. The least technologically advanced—the "least developed," consisting mainly of countries in SSA region—have experienced the greatest annual rate of deterioration. Latin American and Caribbean countries and MENA countries fall somewhere in between, both in their levels of technology and in the degree of their manufactures terms of trade deterioration [14]. Furthermore, countries at early stages of industrial development, with manufactures exports comprising mainly low technology and resource-based goods, sell in highly competitive world markets which operate in much the same way as the markets for primary commodities. By contrast, as we have seen in the discussion above, the exports of the industrially more advanced developing countries (East Asia) include a substantial proportion of sophisticated medium- and high-technology products, where markets are much more influenced by technological innovation, and where prices are determined generally on a "cost plus" basis.

A major part of the current trend in globalization is the development of global production networks (GPNs). Production essentially involves combining inputs to generate final outputs. GPNs are the international systems of optimum production, procuring, marketing, and innovation created through locating production activities, processes, or functions in different countries to maximize benefits from cost, technological, marketing, logistic, and other differences. This process is called by different names: fragmentation, segmentation, production sharing, integrated production, outward processing, or vertical specialization.

Fragmentation refers to the production activities that can be broken down into stages or blocks. Coordination is necessary but proximity helps to bring down its cost. When the production blocks are spatially separated, coordination becomes more complex and costly. Coordination is provided through service links. A service link is a combination of telecommunication, transportation, insurance, quality control, and management coordination to ensure that the blocks interact in the most productive manner. A firm may move the blocks around so that the components can be produced in the best possible location [15].

Advances in transportation and communication technologies, together with recent developments in the world trading system, have opened new opportunities for extending production fragmentation across national borders. A country may import goods from another country, transform them into finished products and export them. For instance, Italian firms import olives from Spain, process and package them, then export them under Italian brand names. Japan exports raw steel to Mexico, where the steel is stamped and pressed. It is then exported to the U.S. where it is manufactured into farm equipment much of which is then exported again. Among the 14 OECD countries, vertical specialization accounted for 21% of their exports and grew almost 30% between 1970 and 1990 [16]. Globalization facilitates fragmentation and helps LDCs specialize in activities or components that they have a competitive edge.

23.3   What Should LDCs Do?

Based on the experience of the past 50 years, the following propositions concerning favorable conditions for growth and development can safely be made:

1. A market economy works better than one planned by the state.
2. An economically free economy works better than a restrictive one.
3. An economy with institutions that protect private property, promote transparency in government, and ensure individual liberty works better than the one with less of these qualities.
4. In case of market failures or strategic sectors, targeted selective government intervention works better than the no government intervention at all.
5. International trade tends to promote growth rather than lessen it.
6. Industrialization success depends on the development of technological capabilities (TC).
7. Less developed countries grow faster with growth in manufactures export: the greater the manufactures export the greater the GDP growth.

By "working better" we mean the achievement of the goals laid out in Section 23.2, namely the development not only of countries but also of people.

23.3.1   The Necessity of a Market Economy

The failure of the economies in which all aspects were planned by the government and the success of those adopting the market system show the virtue of an economically free system. Even the communist countries had to turn to the market system to attain their full potential. Those LDCs which previously had been under heavy government controls are now adopting economic liberalization in one way or another. The well-known Economic Freedom of the World (EFW) index constructed by Gwartney and Lawson [17] shows that increased economic freedom spurs economic growth; not only does it not lead to greater income inequality, but it actually reduces poverty. As defined in the index, economic freedom involves personal choice, voluntary exchange, freedom to compete, and protection of person and property. Institutions and policies are consistent with economic freedom when they provide an environment for voluntary exchange and protection of individuals and their property. This environment includes not only legal and monetary aspects, but also limited interference by government into the private sector, except in the case of market failures and the need for protection and nurturing of infant and strategic industries. To be more specific, economic freedom is reflected in five areas: (1) the size of government in terms of expenditures, taxes, and government enterprises; (2) legal structure and security of property rights; (3) access to sound money; (4) freedom to exchange with foreigners; and (5) regulation of credit, labor, and business. For instance, the 2001 EFW index shows that among the four newly industrializing countries (NICs), Hong Kong and Singapore rank first and second respectively in the123 countries ranked, while the other two, South Korea and Taiwan, both rank 26th.

23.3.2 Opportunity Provided by Globalization

Globalization confers benefits as well as costs to LDCs. Among the former are increased trade and capital flow, which enable many LDCs to improve productivity and to raise income and employment. Those countries, such as the NICs in East Asia, which can take advantage of globalization by implementing policies and establishing institutions compatible with its demands, found themselves on a faster track of economic growth. The rates of economic growth of the four East Asian economies have been among the highest in the world for the last two decades. They are now classified by the World Bank as high income countries in the same league as the advanced industrialized countries. But this achievement is not without costs. Globalization brings instabilities and uncertainties caused by unpredictable and massive financial capital flow, as happened to these countries after the financial crisis in 1997. These speculative attacks revealed the yet-to-be mature institutions of the East Asian NICs and forced them to strengthen the banking systems and to apply correct macroeconomic policies with respect to interest rates and exchange rates.

Unfortunately, the majority of LDCs have been unable to take full advantage of globalization. As a result, the proportion of people in the world in absolute poverty has risen and the gap between the rich and poor countries has widened. The question is what can be done by LDCs to turn the opportunities offered by globalization to their advantage. In what follows we will discuss the strategies and policies derived from lessons learned from the successful countries.

23.3.3 Costs, Prices, Product Qualities, and Technological Innovations

In the global context, LDCs can be seen as peripheral countries clustering around MDCs that provide central markets to the former. Product prices are set in the central markets and those of LDCs must be lower, other things being equal, in order to compete successfully with the incumbent suppliers, who are originally located in the central markets themselves. Market price is equal to producer price plus transport and communications costs. The incumbent sellers have the advantage of zero transport costs. Therefore, the producer price of LDCs must be lower than the market price by an amount at least equal to the transport and communications costs. Obviously the closer the LDCs are to the markets, the lower the transport cost. For instance, in terms of transport cost, Mexico has an advantage over South Korea in selling products in the U.S., which means that the producer price in Mexico can afford to be higher than that in Korea in the competition with American sellers.

The producer price is the cost per unit of output (unit cost). This unit cost is comprised of unit factor costs, unit transport, communication, information, and transaction costs, and unit tax cost. Unit factor cost for each factor, in turn, is the factor payment divided by its productivity. For instance, unit labor cost consists of wage per hour divided by labor productivity, measured in output per hour of work. Tax can be considered as payment to the factor government service, which should also be an argument in the aggregate production function. From this basic relation we can derive policies and institutions that can lower unit cost, i.e., lower factor payment and/or raise factor productivity.

Factors are divided into mobile and immobile ones. Mobile factors are capital and technology while immobile ones are land, governments, and, for all practical purposes, labor. Mobile factors tend to follow the "law of one price," i.e., their returns or payments tend to be equalized across borders due to owners' arbitrage by moving them from countries where they receive low returns to those where they can reap higher returns. The gap between the returns of immobile factors located in the central market countries and in the peripheral countries can be significant. For instance, even when labor is not abundant, LDCs will generally be required to have lower wages, simply to compensate for the distance between the sellers in LDCs and the central markets. Naturally, to minimize the production costs the firms in the central market locations will employ more capital relative to labor, the reverse of what occurs in the peripheral locations.

In order to lower the producer price, LDCs must raise factor productivities which, among other things, come from inflows of capital and technology. But to attract foreign capital and technology, LDCs must raise their returns higher than those they can obtain in central markets, by an amount sufficient to cover the information and transaction costs. Information costs are fixed costs and, in some cases, quite high, as information must be acquired before a firm makes a decision whether to enter production in a new location. After the firm builds production facilities in the new location, transaction costs may be incurred in using and defending property rights such as the buying, selling, and renting of the firm's property and products.

For homogeneous products like cotton and sugar, difference in price, which covers the transport cost, is all it takes for a successful export. For differentiated products such as apparel and footwear, style and quality as fitness for use, which implies customer satisfaction, is also needed. The new trade theory has recently emphasized that aggregate trade shares may depend on the variety and quality of goods produced in the economy [18]. Godfrey and Kolesar [19] consider product quality to be the most important factor in global competitiveness. They demonstrate why Japanese (such as Toyota and Sony) and American companies (such as Xerox and Kodak) which devote their attention to quality management retain their dominance in the marketplace. Greater productivity and lower costs also go hand in hand with improved quality. Less developed countries can compete successfully with American products that have passed through the maturity phase in their product life cycles. LDCs can capitalize on manufacturing strength due to the quality of their disciplined labor but MDCs still lead in exporting sophisticated products with more technology, although the lead has been narrowed over time. Technological innovations may involve process or product design that enhances productivity to compensate for higher wages.

One of the most important innovations in recent years is the new management technology. Computer integrated manufacturing and flexible manufacturing demand a new management method called IPM, as mentioned above [20]. The old management method, which involves a hierarchical command structure, was an answer to a rigid manufacturing system with dedicated assembly lines. With the advent of CIM and FMS, the command hierarchy becomes an obstacle rather than a facilitator because it is embedded in vertical (position oriented) organizational structure. It has to be replaced by the integrated management technique with its horizontal (process oriented) structure. Efficiency and quality problems can be solved by more self-coordination among workers and machines, as the ultimate knowledge of the process rests with the workers. Moreover, as the ultimate knowledge of the product rests with the customer, the latter must be allowed to participate in the production process. Toyota has experimented with this customer–worker participation for some time and has found it quite helpful in its product decisions.

23.3.4 Institutional Factors

Formal and informal institutions, which are called "soft infrastructure" as opposed to "hard infrastructure" like roads and telecommunications, can be established to lower information and transaction costs. This is important as transport and transaction costs tend to make up at least 40% of national output value [21]. Religious or secular institutions set up the normative rules that constrain instinctive, erratic, and opportunistic individual behavior either through legal sanctions or binding individual consciences [21–23a,b]. The rules reduce hold-up risk posed by worker strikes and provide standardized routines that can be used to generate economies of scale.

Formal rules can be imposed from the government to ensure orderly, harmonious, and efficient interactions and transactions among agents. Ethical rules based on customs, metaphysical and religious systems can provide a foundation for instilling in people the virtues of honesty, truthfulness, reliability, trustworthiness, integrity, punctuality, industriousness, diligence, sense of duty, justice, decency, humility, gratitude, prudence, charitableness, self-control, and patience. These are necessary for smooth, economical, efficient interactions among people. They pave the way for efficient, productive behavior among workers and employers and foster the resilience among the agents when the industrial structure has to be adjusted along the line of comparative advantage according to the change in cost conditions.

An example of an ethical system that helped in promoting the discipline and order is the Confucian tradition in the East Asian countries. South Korea, for example, was the major OEM (original equipment manufacturing) producer for footwear ordered by Nike and Reebok during 1980s because of low wages and high quality workers. Korean manufacturers built production facilities and supplied parts to produce footwear. Nike and Reebok just imported shoes carrying their brand names from Korean producers and sold them in America. During the late 1980s and early 1990s, wages started to rise in the Korean footwear industry due to labor shortages and union activities. Nike and Reebok decreased their orders, which precipitated the failure of many large Korean footwear firms [24]. This forced many Korean companies to build their plants in low labor cost LDCs without any protest from local workers. The decline of the Korean footwear industry shows how well this economy adjusts to the changing international division of labor because of a disciplined labor force.

Lack of rules makes interaction between agents less predictable and more uncertain, hence greater transaction costs result. In Latin America, institutional uncertainty has been diagnosed as the central cause of economic stagnation [25]. Institutional infrastructure such as property rights, free markets, stable money, steady macroeconomic policies, political pluralism, conflict resolution institutions and their flexibility is essential to creating a conducive environment for innovation and economic growth [26–28].

One important determinant of industrialization is the technology policy adopted by the government. Among the most practically significant of these policies are the control of technology imports, direct foreign investment, and "mission oriented" research and development (R&D) strategies [29].

23.3.5 Role of the Government

In general, underdevelopment is associated with insufficient knowledge about both technology and attributes [30]. Examples of technical knowledge (know-how) are software engineering, accountancy, and nutrition. Unequal distribution of know-how between countries and within countries creates knowledge gaps. Knowledge about attributes, such as the quality of a product, the diligence of a worker, or the creditworthiness of a firm, is crucial to effective markets. Incomplete knowledge of attributes, referred to as information problems, prevents markets from functioning properly. Information is the lifeblood of markets. Information problems lead to market failures and impede efficiency and growth.

Governments can close the knowledge gaps between LDCs and MDCs by: (1) acquiring knowledge through an open trading system, foreign investment, and foreign licensing; (2) absorbing knowledge through universal basic education and tertiary technical education; and (3) communicating knowledge by using communications technology as well as through increased competition, private sector provision, and appropriate regulation.

Less developed countries can reduce information problems by establishing standards and certification through government, private organizations, laws, or social norms. Without standards and certifications for quality of products, consumers will not buy and markets will fail. For instance, without good accounting and auditing standards, banks may fail and the banking system may collapse. Without certification for food, the consumers may buy spoiled food and get sick, forcing the stores that sold the goods to be closed. Without the approval of the government, some commodities, which proved to be harmful to the users or to the public, may be traded. Thus, in many cases, governments must step in to enforce standards, verify quality, stop harmful products, prevent fraudulent practices to protect consumers, monitor performance, and regulate transactions. Certification informs employers of the skills of the prospective workers and thus facilitates the hiring of workers in the labor markets. Enforcement requires laws and a good judicial system. Without commercial law, there is little incentive for foreign firms to invest in an LDC, which requires joint ownership with local investors. There must be clear law on collecting debt or assigning liability for damages. Foreign investors will not sign contracts that cannot be enforced legally. Setting up a non-profit third-party consumer protection agency may be necessary if governments do not have resources for that purpose. Governments can establish institutions and (public or private) agencies to improve transactions like: finding a job, obtaining a loan, buying food, making investment decisions, etc. Development requires an institutional transformation that improves information flow and creates incentives for effort, innovation, saving, and investment.

The problem of insufficient technical knowledge can be solved by "learning to learn" new technologies. A developing country needs to build learning capability by investing in new skills, technical information, organization methods, and external linkages. This costly learning process, which may be short or long depending on whether the technology is simple or complex, is part of the TC to be developed at the firm level and the national level.

Technological capability is defined in terms of physical investment (plants and equipments), human capital (education and training), and technological effort (e.g. facilities to promote research and development). At the firm level, relevant are capabilities on investment (identify, prepare, design, obtain technology for, construct, equip, and staff plants), production (process optimization, quality control, operation, maintenance, inventory control), and linkages (procurement of inputs and raw materials, absorbing/providing technology from/to input suppliers, subcontractors, consultants, service firms, etc.). At the national level, governments should provide appropriate macroeconomic incentives (interest rates, exchange rates, etc.), incentives to promote healthy domestic competition, and incentives to foster flexible and efficient factor markets. It is the interplay between incentive structures, capabilities, and institutions that determines industrialization success [31].

Government plays a critical role in reducing the uncertainty created by lack of rules mentioned above. Government should provide a framework of clear-cut general rules for doing business, as well as resolving conflict in a free-market setting. It should not favor any industry by special subsidies, tariffs, quotas, or other non-tariffs barriers. Nevertheless, in its early phase of economic development, an LDC may protect infant and strategic industries to be developed based on resource endowments. Coordination failure created by externalities calls for government intervention to organize private entrepreneurs into investments that they might not otherwise have made. For instance, the Korean government masterminded early import-substitution projects in cement, fertilizers, oil refining, synthetic fibers, heavy machinery, chemicals, steel, and shipbuilding. The Taiwanese government initiated and financed the establishment of such industries as plastics, textiles, fibers, steel and electronics [32]. A similar story can be found in the successful leadership and assistance by the Brazilian government in the building of the civil aircraft industry [33] and the automobile industry [34].

More importantly, government may take the lead in providing technological development. The best example is given by Korea which is the most technologically capable among the East Asian NICs. Korea followed the footstep of Japan by forming a close relationship between three sectors: industry, banking, and government. The giant local private firms, the *chaebol*, were given the mission of spearheading the industrialization drive, just as the Japanese counterparts, the *keiretsu,* once were. Korea selectively encouraged activities and firms via credit allocation and subsidization. It provided technology financing in the form of both grants and subsidized loans which were directed by the government to specific activities or firms. Just as once was the case in Japan, FDI in Korea was severely restricted and only permitted when it was the sole way of obtaining technology or gaining access to world markets. Thus it relies primarily on capital-goods imports, technology licensing, and other technology to acquire technology.

Finally, government should provide hard infrastructure such as roads, railways, seaports, airports, communications network, and schools, and soft infrastructure such as legal, political, and educational institutions that support freedom and democracy with considerable citizen participation, ensure property rights, and enhance human capital. The policy conduct should be carried out with transparency and integrity. Correct strategies and policies are essential to development success [35].

23.3.6 *Attractiveness and Competitiveness of a Nation*

A foreign investor compares the estimated rates of profit that can be generated from alternative locations, given the estimated risks and costs. He or she compares net present values of the investment projects in these locations and selects the highest. In other words, he or she compares the rates of return of these projects after setting the net present values to zero, and selects the highest rate. The annual net income of each project is the difference between total revenues and total costs. Normally a firm uses many factors to produce a commodity. This implies that the unit cost of that commodity has to be equal to the ratio of average factor price to the average factor productivity. The average factor price is the weighted average price of all factors in the production of the commodity. The weights correspond to the relative importance of each factor. Similarly, average factor productivity is the weighted average of all these factor productivities. For a sector or a specific industry, the weights could be the average ratio of the expenditure on that factor to the total factor expenditure used in production in that sector.

Next to profit, labor climate is the most crucial factor in attracting foreign investment. Investors look for countries where labor is cheap, and where workers are hard-working, intelligent, and disciplined, with no industrial-wide unions and with as few strikes and walkouts as possible. Additional factors include a business-oriented culture, some form of work ethics, attitude toward thrift, desire for achievement either through education or through business success, propensity for entrepreneurship, and tendency for cooperation and harmonious relations with others (as opposed to tendency for strife).

Finally, global competition requires modern infrastructure, especially in information and communication technology, export processing zones with attractive incentives, high levels of literacy, potential for skills development, provision for upgrading technological and supply capabilities, good business practices which lower transaction costs for producers, proactive promotion and targeting of FDI, economic and political stability, and good governance.

23.3.7 Emphasis on Manufactures and High-Technology Products

Lall et al.[36] identify eight product factors that affect export location: technological capability, marketing capability, logistics and proximity to major markets, fragmentability of production processes, information on and familiarity with different aspects of doing business in the sourcing countries by investors or buyers in major markets, availability of natural resources, and value chain organization. Assuming that a producer, say Motorola, in a major market, say the United States, has marketing expertise in handling the finished product, its choice of outsourcing a product to a developing country depends on whether: the sourcing developing country has the technological capability to produce the good; the logistics are cost reasonable; the product can be fragmented into, say a design phase which can be done in the U.S. and a manufacturing phase which can be done in the developing country; it (Motorola) is familiar with the business-related environment such as labor law, commercial law, bureaucracy, etc., of the country; the country has the needed human and material resources; and it already has established long-term relationships with many subcontractors or suppliers in some other developing countries. Then there are additional economic (Section 23.3.6 above) and policy factors (such as trade restrictions and subsidies, and trading blocs) to consider. To be a successful exporter, an LDC must possess many of these product elements. The easiest and well-trodden path is participation in vertical specialization.

Specialization on a particular component, stage, or block in a production process enables the producing countries to capture economies of scale. In addition, it permits small and medium size firms to operate successfully in the GPN. The implication for LDCs is that they do not have to master entire production processes in order to become viable competitors on the world markets. Each production process may be separated by several stages differentiated by factor intensities. The best locations for different components or activities depend on the relative abundance of resources at the sites. Less developed countries can just specialize in the components that give them the most competitive advantage. Weinhold and Rauch [37] find that productivity growth in the manufacturing sector in LDCs is higher when production is more specialized according to fragmented processes. Take the case of Ireland. Its key costs are between Asia and the industrialized nations. Its electronics industry imports cheaper passive components from Asia and manufactures other electronic components and computers, and assembles printed-circuit-boards (PCBs). The industry is successful in attracting FDI, as it utilizes abundant supplies of medium-skilled, medium-priced labor. In the mid-1990s, while Ireland's share of EU GDP was only around 1%, it received about 25% of all capital expenditures made by U.S. electronics companies in the EU [38].

After the early stage of economic development in which vertical specialization in some low technology components is adopted, LDCs may move on to more sophisticated goods by upgrading TC, an approach that most LDCs take. Consequently, during the past 20 years, exports of manufactures by LDCs were growing faster than those by MDCs in every category of products, especially in high-technology. For instance, exports of manufactures by LDCs grew at about 12% annually, while those by MDCs at about 7%. And while the value of manufactured high-technology exports rose from $20 billion in 1985 to $450 billion in 2000, the growth rate of the LDCs was twice as high as that of the MDCs, at 20% annually compared to10%.

Lall et al. [36] also note that most dynamic exporters are middle income countries, most of which are in East Asia. Technological dynamism is observed if export structure changes from less sophisticated items to more sophisticated ones. Thus while export production is shifting to lower income sites, most low income countries do not benefit that much because they export least sophisticated products such as textile and clothing, footwear, toys, and jute where the growth rate is smallest (2.9% annually during 1990–2000). The success of export among developing countries is concentrated in the top 15 exporters who control 94% of developing countries' total manufactured products, ten of which are in East Asia. These countries are, in descending order of export values in 2001, China, Korea, Mexico, Taiwan, Singapore, Malaysia, Thailand, Indonesia, Brazil, India, Philippines, Turkey, South Africa, and Hong Kong. The reason for their success is that they export highly sophisticated medium- or high- technology products whose growth rate is greatest (13.6% per year during 1990–2000). Among these countries, technological competence varies a great deal. Korea is ranked highest, as it has the greatest capability of designing, manufacturing, and exporting high technology items, followed by Taiwan, Singapore, Malaysia, Thailand, and the Philippines in that order [39]. In the same vein, if the proportion of population enrolled in science and engineering is used as a measure of technological capacity, Korea still leads the LDCs followed by, in descending order, Taiwan, Singapore, Mexico, Hong Kong, Brazil, and India [31].

23.3.8   Environmental Consequence of Growth

Evidence shows that industrialization, at least during the take-off and maturity stages—using Rostow's description for lack of a better term—brings with it declining environmental quality. A conspicuous example is China, whose growth is one of the fastest in the world. Polluting industries, most of which are located in densely populated urban areas, are responsible for over 70% of the national emission of particulates, sulphur oxide, and organic water pollution [40]. According to the 2005 Report by China's State Environmental Protection Administration (SEPA) [41], only 32% of domestic sewage, 58% of domestic garbage, and 60% of hazardous waste (especially waste from hospitals) were treated in the 500 cities surveyed. The untreated sewage was simple flushed into the waterways. As a result, water quality in five out of the seven biggest rivers and 25 out of the 27 major lakes in China was rated poor or dangerous. Some 300 million people drink water that is too contaminated to be consumed safely. Indeed, contaminated water is responsible for the death of more than 30,000 children as a result of diarrhea. China is the world's second-largest producer of greenhouse gases, after the United States. China is on track to add 562 coal-fired power plants-nearly half the world total of plants expected to come online in the next 8 years. The country will surpass the coal-fired generating capacity and the CO_2 emissions of the U.S. in the next couple of years. Sulfur released into the air by burning coal combines with moisture to form acid rain. As a result, acid rain occurred in more than half of the 527 Chinese cities monitored by SEPA. One-third of the urban population is breathing polluted air, often due to coal dust from power plants. On top of this, auto exhaust is expected to get worse over time with 140 million cars to be driven by 2020. Five of the ten most polluted cities in the world are in China. Finally, areas suffering from soil erosion account for 38% of the country's total land areas, a stunning 3.6 million square kilometers. In short, just as urbanization problems arose in the developing countries in a very short time (compared with the similar but prolonged process in developed countries), the environmental problems that developed countries gradually encountered over a span of two centuries overtook China in just two decades.

The case of China is typical of the environmental problems in other LDCs although the latter experience them at a much smaller scale. Most LDCs started their industrial development with the textile industry. But this is one of the worst polluting industries, as the firms, without government intervention, can release dyes, bleaching agents, alkalis, and starch into streams, rivers, and oceans. It is not surprising that China is overloaded with pollutants, as it is becoming the largest producer and user of coal and the dominant exporter of textile and apparel products.

To be sure, many of the environmental problems mentioned above are the results of underdevelopment rather than of growth. We would expect many of them to be corrected when a country becomes more developed. This observation led to a hypothesis which posits that the relationship between environmental degradation and economic development follows the Environmental Kuznets inverted U-curve: environmental degradation increases as the economy changes its structure from predominantly agriculture to predominantly industry, and decreases when the economy moves from being industry-oriented to service-oriented. As the countries become richer, the consumers demand better environmental quality and the governments can afford the cleanup costs and are able to enforce regulations to control emissions. It is also possible that the rich countries, being specialized in services, can move some "dirty" industries to LDCs and import their products. Thus, environmental problems can be redistributed, wittingly or unwittingly, and globalized—as in the case of acid rain, where one country can affect others due to moving clouds.

There are two general measures of pollution: total biological oxygen demand (BOD), which measures organic water pollutants, and total carbon dioxide (CO_2) emission which measures air pollution. The turning point for which the BOD levels off and begins to decline is GDP per capita of $24,000 in purchasing power parity (PPP). But the turning point for CO_2 is much higher, at GDP per capita of $80,000 in PPP [40]. It will take several decades for most LDCs to attain this level of income. In the meantime, the long term effect of high CO_2 levels would be devastating to health and ecosystems. Thus LDCs need to integrate environmental policy into the overall development strategy and to enhance environmental capability along with general capabilities. During the process of expanding technological capability and industry-building, LDCs should adopt, as proposed by UNIDO, environmentally sound technologies (ESTs) in their investment projects. Environmentally sound technologies include: (1) end of pipe (EOP) technologies; and (2) preventive or clean technologies (CTs). End of pipes relate to the treatment of conventional pollutants and recycling of waste products. Clean technologies refer to: (1) product modification or environmentally friendly design of new products; and (2) reduction of the source of pollution by changing the production process itself, which involves technology change, input material change, equipment modification and better process control. To encourage the adoption of these technologies, financial incentives and disincentives in the form of subsidies, low interest loans, investment tax credits, special charges, and waste discharge taxes may have to be instituted.

23.4   A Growth Model as a Guide for Policy Formulation

In the previous section, we discuss supply conditions that should exist in every LDC to promote economic development. In this section, demand conditions are laid out in an extended model à la Thirlwall [42]. It acts as a guide as to what traded goods should be produced and what policies should be made in the face of globalization to achieve balance of payment equilibrium growth.

23.4.1 Demand for Export Function

$$X = A \left(\frac{P}{\bar{P}} \frac{1}{E} \right)^{\eta_x} \bar{Y}^{\varepsilon_x} \tag{23.1}$$

where X=quantity of export; η_x=price elasticity of demand for export with $\eta_x < 0$; P=home price of tradable goods (exports or imports); $\bar{P}$=foreign price of tradable goods; ε_x=income elasticity of demand for exports; E=exchange rate=\$H/\$F; \$H=home country's currency; \$F=foreign country's currency; $\bar{Y}$=income of foreign country; A=a constant.

Taking natural the log of 23.1 and total differential of both sides, we have:

$$\mathrm{dln}\, X = \eta_x (\mathrm{dln}\, P - \mathrm{dln}\, \bar{P} - \mathrm{dln}\, E) + \varepsilon_x \mathrm{dln}\, \bar{Y} \tag{23.2}$$

The result is:

$$x = \eta_x (p - \bar{p} - e) + \varepsilon_x \bar{y} \tag{23.3}$$

where x=percent change in export quantity; p=percent change in the price of export in home (domestic) currency; $\bar{p}$=percent change in the price of import in foreign currency; e=dE/E=percent change in the exchange rate; $\bar{y}$=percent change in foreign income.

23.4.2 Demand for Import Function

$$M = B \left(\frac{\bar{P}E}{P} \right)^{\eta_m} Y^{\varepsilon_m} \tag{23.4}$$

where M=quantity of import; η_m=price elasticity of demand for import with $\eta_m < 0$ and ε_m=income elasticity of demand for imports; Y=home country's income; B=a constant.

Using the same procedure as in 23.2 and 23.3 we obtain:

$$m = -\eta_m (p - \bar{p} - e) + \varepsilon_m y \tag{23.5}$$

where m=percent change in import quantity and y=percent change in home country's income.

23.4.3 Balance of Payments Equilibrium Condition

BP equilibrium requires that total receipts R from exports X and capital inflows K be equal to imports M, i.e.

$$R = PX + K = \bar{P}ME. \tag{23.6}$$

where K=nominal value of capital inflow.

Taking total differential of $PX+K$ and of $\bar{P}ME$, we obtain:

$$X\,dP + P\,dX + dK = ME\,d\bar{P} + \bar{P}E\,dM + \bar{P}M\,dE \tag{23.7}$$

Dividing the LHS of 23.2 by R and the RHS by $\bar{P}ME$, we have:

$$\frac{PX}{R}\frac{dP}{P} + \frac{PX}{R}\frac{dX}{X} + \frac{K}{R}\frac{dK}{K} = \frac{d\bar{P}}{\bar{P}} + \frac{dM}{M} + \frac{dE}{E} \tag{23.8}$$

which becomes:

$$\theta p + \theta x + (1-\theta)k = \bar{p} + m + e \tag{23.9}$$

where θ=share of export in total receipt to pay for import, i.e., $\theta = PX/R$; $1-\theta$=share of capital inflow in total receipt, i.e., $1-\theta = 1 - PX/R = K/R$; k=percent change in nominal capital inflow measured in domestic currency.

Plug x in Equation 23.3 and m in Equation 23.5 into Equation 23.9 and solve for y which is replaced by y_{BP} to indicate the output growth that would satisfy the balance of payment equilibrium. The result is:

$$y_{BP} = \frac{(p-\bar{p}-e) + (\theta\eta_x + \eta_m)(p-\bar{p}-e) + \theta\varepsilon_x\bar{y} + (1-\theta)(k-p)}{\varepsilon_m} \tag{23.10}$$

where y_{BP}=percent change in home output that satisfies the balance of payment equilibrium.

Equation 23.10 shows the four basic components of any country's balance of payments equilibrium growth. The first component $(p-\bar{p}-e)$ represents the pure terms of trade effect on y_{BP}. The second term $(\theta\eta_x + \eta_m)(p-\bar{p}-e)$ measures the volume effect of relative price changes. The third term $\theta\varepsilon_x\bar{y}$ indicates the effect of exogenous change in income abroad. The fourth term $(1-\theta)(k-p)$ denotes the effect of the growth of real capital inflows which finance the growth in excess of balance of payments growth rate. The dynamic law of one price says that $(p-\bar{p}-e)$ should be zero, i.e., the price of a product sold in, say Japan, should be the same as in the United States after the Yen price is converted into the dollar price using the prevailing exchange rate.* Further, the relative purchasing power parity (PPP) theory suggests that $e=p-\bar{p}$, percent change in the exchange rate is equal to the inflation differential between the two countries. In the long run, according to this theory, e will be determined by $p-\bar{p}$,

---

* In the short run, however, the PPP theory does not hold well for any pair of countries as $p-p$ will deviate from e when E is fixed in the fixed exchange rate regime or $p-p$ is at least slow to adjust to a fixed E.

thus we would expect $(p - \bar{p} - e)$ to be negligible.[4] $p - \bar{p}$ represents the change in net barter terms of trade (NBTT).

If we assume that PPP theory holds such that $p - \bar{p} - e = 0$, and that capital inflow is ignored such that $\theta = 1$, then Equation 23.10 is reduced to:

$$\frac{y_{CA}}{\bar{y}} = \frac{\varepsilon_x}{\varepsilon_m} \tag{23.11}$$

A country's growth rate which satisfies the current account balance (y_{CA}) relative to all other countries' growth rates $(\bar{y})$ is equiproportional to the rates of income elasticity of demand for exports (ε_x) and imports (ε_m) [42]. This is called Thirlwall's rule [41] or the 45-degree rule [18].*

Equation 23.11 says that the distinguishing feature between slow-growing economies and fast- growing ones lies in the differences in the structure of production and consumption manifested through the income elasticities of demand for exports and imports. A country that has high income elasticity of demand for imports will have a low rate of GDP growth that maintains the current account balance. Similarly, a country which has high income elasticity of demand for exports will have high rate of GDP growth. Table 23.2 below shows that the LDC income elasticity of demand for exports and the foreign income elasticity of demand for LDC exports are 2.26 and 0.40, respectively. This means that, if the estimation is correct, LDCs on the average can grow more than 5 times as much as MDCs.

These trade elasticities reflect both structures of production and consumption. Countries which export goods that have high income elasticity of demand, such as industrial goods and import goods, that have low income elasticity of demand, such as primary goods, will have higher economic growth relative to others. In particular, primary goods tend to have income elasticities of demand less than 1 and industrial goods more than 1.

These elasticities may reflect the natural resource endowments and consumers' preferences. For exporting countries, however, it is a conscious policy to adopt production structure that would promote the fastest growth, namely high ε_x and low ε_m. To further lower ε_m, the government might have to limit imports of luxury goods and other goods to be protected, altering consumers' preferences. Although import control in the form of quotas and/or high import duties can breed inefficiency, no country has ever been industrialized without some sort of protection. Even now, while developed countries advocate free trade, they still engage in protection of their own markets against many products from LDCs, particularly agriculture and textiles.

---

* This equation can also be used to explain the trade deficit. Take the case of the United States. Hooper et al. [46] in Table 23.1 show that the U.S. income elasticity of demand for imports is 1.8 and the foreign income elasticity of demand for U.S. exports is 0.8. This means that even if real growth levels out at 3% in both the U.S. and the rest of the world, the difference in elasticities would imply that U.S. imports grow at 6% a year vs. 2.7% a year for exports and the U.S. trade deficit is likely to widen (apart from any changes in relative prices). Indeed, the U.S. primary trade deficit has widened steadily since 1990.

23.4.4   Wage Setting Condition

To make the model more realistic, we add the wage-price relation.

$$P = \left(\frac{W}{O}\right) T \text{ which implies that } p = w - o + t \tag{23.12}$$

where W=the wage rate; O=output per worker or average labor productivity; W/O=unit labor cost; T=the markup rate; w=growth in the wage rate; o=growth in the average labor productivity; t=growth in the markup rate which is assumed to be constant (i.e., $t=0$).

Hence

$$p = w - o. \tag{23.13}$$

Similarly for the foreign country:

$$\bar{P} = \left(\frac{\bar{W}}{\bar{O}}\right) T \tag{23.14}$$

$$\bar{p} = \bar{w} - \bar{o} + t \tag{23.15}$$

where $\bar{w}$ is growth in the wage rate in the foreign country, $\bar{o}$ growth in the average labor productivity in the foreign country, t=growth in the markup rate, which is assumed to be zero. Hence

$$\bar{p} = \bar{w} - \bar{o} \tag{23.16}$$

23.4.5   Verdoorn's Law

The second part of Verdoorn's law states that there exists a causal relationship between the growth of manufacturing output and the growth of manufacturing labor productivity. The third part of Verdoorn's law asserts that growth in manufacturing sector is the cause of growth in economy-wide labor productivity.* This has been noticed by UNIDO [40], among others, that rapid industrial growth was the main source of overall labor productivity growth. In our one-sector model, the third part is the same as the second and we assume that productivity growth is proportional to output growth by virtue of static and dynamic economies of scale, that is:

$$o = \lambda y \tag{23.17}$$

$$\bar{o} = \bar{\lambda}\bar{y} \tag{23.18}$$

---

* To be more precise, the growth of the manufacturing sector leads to growth in non-manufacturing labor productivity.

where λ and $\bar{\lambda}$ are the rates at which labor productivity grows with the growth of output in the home country and the foreign country, respectively. λ and $\bar{\lambda}$ are called Verdoorn coefficients.

$$o - \bar{o} = \lambda y - \bar{\lambda}\bar{y} \tag{23.19}$$

23.4.6   Balance of Payment Equilibrium Growth

Thus,

$$p - \bar{p} = (w - \bar{w}) - (o - \bar{o}) = d - (\lambda y - \bar{\lambda}\bar{y}) \tag{23.20}$$

where $d = w - \bar{w}$ which is the differential wage growth between the home country and the foreign country.

Plug 23.20 into 23.10 we have

$$y_{\text{BP}} = \frac{[d - (\lambda y - \bar{\lambda}\bar{y}) - e] + (\theta\eta_x + \eta_m)[d - (\lambda y - \bar{\lambda}\bar{y}) - e] + \theta\varepsilon_x z + (1 - \theta)(k - p)}{\varepsilon_m} \tag{23.21}$$

Rearranging and collecting terms we have:

$$[(1 + \theta\eta_x + \eta_m)\lambda + \varepsilon_m]y$$

$$= (d + \bar{\lambda}\bar{y} - e) + (\theta\eta_x + \eta_m)(d + \bar{\lambda}\bar{y} - e) + \theta\varepsilon_x z + (1 - \theta)(k - p)$$

$$= (1 + \theta\eta_x + \eta_m)(d + \bar{\lambda}\bar{y} - e) + \theta\varepsilon_x\bar{y} + (1 - \theta)(k - p) \tag{23.22}$$

Let $\phi = 1 + \theta\eta_x + \eta_m \cdot 1 + \eta_x + \eta_m < 0$ is the original Marshall–Lerner condition which says that for a successful devaluation (improvement in the balance of current accounts) the sum of (negative) price elasticities of exports and imports must be less than -1. When capital inflow is incorporated into the model, the Marshall–Lerner condition is modified to $\phi = 1 + \theta\eta_x + \eta_m < 0$ where θ is the share of exports in total receipts which include capital inflows and $1 - \theta$ is the share of capital inflows.

After another rearranging, 23.22 becomes:

$$(\phi\lambda + \varepsilon_m)y_{\text{BP}} = \phi(d + \bar{\lambda}\bar{y} - e) + \theta\varepsilon_x\bar{y} + (1 - \theta)(k - p)$$

$$= \phi(d - e) + (\phi\bar{\lambda} + \theta\varepsilon_x)\bar{y} + (1 - \theta)(k - p) \tag{23.23}$$

Finally,

$$y_{\text{BP}} = \frac{\phi(d - e) + (\phi\bar{\lambda} + \theta\varepsilon_x)\bar{y} + (1 - \theta)(k - p)}{\phi\lambda + \varepsilon_m} \tag{23.24}$$

where $\lambda > 0$, $\varepsilon_x > 0$, $\varepsilon_m > 0$, $\eta_x < 0$, $\eta_m < 0$.

23.5   Empirical Estimation of Parameters

Table 23.1 shows that λ ranges from 0.3 to 0.6. Taking the average value for four periods corresponding to low income and middle income country group, λ becomes equal to 0.5 which is the same as other authors' estimate [39].

Our calculation of θ using data from International Monetary Fund Financial Statistics is shown in Table 23.2. Countries are chosen based on available elasticities estimated by other authors. The values for θ are averages of the ratios of current account credits to total current account credits and capital account credits from 1989 to 1998, depending on available data. For instance, for Canada, $\theta = 0.97$, $\varphi = 1 + (0.97)(-0.83) + -1.02 = -0.83$, and $-\varphi\lambda = -(-0.83(0.5) = 0.41$. For the countries listed in Table 23.2, the modified ML condition is satisfied, i.e., $\varphi < 0$. The analysis in the next section is based on this ML condition being met.

23.6   Policy Implication of Globalization

Equation 23.24 indicates what policies are required for economic growth. The following analysis is based on the mathematical derivation presented in Appendix B.

Empirical results presented in Table 23.3 show that an increase in the wage of the home country relative to the rest of the world and inflation, whether it is domestically generated or transmitted from outside, lowers the home country's output growth. Increasing returns to scale, greater capital inflow, expansion of the world economy, and devaluation of the home currency will raise output growth.

Although data on θ are not available for LDCs as a group, we can use South Africa for our purpose as a typical LDC, and given the fact that MDCs' growth is what they aspire to, we may infer that LDCs would benefit from policies that would hold down wage growth, thus increasing returns to scale, greater capital inflow, inflation control, expanding world economy, and currency devaluation. In order to raise λ, the government has to make more effort in

Table 23.1   Estimation of Verdoorn Coefficient λ

Country group	Period	Value of λ
Low income countries	1960–2003	0.48
Low income countries	1981–2003	0.34
Middle income countries	1965–2003	0.63
Middle income countries	1981–2003	0.47
High income countries	1987–2001	0.26
High income OECD countries	1987–2001	0.26
World	1987–2001	0.31

Source: For the computation of λ, see Appendix A.

Table 23.2 Estimation of Long Run Income and Price Elasticity of Imports and Exports, θ, φ, $-\varphi\lambda$

Country	Exports		Imports				
	Income (ε_x)	Price (η_x)	Income (ε_m)	Price (η_m)	θ	Φ	$-\varphi\lambda$
Canada (M2)	1.69	−0.83	1.84	−1.02	0.97	−0.83	0.41
Chile	1.31 (SM)	−1.08 (SM)	1.15 (H1)	−0.15 (H1)	n.a.	n.a.	n.a.
China	1.2 (SM)	−3.13 (SM)	1.2 (H1)	−0.6 (H1)	n.a.	n.a.	n.a.
Finland	2.0 (SM)	−1.05 (SM)	1.56 (H1)	−0.46 (H1)	1.00	−0.51	0.26
Germany (M1)	1.86	−0.66	1.88	−0.60	1.00	−0.26	0.13
Japan	2.11 (SM)	−1.27 (SM)	1.35 (H1)	−0.52 (H1)	1.00	−0.79	0.40
Japan (H2)	1.1	−1.0	0.9	−0.3	1.00	−0.30	0.15
South Africa	0.66 (SM)	−0.51 (SM)	1.06 (H1)	−0.8 (H1)	1.00	−0.31	0.16
U. K. (H2)	1.1	−1.6	2.2	−0.6	1.00	−1.20	0.60
U.S.	1.04 (SM)	−0.73 (SM)	0.98 (H1)	−1.05 (H1)	1.00	−0.78	0.39
U.S. (H2)	0.8	−1.5	1.8	−0.3	1.00	−0.80	0.40
U.S. (M1)	1.54	−0.99	1.94	−0.92	1.00	−0.91	0.46
U.S. (HM)	0.99	−1.51	1.51	−0.54	1.00	−1.05	0.53
U.S. (B)	2.05	−0.69	1.74	−0.72	1.00	−0.41	0.21
U.S. (A)	2.09	−1.07	2.96	−0.84	1.00	−0.91	0.46
U.S. (GK)	1.01	−2.32	1.84	−1.12	1.00	−2.44	1.22
U.S. (M2)	0.92	−1.44	1.26	−0.52	1.00	−0.96	0.48
Rest of OECD (M1)	1.75	−0.83	2.03	−0.49	n.a.	n.a.	n.a.
(LDCs) (M1)	2.26	−0.63	0.40	−0.81	n.a.	n.a.	n.a.
OPEC (M1)	−1.27	−0.57	1.07	−1.14	n.a.	n.a.	n.a.

Source: SM=Senhadji and Montenegro [44], Table 2, 266–271; H1=Hong [45], Table 4.1, 9; H2=Hopper et al. [46], Table 1, 7; HM=Houthaker and Magee [47], Table 1, 113; B=Blecker [48], Table A-4, 148 and Table A-6, 151; A=Alterman [49], Table F and Table G; M1=Marquez [50], Table 2, 75; GK=Goldtsein and Khan [51], Table 4.1, 1078 and Table 4.3, 1082; M2= Magee [52], Table 1, 180; n.a.=not available.

complementary investment in infrastructure and enhancing the coordination of private investment. The crucial condition, however, is that the income elasticity of demand for export must be sufficiently large, which means that the country has to invest in high income-elastic products. The greater the increasing returns to scale or the greater the price elasticities of demand for imports and exports, the greater the required income elasticities. The magnitude of income elasticities

Table 23.3   Effects of Various Economic Variables on BP Equilibrium Income

Country (1)	Wage Increase (2)	Increase in λ (3)	Increase in Capital Inflow (4)	Inflation (5)	Expanded World Economy (6)	Devaluation (7)
Canada (M2)	−	+	+	−	+	+
Chile	−	+	+	−	+	+
China	+	+	−	+	+	−
Finland	−	+	+	−	+	+
Germany (M1)	−	+	+	−	+	+
Japan	−	+	+	−	+	+
Japan (H2)	−	+	+	−	+	+
South Africa	−	+	+	−	+	+
U.K. (H2)	−	+	+	−	+	+
U.S.	−	+	+	−	+	+
U.S. (H2)	−	+	+	−	+	+
U.S. (M1)	−	+	+	−	+	+
U.S. (HM)	−	+	+	−	+	+
U.S. (B)	−	+	+	−	+	+
U.S. (A)	−	+	+	−	+	+
U.S. (GK)	−	+	+	−	+	+
U.S. (M2)	−	+	+	−	+	+
Rest of OECD	n.a	n.a	n.a	n.a	n.a	n.a
LDCs	n.a	n.a	n.a	n.a	n.a	n.a
OPEC	n.a	n.a	n.a	n.a	n.a	n.a

Source: The computation is based on Table 23.2. *Note*: "−"=lower output growth and "+"=higher output growth. The precise conditions are given in Appendix B.

relative to returns to scale coefficient λ and price elasticities holds the key to growth. They reflect the consumer preferences and development strategy adopted by the government which must guide and coordinate investment in the target industries in the initial phase, when the market fails to put the economy on a self-sustaining development path. Emphasis on high technology-intensive products (office/data processing/telecommunications equipment, televisions, transistors, turbines, power-generating equipment, pharmaceuticals, aerospace, optical/measuring instruments, cameras) would offer better growth prospects than low technology-intensive ones (textile fabrics, clothing, headgear, footwear, leather manufactures, travel goods, pottery, simple metal parts, furniture, jewelry, toys, plastic products) because the former have high income elasticities and tend to grow faster in trade [53].

23.7 Conclusion

With the inexorable advance in transportation and communications, the world becomes smaller and smaller every day. The globalization process is a fact and, barring an unexpected economic catastrophe on a worldwide scale, appears irreversible. The question then is whether LDCs can take advantage of it.

Human practices can only be successful and sustainable in the long run if they are compatible with human nature. History shows that socioeconomic systems that are incompatible with human nature, such as slavery and totalitarianism, will eventually fail and disintegrate. Countries which progress far in human development are those establishing a system based on reason, satisfying human aspirations such as individual liberty and security, protection of private property, development of human beings, and participation in honest and transparent government. Less developed countries can do no less in their quest for the same noble goals.

Globalization offers a challenge to LDCs in the sense that it tends to benefit countries with more developed technology and appropriate sociopolitical settings, as mentioned above. However, as human institutions can be developed and refined, any LDC can catch up with MDCs. In principle, if the institutions and economic structures are built correctly, a country's development is merely a matter of time. As trade is an essential of part of globalization, countries generally go through the stages of: first, exporting the least sophisticated products such as agricultural and mineral products or resource-based products such as paper, salted fish, animal fats, or cheese; then, moving on to more sophisticated ones with low technology such as clothing, apparel, textile, footwear, leather; then, more sophisticated products with a medium technology such as radio receivers, electrical equipment and appliances, and high technology ones such as semiconductors, office machines, automatic data processing machines, telecom equipment; and, finally, upgrade to the most sophisticated products such as transportation equipment (aircraft, ships, and automobiles). One reason that some countries can replace others in exporting many products is that the standard of living in the former is lower than the latter, and at the same time the former's growing technological capability is approaching that of the latter. For instance, Japan replaced the U.S. as a top steel exporter during the1960s, but Japan later encountered strong competition from Korea and Brazil because of the latter's lower costs. To remain competitive in steel products, Japan had to move some production blocks to LDCs. The same process applied to Japanese clothing and apparel which were edged out by the Koreans who, in turn, are now being supplanted by the Chinese. The Japanese and Korean apparel makers, in turn found subcontractors in LDCs such as Vietnam, where costs are lower than in China. Similarly, China became a strong competitor of Korea and Taiwan in many electronic components. During the last three decades, the latter two countries had competed successfully with the U.S. and Japan, which are now focusing on more sophisticated high-technology products. As a country progresses economically, its standard of living is rising, and so is its wage level. Although higher standard of living is usually a result of higher productivity, in the long run the wage growth of a high-productivity country may be greater than that of a low-productivity country. Consequently, a country with a higher standard of living becomes less competitive in markets for less sophisticated products. Nevertheless, it may still have competitive advantage in more sophisticated products, as it is continually advancing along the path of technical progress. Thus, we have a succession of countries becoming major exporters based on the dynamic law of comparative advantage driven by the desophistication process. This law can also be applied to knowledge-intensive products such as software. In this case, development of human capital may enable a country like India to be competitive in world trade.

We have seen the evolution in the global competition which benefits a small number of LDCs handsomely. For most LDCs, however, development is a struggle to find the right models for themselves. A practical model is chosen based on the interaction between the three elements of industrialization process: incentives, capabilities, and institutions. Since the interaction occurs in a given unique cultural setting, each country follows its own evolutionary but individual path. In the end, it is found that successful development in the face of globalization requires the right stuff: right institutions, right learning systems, right economic and incentive structures, and right strategies and policies in response to continuing technological advance. Any failure of economic and human development can be attributed, without exception, to the lack of any of these. But first, it is not easy to find the right stuff, due to human weaknesses. So long as exploitation of the underprivileged for personal gain is still attempted by the privileged, and government, instead of acting for the common good, caters to powerful interests, distribution conflict and the resulting insecurity and war could slow down the development process or halt it altogether. Second, the globalization process poses another obstacle, particularly for the least developed economies. A newcomer in the world scene must fit into existing GPNs and the minimum levels of entry are much higher now than 30 years ago [54]. Globalization, then, may actually hinder many countries' integration into the world economy by not providing equal opportunity for the least developed countries. Further, both the global and internal inequality in per capita income has been growing under globalization during the last 40 years [55]. Finally, growing global concern for the environment may force many LDCs to slow down their pace of growth, exacerbating the international inequality. Therefore, all things considered, plus the fact that obstacles to full development appear to be insurmountable for some LDCs, we should not be surprised if they never become fully developed in the narrow (economic) sense, much less in the broader (human) sense.

Appendix A

We wish to estimate the Verdoorn coefficient λ in Equation 23.17. λ is the coefficient that relates the growth of productivity to output growth. It represents the rate of productivity growth caused by output growth. If $\lambda = 0.5$, it means that productivity growth is half of output growth. The procedure of estimating λ is as follows.

The first difference of log of GDP per capita (YPC) was regressed on the first difference of log of MVA for five groups of countries: low income countries (1960–2003), middle income countries (1965–2003), high income countries (1987–2001), high income OECD countries (1987–2001), and the world (1987–2001). The time series data come from the World Bank Development Indicators 2005 and measured in constant 2000 U.S.dollars. Additional regressions are also run for the low and middle income groups for the1981–2003 period. The result is seven equations of the same form: $Y = c + bX + \varepsilon$ where c is a constant, b is the slope coefficient and ε the random error, which is assumed to be independently, identically, and normally distributed with zero mean and constant variance. Let LYPC = log of YPC and its first difference $DLYPC_t = LYPC_t - LYPC_{t-1}$. Similarly for MVA. The form of the seven equations becomes: $DLYPC_t = c + \lambda DLMVA_t + \varepsilon_t$.

For each time period, each variable is tested for unit roots. OLS equations were run only when the null hypothesis of unit root is rejected. In the case of high income countries, high income OECD countries, and the world, the two variables contain unit root, probably because of the shortness of available data. Hence, the second difference of log of YPC and MVA had to be made to induce stationarity before running regressions, i.e., $(DDLYPC)_t = c + \lambda(DDMVA)_t + \varepsilon_t$.

All OLS equations are run using the heteroskedasticity and autocorrelation consistent covariance method of Newey-West. The resulting residuals are tested for serial autocorrelation (Breusch-Godfrey Serial Correlation LM), normality (Jarque-Bera), heteroskedasticity (White), and coefficient stability (Chow and Ramsey). The results are accepted only when the tests show that the residuals are normally distributed, homoskedastic, non-autocorrelated, and that the coefficients are stable. All estimated slope coefficients, i.e., λ, are significant at the 5% level or better, but none of the constant c is significant, which confirms the specification of Equation 23.17. Due to limited space, the detailed results of the seven equations are not presented here. The values of λ for 5 income groups are given in Table 23.2 for seven time periods. Our results confirm many economists' belief that economic growth is achieved by expanding the manufacturing sector.

Appendix B

A. Wage Cost

Taking partial derivative of y_{BP} in 23.24 with respect to d, we obtain:

$$\frac{\partial y_{\mathrm{BP}}}{\partial d} = \frac{\phi}{\phi\lambda + \varepsilon_m} \tag{23.25}$$

Given $\varphi < 0$, there are two cases:

1. $(\partial y_{\mathrm{BP}}/\partial d) < 0$ if $\varepsilon_m > -\phi\lambda$
2. $(\partial y_{\mathrm{BP}}/\partial d) > 0$ if $\varepsilon_m < -\phi\lambda$

A rise in the wage rate in the home country relative to the rest of the world would tend to lower or raise output growth, depending on whether the income elasticity of imports is greater than or less than $-\varphi\lambda$, other things being equal. The results based on data in Table 23.2 and presented in column 2, Table 23.3 indicate case 1 for countries on the list.

B. Increasing Returns to Scale

From Equation 23.24, take partial derivative of y_{BP} with respect to λ, we have

$$\frac{\partial y_{\text{BP}}}{\partial \lambda} = \frac{\phi^2(d-e) - \phi(\phi\bar{\lambda} + \theta\varepsilon_x)\bar{y} + (1-\theta)(k-p)}{(\phi\lambda + \varepsilon_m)^2} \tag{23.26}$$

Assuming that wage growth is the same in two countries and no change in the exchange rate, and ignore capital inflow for the moment and $\bar{y} > 0$, then

$$\frac{\partial y_{\text{BP}}}{\partial \lambda} = -\frac{\phi(\phi\lambda + \varepsilon_x)\bar{y}}{(\phi\lambda + \varepsilon_m)^2} \tag{23.27}$$

Given $\varphi < 0$, there are two cases:

1. $(\partial y_{\text{BP}}/\partial \lambda) > 0$ if $\varepsilon_x > -\phi\bar{\lambda}$
2. $(\partial y_{\text{BP}}/\partial \lambda) < 0$ if $\varepsilon_x < -\phi\bar{\lambda}$

Assuming that $\lambda = \bar{\lambda} = 0.5$, results point to case 1 in column 3, Table 23.3 for countries listed.

C. Capital Inflows

$$\frac{\partial y_{\text{BP}}}{\partial k} = \frac{1-\theta}{\phi\lambda + \varepsilon_m} \tag{23.28}$$

Given $\varphi < 0$, there are two cases:

1. $(\partial y_{\text{BP}}/\partial k) > 0$ when $\varepsilon_m > -\phi\lambda$
2. $(\partial y_{\text{BP}}/\partial k) < 0$ when $\varepsilon_m < -\phi\lambda$

Case 1 is obtained and shown in column 4, Table 23.3 for listed countries.

D. Inflation

$$\frac{\partial y_{\text{BP}}}{\partial p} = -\frac{1-\theta}{\phi\lambda + \varepsilon_m} \tag{23.29}$$

Given $\varphi < 0$, there are two cases:

1. $(\partial y_{BP}/\partial p) < 0$ when $\varepsilon_m > -\phi\lambda$
2. $(\partial y_{BP}/\partial p) > 0$ when $\varepsilon_m < -\phi\lambda$

Column 5, Table 23.3 shows case 1 for listed countries.

E. Expansion of the World Economy

$$\frac{\partial y_{BP}}{\partial \bar{y}} = \frac{\phi\bar{\lambda} + \theta\varepsilon_x}{\phi\lambda + \varepsilon_m} \tag{23.30}$$

To simplify the analysis, assuming that $\lambda = \bar{\lambda}$, then 23.30 becomes:

$$\frac{\partial y_{BP}}{\partial \bar{y}} = \frac{\phi\lambda + \theta\varepsilon_x}{\phi\lambda + \varepsilon_m} \tag{23.31}$$

Computation based on Equation 23.31 indicates positive partial derivative for listed countries (column 6, Table 23.3).

F. Currency Devaluation

$$\frac{\partial y_{BP}}{\partial e} = -\frac{\phi}{\phi\lambda + \varepsilon_m} \tag{23.32}$$

Given $\varphi < 0$, there are two cases:

1. $(\partial y_{BP}/\partial e) > 0$ if $\varepsilon_m > -\phi\lambda$
2. $(\partial y_{BP}/\partial e) < 0$ if $\varepsilon_m < -\phi\lambda$

Case 1 is shown in column 7, Table 23.3 for listed countries.

References

1. Kasper, W., *Global Competition, Institutions, and the East-Asian Ascendancy*, Institute for Contemporary Studies Press, San Francisco, CA, 1994.
2. Stutz, F.P. and de Souza, A.R., *The World Economy*, Prentice-Hall, New Jersey, 1998.
3. Quinlivan, G.M., Multinational corporations: Myths and facts, in *Religion and Liberty*, Acton Institute. Available at: www.acton.org/publicat/randl/article.php?id=364 (accessed 2005).
4. Lall, S., *Benchmarking Pakistan's Competitive Performance*, Asian Development Bank, Seminar Paper. Available at: http://www.adbi.org (accessed 2004).
5. Sen, A., *Development as Freedom*, Anchor Books, New York, 1999.

6. Kaldor, N., *Causes of the Slow Rate of Economic Growth of the United Kingdom*, Cambridge University Press, Cambridge, 1966.
7. Verdoorn, P.J., Fattori che regolano lo sviluppo della produttivita del lavoro, l'industria, No. 1, English translation by Thirwall, A.P., in *Italian Economic Papers*, Vol. 2, Pasinetti, L., Ed., Oxford University Press, Oxford, 1949, 3–10.
8. Michl, T.R., International comparisons of productivity growth: Verdoorn's law revisited, *Journal of Post Keynesian Economics*, 7, 4, 1985.
9. McCombie, J. and de Ridder, J.R., Increasing returns, productivity, and output growth: The case of the United States, *Journal of Post Keynesian Economics*, 5, 3, 1983.
10. Fingleton, B. and McCombie, J., Increasing returns and economic growth: Some evidence from the European Union regions, *Oxford Economic Papers*, 50, 89, 1998.
11. León-Ledesma, M.A., Economic growth and Verdoorn law in the Spanish regions 1962–91, *International Review of Applied Economics*, 14, 55, 2000.
12. León-Ledesma, M.A., Accumulation, innovation and catching-up: An extended cumulative growth model, Cambridge, *Journal of Economics*, 26, 201, 2002.
13. Hansen, J.D. and Zhang, J., A Kaldorian approach to regional economic growth in China, *Applied Economics*, 28, 679, 1996.
14. Panagariya A., Shah, S., and Mishra, D., *Demand Elasticities in International Trade, Are They Really Low?* Policy Research Working Paper no. 1712, The World Bank, Washington DC, December, 1996.
15. Arndt, S.W. and Kierzkowski, H., Eds., in *Fragmentation*, Oxford University Press, Oxford, 2001, 1–16.
16. Hummels, D., Ishii, J., and Yi, K.M., The nature and growth of vertical specialization in world trade, *Journal of International Economics*, 54, 75, 2001.
17. Gwartney, J. and Lawson, R., *Economic Freedom of the World Annual Report*, The Fraser Institute, Vancouver, 2003.
18. Krugman, P., Differences in income elasticities and trends in real exchange rates, *European Economic Review*, 33, 1031, 1989.
19. Godfrey, B.A. and Kolesar, P.J., Role of quality in achieving world class competitiveness, in *Global Competitiveness*, M.K. Starr, Ed., Norton, New York, 1988, 213–238.
20. Hessel, M.P., Mooney, M., and Zeleny, M., Integrated process management: A management technology for the new competitive era, in *Global Competitiveness*, M.K. Starr, Ed., Norton, New York, 1988, 121–158.
21. North, D.C., *Transaction Costs, Institutions, and Economic Performance*, Occasional Paper no. 30, International Center for Economic Growth, San Francisco, CA, 1992.
22. Hayek, F.A., *Political Order of a Free People*, Law, Legislation and Liberty, Vol. 3, Routledge & Kegan Paul, London, 1979.
23a. Hayek, F.A., *The Fatal Conceit*, University of Chicago Press, Chicago, 1988.
23b. North, D.C., *Transaction Costs, Institutions, and Economic Performance*, Occasional Paper no. 30, International Center for Economic Growth, San Francisco, CA, 1992.
24. Clark, G.L. and Kim, W.B., *Asian NIEs & the Global Economy*, Johns Hopkins University Press, Baltimore, MD, 1995.
25. Borner, S., Brunetti, A., and Weber, B., *Institutional Obstacles to Latin American Growth*, Occasional Paper no. 24, International Center for Economic Growth, San Francisco, CA, 1992.
26. North, D.C. and Thomas, R.P., *Rise of the Western World*, Cambridge University Press, Cambridge, 1973.
27. Jones, E., *The European Miracle*, 2nd ed., Cambridge University Press, Cambridge, 1987.

28. Rosenberg, N. and Birdzell, L.E. Jr., *How the West Grow Rich: The Economic Transformation of the Industrial World*, Basic Books, New York, 1987.

29. Lall, S., *Learning from the Asian Tigers*, St Martin's Press, New York, 1996.

30. World Bank. *World Development Report 1998/99*, The World Bank, Washington, DC, 2000.

31. Lall, S., Technological capabilities and industrialization, *World Development*, 20, 165, 1992.

32. Rodrik, D., Getting intervention right: How South Korea and Taiwan grew rich, *Economic Policy*, 20, 78, 1999.

33. Marques, Rosane A., Evolution of the civil aircraft manufacturing system of innovation: A case study in Brazil, in *Innovation, Learning, and Technological Dynamism of Developing Countries*, S. Mani and H. Romijn, Eds., United Nations University Press, New York, 2004, 77–106.

34. Kesidou, E., The Political economy of technology policy: The automotive sector in Brazil (1950–2000), in *Innovation, Learning, and Technological Dynamism of Developing Countries*, S. Mani and H. Romijn, Eds., United Nations University Press, New York, 2004, 107–134.

35. Vietor, R.H.K., *Globalization & Growth,* South-Western, Mason, Ohio, 2005.

36. Lall, S., Weiss, J., and Zhang, J., *The* "sophistication" of exports: A new measure of product characteristics, ADB Institute Discussion Paper no. 23, Asian Development Bank, Tokyo, Japan, January, 2005.

37. Weinhold, D. and Rauch, James E., Openness, specialization, and productivity growth in less developed countries, *Canadian Journal of Economics*, 32, 1009, 1999.

38. Ruane, F. and Görg, H., Globalization and fragmentation: Evidence for the electronics industry in Ireland, in *Fragmentation*, S.W. Arndt and H. Kierzkowski, Eds., Oxford University Press, Oxford, 2001, 144–164.

39. Mani, S. and Romijn, H., Eds., in *Innovation, Learning, and Technological Dynamism of Developing Countries*, United Nations University Press, New York, 2004, 1–11.

40. United Nations Industrial Development Organization, *Industrialization, Environment and the Millennium Development Goals in Sub-Saharan Africa*, UNIDO Industrial Development Report, Vienna, 2004.

41. *China Daily*, Available at: http://www.chinadaily.com.cn (accessed September 12, 2005).

42. Thirlwall, A.P., *The Nature of Economic Growth*, Edward Elgar, Northampton, MA, 2002.

43. Thirlwall, A.P., The balance of payments constraint as an explanation of international growth rate differences, *Banca Nazionale del Lavoro Quarterly Review*, March, Vol. XXXII, No. 128, 45–53, 1979.

44. Senhadji, A.S., and Montenegro, C.E., Time series analysis of export demand equations: A cross-country analysis, *IMF Staff Papers*, 46, 3, International Monetary Fund, Washington DC, 1999.

45. Hong, P., *Import Elasticities Revisited*, DESA Discussion Paper No. 10, United Nations, 1999.

46. Hooper, P., Johnson, K., and Marquez, J., Trade elasticities for the G-7 countries, *Princeton Studies in International Economics,* No. 87, 2000.

47. Houthakker, H. and Magee, S., Income and price elasticities in world trade, *Review of Economics and Statistics*, 51, 111, 1969.

48. Blecker, R.A., *Beyond the Twin Deficits*, Economic Policy Institute, Washington DC, 1992.

49. Alterman, W., Using disaggregated data to dissect the U.S. trade deficit, *Papers and Proceedings-Tenth Annual Meeting*, Korea–America Economic Association, 1995.

50. Marquez, J., Bilateral trade elasticities, *Review of Economics and Statistics*, 72, 70, 1990.
51. Goldstein, M. and Khan, M., in *Income and Price Elasticities in Trade, in Handbook of International Economics*, R.W. Jones and P. Kenen, Eds., Vol. 2, North-Holland, Amsterdam, 1985, 1041–1105.
52. Magee, S.P., Price, income, and foreign trade, in *International Trade and Finance*, P.B. Kenen, Ed., Cambridge University Press, Cambridge, 1975, 175–252.
53. Lall, S., The technological structure and performance of developing country manufactures exports, 1985–98, *Oxford Development Studies*, 28, 337, 2000.
54. Lall, S., Albaladejo, M., and Zhang, J., Mapping fragmentation: Electronics and automobiles in East Asia and Latin America, *Oxford Development Studies*, 32, 407, 2004.
55. Ocampo, J.A. and Martin, J., Eds., in *Globalization and Development*, The World Bank, Washington DC, 2003, 99–128.

Chapter 24

Complexity and the Science–Policy Interface

Kathi K. Beratan
Duke University

24.1   Introduction

Negative trends observed in both social and ecosystem conditions around the world raise increasing concern about converging crises that human communities will be facing in coming decades. Arguably the most alarming set of observations involve changes, such as shifts in growing conditions for crops and in pathways for transmission of plant and animal diseases, that have been linked to global climate change. Thoughtful people, scientists, policy makers, and citizens alike, are increasingly expressing a sense of urgency regarding the need to take effective action to mitigate the threats. However, it is not at all clear how to do this. Although there have been some notable successes, several decades of research into natural resource management have proven disappointing in terms of halting degradation of stressed environments and fragile ecosystems [1]. Many resource and environmental problems are proving resistant to solutions [2]. Too many policies and management actions are not only ineffective, but also produce a whole new set of problems that often prove to be more damaging than the original one. In short, traditional approaches to both science and policy making do not appear to be providing the answers we need.

In recent years, significant progress has been made towards understanding the challenges we face. Innovative collaborative efforts, such as the Research Alliances research informing practice [1,3] have shown that the big problems policy makers and managers are wrestling with emerge from complex interactions among innumerable components and processes within intimately interlinked human and natural systems—social–ecological systems. New approaches to environmental policy making and resource management, such as adaptive management and adaptive governance [4,5] have shown promise for addressing such problems. However, it has proven extremely difficult to put these promising concepts into practice. How can we modify the science–policy interface so that we more effectively put knowledge to *work* towards addressing significant problems?

There is a critical need for translation from theory into practical guidelines for practice. In this chapter, I seek to contribute to this translation process. I first provide an overview of the nature of the problems we face and the difficulties encountered in trying to address them. This summary draws from a wide range of literatures, and includes illustrative examples drawn from my own experiences with collaborative efforts to integrate science into real-world decision situations related to environmental problem-solving. Finally, I present some practical ideas that people on the front lines—policy makers, planners, and managers—can use to assist in developing strategies that are both scientifically sound and achievable in real-world settings.

24.2 Complex and Contentious Problems

Coupled social and ecological systems (SES) are complex and adaptive. Conditions in such systems are the products of countless processes that operate simultaneously at a range of scales on innumerable individual elements (people, plants, animals, water, etc.). Processes commonly are non-linear, meaning that equal amounts of stress or disturbance can produce very different amounts of response; feedback relations and lagged responses contribute additional unpredictability. Events affecting an SES rarely have a single, well-defined cause with clear links to effects; instead, there are many factors that contribute indirectly and in concert, and thus it is very difficult to trace any event back to its causes [6]. These abundant and complex interlinkages mean that perturbations to one part of the system will be felt throughout the system, often in unexpected and surprising ways. As a result, major changes in system conditions and behavior tend to occur abruptly and with very little advance warning, and those changes are likely to be irreversible [3,7]. An important consequence of complexity is that it is impossible for scientific and technical studies to fully and accurately predict the results of alternative policy options [8]. In particular, the system-wide consequences of decisions about a particular system element cannot be fully anticipated. Even in those rare situations where we have a reasonably good understanding of the natural system dynamics, we still must contend with the largely unpredictable realm of human behavior. In short, uncertainty is inherent, and surprise is inevitable.

The process of addressing problems affecting an SES is further complicated by the unavoidable fragmentation of decision-making authority and responsibility. Many people are impacted by events affecting the system, and many organizations and jurisdictions share responsibility for decision making; all have their own beliefs and values, and so decision making requires negotiation among competing viewpoints. When dealing with such uncertain decision situations, often termed "wicked" problems, decision makers commonly turn to scientists and other technical experts, seeking definitive knowledge about what should be done, and thus what policies should be put into place. Despite the best efforts of both scientists and decision makers, however, painfully little progress has been made in solving the most serious problems, such as poverty and environmental degradation. For example, decades of environmental regulation and focused management efforts in the United States have not succeeded in reversing the trends of accelerating loss of biodiversity and overall ecosystem integrity—things continue to get worse instead of better.

The boundary between policy makers and scientists has typically resembled a chasm rather than a semi-permeable membrane. One source of tension is the commonly-observed lack of agreement between science-based predictions and real outcomes. Numerous examples have been documented in which policies based on the best available science have produced unanticipated consequences that are as bad, or worse, than the original problem. For example, attempts to eliminate flood hazard along rivers using engineered structures such as levees have instead increased the frequency of large, damaging floods. Likewise, the effort to prevent all forest fires has created conditions favoring larger, hotter, and more destructive fires. The flood control and fire suppression strategies of the past century are examples of the "command-and-control approach" to natural resource management. This approach assumes that each system of interest has a particular configuration that is stable (e.g., "climax forest"), and that scientists can develop precise and accurate predictive models of future system conditions. These assumptions are not valid when dealing with complex adaptive systems, which are characterized by multiple semi-stable states and large inherent uncertainties [9]. In other words, command-and-control management actions are based on inaccurate or inappropriate models and assumptions, and so actual outcomes are almost certain to be very different from predictions.

The assumption of stability and predictability fosters misinterpretation of uncertainty as error or incompetence, and limits the effective use of science in decision making. Competing interests can readily produce conflicting "expert" information and predictions that supports their particular arguments and objectives [10,11]. A focus on scientific disagreements often serves as a cover for differences in values and priorities among individuals and groups, since arguing about science is relatively risk-free in comparison to talking openly about values [12]. Even when decision makers are honestly trying to find a solution to a problem, they frequently find themselves faced with seemingly contradictory information, and they tend to place especially heavy weight on scientific advice that happens to support a decision they prefer for other reasons [10].

24.3 Shifting Views of Science

Humans, like other organisms, are directly and indirectly impacted by the behavior of natural systems. Unlike other organisms, humans can anticipate the potential impacts of events and take actions intended to alter those impacts [13]. These actions constitute management activities. Political-managerial systems are the mechanisms through which actions that impact SESs are designed and implemented. The behavior of political-managerial systems, like human culture and collective behavior in general, are structured by *institutions*, the sets of routines, norms and incentives that shape and constrain people's preferences and behavior. Institutions constitute a form of collective memory, a way of integrating experiential knowledge across a time span greater than a single human lifetime.

Our institutions for the creation and use of scientific information have evolved in response to our changing understanding of how natural and human systems function. Through the 1970s, the problems being addressed in areas like the environment and public health were thought to be simple and easily definable, with obvious and readily implementable solutions [14,15]. This view was supported and strengthened by impressive results obtained from researchers applying reductionist methodologies within increasingly specialized disciplines. In the reductionist approach to science, complex systems or problems are analyzed by identifying and exploring the parts, or examining the effect of one variable at a time [16]. Within the reductionist tradition, the view of scientists in policy making is that of dispassionate experts, free of the influence of politics, who objectively identify "best" actions—those that can be shown through quantitative analysis to produce the greatest benefits with the least costs.

The idealized notion of science as the disinterested pursuit of knowledge translates to the norm of *objectivity* in the practice of science. Objectivity can be defined as the ability to perceive or describe something without being influenced by personal emotions or prejudices. The norm of objectivity is so integral to our mental model of the practice of science, and to the self-image of scientists, that it is difficult for us to critically assess. However, evidence is mounting that true objectivity may be unattainable in practice. Cognitive neuroscience research has shown that emotion is an important component of human experience and behavior [17], with emotional processes playing a critical role in reducing to a manageable number the nearly unlimited considerations that enter into any choice [18]. Emotions and related subjectivity appear to be essential to making sound decisions; research on individuals with damage to emotion-processing parts of the brain shows that lack of an emotional contribution to high-level decision making results in patients making personally disadvantageous decisions [19]. Emotion processes appear to be most important under conditions of uncertainty and incomplete knowledge [20,21], conditions that apply to any worthwhile research project. As Cortner points out, subjective value interpretations are made by scientists at every step of the scientific process [22]. It appears that meaningful description and analysis, the core activities of science, are not possible without personal emotions and prejudices, less pejoratively known as biases based on experiential knowledge.

Separating science and policy making into different categories has served a useful purpose, as shown by the tremendous growth in scientific knowledge over the past fifty years. The development of explanatory and predictive hypotheses and the testing of those hypotheses through experiments and observations are and will remain the definitive elements of science. Nonetheless, this separation is somewhat arbitrary; the two activities are endpoints in a continuum, with no clear and natural dividing line between them. The unfortunate negative consequence of the useful division between science and policy is that it has discouraged scientists from participating appropriately in the policy process. The belief in the absolute separation of science and policy has become institutionalized to the point that scientists can damage their careers if they attempt to make the link [22].

Notable failures of efforts to deal with serious problems at local to global scales suggest that a different approach to science is needed to deal effectively with complexity. As Rapport editorialized, "In a world imperfectly known, laboratory-driven, tightly-controlled experimentation no longer applies and deterministic models must give way to pluralism in which contributions from many fields of knowledge are given their due. Through much of the 20th century, progress in science has been measured by going deep into more specialized areas of knowledge. Environmental challenges call for another standard, measured by the degree of synthesis or integration among the parts" [23].

The new approach to science that is beginning to develop is both *transdisciplinary* and *holistic*. A transdisciplinary approach recognizes that, for science to contribute to the resolution of societal issues, it must be situated in its social and political context. Thus problems are defined in the context of specific applications rather than in a disciplinary framework, and research is intended to be useful to someone, whether in industry or government, or to society more generally [24]. Holistic or system-based approaches recognize and seek to account for real-world system complexity [25], and thus involve placing as much emphasis on identifying and describing the connections between objects and events as on identifying and describing the objects and events themselves [26]. As Laszlo points out, a complex system is a divisible whole, but functionally it is an indivisible unity with emergent properties [27]. In practice, this means that scientific exploration of a complex SES should, at least initially, focus more on the interactions among objects and events than on the objects and events themselves, and on the dynamic behavior of the system as a whole rather than on its structural details.

In order for scientists to develop problem-focused knowledge that is useful to policy makers, they must recognize that social interactions contribute at least as much as biophysical processes to the emergent behavior of an SES, and thus that any forward-looking assessment and management effort involving an SES must focus as much on social dynamics as on biophysical processes. Thus far, our research institutions have largely addressed the socio-economic and biophysical components of systems separately. Typically the agenda is set by biophysical scientists who want information from social scientists that will fit neatly into their models [28]. Such an approach fails to recognize the critical cross-linkages between human and natural system elements, and the difficulties inherent in altering the social and political processes through which societies address complex problems. Too often, it is assumed that social interactions will take care of themselves, or some token guidelines may be tacked on to agreements as an afterthought.

Effective transdisciplinary research requires good communication among a diverse array of scientists, practitioners, and citizens. As Mohrman and colleagues argue, attention must be paid to the relationship between researchers and practitioners, not simply to the content of the research, if that research is to be useful [29]. Scientists and policy makers come from very different cultures with different norms and expectations that produce different mental models and, thus, worldviews. All communication, both the words themselves and clues to underlying meanings such as body language, gets filtered through and interpreted according to the recipient's mental models. Therefore, it is very difficult for both scientists and policy makers to recognize exactly *what* gets communicated during interactions. All too commonly, participants come away from meetings with very different understandings of what happened. I encountered an instructive example of this while researching cooperative watershed management in the San Francisquito Creek Watershed in the southern San Francisco Bay area of central California. Following a damaging flood in 1998, the local water district developed a plan, in collaboration with the Army Corps of Engineers, to raise and strengthen deteriorating flood control levees in the lower watershed. The proposed construction activities would have a particularly large impact on one neighborhood. In order to answer residents' questions and ease concerns over the impacts of construction, the flood control agencies set up a meeting with the neighborhood association at which an engineer described the construction plan and then answered questions. This well-intentioned public information effort backfired badly because the audience received a very different message from that which the speaker intended to send. A resident asked a question about why a different and less disruptive approach (reinforcing the levee with sandbags) had not been selected. As related to me by several meeting attendees, the engineer "rolled his eyes," sighed audibly and with "exaggerated patience" began to explain why the sandbag approach was not technically or fiscally feasible. A year after that meeting, attendees remembered the engineer's body language much more clearly than any of the words he spoke. The message received by the residents was that the flood control agencies were arrogant and considered the residents to be "stupid," and that the meeting was intended to control public response to an already-selected plan rather than an honest attempt to include the neighborhood in the planning process. As a direct result of this meeting, the neighborhood association mounted a vigorous campaign against the levee renovation plan. Although the plan was eventually implemented, the neighborhood's opposition delayed the start of the project, and has been cited as one factor (among many others) that limited progress towards cooperative management of the watershed.

24.4 Institutional Change

All human activities, including science, are essentially social in nature [14]. It is often an unpleasant shock to science students to learn that effective presentation of their results in talks and professional papers is as important (if not more so) to their careers as is the quality of the science they do. The information communicated through these peer activities is as much about the character and ability of the researchers as about the research findings. As Miller notes, social scientists studying the practice of science have found that science "turns out to look a lot like other social institutions, full of norms, beliefs, ideologies, practices, networks, and power and deeply engaged in the production and management of social order" [30].

When reformers attempt to introduce new institutional frameworks, they are faced with the task of *deinstitutionalizing* old rules and norms [31]. At a fundamental level, changing institutions translates into changing collective human behavior. This is an extremely difficult task [32,33]. Established patterns of behavior are habitual, and require little conscious thought. Uncertainty is relatively low because past experience provides good information about other people's reactions and responses, and about localized, short-term results. Any change to established behaviors and procedures introduces uncertainty about responses and outcomes, and thus is inherently risky for the responsible individuals and organizations. At organizational and societal levels, this resistance to change is referred to as *institutional inertia*. Three very common and powerful sources of institutional inertia are sunk costs, uncertainty, and political conflict. These reduce the attractiveness of institutional alternatives and act as a barrier to any switchover to new institutions [34]. Institutional inertia is not always a bad thing; it can be useful in "normal" situations, when past experience is a good predictor of future outcomes. Institutional inertia helps guard against changes that seem good over the short term, but which produce negative outcomes over longer time periods. However, this resistance to change also hinders our ability to recognize and implement necessary adaptations when dealing with novel events and circumstances.

Our science institutions are slowly beginning to change in response to changes in our understanding of complexity, as well as to related changes in the demands of both public and private sector funding sources. Transdisciplinary, systems-based approaches to science research are beginning to gain a foothold in academia, through the boundary-spanning activities of programs located outside of individual departments and disciplines, such as research centers and institutes that are organized around particular societal problems and research questions. Such programs are not replacing the traditional departments and disciplines, but instead are augmenting them. The increasing importance of such programs is a promising sign that the institutional adaptations needed to deal with complexity are beginning to occur. However, the adaptations are progressing very slowly, as any junior faculty member who is attempting to conduct transdisciplinary research can attest. The reductionist paradigm still dominates in the organizational practices of universities, most notably in those related to hiring, promotion, and tenure decisions.

Changes in public sector management institutions are occurring even more slowly than in science institutions. The organizational structure of modern academic institutions has evolved to maintain stability of the organization as a whole, while supporting individual creativity and innovation. Although intellectual orthodoxies have an undeniable influence, academic institutions inherently value the concept of adaptation to new knowledge. In contrast, governmental management institutions tend to be cautious and risk-averse, and are strongly influenced by political and legal considerations. Any change in the *status quo* will produce "winners" and "losers," particularly in the short-term. Those who currently have wealth, power, and influence will resist changes that they believe will shift that wealth, power, and influence from them to others. Thus, special conditions are required for real change to occur.

Example: Science Impact Program (SI), United States Geological Survey (USGS).

Overcoming the considerable barriers to institutional change requires both dedicated champions and strong support from above. The SI of the USGS provides an example of the challenges facing institutional change efforts. Science Impact Program is described as a focused research effort to increase the use and value of USGS science in decision-making. The strategy for accomplishing this is for SI staff and collaborators to "develop methods, tools, and techniques to build explicit linkages between science and societal decision makers." A feature of SI that distinguishes it from USGS standard practice is active engagement of community decision makers and stakeholders in all phases of project planning and implementation. Another difference is an increased attention to integrating the social and economic aspects of the problem situation into the scientific analysis.

After receiving minimal funding for approximately three years through the Director's Venture Capital Fund, SI became a formal Program within the Survey's Geography Discipline in September of 2004, as part of a major reorganization of the USGS by outgoing Director Charles Groat. Acknowledging a lack of needed expertise in some areas, SI has established external partnerships with five academic institutions. Most relevant to this paper is the partnership with Massachusetts Institute of Technology (MIT). The MIT–USGS Science Impact Collaborative (MUSIC) is based in the Department of Urban Studies and Planning at the MIT. MIT–USGS Science Impact Collaborative is testing ways in which joint fact finding (JFF) can be used to promote collaborative planning in science-intensive policy disputes.

U.S. environmental agencies are supposed to maintain a separation between the technical and political (or policy) aspects of their decisions. Agencies have had to determine when they are doing science (which is permitted) and when they are doing policy (which is not) [35]. MIT–USGS Science Impact Collaborative has addressed this issue, arguing that:

> By initiating the Science Impact program, the USGS becomes a champion for using science in decision making, without being an advocate for specific decisions. Although this boundary may appear to be less distinct as we attempt to cast our science more in a decision-making framework, the USGS must preserve its non-advocacy policy. We can act neither as advocates nor as consultants in this effort. The high degree of trust that our agency enjoys derives largely from our impartiality and our commitment to providing broad public benefits through our work. Admittedly,

> the boundary between supplying scientific information for decision making and recommending a course of action sometimes becomes somewhat difficult to delineate. Even when our scientific information seems to lead toward a certain solution or decision, however, we must present the scientific information in such a way as to refrain from making specific policy recommendations [36].

One way in which MUSIC is seeking to implement this vision is by providing training to USGS scientists in skills such as facilitation, mediation, and communication.

The SI champions and partners have encountered a number of barriers to institutional change, primarily linked to lack of funding coupled with limited opportunities for discourse among SI champions and the majority of the research staff. Science Impact Program has not been a line item in the USGS budget, therefore the very limited funding given to SI for program development was taken from established programs. Given the internal competition among programs and projects for limited funds, resentment of SI from within the organization developed before SI had a chance to introduce itself and its mission to potential partners and collaborators within the organization.

A related barrier involves cultural differences between researchers in the biophysical and the social sciences, as well as between researchers and practitioners. U.S. Geological Survey researchers, who overwhelmingly come from biophysical science backgrounds and institutions, have expressed difficulty in recognizing the differences between the SI approach and their past practice. My SI colleagues and I have frequently encountered statements along the lines of "we're already doing that." In the few instances where the SI champions have had the opportunity to explore the question with their colleagues through extended face-to-face interactions, the differences were made clearer, greater shared understanding was achieved, and resistance to SI concepts was reduced [37].

Another major barrier to success for SI is lack of an active champion within the highest echelons of the Survey. Interviews of USGS researchers that I have conducted suggest that SI has, in effect, received official *permission* to proceed from the USGS leadership, but with little concrete evidence of true *commitment* to the program. Few who were not directly involved with the program's inception knew that it exists. When known of at all, SI was lumped in with a number of organizational changes announced by former USGS Director Charles Groat soon before his departure from the Survey. Several of the people interviewed said that they did not understand the reasons for the whole suite of changes, or how they are to be implemented. Thus, SI has been buried within an internally controversial cluster of bureaucratic changes rather than being highlighted by the leadership as a positive addition to the methods and approaches available to Survey personnel. Unless active steps are taken to shift this situation, SI's long-term survival is in doubt.

Adaptive Management has been proposed as an integrated, multidisciplinary approach for confronting uncertainty in natural resource issues [38–40]. Adaptive management assumes that scientific certainty cannot be achieved prior to taking action, and thus treats every management plan as a set of testable hypotheses and every management action as an experiment. In any adaptive management effort, the role of science is primarily that of monitoring progress toward predefined goals. In other words, science steps in *after* the problem is well-defined and after desired goals are identified through political means [16].

Although appealing in theory, adaptive management has proven very difficult to implement, and has been repeatedly misapplied or misappropriated [41,42]. Many applications of adaptive management have stopped at the assessment phase and have failed to implement meaningful changes in management. The most promising adaptive management experiments in the United States mainly involve relatively simple institutional settings, with a single lead management agency and a few dedicated people who have organized and maintained the experimental initiative. Adaptive management has been more problematic in complex institutional settings such as those connected to the Florida Everglades, Columbia River, and Upper Mississippi River, where management, research, and policy change involve collaboration among several agencies with complicated, overlapping historical responsibilities and legal mandates [42]. Various reasons have been offered for low success rates in implementing adaptive management, most of which have to do with cost and institutional barriers [41,43–46].

It takes a long time to develop and implement an effective adaptive management effort, and even longer before positive outcomes are observed. In what Lee considers adaptive management's high-water mark, a project to deal with a declining ground fish fishery off northwest Australia, the adaptive learning program took about a decade to yield practical results [47]. Two factors contribute towards this slow progress. First, many of the critical processes that impact the natural system components and conditions of interest operate at timescales that are very long compared with those of management and decision making processes. Secondly, implementation of collaborative and adaptive processes requires a good working relationship among the responsible organizations and individuals. The necessary trust-based relationships are built through repeated interaction, and take time to develop. Lee argues that a collaborative structure should be in place before an adaptive exploration of the landscape gets underway. Too often, however, adaptive management efforts concentrate on developing models of biophysical processes and essentially ignore social dynamics.

24.5 Practical Strategies for Managing the Interface

The most important point for practitioners to take away from the previous discussion is that social interactions are of critical significance when addressing problems affecting complex social–ecological systems. In these complex decision situations, integrating sound science into the decision-making process—managing the science–policy interface—in essence consists of organizing and managing a set of social interactions, and thus is an exercise in institutional design. In this section, I discuss some practical strategies for getting from here to there. The section is organized around three basic recommendations: broaden involvement in question-framing; put greater emphasis on qualitative, conceptual models, particularly during the early phases of the decision process; and use boundary organizations, neutral third-parties, as science facilitators and integrators.

24.5.1 Question-Framing

Question-framing is arguably the most important, and the least considered, part of the decision process. Asking the right question is crucial to constructing a problem definition [30]. When dealing with science-intensive decision situations, there are two interrelated sets of questions that need to be defined: what are the specific *problems* being addressed, and what are the relevant *scientific research* questions that need to be tackled? The two question sets are different, and I discuss them separately in this section, but they share a key characteristic: because of the dynamics of complexity, diversity of viewpoints is needed in order to devise questions that lead to *useful* answers.

24.5.1.1 Problem Definition

Problem definition is a subjective process: a particular event or set of conditions is recognized as a "problem" only if it impacts humans sufficiently to gain a threshold level of attention. In most complex decision situations, relatively little thought is given to problem definition. The decision makers assume that they know what the problem is, and seldom examine that assumption in any depth. However, it is likely that the "problem" the decision makers are responding to is but one facet of a problem situation, an emergent manifestation at a particular observational scale of a multiscale set of interacting processes.

There can be many different but equally valid interpretations of a situation, based on different viewpoints, values, and experiences. The same problem situation will be described very differently by a civil engineer, a social worker, and the CEO of a manufacturing firm. Each description is equally valid, and equally incomplete. Only by integrating a diverse set of descriptions can an accurate picture of the situation be developed. This process is analogous to the way in which a police officer pieces together an accurate picture of an automobile accident from a number of eyewitness descriptions, each of which is limited by factors such as the angle of view (viewpoint), and attentional biases based on prior experience (e.g., an observer noticing that the car was red because it reminded her of a friend's red car). Each organization, and each individual, sees the world through the filter of different experiences and assumptions. Inclusion of this diversity in the decision making process can enhance the ability to recognize unexpected patterns, and encourages creativity and innovation.

The challenge of developing policies openly in contexts where there are many conflicting interests, often with little initial trust among interest groups or in government agencies, is driving interest in addressing environmental concerns through development of collaborative consensus-building policy arenas [48]. Based on a comparative evaluation of large-scale ecosystem restoration projects in the U.S., Van Cleve and colleagues concluded that the public has to be involved in defining the problem, since public buy-in at the problem-definition stage of the project is "tied to many aspects of the potential for progress towards meeting restoration goals" [49]. In the United States there is evidence that the rise of participatory mechanisms for addressing environmental problems is beginning to replace top-down, command-and-control approaches that require authoritative knowledge as a precondition for action [12]. The U.S. Congress has mandated a role for public participation in governmental decisions through the National Environmental Policy Act (1969) and the National Forest Management Act (1976), which require agencies to allow the public access to national resource decision making. Community engagement has also been seen as a means of reducing vulnerability in the area of disaster planning [50].

Despite official sanction, the actual level of public involvement achieved has been modest [30]. Public participation in environmental issues is too often an afterthought or the result of a crisis [51], in part because decision making organizations believe that citizen involvement accomplishes little more than complicating an already difficult task that is best left to professionals. All too often, stakeholders are brought into the process only after key decisions have been made, in an attempt to obtain public support for the "expert" decision. Many of these efforts are, in effect, public relations exercises aimed at defusing public resentment rather than genuine efforts to develop adaptive problem-solving processes [30]. Such insincere public-participation processes seem to weaken the relationship between citizens and their government [52], doing more harm than good and significantly reducing the likelihood of finding an effective solution to an environmental problem.

The Comprehensive Everglades Restoration Plan (CERP), a large-scale ecosystem restoration effort in southern Florida, provides an example of problems created by lack of broad participation in question framing. An assessment of "lessons learned" from existing large-scale ecosystem restoration projects in the United States found that in the CERP "the organizational structure was fixed and the range of restoration options already pre-determined before science began to play a role. This situation constrained innovative science and limited the power of science to influence decisions. Also, this program has often been frustrated by tensions between state and federal agency partners. This may be a result of the USACE's tendency to rely on engineering solutions to solve environmental problems or the highly political nature of the problem. At times, this conflict has hindered progress and consumed resources" [49]. Too little effort was made to develop a consensus view of the specific causes and effects of the problem, and thus about the appropriate strategies. As a result, project activities have been slowed by controversy and legal challenges, and it has proven extremely difficult to gain sufficient support for implementation of any significant management activities.

24.5.1.2   *Formulation of Scientific Research Questions*

In order for scientists to conduct research that is relevant to the policy process, the process of framing the research question—deciding what to study—must be modified to incorporate the requirements imposed by complexity. Scientists doing fundamental research (as opposed to those developing products for commercial purposes) generally select questions to study based on their own particular interests and expertise. Deep knowledge leads to narrow questions, leading to deeper knowledge. This individualistic approach to question framing has been effective in providing basic knowledge of the fundamental workings of the universe, and will continue to be important to the advancement of scientific knowledge. However, it is ill-suited to the process of developing research aimed at addressing problem conditions within a SES.

Involving a greater diversity of viewpoints in the process of framing research questions can provide a more complete picture of how a particular issue or condition fits within the larger system. It can shift the selection process from "what is important to me, as a research scientist, for understanding my particular piece of the puzzle" to "what is important to know about the whole system, in the context of a recognized set of issues and concerns?" For example, Mohrman and colleagues, in a study of organization design activities within a group of organizations attempting to adapt to a changing business environment, found that *joint interpretive forums* increased the likelihood that research results would be useful to practitioners [29]. They found that such forums enabled the surfacing of different knowledge structures for collective examination, and created a collective long-term memory consisting of information as discussed and labeled by the group rather than as separately perceived by each individual participant. However, it is uncommon for scientific researchers to consult with non-scientists, such as decision makers, when selecting and developing research projects. Consequently, despite the scientific merit of a particular study, the results commonly are of little use to decision makers. The common mismatch of research focus to practical needs tends to be compounded by communicative disconnects. As Willtshire points out, "Quite often scientific researchers produce complex results, they do not communicate those results simple and concisely— they do not seem to be able to convey the essence of what their research is saying in language the policy maker can understand" [53].

Many have argued for the need to break down the wall between the practice of science and policy making. For example, McDougall and Braun note that "Clearly, classical 'rigor' is not in itself sufficient if the science cannot transfer into real world, complex systems, and ultimately to benefits" [54]. However, there is strong uneasiness within the scientific community at the prospect of making so large a change in the fundamental institutions that have governed and guided modern science. For example, I have participated in or listened to many discussions among scientists affiliated with the USGS about "participative," "collaborative," or "democratic" approaches to science. The scientists expressed strong concerns about risking their reputations for objectivity if they participate in such an exercise. Quite reasonably, they fear that the validity of the research findings will be compromised if subjective experience and value judgments are allowed to play a role in analysis and interpretation of results. Likewise, Mohrman and colleagues found that some segments of the organizational science research community had grave reservations about conducting research in a close relational context with the business community, due to the fear of violating objectivity and jeopardizing the ability to generate "truth" [29]. However, the authors argue that a close relational context may be necessary if research is to be perceived as useful by practitioners. I believe that this is even more important when dealing with science-intensive decision situations in the public sector, where conflicting interests and lack of trust are barriers to learning. In addition, broader involvement can serve as a source of information and knowledge about the system of interest that is not otherwise available to the researcher.

Institutions for establishing the validity of findings and appropriateness of methodologies, such as peer review, are even more important for this more inclusive approach to science than for traditional "deep" science approaches. As de Bruihn and ten Heuvelhof suggest, "the risk of ending up with 'negotiated nonsense' instead of 'negotiated knowledge' can be kept within acceptable bounds by routinely submitting the results of the investigation to experts for peer review" [55]. These institutions do need some adjustments to adapt to complexity, but they play a vital role in establishing the boundaries of sound practice.

24.5.2 Models as Tools to Assist Development of Shared Understanding

Models are the means by which humans translate perceptions into information, knowledge and institutions [56], and they are the workhorses of modern science and management activities. When we think of models, we most commonly think of quantitative predictive models. However, models have multiple roles and functions: model development can assist researchers in understanding the structure and processes that contribute to emergent system behaviors; models can help define an envelope of possibilities, a range of possible outcomes, for selected policy options and future conditions; models can provide insight into the sensitivity of the system to particular actions and changes, thus allowing managers to make the most effective use of scarce funds and staff time; and models can serve as a means to communicate and integrate diverse viewpoints.

Selection of policy and of management actions is based on "If-Then" hypotheses, whether explicit or implicit. These hypotheses are derived from models: sometimes the models are quantitative and precise; more often we unconsciously rely on our mental models. Any model is a *simplification* of a complex reality, and thus is inherently incomplete and approximate. Such simplification is a fundamental element in the function of the human brain, which filters an effectively infinite amount of data in the form of sensory input and puts the most significant bits together to form a mental model, or schema, that approximates the momentarily significant attributes and behavior of the real world. The critical question for evaluating a particular model in a particular situation, whether a mental model or a quantitative predictive model is whether or not it offers a *useful* simplification. When developing an explicit model intended to guide policy development and collective behavior, a consensus on simplifying assumptions is required in order for people to trust the model, and to accept any decisions based on the model and/or the modeling process. Strategic filtering of information—identifying what can be *left out* of the model—involves judgment calls based in large part on tacit knowledge and creative insights. Confidence in the result of the filtering process comes from direct involvement of end-users and stakeholders in the filtering process.

In many management situations, reasonableness and believability are more important criteria than predictive precision for model selection and development. There are inevitable trade-offs between accuracy and precision in modeling, and increasing model detail will not necessarily result in more accurate predictions or reduce the risk of making a bad prediction. Walters discusses three reasons for distrusting detailed models as much or more than simple ones [42]. First, critical interactions or events can be highly concentrated in space and time at scales, locations, or times that have been ignored, or over which a simple averaging process has incorrectly been assumed. Second, adding more detail adds more parameters to the model structure, and it is probable that there will be inadequate data available for at least some of these added parameters. Finally, because of feedbacks and cross-scale interactions, we seldom have accurate enough data on process rates and initial spatial pattern to accurately simulate the outcomes of events [57]. As a result, models are rarely fully predictive, and that they are best thought of as illustrative [11].

For example, a cause–effect relationship identified by biophysical scientists is that an increase in the proportion of impervious surface in a watershed will result in increased levels of pollutants in stream water and an increase in extreme water flows, both high and low. This relationship is relatively easy to express as a quantitative model which can be used to predict the approximate reduction in surface water pollution that will result from removal of a given amount of impervious surface. Effective policy aimed at improving surface water quality and water flow based on this relatively straightforward relationship is not simple to formulate, however, and the quantitative model provides little guidance. The amount of impervious surface in a watershed is a consequence of decisions made by a large number of people and organizations. Rather than a single cause–effect relationship and a single if-then hypothesis, there are a number of linked relationships and hypotheses that can be thought of as a causal chain. Some links in the chain are purely social in nature, some are purely biophysical, and some connect the two. A more comprehensive model is needed by policy makers, one that includes information about the driving forces behind the choices that people make related to impervious surfaces. The inclusion of human behavior means that such a model cannot be quantitative and fully predictive, but it can provide policy makers with important insights that can assist them in crafting effective policies.

Management actions based on an invalid or inaccurate model are likely to produce unexpected and undesired outcomes. The effectiveness of a model in capturing a particular aspect of dynamic system behavior depends on the appropriateness of the assumptions used to filter and prioritize the flood of potentially relevant information. Because every complex SES is unique, reliance on the general knowledge of experts over the specific experiential knowledge of local peoples is likely to produce an inappropriate (or, at least, non-optimal) set of assumptions, particularly those related to human behavior, and the resulting model is likely to be a poor predictor of system behavior. In other words, development of useful and accurate models of SES behavior requires the participation of people with diverse experiential knowledge of the specific SES of interest. Given the extreme complexity of SESs, *everyone* can be considered "non-expert," since even technical and scientific experts will be expert in only part of the whole system. Knowledge about a given SES's structure and behavior is distributed among a large number of organizations and individuals. Therefore, it is critical to include a diverse group of people, with a wide range of expertise and experiential knowledge, in the model development process. Finding effective ways of integrating data has proven to be a continuing headache, however, because of the volume and disparate nature of the information generated by the problem-solving process [30].

Collaborative development of a conceptual system model is an effective starting point for building both knowledge of what to do and the collective capacity to act. Walker and colleagues suggest that development of a conceptual model of an SES based strongly on stakeholder inputs can serve to bound the problem and to elicit information on the important issues, the major drivers, and to identify key areas of uncertainty [8]. A conceptual system model can assist in recognition of cross-scale interactions and human scale biases.

Model development should an iterative and long-term process. A model is a snapshot, a summary statement of what is understood about a particular system at a particular time. The system will change over time. In addition, our collective knowledge of a given system will always be incomplete, and so our understanding of the system structure and dynamics will evolve through experience and new scientific findings. Updating the conceptual model can be an effective means of integrating new knowledge into ongoing and future decision processes.

24.5.3 Boundary Organizations

When the objective is decision-making that actually contributes to improved conditions, focused attention on relationship-building and careful design and facilitation of decision processes is of fundamental importance. As Bardach points out, development of trust, a problem-solving ethos, and consensus-building processes takes time, effort, skill, and a mix of constructive personalities who are around long enough to build effective relationships [58]. The skills and abilities that are required for excellence in research are different from those that are required for integrating research results into the policy sphere. As demonstrated by the San Francisquito Creek Watershed example discussed above, not everyone involved in a planning/management effort can or should reach across the science–policy interface, or even across disciplinary divides. Both scientists and policy makers use specialized language, or jargon, that hinders communication across the science–policy boundary. An engineer who develops quantitative predictive models and a political scientist studying public policy may understand that they need to collaborate in order to achieve a common goal, but they are likely to be too far apart in worldviews, interests, language, and methodology to have a meaningful exchange of ideas. Knowledge exchange and relationship-building can be greatly enhanced by participation of an intermediary, someone with sufficient knowledge about both disciplines to be able to translate and integrate the disciplinary ideas and concepts. Jargon serves an important function among a community of practice, in that it facilitates concise and precise communication of complex and multi-faceted concepts. New terms which prove useful to the community will enter the common language of that community; such terms become shorthand references to all of the assumptions and negotiated meanings and implications that have accumulated around the term. People who are not members of that particular community of practice will not be familiar with those assumptions and meanings, and thus will not be able to fully understand the intended message.

Work in the area of mediation and dispute resolution has demonstrated the effectiveness of a neutral third-party in facilitating processes aimed at developing shared understanding. Taylor and colleagues suggest that science and policy translators are needed in order for scientists and policy makers to effectively engage with one another [16]. Likewise, Williams considers the role of catalysts or informational intermediaries to be highly influential in shaping and facilitating partnerships, because they help overcome informational asymmetries between social groups, establish a common set of expectations, and facilitate goal adjustment, foster co-operation and exchange, act as neutral arbitrators in conflict resolution, and reduce communication costs and uncertainty [6].

In every successful organization, there are people who are catalysts, who have a 'knack' for making things happen. They are adept at getting the "right" people talking to each other, they see connections between things that other people miss, and they ask the types of questions that spark creative and innovative thinking among colleagues. These key individuals are referred to as 'boundary spanners', since they are effective at building bridges across institutional and disciplinary boundaries. Boundary spanning activities can be carried out by a group of people (for example, one department in a larger organization) or by an organization (in a multi-organizational context). Drawing on the common concept of boundaries in social studies of science, David Guston in 1999 coined the term "boundary organization" to describe institutions that straddle yet join the relatively distinct domains of politics and science [59]. To effectively conduct boundary spanning activities, an organization must be perceived by all participants as expert (and thus credible), apolitical and unbiased (and thus trustworthy), stable and long-lived, and flexible and responsive (and thus able to adapt to changing circumstances). The presence of boundary organizations is thought to facilitate the transfer of usable knowledge between science and policy [60]. The U.S. Department of

Agriculture's Extension Service is an example of a boundary organization [61]. Extension agents act as a bridge between individual farmers and research scientists, providing a two-way link between research and day-to-day management activities.

Participants in a decision process must *trust* an intermediary organization in order for it to be effective as a boundary organization. Both perception and reputation are important components. Trust includes several components:

- *Agenda*: There is no such thing as an individual or organization without an agenda. It is important that the boundary organization's agenda be transparent (i.e., readily identifiable by the participants), and perceived by participants as not being in conflict with stakeholder agendas. Schneider emphasizes that institutions placed between citizens and scientists must be open and transparent to all citizen groups, including special interests, in order to be credible [62].
- *Ethics*: The boundary organization must earn a reputation for ethical behavior. Participants must feel as if they can believe what the boundary organization tells them.
- *Competence*: The boundary organization must earn a reputation for adding value to a decision process. Its members have to have, and be recognized as having, the necessary skills to do the job. Both the scientists and the policy makers must recognize that they will receive benefits from boundary organization participation before they will be willing to cooperate.

Academic institutions and respected non-profit organizations can serve as boundary organizations. Policy makers, resource managers and other practitioners can assist in identifying potential boundary organizations, and take steps to foster and support that organization's effectiveness as a trusted intermediary.

Example: Digital Comprehensive Planning Process.

One of the most effective examples I have seen of a boundary organization that facilitates collective cognition is the collaborative inquiry process conducted by the Prescott College/Blueline Consulting Group, LLC (BLC) based in Arizona. BLC provides scientific and technical support for development of comprehensive plans by local governments. BLC develops computer-based modeling and visualization tools tailored to the local situation. What distinguishes the BLC approach from standard approaches to technical consultancy is its focus on consensus-building through collaborative inquiry—computer-based decision tools are designed to facilitate rather than replace dialogue. The BLC works closely with decision makers, local experts, and stakeholders to frame a specific question, develop appropriate integrative models that directly relate to the local planning process, and explore the potential long-term impacts of alternative development scenarios. A central element of BLC's agenda is encouraging communities to make better, more sustainable decisions through fostering *informed* collective dialogue about values, assumptions, and alternative futures. Municipalities are willing to participate because the process is designed to generate a product of tangible value to them, a comprehensive plan that satisfies requirements, at a lower cost than the standard comprehensive planning process. Most of the municipal staff and stakeholders who have participated in BLC Digital Comprehensive Planning projects have indicated that they believe that the consensus-building process produced better decisions, and more effective implementation [63].

A key reason for the effectiveness of this group is its members' understanding of their target audience, municipal planners. One of the program's developers had past work experience as a municipal planner, and thus had first-hand knowledge about the needs of and constraints on planners. Early in the development process, the BLC group members gave careful thought to what would constitute a "successful outcome" both for themselves and for their target audience; this allowed them to design processes and tools that met both sets of needs and agendas. This strategic approach was championed by the project's leader, Wil Orr, who encouraged innovation among the BLC team, and who was able to communicate effectively both to the leadership of their host institution, Prescott College, and to outside funding agencies such as NASA.

24.6 Process Design Considerations

Successful implementation of an adaptive and collaborative process for making and implementing policy requires careful attention to process design. A poorly designed project will almost always fail [64]; a carefully thought-out and agreed-upon procedural framework is a necessary prerequisite for substantive and constructive discussion and negotiation. Process design must take into account the unique dynamic of a particular situation's issues, history, technical information, players and relationships, as well as regulatory, legal, and community contexts. Most importantly, all of the organizations with decision-making responsibility, and most of the key stakeholders, must be supportive of the process and willing to invest the time necessary to make it work.

In this section, I describe some guidelines for practitioners seeking to establish an adaptive and collaborative problem-solving process. This is not intended to be a complete or detailed blueprint for action. Instead, I highlight aspects of process design that relate to more effectively managing the science–policy interface in decision situations marked by complexity and uncertainty.

The first and most important consideration in process design should be a focus on developing trusting relationships among participants. No real progress can be made unless and until participants develop trust and respect for each other, so sufficient time must be set aside at the beginning of the process for relationship-building among partners. People need to know each other as individuals, not just as scientists, community members, or representatives of organizations. If people do not know each other, they will not trust each other and will revert to fear-based interactions [65]. The necessary changes in attitudes and protocols will not occur overnight. Change will be incremental and will require persistent and tender nurturing.

The initial stage of relationship building is a delicate one, because trust is usually at a minimum. Thus, it is important that the initial relationship building be a facilitated process. A neutral facilitator, perhaps from a widely accepted boundary organization, can help the participants develop ground rules and serve as a mediator between actors divided by past problems. The particular role played by the facilitator will vary according to the particular situation—the more contentious the issue or the weaker the institutions (for example, in a country with weak democratic traditions), the more critical the mediation function. In other cases, process management will be key (making sure meetings run smoothly, for instance). Mediation and dispute resolution practitioners have developed an extensive toolkit that can be used for this very important capacity-building effort [11,64,66].

For example, during the first two years of an ongoing effort to facilitate evolution of a collaborative multi-municipal watershed management process in southwestern Pennsylvania, staff from Duquesne University's Center for Environmental Research and Education (CERE) concentrated on developing trust-based relationships with several of the socially and economically diverse municipalities. Center for Environmental Research and Education has built upon these relationships by conducting watershed management-related events at which representatives from the municipalities had an opportunity to work with each other and thus begin to establish inter-municipal connections [67]. The investment made by CERE in relationship building has played a significant role in building support for collaboration in this highly fragmented jurisdictional setting. The process is continuing and ultimate success is not yet assured, but a noticeable change in attitudes has been reported by several key decision makers in the watershed [68].

Process design must take into account the commonly overlooked fact that participation is a scarce resource [64]. All potential participants—decision makers, managers, technical experts, formal stakeholders, and the general public—have limited time to spend on a collaborative process. Potential participants are usually very busy, with many important tasks competing for too little time, and a decision to do one thing may result in something else being left undone. A truly collaborative process will only develop if the agency seeking others' involvement demonstrates through careful process design that there is respect for and appreciation of the participants' time. An important design component is a clear connection between the collaborative process and actual policy development and implementation—people will not make the time to be part of a "dead-end" process that does not influence decision making. For example, many (if not most!) opportunities for "citizen input," such as public hearings, are too divorced from the actual decision-making process to have any significant impact. In practice, an obviously inconsequential participative experience can do more harm than good, producing suspicion and resentment that discourages rather than encourages collaboration. Bierle and Konisky found that success in public participation efforts was highly related to the lead agency's commitment to the participatory process, as demonstrated by provision of adequate funding and staffing, lack of turnover, and sustained interest in the process [69]. In other words, the leading agencies and organizations must demonstrate sincerity and commitment to the process in order for people to choose to participate.

Effective policy development, implementation and evaluation require a broad consensus on the specifics of the problem being addressed, and on basic cause–effect relationships responsible for the problem. Achieving this consensus is the most difficult challenge in the entire process; as discussed above, problem definition brings into play differences in values and interests. It is tempting to avoid open discussion of values and interests, or at least to postpone the discussion for as long as possible, particularly in situations where relationship building has not been a focus. However, in the absence of such a consensus, it is almost a surety that the process will fail to improve the problem situation. Development of a conceptual model during collaborative problem definition can greatly simplify formulation of specific policies, implementation strategies, and monitoring activities.

A critical, arguably defining, characteristic of an adaptive process is formalized feedback mechanisms that use monitoring and evaluation of the effects of imposed management activities as criteria for modifying the management plan. Unfortunately, post-implementation monitoring is commonly inadequate or omitted. Once actions have been taken (implementation), the usual scenario is that the issue fades from public awareness, funding dries up, and the responsible agencies wish to avoid the negative consequences that might follow if monitoring exposes inadequacies in policies or implementation. An important psychological and strategic factor that has limited post-implementation review is reluctance to acknowledge errors. Particularly in the litigious climate of the United States, organizations and individuals have a realistic fear that admission of error will lead to liability claims and legal challenges. Thus, it is important for the participants to make a strong formal commitment to monitoring and evaluation at the very beginning of the project, and to set up agreements and understandings that limit the hazards of transparency.

24.7 Conclusion

Sound science is an essential element in sound decision making, but science alone cannot solve problems. Lack of knowledge about the natural world is not the principal limiting factor in dealing with the problems that confront us [30]. There certainly are significant gaps in our scientific knowledge, but we do not seem to be doing a good job of translating the considerable amount of basic knowledge that we *do* have into policy and action; as Sarewitz had argued, "the capacity of science to provide predictive information that serves the needs of policy makers has yet to be demonstrated" [12]. Science, commonly in the form of a quantitative model, may point to a particular set of management actions as appropriate. However, the science provides little insight into the implementability of those actions. Sarewitz identifies the two principal roles for science in environmental controversies as being diagnosis and assessment rather than choice of actions.

It is not facts that convince people who are not experts in a given area; instead, they accept or reject information based on their evaluation of the *people* who deliver that information. For trust to develop, there needs to be an ongoing dialogue between the information providers (scientific researchers and other technical experts) and the other participants (decision makers, managers, stakeholders, citizens). A dialogue is a two-way exchange, a give-and-take in which both sides learn from each other. Typically, however, information flows in only one direction, from the scientists and technical experts towards the decision makers and managers. As a result, the information all too often does not answer the most pressing questions, is in a form that does not convey meaning to the participants, and does not get to the people who need it in time to be of use. Cash and colleagues point out that scientific information is only likely to influence public perceptions and policy development to the extent that the information is perceived to be not only credible, but also salient and legitimate [70]. The common failure of technical experts to address one or more of these three criteria results in production of information and recommendations that gather dust on shelves and that are not followed up on—a waste of resources that is frustrating to experts, decision makers and citizens alike.

Scientists are also citizens, and thus have just as much (but no more) of a say as other citizens regarding value judgments that must be made. What scientists are in a unique position to provide is insights into the strengths and limitations of scientific knowledge, and training in recognizing when science is being misused or misinterpreted. Cortner argues that a new approach to the practice of science requires a rethinking of the traditional debate about advocacy and its relationship to public policy [22]. I believe that scientists can and should be advocates for the *process* of integrating sound science into policy making, without endorsing one particular opinion over another.

Acknowledgments

First and foremost, I want to thank Herman Karl, a Senior Scientist with the U.S. Geological Survey. He has been a long-time collaborator, and a fellow traveler on the fascinating and challenging road from the physical towards the human sciences. He has also provided funding for my work, through the U.S. Geological Survey's Director's Venture Capital Fund. I want to thank Sung-Jun Myung, who provided me with much enlightenment about how to read and interpret social science literature. My thinking about the science–policy interface has been greatly enriched by conversations with Steve Light and Christine Turner. Finally, thanks to the School of Arts and Sciences at Duke University for their support of my work.

References

1. Ashby, J., Introduction: Uniting science and participation in the process of innovation—research for development, in *Managing Natural Resources for*

Sustainable Livelihoods: Uniting Science and Participation, B. Pound, S. Snapp, C. McDougall, and A. Braun, Eds., Earthscan Press, London, 2003, 1–18.

2. Berkes, F., Colding, J., and Folke, C., Introduction, in *Navigating Social–Ecological Systems: Building Resilience for Complexity and Change*, F. Berkes, J. Colding, and C. Folke, Eds., Cambridge University Press, New York, 2003, 1–29.

3. Gunderson, L.H. and Holling, C.S., Eds., in *Panarchy: Understanding Transformations in Human and Natural Systems*, Island Press, Washington, DC, 2002, 507.

4. Brunner, R.D., Steelman, T.A., Coe-Juell, L., Cromley, C.M., Edwards, C.M., and Tucker, D.W., Eds., in *Adaptive Governance: Integrating Science, Policy, and Decision Making*, Columbia University Press, New York, 2005, 319.

5. Koontz, T.M., Steelman, T., Carmin, J., Korfmacher, K., Moseley, C., and Thomas, C., *Collaborative Environmental Management: What Roles for Government?* Resources for the Future, Washington, DC, 2004.

6. Williams, P., The competent boundary spanner, *Public Administration*, 80, 103, 2002.

7. Dooley, K.L., A complex adaptive systems model of organization change, *Nonlinear Dynamics, Psychology, and Life Sciences*, 1, 69, 1997.

8. Walker, B., Carpenter, S., Anderies, J., Abel, N., Cumming, G., Janssen, M., Lebel, L., Norberg, J., Peterson, G.D., and Pritchard, R., Resilience management in social–ecological systems: A working hypothesis for a participatory approach, *Conservation Ecology*, 6, art14, 2002, Available at: http://www.consecol.org/vol6/iss1/art14 (accessed on December, 2005).

9. Holling, C.S. and Meffe, G.K., Command and control and the pathology of natural resource management, *Conservation Biology*, 10, 328, 1996.

10. Ozawa, C.P. and Susskind, L., Mediating science-intensive policy disputes, *Journal of Policy Analysis and Manangement*, 5, 23, 1985.

11. Adler, P.S., Barrett, R.C., Bean, M.C., Birkhoff, J.E., Ozaawa, C.P., and Rudin, M., *Managing Scientific and Technical Information in Environmental Cases: Principles and Practices for Mediators and Facilitators*, Resolve, Inc., Portland, OR, 2000.

12. Sarewitz, D., Science and environmental policy: An excess of objectivity, in *Earth Matters: The Earth Sciences, Philosophy, and the Claims of Community*, R. Frodemen, Ed., Prentice Hall, Saddle River, NJ, 2000, 79–98.

13. Westley, F., Carpenter, S.R., Brock, W.A., Holling, C.S., and Gunderson, L.H., Why systems of people and nature are not just social and ecological systems, in *Panarchy, Understanding Transformations in Human and Natural Systems*, L.H. Gunderson and C.S. Hollings, Eds., Island Press, Washington, DC, 2002, 103–120.

14. Addleson, M., Resolving the spirit and substance of organizational learning, *Journal of Organizational Change Management*, 9, 32, 1996.

15. Kraft, M.E., *Environmental Policy and Politics*, 2nd ed., Addison-Wesley Ed. Pub. Inc., New York, 2001.

16. Taylor, B., Green, W., and Cooper, R., *Illuminated or Blinded by Science? A Discussion Paper on the Role of Science in Environmental Policy and Decision-Making*, Office of the Parliamentary Commissioner for the Environment, Wellington, NZ, 2003.

17. Dolan, R.J., Emotion, cognition, and behavior, *Science*, 298, 1191, 2002.

18. Lemerise, E.A. and Arsenio, W.F., A integrated model of emotion processes and cognition in social information processing, *Child Development*, 71, 107, 2000.

19. Bechara, A., Damasio, H., and Damasio, A.R., Emotion, decision making and the orbitofrontal cortex, *Cerebral Cortex*, 10, 295, 2000.

20. Damasio, H., Grabowski, T., Frank, R., Galaburda, A.M., and Damasio, A.R., The return of Phineas Gage: Clues about the brain from the skull of a famous patient, *Science*, 264, 1102, 1994.

21. Oatley, K. and Jenkins, J.M., *Understanding Emotions*, Blackwell, Cambridge, MA, 1996.

22. Cortner, H.J., Making science relevant to environmental policy, *Environmental Science and Policy*, 3, 21, 2000.

23. Rapport, D.J., Transdisciplinarity: Transcending the disciplines, *Trends in Ecology and Evolution*, 12, 289, 1997.
24. Gibbons, M., Limoges, C., Nowotny, H., Schwartzman, S., Scott, P., and Trow, M., *The New Production of Knowledge*, SAGE Publications, Thousand Oaks, CA, 1994.
25. Bossel, H., Assessing viability and sustainability: A systems-based approach for deriving comprehensive indicator sets, *Conservation Ecology*, 5, art12, 2001, Available at: http://www.consecol.org/vol5/iss2/art12.
26. Clayton, A.M.H. and Radcliffe, N.J., *Sustainability: A Systems Approach*, Earthscan, London, 1996.
27. Laszlo, E., The contribution of the systems sciences to the humanities, *Systems Research and Behavioral Science*, 14, 5, 1997.
28. Jamieson, D., Problems and prospects for a Forest Service program in the human dimensions of global changes, in *Breaking the Mold: Global Change, Social Responsibility, and Natural Resource Management*, K. Geyer and B. Shindler, Eds., USDA Forest Service, Portland, OR, 1994, 23–28.
29. Mohrman, S.A., Gibson, C.B., and Mohrman, A.M. Jr., Doing research that is useful to practice: A model and empirical exploration, *Academy of Management Journal*, 44, 357, 2001.
30. Miller, A., *Environmental Problem Solving: Psychosocial Barriers to Adaptive Change*, Springer, New York, 1999.
31. Lowndes, V. and Wilson, D., Social capital and local governance: Exploring the institutional design variable, *Political Studies*, 49, 629, 2001.
32. Rogers, E.M., *Diffusion of Innovations*, 5th ed., Free Press, New York, 2003.
33. Anderson, A.R., *Marketing Social Change: Changing Behavior to Promote Health, Social Development, and the Environment*, Jossey-Bass Publishers, San Francisco, CA, 1995.
34. Genschel, P., *The Dynamics of Inertia: Institutional Persistence and Institutional Change in Telecommunications and Health Care*, MPIFG Discussion Paper 95/3, Max-Planck-Institut für Gesellschaftsforschung, Köln, 1995.
35. Yearley, S., Environmental challenges to science studies, in *Handbook of Science and Technology Studies*, S. Jasanoff, E. Markle, J.C. Petersen, and T. Pinch, Eds., Sage, Thousand Oaks, CA, 1995, 457–479.
36. MIT-USGS Science Impact Collaborative, Available at: http://web.mit.edu/dusp/epg/music/ (accessed on December, 2005).
37. Karl, H., personal communication, 2004.
38. Holling, C.S., *Adaptive Environmental Assessment and Management*, Chichester, New York, 1978.
39. Walters, C., *Adaptive Management of Renewable Resources*, McMillan, New York, 1986.
40. Gunderson, L., Resilience, flexibility and adaptive management—antidotes for spurious certitude? *Conservation Ecology*, 3, art7, 1999, Available at: http://www.consecol.org/vol3/iss1/art7/ (accessed on December, 2005).
41. Halbert, C.L., How adaptive is adaptive management? Implementing adaptive management in Washington State and British Columbia, *Reviews in Fisheries Science*, 1, 261, 1993.
42. Walters, C., Challenges in adaptive management of riparian and coastal ecosystems, *Conservation Ecology*, 1, art1, 1997, Available at: http://www.consecol.org/vol1/iss2/art1 (accessed on December, 2005).
43. Ludwig, D., Hilborn, R., and Walters, C.J., Uncertainty, resource exploitation, and conservation: Lessons from history, *Science*, 260, 36, 1993.
44. Gunderson, L.H., Holling, C.S., and Light, S.S., Eds., in *Barriers and Bridges to the Renewal of Ecosystems and Institutions*, Columbia University Press, New York, 1995.

45. Castleberry, D.T., Cech, J.J., Erman, D.C., Hankin, D., Healey, M., Kondolf, G.M., Mangel, M. *et al.*, Uncertainty and instream flow standards, *Fisheries*, 21, 20, 1996.
46. Van Winkle, W., Coutant, C.C., Jager, H.I., Mattice, J.S., Orth, D.J., Otto, R.G., Railsback, S.F., and Sale, M.F., Uncertainty and instream flow standards; perspectives based on hydropower research and assessment, *Fisheries*, 22, 21, 1997.
47. Lee, K.N., Appraising adaptive management, in *Biological Diversity: Balancing Interests Through Adaptive Collaborative Management*, L. Buck, C.C. Geisler, J. Schelhas, and E. Wollenberg, Eds., CRC Press, Boca Raton, FL, 2001, 3–26.
48. Innes, J.E., Gruber, J., Neuman, M., and Thomopson, R., *Coordinating Growth and Environmental Management Through Consensus Building*, CPS Report: A Policy Research Program Report, University of California at Berkeley, California Policy Seminar, 1994.
49. Van Cleve, F.B., Simenstad, C., Goetz, F., and Mumford, T., *Application of "Best Available Science" in Ecosystem Restoration: Lessons Learned from Large-Scale Restoration Efforts in the U.S.* Puget Sound Nearshore Ecosystem Restoration Project, 2003, Available at: http://www.adaptivemanagement.net/pugetlessons.pdf (accessed on December, 2005).
50. Tompkins, E.L. and Adger, W.N., Does adaptive management of natural resources enhance resilience to climate change? *Ecology and Society*, 9, art10, 2004, Available at: http://www.ecologyandsociety.org/vol9/iss2/art10/ (accessed on December, 2005).
51. Chess, C., Evaluating environmental public participation: Methodological questions, *Journal of Environmental Planning and Management*, 43, 769, 2000.
52. Moore, J.L., What is stopping sustainability? Examining the barriers to implementation of "Clouds of Change", in *Fatal Consumption: Rethinking Sustainable Development*, R.F. Woollard and A.S. Ostry, Eds., UCB Press, Vancouver, WA, 2000, 101–129.
53. Willtshire, K., Scientists and policy-makers: Towards a new partnership, *International Social Science Journal*, 53, 621, 2001.
54. McDougall, C. and Braun, A., Navigating complexity, diversity and dynamism: Reflections on research for natural resource management, in *Managing Natural Resources for Sustainable Livelihoods: Uniting Science and Participation*, B. Pound, S. Snapp, C. McDougall, and A. Braun, Eds., Earthscan Press, London, 2003, 20–47.
55. de Bruihn, J.A. and ten Heuvelhof, E.F., Scientific expertise in complex decision-making processes, *Science and Public Policy*, 26, 179, 1999.
56. Davidson-Hunt, I.J. and Berkes, F., Nature and society through the lens of resilience: Toward a human-in-ecosystem perspective, in *Navigating Social–Ecological Systems: Building Resilience for Complexity and Change*, F. Berkes, J. Colding, and C. Folke, Eds., Cambridge University Press, New York, 2003, 53–82.
57. Holling, C.S., Cross-scale morphology, geometry, and dynamics of ecosystems, *Ecological Monographs*, 62, 447, 1992.
58. Bardach, E., *Getting Agencies to Work Together: The Practice and Theory of Managerial Craftsmanship*, Brookings Institution Press, Washington, DC, 1998.
59. Guston, D.H., Stabilizing the boundary between U.S. politics and science: The role of the office of technology transfer as a boundary organization, *Social Studies of Science*, 29, 87, 1999.
60. Guston, D.H., Clark, W., Keating, T., Cash, D., Moser, S., Miller, C., and Powers, C., *Report of the Workshop on Boundary Organizations in Environmental Policy and Science*, Belfer Center for Science and International Affairs, Discussion Paper 2000-32, Harvard University, Cambridge, 2000.
61. Cash, D.W., *'In Order to Aid in Diffusing Useful and Practical Information…': Cross-Scale Boundary Organizations and Agricultural Extension*, Belfer Center for Sconce and International Affairs, Discussion Paper 2000-10, Harvard University, Cambridge, 2000.

62. Schneider, S.H., The role of science: Guidance and service, in *Sustainable Development: The Challenge of Transition*, J. Schmandt and C.H. Ward, Eds., Cambridge University Press, New York, 2000, 131–152.

63. Orr, W., personal communication, 2004.

64. Andrews, C.J., *Humble Analysis: The Practice of Joint Fact Finding*, Praeger Publishers, Westport, CT, 2002.

65. Adler, P. and Birkhoff, J., *Building Trust: When Knowledge From "Here" Meets Knowledge From "Away,"*, The Policy Consensus Center, Portland State University, Portland, OR, 2003.

66. Susskind, L., McKearnan, S., and Thomas-Larmer, J., *Consensus Building Handbook: A Comprehensive Guide to Reaching Agreement*, Sage Publications, Thousand Oaks, CA, 1999.

67. Kabala, S., personal communication, 2004.

68. Myung, S.-J., personal communication, 2004.

69. Bierle, T.C. and Konisky, D.M., Values, conflict, and trust in participatory environmental planning, *Journal of Policy Analysis and Management*, 19, 587, 2000.

70. Cash, D.W., Clark, W.C., Alcock, F., Dickson, N.M., Eckley, N., Guston, D.H., Jäger, J., and Mitchell, R.B., Knowledge systems for sustainable development, *PNAS*, 100, 8086, 2003.

Chapter 25

Multi-Party Environmental Negotiations: the Democratizing Nations of Mexico and Ecuador

Jennifer E. Horan
University of North Carolina at Wilmington

Donna L. Lybecker
Pennsylvania State University

25.1 Introduction

Environmental problems have a distinct importance for societies. This importance rests on the fact that ecological concerns simultaneously present a challenge at the ethical, social, economic, political, and scientific levels. Thus, when resolving today's environmental problems, it is necessary for governments to not only address the strictly cognitive concerns at play, but also to manage the ethical uncertainties derived from conflicting values in society.

In democratic societies attempting to resolve complex issues, it is not uncommon for political decisions to be made within a relatively broad communicative forum. The hyper-complexity of many environmental problems obliges governments to engage in dialogues concerning existing pieces of scientific, economic, and political knowledge, as well as values held by a wide range of interests. Not infrequently, if these dialogues can be initiated and sustained, it is possible to reveal that much of the knowledge and many of the interests complement each other [1]. Ideally, these communicative forums are multi-party, comprised of government officials, scientists and technicians within the bureaucracy, traditional economic actors, and representatives of the broader civil society—including the private business sector, non-governmental organizations (NGOs), and spokespersons for social movements. This framework for a negotiation-based forum for decision-making has been gaining attention and support within the international community in recent years [2–4]. This broad endorsement suggests that complex issues such as environmental concerns, within both democratic and democratizing countries, need to be addressed in an open process that counts on the participation of all sectors of society [2–4].

Despite increasing international pressure for an open forum format for discussions of environmental problems in all countries, this approach is less common within societies transitioning to democracy than in established democracies. However, in many nations there is increasing transparency in public policy processes; it has been forced by greater global awareness due, in part, to the speed at which we receive detailed information on events and environmental developments through the World Wide Web. Additionally, there is increased public participation, partially advanced by public participation requirements for receiving World Bank and Inter-American Development Bank monies. And there is greater pluralism in the voices of advocacy, a consequence of pressure from domestic democracy movements. These changes, and the public support behind them, are compelling governments to make greater use of multi-party negotiations. Despite these advances, some governments making the transition to democracy are holding back from negotiation-style decision-making [3,4]. Reasons behind this reluctance vary, but often include the desire to maintain decision-making power in the hands of the traditional decision makers (including government officials, top businessmen, and the military), and lack of experience with greater pluralism. Consequently, in the nations where there is limited negotiation-style decision-making, stakeholders not involved with one of these traditional decision-making groups often play largely symbolic roles. An examination of negotiations for environmental decision-making in two Latin American countries reveals the variation in negotiation processes that is present in Latin American nations transitioning to democracy.

The objective of this chapter is to characterize the status of communicative forums featuring multi-party environmental negotiations within countries transitioning into greater democracy. More specifically, this chapter describes actions taken by both traditional and non-traditional actors interested in environmental decision-making, and notes the consequences of these actions on environmental negotiations in their respective countries. This paper focuses on two countries "transitioning to democracy" in Latin America—Mexico and Ecuador.

Mexico and Ecuador were selected for comparison both because of their similarities and because of their differences. Both countries are transitioning to democracy—working to improve upon the democratic institutions that exist—

and both have serious environmental problems—problems of concern to not only their citizens, but to the international community. Mexico is an economically and socially diverse, relatively wealthy developing nation with newly formed North American Free Trade Agreement (NAFTA) ties to the developed western countries of Canada and the United States. Ecuador, in contrast, is one of the geographically smallest, most densely populated, and economically challenged countries of Latin America. A comparison of these two countries will highlight the degree of diversity present within the overall progress toward the use of multi-party environmental negotiations in countries transitioning to democracy.

25.2   Negotiations within Latin American Countries

In the past, some negotiated decision-making existed within Latin America's traditional, centralized decision-making framework. The interests represented within these negotiations were commonly limited to a select group, and they functioned within the prominent system of *corporatism* that has existed in the governments of Latin America for many years. Furthermore, the traditional negotiation style within Latin America is associated with nonverbal, informal, high-context communication, stressing long-term relationships among the parties involved and preoccupation with status and saving face [4–7]. Within Latin America, this style of negotiated decision-making, relying on informal relations and politico-technical methods rather than truly inclusive negotiations, has been institutionalized due to traditional political actors' practice of imposing their will and the absence of widespread political participation by the public [4].

Although many of these characteristics of governance still exist, much of the recent literature focuses on Latin American countries' movement toward greater democracy and the associated societal pluralism [8–14]. Compared to the situation 30 years ago, the majority of Latin American countries have made substantial progress toward greater transparency and increased public participation in their public policymaking process [12–14]. That said, it is also true that much of Latin America is still early in democratic transition, functioning under a system that is a combination of the traditional, centralized, elite-controlled decision-making and the more democratic, pluralistic decision-making that includes negotiations [15,16]. Our research adds to the existing literature on negotiations by expanding the discussion on democracy and negotiations with the inclusion of the Mexican and Ecuadorian cases. We examine the expansion of democratic legitimacy in two Latin American countries in the midst of complex transitions toward democracy and thus undertaking increasingly more inclusive multi-party environmental negotiations.

25.3   Mexico

Although Mexico is a developing and democratizing country like many of its neighbors to the south, it has made rather uncommon progress toward both greater democracy and economic development. Movement toward greater democracy has included fair(er) elections, more clearly developed division of power among the branches and levels of government, and continuing professionalization of the bureaucracy [16,17]. Additionally, Mexico features the second largest economy in Latin America, and according to the World Bank [18], Mexico is solidly ensconced among the world's upper-middle income countries—one of only eight of the twenty Latin American countries so ranked by the World Bank. These characteristics were, in some measure, forced upon Mexico with the advent of the North American Free Trade Agreement. However, increasing domestic pressures have also shaped the expansion of democracy and reform of the economic sector—important changes that have led to a society featuring a growing emphasis on public participation and societal acceptance of greater pluralism and diversity of viewpoints. It is these characteristics that are affecting many issue areas within Mexico, including the area of environmental politics [19,20].

25.3.1 Mexican Environmental Politics and Management

For Mexico, economic development has come at a rather high price in environmental degradation—a cost that Mexico has only begun to deal with in the past 15 years. In 1988, Mexico's out-going president, Miguel de la Madrid, responded to rising public and international concern about environmental problems by revamping the national environmental laws to include greater emphasis on minimizing environmental degradation [19–21]. Madrid's successor, Carlos Salinas, further emphasized the need to address environmental concerns with a broad reorganization of Mexico's environmental and natural resources administration and an escalation of Mexico's cooperation for international environmental protection—spurred in part by economic liberalization and Mexico's initiative to enter into a North American free trade pact [19–21]. Under President Ernesto Zedillo, Mexico's president from 1994 to 2000, the national environmental law was extensively revisited to emphasize sustainable development as a national priority, to clarify significant ambiguity in the law with respect to intergovernmental responsibilities, and to provide greater opportunities for both public access to environmental information and public participation in environmental policy implementation [19,22]. Finally, the administration of President Fox laid out a number of new strategies for dealing with environmental concerns in the "National Program of Environment and Natural Resources 2001–2006." This document placed emphasis on federalism to encourage clear, efficient and up-to-date regulations and promote efficient environmental performance, increased social involvement and accountability, and creation of an ecological culture that takes into account both care for the environment and influence from all levels and sectors of environmental decision making [23]. In addition to specifically environmental policies, a more general piece of legislation that is impacting Mexico's environmental issues and management is the 2003 Governmental Public Information Access Law. This measure is similar to the United States' Freedom of Information Act. On paper, this law is key to accessing official information surrounding environmental concerns—granting public access to federal documents, and strengthening the 1996 national environmental law's statements that everyone merits access to ecosystem information. In addition, promising actions taken include a U.S. $20 million annual budget for the federal institute established to operate the freedom of information act, and in 2004 a coalition including environmental groups signed a covenant with the federal right to know institute to help citizens make use of the mechanisms now available to access government records. That said, the law has yet to be fully tested, and according to case studies conducted by the Mexican nonprofit *Presencia Ciudadana Mexicana*, although the law grants access to government agencies, these agencies do not have much of the information that environmentalists seek [24]. Overall, many of the new environmental policies can accurately be described as incipient and still under trial. However, these measures have strengthened Mexico's capacity to address environmental concerns. Moreover, these initiatives have unfolded in a context of both economic liberalization and democratic transformation of national political institutions, changes that offer great potential for the long run, but that complicate both policy development and implementation and cloud efforts to assess the consequences of current policy reform accurately in the short run.

25.3.2 *The Mexican State*

Traditionally, Mexico was considered a semi-authoritarian government and a "presidential regime." These labels were fairly accurate because the government's three-branch system did not function in practice. Instead, the executive branch's formal and informal powers overshadowed the legislative and judiciary branches, leaving these latter two branches to accept presidential decisions without any power of review or veto. Furthermore, prior to 1997 the system of political parties consisted of a hegemonic party, the National Revolutionary Party(PRI [*Partido Revolucionario Institucional*]) that controlled the presidency, Congress, and most of the states' governorships, and a few weak opposition parties, most notably the National Action Party (PAN [*Partido Accion Nacional*]) and the Democratic Revolutionary Party (PRD [*Partido Revolucionario Democratico*]). In addition, although electoral processes existed, they were not fundamental to defining political representation or distributing power among political groups [16,25]. The ties between the government and the PRI were such that they were considered one and the same throughout the country. The expansive power of the PRI ruling elite solidified its influence within many sectors of society, eventually resulting in the near complete cooptation of most significant groups.

The unchallenged power of the Mexican presidency (and PRI) as an institution affected the administrative structure and procedures operating within the federal government. Without real opposition at the national level, executive power determined the framework of political institutions and the procedures they employed in their work. Consequently, public policy decision-making within Mexico has been controlled for a long time by a small group of political and economic elites [17]. These elites debated among themselves at times, but did not open their internal negotiations on issues such as environmental concerns to diverse parties or voices until very recently.

Currently, Mexico is undergoing an intense political transition. After more than 70 years of PRI domination, the PAN (opposition party) took control of the presidency in 2000. This political transition means a great deal, not the least of which is greater democracy in the long run [25]. It also means a new expectation for reforms within the Mexican state administrative apparatus—reforms to include new ideas and tools for public management that were first introduced in the mid-1990s [17,26]. The ideas and tools introduced include a framework for increasingly open discussions or negotiations and a commitment to greater pluralism in decision-making. Among the groups attempting to take advantage of these changes and consequently play a part in multi-agency bargaining within environmental negotiations are: government and political party representatives, including members of the PRI and of political parties previously excluded, domestic non-governmental actors, including environmental NGOs and the so-called "green enterprises," and international actors.

As the end of the Fox administration nears, rumors abound of a possible strengthening of Mexico's traditional decision-makers. Although the resulting changes cannot be known until the next president is elected, it is unlikely that all advances will be reversed. Now that diverse groups have experienced the power of more inclusive decision-making, they are likely to continue their fight for greater representation within policy making.

25.3.3   Mexican Environmental Negotiations: the Actors

Government agencies and political parties constitute a diverse group of environmental policy proponents. Although the traditional players (President, major government officials, PRI) comprise a part of the group, with the advent of an opposition party president and more diverse actors elected to Congress (including the Green Party candidates), the variety of interests represented within this group is growing [16,25]. Political parties are increasingly important in addressing environmental concerns—nearly all parties now include environmental issues in their platforms—and are pushing for greater representation within environmental negotiations. Finally, government agencies are also included within the environmental decision makers, although severe budget cuts and shortfalls have recently limited the power of these agencies within environmental discussions.

A second set of actors involved with environmental concerns is the domestic NGOs. The number and importance of environmental NGOs has grown steadily since the late 1980s, totaling over 400 accredited organizations active in Mexico [27]. Additionally, companies and farmers who benefit from green markets, through either ecotourism, organic products, or goods gathered from sustainably managed forests, also attempt to influence environmental policies and decision-making [27]. These groups have used the emergence of environmental concerns as an opportunity to construct new alliances. The resulting networks have been able to bring together the middle-class, urban-based environmental activists, grassroots indigenous and community-based groups, along with the green industries and farmers [27]. With increasing numbers of supporters and thus increasing levels of attention, these groups are beginning to garner consideration from the government for inclusion in some environmental discussions—at least in public forums held prior to the continuing "behind closed doors" negotiations and elite-controlled decision-making.

Finally, international actors also play a noteworthy role in Mexico's management of environmental concerns. The NAFTA institutions, following their environmental side agreement, have influenced and are influencing environmental decision-making events and procedures in northern Mexico. This influence is accomplished through developing regulations and enforcing greater compliance—spurring both administrative and legislative reforms along with greater public participation throughout Mexico. Additionally, international development agencies such as the Inter-American Development Bank (which is responsible for financing and influencing environmental conservation projects and policies) and international organizations such as the Organization for Economic Co-operation and Development, or OECD, (which requires commitment to moving toward a more comprehensive and transparent approach to environmental management), have become more involved in Mexican decision-making processes. Likewise, international NGOs such as the Nature Conservancy and the World Wildlife Fund have also become involved in Mexico. The strength of these international actors, through their fiscal resources and access to international media and supporters, have helped put Mexico's environmental concerns into the public realm, drawing attention to both the voices that are heard and those that are not heard without some external assistance [21]. The involvement of these international actors is forcing Mexico's elite to include other actors, at least superficially, within the bargaining and negotiation arena involving environmental concerns.

25.3.4   Genuine Inclusion or Superficial Change? The Gray Whale Controversy

As the above describes, within Mexico there is a movement for greater recognition of diverse interests concerning environmental issues. However, a lack of transparency and minimal access to information, the weak supervision from Congress and society, and the capacity of powerful bureaucrats to undermine many management reform efforts leaves many people questioning how these new tools for public management have been put into practice. Some critics maintain that they are utilized simply for superficial administrative reform [28].

As is the case in every country, the level of inclusion of diverse interests varies, depending on the issue at hand. Within Mexico, there are numerous cases that substantiate the proposition that the change to include more interests within environmental negotiations is simply a superficial pretense [27,29,30]. However, on the other side of this discussion and in support of Mexican advancement in multi-party bargaining in environmental negotiations, there are a few cases, such as the protection of the gray whale, that attest to Mexico's genuine progress toward the meaningful inclusion of diverse parties in multi-agency environmental negotiations. This inclusion has occasionally occurred not only in the so-called bargaining phase, but also with the actual decision-making surrounding environmental concerns. It is this movement toward greater inclusion that is discussed next.

25.3.5 Mexican Environmental Negotiations: Gray Whales and the Desert Biosphere Reserve

In January of 1995, the Mexican public learned of a project to build a massive salt mining operation at Laguna San Ignacio in Baja California Sur, the last pristine mating and calving ground of the gray whale. Mexico's National Ecology Institute (INE) was poised to give the green light to Exprotadora de Sal (ESSA), a joint venture owned by the Japanese firm Mitsubishi and the Mexican government, to develop 525,000 acres of the Vizcanio Desert Biosphere Reserve (Latin America's largest protected natural area) into a massive saltworks. The proposed operation threatened more than two-thirds of the Biosphere Reserve, along with local human populations at Punta Abreojos, whose lobster and abalone fisheries would be destroyed, and communities surrounding the lagoon, whose residents base their livelihood on whale-watching and fishing. The saltworks would bring 200 permanent jobs to the region, although the majority of these would be for skilled outsiders [31].

Following the exposure of the plan, on February 27, 1995 the INE recommended against the saltworks project's (first) environmental impact assessment on the grounds that it now viewed the assessment as incompatible with the Biosphere Reserve's objectives. Within weeks of this change, battle lines were drawn. Numerous Mexican environmental groups, along with international supporters, challenged Herminio Blanco, head of Mexico's Ministry of Commerce and Industrial Development and the president of the ESSA board of directors, along with almost every politician in Baja California Sur [32]. So began a struggle for increased transparency and pluralism within Mexico's environmental decision-making, and so also began the informal negotiations and bargaining for effective environmental conservation among governmental and non-governmental, domestic and international groups within Baja California Sur.

Soon after the INE's recommendation against the saltworks project's environmental impact assessment, 60 environmental organizations from around the world, including many well-known figures such as Homero Aridjis, Carlos Fuentes, Allan Ginsberg, and Robert F. Kennedy Jr., publicly supported the Mexicans opposing the ESSA's saltworks. Alliances were formed between these environmental groups, Mexico's Green Party, local fishing cooperatives, and regional whale watching businesses. The combined environmental/grassroots group utilized the Mexican and international press to garner support, share information, and maintain a degree of pressure on the Mexican government and the ESSA [32]. Additionally, in 1996 the members of this group utilized another tool in their "bargaining" process; they filed suit against the Ministry of the Environment [31,32]. This suit brought about an acknowledgement by the Mexican federal court of the right of an organization to challenge environmental regulations, the first time such a verdict had been handed down[*] [31]. Through this maneuver, the environmental/grassroots group was "negotiating" with the government in a non-traditional manner. The group's members believed that they would not be heard if they spoke directly with government officials, thus they chose to do their speaking through the legal arena and through the press coverage surrounding the lawsuit [31,32]. Utilization of these non-traditional arenas compelled the government to address the concerns of the group and thus opened a door for these non-traditional interests to participate in environmental negotiations.

During the time these actions were taken by the environmental/grassroots group, those holding the pro-saltworks position were attempting to maintain control through established political channels. A former governor of Baja California Sur, Guillermo Mercado, who staked his political career on the saltworks, became the leader in shoring up support for the project [31]. Mercado made sure members of the ruling establishment, including the legislative and municipal president (mayoral) candidates, were loyal team players who supported the saltworks. Utilizing the politicians, along with pro-government press channels, Mercado made the argument that the controversy was a battle against elitist and international interests using the gray whale as a screen to stop Mexican workers from securing decent jobs. By taking this stance, Mercado and his supporters were attempting to discredit the other voices, thus "eliminating" the need for negotiations, and once again maintain elite control of the environmental decision-making processes.

In the past, this type of move by politicians and the ESSA would likely have worked; however, in response to these actions and the irregular project acceptance practices being brought to light, actors within Mexico's federal environmental agencies were persuaded to add their voices to this informal bargaining [31,32]. In support of greater transparency and public participation, and greater accountability for following decision-making procedures, Julia Carabias, head of Mexico's federal environmental agency (SEMARNAP), made a concerted effort to open up the environmental review process to guarantee greater objectivity. First, Carabias posted the project on the Internet—in contrast, federal authorities in charge of the first environmental impact assessment never did release the report to the public. Second, Carabias made the decision to convene a scientific advisory committee to oversee the new (second) environmental impact assessment. This advisory committee included seven distinguished scientists, some of whom were recommended by the environmental/grassroots group [31,32].

Carabias' actions were unheard of for the head of a Mexican government agency. They allowed non-traditional actors to be present and involved in environmental decision-making. Moreover, the appointed scientific advisory committee decided to hold a 6-hour meeting to receive public input on the

---

[*] Under Mexico's federal environmental law, any NGO or individual has the right to contest an environmental impact assessment and request that the government halt the project. In practice this almost never occurs, and government technocrats are highly suspicious and resistant to any public participation in the decision-making process [31].

effects of the saltworks project. This constituted the first time that federal officials in Baja California Sur bothered to solicit public input about a development project in that region of the country.

By establishing a public review process for environmental impact assessments, Carabias and the scientific advisory committee contributed to both increasing transparency in environmental decision-making and to the democratization of Mexico. Opening a government process to the public is a substantial achievement for a country where information is guarded as fiercely as the public treasury [31]. Both of these characteristics contributed to the expansion of true multi-party discussions, or informal negotiations, for environmental concerns within Mexico.

On March 2, 2000, in the face of pressure both domestic and international, government and non-governmental, and legal and social, President Zedillo announced that the saltworks project would be canceled. Although the publicly stated reason for cancellation of the project focused on economic concerns, in reality most spectators believe that the environmental/grassroots group (along with help from Mexico's environmental agency) had forced its entrance into negotiations, played hard ball, and won [31,32]. Despite the formal reason behind the cancellation of the saltworks project, the very announcement that it had been canceled revealed that a noteworthy precedent had been set. Non-traditional political actors had not only been a part of an environmental bargaining process, but had also succeeded in exercising influence in environmental decision-making within Mexico.

Since that time, the question of the saltworks plant has reemerged. As the presidency of Fox comes to a close, political momentum in Mexico's capital appears to be shifting toward a vision of greater industrialization for San Ignacio Lagoon and its surrounding territory [33]. Many local residents and a number of environmental groups are bracing themselves for a possible government resurrection of the saltworks project; whether Mexican politics will accommodate diverse interests remains to be seen. However, those who have now influenced the policy-making surrounding this project, who have seen elements of public-participation in a vibrant democracy, may not be willing to return to a position of silence.

25.3.6 Mexican Environmental Negotiations: Lessons from the Gray Whale Controversy

The gray whale controversy reveals that more diverse interests are making their voices heard within environmental "negotiations" and the decision-making process in Mexico. Although these are not formal negotiations as conceptualized within developed, democratic nations, this informal bargaining on the part of non-traditional actors has opened the door to greater transparency and public participation within Mexico's environmental decision-making. Additionally, as governmental agencies expand their powers and as non-traditional actors take advantage of opportunities within the press and legal systems, more voices will be included in environmental negotiations, possibly leading to a more formally inclusive negotiation process in the future.

Within Mexico, a continuing transition to greater democracy, and thus more transparency and public participation, insures a changing constellation of actors as new groups and organizations come onto the scene. Increasing levels of interaction among these organizations, and the taste of success, has brought increasing pressure for more widely distributed information about environmental conditions. This advancement of public access to information has further increased public participation in environmental policy. Ultimately, an increase in public participation in Mexico is as much a function of advancing public access to information and establishing a right to information (transparency) as it is strengthening political access to the government itself. With access to more information, concerned interests can utilize international and now legal pathways within Mexico to force the government to include more voices within environmental negotiations. At the systemic level there is little doubt that the strengthening of the democratic transition is integral to strengthening multi-party bargaining in Mexico's environmental negotiations.

Finally, it is important to note that the gray whales and Desert Biosphere Reserve controversy may be an unusual case. Other environmental concerns in Mexico do not draw the level of international or domestic attention garnered by this case. Government administrators have not been forced to increase transparency and pluralism to the same degree for other environmental concerns. That said, this case does show change, and thus the possibility of greater openness and pluralism in the future. Furthermore, since the conclusion of the gray whale dispute, Mexico has passed freedom of information legislation for environmental concerns. Although this legislation is not fully equivalent to the U.S. Freedom of Information Act, it is still a vast improvement for Mexico and opens the door to even greater transparency and public participation.

25.4 Ecuador

In comparison to Mexico, countries such as Ecuador retain a weaker hold on democracy, and progress toward democratic consolidation seems to be primarily focused on emerging pluralism in the context of fragile political institutions [34–36]. Within Ecuador, the emergence of numerous interest groups acting in the political system has not necessarily diversified the strata of elites who have historically retained political control. As a result, the executive branch continues to make many of Ecuador's most environmentally significant political and economic decisions. The absence of strong, effective and stable political institutions (executive, legislature, political parties, judiciary) and the continued problem of political corruption within each of these institutional structures remains an important barrier to democratic consolidation and the emergence of multi-party environmental negotiations [35].

Politically, Ecuador can be characterized as a country in democratic transition, as host to oligarchic democracy [37], and as driven (and victimized) by political corruption[*] [38]. If there is a consistent policy message coming from the Ecuadorian political system across governments, it is the emphasis on following any path necessary to accomplish economic development. Because the modern Ecuadorian economy continues to rely on primary commodities such as bananas, flowers, shrimp, mining and petroleum, these sectors have successfully resisted efforts to moderate environmental impacts. Today, the most serious environmental problems come from two critical sectors for the Ecuadorian economy, shrimp mariculture and petroleum [39,40].

The initial discovery and extraction of significant oil reserves in Ecuador coincided with the emergence of international interest in environmental conservation. The Ecuadorian government came under pressure from the international environmental community, in particular the United Nations, to protect some segments of its natural environment. The United Nations argued that Ecuador could establish a system of protection that would provide a hierarchy allowing strict conservation at one end and sustainable development with positive economic benefits on the other. Subsequent to the discovery and first large scale extraction of oil reserves in 1964, a national system of protected areas was created in 1976 and formalized in national legislation in 1981 [39,41,42].

25.4.1 Ecuadorian Environmental Politics and Management

Environmental management in Ecuador today is a result of policies pursued by central authorities that have in turn produced a convoluted structure of environmental management. One way it manifests itself is through governmental action in the form of legislation and bureaucratic structures oriented toward environmental protection and sustainable management of ecologically sensitive areas. In this vein, the government has maintained a minimally consistent profile of legislation, combined with bureaucratic action and development. For example, the agency originally created to oversee the park system was elevated from one located within the Ministry of Agriculture to the ministerial level in 1996. The Ministry of the Environment existed through the remainder of the 1990s as a centralized bureaucratic entity but in the 2000s has begun to formally shift park and protected area management to provincial government and to private non-profit organizations. This organizational growth has both positive and negative implications. First it indicates the increasing relevance and attention to environmental concerns at the local level within the political system. Second, it demonstrates the expanding power domestic environmental non-profits and international non-governmental actors have on this policy area. Third, the expansion of laws, regulations and other administrative rules has been

---

[*] In the 1960s, private investors sold exploration concessions to the Gulf of Guayaquil for hundreds of dollars; those concessions later proved the existence of 4 trillion cubic feet of natural gas reserves. Currently one ex-Vice President, Alberto Dahik (1992–1996) and one ex-President, Abdala Bucaram (1996–1997) are living in exile as a result of allegations of financial misconduct. The Quito Chamber of Commerce has estimated that political corruption costs 2 billion dollars annually out of a GNP of 39.6 billion.

large enough to result in a level of complexity that has had the unintended consequence of making application and enforcement of the rules difficult. The result has been only partial implementation [39].

Ecuador's statement of environmental conservationist intent is characterized by a variety of elements, ranging from the domestic legal structure of the system of protected areas, constitutional statements of "rights" of citizens to live in a clean environment, participation as a signatory to international environmental treaties and contractual commitments to international organizations such as the United Nations' Educational, Scientific and Cultural Organization (UNESCO). An excellent example of this type of commitment can be seen in the World Heritage agreements that require participating nations to fulfill specific obligations to the natural environment. It is therefore not accurate to dismiss Ecuador's governmental commitment to management and conservation of its natural resources as trivial. However, formally stated governmental intent to either conserve or manage environmental resources has not translated into either systematic or effective action to implement either conservation or sustainable management goals. Moreover, the efforts made to build a domestic structure that will aid the government in achieving either of these objectives can be characterized as largely unsuccessful. The reasons for this are complex, but they are rooted in the domination of the state apparatus by elites who use their power to centralize political authority and then wield that authority primarily in the interest of economic development, with little attention being paid to social services, economic redistribution, and the long-term environmental health of the nation.

Despite the continued institutional movement toward political centralization, the past 25 years have seen the emergence of two important groups of environmentally significant actors on the Ecuadorian political scene. First, since the creation of the system of protected areas and the formal transition to democracy, a broad spectrum of environmental interest groups has emerged as highly organized activists focused on monitoring the management of the system as well as actively tracking environmental issues facing Ecuador. Second, the establishment of the system of protected areas was an important factor in the general politicization of Amerindians in Ecuador. Amerindian political organization has focused on the human and civil rights of Amerindian citizens of Ecuador. For some of the more traditional and isolated tribal groups, the status of the environment, and its conservation, has been a fundamental component of their political demands.

25.4.2 Problems of Institutional Legitimacy

Ecuador clearly falls into the category of "uncertain democracy." Since its transition from military rule in 1979, there have been multiple occasions when the prospect of a military coup seemed imminent. In January of 2000, an alliance between the military and the indigenous-based political party Pacha-kutic led to the overthrow of democratically elected president Jamil Mahuad and installation of his Vice-President, Gustavo Noboa. In the most recent presidential elections of 2003, the winner, Lucio Gutíerrez, was the leftist Colonel who engineered the coup against Mahuad. His election victory was assured, at least in part, by the strong support of the indigenous movement. This alliance was quickly broken when, shortly after taking office, Gutíerrez implemented economic austerity programs opposed by the indigenous groups. The Gutierrez era came to a dramatic end in April of 2005 when Gutíerrez was forced to flee the country, after a scheme to restructure the Supreme Court with the backing of exiled former President Abdalá Bucaram and his political party the Roldosista Ecuadorian Party (PRE) failed. The events of early 2005 demonstrate the low levels of institutional legitimacy accorded the office of the President, the judiciary and, despite its uninterrupted status, the legislative branch. In addition, the newly powerful indigenous movement has lost credibility as a political entity that was better, i.e., less corrupt, than traditional elites. While popular participation and freedom of speech seem to have expanded, institutional legitimacy as viewed by citizens and international observers has not.

While oligarchic democracy continues to persist in Ecuador, and institutional legitimacy is at low ebb, it is interesting to note the growing importance of emerging, politically effective advocacy groups. In particular, indigenous groups have succeeded, despite recent setbacks, in taking the members of a previously disenfranchised segment of the population and mobilizing them to the status of national level policy actors [43]. The question is, to what end? For some observers, that question has been negatively answered by the movement's participation in the coup of 2000 and the subsequent downward spiral. Is there an emerging plural democracy that can survive despite institutional fragility? There are three possibilities in this regard. First, the alliance between grassroots indigenous groups and the military may have been merely a vehicle for a traditional elite group (the military) to attain power. This seems unlikely, given their unwillingness to assume power in late April 2005. Second, the 2003 election results could signal the weakening of traditional oligarchs in Ecuador and the emergence of a fledgling competitive democracy. This possibility seems limited, however, given the collapse of the electoral alliance between indigenous groups that the resurgence of traditional elites embodied in their efforts to remove Gutierrez from office. Currently, Alfredo Palacio, the more left-leaning of the two and former Vice-President, retains tenuous control of the government. The final possibility is that an extreme version of pluralism has taken hold in the context of Ecuador's democratic framework, indicating the continuance of severe political fragmentation, which could work in favor of elite political interests and against the process of democratic consolidation.

25.4.3 Ecuadorian Environmental "Negotiations": the Actors

The government's attempts at organizing a system of protection in the context of weak political institutions, low levels of citizen trust in government and strong economic motivations to access all exploitable environmental resources have led to the emergence of a privately held system of protected areas, in addition to the state system.* Both private and public efforts at conservation suffer from problems that can be linked to the economic, social, and political characteristics of Ecuador. Exploitation of environmental resources that the national system of protected areas is intended to protect has accelerated and likely surpassed the pace of either conservation- or sustainable management-oriented policies. This is partly because the government will not provide adequate resources to the Ministry of Environment and the devolution of authority to the provincial level is as yet unproven in terms of increasing or decreasing resources to protected areas across the system. Clearly the possibility exists for this approach to increase and improve responsibility, cooperation, access and investment at the local level. Recent research indicates the relevance of two considerations. First, citizens evaluate local government as less corrupt and more effective than national government. This bodes well for environmental management efforts focused at this level. The second consideration is more problematic, in that when we look at the level of citizen participation in local government, it is among the lowest in Latin America—a mere 11% [38]. Additionally, unitary states such as Ecuador are not generally interested in giving up responsibilities they view as important to the state. Thus we can infer that in terms of budget allocations, local governments may be the recipients of an unfunded mandate, i.e., the responsibility without attendant resource support. Complicating the issue even more is the problem of institutional legitimacy. Legal institutions, especially the judiciary, are so weak in Ecuador that even private areas are "protected" only to the degree that owners are able to police their own holdings. Private groups must also be able to defend themselves against the government should it decide it wants access to something within their private holdings.

Multi-party negotiations are key in the development of existing environmental policy in Ecuador today. Such participation on the part of various groups is not solely a result of greater openness by the government. It is apparent that in Ecuador the government is not recognized as either the most important force or the final arbiter of environmental policy. Governmental ambivalence on the environment, institutional weakness and citizen expectations in the face of the establishment of democratic institutions have created a political context in which groups of all kinds can become relatively powerful. In fact, there are multiple groups functioning in support of and in opposition to governmental interests; most follow their own agendas. The problem is that without an effective state apparatus to coordinate these efforts, policymaking and, most importantly, the process of implementation and enforcement, are severely fragmented, leaving environmental management in a similar state of inconsistency.

At the international level, multi-party negotiations are indeed common. We see them as international environmental treaties which are written and re-written. They are observable in the Ecuadorian context during the processes of rulemaking for environmental regulations, issuing environmental permits and licenses, planning for mineral extraction, and developing land management

---

* Ecuador has a long tradition of allowing native people to continue to hold "in common" native lands. The common lands tradition co-exists today with a new practice of selling state property to in-debt conservation groups for nature arrangements [47].

plans. When we look to the experiences of other political systems, it is possible to observe organizations assigning teams of employees to develop solutions that are consistent with the agency mission and oriented toward enhancing the public welfare [44]. In Ecuador, the multiple groups form a diverse spectrum ranging from the domestic to the international, but they do not necessarily function with the goal of "enhancing the public welfare."

25.4.4 *Ecuadorian Environmental Negotiations: the Case of Cayapas–Mataje*

One example of problems facing Ecuador's environmentally sensitive areas can be seen in the case of the Cayapas–Mataje region of Ecuador. In 1995 this area, located in the coastal province of Esmeraldas on the northern border with Colombia, was identified as a significant environmental resource and therefore eligible for protection. Environmental groups viewed the extension of reserve status to Cayapas–Mataje as one of the few remaining tools available to stop or delay the wholesale destruction of the remnants of the broader mangrove ecosystem that once existed along the entire Ecuadorian coast [45]. Several environmental groups active in the area had influence with then Vice-President Alberto Dahik and were successful in gaining his support for the extension of reserve status to this area, an action which would bring it into the national system of protected areas. The region supported a wide variety of wood resources as well as coastal territory and was being aggressively utilized by private entrepreneurs for both wood and shrimp development [46].

The work to accord Cayapas–Mataje protected reserve status was intensely political and followed an informal bargaining approach. Activist environmental groups were closely allied with the then-Vice-President of Ecuador. Dahik supported reserve status for the region, but the major barrier to protecting Cayapas–Mataje was the Ecuadorian Institute of Forestry, Natural Areas and Wildlife (INEFAN), which had to approve the extension of protection. According to critics of the Ecuadorian bureaucracy, the reserve status for the Cayapas–Mataje region was not approved by INEFAN because it was protecting its ministerial territory, presumably against other components of the executive branch. As a consequence, despite the support and signature of the Vice-President on a plan to extend reserve status, the plan failed. Forty days later, the INEFAN came forward with a proposition for a reserve based on scientific study [46].

This process did open the way for an actual study by an environmental group that concluded that Ecologic Reserve status was the best alternative. This category of protection allows minimal human activity. Specifically, the Ecologic Reserve guidelines state that sustainable development projects, educational research and recreational activities are allowed. The Ecuadorian Institute of Forestry, Natural Areas and Wildlife's report recommendations included directives to prohibit the development of new farming operations and to remove existing shrimp farm operations. The report also recommended the adoption of a new perspective on forests that would treat them as important in and of themselves.

Shrimp farmers operating in the region responded to the report with opposition, and committed to perform their own study in which they determined that their industry was not a problem within the Reserve. A key element of the shrimp industry position was that shrimp farming would create jobs for the local economy. Industry proponents argued that the existence of a local job base would provide a complementary economic foundation to eco-tourism to the Reserve. These combined benefits would theoretically generate the economy necessary to increase the protection of mangrove forests. This assertion was questioned by environmental groups led by Acción Ecologica [46].

The Ecuadorian Institute of Forestry, Natural Areas and Wildlife next came forward with yet another plan responding to the shrimp industry's claims of sustainable management, in which they exempted private property from conservation recommendations. In effect, they would declare the total territory an Ecologic Reserve, but the agency allowed existing shrimp farming operations and the designation of exempt private property, rendering them free from conservation oriented environmental regulations. The activist environmental group, Acción Ecologica, challenged this compromise because the exclusion of private property would benefit the shrimp farmers, who were already working on eight new farm projects. The conflict between groups and the government continued another three to four months. The Ecuadorian Institute of Forestry, Natural Areas and Wildlife was particularly intransigent on the issue of the shrimp farms. As a result of the continued unwillingness of INEFAN to regulate the shrimp farms and to restrict the expansion of future shrimp farming operations, Acción Ecologica decided to stage a sit-in at the INEFAN offices in November of 1995. The primary consequence of the sit-in was to bring the national legislature into the picture. The legislature questioned the activities of INEFAN and influenced subsequent discussions about the reserve area. In the end, a compromise agreement was reached in which segments of the reserve were set aside for conservation, and shrimp farming operations were prohibited in these particular areas. The question that remained after the final round of negotiations was this: How would the protections be enforced? In 1996 the reports coming out of the region were that this agreement was not being systematically enforced and that shrimp farming continued to expand illegally. At the time, Acción Ecologica estimated that the mangrove deforestation of the region had reached 85% of what existed in 1985 [46].

25.4.5 Ecuadorian Environmental Negotiations: Lessons from the Case of Cayapas–Mataje

In this example, a variety of relatively well-organized actors debated the merits of environmental conservation versus exploitation. Each group focused on the promotion of its respective political or economic agenda. One consequence of these varying foci was that potential compromises, such as managing access to mangrove reserves or investigating alternative methods of shrimp farming, were never attempted. The explanation for how events surrounding the Cayapas–Mataje controversy unfolded is primarily about the power of the different groups functioning in the Ecuadorian political system, but it is also about the relative weakness of the state apparatus charged with the formulation and implementation of environmental plans—whether they are extractive or protective in nature. Thus, the two primary problems for the state, its agencies and its bureaucratic ministries are first, the relatively weak commitment to protect environmental resources when those resources are exploitable for economic gain; and second, the unwillingness to allocate power and resources for the implementation and enforcement of environmental law.

25.5 Conclusion

Many countries are facing the transition to democracy at the same time they are being called upon to address environmental concerns. The combination of these pressures is forcing governments to take another look at the decision-making surrounding environmental issues. More commonly, for democratizing countries such as those in Latin America, the traditional manner of negotiating projects with environmental components within a closed group of elite interests is no longer seen as an acceptable standard operating procedure. With increasing interest from domestic and international groups, democratizing governments are faced with pressure for greater inclusion in environmental decision-making.

This chapter has explored the status of changes occurring within the communicative forums of two Latin American countries, Mexico and Ecuador. Comparing the manner in which these two countries address the changes in environmental decision-making allows for a number of tentative inferences to be drawn, although more extensive investigation is needed before definitive conclusions can be formulated.

First, the cases from Mexico and Ecuador reveal that there are changes taking place within environmental decision-making. Although Mexico appears to be more inclusive than Ecuador, citizens and organizations in both countries are pushing their respective governments for more inclusion in decision-making. The act of pressuring the traditional decision-makers has two implications: (1) it opens the door (if only a crack) to greater involvement in decision-making; and (2) it draws in and energizes increasing numbers of concerned individuals and groups, thus increasing the level of public participation.

Second, the citizens and organizations in these countries are not pursuing negotiations within the traditional, developed, democratic model. Rather, the manner of becoming a part of formal negotiations and decision-making is to force entrance through informal bargaining in the public and international arenas. By compelling the revelation of traditionally suppressed information, non-traditional actors are pushing the governments to at least acknowledge a wider array of voices. Additionally, diverse groups within Mexico and Ecuador are utilizing the power of international connections to draw attention to their environmental concerns. This strategy puts pressure on governments and other agencies to at least superficially address a broader range of concerns. The case studies demonstrate that environmental groups in Mexico and Ecuador are utilizing these non-traditional strategies to become part of formal "multi-party negotiations." Furthermore, these groups are personalizing the use of non-traditional strategies, creating approaches that are effective for their individual situations.

Third, the case studies reveal that Mexico and Ecuador are both experiencing the emergence of environmental groups as important players able to make an important impact on policy development. This development in Mexico appears to be an indicator of expanding pluralism in the context of an increasingly strong and capable state. The agencies charged with environmental management are being impelled to take environmental and grassroots actors into account. Interestingly, this does not appear to be weakening government institutions; rather, it is allowing them greater independence within the government structure and forcing traditionally powerful institutions to share power. For example, the gray whale case revealed growing independence of the judicial branch and the federal environmental agency SEMARNAP. These events are not only allowing more seats at the negotiation table, but they strengthen democratic processes within the Mexican government. Such events, in turn, open doors for even more interests to push their agendas.

By contrast, in Ecuador the emergence of environmental groups as important players able to make an impact on policy formulation is occurring in a different context. The Ecuadorian state and its bureaucratic agencies are weak, generally controlled by special interests. The environmental group in the Ecuadorian case study achieved a legal protective status for the coastal mangrove ecosystem, but was not able to remove the shrimp operations because of the strength of the shrimp "lobby" in Ecuador. The powerful economic position of interests such as the shrimp farmers overrode other interests in that case. Thus, the developmentalist orientation of the state continues to triumph; rather than strengthening democracy with increased pluralism in negotiations, the state enforces its power to sustain the pre-development initiative. Long term economic goals are not achieved because a pro-development orientation requires stronger political institutions able to more completely implement and enforce laws. Ecuador's systematic weakness in these areas has left the multi-parties operating in a political context that overemphasizes the short term. Environmental groups are able to achieve some goals, but because of these problems the long term benefit for either conservation or sustainable management is unknown.

Although there are changes taking place in both of these "transitioning to democracy" countries, the changes are not following the same path. Positive changes are more prominent and more institutionalized in Mexico than Ecuador, revealing diversity within the process of initiating multi-party environmental negotiations for countries in transition. However, ultimately, the fact that the more developed Mexico has made strides toward greater inclusion in decision-making gives hope that as Ecuador develops economically and democratically, Ecuadorians, too, will modify their environmental policy decision-making style to one of more inclusive negotiated decision-making.

References

1. Funtowicz, S. and Ravetz, R. *Epistomología Política*, Centro Editor de América Latina, Buenos Aires, Argentina, 1993.
2. World Commission on Environmental and Development. *Our Common Future*, Oxford University Press, Oxford, 1987.
3. United Nations. *Agenda 21: The United Nations Programme of Action from Rio*, United Nations, New York, 1992.
4. Leis, H.R., A politico-communicative model to overcome the impasse of the current politico-technical model for environmental negotiation in brazil, in *in The Environment, Sustainable Development and Public Policies: Building Sustainability in Brazil*, C. Cavalcanti, Ed., Edward Elgar Publishing, Northhampton, 2000, 94.
5. Cohen, R. *Negotiating Across Cultures: Communication Obstacles in International Diplomacy*, United States Institute of Peace Press, Washington, DC, 1991.
6. Acuff, F. *How to Negotiate Anything with Anyone Anywhere around the World*, AMACOM, New York, 1997.
7. Cohen, R., Negotiating across cultures, in *in Turbulent Peace: The Challenges of Managing International Conflict*, C.A. Crocker, F.O. Hampson, and P. Aall, Eds., United States Institute of Peace Press, Washington, DC, 2001, 469.
8. O'Donnell, G., Schmitter, P.C., and Whitehead, L. *Transitions from Authoritarian Rule: Comparative Perspectives*, The Johns Hopkins Press, Baltimore, 1986.
9. Wiarda, H.J. *The Democratic Revolution in Latin America: History, Politics and U.S. Policy*, Holmes and Meier Publishers, New York, 1990.
10. O'Donnell, G. and Schmitter, P.C. *Transitions from Authoritarian Rule: Tentative Conclusions about Uncertain Democracies*, The Johns Hopkins University Press, Baltimore, 1991.
11. Mainwaring, S. and Scully, T.R. *Building Democratic Institutions: Party Systems in Latin America*, Stanford University Press, Stanford, 1995.
12. Diamond, L. *Developing Democracy toward Consolidation*, The Johns Hopkins University Press, Baltimore, 1999.
13. Grindle, M.S. *Audacious Reforms: Institutional Invention and Democracy in Latin America*, Johns Hopkins University Press, Baltimore, 2000.
14. Adams, F. *Deepening Democracy: Global Governance and Political Reform in Latin America*, Praeger, Westport, 2003.
15. Ottaway, M., Facing the Challenge of Semi-Authoritarian States, *The Chronicle of Higher Education Online*, February 2003, Available at http://www.chronicle.com (accessed on February 7, 2003).
16. Beer, C. *Electoral Competition and Institutional Change in Mexico*, University of Notre Dame Press, Notre Dame, 2003.
17. Camp, R. *Politics in Mexico: The Democratic Transformation*, 4th ed., Oxford University Press, New York, 2003.
18. World Bank. *World Development Report, 1997*, The World Bank, Washington, D.C., 1997.
19. Rodríguez, V. *Decentralization in Mexico: From Reforma Municipal to Solidaridad to Nuevo Federalismo*, Westview Press, Boulder, 1997.
20. Mumme, S.P., Environmental policy and politics in Mexico, in *Ecological Policy and Politics in Developing Countries: Economic Growth, Democracy, and Environment*, U. Desai, Ed., State University of New York Press, Albany, 1998, 183.
21. Lybecker, D.L., Decentralization of Environmental and Water Policy in Northern Mexico: Sonora and Baja California, Ph.D. dissertation, Colorado State University, Fort Collins, 2003.
22. Alanis Ortega, G. 1996—el año de la Reforma a la Legislación Ambiental, *Teorema*, 8, 48, 1996.

23. SEMARNAT, National Program of Environment and Natural Resources 2001–2006, Available at http://www.semarnat.gob.mx/dgeia/web_ingles/programa/indice.shtml (accessed on November 19, 2005).

24. Naumann, T., Counter Punch, *SpinWatch*, April 2005, Available at http://www.spinwatch.org/modules.php?name=News&file=article&sid=760 (accessed on December 9, 2005).

25. Ard, M. *An External Struggle: How the National Action Party Transformed Mexican Politics*, Praeger, Westport, 2003.

26. Dominguez, J.I. and Fernández de Castro, R., *The United States and Mexico: Between Partnership and Conflict*, Routledge, New York, 2001.

27. Umlas, E., Environmental Non-Governmental Networks: The Mexican Case in Theory and Practice, Ph.D. dissertation, Yale University, New Haven, 1996.

28. Arellano-Gault, D., The Mexican Political Transition: Background, *American Political Science Association Online Columns*, August 17, 2001, Available at http://www.apsanet.org/publications/COLUMNS/archives/2001/Aug/arellano0817.html (accessed on September 22, 2003).

29. Brown, C., A Watershed and Bio-regional Approach to Transboundary Water Management in the Tijuana River Watershed, Ph.D. dissertation, University of California, Santa Barbara and San Diego State University, 1998.

30. Hipple, A., The environmental movement in Mexico and cross-border organizing today: Where do things stand?, *Borderlines*, 74, 9, 2001,, Available at http://www.americaspolicy.org/borderlines/2001/bl74/bl74_body.html (accessed on January 24, 2004).

31. Dedina, S., *Saving the Gray Whale: People, Politics, and Conservation in Baja California*, The University of Arizona Press, Tucson, 2000.

32. Aridjis, H., Anatomy of a victory: The saving of St. Ignacio lagoon, *Earth Island Journal*, 15, 3, 2000,, Available at http://www.earthisland.org/eijournal/fall2000/fe_fall2000whales.html (accessed on October 1, 2003).

33. Weiss, K.R., Still not home free, *Los Angeles Times*, March 23, A1, 2005.

34. Hurtado, O., *Political Power in Ecuador*, University of New Mexico Press, Albuquerque, 1980.

35. Kimerling, J., Disregarding environmental law: petroleum development in protected natural areas and indigenous homelands in the Ecuadorian Amazon, *Hastings International and Comparative Law Review*, 14, 849, 1991.

36. Isaacs, A., *Military Rule and Transition in Ecuador, 1972–1992*, University of Pittsburgh Press, Pittsburgh, 1993.

37. Conaghan, C.M., *Restructuring Domination: The Industrialist and the State in Ecuador*, University of Pittsburgh Press, Pittsburgh, 1988.

38. Seligson, M. and Recanatini, F., The environment and governance and corruption, in *Ecuador: An Economic and Social Agenda in the New Millennium*, V. Fretes, M. Cibils, M. Giuglae, and J.R. Lopez, Eds., World Bank, Washington DC, 2003, 411.

39. Escobar Cárdenas, R. and Vásquez, C., *Plan de Manejo Estratégico de la Reserva Ecológica Manglares Cayapas–Mataje, Proyecto INEFAN/GEF*, Direccion Nacional de Areas Naturales y Vida Silvestre DNANVS/INEFAN, Quito, Ecuador, 1999.

40. Beckerman, P. and Solimano, A., *Crisis and Dollarization in Ecuador: Stability, Growth, and Social Equity*, International Bank for Reconstruction and Development, Washington, DC, 2002.

41. Putney, A.D., *Informe Final: Estrategia Preliminar Para La Conservación de Areas Silvestres Sobresalientes del Ecuador*, Food and Agriculture Organization of the United Nations, Rome, Italy, 1976.

42. Fundación Natura. *Acciones de Desarrollo en Zonas de Influencia de Áreas Protegidas*, Fundación Natura, Quito, Ecuador, 1991.

43. Selverston-Scher, M., *Ethnopolitics in Ecuador: Indigenous Rights and the Strengthening of Democracy* North–South Center Press, Coral Gables, 2001.
44. Lamb, B.L. and Lybecker, D.L., Legal consideration in inland fisheries management, in *Inland Fisheries Management*, C.C. Kohler and W. Hubert, Eds. 2nd ed., American Fisheries Society, Bethesda, 1999, 83.
45. Robadue, D., Jr. *Eight years in Ecuador: The road to integrated coastal management, Coastal Resources Center, University of Rhode Island, and the Global Environment Center, Narragansett*, U.S. Agency for International Development, 1995.
46. Chavez, G., personal communication with Jennifer Horan, 1996.
47. Gibson, C.C., McKean, M.A., and Ostrom, E., *People and forests: communities, Institutions, and Governance*, MIT Press, Cambridge, 2000.

Index

equity, 473
ESA *see* Endangered Species Act
ESD *see* Decade of Education for
    Sustainable Development
ESTs *see* environmentally sound
    technologies
Europe
    global warming policy, 43–60
    transborder air pollution, 63–64
European Court of Justice (ECJ), 488
European Environment Agency, 46
European Parliament, 44
European Union
    desertification, 83
    eco-terrorism, 436
    global warming, 48–50
    history, 45–46
European Union Commission, 43–46
Executive Orders, green procurement,
    263–268
exobiology, 109–110
expansion of world economy, 522
exports, 516

F

FBI *see* Federal Bureau of Investigation
FDI *see* foreign direct investment
Federal Bureau of Investigation (FBI),
    433–436
Federal Environmental Executive,
    263–266
federal government, 262–268, 282
feedback loops, 300–301
foreign direct investment (FDI), 492–493,
    497, 507
forest-related actions, 440
formal institutions, 343–346, 351
foundation strength, 300
fragmentation, 141–142, 146–147,
    498–499
Framework Convention on Climatic
    Change, 226
free market, 296
free trade, 177–216
Friends of the Earth, 51
frontiers
    space, 7, 95–112
    space as environmental frontier,
    7, 95–112

G

G-8 Summit, 452
G-77 Summit, 462–463, 465, 468
GATS *see* General Agreement on Trade in
    Services
GATT *see* General Agreement on Tariffs
    and Trade
GDP *see* gross domestic product
General Agreement on Tariffs and Trade
    (GATT), 178, 183, 185–187
General Agreement on Trade in Services
    (GATS), 185–186
geographic context, regulation, 294
geologic repository for nuclear waste,
    387–391
geosynchronous/geostationary orbits,
    102–105
globalization
    challenges, 449–468
    claims, 167–168
    colonization, 449
    conceptual meaning, 2
    culture, 492
    decolonization, 449
    developing countries, 491–522
    effect, 65–67
    enrichment, 452–453
    environment, 1–14, 433–445
    impoverishment, 452–453
    modernization, 450–452
    North-South issues, 449–468
    policy implication, 515–517
    process, 491–495
    re-colonization, 450–452
    spontaneous, 455–457
    sustainable economic growth/environ-
        ment, 2–5
    tourism, 495
    United Nations, 8
    World Trade Organization, 456
global media, 454, 456
global warming, 43–60
goals, green procurement, 275, 279–280
good faith bargaining, 424–425
Gore, Vice President Al, 47
governance, 8, 464–467
    federal states, 35
    global, 137–154
    local and regional, 35–36
governing, desertification, 85–89